Railroads
for
Michigan

Railroads for Michigan

Graydon M. Meints

Michigan State University Press • *East Lansing*

⊚ The paper used in this publication meets the minimum requirements of ANSI/
NISO Z39.48-1992 (R 1997) (Permanence of Paper).

 Michigan State University Press
East Lansing, Michigan 48823-5245

Printed and bound in the United States of America.

19 18 17 16 15 14 13   1 2 3 4 5 6 7 8 9 10

LIBRARY OF CONGRESS CATALOGING-IN-PUBLICATION DATA
Meints, Graydon M.
Railroads for Michigan / Graydon M. Meints.
pages cm
Includes bibliographical references and indexes.
ISBN 978-1-61186-085-6 (cloth : alkaline paper)—ISBN 978-1-60917-374-6 (ebook) (print)
1. Railroads—Michigan—History. 2. Railroads—Michigan—History—Pictorial works.
I. Title.
TF24.M5M43 2012
385.09774—dc23
2012028524

Book design: Charlie Sharp, Sharp Des!gns, Lansing, Michigan
Jacket design: Erin Kirk New
Jacket art: *(front)* Library of Congress, Prints & Photographs Division, Detroit
Publishing Company Collection, lc-d4-39785. *(back)* Sam Breck collection. *(upper front
flap)* Illustration from *The American Railway* (New York, 1897), 111. *(lower front flap and
lower back flap)* Graydon M. Meints Collection. *(upper back flap)* Burton Collection,
Detroit Public Library.

g green Michigan State University Press is a member of the Green Press Initiative
press and is committed to developing and encouraging ecologically responsible
publishing practices. For more information about the Green Press Initiative and the
use of recycled paper in book publishing, please visit *www.greenpressinitiative.org*.

Visit Michigan State University Press at *www.msupress.org*

Contents

The Pioneer Years, 1830–1855

The New Michigan

"I have no hesitation to say that it would be to the advantage of Government to remove every inhabitant of the Territory, pay for the improvements and reduce them to ashes. . . . From my observation the Territory appear[s] to be not worth defending and merely a den for Indians and traitors. The banks of the Detroit River are handsome, but nine-tenths of the land in the Territory is unfit for cultivation." General Duncan McArthur wrote his candid opinion to William Woodbridge in late 1814. President James Madison had offered Woodbridge the post of secretary of the Michigan Territory. Then thirty-four years old, Woodbridge had lived in Marietta, Ohio, since his family moved there in 1791 when he was only eleven. He was admitted to the bar in 1806 and the next year ran for a political office, won election, and discovered his vocation in life. Territorial governor Lewis Cass, an old friend, was away from Detroit at the time, so Woodbridge wrote instead to McArthur to get a feel about Detroit and the territory. McArthur did not much care for Detroit, but despite his feelings he encouraged Woodbridge to come up and take a look for himself. Woodbridge did not make the trip but did decide to accept the job. He moved to Detroit in 1835 to start a lifelong career of public service to Michigan, first as territorial secretary, then as territorial delegate to Congress, justice of the territorial supreme court, its second governor, U.S. senator, and finally an attorney in private practice until his death in 1861.

McArthur's feelings mirrored those of the U.S. surveyor general, Edward Tiffin. "Not more than one acre in a hundred, if there were one out of a thousand that would in any case admit of cultivation," was his blunt opinion. In 1815 the federal government had put Tiffin in charge of a survey of the Michigan Territory that was to provide land that could be awarded to the veterans of the War of 1812. His men tramped around southeastern Michigan all summer finding lakes, swamps, hordes of mosquitoes, and a lot of sandy soil, but nothing they thought was appealing. His final report repeated all of the bad feelings his crew had about Michigan. Official Washington took Tiffin's report at face value, passed over Michigan and selected instead land in Illinois and Missouri. Only a few of those embattled veterans ultimately came to pioneer in Michigan.

President Madison named Lewis Cass governor of the Michigan Territory on 29 October 1813 as a reward for his military service in Michigan during the War of 1812. In 1799, when he was seventeen, the Cass family had moved from Exeter, New Hampshire, to Marietta, Ohio, arriving eight years after the Woodbridge family. Cass also studied law, was admitted to the bar, and soon was in the thick of Ohio politics. During the War of 1812 he rose from colonel to brigadier-general in the regular army, gaining in the process a feisty personality. When Cass moved permanently to Michigan in 1814 he became an aggressive booster of anything and everything that might benefit the young territory. A short, portly man, he was at ease with politicians, pioneers, and the Indians of the territory. He had a wide curiosity and involved himself in everything political, social, and economic. If Cass can be faulted for anything while governor it was that he was frequently away from Detroit, gone on trips to Washington or on one of his periodic excursions of exploration.

Cass could not suppress Tiffin's report, but he worked to offset it with more favorable reports and articles in the *Detroit Gazette* that began to appear in July 1817. Other newspapers in the East copied these articles, and a more favorable picture of Cass's territory began to reach the public. Michigan at this time consisted of only a few thousand French and Americans at Detroit, an army garrison at Mackinac Island, and small settlements at Sault Ste. Marie, Monroe, Mt. Clemens, and Fort Gratiot outside present-day Port Huron. Pontiac was platted in 1818. French farms lined the Detroit River and inland along the River Raisin and some other streams. A few small farmsteads were clearings in the woods, but most of Michigan was heavily forested.

Cass's favorable press did not mitigate the fact that getting to Michigan was a journey not to be undertaken lightly. For New Englanders and New Yorkers, it involved a wagon and horseback trek overland to Buffalo, then a choice whether to go by dangerous sailing ship across Lake Erie or to continue by land through southern Ontario or northern Ohio. Immigrants from Virginia and Pennsylvania more often came across the Appalachians by road to Pittsburgh and into Ohio, over the trails and across the trackless wilderness of Ohio and Indiana, then up into Michigan. Sprawling between Toledo and Sandusky, Ohio, the Black Swamp was a nearly impassable obstacle for travelers until well into the 1830s when a half-decent road was finally completed. A wide swath of land south, west, and northwest of Detroit was a clay lake bottom full of swamps and easily flooded by rains. The only formally established road in the territory was the Maumee Road between Toledo and Detroit, which soldiers built after the War of 1812.

A trickle of settlers came to Michigan despite the daunting and arduous journey. Almost 4,000 of them settled during the decade of the 1810s, increasing the total population in the Michigan Territory to nearly 9,000. Of these, some 2,000 lived west of Lake Michigan in what eventually became other states. *Walk-in-the-Water*, the first steamship on Lake Erie, was launched in 1818. The fare from Buffalo to Detroit in steerage was $7, while a cabin cost an impressive $18. In 1825 two more steamships began plying Lake Erie, and every year after more were added. By 1827 the territory's population grew to 17,411, and in the next three years to 31,639. What had been a trickle became a swell.

The Michigan Territory had become a much more attractive place. By 1821 the Indians, under the influence and duress of Governor Cass, had signed treaties ceding virtually all of their lands in the Lower Peninsula, which allowed the federal government to begin surveying the new territory and selling the land to the public. In 1820 it reduced the selling price of land down to $100 for an eighty-acre parcel, a family-size farm, and allowed buyers to pay with a variety of bank notes, including those of some of the territorial banks. In 1823 a land office was opened at Monroe to handle the increasing volume of government land sales. With the completion of the Erie Canal in 1825, between Albany and Buffalo, it became considerably easier to reach Michigan, if one had the fare for the canal boat. Lake travel improved more when the Canadians opened the Welland Canal between Lake Erie and Lake Ontario in 1829. The cost of travel and land, to say nothing of the physical exertion of homesteading, required aggressiveness and thrift by the new settler. The lazy stayed at home. Nor did many of the new arrivals stay long in Detroit. They came to start a new life farming a new homestead, not to be city dwellers. A common practice among pioneer families, on arrival in Michigan, was for the men to go on horseback looking for suitable land to buy, an effort that often took weeks and sometimes months. Then the rest of the family, with children and wagons and livestock, ventured off to their remote new home.

Cheaper land and the Erie Canal provided only a part of the impetus for new settlers to come Michigan. A new feeling was bubbling up into the mainstream of American life. It came to be called "Jacksonian Democracy," following the election of Andrew Jackson as president in 1828. Throughout the earlier terms of the more patrician Washington, Madison, and the Adamses, this feeling was fairly subdued, while Jefferson's eight years in office changed it very little. The raucous, mudslinging of 1828 that Jackson waged against John Quincy Adams was a completely different type of campaign. Jackson's strong rhetoric struck a new chord; the government was more for the benefit of the citizenry and less for the country. This was completely different from the approach of more patrician earlier presidential candidates. The excitement Jackson brought was infectious, particularly to the newly franchised voters. What started as a political movement became much more upon his inauguration. For the workers and farmers, Jackson's term came to express a new general enthusiasm about politics, but also a general optimism about the future of the United States and its development. The business depression of 1828–29 was beginning to fade. It became easier to borrow money to try starting some new economic venture. Jackson was pushing the Indians west to allow Euro-American settlers more land.

Easterners began to discover that the Michigan Territory was a place with an abundance of farmland for sale at bargain prices, an opportunity to get in on the ground floor for a fresh start, a chance to do something important for one's self. With the Erie Canal and the growing number of Lake Erie ships, it became easier to get to Michigan. Recent immigrants from New York State and from New England, full of Yankee aggressiveness, wrote back to relatives and neighbors and bragged up the prospects of Michigan. The land was fertile and good for all kinds of crops, which encouraged more would-be farmers to come to Michigan. With the farmers came the speculators, both elbowing each other to get the best land. New territorial banks were eager to make loans to buy land. Sales of government land shot up from 70,000 acres in 1830 to 217,000 in 1831, to 405,000 acres in 1835, and topped out at 1,500,000 acres in 1836. Michigan's population grew as fast, from 31,600 in 1830 to 87,200 in 1834, to 174,600 in 1837, and to 212,200 in 1840. Cheered on by Jacksonian Democracy, "Michigan fever" was a growth unmatched anywhere else in America.

SOURCES

Bald, F. Clever. *Michigan in Four Centuries*. New York: Harper & Row, 1961.

Buley, R. Carlyle. *The Old Northwest*. 2 vols. Bloomington: Indiana University Press, 1951.

Fuller, George N. *Michigan: A Centennial History*. 2 vols. Chicago: Lewis Publishing, 1939.

Gilpin, Alec R. *The Territory of Michigan, 1805–1837*. East Lansing: Michigan State University Press, 1970.

A New Kind of Road

Early in the 1820s, well before the explosion of growth, territorial officials joined with residents trying to improve travel in Michigan by asking the federal government for new roads. The response from Washington was meager, with just a few roads authorized, but the work on them went slowly, and their usefulness depended more on good weather than on the quality of their construction. The territorial government also tried its hand at building some roads, but it had little money to do very much. Individual counties and townships also authorized local roads, but it was easier to authorize them than to get them built.

Travel within Michigan remained far from easy. The choice was either to use one of the few ships that sailed the Great Lakes coastwise or go on horseback along the narrow Indian trails. The territory's roads were little more than primitive tracks, a path through the woods with tree stumps cut short enough to allow a wagon to pass over them. They became a sea of mud after each rainfall. Cuts, fills, bridges, and road surfacing were improvements that were deferred to the future. In 1824 Congress authorized a survey of the Chicago Road, which was to extend from Detroit, through Ypsilanti, the Irish Hills, Jonesville, Coldwater, Sturgis, and White Pigeon, through Bertrand south of Niles, then through Indiana and along the Lake Michigan shore, to Fort Dearborn at Chicago. The surveyors followed the Sauk Trail that American Indians had used for time unrecorded, but little work was done to the road before 1829. This road is now Highway U.S. 12 between Ypsilanti and Edwardsburg. The federal government also rebuilt the Maumee Road between Toledo and Detroit in 1827. In 1829 Congress appropriated funds for a road from Detroit to Saginaw, on what is now Woodward Avenue and the Dixie Highway, but by 1835 it was finished only as far as a little north of Flint. Congress also authorized a military road from

Port Sheldon & Grand Rapids

The Port Sheldon & Grand Rapids was chartered in 1837. The railroad that was proposed was part of a larger plan to found a Lake Michigan port city named Port Sheldon at the mouth of the Pigeon River, about halfway between Holland and Grand Haven. The promoters, mostly from New York State, may have thought that by building from Lake Michigan their railroad would reach Grand Rapids sooner than the roads building from the east.

They cleared some land and built a large hotel at Port Sheldon, then laid a few yards of railroad track. This much done, the promoters printed an impressive map of the entire undertaking and set out to sell lots in their new and soon-to-be prosperous city. The panic of 1837 arrived but purchasers did not, the lots did not sell, and the railroad was never built farther. Eventually the hotel decayed and disappeared, except its columns, which were taken to Grand Rapids and used on a new residence.

Detroit to Port Huron, now Gratiot Road, but work on it proceeded so slowly that it was easier for those bound for Port Huron to go by ship. In 1829 the territorial council established the Territorial Road. It split from the Chicago Road at Ypsilanti, passed through Ann Arbor, Jackson, Battle Creek, and Kalamazoo, and ended at St. Joseph. At Pontiac the Grand River Road branched off the Saginaw Road, but during the first ten years it was barely passable for the journey to Lansing and Grand Rapids. These roads may have existed on paper, but were little more than paths through the forest.

In November 1827 Detroit residents sent off a petition asking Washington to build a canal to connect Lake Michigan with Lake Erie at Detroit. Clearly the two-year-old Erie Canal across New York State was a success, and the petitioners tried to persuade the federal government that a similar canal across the base of Michigan's Lower Peninsula would be equally successful. Since Michigan was not yet a state, they thought it should fall to Washington to build the canal. In February 1828 residents of Monroe, not to be outdone by the Detroiters, sent their own petition, its only difference being that they wanted the canal to begin at Monroe rather than at Detroit.

In 1830 these requests took a subtle but important shift. In his annual message to the legislative council, Governor Cass stated that "there is one obvious and signal improvement, which could be made, which no doubt eventually will be made. And that is, to unite the mouth of the St. Joseph with our eastern coast, by a canal or rail-road, as experience may establish the superiority of either, across the base of the Peninsula." What Cass envisioned was a Michigan replica of the Erie Canal, but now he also allowed that the newly popular idea of a "rail-road" would be an acceptable substitute for the waterway. Remembering the closeness of both the French and the recently defeated British, he suggested that this project would be important to national defense as well as to trade; he encouraged Washington to make a survey of a possible route. He was confident that the program not only would pay for itself but also could provide a continuing stream of revenue for years to come. Since neither the territory nor its residents had the funds to construct it, he thought it only reasonable that the federal government provide the money.

At the time Cass spoke the railroad was a new and mostly unproved form of transport. In the United States the Baltimore & Ohio had completed thirteen miles of track in May 1830 and used horses to pull its diminutive cars. The six-mile Charleston & Hamburg was being built in South Carolina and planned to use a steam locomotive. The only other railroad of any size was the Mohawk & Hudson, which was then being built between Schenectady and Albany, New York. Despite little practical knowledge of them and even less experience with them, the railroad was a frequent topic of conversation. Newspapers printed long articles describing the developing new railroad technology. Copies of these articles appeared in newspapers throughout the Northwest Territory to enlighten readers who had never seen a train.

Canal developers continued to insist, of course, that river transport was the proven means of carrying passengers and freight. In 1826 the state of Ohio undertook an extensive canal-building program. Indiana was not far behind, although it soon became mired in a dispute over where the canals should be dug. Illinois, moving a little less quickly than the others, made plans for its own Illinois and Michigan Canal to connect Lake Michigan with the Illinois River and make that navigable to the Mississippi. Both Indiana and Illinois received grants of federal land to assist them in financing their canal projects. Despite canal support elsewhere, Michigan petitioners hedged their bets by asking for either a railroad or a canal, and leaving the choice to the federal government. By 1834, reflecting the development of the rail system in the East, petitions from Michigan began asking for railroads to the exclusion of canals.

All this time Governor Cass continued to support anything that would improve travel in the territory. On 31 July 1830 he signed a farsighted piece of legislation that provided for the incorporation of the "President, Directors and Company of the Pontiac and Detroit Railway." This was the first railroad charter granted in the Michigan Territory and probably the earliest charter in the Northwest Territory. It came just

Territorial governor Lewis Cass signed the law that chartered the first railroad in the Northwest Territory and for Michigan—the Pontiac & Detroit in 1830.

Archives of Michigan.

nine months after Robert Stephenson's pioneering steam locomotive *Rocket* made its trial runs on England's Liverpool & Manchester, and just five years after that country's first true railroad, the Stockton & Darlington, was built. In 1830 the state of Ohio also chartered its first railroad, the Ohio & Steubenville. The next charter in any part of the Northwest Territory did not come until 1832, when another Michigan road was chartered and the first charters were granted in Indiana.

The developers of the town of Pontiac organized the Pontiac & Detroit Railway to help the sale of town lots in their new community. Pontiac was more than twenty miles inland from the Detroit River, and a railroad would make it far easier for settlers to get to it and the surrounding Oakland County. Once there and settled, and with their farms and factories producing, the railroad would be an easy way to ship produce and goods to the outside world at a reasonable cost. In 1830 it cost as much to move grain from Pontiac to Detroit as to ship it from Detroit to New York City. To solve this local problem much of the grain raised around Pontiac was consumed at home, most often after it was converted into whiskey at a local distillery. But with a charter in hand and a will for success, nothing happened. Not enough money could be found to build the railroad. The stock was priced at $100 per share, and investors could buy in with 10 percent down and the balance payable in $10 installments. The company was given five years to build its line. One troubling clause stipulated that after twenty-eight years the company's rights would revert back to the territory. The years slipped by, and the railroad was never built.

In August 1831 Lewis Cass left Michigan to become Andrew Jackson's secretary of war. George B. Porter replaced him, but did not want the job. A little earlier Jackson had appointed John T. Mason as secretary of the territory, but Mason resigned the job in 1831 to go off to Texas to find his fortune. Mason persuaded Jackson to replace him with his nineteen-year-old son, Stevens T. Mason. During Porter's frequent and extended absences from Michigan, and after his death in 1834, the young Mason was the acting governor of the Michigan Territory.

In 1832 Governor Porter signed the charter legislation for the Michigan Territory's second railroad. The Detroit & St. Joseph Railroad evolved from the frequent, albeit ignored, petitions to Washington for a cross-peninsula railroad. It seemed possible that private capital might do what the federal government would not. It was created by a group of Detroiters: Oliver Newberry, Charles Larned, Eurotas P. Hastings, DeGarmo Jones, John R. Williams, and John Biddle were among the commissioners named to sell stock. A number of non-Detroiters also were named, men who could lend visible prestige and their money-raising talents to the project. The D&SJ line was to strike directly across the Lower Peninsula from Detroit, through Ann Arbor, Jackson, Albion, Marshall, Battle Creek, Kalamazoo, and Paw Paw, to Lake Michigan at St. Joseph. Its route would parallel the barely passable Territorial Road and the earlier talked-about canal. The promoters were sure that their more modern railroad would duplicate the success of the Erie Canal.

When it came time to raise funds to start building, the money could not be found. Not enough could be collected even for a survey of the route. A meeting in Ann Arbor in September 1834 raised only $400. The territorial government saw merit in the proposal and did some of its own badgering. The War Department planned to send Colonel John MacPherson Berrien to Michigan to do some lake port surveying, and, since he was in the territory, he was authorized to survey a railroad line for the D&SJ. In December 1834 Berrien turned in his favorable report. He suggested the line could run along the Chicago Road from Detroit to the Rouge River in Dearborn, then go toward Ypsilanti. West of Ypsilanti it could follow the valley of the Huron River to Ann Arbor and the Territorial Road to Jackson. West of Jackson it could follow the south side of the ridge of land lying between the Kalamazoo and St. Joseph Rivers as far as Prairie Ronde, near Schoolcraft. His route then proceeded down a rather steep grade to Paw Paw, and finally along the Paw Paw River to St. Joseph. The surveyed line was 192 miles in length and with no heavy grades except the one west of Prairie Ronde. He claimed that could be solved either by an "inclined plane" or a longer route with an easier grade. Berrien found an adequate supply of timber along the route, enough to provide all that would be needed for the wooden superstructure of the line. Berrien did not provide a cost estimate, but others estimated it would cost $3,200 per mile to build the section from Detroit to Ann Arbor. The fact that Berrien's survey did not coincide with the route authorized in the D&SJ charter was of no concern but rather a detail that could be taken care of when the time came.

The D&SJ promoters promptly assembled a convention of rail supporters on Christmas Eve day 1834 in Detroit, endorsed the Berrien report, and sent it to Congress with a request for a grant of land to finance construction of the railroad. To improve the prospects they threw in a branch line to Monroe and would allow any other branches that the legislature might order. Washington kept silent.

In 1833 the territorial legislature chartered two more railroads, the

MIXED TRAIN ON DETROIT & PONTIAC RAILWAY, 1843

This may or may not be an accurate drawing of an early-day Detroit & Pontiac train. It is, however, the only one that has been found of this pioneer Michigan railroad.

Illustration from George B. Catlin, *The Story of Detroit* (Detroit, 1923), 366.

Romeo & Mount Clemens and the Erie & Kalamazoo. In 1834 charters were granted for the Shelby & Detroit and the Detroit & Pontiac. Of these four only the Romeo & Mount Clemens failed to build a railroad. The Detroit & Pontiac's charter was an attempt by new owners to put new life into the 1830 Pontiac & Detroit. Since its original charter called for the line to be built by 1835 and no work of any sort had been started, the charter would expire soon.

By 1835 railroads were no longer a novelty; the technology of moving freight and passengers by rail improved rapidly. The roads developed enclosed cars for passengers that protected riders from sparks and the elements, although freight continued to be carried on open flat cars. The steam locomotive was imported from England, and American ingenuity developed and improved it substantially. Every road adopted the locomotive, and soon it replaced all use of horses. Early track-laying technique used a raised wooden base and superstructure with iron "strap rail" strips as the surface for the car wheels to roll; wooden ties laid directly on the ground slowly superseded this. Eventually an upright iron rail that rested directly on the ties replaced the strap rail, long strips of iron nailed onto the wooden rails. For passengers, a train ride may have been a convenience but often was not a pleasant experience. The train was dirty from wood smoke, usually erratic, often late, and subject to breakdowns and derailments that the male riders were expected to help repair. The cars were crowded with every sort of traveler, the haughty hoi polloi, the dignified and the unkempt, the dandy and the bumpkin. Despite all of its failings, and if one could abide the character of one's fellow riders, the train most certainly was an improvement in speed and convenience over all other forms of transport.

By 1835 the demand for railroads in Michigan had not diminished but was overshadowed by a new set of political events. The first came in 1832 when the legislative council petitioned Congress for an act that would allow drafting a state constitution. Congress refused to act, claiming Michigan's proposed southern boundary infringed on the rights of the state of Ohio. Eventually Michigan's legislative council ordered a census be taken in October 1834 to find out if the territory had enough residents to become a state under the terms of the Ordinance of 1787, which created the Northwest Territory. The final count was just over 87,000, well more than the 60,000 needed to qualify for statehood. A convention assembled in May 1835 in Detroit to draw up a state constitution. On 5 October the voters ratified this constitution, elected Stevens T. Mason as governor, and chose all of the requisite state and federal political officers. But Congress refused to accept the result and continued adamant in its support of Ohio's boundary claim that the site of Toledo should be in Ohio. A new survey to locate the state boundary, ordered by Ohio governor Robert Lucas, satisfied no one in Michigan and changed nothing. In May 1835 men went to arms in an opéra bouffe belligerence called the Toledo War, notable for its lack of casualties, in Michigan's very brief attempt to defend its border claims against Ohio. Finally, in December 1836 another convention, brought together under rather unusual and such questionable circumstances that it was called the "Frostbitten Convention," adopted a proposed deal conceding a boundary line satisfactory to Ohio and accepting much of the Upper Peninsula as a trade-off. On 26 January 1837 Michigan was formally admitted to the Union as the twenty-sixth state.

Money, in the form of a surplus in the federal treasury, was behind the rush to statehood. President Jackson proposed to distribute this surplus to the states, and Michigan's share was estimated at $500,000. As a territory there would be no money, but as a state it could gain in this windfall. Also, it might become possible to obtain a portion of the proceeds from the sale of government land in Michigan. Land sales at the federal land offices at Monroe, Kalamazoo, and Ionia were reaching new highs each year.

Another important reason for supporting statehood came from a collection of ideas called "internal improvements." Under this catchall term a state could undertake a wide variety of public works projects, such as building roads, canals and locks, dams, and railroads, activities that were prohibited to a territory. A state could borrow money to build what it chose and repay the loans with the profits from operating the works; when they became free and clear the state would have a never-ending stream of revenue. Ohio already had its canal-building projects under way. Indiana and Illinois were eager and ready to start. As a territory Michigan had to stand aside, while as a state it could be as progressive as the rest of the Old Northwest.

Stevens T. Mason became Michigan's first governor at the age of twenty-five. He enthusiastically promoted an "internal improvements" program to bring railroads to Michigan. While he was governor the state built two railroads, from Detroit to Kalamazoo and from Monroe to Hillsdale. The program eventually became a complete financial fiasco.

State Archives.

River Raisin & Grand River

In 1835, when railroads were still very new and before the internal improvement program was a reality, the citizens of Monroe wanted their community to be the eastern terminal of a railroad that would extend across the state. Both Detroit and Toledo had announced plans for such lines; therefore Monroe must have one, too. The result was the River Raisin & Grand River, an ambitious attempt to build from Monroe, through Tecumseh, Clinton, and Marshall, to the rapids of the Grand River, a distance of about 150 miles. The state's charter named eight men from Monroe, Tecumseh, and Marshall as commissioners to sell stock, and allowed them a generous thirty years to get their railroad built. It also allowed the railroad to open a bank to help it raise money for construction.

But no railroad building started. One report has it that the stock had been subscribed, probably with minimal down payments, and that the company had surveyed a line between Monroe and Marshall. Apparently the bank absorbed most of the time and talents of the railroad's promoters. The bank soon gained a reputation as a "wildcat" bank by issuing bank notes without much hard currency for collateral behind them. Not long after the state brought such banking practices to a halt, both the bank and the railroad dropped from view.

In three days in August 1835 Governor Mason signed charters for four more railroads: the River Raisin & Grand River, which was to be a cross-peninsula road beginning at Monroe; the Macomb & Saginaw; the Maumee Branch; and the Detroit & Maumee. This last road was proposed to extend into the now-hated Ohio river port at Toledo and there would connect with the Maumee Canal to the Ohio River and with the Erie & Wabash Canal into northern and western Indiana.

Money to build these proposed railroads continued to be difficult to find. The state hit on the novel idea of allowing a railroad company to form a bank that would help it raise money. Requests for "railroad banks" came in, and the legislature obliged by authorizing the Detroit & Pontiac to open a bank at Pontiac, the Detroit & St. Joseph at Ypsilanti, the Erie & Kalamazoo at Adrian, the Macomb & Saginaw at Mount Clemens, and the River Raisin & Grand River at Tecumseh. The first three were successful to the extent that apparently they helped raise money to start building the associated railroad. Of the latter, the associated rail line was never built, while the bank itself became a full-size financial nuisance as a true "wildcat" bank that lasted until the state forced it closed in 1844.

As the excitement of organizing a new state faded a little, some men of affairs turned their attention back to making money with new railroads. In March 1836 the legislature granted charters to eleven more lines: the Allegan & Marshall, the Shelby & Belle River, the St. Clair &

Romeo, the Constantine & Niles, the Monroe & Ypsilanti, the Clinton & Adrian, the Palmyra & Jacksonburgh, the Kalamazoo & Lake Michigan, the Havre Branch, the Monroe & Ann Arbor, and the River Raisin & Lake Erie. All of these were very local undertakings whose names described what lines their local promoters intended to build. Several of them did manage to survey a line, and a few did grade a bit of line, but of all of them, only the Palmyra & Jacksonburgh ever completed any railroad line or ran a train.

Construction started on three rail lines in the spring of 1836. Early in the year the Detroit & St. Joseph let contracts for grubbing and clearing out trees and underbrush for its line between Detroit and Ypsilanti. By November the line was graded west from Detroit to about Dearborn. In April the Detroit & Pontiac awarded contracts for grubbing for the first fifteen miles out of Detroit. By 1836 the Erie & Kalamazoo already had graded some of its line between Toledo and Adrian, put in timbering and superstructure during that summer, and operated its first train through to Adrian apparently in late October. The only definitely stated date for the official start of service is 2 November, but contemporary supporting evidence is missing.

In any event, the Erie & Kalamazoo was the first railroad to run trains in Michigan, was the first railroad in the states of the Northwest Territory, and was the line located farthest away from the eastern

Darius and Addison J. Comstock

Darius Comstock: Born 12 July 1768, Cumberland, R.I.; died 2 June 1845, Raisin Twp., Lenawee Co.

Addison J. Comstock: Born 17 October 1802, Palmyra, N.Y.; died 20 January 1867, Adrian.

The Comstocks, father and son, moved to Lockport, New York, in 1820, and were contractors building part of the Erie Canal in that area. The family moved to Adrian in 1826. Darius was a devout Quaker, and throughout his life his home served as a station on the Underground Railroad. Addison bought land that in 1828 he platted into the city of Adrian. He built the first house in Adrian, a sawmill, and a grist mill; served as postmaster, town clerk, and mayor; and eventually became a banker.

In 1833 the Comstocks obtained a charter for the Erie & Kalamazoo Railroad to build from Port Lawrence (now Toledo) on Lake Erie, to some point on the Kalamazoo River. The first train, a couple of cars pulled by horses, arrived in Adrian from Toledo on 2 November 1836. The E&K was the first railroad to be built in Michigan and in the Northwest Territory that has remained in continuous operation. A part of the original route remains in use today in the Palmyra and Blissfield area.

This 1837 newspaper ad announced the arrival of the Erie & Kalamazoo's first steam locomotive. It gives no schedule times for the trains, probably because the road assumed everyone knew when the trains ran.

seaboard. A cannon shot at Port Lawrence, as Toledo was then known, announced the train's departure. One reporter wrote:

> The first train on the Erie & Kalamazoo railroad was brought in by John Barragar. He drove his horses tandem between the wooden rails. It was a slow, tedious and unpleasant trip of thirty-three miles. The Cottonwood swamp was under water most of the year, the mud between the rails almost impassable. "If the fates were propitious" the journey could be made from sun to sun but it often required the most of two days to make the trip one way.

A new pair of horses took over every four miles. The first passenger cars were stagecoachlike carriages with flanges on the wheels to keep them on the rails. The first train into Adrian called for a celebration. "Cannon boomed, the militia paraded, the band played, the people went wild with excitement and the festivities lasted far into the night," a kind of celebration that became a standard to mark the arrival of a new rail line. The Erie & Kalamazoo received its first steam locomotive in early summer 1837, and it began running trains of three cars on a much faster schedule, leaving Toledo in early morning and returning from Adrian in early afternoon.

SOURCES

Blois, John T. *1838 Gazeteer of the State of Michigan*. Detroit: Sydney L. Rood, 1838. Reprint, Knightstown, Ind.: Bookmark, 1979.

Dodge, (Mrs.) Frank P. "Marking the Terminus of the Erie and Kalamazoo Railroad." *Michigan Pioneer & Historical Collections* 38. Lansing, Mich.: Wynkoop, Hallenbeck, Crawford, 1912.

Fuller, George N. *Michigan: A Centennial History*. 2 vols. Chicago: Lewis Publishing, 1939.

Michigan Legislature. *Acts of the Legislature*. Various years. Lansing, Mich.: various publishers.

Waggoner, Clark, ed. *History of the City of Toledo and Lucas County, Ohio*. New York and Toledo, Ohio: n.p., 1888.

"To Lead to Lasting Prosperity"

When Stevens T. Mason took the oath of office in 1836, Michigan was a much different place from that of 1831 when he first came to the Territory. Its population had exploded as immigrants poured off the boats at Detroit and Monroe. It would be estimated that 200,000 people would pass through Detroit, most of them new arrivals. Small settlements could be found along Lake Michigan at Muskegon, Grand Haven, South Haven, St. Joseph, and New Buffalo. The roads inland from Detroit, bad as they were, were crowded with wagonloads of new settlers moving to their new homesteads. There were new towns strung along the Chicago and Territorial Roads, with the new communities of Jonesville, Sturgis, Niles, Ypsilanti, Ann Arbor, Jackson, Albion, Marshall, Battle Creek, and Kalamazoo growing in importance. Between them smaller settlements had started. Stagecoaches ran regularly on both roads, a few of them going as far as the fledgling village of Chicago. Outside Detroit and off the two major roads, new communities were founded at Adrian, Tecumseh, Brighton, Howell, Ionia, and Grand Rapids. Port Huron, Mt. Clemens, and Saginaw were growing, as was a new community at Bay City. Water-powered sawmills and flour mills were everywhere, and merchants and traders and bankers found ready customers. Anyone who built a factory that produced something could sell it readily in the local market. There was no shortage of brewers and distillers.

Governor Mason and the farmer in his remote field held the same opinion about internal improvements. They were not just important, they were crucial and they had to be built. Once built they would bring the prosperity of the future, and profits would flow in a stream that reached to the horizon. This sentiment had been growing since the early 1830s. Ohio's canal-building program already was well under way, Indiana also had started digging canals and had some railroads on the drawing board, and Illinois was poised to start. There was no reason for Michigan to come in last; it should take a leading place in providing not only roads, ports, and canals but railroads as well. The state's new constitution put it plainly:

> Internal improvements shall be encouraged by the government of this state; and it shall be the duty of the legislature, as soon as may be, to make provisions by law for ascertaining the proper objects of improvement, in relation to [roads], Canals, and navigable waters; and

it shall also be their duty to provide by law for an equal, systematic, and economical application of the funds which may be appropriated to these objects.

The document did not mention railroads specifically, but the term "roads" certainly could be interpreted broadly enough to include them. Governor Mason more than warmed to the subject in his annual message to the legislature in February 1836.

The spirit and enterprise which has arisen among our citizens, if fostered and encouraged by the State, cannot fail to lead to lasting prosperity. Your liberal legislation should embrace within its range every section of the state. No local prejudice or attachments should misdirect the equal liberality with which you should guard the interests of your constituents.

The governor suggested that an engineer, or a commissioner, or a board of commissioners, could manage the entire undertaking, and they should report to the legislature annually. Mason did not mention borrowing any money for all of this, but many Michiganders were eager to push ahead and were willing to speed up success by borrowing needed funds. Throughout 1836 the lawmakers discussed and wrangled over how best to start and manage the program, what projects to build, and how to fund them. New York State provided one example when it had constructed the Erie Canal for $7,000,000 and, with the tolls it charged, had recovered that cost and interest charges in nine short years. The grand total cost of Ohio's program was not known, since it had been put together year by year. Indiana had just enacted a $13,000,000 program, and Illinois was in the process of enacting one planned to cost $10,250,000. The Illinois program had some of everything: the Michigan and Illinois Canal, 1,300 miles of railroad, road building, and river improvements. Each of those three states' programs was more ambitious than anything Michigan was considering. The cost of Michigan's proposed program was never calculated accurately, but it was estimated to be about $8,000,000. This came down to about $50 for each resident of the state, few of whom had that kind of money or even paid that amount in taxes. This made no difference, for it was a certainty to all that the tolls and the profits would pay for the whole thing.

In early 1837 Michigan's first legislature took up the internal improvements program and on 21 and 22 March passed a group of bills to establish it. It set up a seven-member board to manage it. Initial funding was to come from the anticipated federal surplus that was to be loaned to it, and it authorized Governor Mason to obtain a loan of $5 million to fund the program. One bill listed the specific projects that were to be undertaken, and this list demonstrated the fundamental difficulty that was to plague the program throughout its life. To get any part of the package passed there had to be something in it for everyone. What had been conceived as a program having the support of all the people turned quickly into a political horse-trading free-for-all. No district was happy if it failed to get as much benefit as was given to other areas. It proved impossible to gain enough votes for any one project. Multiple projects were the only way to satisfy the legislators from each of the different sections of the state. In its final form three railroads were to be built across the state: from Monroe to New Buffalo, from Detroit to St. Joseph, and from Port Huron to the Grand River in Kent County. The board was authorized to purchase the rights of the Detroit & St. Joseph, the Detroit & Pontiac, and the Havre Branch railroads. Three canals were included: one connected the Clinton River near Mt. Clemens with the mouth of the Kalamazoo River, one was to bypass the rapids of the St. Marys River at Sault Ste. Marie, and the last was to connect the Saginaw River with the Maple or Grand River, southwest of Saginaw. For good measure, a number of improvement projects were planned for the Grand, Kalamazoo, and St. Joseph Rivers.

The governor nominated Justus Burdick of Kalamazoo, David C. McKinstry of Detroit, Hart L. Stewart of Mottville, John M. Barbour of Bertrand, Gardner D. Williams of Saginaw, Levi S. Humphrey of Monroe, and Daniel LeRoy of Pontiac to be members of the newly established board. All were confirmed by the legislature except for LeRoy, and James B. Hunt of Pontiac was named in his place.

With the program set up, Governor Mason sailed to New York City to negotiate the $5 million loan. Detroiter Oliver Newberry immediately agreed to buy $500,000 of the bonds when they were issued. When Mason departed, the financial times were still reasonably good in Michigan, but on the East Coast he found new difficulties. The severe economic constriction of the financial panic of 1837 was beginning to take hold. The nation's boom times, which had brought heady growth to Michigan, probably had gone too far. Eighteen states had started or were considering internal improvement programs, most of which well exceeded their ability to repay. To dampen down affairs a bit President Jackson issued his Specie Circular to federal land offices requiring land sales be paid for in hard currency and disallowing the more commonly used bank notes. Jackson's dislike of central banks led to his campaign to let the charter of the Bank of the United States expire. This bank was the closest institution in the United States like a central bank, and it did exercise some restraint on local banks. At the same time a number of British bankers began to consider their loans to be at risk and, to protect themselves, slammed shut the lending window.

Mason could not find takers for the bonds and headed back to Detroit empty-handed. On a return visit in September Mason was no more successful, but he was advised that if the interest rate was raised to 6 percent and made payable in Europe, the bonds would be more salable. Mason called a special session of the legislature, and it obliged with the suggested changes. In June 1838 the governor finally reached an agreement with the Morris Canal and Banking Company of New York. It would take one-quarter of the bonds, and the United States Bank of Philadelphia the remaining three-quarters. They would pay the state in installments of $250,000 each quarter. Mason decided there was no better deal to be made and agreed to the arrangement.

In April 1837 the internal improvements board purchased the assets of the Detroit & St. Joseph for $322,321. The board made surveys of routes for the three railroad lines and inspected the rivers scheduled for improvement. The route for the "Central" line used that of the D&SJ franchise, and was set to be from Detroit, through Ypsilanti, Ann Arbor, Jackson, Albion, Marshall, Battle Creek, Kalamazoo, and Paw Paw, to St. Joseph. It continued the construction already started by the D&SJ.

The "Southern" line was a much more difficult story. The first route survey was completed in late summer of 1837. The board held hearings in Jonesville in October and then ordered three more surveys in Lenawee County based on the responses. More hearings were held at the end of November, and after those the board decided the route would be from Monroe, through Adrian, Hillsdale, Coldwater, Mason (in Branch County), Branch, and Centreville, along the St. Joseph River to Constantine and Mottville, then west through Adamsville, Edwardsburg and Bertrand to New Buffalo. The legislature got into the act in March 1838 when it directed the board to alter the route between Edwardsburg and Bertrand so it would pass through Niles, and in April it ordered a curve in the road or a branch to reach Dundee. Also, it ordered the board to restudy the route west of Centreville and to consider routing the line through Three Rivers and Cassopolis to Niles, and caused still one more survey. The board obliged a citizen

COPYRIGHT 1890 BY SILAS FARMER

By 1838 the state of Michigan built this small passenger depot and freight house on the southeast corner of Michigan and Griswold in Detroit. Train tracks ran out Michigan Avenue as far as Fourteenth Street before going onto a private right-of-way.

Silas Farmer, *History of Detroit and Wayne County and Early Michigan* (Detroit, 1890), 898.

who persuaded the board the line should go through Hudson rather than bypassing it to the north.

The board had some of the same problems about the "Northern" line's route. Several possible routes west from the St. Clair River were surveyed in the last half of 1837. In October the board decided the route would start from Port Huron rather than St. Clair, then run through Lapeer, Flint, and either Corunna or Owosso. It was then to continue west to the mouth of the Maple River at Muir, cross the Grand River and follow its south bank through Grand Rapids to Grand Haven. The owners of the St. Clair & Romeo Railroad objected to the route as an infringement on their charter right to build from St. Clair to Lake Michigan on much the same route as that adopted for the Northern. The legislature directed the board to have the road run through both Corunna and Owosso instead of just one of them. In Port Huron it wanted the terminal relocated from the north to the south side of the Black River.

The other projects soon developed problems. One short segment of the Clinton & Kalamazoo Canal was dug between Frederick and Utica, used just once, and then abandoned. The Saginaw-Maple Rivers Canal had some digging done, but it, too, was never completed. The ship canal at Sault Ste. Marie was surveyed and work started. When the U.S. Army quartermaster at Fort Brady learned the details of the board's plans he notified Washington, which in turn notified the state that it would be interfering with an improvement made by the U.S. government. A compromise was finally worked out that required the board to restore an unused mill race when the canal was completed. The state's contractor refused to proceed, possibly because he was more interested in suing the state for damages than being sued for failure to live up to his contract. Only a little work was done on the river improvements.

In January 1838 trains began running on the Central line from Detroit to Dearborn. The station in Detroit was at the corner of Griswold and Michigan, and trains ran down the center of Michigan Avenue for about a mile before moving onto a private right-of-way. William Nowlin described his impressions of the first train into Dearborn in his reminiscence, *The Bark Covered House*:

> He came prancing and pawing upon the iron track, and he disdained to touch the ground. His body was as round as a log. His bones were made of iron, his veins were filled with heat, his sinews were of brass, and "every time he breathed he snorted fire and smoke." He moved proudly up to the station. . . .
>
> I went home and told the wonderful story of the sight I had seen. There was but little talked about, in our house, except the cars, until the whole family had been to see them. We thought, surely, a new era had dawned upon us, and that Michigan was getting to be quite a country.

When the line was completed to Ypsilanti, twenty-eight miles from Detroit, the board pulled out all the stops. The road's lone locomotive, named for Governor Mason, and one passenger car were polished up for a celebratory first run on Friday, 2 February 1838. A second car was built for the excursion and suitably named *Governor Mason*. A few freight cars rounded out the train to provide enough seating for the dignitaries. It took three hours to make the trip from Detroit to Ypsilanti. The grand callithumpian event that followed—with the airs of a brass band and a banquet, which was followed by speech after speech, all of which, one suspects, were encouraged by ample refreshments—set down a standard to celebrate line openings in the decades that followed. On the trip back to Detroit the engine broke down at Dearborn. Some weary dignitaries walked the remaining ten miles into Detroit while others waited for horses to pull the train. In October the board finally got around to reimbursing Joel Collier and Luther Dean the grand sum of $65 for hauling the train back to Detroit.

Construction pushed on. The eight miles into Ann Arbor were completed on 17 October 1839, and another celebration took place, this time with the Detroit city council, the Brady Guards, and 800 citizens on the excursion train. Dexter was reached on 4 July 1840, and the remaining forty miles to Jackson were pretty much completed by the end of the year, although the board reported some work still had to be done to put the road into proper operating condition. The whole project was far from easy work; everything took longer than expected, everything cost more than planned, and the funds needed were greater than the proceeds of the bond sale that trickled in.

Things were even more difficult on the Southern line. The commissioner in charge, Levi S. Humphrey, had his own ideas about how things should be done, some of them a bit unconventional. He awarded construction contracts to some friends of his without properly advertising for bids, and also to a company in which he appears to have had a financial interest. Some legislators wanted the contracts canceled and republished. Humphrey refused to do this because he considered the contracts valid. A legislative committee found Humphrey's chosen insiders were overcharging for materials. Also, he was found to be arbitraging between state funds and the wildcat bank currency that he used to pay contractors. Work came to a halt when an epidemic laid workmen low during the summer. Humphrey decided that the line should be built above ground, with the superstructure for track and rails resting on pilings. There was some justification for this approach, given the swampy character of much of the land outside Monroe. But by the end of 1839, although work was started and more than two years had passed, the road was not yet ready for trains between Monroe and Adrian. Humphrey thought it would not be profitable to begin operations until the line was completed to Hillsdale, which was a potential source of a considerable amount of freight. As the board pondered this it became obvious that the Southern would be hampered by its lack of direct access to the waterfront in Monroe, a situation everyone seems to have overlooked. The board had bought the Havre Branch Railroad to provide the Southern with direct access to Lake Erie, but that project met with nothing but delays and in the end was never built. The legislature later authorized buying the River Raisin & Lake Erie to gain access to the Monroe harbor. To improve this access the board made an agreement with the LaPlaisance Bay Harbor Company to use its wharf, but the legislature would not approve that deal and thereby negated the advantage of the RR&LE purchase. At last, on 23 November 1840, trains

The Havre Branch Railroad

Havre never was a real place except in the mind of some visionary politicians. They realized that as a price of admission to the Union, Michigan might have to give up a strip of northern Ohio that included Toledo. To offset Ohio's ill-gotten advantage, the Lake Erie port city of Havre was created about a mile and one-half north of the state line on North Maumee Bay. In March 1836 the state legislature granted a charter for "The Havre Branch rail-road company," which authorized a line from Havre westerly to a connection somewhere with the Erie & Kalamazoo. If Ohio won the Toledo area, E&K shippers would still be able to ship to Lake Erie boats docking in Michigan.

In 1837 the legislature authorized the newly created board of internal improvement to purchase the Havre Branch's charter, which it did within a few months. By the end of the year the line was surveyed, but the panic of 1837 stopped the award of any contracts for construction. Nothing happened until 1840, when the legislature authorized a change of the western terminus to a connection with the Southern line in the city of Monroe instead of with the E&K, and authorized another railroad, the Maumee Branch, to build the line. This could have allowed the Southern a direct line to Lake Erie shipping, something it later achieved only with difficulty.

Nothing ever came of any of this. The community of Havre disappeared quickly and quietly, and its namesake railroad was as soon forgotten.

began running on the Southern line between Monroe and Adrian. At Adrian, the Southern competed with the Erie & Kalamazoo and often came out second-best. The E&K's trains ran to a much superior harbor at Toledo, a port that was nearer to Buffalo by boat than was Monroe.

Charges of favoritism also were alleged about the contracts the board let for the Northern line. In 1838 contracts were let to clear and grade 130 miles of road between Port Huron and Lyons, and some grading was done on short segments at Lyons and west of Flint.

Commissioner Humphrey departed the board and the Southern at the end of his term in April 1840. As money grew even tighter the following winter, the board wanted to move a shipment of strap rail from Monroe to use on the Central. The mayor of Monroe issued an alarm about the intended "theft." A group of men gathered in the dark of night, loaded the rails on cars, roused the locomotive engineer to pull the cars into the country, and unloaded and secreted the rails under logs and brush. Months later, after yet another change in commissioners, the rails were returned to be installed on the Southern. When the line finally pushed into Hudson in 1843, some of the wood rails had been exposed to four years of Michigan weather and already were beginning to deteriorate. The line finally reached Hillsdale on 25 September 1843, but it was not until October that the strap iron rails were put on to make the road ready for full operation.

The Central was completed to Albion on 25 June 1844, to Marshall on 12 August 1844, and to Battle Creek on 25 November 1845. By one means or another the Central was officially completed into Kalamazoo on 2 February 1846. The engine *St. Joseph* ran into town on the first, on a Sunday morning during church services, and members rushed from their pews to see the new wonder. As the Central was built this far west it tapped new and fertile farmlands, which provided increased revenues for the road. Only this income kept alive any hope of completing any of the internal improvement projects.

SOURCES

Dunbar, Willis F. *All Aboard! A History of Railroads in Michigan.* Grand Rapids, Mich.: W. B. Eerdmans, 1969.

Elliott, Frank N. *When the Railroad Was King.* Lansing: Michigan Historical Commission, 1966.

Fuller, George N. *Michigan: A Centennial History.* 2 vols. Chicago: Lewis Publishing, 1939.

Parks, Robert J. *Democracy's Railroads.* Port Washington, N.Y.: Kennikat, 1972.

Wing, Talcott E. *History of Monroe County.* New York: Munsell, 1890.

New Roads and Old Problems

The internal improvement board considered buying the privately owned Detroit & Pontiac when that road was in its infancy in 1837. Nothing came of it, apparently because the railroad rejected the deal. The road's owners, Sherman Stevens and Alfred L. Williams, with their training as currency traders, promoters, and speculators, were able to build their road by using their railroad bank to raise money. South of Royal Oak the grading turned the long-undisturbed earth into a bog. It took months to fill in the sinkholes that caused tracks laid during the day to disappear overnight. After nearly two years, on 19 May 1838, the section between Royal Oak and the Detroit station at Jefferson and Dequindre was completed. Horses pulled the lone passenger car and the few freight cars the company owned. Passengers paid $1 for the ride; freight was carried at 50 cents per hundred pounds. The line was so popular that it had to run two trains each way to handle the demand.

This ad for the state's Southern Railroad announced the 1842 season of service. The trip to Adrian included a free transfer from Lake Erie ships at Monroe. Passengers were assured of a ride that was safer than one provided by an unnamed competitor—the Erie & Kalamazoo.

Talcott E. Wing, *History of Monroe County* (New York, 1890), 225.

Sherman Stevens and Alfred L. Williams

As young men Stevens and Williams moved to Pontiac when the community was not much more than a dream of the future. Stevens had been a currency trader in Buffalo for several years, while Williams had been one of John Jacob Astor's agents. In 1835 the owners of the Detroit & Pontiac invited the two to help start up their railroad. To raise money they organized the railroad's bank that same year in Pontiac. The bank made money for the two; they bought land for a right-of-way, and between 1837 and 1843 built the twenty-four-mile line. The record implies that there was chicanery behind Williams and Stevens's every move, and hardy any duplicity they would not resort to. They built tracks where they wished, economized on construction, borrowed without regard to repaying, and spent a great deal of time in court. When the state forced their bank to close in 1839, it had at least $200,000 of notes in circulation, all of which became worthless. Both men filed for bankruptcy in 1842. Stevens was forced out of the railroad and had to watch the road's first locomotive, *Sherman Stevens*, being renamed *Pontiac*. Williams maintained a minimal involvement with the railroad until 1851, when he, too, was forced out.

The Pontiac road was completed into Birmingham on 16 August 1839. The year before it had received a state loan of $100,000, which Stevens said was used to buy strap iron for the rails. Somehow he obtained another loan of $100,000 from the state of Indiana. In 1839 Stevens traveled to Philadelphia to buy the road's first locomotive from Matthias Baldwin. When it was delivered, it came complete with a brass plaque on each side displaying its name, *Sherman Stevens*. According to Stevens, it replaced a black horse, Old Pete, who stayed with the road for twenty-five years. He worked during construction, pulled the first passenger cars, and ended his career switching cars at Pontiac. If Old Pete felt there were too many cars for him to pull at one time, he would not move until some of them were uncoupled.

Service was quite informal since the train would stop anywhere to pick up or drop off a passenger. Trains were reputed to be so slow that one story has it that a middle-age man going to Pontiac died of extreme old age during the ride. Another claimed there were so few prisoners at the Pontiac penitentiary because those who were sent there by train completed their sentence before they arrived. At times the strap rail would work loose, bend up, and pierce the floor of the passenger car. Rather than spend money to buy better rails, the line applied metal sheeting to the bottom of the car and touted this feature of the new car as well as its heating system. Eventually the company defaulted on its interest payments to the state. The state made a few threats against Stevens and Williams but had no stomach for legal action, and eventually settled for $32,000. Indiana got nothing back on its loan. Baldwin had to sue to get paid for his locomotive and finally settled in 1846 for $5,150. Stevens was forced out of the company in 1842 and dodged his debts by filing for bankruptcy. Williams also went bankrupt, but remained with the road until 1851. Despite a host of problems, the line was finally completed into Pontiac on 4 July 1843.

In 1842 the Pontiac line laid tracks on Gratiot Avenue from Dequindre into downtown Detroit on Farmer Street. Property owners complained that the street became a sea of mud after each rain because the railroad did not maintain it properly. Years of complaints and agitation brought no results until exasperated citizens, armed with tools, tore up some of the track in 1849. The tracks were put down again, torn up, and again restored. After several years of this sort of standoff, the company in 1852 built a new line to the Detroit River into a new station at Brush Street and permanently removed the tracks from Gratiot Avenue.

The Erie & Kalamazoo received its first steam locomotive, the *Adrian*, from Baldwin in the summer of 1837. The company appears to have been a popular success from the beginning. It tapped a fertile farming area in Lenawee County and connected it to the Lake Erie port at Toledo. But the road also suffered after Toledo was placed within Ohio, so that Michiganders viewed the E&K as a "foreign" road. It is likely that the panic of 1837 made it difficult for the line to raise more money to continue building to the Kalamazoo River, but its success did lead its owners to support the formation of a connecting line, the Palmyra & Jacksonburgh, in 1836. The P&J was to run from Palmyra to Tecumseh and Clinton, and eventually was to be built to Jackson. Most important, it would feed profitable traffic to the E&K. The state made a loan of $20,000 to the P&J to help it along. Operations started on the section from Palmyra to Tecumseh on 9 August 1838. An extension to Clinton apparently was built either that year or the next, but was operated for only a year or so and then abandoned back to Tecumseh. By 1840 the P&J was moving so much business that it wanted to use a steam locomotive instead of horses. To make the change it had to put down strap iron on its wooden rails, which it talked the state into lending it. Eventually the company defaulted on the terms of the loan, and, in 1844, the state took over the Palmyra line, severed its connection to Palmyra, and made it a branch of the Southern line.

The state also loaned $60,000 to the Allegan & Marshall Railroad,

This classic engraving shows the *Adrian*, the Erie & Kalamazoo's first locomotive, pulling the road's "palace" passenger car. Note that the engineman and fireman had to stand exposed to the elements. Passengers were expected to help load wood and carry water when the engine refueled. As fanciful as the 1837 scene appears, railroad officials of the era vouched for its accuracy.

Talcott E. Wing, *History of Monroe County* (New York, 1890), 218.

but that company never did more than grade a few miles of road. The state's money was lost. Also, the state loaned $75,000 to the Ypsilanti & Tecumseh. It graded much of its line, and contracted for two locomotives, but by about 1840 the company disappeared from view. One other obscure company appeared at this time. The Shelby & Detroit was in business by September 1839 from Utica south to within five miles of the Gratiot Road, in the vicinity of Seven Mile or Eight Mile Road. Apparently it used only horses for motive power until it ended operations in 1844. Several attempts were made to revitalize the road, but it never operated again.

Soon after the internal improvement program was started legislators began grumbling about how it was being handled. It appears that legislators with influence got favors, while others were made unhappy when a pet project was not included. Once work was under way, charges of all sorts—alleging mismanagement, financial improprieties, self-dealing, favoritism, and collusion with friends and business partners—were leveled against the internal improvement board members. Some of these allegations were politically motivated and some not, but they produced evidence strong enough that resignations and lawsuits followed. Dozens of reports and studies were printed in House and Senate documents, and few were supportive of how things were being done. Also, there was a feeling that Governor Mason had not handled the state's financial affairs properly. The problems with the internal improvement program were laid at his desk. Questions continued to dog him about the $5 million bond sale. By 1839 most of the state's wildcat banks had been closed by state bank examiners and by the panic of 1837, but there remained a generalized distrust even of the sound banks that handled the state's money.

In the election of November 1839 disillusioned voters put Mason out of the governor's office and replaced him with the Whig candidate, William Woodbridge. It fell to Woodbridge to figure out what internal improvement projects to keep going, how to raise money to do them, and how to discontinue the rest. In his January 1840 address to the legislature he said, "This scheme, so bold in its inception, so splendid in its design, so captivating to a fervid imagination, but yet so disproportioned to our present local wants, and so utterly beyond our present means, must, I fear, as a whole at least, be given up."

He tried to tighten controls and reduce costs by canceling all of the canal projects and stopping work on the Northern line. The only projects retained were the Central and Southern roads, steps that made Woodbridge no friends. In January 1840 the state had to borrow $605,000 from the Bank of Michigan to meet obligations for work already completed.

In April 1840 the Morris Canal and Banking Company defaulted on its payments to the state for its share of the $5 million bond sale, and went into bankruptcy. The United States Bank of Philadelphia continued its payments until October 1841, defaulted, and soon after it failed as well. By this time the two banks had sold nearly all of the $5 million in bonds to investors, for which they paid the state about $$2.3 million in cash. Woodbridge, then age sixty-one, had had enough. He resigned the governorship on 23 February 1841 when the legislature appointed him U.S. senator.

In the 1841 fall election John S. Barry of Constantine was chosen governor. He took over wrestling with the same problems as well as dealing with the default of the eastern banks on the $5 million loan. Even before he had taken office Barry had the good fortune to get some help from the federal government. Congress gave Michigan a grant of 500,000 acres of public land to be used to fund internal improvements and also began paying the state 10 percent rather than 5 percent of the proceeds from the sale of federal lands in Michigan. Both of these helped a little, but not much. The state started to issue warrants in anticipation of the sale of this land to pay contractors. In his first message to the legislature in 1842 Barry admitted that the "system, so called, was altogether beyond our means, and, indeed, embraced projects of improvement that were not at the time required for the public good."

In early 1842 Barry made an announcement for which he received both cheers and jeers: the state would be responsible only for those bonds for which it had received payment, and the rest he ordered returned to the state for cancellation since that state had received no payment. Many considered the idea of "repudiation" an ugly thing that would damage the state's reputation. It became a delicate political issue, but Barry remained determined not to pay for something not received.

Throughout both the Woodbridge and Barry administrations there was some talk of selling the state's two railroads, but more often it was a search for ways to finish the projects rather than to dispose of them. In 1844 the legislature finally brought to the floor a bill to sell both the Central and Southern railroads, but it did not pass. The state's large debt, taken on to build the projects and even as reconfigured by Barry, remained a worrisome burden that had to be dealt with. A constant undercurrent was the feeling that the whole affair had been misman-aged. Barry's 1845 message to the legislature asked that the decision to sell be delayed because there was some possibility of increased revenues and of some new federal help to aid in building the two railroads. The legislature could not muster enough votes to decide anything. By spring 1845 both Detroit newspapers were printing articles solidly in favor of the sale of the two railroads, and a few non-Detroit journals joined them. In 1845 the legislature passed a new package of small internal improvements projects that would use up about half of the proceeds from the sale of the federal land grant. Governor Barry promptly vetoed the whole package.

In January 1846 newly elected governor Alpheus Felch delivered his annual message to the legislature and in plain language recommended the sale of both of the state's railroads. In the ten years since the internal improvements were considered, public opinion and political sentiment had completely deserted the old enthusiasm and now favored selling the railroads and getting out of the transportation business.

The events of the last half of 1845 and early 1846 are not completely

Henry N. Walker

Born 30 November 1811, Fredonia, N.Y.; died 24 February 1886, Detroit.

Walker came to Detroit in 1834 or 1835 and set up a law practice. He was the sort of person who was interested in everything and involved in everything. He held several positions in the court system. For short periods he was the postmaster at Detroit and the state's immigration agent. From 1845 to 1847 he was Michigan's attorney general under Governors John S. Barry and Alpheus Felch. From 1843 to 1855 Walker was the historiographer for the city of Detroit, in 1849 he was one of the founders of the Detroit Savings Bank, and from 1861 to 1875 he owned and edited the *Detroit Free Press*. He worked on behalf of the temperance movement and was a major benefactor of the Detroit Observatory at the University of Michigan.

In 1845 Walker became involved in the state's efforts to sell its two railroads, especially in the sale of the "Central" line to the Michigan Central. He played a part in the formation and early life of the Great Western Railway of Canada and was a director of the Detroit & Pontiac. In 1852 and again in 1855 he traveled to London to raise money to build the Oakland & Ottawa, in which he was a major stockholder. After the D&P and O&O companies merged to become the Detroit & Milwaukee, he became the new road's president. To get the D&M completed to Grand Haven, he found help from the Great Western, which took control of the road in exchange for the financial aid.

Walker rounded out his railroad career as one of the founders of the Upper Peninsula's Houghton & Ontonagon in 1870, and in 1872 he served a short term as president of its successor, the Marquette, Houghton & Ontonagon.

clear, although the basic outline is known. Apparently Governor Barry saw some merit in the sale of the railroads and sent his attorney general, Henry N. Walker, out East to see if there were possible purchasers. Walker stopped at Albany, New York, to confer with Erastus Corning. Corning owned an iron works that produced most of the strap rails used by railroads, was president of the Utica & Schenectady Railroad, and was involved in almost everything that might make money. He grew interested in Walker's topic and brought in John W. Brooks. Brooks, then twenty-six years old, was the superintendent of the Auburn & Rochester who had started his career as a civil engineer on the Boston & Maine. He came to Michigan to inspect the state's Central railroad, found that much of it needed to be rebuilt and that nearly everything else needed repairs. But what he saw excited him and made him certain that the road had real possibilities. While in Detroit Brooks made contact with James F. Joy, a thirty-six-year-old attorney who was a sort of power behind the throne and a strong supporter of the sale of the state's railroads. Brooks assembled a pamphlet, *Report Upon the Merits*

John Woods Brooks

Born 2 August 1819, Stow, Mass.; died 16 September 1881, Heidelberg, Germany.

After his academy education and an apprenticeship in engineering, Brooks became chief engineer of the Boston & Maine Railroad in 1839, and four years later became superintendent of the Auburn & Rochester Railroad. In April 1842, just before his move to the A&R, he married Charlotte Louisa Dean. In 1845 he came to Detroit, apparently at the urging of Erastus Corning of the Mohawk & Hudson, to investigate a railroad that the state of Michigan wanted to sell. Brooks's report recommended buying the line; Corning found considerable merit in the idea and encouraged using the report to raise money for the purchase. Brooks, with Corning's support, eventually went to Boston, where he met John Murray Forbes, who was looking for new investments. Forbes became interested in Brooks's railroad idea, and became the leading backer.

In 1846 Brooks became general superintendent and on-site manager of the newly formed Michigan Central Railroad. He had charge of the complete renovation of the entire line and encouraged its extension into Chicago, which was completed in May 1852. It was his exceptional talents that made the Central into a profitable railroad. In 1855 Brooks became the road's second president, following John Murray Forbes. At that time many of the Central's founders had invested in a ship canal at Sault Ste. Marie, and to protect their investment Brooks eventually had to take charge of construction, finishing it in 1855. In 1862, while serving as MC president, Brooks was named a commissioner for the Hoosac Tunnel in Massachusetts and spent three years in an unsuccessful attempt to complete it. All this time Brooks was heavily involved with Forbes and James F. Joy in the development of the Chicago, Burlington & Quincy Railroad. In May 1866 he was paralyzed to the degree he had to give up the Michigan Central presidency.

Three years later Brooks was recovered sufficiently to assume presidency of a subsidiary of the Burlington. In 1875 Forbes discovered some questionable financial dealings and forced both Brooks and Joy from the Burlington management. Brooks's health began to fail, and when his death came he and Forbes had never reconciled. As an exceptionally capable engineer he was called by railroad authority Charles Francis Adams Jr. "the most thoroughly competent man in the United States."

of the Michigan Central Rail-Road as an Investment for Eastern Capitalists, to sell the idea to investors.

At Corning's suggestion Brooks went first to New York City to look for money. He found little interest there, went on to Boston, and there met John Murray Forbes. Then age thirty-three and a millionaire shipowner and semiretired from the China trade, Forbes was speculating in Western land and looking for some new ways to put his money to work. Forbes was very much interested in Brooks's idea and met with enough of his friends that he was able to assemble the capital needed to buy the Central line.

When the legislature convened in January 1846 it was at last ready to sell the railroads, a move that had the complete support of Alpheus Felch, the new governor. The internal improvement board reported that $30,000 was needed each year just to keep the Central road in operation. A new tax would have to be levied to pay the interest on the state's bonds since the railroads were not yielding enough revenue to pay it. Against this backdrop James F. Joy was lobbying for the sale. The resulting legislation, signed by Felch on 28 March 1846, provided a charter to create the Michigan Central Railroad and set the terms of the sale of the Central line to the MC. The new company had six months in which to pay a $500,000 down payment and then a year to pay the remaining $1.5 million, using either cash or state bonds. The provision for payment by state bonds allowed the incorporators to buy up Michigan's internal improvement bonds at a heavy discount and have them count at face value toward the purchase price. The $2

John Murray Forbes

Born 23 February 1813, Bordeaux, France; died 12 October 1898, Milton, Mass.

After only a few years of formal schooling, at age fifteen Forbes began working in his uncle's trading firm and two years later was sent to China to manage the business there. His business acumen developed quickly. In February 1834 he wed Sarah Hathaway, a marriage that produced six children. By his early thirties, married and now quite wealthy, Forbes began to look for other investments for his money. In 1846 he was attracted to a proposal to buy the "Central" railroad from the state of Michigan. He led the group that organized the Michigan Central Railroad and formed the triumvirate, with John W. Brooks and James F. Joy, that ran it for more than twenty years. He was the road's first president and continued as a leading figure in the company for twenty-five years.

When the MC was completed to Chicago in 1852, the three men started investing in a number of small Illinois railroads, which became, in 1856, the nucleus of the Chicago, Burlington & Quincy. Within two years he tried to retire from active management to a new home at Buzzards Bay, remaining content to serve as director of many of the roads in which he had invested. Throughout the Civil War he was aggressively involved in the war effort, and he continued to support the antislavery movement and claimed he had John Brown visit his home. By 1867 he was forced into more active involvement in the Burlington, to protect the investment he and his friends had made. In 1875 he discovered some of James Joy's financial and management practices on the Burlington, and in disapproval forced Joy from the presidency of the railroad. In 1878 Forbes became the road's president, and later its chairman, and held that position until 1892.

When death came, after several years of failing health, he was eulogized for his early realization of the potential of railroads and for the integrity and Boston conservatism that characterized him throughout his life.

million purchase price was about $200,000 less than the cost to build the road to Kalamazoo. The new owners were required to rebuild the first fifty miles of line west of Detroit with new rail within two years and complete the line to Lake Michigan within three years. It was allowed to operate steamboats that connected with its line. The state reserved the right to buy back the road after 1866 for the market value of its stock plus 10 percent.

A similar bill passed on 9 May to authorize the sale of the Southern line and create the Michigan Southern Railroad. It was similar to the Central's bill in most respects except the sale price was a modest $500,000, with only a $10,000 down payment and the balance in $25,000 semiannual installments. The new company was given four years to build to Coldwater, another four to build to the St. Joseph River, and yet another four to build to Niles. The Tecumseh Branch was to be completed to Jackson within three years. Two bidders came forward, one a group of New York State men, apparently connected with the Erie & Kalamazoo, who bid $600,000, and another group from southern Michigan headed by Detroit attorney Elisha Litchfield that bid $500,000. The first group wanted the right to connect the Southern line to the Erie & Kalamazoo, probably realizing a route into Toledo was more valuable than one into Monroe. The Litchfield group's lower bid was accepted although it was less than half the amount spent to build the line. Apparently the state drew the line at tolerating any possible benefit to the "foreign" Erie & Kalamazoo road.

The Michigan Central paid its down payment just under the wire, on 23 September 1846, and took over the next day. John Murray Forbes became the new road's president, John W. Brooks its superintendent, and James F. Joy its chief counsel. The Michigan Southern began operations on 28 December 1846, headed by James J. Godfroy of Monroe, Elisha Litchfield as treasurer, and Thomas G. Cole from the internal improvement days as the first superintendent.

Once the lines were sold, the state was glad to be out of the railroad business. The internal improvement program was conceived with high hopes during affluent if speculative times. Each of the three railroad projects was justifiable by some criteria. The rival demands of legislators from different areas of the state ultimately weakened then entire undertaking and then speeded its downfall. Each section insisted on a project for itself and demanded it be continued even after financial difficulties began to appear. If the state had been able to concentrate its efforts after 1841 on its most promising project, the Central line, it might have been able to avoid many of the difficulties and much of the embarrassment that ensued. The political situation of the day, however, would not allow this sort of reasonableness. The result was the partial completion of only two railroads and the sale of both at less than their cost of construction. The canal projects were abandoned and the river improvements only partially completed. Taking the positive side, the state had been able to build part of two railroads, and left to private enterprise it is questionable if they could have been built as early as they were. The life of the Detroit & Pontiac under private ownership and saddled with its own peculiar difficulties, and the later example of the Erie & Kalamazoo, shows that it was just as difficult to build a pioneering railroad with private capital.

SOURCES

Dunbar, Willis F. *All Aboard! A History of Railroads in Michigan*. Grand Rapids,
    Mich.: W. B. Eerdmans, 1969.

Farmer, Silas. *History of Detroit and Wayne County and Early Michigan*. 3rd ed.
    Detroit: Silas Farmer, 1890. Reprint, Detroit: Gale Research, 1969.

Fuller, George N. *Michigan: A Centennial History*. 2 vols. Chicago: Lewis Publishing,
    1939.

Michigan Railroad Commission. *Aids, Gifts, Grants and Donations to Railroads . . .*
    Lansing, Mich.: Wynkoop, Hallenbeck, Crawford, 1919.

Parks, Robert J. *Democracy's Railroads*. Port Washington, N.Y.: Kennikat, 1972.

Trap, Paul. "The Detroit and Pontiac Railroad." *Railroad History* No. 168 (Spring
    1993).

Wing, Talcott E. *History of Monroe County*. New York: Munsell, 1890.

Success and a Conspiracy

The Michigan Central, with Forbes, Brooks, and Joy in charge, had a great deal of work to do on the road, and had to do it in a hurry. The east end of the line was then eight years old but had received only enough maintenance to keep the trains running. Forbes wrote his wife that "we found the road in a most deplorable condition, the iron broken up often into pieces not a foot long, and sometimes we could not see any iron for some feet, only wood; in other places short pieces of iron, almost athwartships. . . . This bad road last about eighty miles." Brooks bought a parcel of land on Third Street close to the Detroit River for

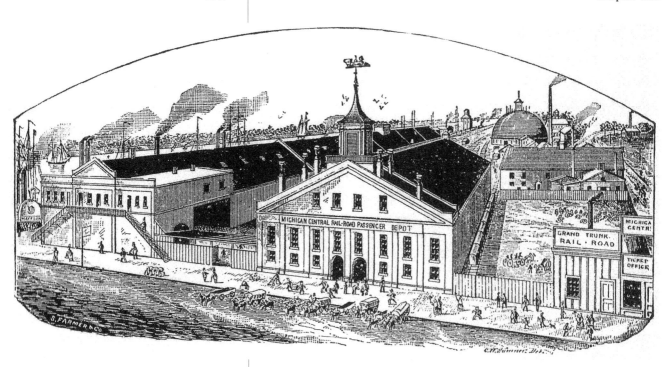

The Michigan Central built a new and much larger Detroit station in June 1848 to replace the state's downtown facility. Located along the Detroit River on the west side of Third Street, the freight house was on the left near the river, the waiting room in the center, and a ticket office on the right. The domed building behind the station was the roundhouse for locomotives.

Silas Farmer, *History of Detroit and Wayne County and Early Michigan* (Detroit, 1890), 899.

a new Detroit station and had it open on 30 May 1848. A new freight house and new shops buildings were built nearby. Running trains down Michigan Avenue ended, with the depot grounds eventually used for a new city hall. By the end of 1849 the line between Ypsilanti and Dexter was relocated from the south bank of the Huron River, and was shortened and straightened, with several new bridges crossing the river. New sixty-pound T-rails were put in on forty-five miles of road, and bridges were rebuilt to handle heavier trains. It fell to Brooks, as both an experienced civil engineer and a capable executive on the ground, to direct the many projects.

The Michigan Central's charter required it to build to Lake Michigan by early 1849. In June 1847 Forbes came out from Massachusetts and with Brooks scouted possible Lake Michigan ports for the Central. Forbes rejected St. Joseph as being too swampy and much preferred either New Buffalo or Michigan City, Indiana. Brooks already had started grading west of Kalamazoo when the directors decided to build to the small, undeveloped port of New Buffalo. This would put the end of the line only a few miles north of the Indiana state line and was the Michigan port the shortest distance to Chicago. Forbes kept the money coming to keep up construction so that in October 1848 the line was finished into Niles. On 23 April 1849 the MC began to run trains into New Buffalo.

Brooks had already arranged for Captain Eber Brock Ward of Detroit to provide two steamships to meet the trains and take passengers to Chicago. Another sailed daily to Waukegan, Illinois, Racine, Kenosha, and Milwaukee, Wisconsin. That same year the Central built the *May Flower* to carry passengers between Buffalo and Detroit. It was probably the largest steamship on the Great Lakes at the time and was advertised as the most luxurious. Put all together the Michigan Central now operated a through service between Buffalo and Chicago. Great Lakes ship owners reacted to this invasion of their territory by setting a $5 fare for the Buffalo-Chicago trip via the Straits of Mackinac, with four or five days bed and board included. The MC met this with the same rate for a trip that took one-third the time. Chicago may have been the destination of many of the Central's passengers, but the conservative Forbes was unwilling to extend the MC tracks there, preferring to wait for some other line to build out from Chicago to his road.

James F. Joy

John W. Brooks

John Murray Forbes

George Bliss

James F. Joy, John W. Brooks, and John Murray Forbes completed the Michigan Central's road into Chicago in 1852, and then developed it into an important and prosperous railroad. George Bliss built the Michigan Southern into Chicago that same year.

Railroad History.

Brooks's new rails brought increased train speeds, up to a dazzling thirty miles per hour, which developed into a thorny new problem. When the state had operated the line, train speeds were relatively low. The right-of-way was unfenced, allowing livestock to roam freely, and occasionally a passing train caused the untimely demise of one of them. To placate the farmers the state paid full value for any stock it killed. It has been said that some farmers purposely fed their livestock along the tracks in hope of fetching a better price from the state than on the open market. Brooks built some fences along the tracks, but a few of these were torn down to keep the money coming. Brooks's position was that the animals were trespassing on railroad property and that their owners were negligent in the care of their livestock. He announced that in the future the railroad would admit no liability of any sort, but would offer to pay half the appraised value of any livestock it killed through its negligence. The farmers saw this as an admission of liability and demanded full value. Brooks refused. He had money problems enough without trying to enrich local husbandmen as well.

Farmers between Dowagiac and Niles retaliated by derailing a locomotive. On the stiff grade west out of Kalamazoo the tracks were greased with lard. At Marshall, evening trains found switches set toward sidetracks or, worse, sometimes were shot at. John D. Pierce of Marshall, a member of the legislature and the state's first superintendent of public instruction, fulminated. He justified the acts against the Michigan Central when he said, "The road has been for a long time one gore of blood. No heathen altar ever smoked more continually with the blood of its victims." Brooks's response was that the cattle owners were trespassers.

The reaction was most violent east of Jackson, between Michigan Centre and Grass Lake. A number of public meetings resulted in requests that Brooks pay full damages until the right-of-way was completely fenced. From one of these meetings a committee of three sent Brooks a letter that described the state of mind of the farmers and implied further action might take place. Brooks responded that the road had no liability to pay anything, that it would continue its one-half payments, and that if the committee wanted to take a test case to the state supreme court, the Central would pay some of the legal costs incurred. He also said that he would hold the three writers responsible for any injury done to his company in an attempt to coerce it to change.

At the forefront of the Jackson County farmers was Abel F. Fitch. Then forty-three years old, Fitch was one of the founders of Michigan Centre, a land speculator who had been involved with the "wildcat"

Jackson County Bank, was Leoni Township supervisor, owned 500 acres of land, and in all was probably the richest and most successful man in the vicinity. Fitch took up the fight of those he believed were wronged by what he thought was an uncaring, money-driven monopoly owned by greedy eastern capitalists. In Fitch's home, and in the tavern run by his brother-in-law Ammi Filley, residents aired grievances and formulated plans that would gain the rightful redress that the heartless railroad denied. Supported by ample alcoholic encouragement, "the boys" forayed into the night to stone trains, shoot at them, set fire to wood piles used for locomotive fuel, place logs and iron bars across the rails, and change switches to derail trains. Brooks slowed his trains to a crawl and put up a $500 reward for any perpetrator, but no one was arrested.

In the spring of 1850 the campaign against the railroad resumed. A moral tone was added to all the grievances: the railroad was a monopoly that set its rates unfairly against Jackson County shippers. The whole contretemps was overblown into "the great railroad conspiracy." Businessmen from Jackson agitated to get the Michigan Southern branch from Tecumseh completed, which would provide them a second rail outlet. But nothing worked for the conspirators. That summer Brooks took new steps to protect his railroad. He hired Darius Clark, a Marshall businessman, a quiet unlikely sort, to take on the job of finding out the culprits and bringing them to trial. Clark hired several men as undercover agents, and they successfully infiltrated Fitch's network. Working carefully Clark began accumulating evidence, reporting it directly to Brooks. Brooks and Joy finally were satisfied that they had enough to take the case to court, although Clark still urged caution. Events came to a head on 19 November when the MC freight house in Detroit was burned. Arson was suspected. Clark eventually learned that George Gay, who ran a Detroit brothel, had been hired by Fitch to set the fire and that another man had been given an "incendiary match" to burn the Niles depot. Fitch already knew that the railroad had penetrated "his boys," but that did not stop his boasting about the fire at Detroit. Joy got warrants against Fitch and forty-three others. On 19 April 1851 one train left Niles and another left Detroit, and by midnight the deputies had gathered up most of the gang. The next morning, after an all-night train ride, Fitch and the others were paraded through the streets of Detroit en route to jail.

The trial began on 14 May with William H. Seward, a leading New York attorney (who as Andrew Johnson's secretary of state bought Alaska in 1866) heading a smallish team for the defense, with eight attorneys led by Joy for the prosecution, and presided over by Judge Benjamin F. H. Witherell. The trial lasted over four months, until 25 September, with much of the testimony centered on the credibility of witnesses for both sides. None of the accused was able to provide the relatively high bail before or during the trial. Fitch died in a hospital on 24 August after contracting dysentery in jail, and another defendant also died in jail. The jury deliberated for nine hours and returned a verdict of guilty against twelve of "the boys" and a not guilty verdict against the other twenty. One of the twelve found guilty died while in prison, while all the others were pardoned by 1855. Although the railroad can be said to have won the trial, it also caused a good deal of public ill will against the company.

The new owners of the Michigan Southern lacked one advantage that the rival Michigan Central had. Money! They soon found out what others before and after learned—that it is exceptionally difficult to raise money to build a railroad. The tracks and equipment of the Southern were, if possible, in worse condition than the Central's. Soon after the purchase, some New York State money, most likely through Elisha Litchfield's influence, began trickling into the company, accompanied by his aggressive brothers, Edwin C. and Electus. Teunis VanBrunt, a relative of the Litchfields, and Jacob Ten Eyck bought into the company, with VanBrunt becoming the new president. The Michigan Southern's competitor into Adrian, the Erie & Kalamazoo, after only a few years fell on hard financial times of its own. After several chaotic years with no one seeming to manage anything, Washington Hunt and railroad executive George Bliss Jr. bought the E&K in 1848 for $60,000. They changed its gauge from four feet ten inches (the Ohio gauge) to standard gauge of four feet eight-and-a-half inches, cleaned up the balance sheet, reduced its debt, and put it up for sale. In August 1849 they leased it to the Southern, in perpetuity, for a very profitable $30,000 per year. As part of the deal, and very likely because of the new money he and some of his friends were willing to bring to the company, Bliss joined the board of directors and soon after became president of the Michigan Southern. Bliss had solid railroad credentials that took him from the early construction days of the Western Railroad of Massachusetts to its presidency. Bliss saw more promise in Toledo than Monroe as a Lake Erie port, and by 1850 had several steamboats sailing under the Southern's flag between Buffalo and Toledo, and not long after completely dropped those to Monroe.

Bliss also saw potential in the growing city of Chicago and believed

George Bliss Jr.

Born 16 November 1793, Springfield, Mass.; died 19 April 1873, Springfield, Mass.

After Bliss graduated from Yale University he set up a law practice, and over the years became active in state politics. He was elected state representative and state senator for a number of terms, and sat on the governor's council. He began his railroad career in 1836 as general agent on the Western Railroad of Massachusetts, and by 1842 worked his way up to be its president. In 1848 he and his partner, Washington Hunt, bought the bankrupt Erie & Kalamazoo Railroad at distress-sale prices, tidied up the road, and were able to lease it in perpetuity to the Michigan Southern under very favorable terms.

Apparently because of the money he and some of his friends could bring to the Michigan Southern, he became president of that road in August 1849. One of his first acts was to make Chicago rather than Lake Michigan the road's western goal. In May 1852 he completed the western extension that made his road into an important route between Lake Erie at Toledo and Chicago, and then retired from the presidency. Conditions at the Michigan Southern and its successor, the Michigan Southern & Northern Indiana, grew progressively worse, so much so that Bliss was called back to the presidency in 1858. By then the road's affairs were in such disarray that even Bliss's genius could not repair the damage. He resigned again in 1860, ending his active involvement in railroad management.

the Southern should build there. In May 1849 he persuaded the Michigan Southern board to authorize extending the road from Hillsdale to Chicago. The board met with the board of the Buffalo & Mississippi Railroad, a company that held rights to build across northern Indiana, to work out some sort of agreement. In November 1849 the Michigan Southern created the Northern Indiana to build a line across Indiana, and then bought the rights of the B&M . The Northern Indiana announced it would build from LaPorte east toward Michigan to connect with the Southern. At the same time the B&M was preparing to build a line between Michigan City and Illinois.

During its short life the Michigan Southern had to go back to the Michigan legislature several times to get extensions of its payment schedule and its anticipated construction deadlines, most of these caused by a chronic lack of funds. In 1849 it got an extension of the final payment date to 1854 as well as a further delay building its line to Lake Michigan. Soon afterward it got an extension to complete its branch between Tecumseh and Jackson. In 1850 again it was allowed more time, but this time an impatient legislature forced it to accept new specifications for the location of its line west of Hillsdale. The money that Bliss brought with him did allow the Southern to start construction in the spring of 1850. By September contractor Ransom Gardner had jogged a line north from Hillsdale and built the four miles into Jonesville. There it curved west, and building began in earnest. By December the line was completed to Coldwater, to Sturgis in March 1851, and to White Pigeon in July.

Once into White Pigeon Bliss had to deal with what the legislature had forced on him. The Michigan Southern's much-amended charter now stipulated that the line be built to the St. Joseph River at Constantine before it could cross the state line into Indiana. Bliss was certain he detected the hand of the Michigan Central's James F. Joy in this hindrance, and tried to figure out a way to get around the mandated detour. South Bend railroad booster Thomas S. Stanfield provided Bliss with the solution. If Bliss would build a direct line between White Pigeon and the Indiana state line at Vistula for Stanfield to own privately, he would allow the Southern to use it. Bliss jumped at the offer, built the short piece, and on 4 October 1851 the locomotive *John Stryker*, named after one of the Southern's directors, puffed into South Bend with the first train from the East. The Michigan Southern was now in business between Toledo and South Bend, and it was an important step closer to Chicago.

The Michigan Central at New Buffalo continued content to wait for a friendly Chicago connection to build out to it. William Butler Ogden, businessman, speculator, first mayor of Chicago, and founder of Chicago's first railroad, then owned the B&M and was interested in some sort of deal. In 1848 Joy and Brooks got the Michigan legislature to allow the MC to help other companies that were building to Chicago. This appears to have been an attempt to allow the Central to assist Ogden's B&M well before Bliss bought that road in November 1849. The MC apparently also made a deal with the B&M to use its rights to build an extension from New Buffalo to Michigan City, Indiana. Construction began in late 1849 and the MC ran its first train into Michigan City on 29 October 1850, although it continued its steamship connections from New Buffalo.

Forbes felt his relationship with Ogden's Buffalo & Mississippi was good enough that the Central could rely on the B&M for access to Chicago. When the Michigan Southern bought the B&M's rights, that approach fell apart. With its friendly connection now owned by its arch competitor, Forbes was forced to agree that the Central had to build its own line to Chicago. Joy headed to Indianapolis to persuade the Indiana legislature to give the MC the needed charter rights, but he came away empty-handed thanks to Bliss's Northern Indiana lobbyists. James Brooks, president of the New Albany & Salem and no relation to the Central's John Brooks, sought out Joy to try for a deal of his own. His New Albany had built thirty-five miles of line in southern Indiana but needed a lot more money to complete its hoped-for line all the way to Michigan City. The New Albany had rights to build almost anywhere it wanted in Indiana, and this was just what Joy needed. The two struck a deal, with the MC giving the New Albany some $500,000 in financial aid, and in exchange it used the New Albany's rights and name to begin to start building a line from Michigan City to the Illinois state line. Bliss got wind of the deal and got an injunction against the New Albany road arrangement; he sued to force observance of his charter, and in fact sued for any other reason he could think up. Joy countered with his own suits charging that MC rights were violated by the Southern building within five miles of the Central and tried to get the Michigan legislature to revoke the Southern's charter. No attempt to stop the other was too frivolous, but in the end all of the maneuvering by both of them accomplished nothing.

Bliss worked as ferociously to get his Northern Indiana built as Brooks and Joy did their Michigan Central. To thwart the Central Bliss used the B&M charter to start building a line from Michigan City west to Illinois, apparently in 1851. It hugged the shore of Lake Michigan through the sand dunes and beaches of the barren country. Brooks went farther inland as he pushed the Central's line from Michigan City to Illinois.

By the end of 1851 both roads were nearing the Illinois state line. For some reason the city fathers of Chicago were certain in their knowledge that both Michigan railroads planned to bypass their city completely and instead head west and southwest over connecting rail lines. To build in Illinois Bliss already had formed a subsidiary, the Northern Indiana & Chicago. Forbes had no similar rights for his road, and when Joy went to the Illinois legislature he came away with nothing, thanks again to Bliss's lobbying efforts.

When the Northern Indiana was ready to start building in Illinois, Bliss found that much of the land he needed was already owned by the Chicago & Rock Island Railroad, a line that was just starting to build from Chicago to the Mississippi River. The Rock Island's president, Joseph Sheffield, had been a construction contractor for Bliss on part of the Northern Indiana. Bliss proposed the two roads build a joint line into Chicago, and Sheffield agreed. On 20 February 1852 the Southern ran its first train into Chicago to a temporary station on Twenty-Second Street, just outside the Chicago city limits. By January 1852 bliss had extended his main line from South Bend to LaPorte, Indiana, and had completed the B&M from Michigan City into Illinois. This left a gap in the main line between LaPorte and Michigan City. Passengers had to use stagecoaches to get from one train to the other. Bliss continued to push main-line construction between LaPorte and Baileytown. That gap was closed, and trains began running through from Toledo to the Twenty-Second Street station on 22 May. The next year the Rock Island and the Michigan Southern began building a new permanent station at LaSalle and Van Buren Streets in downtown Chicago, a site that is still one of Chicago's railroad stations.

The Michigan Central still lacked rights to build in Illinois. Through the efforts of David A. Neal, a director of the Illinois Central Railroad and an incorporator of the Michigan Central, the IC was willing to provide a route for the MC. In exchange it asked the MC to help it out with money it needed desperately to build its own line. Chicago's city fathers were driving a hard bargain before allowing the IC into the city. The prospect of locomotive smoke interfering with the citizenry's serene view of Lake Michigan aroused civic ire. To assuage the upset citizens, the city demanded the IC build along the waterfront and put in substantial breakwaters to keep Lake Michigan out of the city streets. MC money picked up a share of the cost for this work, and in return the MC received running rights over the IC from Kensington into Chicago.

All that remained now was a few miles of line from the Indiana state line to the Illinois Central tracks. Brooks and Joy tried to persuade Forbes to build the piece in the hope they could get everything legalized later. After several months Forbes realized that there was no other alternative to be found, and authorized the construction. The MC made its connection with the IC at Kensington and began operating trains from Detroit to the IC station on Thirteenth Street on 21 May 1852. In April 1856 the IC and MC completed a new and much larger station at Lake Street. The New Albany & Salem, thanks to MC money, completed its line from the Ohio River into Michigan City in 1854 and began operating a through train between Chicago, Michigan City, and Lafayette, Indiana, which made connections with trains to Indianapolis and Cincinnati.

Once into Chicago both the Michigan Central and the Michigan Southern worked to improve their connections to the East. Both roads already owned and chartered steamships that ran from Buffalo to their respective eastern terminals, Detroit and Toledo, and both roads

Michigan Central Rail Road Company's
STEAMER MAY FLOWER,
In connection with the
STEAMERS ATLANTIC AND OCEAN,
MICHIGAN CENTRAL RAIL ROAD LINE BETWEEN BUFFALO AND DETROIT AND PORTS ON LAKE MICHIGAN.
The above Boats are built expressly for this Line and are not excelled for speed and accommodations by any Line in America
Time: From Buffalo to Detroit 16 hours, Buffalo to Chicago 35 hours, to Milwaukee 45 hours.

continued to expand their fleets. Both roads sent out traffic solicitors, who cut rates and gave rebates and cash to induce shippers to abandon the other road. Each company complained about the other's tactics but never stopped its own agents. In the long run what each road gained was at the expense of the other. The agents of both lines were more skilled at cutting rates than they were at adding to their employers' profits.

Both roads knew that the Lake Erie ship connection to the East was inadequate, and the amount of traffic handled after completion to Chicago proved it. To make it worse, when the lakes were closed to shipping in the winter, the ships were of no value. A rail line across southern Ontario had been talked about during the 1840s, and late in that decade the Great Western Railway was formed to build from the Niagara River to the Detroit River. James F. Joy and Henry N. Walker visited Toronto and Niagara Falls with Great Western and New York Central officials in an attempt to build up financial support. Not much money was forthcoming, so the Great Western turned to England, and the British appear to have been more supportive. Construction began in October 1849 at London, Ontario. The start of any building brought

Until rail connections to the East were built, both the Michigan Southern and the Michigan Central had steamships on Lake Erie to reach Buffalo and eastern railroads. The Michigan Central's *May Flower*, with its sister ships *Atlantic* and *Ocean*, steamed along the north shore. The Southern's *Northern Indiana*, *Southern Michigan*, and *Empire State* sailed along the south shore into Toledo, and called at ports along the way. Both roads dropped all of their Lake Erie ships by 1856.

May Flower: The Mariner's Museum, Newport News, Va.

out more American money, enough to ensure completion of the road. John W. Brooks and Erastus Corning joined the Great Western's board of directors. The line was completed between Niagara Falls and Windsor by Christmas 1853, and regular service began on 17 January 1854. Detroit celebrated its first rail connection to the East as much as any community in Ontario. The MC instituted a ferry service across the Detroit River, although the difference in Canadian and U.S. track gauges still required that freight cars be unloaded at the border, then reloaded into cars of the other gauge. The first suspension bridge near Niagara Falls was completed in March 1855, replacing a ferry service and improving the direct rail connection with the East.

On the south shore of Lake Erie, in the early 1850s a through rail line was not even being talked about. Two lines were building slowly between Cleveland and Toledo, another east from Cleveland, one out of Erie in the state of Pennsylvania, and one west from Buffalo. End to end these could be assembled into a line between Toledo and Buffalo, except that each went ahead quite independently of the others. The state required the road in Pennsylvania to be built with a different track gauge. Eventually they built up to each other's lines, and then they did begin to work together more closely. The Cleveland, Ashtabula & Painesville began calling itself the "Lake Shore Road," a name that eventually was used for all of the roads on the between Buffalo and Toledo. By January 1853 it was possible to get from Buffalo to Toledo, using four different rail lines. Riders had to change trains several times, and there was no coordination of schedules, but it was possible. At Toledo, travelers transferred to the Michigan Southern for a train ride straight through to Chicago.

When the Great Western was completed in 1854 the Michigan Central dropped its Lake Erie sailing ships in favor of the faster year-round rail service across Ontario. When the lines along the south shore finally assembled themselves into a feasible through route in 1856, the Michigan Southern discontinued its Lake Erie fleet.

The Detroit & Pontiac was out of money by the time it reached Pontiac in 1843. The railroad's bank closed, and both of its promoters were bankrupt. Alfred Williams stayed on, and the road kept running. With Sherman Stevens's departure from the company, its corporate records become murky and still more incomplete. There were several reorganizations and attempts to get money to pay on its debts, none of which succeeded. In 1843 Henry N. Walker, who later became Michigan's attorney general, joined the Pontiac road's board of directors. Walker came with railroad experience going back to the first days of the internal improvements program.

In 1848 Alfred Williams, Gurdon O. Williams, Horace C. Thurber, and several other Detroiters incorporated the Oakland & Ottawa Rail Road to build a line from Pontiac, via Fenton, to Lake Michigan in Ottawa County. In 1849 Walker and several of the same men bought complete control of the Detroit & Pontiac, and in 1850 the legislature authorized a connection between the two companies. Walker must have believed that the completion of the Great Western, despite its close ties with the Michigan Central, would also benefit his new purchase. In 1852 Walker once again started up construction, but money was in such short supply that very little got done. He made a trip to England in 1852 and another in 1855 in an effort to sell bonds, but had only moderate success. In 1855 he merged the Oakland & Ottawa and the Detroit & Pontiac into a new company named the Detroit & Milwaukee, a name that gave evidence of its owners' ambitious goals. Walker managed to continue to push construction so that on 2 October 1855 the line was completed from Pontiac to Fenton, the next July to Owosso; by 14 January 1857 it was running to St. Johns and by 12 August to Ionia. There the company ran out of money completely, and Walker went back to his friends at the Great Western.

The Great Western's president, Charles J. Brydges, with his road newly completed from Niagara Falls to Windsor and using the Michigan Central to reach Chicago, was interested in gaining another western connection at Detroit, and if he controlled it, all the better. Only twenty-nine years old, Brydges was both ambitious and visionary, and saw the potential in a deal with the Detroit & Milwaukee. With it he could extend his railroads far into the American Midwest. He arranged a loan to the D&M, and in exchange the Great Western took control of that road. On 2 July 1858 the D&M locomotive *Empire* steamed into Grand Rapids, and by 22 November its line was complete to the Lake Michigan shore at Grand Haven. Michigan now had a third railroad line crossing the state, and Canadian and British money got it built.

SOURCES

Dunbar, Willis F. *All Aboard! A History of Railroads in Michigan*. Grand Rapids, Mich.: W. B. Eerdmans, 1969.

Farmer, Silas. *History of Detroit and Wayne County and Early Michigan*. 3rd ed. Detroit: Silas Farmer, 1890. Reprint, Detroit: Gale Research, 1969.

Fuller, George N. *Michigan: A Centennial History*. 2 vols Chicago: Lewis Publishing, 1939.

Harlow, Alvin F. *The Road of the Century*. New York: Creative Age Press, 1947.

Hirschfield, Charles. "The Great Railroad Conspiracy." *Michigan History* 36:2 (June 1952).

Meints, Graydon M. "Race to Chicago." *Railroad History* No. 183 (Autumn 2000).

Parks, Robert J. *Democracy's Railroads*. Port Washington, N.Y.: Kennikat, 1972.

Pearson, Henry G. *An American Railroad Builder: John Murray Forbes*. New York: Houghton Mifflin, 1911.

Trap, Paul. "The Detroit and Pontiac Railroad." *Railroad History* No. 168 (Spring 1993).

Wing, Walcott E. *History of Monroe County*. New York: Munsell, 1890.

The Railroads Come of Age, 1855–1875

A New Success

By the middle of the nineteenth century the railroad was no longer a source of wonder or even a novelty. As more people rode trains, the railroad entered the flow of usual American life. This could not have been otherwise since no other form of land conveyance provided such speed, convenience, and affordability. There was no other technology on the horizon that matched it. Nor was it any longer so much a pioneering business. Railroads began to develop standardized methods of operations and types of equipment and, most important, had created an ideal method of financing. The design of trackwork and the mechanics of steam locomotives were no longer objects of experimentation. The basic design of rolling stock for passengers and freight was settled. Samuel F. B. Morse's new telegraph was used first in intercity communications and was being applied to direct the movement of trains. Other technological advances were to come in the future, but the basic structures and designs were in place. New styles of corporate management were introduced, and new stock- and debt-financing techniques became common and were found valuable. By 1855 three railroads were built west into Chicago. The Pennsylvania Railroad was built from Philadelphia to Pittsburgh, and the Baltimore & Ohio was in operation to Wheeling, West Virginia. Tracks reached nearly every major city east of the Mississippi River.

Twenty-five years of experience had shown that the most critical need in building a railroad was finding and luring in outside capital. The successful companies located needed financing, with most of it coming from New England and New York City, but often only after local capital had started but failed to complete the project. The promoters came to rely much more heavily on debt financing, which allowed them to reserve stock ownership partly to themselves and partly to use as an incentive gift to financiers. The panic of 1854 brought a modest slowdown in economic activity that was short-lived, but the ensuing panic of 1857 was the most severe in twenty years. This panic began with the failure of the Ohio Life Insurance & Trust Company in August 1857, and grew into a financial panic with an international reach. The earlier stimuli that followed the victory in the Mexican War in 1846 and the discovery of gold in California in 1849, and accompanied by an increasing population and westward expansion that came afterward, proved to be a frail defense against the financial stampede.

The panic of 1857 caused a temporary slowdown in the enthusiasm for building railroads. Local banks began to demand the return of their deposits from New York City banks. To meet this demand the major banks began to call in and cancel loans, some of which had been made to stock market speculators. This led to a sharp drop in the prices of stocks generally, with railroads not at all exempt. In just months deposits at New York City banks dropped by a third, and loans went down by a quarter. Against this somber economic backdrop Michigan continued to grow. The state's population rose from 507,000 in 1854 to 749,000 in 1860, a 50 percent increase.

SOURCES

Cochrane, Thomas C., and William Miller. *The Age of Enterprise*. Rev. ed. New York: Harper & Row,. 1961.

Morison, Samuel Eliot. *The Oxford History of the American People*. New York: Oxford University Press, 1965.

Land Grants to the Rescue

When the state sold its two railroads in late 1846 only 271 miles of railroad line operated in Michigan. The Michigan Central extended from Detroit to Kalamazoo, the Michigan Southern's main line extended from Monroe to Hillsdale and a branch ran from Lenawee Junction to Tecumseh, the Erie & Kalamazoo's line ran from Toledo to Adrian, and the Detroit & Pontiac's line ran between those points. Both the Michigan Central and the Michigan Southern had a legal requirement to finish building west to Lake Michigan. The pioneer road, the Erie & Kalamazoo, had charter authority to build farther west but was in no financial condition to do any more.

Money, of course, was the problem. Both the MC and the MS

UPPER PENINSULA LAND GRANTS

—— Existing railroads, 1857

—— Land grants, 1857

LAKE SUPERIOR

KEWEENAW

HOUGHTON

KEWEENAW BAY

LAKE SUPERIOR

ONTONAGON

BARAGA

WHITEFISH BAY

GOGEBIC

MARQUETTE

ALGER

LUCE

CHIPPEWA

IRON

SCHOOLCRAFT

DICKINSON

DELTA

MACKINAC

TO MACKINAC COUNTY

MENOMINEE

GREEN BAY

TO LEELANAU COUNTY

TO CHARLEVOIX COUNTY

GRAND TRAVERSE BAY

EMMET

CHEBOYGAN

LAKE

CHARLEVOIX

PRESQUE ISLE

LEELANAU

ANTRIM

OTSEGO

MONTMORENCY

ALPENA

BENZIE

GRAND TRAVERSE

KALKASKA

CRAWFORD

OSCODA

ALCONA

LAKE MICHIGAN

MANISTEE

WEXFORD

MISSAUKEE

ROSCOMMON

OGEMAW

IOSCO

MASON

LAKE

OSCEOLA

CLARE

GLADWIN

ARENAC

SAGINAW BAY

HURON

LAKE HURON

OCEANA

NEWAYGO

MECOSTA

ISABELLA

MIDLAND

BAY

TUSCOLA

SANILAC

MUSKEGON

MONTCALM

GRATIOT

SAGINAW

LOWER PENINSULA LAND GRANTS

—— Existing railroads, 1857

—— Land grants, 1857

- - - Additional grant, 1864

· · · · · Additional grant, 1871

OTTAWA

KENT

IONIA

CLINTON

SHIAWASSEE

GENESEE

LAPEER

SAINT CLAIR

ALLEGAN

BARRY

EATON

INGHAM

LIVINGSTON

OAKLAND

MACOMB

LAKE ST. CLAIR

VAN BUREN

KALAMAZOO

CALHOUN

JACKSON

WASHTENAW

WAYNE

CANADA

BERRIEN

CASS

ST. JOSEPH

BRANCH

HILLSDALE

LENAWEE

MONROE

LAKE ERIE

INDIANA

OHIO

Two Michigan maps of land grants
made to railroads, 1857-71.

had to finish paying the state for their roads and also had to face the substantial costs of overhauling and upgrading tracks to meet the terms of their state charters. Both needed more locomotives and cars to handle their increasing traffic. Both would need even larger sums to begin construction to extend their lines.

The Michigan Central had a somewhat easier time of it. Using John Murray Forbes's connections in Boston and New Bedford, it managed to raise enough money to meet its needs. Forbes complained about having to spend so much time raising money, but he was able to get the MC built to Chicago in May 1852. The Michigan Southern had a far more difficult time of it. Ownership passed completely out of Michigan to men from New York State, and even with their circle of friends it appears to have been a challenge to have money enough to meet all the bills as well as make the required payments to the state. Both companies also owned and chartered ships on Lake Erie to provide critically needed eastern connections to Buffalo for more traffic. The newly formed Oakland & Ottawa sent Henry N. Walker to Great Britain in an attempt to raise financing for construction west of Pontiac. Between 1846 and 1854 nearly all the railroad construction in Michigan was done by the Michigan Central and the Michigan Southern in building their extensions to Chicago. The poorer roads had a much harder time of it.

Two men from Illinois changed this. In 1847 Stephen A. Douglas, the "Little Giant," was elected U.S. senator, and Abraham Lincoln was elected to the House of Representatives. Both men were strong supporters of the Illinois Central Railroad, but it was going nowhere for a lack of money. In December 1847 Douglas spoke out to support his idea of a grant of land to aid a railroad that would connect the "Upper and Lower Mississippi Rivers with the chain of lakes at Chicago." Lincoln agreed. But this sort of aid, or any sort of aid, had been difficult to get ever since the 1830 controversy when President Jackson vetoed assistance for the Maysville Road. Douglas thought that times had changed and that Congress might now pass some sort of local aid bill. First he worked out differences with Sidney Breese, the other Illinois senator, who wanted support only for a local line from Cairo to Galena, Illinois. Douglas retained Breese's line while keeping a branch he wanted to Chicago. Next he dealt with the objections of senators from the East and the South. These were colored by the sectional disputes between North and South and had to be smoothed enough to allow Douglas to get the land grants through the Senate. The interplay of abolition and slavery, the new Republican Party, states' rights, and much more are complexities that are discussed better in other works. To get his measure passed Douglas gave easterners a compromise on some tariff issues that were of no importance to midwesterners. For the southerners, he put in William R. King's pet project, the Mobile & Ohio Railroad, giving it land grants in Alabama and Mississippi. All of this horse-trading paid off when, on 3 May 1850, Douglas's proposal passed the Senate. On 17 September it passed the House, and Millard Fillmore, newly installed as president after the death of Zachary Taylor, signed the bill three days later.

The basic pattern of the land grant was for the federal government to convey to the state alternate mile-square sections of land extending for six miles out from both sides of the railroad line. If the land had already been sold, the railroad could other pick sections of land as much as fifteen miles from its line. The unsold land that was not granted to the railroads was increased in price from $1.25 to $2.50 per acre, very neatly offsetting any potential loss of federal revenue. The bill left it to the state legislatures to decide which railroads would receive the grants. To ensure performance, a railroad could get title to the grant land only in twenty-mile segments as sections of its line were built.

This grant provided just the boost that the Illinois Central needed. Construction started quickly. Supplemented with financial help from the Michigan Central, the IC put into service its first fourteen miles of road between Chicago and Kensington in May 1852, and by August finished it as far as Kankakee. The following July it built into Carbondale, and in January 1855 the IC completed the line between Chicago and Cairo.

Seeing the speedy construction of the Illinois Central that followed the passage of Douglas's land-grant legislation, other states submitted a legion of requests for grants of their own. They assured Congress that the lure of free land would encourage railroads to build, and the presence of a railroad would bring settlers. Once built, these railroads would connect with other lines to provide an outlet for commerce and be a source of prosperity. Even President Franklin Pierce could no longer hold to his views and continue to lean against the gale of this demand. During 1856 and 1857 Congress granted nearly 20,000,000 acres of federal land in eight states to promote 4,649 miles of line for forty-five different railroad projects. One-quarter of this subsidized mileage was in Michigan, and 3,775,000 acres of land were transferred to the state for the subsidy. The bill that Congress passed and that President Pierce signed on 3 July 1856 was not at all what the Michigan railroads had hoped for. First, Congress made the grants of land directly to the state rather than to any railroad company. Second, Congress identified only general routes and did not name any eligible company. Third, twenty miles of rail line had to be completed and ready for operation before the company was entitled to its initial grant of 120 sections of land, and additional twenty-mile segments had to be completed to be eligible for more. Fourth, any corporation's capital stock had to be paid for in full by its owner, not just subscribed to with a down payment. None of these was an impossible obstacle; they simply brought forth different tactics.

Congress named six routes in Michigan. In the Upper Peninsula grants were designated for lines from Little Bay de Noquet in the vicinity of Escanaba to Marquette and then to Ontonagon, and from both Marquette and Ontonagon to the Wisconsin state line. Lower Peninsula routes were to be from Amboy (township) via Hillsdale and Lansing to some point on or near Little Traverse Bay, from Grand Rapids to the same point, and from both Grand Haven and Pere Marquette (now Ludington) to Flint and then to Port Huron. Each of the routes, with the partial exception of the Port Huron–Grand Rapids–Flint–Grand Haven line, reached into remote, largely uninhabited territory. The Marquette range by then had the beginnings of an iron-mining industry, but most of the Upper Peninsula and the northern Lower Peninsula remained covered by thick forest.

At the time, only a few companies were in business that could take advantage of the land grants. The prospect of grants of free land brought out more than a dozen new companies. In the Upper Peninsula the first of five companies into the scramble was the Ontonagon & State Line, formed by mostly men from Ontonagon who were joined by Chicago pioneer William Butler Ogden. Next came the Iron Mountain & Wisconsin State Line that Heman B. and George H. Ely and Lewis H. Morgan promoted to build from Little Bay de Noquet to Marquette. The Bay de Noquet & Marquette, formed by Samuel P., George H. and John F. Ely, along with Lewis H. Morgan and John, Wells, and Austin Burt, was to build over that same route from the Marquette iron range. Morgan and the Elys already controlled the Iron Mountain Railroad that was then being built from Marquette to the iron mines near Ishpeming and Negaunee. The Iron Mountain's line was completed in August 1857, the first steam railroad in the Upper Peninsula. The same men also formed the Marquette & State Line to go after another grant. The Marquette & Ontonagon was the only candidate formed to go for

William Butler Ogden

Born 5 June 1805, Walton, N.Y.; died 3 August 1877, Chicago.

Ogden began operating a sawmill at age fourteen due to his father's poor health. At age thirty his brother-in-law, Charles Butler, persuaded him to move to Chicago to plat and sell some land he owned. Ogden took one look at the primitive village of 1,500 and knew he had found his life in the new community. He became an enthusiastic booster of Chicago, was elected its first mayor in 1837 when it was incorporated, started buying up land for himself while he sold off Butler's lots, and all the while involved himself in any sort of project that would develop the town. He became a strong supporter of the Illinois & Michigan Canal to link Chicago to the Mississippi River. In 1845 Ogden picked up the ten-year-old unused franchise of the Galena & Chicago Union Railroad. Seeing the volume of grain, produce, and livestock moving over bad roads into Chicago, he knew it would increase even more if better transportation was provided. He managed to raise enough money locally to start building the road, and in October 1848 the first train traveled the nine miles from Chicago to Oak Park. He left the Galena in 1851 but kept his zest for railroads.

One effort Ogden made to extend the Galena came in 1847, when he bought the franchise for the Buffalo & Mississippi, a road that was planned from Chicago to Goshen, Indiana. He thought this would provide an ideal entry for the Michigan Central to get into Chicago. The MC declined to buy, and Ogden eventually sold it to the competing Michigan Southern. Then he involved himself with a line into Wisconsin to tap his lumber holdings. In 1859 this road became the Chicago & North Western, and five years later it bought the Galena road. In 1862 he was one of the organizers of the Peninsula Railroad, which built a line between Negaunee and Escanaba to haul iron ore to Lake Michigan. The line soon was added to the Chicago & North Western.

Ogden retired from railroading in 1868 to manage his many other businesses, particularly his Wisconsin lumbering operations. He died after a short illness.

the land grant between its named terminals. Later in 1856 Congress added to the bonanza by granting four additional sections of land per mile for three of the Upper Peninsula land-grant routes but left out the Ontonagon-Wisconsin state line route. Lewis H. Morgan and the Elys did quite well for two of their companies.

In the Lower Peninsula two companies were formed that went after the Amboy–Lansing–Traverse Bay land grant, the Amboy & Traverse Bay, which was formed by a group from Jackson, and the Amboy, Lansing & Traverse Bay, which was organized by men most of whom were from Owosso. To help themselves the two companies put as many influential politicians on their boards of directors as they could find. Three companies went after the Grand Rapids–Traverse Bay grant. The Grand Rapids & Northern was a Grand Rapids creation headed by

William A. Richmond and Daniel Ball. The Grand Rapids, Traverse Bay & Mackinac had mostly Kalamazoo and southern Michigan men behind it, as well as some support initially from the Grand Rapids & Indiana Railroad. At the last minute the GR&I's promoters formed their own candidate, the Grand Rapids & Mackinaw.

Three existing companies competed for the Port Huron–Flint–Grand Haven land grant. The Port Huron & Lake Michigan was an ambitious cross-state project that had very little money. The second was the Detroit & Milwaukee, then under active construction from Detroit through Owosso and Grand Rapids to Grand Haven. The other was the Port Huron & Milwaukee, which was proposed from Port Huron to Owosso and there to connect with the Detroit & Milwaukee. Thanks to Canada's Great Western Railway the D&M had enough financing to get built nearly into Ionia by the time the land grants were awarded. The Flint-Ludington land grant attracted two companies, the Lake Superior Railroad that was formed by Pontiac businessmen and which proposed to build from Pontiac to Ludington, and the Flint-based Flint & Pere Marquette, which planned to build from Flint to Ludington.

The lobbying was furiously intense. When the legislature met in January 1857 it could not even decide how to dispose of the land grants, much less which of the clamoring competitors should have them. Soon after, and nearly a year after Congress had made the grants, the lawmakers made up their minds, deciding how to award the grants and setting up a board of control to manage the program. The Upper Peninsula grants went to the Bay de Noquet & Marquette, the Marquette & Ontonagon, the Marquette & State Line, and the Ontonagon & State Line. In the Lower Peninsula the Port Huron–Grand Haven grant went to the Port Huron & Milwaukee and the Detroit & Milwaukee, the one to Ludington to the Flint & Pere Marquette. By this time the Grand Rapids & Indiana had absorbed its Grand Rapids & Mackinaw subsidiary and received a grant as well. The legislators chose the Amboy, Lansing & Traverse Bay for the grant through the center of the state.

Congress supplemented the Grand Rapids & Indiana's grant in 1864 by adding grant lands for its proposed line between Fort Wayne, Indiana, and Grand Rapids, although with some restrictions on the land available in Indiana. In 1866 Congress allowed the Flint & Pere Marquette to pick a destination on Lake Michigan rather than requiring Ludington as the western terminus, but the road eventually did build to Ludington anyway. In 1871 the grant made to the Amboy, Lansing & Traverse Bay, which by that time had been bought by the Jackson,

Between 1862 and 1874 the Flint & Pere Marquette grew from just a short line out of Saginaw to Flint into a road that extended from Monroe to Ludington.

Lansing & Saginaw, was modified to allow the Straits of Mackinac as the northern terminus.

By 1879 a total of just over 3,100,000 acres of land, equaling nearly 4,900 square miles, had been transferred to Michigan railroad companies. Most of the lines named by the grant legislation had been built. The railroads had not claimed about 700,000 acres, and Congress transferred this land to the state without restrictions.

Was the land-grant program worth its cost? The answer is a qualified yes. The program has often been characterized as a giveaway, but it was far from that. The federal government received 50 percent reductions in freight and passenger rates over land-grant lines, while the mail was carried at 80 percent of the rate paid on other railroad routes. These lower rates finally ended in 1945, after giving nearly ninety years of benefit to the government. Most important of all, most of the lines on the grant routes did get built. They extended into largely unsettled areas with no traffic base and long before there was any economic justification for them. Many Lower Peninsula lines eventually did become lumber haulers, so long as that boom lasted. Several of the Upper Peninsula roads developed into important iron ore haulers after mining developed. It is impossible today to set a precise dollar value on the value of land grants versus the reductions in charges and increased salability of adjoining government land. On balance, it appears that the federal government did get sufficient reductions in charges to offset the income it might have received from the sale of the lands to the public. Access to a rail line did help sell the government's remaining land. The state and municipalities certainly benefited from the increases in the value of land and from the property taxes received. The railroads had difficulty disposing of some of the grant land, some of which stayed on the books for years, and very likely did not receive as much as they had hoped for when the grants were first made.

SOURCES

Bliss, A. N. "Federal Land Grants for Internal Improvements in the State of
    Michigan." *Michigan Pioneer & Historical Collections* 7 (1886). Lansing, Mich.:
    Thorp & Godfrey, 1886.

Corliss, Carlton J. *Main Line of Mid-America*. New York: Creative Age Press, 1950.

Donaldson, Thomas. *The Public Domain: Its History, with Statistics*. Washington,
    D.C.: Government Printing Office, 1884.

Dunbar, Willis F. *All Aboard! A History of Railroads in Michigan*. Grand Rapids,
    Mich.: W. B. Eerdmans, 1969.

Michigan Railroad Commission. *Aids, Gifts, Grants and Donations to Railroads . . .*
    Lansing, Mich.: Wynkoop, Hallenbeck, Crawford, 1919.

A New Constitution and New Railroad Law

During the late 1840s several of the states around Michigan called constitutional conventions and wrote new state constitutions. In November 1849 Michigan's voters, imbued with the spirit of President Andrew Jackson and the "Jacksonian Democracy" he inspired, called for a similar convention by a nine-to-one margin to reconsider the 1835 constitution. Some voters thought that temperance measures were too weak, others that women and blacks were entitled to the vote, some that more office holders should be elected rather than appointed. Many believed that the legislature and its actions should be reined in and brought under firmer voter control. The convention met for nearly a year; the voters handily approved the final product.

There were two important new provisions affecting railroads. One provision barred any state involvement in internal improvement projects by stating, "The State shall not be a party to or interested in any work of internal improvements, nor engage in carrying on any such work, except in the expenditure of grants to the State of land or other property." The final outcome of the 1837 internal improvement program left a very bitter aftertaste with the voters, and left Michigan with a tarnished reputation for its refusal to honor some of the internal improvement debt. The drafters attempted to close the barn door on the whole matter. That the voters had vigorously demanded these improvements earlier in the 1830s did not keep later voters from blaming the legislature for the final result. This bitterness showed through in a paper given in 1875 by Dr. Oliver C. Comstock of Marshall to the Pioneer and Historical Society of Michigan. Thirty years after the events he remarked that, following the sale of the Central and Southern lines, "Nothing but the debris of our air castles remain, and they only to plague our recollections." The precise language in the constitution did leave the door slightly ajar. Through this gap the state allowed itself to use grants of land to assist the Detroit, Mackinac & Marquette in building its line in the Upper Peninsula in the 1870s.

A second provision said the state could no longer "subscribe to, or be interested in, the stock of any company, association, or corporation." The voters had grown skeptical of the legislature's ability to control what it created and in this way attempted to keep legislators from giving special benefits to their friends. Legislators were prohibited from writing special acts of incorporation to form privately owned businesses. In part this came from a wish to prevent a reoccurrence of the abuses associated with "wildcat" banking. But there was also a fear of the advantages of "railroad monopolies," a charge that was at times leveled at the Michigan Central as part of the "Great Railroad Conspiracy," and a feeling that lawmakers had in the past and might again confer some special advantage on some favored company. The new constitution applied this blanket prohibition to all forms of incorporations. Because of this well-intentioned proviso promoters of railroads or any sort of company no longer could have an attorney draw up favorable articles of

James Frederick Joy

Born 2 December 1810, Durham, N.H.; died 24 September 1896, Detroit.

After Joy graduated from Dartmouth College at the head of his class, he attended Harvard Law School. At age twenty-five he moved to Detroit in 1836 to join with George F. Porter in a very successful practice. He agitated in the state legislature for the sale of the state's internal improvement railroads, and then guided the legislation leading to their sale to the Michigan Southern and the Michigan Central. He was an important participant in forming the latter company in 1846.

From 1846 on he was the Michigan Central's attorney, lobbyist, and director, and served as president of the road from 1867 to 1877. He arranged money to build several important feeder lines that became subsidiaries of the MC and later were merged into it. Once the MC was completed into Chicago in 1852, he and his MC associates invested in and developed lines west of Chicago that were the nucleus of the Chicago, Burlington & Quincy. He managed the construction of several important parts of the Burlington road and its subsidiaries between 1853 and 1871 and was president and director of a number of these companies during that time. John Murray Forbes forced Joy from the Burlington road's presidency in 1875 after a disagreement about Joy's financial dealings. Joy left the MC when William Henry Vanderbilt gained control of the road in 1877.

Joy was a principal in the company that built the St. Marys River locks and canal at Sault Ste. Marie in 1855. As the MC president, he strengthened his road by helping a number of connecting lines raise construction money, then leased them to the MC when they were completed. He was president of both the Chicago & West Michigan (New Buffalo–Holland–Grand Rapids and Holland-Muskegon-Pentwater) from 1870 to 1876 and the Detroit, Lansing & Lake Michigan (Detroit–Lansing–Ionia–Howard City) from 1874 to 1879. He advanced the construction of both companies by his ability to raise money. In 1879 Jay Gould gained control of the Wabash Railroad. He and Joy joined forces to build a Wabash line into Detroit. Recognizing Joy's talents, Gould made him president of the Wabash, St. Louis & Pacific from 1884 to 1887, during which time he worked at an unsuccessful reorganization of the road.

Throughout his life Joy was active in politics, first as a Whig and later was one of the founders of the Republican Party at Jackson; he served one term as a state representative, and for many years was an important influence in the Republican Party at the state level. He married twice, and had seven children. His son, Henry B. Joy, became president of the Packard Motor Company.

incorporation, locate a willing legislator to introduce the bill, and once passed start up the company. But the framers of the new constitution did not anticipate the explosion in the number of new corporations that would be formed or needed in the coming decades.

Problems arose quickly. Pressing economic activity soon began to demand new mining, banking, and railroad companies, but no legal means existed to form them. In 1851 the legislature solved part of the problem by passing general incorporation laws for mining, toll bridge, telegraph, and plank road companies. A law for manufacturing corporations finally was passed in 1853. A similar law for railroads drew strong objections from the Michigan Central's James F. Joy. The MC, with its charter and its commanding railroad line, saw no need to allow potential competitors into its territory. Several other attempts were drafted in the next five years and were passed by at least one house of the legislature, but through Joy's formidable influence no bill reached the governor's desk. That John Stryker, the Michigan Southern's lobbyist, favored a bill was not enough to persuade the legislature to act.

In 1855 Michigan's new Republican Party, founded a year earlier "under the oaks" in Jackson, took control of both houses of the state legislature, and Republican Kinsley S. Bingham gained the governor's chair. Despite continued aggressive lobbying by the Michigan Central, the two houses of the legislature passed a railroad incorporation bill that Bingham signed on 12 February. During the four years before its passage Joy had been able to argue and lobby for enough changes in the bill that there was little in it that the Central opposed strongly. The statute allowed mergers between companies to form trunk lines, and placed no restrictions on capitalization, debt, or pooling arrangements with other railroads. The new law provided that twenty-five or more stockholders could file articles of incorporation with the secretary of state after they had subscribed to company stock at the rate of at least $1,000 per mile and paid cash for at least 5 percent of their subscribed stock. This payment could be in cash or some other asset of equivalent value. Construction could begin when at least $8,000 of stock per mile of road (on roads that used T-rails) had been sold. Railroads had the right to buy, acquire by gift, or obtain by condemnation any land they needed for a right-of-way. The legislature retained some control over the rates the railroad charged. All companies had to equip their locomotives with a bell and a steam whistle to be used when approaching every road crossing, had to erect warning signs at each crossing, had to fence the right-of-way, and had to provide cattle guards where needed. A tax of 1 percent on the capital stock was levied in lieu of all other state and local taxes. Employees working on passenger trains and in stations were required "to wear upon his hat or cap a badge, which shall indicate his office, and the initial letters of the style of the corporation." Railroad companies were forbidden to hire employees who "use intoxicating drinks as a beverage."

With the railroad incorporation law came passage of another that provided for "the construction of train railways." This provided a much simpler corporate structure with fewer stipulations and was designed specifically for roads used in connection with mining and lumbering operations. The legislature also passed a similar incorporation law for street railways, which anticipated rail lines that would be operated on city streets. The first train and street railways were not formed until 1863.

The first company formed under the new railroad incorporation law was the Ely brothers' Iron Mountain Rail Road on 15 February 1855. It was to build from Marquette to the west line of Ely Township in Marquette County to tap several iron mines. The second company incorporated was the Detroit, Monroe & Toledo on 6 March, which planned to build between its namesake cities. The third was the Iron Mountain Railway on 10 March, which proposed to build a line between Marquette and the iron mines owned by the Jackson Mining Company.

SOURCES

Comstock, Oliver C. "Internal Improvements." *Michigan Pioneer and Historical Collections* 1 (1875).

Dunbar, Willis F. *All Aboard! A History of Railroads in Michigan.* Grand Rapids, Mich.: W. B. Eerdmans, 1969.

Elliott, Frank N. *When the Railroad Was King.* Lansing: Michigan Historical Commission, 1966.

Fuller, George N. *Michigan: A Centennial History.* 2 vols. Chicago: Lewis Publishing, 1939.

McClintock, William R., Jr. "Early Railroad Regulation in Michigan: 1850–1863." Ph.D. diss., University of Wyoming, 1976.

Michigan Legislature. *Acts of the Legislature, 1855,* Nos. 82, 148.

Seavoy, Ronald E. "Borrowed Laws to Speed Development: Michigan, 1835–1863." *Michigan History* 59:1–2 (Spring–Summer 1975).

Utley, Henry M., and Byron M. Cutcheon. *Michigan as a Province, Territory and State* . . . New York: Publishing Society of Michigan, 1906.

Building the Detroit & Milwaukee

In 1848 the state legislature granted a charter to the Oakland and Ottawa Rail Road Company authorizing it to build a line from Pontiac, via Fentonville, to Lake Michigan in Ottawa County. Among its promoters from Pontiac and Detroit were Horace C. Thurber of Pontiac and Alfred

L. Williams, who owned the Detroit & Pontiac Railroad. The next year Thurber and Williams, joined by Dean Richmond and Henry N. Walker, purchased the Detroit & Pontiac. Richmond, a resident of Buffalo, was involved in New York state politics and from the early years also in its railroads. He worked himself up to the presidency of the New York Central in 1864. Walker served as Michigan's attorney general from 1845 to 1847, and also worked with James F. Joy and John W. Brooks to raise money to build the Great Western Railway in Canada. When, in 1851, they were able to persuade Erastus Corning of Albany to become involved, the Great Western became a reality.

In 1848 the legislature authorized the Detroit & Pontiac to connect with the Oakland & Ottawa and the next year authorized it to issue mortgage bonds up to $2,500,000. By 1852, when the O&O was ready to start building, it still had not raised much of the needed money. Walker went to England in an attempt to sell the company's bonds and made a second, more successful trip in 1855. Construction finally started, and the line finished to Fenton in 1855 and to Owosso in 1856. The O&O and the D&P merged in 1855 to form a new company with much more ambitious name, the Detroit & Milwaukee.

By the time the Detroit & Milwaukee reached Ionia, in 1857, it was again out of money. Walker, now president, went to see his friend Charles J. Brydges, of the Great Western Railway. Brydges, then only twenty-nine years old, was a young and energetic man full of ambition to make the Great Western into an important carrier. Adding a completed D&M would give him a railroad that extended from Niagara Falls to Lake Michigan. It is possible that Brydges dreamed of much more. He appears to have had some involvement with a line in Wisconsin that was to build across the state to the Mississippi River. He even talked of controlling a line that extended as far as Saskatchewan. In November 1857 Brydges agreed to loan Walker's D&M the funds it needed, took a mortgage on the line as security, and with that gained control of the company.

With the Great Western's money the D&M pushed into Grand Rapids and was opened for business on 4 July 1858, the first rail line to Grand Rapids. On 22 November it completed its line into Grand Haven and by building along its north bank avoided having to build an expensive bridge across the Grand River. Opposite the village the railroad built an impressive two-story depot, part of which served as a hotel. A ferry brought passengers and freight across the river into the village. Soon after, it began handling traffic to and from Lake Michigan

Charles J. Brydges was the guiding genius behind the growth of the Great Western Railway of Canada between 1853 and 1862. To fulfill his dream of a railroad that would extend from Ontario into the American Midwest, he arranged for the money that allowed the Detroit & Milwaukee to complete its line from Detroit to Grand Haven.

American Phrenological Journal, August 1866.

ships. Throughout its life the Detroit & Milwaukee rarely showed a profit, and for Brydges's Great Western, it proved to be more of a burden than an asset.

SOURCES

Currie, A. W. *The Grand Trunk Railroad of Canada*. Toronto: University of Toronto Press, 1957.

Dunbar, Willis F. *All Aboard! A History of Railroads in Michigan*. Grand Rapids, Mich.: W. B. Eerdmans, 1969.

Percival, John J. "Railroads in Ottawa County." *Michigan Pioneer & Historical Collections* 9 (1886). Lansing, Mich.: Thorp & Godfrey, 1886.

Stevens, G. R. *Canadian National Railways: Sixty Years of Trial and Error, 1836–1896*. 2 vols. Toronto: Clark, Irwin, 1960, 1962.

Growth and Panic

The panic of 1854 caused some slowdown in economic activity, some relief from the national euphoria that had been building up for the ten years since 1844. Railroads were capturing the public's imagination and were being built in every direction. The completion of the Michigan Central and the Michigan Southern to Chicago in 1852 brought new revenues to these two roads. The land-grant law of 1850 provided still more stimulus. All of these new railroads needed capital, and lots of it. As railroad stocks became a popular and more widely held form of investment, they also created new methods of speculation. Players, both inside and outside of the companies, found they could shade things a little and make substantial profits for themselves. Several years of relatively good times began to bring on the inevitable abuses. The president of the New York & New Haven Railroad issued $2 million of unauthorized stock in his own company. The Harlem Railroad issued $300,000 of forged stock. The Vermont Central's president put out 10,000 shares of his company's stock and pocketed the money.

When these railroad frauds, and others by other companies, were discovered, the market reacted dramatically. Money for stocks, but particularly railroad stocks, suddenly became hard to find. Share prices dropped sharply. But the bear market did not last, and within months the ebullience returned.

In early 1855 a group of Detroit, Monroe, and Toledo men formed the Detroit, Monroe & Toledo. One of the founders was Zachariah Chandler, who served one term as mayor of Detroit and would develop into an important voice in national Republican Party politics. Building began from a connection with the Detroit & Milwaukee north of Ferry Street in Detroit, made a U-turn, and headed south. By the end of the year the line was open as far as Monroe, and in July 1856 the road was completed into Toledo. There it connected with the Michigan Southern to Chicago and with the Wabash that was building to St. Louis. The Southern's owners considered the line's good connections in Toledo, and leased the road in perpetuity in 1856. The Detroit line provided more traffic that fed to the Michigan Southern to haul the rest of the way to Chicago and to the lines between Buffalo and Toledo that were beginning to work together.

Although the panic of 1854 evaporated quickly, some of its effects remained. Railroad stock prices fluctuated sharply, but over several years their trend was down. Interest rates remained high, even as the speculators boomed ahead. Railroad construction continued to demand large amounts of the nation's capital. That need went unmet, partly because of a lack of dividends on the stock and partly because the Crimean War in Europe shut off most money from that source. Bonds developed into a more important vehicle than capital stock for raising money. The bonds offered better security than the stocks, usually by a mortgage on the rail line itself. The road paid the interest on bonds if at all possible. In a bankruptcy or reorganization bondholders had rights ahead of stockowners. Dividends to the owners had to wait.

Investors and citizens grew a bit worried, then more concerned, developed the jitters, and finally decided to seek the safety of cash. The ensuing panic of 1857 was the most severe in twenty years. In August 1857 the Ohio Life Insurance & Trust Company had to sell its railroad stocks to meet its depositors' demands. The snowball began to roll downhill, gathering momentum as one bank after another failed. The early stimulus that followed the victory in the Mexican War in 1846 and the discovery of gold in California in 1849, and accompanied by the increasing population and westward expansion that came afterward, proved to be a frail defense against the financial stampede. The country soon fell into the worst depression since 1837. European countries were in no better shape. Money was not only expensive but came to be nearly impossible to find.

Two pieces of railroads were built in Michigan in the three years between the two panics. The Michigan Southern & Northern Indiana, which was the result of the April 1855 merger of the Michigan Southern and the Northern Indiana, was obligated by the Southern's 1846 charter to build a branch to Jackson within three years. This political requirement was a nuisance that the road tried to put off, but which did not go away. With the Michigan Central already built into Jackson, there was little appeal in competing for the traffic from that one city. Jacksonites, on the other hand, were eager to have a second line to break what was considered the MC's monopoly on traffic. In 1849 the legislature gave the Southern three more years. In 1850 the legislature got even tougher and forced the company to begin construction on its main line, but that left the company with no money for work on the Jackson Branch. In 1855 the Southern finally extended the branch as far as Manchester. With help from the citizenry, who went out and worked in the field, it completed the branch to Jackson in July 1857.

The Amboy, Lansing & Traverse Bay Railroad first saw life in January 1857. A group of Owosso businessmen formed the company to go after one of the state's land grants. The road's president, Alfred L. Williams, led the lobbying effort in Lansing to get the land grant for his road. Having Amos Gould and Alvin N. Hart as directors did not harm the effort. Gould was an Owosso lawyer and land speculator and had served a term in the state senate. Lansing resident Hart had served in the first state house back in 1835 and several terms as senator as well, and had been involved with railroads since their earliest days in Michigan. The Amboy, Lansing & Traverse Bay line was so meandering that the road soon was called the "Ramshorn." It was so well known by that name that its caustic nickname, "Awfully Long and Terribly Bumpy," never got much use.

In early 1857 it beat out the Jackson-created Amboy & Traverse Bay for the prized land grant. With this and a bit of cash in hand, and probably prodded by some political influence, the company began construction in the spring of 1858 from Owosso, where it connected with the newly built Detroit & Milwaukee, toward Lansing. During the year it was completed into Laingsburg and into Bath the next year. From wherever the end of the line was, passengers boarded a stagecoach to complete their journey to Lansing. The road finally reached Grand River Avenue in North Lansing in 1861. By that time it had built the requisite twenty miles of road and was the first company to apply for part of its land grant.

The Civil War and a continuous shortage of funds made the Ramshorn into a "poor relations" kind of railroad. Its first locomotive was a diminutive cast-off that had been used in constructing the Detroit & Milwaukee. Its employees built the road's freight cars and completed its only passenger car. David Gould was the line's general manager and superintendent, and he also ran one of the locomotives. The Ramshorn had so much difficulty completing its last mile of road from North Lansing into Lansing that in April 1862 the *State Republican* urged residents to go out and help with grading the line. The Civil War had so depleted manpower and the availability of supplies that it took more than a year, in August 1863, to finish the road to Michigan Avenue in Lansing and become the first rail line to reach the state's new capital.

Getting to Lansing forced the company to decide whether to build south to Jackson or north to Saginaw and Bay City. As an incentive the legislature authorized the city of Saginaw to issue $40,000 in bonds to aid in the construction of the Ramshorn to that city. Also in 1863 the legislature authorized the city of Jackson and townships in Jackson County to issue bonds to assist any railroad to build between Jackson and Lansing. Unfortunately this aid more likely would go to help the newly formed Lansing & Jackson rather than the Ramshorn. In the end the Ramshorn may have done a little grading south of Lansing toward Eaton Rapids, but it did considerably more grading for its line between Owosso and Saginaw. When the money ran out in 1864 the company stopped all work and soon slid into receivership. The Jackson, Lansing & Saginaw, formed in February 1865, bought all the Ramshorn's franchise rights north of Lansing in October 1866, including the larger part of its land grant. The JL&S promptly amended its corporate articles to allow it to build first to Little Traverse Bay and then to the Straits of Mackinac. The legislature modified the land grant to fit the change. The JL&S bought the Ramshorn line between Owosso and Lansing, and the grading north of Owosso, when the road was sold at foreclosure early in 1867.

Only one railroad was built immediately after the panic of 1857, the Chicago, Detroit & Canada Grand Trunk Junction. It was built by the Grand Trunk Railway of Canada, partly in an effort to meet the competitive threat that came from the Great Western's completion into Windsor in January 1854, and partly to fulfill its own broader goal of reaching the American Midwest. The GW had through traffic arrangements for freight and passengers as the eastern connection of the friendly Michigan Central. The Grand Trunk built a line to Port Edward, opposite Port Huron, and had no connections to the west. The solution was a line from Fort Gratiot, just north of Port Huron, to

Detroit. The Grand Trunk was an established company financed almost entirely by the British, and it was somewhat easier for it to raise the needed capital than it was for its American counterparts. The line was built quickly and completed in November 1859. Its south terminus was West Detroit, where it connected with the Michigan Central for points west, and also a connection with the recently built Detroit, Monroe & Toledo. The Grand Trunk made its own agreement with the Michigan Central and also gained access to Chicago.

Thomas Alva Edison became the Grand Trunk's most famous employee. Not long after the road began operations the twelve-year-old was selling snacks on the morning train to Detroit and on the afternoon train back. As business improved he hired other boys to work on the road's other trains. In 1863 he saved the son of the Mt. Clemens's telegraph operator from being struck by a train, and in gratitude the operator agreed to teach young Edison telegraphy. Edison also began publishing the *Grand Trunk Weekly Herald* newspaper in the baggage car of the train. His publishing efforts were cut short when some chemicals spilled, burst into flames, and set fire to the car. At Smiths Creek the conductor threw the printing press and the chemicals off the train, then followed them with Edison himself.

SOURCES

Cochrane, Thomas C., and William Miller. *The Age of Enterprise*. Rev. ed. New York: Harper & Row, 1961.

Dunbar, Willis F. *All Aboard! A History of Railroads in Michigan*. Grand Rapids, Mich.: W. B. Eerdmans, 1969.

Ellis, Franklin. *History of Shiawassee and Clinton Counties*. Philadelphia: D. W. Ensign, 1880.

Gould, Lucius E. "The Passing of the Old Town." *Michigan Pioneer & Historical Collections* 30 (1906). Lansing, Mich.: Wynkoop, Hallenbeck, Crawford, 1906.

Harlow, Alvin F. *The Road of the Century*. New York: Creative Age, 1947.

Michigan Railroad Commission. *Aids, Gifts, Grants and Donations to Railroads . . .* Lansing, Mich.: Wynkoop, Hallenbeck, Crawford, 1919.

Iron Mines and Iron Rails

The Upper Peninsula and Isle Royale were a gift by the federal government in 1836 in an attempt to soothe the feelings of Michigan politicians over the loss of Toledo to Ohio. Trader Alexander Henry had heard of copper there as early as 1763. Still earlier, American Indians had used it for tools and weapons. State geologist Douglass Houghton's 1841 report to the legislature about copper started a full-scale copper boom in 1845.

In September 1844, while surveying near Teal Lake near Ishpeming, William A. Burt saw his compass go wild. He sent out his crew to determine the reason, and they found outcrops of iron ore. When Burt's findings were published the next year it touched off another rush of fortune seekers. In July 1845 Philo M. Everett and a dozen other residents of Jackson formed the Jackson Mining Company. As a group they knew little or nothing about mining, which minerals to mine, or where the minerals were located. But Everett and several others started off immediately, and by using train, stagecoach, wagon, canoe, and boat they got from Jackson to Marquette in twenty-one days. With the help of Chippewa chief Marji-Gesick, Everett was able to find the Teal Lake iron ore deposit.

In 1846 Jackson Mining Company president Abram V. Berry was back at the site and sent some of the ore to a Branch County ironmaker. The ore produced superb-quality iron, and the Jackson Mine was in business. The company shipped in material to build the Carp River forge. Using charcoal for fuel, it soon began producing iron. The finished product, in blooms two feet long and four inches square, was hauled to the waterfront in Marquette and shipped out. Abram's only problem was that the operation lost money.

In 1846 a Cleveland, Ohio, group formed the Cleveland Mining Company and set up operations on "Cleveland Mountain," not far from the Jackson Mine. Two of its founders, Samuel L. Mather and Morgan L. Hewitt, became important mine owners as the industry grew. The next year Robert Graveraet, another mining pioneer, formed the Marquette Mining Company and tried taking over the Cleveland location by squatting on it. Graveraet had the stamina of several men and the ambition of a good many more, but his maneuver ultimately failed. He did interest Waterman A. Fisher of Worcester, Massachusetts, in iron mining, and with Fisher's backing Graveraet built an iron forge on the Lake Superior shore at what is now Marquette. Graveraet originally named the place Worcester after Fisher's home, but the missionary's name soon replaced it. It took herculean effort to haul wagonloads of iron ore down the twelve miles of trail from the Jackson and Cleveland Mines to Marquette. As a result Fisher lost $120 on every ton of iron that was made at the forge. But Graveraet did have the good fortune to hire a young lad named Peter White to work for him, and White became the founder of the city of Marquette. Later on Graveraet established the Lake Superior Mine southwest of Ishpeming.

Early on it became obvious that forging iron near the mine was not a profitable method of operation. Labor was difficult to keep, and charcoal was the only fuel available to produce sufficient heat to produce iron, and it also was expensive. Despite every effort no forge ever made money for its owners. The only reasonable alternative was to ship the ore down lake to the mills where it was to be used. This required hauling the ore from the mine to a ship at Marquette, piling it on the open deck, unloading it at Sault Ste. Marie to be hauled around the rapids, then reloading it for final leg by ship. Ships that could carry ore on the open waters were relatively small.

The first locks at Sault Ste. Marie were built in 1797, but they could not handle anything much larger than a voyageur's canoe. In 1837 Governor Mason included a locks on the St. Marys River in his internal improvement program, but the contractor ran afoul of the commandant at Fort Brady. Bills were introduced in Congress several times for a grant of federal land to aid in constructing the locks, but each came to nothing. The production of both iron ore and copper grew in quantity, large enough to demand improved shipping. In August 1852 Congress authorized a grant of 750,000 acres of land to the state and also granted a right-of-way over remaining federal land as assistance to build the locks. In Michigan Charles T. Harvey, a salesman for the Fairbanks Scale Company, saw a grand opportunity. He went to Detroit to interest James F. Joy, and they formed the Saint Marys Falls Ship Canal Company in February 1853. The Fairbanks brothers, August Belmont, and from the Michigan Central Erastus Corning, Joy, John Murray Forbes and John W. Brooks. Harvey was the company's agent, and he presented himself as a whirling dervish in getting the canal built. Much of getting the actual construction done fell to the engineering skills of John W. Brooks. But Harvey worried and badgered and cajoled the project through. The canal and locks were completed on 31 May 1855, just days short of the two-year requirement.

With the Soo locks and canal open the mine owners then had to deal with the challenge of getting iron ore from the mines to the ships as Marquette. It cost $3.00 a ton to move ore from Marquette to the Lake Erie ports, and another $5.00 to move it the first dozen miles from the mines to Marquette. At first the ore was hauled by wagon down steep trails and dangerous narrow pathways. Next they tried stockpiling it

Heman B. Ely

Born 15 March 1815, Rochester, N.Y.; died 14 October 1856, Marquette.

Ely was the son of judge Elisha Ely, the 1833 founder of Allegan. First he practiced law, then in 1849 he became a contractor constructing telegraph lines. By 1850 he had moved to Cleveland and was named the first president of the Cleveland, Painesville & Ashtabula, the central link in the line of roads between Buffalo and Toledo. In 1852, after completing the CP&A, he moved to Marquette to survey a railroad line that would connect Lake Superior with the iron mines near Negaunee and Ishpeming. He also was a contractor in building the ship canal and locks at Sault Ste. Marie.

After those locks were completed in 1855 he returned to Marquette and his railroad project. As a member of the state legislature, he promoted passage of the general railroad incorporation bill. This done, with his brothers George H. and Samuel P. he organized the twenty-five-mile Iron Mountain Rail Road in February 1855 to connect the Marquette Range iron mines with Lake Superior at Marquette. Soon after he began building a line that many said could not be built. His untimely death came before the railroad's completion in August 1857, and it fell to his brothers to finish this first part of the Duluth, South Shore & Atlantic.

at the mine and, come winter and with the ground frozen, sledding it to Marquette, an equally daring undertaking, assuming the teamsters could be persuaded to the work in the winter.

Mine owner Heman B. Ely had built a railroad in Ohio a few years earlier, and he knew that a railroad would be a better way to move the ore. He had been talking up his idea since 1851. The obstacles to be overcome were a lack of money and, without a general railroad incorporation law, a legal way to start up a company. The mine owners met this stalemate by building a plank road. It took two years to construct, and it was not opened to the Jackson and Cleveland Mines until the fall of 1855. Using the plank road presented its own unique perils. A wagon's brakes did not always hold on the steep downgrades, and often the result was expensive mules being crushed or killed. The wagon wheels damaged the plank road so quickly that the owners put wooden rails on the road and nailed a strip of iron on top. This improvement increased the tonnage that could be hauled and increased the accident rate as well.

Ely did not give up. He had worked on the construction of the Soo canal and built up some capital of his own for a railroad. In February 1855 Ely, with his brothers Samuel P. and George H., and with Lewis H. Morgan, formed the Iron Mountain Rail Road. Heman Ely died in

ABOVE: An 1861 view of the first ore dock
built at Marquette by a railroad to transfer
iron ore from railcars to lake ships.
Built in 1855, the increasing volume of
ore soon forced its replacement with a
substantially larger one.

Ralph D. Williams, *The Honorable Peter White* (Cleveland, 1907),
173.

RIGHT: The *Yankee*. Many claim this was
the first steam locomotive to be built
specifically for use in iron mines. This
one worked at the Jackson Mine, near
Negaunee, from 1868 to 1895.

Sam Breck collection.

October 1856 before the railroad was completed, and it fell to his brother
Samuel to finish it. Construction was completed from Marquette to the
Jackson, Cleveland, and Lake Superior Mines in August 1857, and the line
formally opened in September. A dozen tons of ore was a day's traffic
on the plank road; Ely's railroad brought down 1,200 tons daily. The
Cleveland company built a 400-foot dock at Marquette in June 1859 and

could load four ships at one time. Iron ore tonnage quintupled between 1858 and 1860, and lake shipping costs dropped by a third to $2.07 a ton. The cost of moving ore from the mine to Marquette dropped even more dramatically, from $5.00 to 87 cents per ton.

SOURCES

Boyum, Burton H. *The Saga of Iron Mining in Michigan's Upper Peninsula*. Marquette, Mich.: John M. Longyear, 1983.

Dunbar, Willis F. *Michigan: A History of the Wolverine State*. Grand Rapids, Mich.: W. B. Eerdmans, 1970.

Hatcher, Harlan. *A Century of Iron and Men*. Indianapolis: Bobbs-Merrill, 1950.

Williams, Ralph D. *The Honorable Peter White*. Cleveland: Penton, 1907.

The Civil War and the Railroads

The Civil War came home to Michigan when President Abraham Lincoln asked the states to furnish 75,000 men for ninety-days duty to "suppress" the rebellion. Michigan's share was one regiment of ten companies, about 1,000 men. This modest number came forward quickly in southeastern Michigan; the Detroit Light Guard, Jackson Greys, Coldwater Cadets, Burr Oak Guard, Ypsilanti Light Guard, and Manchester Union Guard were among those mustered into service. A month and a day after the firing on Fort Sumter the unit left Detroit by ship for Cleveland. From Cleveland they went to Washington by train, probably the first such ride for many of the volunteers.

By war's end, four years later, some 90,000 Michigan men had joined the Union army. Many of them traveled by train to Detroit, then moved by ship to Cleveland and on by train to Washington. Those assigned to the western armies most often went by train to Chicago, down the Illinois Central to Cairo, and then by ship to their units. These 90,000 were nearly 25 percent of Michigan's 1860 male population. Farming was most affected since Michigan was still a largely agricultural state. With the husbands gone it fell to wives, children, and the elderly to keep the farms going. The railroads made it easier to ship their produce to market. The war caused higher prices that increased the income of farm families and made it possible to buy more sophisticated farm machinery—mowers, reapers, threshers, and better plows—that were sorely needed to keep the farms going. Inside the home the homemaker

got some relief from her demanding tedious duties with the introduction of sewing and washing machines.

Railroad construction in Michigan came almost to a halt. With one
exception only bits and pieces of a few lines were built between 1861
and 1865. Thankfully, the ravages and sabotage that were inflicted on
the Baltimore & Ohio and railroads in the South never took place in
Michigan. Recognizing their importance to the war effort, the government exempted locomotive enginemen from the military draft that
applied to most other male citizens.

The war brought boom times to the Upper Peninsula. There were
large increases in the demand for both iron and copper. Mining was
not only crucial to the war effort, but it also became quite profitable.
The price of copper rose from 17.0 to 46.3 cents a pound, and iron
ore prices also jumped. The increased demand and the sharply rising
profits resulted in an acute labor shortage. Mine workers were drafted
into the military or simply walked away to volunteer. In an effort to
keep up production, companies increased wages, but the cost of living
rose faster. Congress passed a law that encouraged mine workers to
immigrate and went so far as to exempt them from the draft. The mine
owners sent out recruiters to attract workers, often to the Scandinavian
countries, but in the end these efforts did not accomplish much.
Once here many of these new workers walked away from their new
jobs and enlisted in the military, possibly to get the federal and state
bounties offered.

During the Civil War Chicago developed into an important iron-
manufacturing center. The route to ship iron ore from Marquette
through the Straits of Mackinac to reach Lake Michigan was roundabout at best. To avoid this the owners of the Chicago & North Western
formed the Peninsula Railroad in February 1862. The new road was
built from the mines at Negaunee and Ishpeming to haul iron ore to
ships at Escanaba. Work started promptly, but shortages of labor and
materials slowed completion. The Peninsula built a dock at Escanaba
to handle its construction supplies and then added a second dock to
load Marquette range iron ore onto ships. The line finally opened for
business in September 1864 and was merged into its owner the next
month.

In 1863, while building was under way, the Chicago & North
Western amended the Peninsula's articles to provide for an ambitious
expansion program. These new rights extended the main line south to
the Wisconsin state line and west from Ishpeming to Ontonagon, and

authorized a branch to Marquette and another branch to Portage Lake in Houghton County. During the Civil War, and immediately after it, the Chicago & North Western did build a few spurs and branches to new iron mines in the Ishpeming and Negaunee area, but with one exception none of the ambitious projects was ever completed.

During the war both the Michigan Central and the Michigan Southern increased their freight traffic, particularly in grain and livestock shipped from Chicago. But this business was heavily eastward and resulted in trains of empty cars moving west. The MC was further handicapped by the government prohibition on troop movements across Canada; southern Ontario was considered so much a home for Confederate sympathizers that the United States required passports for through travelers.

A railroad extending to the Pacific coast was a dream that found increasing support in the decade before the Civil War. Southern congressmen vigorously opposed any route except one that ran through the Southern states. Secession removed that obstruction. In the 1860 election campaign the Republican Party platform and candidate Abraham Lincoln both supported the Pacific railroad. Illinois senator Stephen Douglas boosted the central route idea and said the line should start at Chicago. On 1 July 1862 President Lincoln signed the Pacific Railway Bill. Two companies were named to build the line, the Union Pacific from Council Bluffs, Iowa, on the Missouri River westward, and the Central Pacific eastward from Sacramento, California. The CP had been organized in 1861, and the UP came to life in the fall of 1863. Ground was broken at Omaha, Nebraska, on 2 December, but little work was done before 1866. That year the now-infamous Crédit Mobilier of America was formed to be the UP's construction contractor. Its owners lined their pockets handsomely and in the process did build the Union Pacific. The four owners of the CP used Crocker and Company as a similar tool. On 10 May 1869 the Pacific railroad was proclaimed completed at a "golden spike" ceremony at Promontory Point, Utah. On 4 July 1864 Congress granted a charter for the Northern Pacific, a second transcontinental rail line from Lake Superior to some port in the Pacific Northwest. Construction did not start on this line until well after the end of the Civil War.

The Civil War worked horrific social damage. The loss of life and the maimed bodies were a legacy not soon overcome. Old animosities rankled, and Reconstruction added more of them, an effect that has taken generations to quiet. For the railroads, the war brought positive results. It brought new prosperity and new procedures. New techniques were developed for track and bridge construction. The telegraph was adapted to facilitate the movement of trains. A new level of cooperation between connecting railroads developed, encouraged by more uniformity in track gauge between companies. The war promoted and then speeded up the changeover from iron to more durable steel rails, and started the development of larger locomotives that used coal instead of wood as fuel. In short, American railroads came of age so that at the war's end they were ready to move into a new and far more prosperous era.

President Ulysses S. Grant's administration, which began in March 1869, mirrored an attitude toward business that many Americans of the time accepted: erect few obstacles and enjoy the benefits. Michigan's newest industry, lumbering, came into its own after the Civil War, and grew by leaps and bounds as eastern timber played out. The great Chicago fire of October 1871 opened a market bonanza for Michigan loggers as Chicago grew to become the most important distributor of their lumber. The burst of railroad construction in the ten years after the end of the Civil War was astounding. East of the Mississippi River a network of lines developed almost overnight that provided an ease and economy of travel that no society in history had ever seen. Michigan's rail mileage doubled from 462 in 1855 to 931 in 1865, then exploded to 3,347 by the end of 1875. Old companies expanded and new ones were created to take part in this railroad boom. Construction went on everywhere in Michigan in the ten years after the war. For the sake of clarity it is easiest to present this explosive growth by describing each company separately.

SOURCES

Blum, Albert A., and Dan Georgakas. *Michigan Labor and the Civil War*. Lansing: Michigan Civil War Centennial Observance Commission, 1964.

Fuller, George N. *Michigan: A Centennial History*. 2 vols. Chicago: Lewis Publishing, 1939.

Marks, Joseph J. *Effects of the Civil War on Michigan Farming*. Lansing: Michigan Civil War Centennial Observance Committee, 1965.

Stover, John F. *American Railroads*. Chicago: University of Chicago Press, 1961.

Weber, Thomas. *The Northern Railroads in the Civil War, 1861–1865*. New York: King's Crown Press, 1952. Reprint, Bloomington: Indiana University Press, 1999.

The Railroad Boom: The Grand Rapids & Indiana

The Grand Rapids & Indiana Railroad was part of a grand scheme for two railroads that centered in Hartford City, Indiana. One was the Fort Wayne & Southern, which was to build a line from Fort Wayne, through Hartford City and Muncie, to either Jeffersonville or Louisville. The FW&S was to be a link between the Ohio River and the Wabash & Erie Canal, then being built through Fort Wayne. The GR&I was chartered on 18 January 1854 to build a line from Hartford City, and the FW&S through Warren, Huntington, Columbia City, Albion, LaGrange, and Howe, Indiana, and in Michigan through Sturgis, Centerville, and Kalamazoo to Grand Rapids. The GR&I was to be the important route to haul northern Michigan timber to the Ohio River. The line was unique in that it was planned as a north-south route through Grand Rapids and would be the first interstate road of its length in Michigan.

GR&I president Joseph Lomax moved to Sturgis and in May 1855 incorporated the Grand Rapids & Southern Railroad to build the eighty-seven-mile section between Grand Rapids and the Indiana state line south of Sturgis. The GR&S and the Indiana-organized GR&I were merged in August 1855 as the Grand Rapids & Indiana Railroad. At about this time the GR&I's southern terminus was changed from Hartford City to Fort Wayne. The Ohio & Indiana was now running into Fort Wayne from Pittsburgh, while the FW&S had not yet started construction. The first train of the O&I arrived in Fort Wayne in November 1854, and soon after that road became the middle section of the Pittsburgh, Fort Wayne & Chicago road. The PFW&C later came under the control of the Pennsylvania Railroad and became part of its New York–Chicago main line.

Shortly after the August 1855 merger, the GR&I joined the crowd of railroad companies petitioning Congress for a land grant to help build its road. In the final bill, passed in September 1850, Congress made a grant to the state of Michigan for a railroad line between Grand Rapids and a point on or near Little Traverse Bay, in the vicinity of what is now Petoskey. The law also required that the company's capital stock had to be paid for in full by the owners, not just subscribed to with a down payment. More disappointing, there was no grant for a line south of Grand Rapids.

None of these obstacles was insurmountable, and President Lomax set to work. In Lansing he found two other bidders for the grant he wanted, the Grand Rapids–based Grand Rapids & Northern and the Kalamazoo-based Grand Rapids, Traverse Bay & Mackinac. At first Lomax supported the latter company, but at the last minute decided to form his own Grand Rapids & Mackinaw to go after the grant. The draft of the bill awarding the grants named the Grand Rapids & Northern, but by the day the bill came out of the legislature the Grand Rapids & Indiana had replaced it. Lomax had more than three years to complete the first twenty miles of line by 1 December 1860, build twenty additional miles annually thereafter, and complete the line by 15 November 1864. But the GR&I had no corporate rights for a line north of Grand Rapids or any fully paid stock. Lomax solved both problems in one stroke. The stock of the new Grand Rapids & Mackinaw Railroad was recast as fully paid. In June 1857 he merged the GR&M and another Indiana road with the GR&I. Using a financial sleight of hand in the merger agreement, the stock of the consolidated company was recorded as fully paid although no cash had been received and the right to build was transferred.

Getting the land grant solved none of the GR&I's money problems. The panic of 1857 made raising money impossible. Lomax received some donations and gifts of right-of-way and depot grounds but still had no money to grade a line, much less to lay tracks and begin operations. By 1861 the other contenders tried to wrest the grant away since the GR&I had not started construction. Lomax asked the English engineer James Samuel and the American railroad expert Henry V. Poor to make a report on the prospects of the company and its land grant. The two prepared a twenty-four-page report that of course supported the company's plans. It recommended first building from Grand Rapids to Cedar Springs to take advantage of the land grant, then to build from Grand Rapids to Kalamazoo to connect with the Michigan Central for through traffic. With proper management they believed the line could be completed in two and a half years. Fate intervened as the Civil War's first major battle, Bull Run, was fought in July 1861 as the report was issued. Some small amount of work was done during the next few years, but there was little cash to accomplish very much. The board of directors often did not bother to meet. The land-grant law's deadlines for construction came and went and were extended by an obliging Michigan legislature. In 1864 an Indiana congressman was able to increase the GR&I's land grant to include that part of the line between Grand Rapids and Fort Wayne. Even this bonus did not provide enough spark to start construction.

At the end of the Civil War some Fort Wayne businessmen became more interested in the GR&I. They may have thought that Lomax had accomplished too little. In the spring of 1866 Lomax resigned the GR&I presidency, although the circumstances surrounding his departure are not clear. Judge Samuel Hanna replaced him, then soon fell ill and died after just three months in office. Joseph K. Edgerton, a Fort Wayne attorney and landowner, succeeded Hanna. Edgerton, like Hanna, was an early settler of Fort Wayne, and both were heavily involved in the construction of predecessor lines of the Pittsburgh, Fort Wayne & Chicago. Both also had dealings with the Pennsylvania Railroad in the mid-1850s to get financial assistance for the Fort Wayne road. In August 1867 Edgerton persuaded some of his friends in Fort Wayne and Chicago to take a contract to build the GR&I between Fort Wayne and Paris, Michigan. Mancel Talcott headed the construction company, and he agreed to advance his own money toward the project in exchange for operating the road as it was completed.

On Christmas Day, 1867, the GR&I completed the first twenty-mile section between Bridge Street in Grand Rapids and Cedar Springs. It bought two locomotives, the *Pioneer* and the *Muskegon*; two passenger cars; and a handful of freight cars to operate the road. The GR&I just met the end-of-the-year deadline and managed to hold on to its land grant.

In 1868 the company started building toward Kalamazoo. It bridged the Grand River and built south some four miles before it once again ran out of money. The GR&I had counted on $100,000 in aid promised by the city of Grand Rapids, but now the city refused to pay. The city also had authorized $100,000 to aid the Grand River Valley line that was being built from Jackson, and that road may have appeared to have better prospects. The Michigan Supreme Court upheld the city's claim and declared the GR&I bond issue to be void; it was not until 1872 that a federal court upheld the GR&I's appeal and forced the city to pay the aid money.

Throughout the appeal no more money came in, and creditors began demanding payment. Some alleged that Ransom Gardner, who was building a competing line between Kalamazoo and Grand Rapids, encouraged this. In January 1869 the GR&I agreed to a "friendly" receivership to resolve some of its financial problems. Jesse L. Williams, one of Edgerton's longtime associates from Fort Wayne, was named receiver. Williams then was doing engineering work as a government-appointed director of the Union Pacific and also served on the board of the Pittsburgh, Fort Wayne & Chicago. He went to work immediately to preserve the GR&I land grant and deal with a host of problems. The legislature's most recent extension gave him until 1 July 1869 to build

Between 1867 and 1875, after a dozen years of trying on its own, the Grand Rapids & Indiana had the Continental Improvement Company build its line from Fort Wayne, Indiana, to Petoskey, as well as a branch to Traverse City for a subsidiary company.

twenty miles of line north from Cedar Springs. Michigan's attorney general had filed suit to determine if the GR&I was solvent and entitled to keep its grant. A committee of the legislature was investigating it as well. In March 1869 the Michigan legislature passed a bill that kept the July 1869 deadline for the second twenty-mile section but did give the GR&I until the beginning of 1871 to complete the third twenty-mile section. After that the road had only to build twenty miles each year to keep its grant. The state law did not affect the congressional completion deadline of 1 January 1874.

Williams began meeting with George W. Cass, president of the Pittsburgh, Fort Wayne & Chicago, to see if he could find more help. Williams showed off the potential of the GR&I as a valuable connection for the Fort Wayne road. With a direct route between the lumbering area in northern Michigan and the markets in the East, the GR&I could furnish a considerable amount of traffic to the Fort Wayne road. Cass became interested and brought in railroad builder William Thaw and Pennsylvania Railroad vice president Thomas A. Scott. Scott was the genius behind the Pennsylvania's aggressive expansion into the Midwest, and he must have seen another opportunity.

Scott, Thaw, and Cass formed the Continental Improvement Company, brought in a few outsiders for added capital, and on 1 May 1869 signed a contract to build the GR&I. The construction deadlines of the state and Congress were written into the contract. As security Continental took $8 million in GR&I bonds that were to be issued, which were secured by a mortgage on the projected line. It also took all of the $2.8 million in GR&I common stock and the rights to about one million acres of grant land that the GR&I was eligible to get.

Continental moved quickly. It took over the work already started north of Cedar Springs and pushed it ahead at a frantic pace. In fifty-one days Continental completed the twenty miles between Cedar Springs and Morley and kept the land grant alive. Then it began working in two directions, from Morley north and from Grand Rapids south to Fort Wayne. A year later, by June 1870, the GR&I was running trains between Fort Wayne and Sturgis, in August to Kalamazoo, and in September to Grand Rapids. In August the line was extended from Morley to Paris, and on 1 October through service began from Fort Wayne to Paris.

By the end of 1871 the GR&I completed its line to Cadillac. The first survey of the road went between Lakes Mitchell and Cadillac. When GR&I director George A. Mitchell decided he wanted to extend the line to along the east shore of Lake Cadillac through the hamlet of Clam Lake, the company obliged. Mitchell thought he could pick up the GR&I's grant land for its timber. He stayed, renamed the community Cadillac, and became its most important citizen. Through his influence the town became an important sawmill center. In June 1871 the GR&I leased a southern connection, the Cincinnati, Richmond & Fort Wayne, which was being built between Richmond and Fort Wayne. The GR&I also encouraged another company in building a line between Richmond and Cincinnati.

Once Continental had started work Cass and Scott made a deal to ensure their profits. In September 1869 Cass had his Fort Wayne road agree to guarantee half of the interest on the $8 million bond issue in exchange for a majority of the GR&I common stock. The Fort Wayne also agreed to cover the personal risk of Cass and his friends at Continental. The Pennsylvania Railroad already had leased the Fort Wayne road,

Thomas A. Scott climbed through the ranks to become president of the Pennsylvania Railroad from 1874 to 1880. A hardworking and hard-driving man, he also was president of the Union Pacific for a year and promoted building the Texas & Pacific. For Michigan, he was a founder of the Continental Improvement Company, which built most of the Grand Rapids & Indiana.

Centennial History of the Pennsylvania Railroad Company (Philadelphia, 1949), facing 341.

and the next day it assigned its GR&I agreement to the Pennsylvania. This locked up the Continental's owner's profits and made the GR&I a property of the Pennsylvania.

Perry Hannah, Traverse City's most important lumberman, decided he wanted a rail connection with the GR&I. In 1870 he contacted George Cass, who had the line surveyed, and Hannah eventually contracted with Continental to build his Traverse City Railroad as well. The GR&I operated the road for Hannah and began running trains between Traverse City and Walton Junction in November 1872. GR&I rails reached Petoskey by November 1873, although the line was not opened formally until the following spring.

SOURCES

Baxter, Albert. *History of the City of Grand Rapids, Michigan*. New York: Munsell, 1891.

Burgess, George H., and Miles C. Kennedy. *Centennial History of the Pennsylvania Railroad Company, 1846–1946*. Philadelphia: Pennsylvania Railroad, 1949.

Dunbar, Willis F. *Michigan: A History of the Wolverine State*. Grand Rapids, Mich.: W. B. Eerdmans, 1970.

Johnston, Marie. "The Building of the Grand Rapids and Indiana Railroad." *Indiana Magazine of History* 41 (1945).

Peterson, William R. *The View from Courthouse Hill*. Philadelphia: Dorrance, 1972.

The Railroad Boom: The Flint & Pere Marquette

The Flint & Pere Marquette Railway was formed in Flint on 21 January 1857 to go after the land grant between Flint and the mouth of the Pere Marquette River, now the location of the city of Ludington. Even with the grant in hand the panic of 1857 made raising money difficult, and the company was forced to go back to the state legislature for extensions of time. Enough local capital finally was found to allow the company to begin some construction in 1859, but that soon ran out, and outside money was needed to keep the building going and to preserve the land grant. By 1860 the company was able to raise some construction money in New York, which was added to by Captain Eber Brock Ward of Detroit, who became the road's president. On 20 January 1862 the road ran its first train to celebrate completion of the first section. The engine *Pollywog* hauled two cars of dignitaries and celebrants from Saginaw the twenty-six miles to Mt. Morris, four hours down and five hours back. It then received its first section of its land grant, enabling it to finish the road into downtown Flint by the end of 1863. The road brought new supplies of logs into Flint's sawmills and tripled revenues as well.

Construction started up again after the end of the Civil War. By the end of 1867 tracks were laid from Saginaw into Midland and in 1868 to Averill. As each twenty miles of line was finished more grant land moved to the road's assets. By the end of 1868 the F&PM had received 307,200 acres of grant land. The railroad's land department reported it was receiving many inquiries from prospective settlers and believed its land would sell readily. William L. Webber, the company's land agent, spent the next twenty years selling this land by promoting it widely with testimonials, advertising, pamphlets, and newspaper articles. Most of the land eventually sold for an average of $5 an acre, and much of that was paid for in installments over three to five years. But the land sales provided the F&PM with a source of revenue, and the road could not have been built as quickly without it.

Each year brought another extension west. Lumber began to come down the Tittabawassee River to Sanford and the Tobacco River to Clare, providing traffic that the road hauled to Saginaw sawmills and very welcome income as well. When the line reached Evart it touched the Muskegon River, and this added a new stream of logs. Between 1863 and 1868 lumber production at Saginaw increased from 133,500,000 to 457,396,000 board feet, much of this from logs hauled in by the F&PM. Most of the towns along the line were founded as the railroad was built. Reed City was reached in 1871, and here the F&PM connected with the Grand Rapids & Indiana.

In 1864 Henry H. Crapo, a Flint lumberman, thought he had to have a rail outlet to move his lumber production more reliably to a connection with the Detroit & Milwaukee at Holly. He built the Flint & Holly between those points in November 1864. To build up more revenue Crapo and the D&M got together with the connecting F&PM to operate trains through from Saginaw to Detroit. In 1868 the F&PM bought the Flint & Holly and obtained direct access to a valuable rail outlet.

The city of Monroe was the major impetus behind the Holly, Wayne & Monroe. The city's leaders thought that a new competitor would encourage better service than that offered by the Lake Shore & Michigan Southern. The HW&M was organized in 1865 to build a line from Monroe to Holly. At Holly it would connect with the Detroit & Milwaukee's line to Grand Haven and with the Flint & Pere Marquette

Eber Brock Ward was said to be the richest man in Michigan when he died in 1875. He made his fortune first in building and sailing Great Lakes ships, then later in making steel and in lumbering. He led a group of investors who bought control of the Flint & Pere Marquette and built much of its line. He was the road's president from 1870 to 1874.

George Kemp Ward, *Andrew Warde and his Descendants, 1597–1910* (New York, 1910), facing 296.

Henry Howland Crapo

Born 22 May 1804, Dartmouth, Mass.; died 22 July 1869, Flint.

Born into a farm family, Crapo taught himself surveying and then prepared himself to become a teacher, eventually qualifying himself to be the school's principal. In 1832 he moved to New Bedford, Massachusetts. Over time he was elected to every public office, found time to start a variety of businesses, and interested himself in everything else. By 1837 he started investing in Michigan pinelands, and moved to Flint in 1856 to further develop and manage his growing involvement. He logged timber from his land, sawed it in his own mills, and then personally managed selling it. Well away from a lake port, he wanted railroad service to improve his success and built the Flint & Holly to a connecting road to move his lumber to market.

Originally a Whig, Crapo changed to the Republican Party when it was formed in 1854. He involved himself in municipal life in Flint and served a term as mayor. He served as state senator during 1863 and 1864, then was governor of Michigan for two terms from 1865 through 1868. By 1866 he was so ill that he had to conduct most of his work from his sickbed. As governor he encouraged the development of European immigration to Michigan and strongly supported the growth of the agricultural college that now is Michigan State University. Most controversial were his vetoes of a series of bills that authorized municipalities and townships to issue bonds to aid building new railroads. The state senate supported his veto by just one vote. Eventually the state supreme court declared the entire practice unconstitutional.

Henry Crapo's physical condition continued to deteriorate during his second term as governor. He underwent surgery a few months after leaving office, but it appears he did not allow himself to recuperate fully, and died just a few weeks later.

In 1825 Crapo married Mary Ann Slocum and with her had ten children. The first was their only son, William Wallace Crapo, who continued his father's businesses and also became an important railroad official in his own right. One grandson was William Crapo Durant, who founded General Motors Corporation in 1908 and was its president from 1916 to 1920. Another grandson, Stanford Tappan Crapo, was a cofounder of the Huron Portland Cement Company, and followed with a career with the Flint & Pere Marquette, eventually serving as its general manager from 1899 to 1901.

for its lumber traffic. Even with financial help from the F&PM it was several years before construction started. Once begun, the line was finished in short order and opened for service at the beginning of 1872. But the citizens of Monroe were disappointed, for they expected the HW&M to provide a third railroad passing through their town. That did not happen because the easiest route for the new HW&M was to swing over to a connection with the Lake Shore & Michigan Southern on the far north side of Monroe and use its tracks into the city. The HW&M ran its trains through to Toledo over LS&MS tracks. The Holly road also had a friendly connection with the Michigan Central at Wayne and used that line to run its trains into Detroit. Through passenger trains into Detroit over the Detroit & Milwaukee tracks from Holly were discontinued and replaced by four runs each way between Bay City and Detroit via Wayne. The Flint & Pere Marquette bought the Holly, Wayne & Monroe in February 1872.

When the F&PM merged with the Holly road, it also merged with three other small companies. The Bay City & East Saginaw was started with local money, finished with financial help from the F&PM, and completed in 1867 as a friendly connection between its namesake cities. The Flint River, built in 1872 by the owners of the F&PM, was a lumber-hauling line that extended from Flint to Otter Lake. The F&PM's owners also formed the Cass River, but it is uncertain that it ever built any line before it was absorbed. The F&PM also acquired control of the East Saginaw & St. Clair, which owned a short belt line railway in Saginaw.

When its outlet to Monroe was completed the F&PM was in the enviable position of being able to move logs to the sawmills at Saginaw and Flint, and finished lumber to Detroit and, more important, to Toledo, where it connected with rail lines to all of the nation's major cities.

Henry H. Crapo came to Flint in 1856, at age fifty-two, to improve the profits of his logging business. He built the Flint & Holly between those points in 1864 to improve shipping his lumber. With a fortune made in lumbering, he went into politics and served two terms as Michigan's governor, from 1865 to 1869.

Henry M. Utley and Byron M. Cutcheon, *Michigan as a Province, Territory and State* (New York, 1906), facing 44.

SOURCES

Dunbar, Willis F. *All Aboard! A History of Railroads in Michigan*. Grand Rapids, Mich.: W. B. Eerdmans, 1969.

Elliott, Frank N. *When the Railroad Was King*. Lansing: Michigan Historical Commission, 1966.

History of Saginaw County, Michigan. Chicago: Chas. C. Chapman, 1881.

Ivey, Paul Wesley. *The Pere Marquette Railroad: An Historical Study of the Growth and Development of One of Michigan's Most Important Railway Systems*. Lansing: Michigan Historical Commission, 1919.

Lewis, Martin D. *Lumberman from Flint: The Michigan Career of Henry H. Crapo*. Detroit: Wayne State University Press, 1958.

Wing, Talcott. *History of Monroe County*. New York: Munsell, 1890.

The Railroad Boom: The Jackson Roads

At the end of 1841 the first little engine hauled the few cars of the first train into Jackson on the state's new "Central" line. There was no depot for the village passengers and no warehouse to store freight. In fact, regular service would not begin until early the next spring. Despite this slow start, within the next thirty years Jackson would grow into a major railroad center. This came about through the efforts of a group of eight Jackson businessmen.

The first of the group to arrive in Jackson was William D. Thompson, who came from Chenango County, New York, and settled in his new home in 1831. (William D. Thompson is not to be confused with William R. Thompson, who came to Jackson in 1830 and was one of the stock commissioners of the pioneering Detroit & St. Joseph Railroad, and later was named a member of Michigan's Board of Internal Improvement.) Thompson promptly opened a store. When the railroad arrived he was appointed freight agent. He moved to Niles as the Michigan Central's general freight agent when the road was completed there in the fall of 1848. The next spring he bought two used steamships and several keelboats and went into the river shipping business on the St. Joseph, going as far upriver as Constantine. He prospered for two years until the Michigan Southern was built into South Bend. In 1851 he sold out and moved back to Jackson to found what eventually became the Jackson City Bank.

Hiram H. Smith moved to Summit Township in August 1835 from Malone, New York. The next year he moved to a farm near Mason and by 1838 was deep into the county's political life, serving first as county treasurer, then as clerk. Smith moved to Lansing in 1847, built its first flour mill, and in 1859 was elected Lansing's first mayor. Smith moved back to Jackson in 1864.

Henry A. Hayden came to Michigan from Otsego County, New York, in 1837 and moved to Jackson in 1838. Like Thompson, he worked on the Central, first as a civil engineer, then as superintendent of repairs, and eventually as paymaster. In 1842 he left the railroad and bought the first of a series of flour mills that he was to own.

Amos Root arrived in Michigan Center in November 1838 from Fort Ann, New York, and began the first mercantile business there. Prospects must have been more promising in Jackson, for he moved to that village in 1841.

Dr. Moses A. McNaughton came to Jackson in April 1841 from Washington County, New York, and set up a medical practice.

Jerome B. Eaton was born in Herkimer County, New York. He began teaching at age thirteen and at age twenty went out "peddling." He moved to Adrian in 1833 and set up a dry goods business. In 1842 he moved to Jackson and took on a barrel-making contract using Jackson's prison residents as employees.

Peter B. Loomis came from Amsterdam, New York, in the spring of 1843 and set up a dry goods business. Later he went into milling and in 1856 established a private bank. In 1857 he was one of the organizers of the Jackson City Gas Company and became its president.

Eugene Pringle was the last of the eight to come on the scene, moving from Richfield, New York, in 1850. He had a strong legal education, and immediately set up his practice and continued it until his death.

When the state put the Central line up for sale in the spring of 1846, Amos Root realized that the new owners of the Central would be bringing substantial sums of money into that venture. He reasoned that it would be a good thing to build some sort of branch line that could feed traffic for his and the Michigan Central's mutual benefit. Grand Rapids was becoming *the* important city on the Grand River, and it had no railroad. Root talked with some men he knew along a possible route and then went off to the legislature to get a charter for his project. On 4 May 1846 he obtained a charter for his Grand River Valley Railroad. Root could not find money at the time to build his road, but he kept his charter alive for years with time extensions from an indulgent legislature.

In May 1852 the Michigan Southern Railroad finished building its line from Hillsdale into Chicago. Its charter also required that it build a line from Tecumseh into Jackson. Root and Peter Loomis thought the company was taking too long to get around to the Jackson Branch. Root used his seat in the legislature to pressure the Southern's lobbyists about the Jackson Branch every time they came asking for a state favor. Root's prodding paid off eventually when, in 1855, the Southern extended the line from Tecumseh as far as Manchester. Still the MS had no enthusiasm for spending good money to build a branch that would invade the Michigan Central's territory. At the same time, the Central objected loudly to a potential violation of its franchise. To get around these problems Root and Henry Hayden formed a small company named the Jackson Union Railroad in July 1855 with rights to build from Jackson to Napoleon. Apparently all it ever did was acquire some of the land that the Michigan Southern needed. In July 1857 the Southern finally finished building its branch into Jackson. The Michigan Central would not tolerate a connection with this interloper, forcing the Michigan Southern to build its own depot on South Milwaukee Street. It was not until 1878, when William Henry Vanderbilt had firm control of both roads, that the Southern's passenger trains began running into the MC depot on East Michigan Avenue.

When Michigan received the federal grant lands in June 1856 one of the routes stipulated was from Amboy Township, on the Ohio state line due south of Hillsdale, through Lansing to Little Traverse Bay in the vicinity of Petoskey. Two companies were formed to go for the grant. The Amboy & Traverse Bay Railroad was organized in December 1856, and it was followed in January 1857 by the Amboy, Lansing & Traverse Bay. The A&TB proposed to build from Amboy, via Hillsdale, Jackson, and Lansing to Traverse Bay; the AL&TB proposed to build from Amboy, via Hillsdale and Lansing, to Traverse Bay. Jackson was heavily represented on the A&TB with Hayden, Loomis, and McNaughton as directors, and with former state senator Michael Shoemaker as president. Mostly Owosso residents and no Jackson men were involved in the AL&TB, but Hiram Smith, who then lived in Lansing, was a director. In February 1857 the land grant was awarded, but the Jackson group lost out to the AL&TB.

At the outbreak of the Civil War in 1861 seven of the "Jackson Eight" were well settled in the community; Hiram Smith moved back from Lansing in 1864. The group was influential and had profited from Jackson's growth as a commercial center. Pringle was the youngest of the group at age thirty-four; the rest were in their forties, except for Smith, who was fifty-one. McNaughton closed his medical practice in 1851 and devoted himself entirely to his real estate business. Root sold his shop and after 1857 dealt only in real estate while managing his farm. Most of the group saw service in the Union army, some of them in William Withington's Jackson Grays.

In December 1863 some of the group edged into railroading when they organized the Lansing & Jackson Railroad. The company headquarters was in Jackson, with Hayden, Loomis, Smith, and Thompson among the first directors; they were joined by others who had been involved with the Amboy & Traverse Bay back in 1856. Smith brought in James Turner, of Lansing, who had been a moneyed backer of the AL&TB. Turner was named treasurer and Hayden president of the L&J. The AL&TB, usually called the "Ramshorn" in tribute to its roundabout route to Little Traverse Bay, was having trouble making a go of it. Despite its land grant it was out of money and went into receivership in 1864. The Lansing & Jackson had not made any more progress. In February 1865, as the Civil War was ending, President Hayden, probably encouraged by James Turner, changed the L&J's name to the more ambitious name of Jackson, Lansing & Saginaw. With this change came new authority for a line from Jackson to the Saginaw River, a route that could include the AL&TB's existing Owosso–Lansing line. By the end of 1865 the JL&S was built from Jackson to Mason and in June 1866 was finished into Lansing at Michigan Avenue, where it connected with the Ramshorn. In October 1866 Charles C. Trowbridge, the AL&TB's receiver, sold the AL&TB franchise from Lansing to Traverse Bay, its land-grant rights north of Lansing, and the completed Owosso–Lansing line to the JL&S. Hayden and Smith resumed construction immediately, and the JL&S was completed through Saginaw into West Bay City by the end of 1867.

The end of the Civil War caused a new surge of enthusiasm for railroads that brought with it a new scheme to raise money to build them. Cities, villages, and townships that wanted lines were willing to go into debt to get them. Eugene Pringle is given credit for writing some of the early legislation that provided the JL&S with this source of funds. The Grand River Valley benefited in the same way.

Amos Root's Grand River Valley charter had lain dormant for nearly twenty years, but in 1865 he brought it back to life. He made arrangements with the JL&S to operate that road's line between Jackson and Rives Junction. By 4 July 1868 the GRV line had been built from Rives Junction as far as Eaton Rapids, later that fall to Charlotte, and by February 1869 to Hastings. In the spring of 1870 the entire line was finished into Grand Rapids. In August the Michigan Central leased the company in exchange for financial help from the MC's president, James F. Joy. The MC also leased the Jackson, Lansing & Saginaw in September 1871 in exchange for Joy's help.

The Michigan Central then operated the only east-west line through Jackson to Chicago, but the owners of the Grand Trunk Railway of Canada had considered, for a dozen years, having their own line from Chicago to Port Huron. In December 1866 a group of Michiganders formed the Grand Trunk Railway of Michigan to build a line from Ridgeway, now known as Richmond, through Pontiac, Jackson, Three Rivers, and Niles, to Chicago. They also formed the Grand Trunk Railway of Northern Indiana to build there. It was entirely possible that the promoters thought they could build the road and sell it to the Grand Trunk or at the least sell their franchise. McNaughton and Eaton were

members of both companies' first board of directors, with Eaton named
president of the Michigan company. Nothing came of this project, or
of the Grand Trunk Railroad of Michigan, which the two men formed
in May 1868 to build on a more northern route through Lansing to
St. Joseph. In July 1868 McNaughton and Eaton formed yet another
company, the Michigan Air Line Railroad, to merge with their two 1866
Grand Trunk companies in Michigan and Indiana. They brought in
Chicago railroad builder Joseph E. Young. In 1869 they finished a short
piece of line between Richmond and Romeo. This done, the company
shifted its attention to that part of its line west of Jackson. It is not
recorded, but this change may well have been influenced by James F.
Joy's attempt to persuade the MAL's officers with an offer of some
Michigan Central construction money. Joy may have been trying to keep
the Grand Trunk from becoming a competitor, or he may have wanted
the extra track capacity between Jackson and Niles. In any event, work
on the section between Romeo and Jackson stopped and began west
from Jackson. Rails were laid to Homer by the summer of 1870, by fall
into Three Rivers, and finished into Niles in February 1871. In October
1870 the MAL acquired the franchise of the St. Joseph Valley Railroad,
which held rights in Indiana to build between Niles and South Bend,
and extended its line there the next year. When it was completed the
Michigan Central leased the route from Jackson to South Bend.

Into all of this activity a fourth Jackson railroad project was brought
forward. In July 1868 Jackson men formed the Jackson, Fort Wayne &
Cincinnati. Hayden, Loomis, Root, Smith, and Thompson were on the
first board of directors, with Smith as president, Loomis as treasurer,
and Pringle as secretary. Other Jackson men rounded out the first board.
A month later they formed the Fort Wayne, Jackson & Saginaw in the
state of Indiana, and in January 1869 merged the JFW&C into the FWJ&S.
The road was built in short order. Smith was in charge of construction,
and the road was completed from Jackson to Reading by November
1869, and to Fort Wayne on Christmas Day, 1870. Smith resigned the
presidency at the end of 1870, and Loomis took his place.

Between the end of the Civil War, in 1865, and February 1871 the
eight Jackson men built nearly 400 miles of railroad line: from Jackson
to Lansing, Owosso to Bay City, Rives Junction to Grand Rapids, Jackson
to Niles to South Bend, and Jackson to Fort Wayne. They also built 14
miles between Richmond and Romeo and had bought 27 miles of the
Ramshorn for one of their properties. The group transformed Jackson
into an important railroad center. Jackson replaced Marshall as the

division point for changing crews and locomotives. On the east side of the city the railroad built the beginnings of a major switching yard. In June 1873 the Michigan Central moved its shops from Marshall to Jackson and added more than 1,000 workers to company payrolls. Eaton is credited as helping to persuade the railroad to make this move.

Hiram Smith continued to build railroads. After leaving the Fort Wayne line in 1871, he and James F. Joy became involved in the Detroit, Lansing & Lake Michigan. Smith became its president until 1873 and was in charge of constructing its line between Detroit and Lansing. In 1872 Joy asked Smith to take charge of building the Detroit & Bay City, another road Joy was helping financially. That line was completed in July 1873.

In November 1873 Hiram Smith and several others turned their hands to city transportation by forming the Main Street Railway to operate horse-pulled cars the length of Main Street in Jackson. Smith, Eaton, Loomis, and Thompson were the organizing directors. Nothing came of this attempt, but Loomis and Smith tried again in August 1881 when they formed the Jackson City Railway. With Smith as its first president, and his son Henry as general manager, the company ran its first horse-drawn streetcars in 1886. When electric operations became practical Smith and his sons Henry and Dwight founded the Jackson Street Railway and took over the lines of the horse company. Hiram Smith died in May 1898.

Henry Hayden served as president of the Jackson, Lansing & Saginaw until 1895, and continued on as director until 1898. He was one of the founders of the Peoples National Bank and was its president until his death in 1899.

Peter B. Loomis served as president and general manager of the Fort Wayne, Jackson & Saginaw until the end of 1879. The road managed to stay independent for a time, but that was not done easily. The panic of 1873 brought deficits to the company, and eventually it defaulted on its bond interest. It was reorganized with New York money in December 1879 as the Fort Wayne & Jackson. Loomis, Thompson, and Smith left the company, but Pringle remained as the road's attorney. In 1882 the Fort Wayne was leased to the Lake Shore & Michigan Southern. Loomis continued as a director of the Jackson, Lansing & Saginaw until 1896. He died in December 1905.

William D. Thompson served as treasurer and director of the Jackson, Lansing & Saginaw until 1899.

Amos Root continued as president of the Grand River Valley almost to his death in 1891. He also served as a director of the Fort Wayne &

Jackson from 1879 until 1891. John M. Root became the GRV president upon his brother's death and held the office until 1898.

Jerome B. Eaton served as president of the Michigan Air Line Railroad from 1872 until his death in August 1887. The MAL was split into two companies in 1875, with the MAL Railroad owning the line from Jackson to South Bend, and the MAL Railway eventually building a line from Richmond, through Pontiac, to Jackson in January 1884. Eaton also held the presidency of the MAL Railway until 1878, when the Grand Trunk of Canada took ownership.

Moses A. McNaughton was treasurer and a director of the MAL Railroad from 1872 until 1887. He also served as a director of the MAL Railway from 1875 until 1891.

Eugene Pringle remained the attorney for the Fort Wayne line until 1883. He served as a director of the MAL Railroad until 1889.

The railroad network that the eight men from Jackson built was an important employer the community. It was an asset for James F. Joy's Michigan Central and later for the Vanderbilts and their New York Central Railroad. The network provided the first Lower Peninsula railroad to reach the Straits of Mackinac. Jackson itself became a preeminent railroad town in Michigan. As a division headquarters and with its major shops, much of the New York Central in Michigan, away from Detroit, was managed from Jackson.

SOURCES

DeLand, Charles V. *History of Jackson County*. Indianapolis: B. F. Bowen, 1903.

Michigan Railroad Commission. *Aids, Gifts, Grants and Donations to Railroads . . .*
     Lansing, Mich.: Wynkoop, Hallenbeck, Crawford, 1919.

The Railroad Boom: The Grand Trunk Lines

By 1858 twenty years had passed since the start of the state's internal improvement program, but Port Huron still had no railroad. That year the Great Western Railway completed a line from London to Sarnia on the east bank of the St. Clair River. At the same time, the Grand Trunk Railway of Canada was busy extending its own line from Portland, Maine, westward through Toronto, and completed it to Port Edward, Ontario, by the end of 1859. In November 1859 a Grand Trunk subsidiary completed a connecting line from Fort Gratiot, just north of Port Huron, to the west side of Detroit, where it made valuable connections with the Michigan Central to Chicago and with the Michigan Southern to Toledo.

Ten years earlier a local group had formed the Port Huron & Lake Michigan Rail Road to build a line from Port Huron to Lake Michigan in the vicinity of Grand Haven. This used the same route that the state's internal improvement program had chosen for its "Northern" railroad line. In 1847 the PH&LM bought the rights of the Northern from the state, but nothing more happened. The road's charter lapsed for a lack of activity, forcing the promoters to get a new charter for the road in 1855. Also in 1855 another group, headed by Nelson P. Stewart, who was the president of the Detroit & Pontiac, incorporated the Port Huron & Milwaukee Railway to build from Port Huron to some connection with the Detroit & Milwaukee road, a road that was just starting construction west from Pontiac. The PH&M did manage to do some grading west from Port Huron but not much else. In 1857 the Lake Michigan company was awarded the state land grant for a line from Port Huron to Flint and Grand Haven. In an effort to improve its own prospects, the state permitted the Port Huron & Milwaukee to be sold to the Detroit & Milwaukee. The sale of the PH&M never took place, and financial difficulties eventually forced

William L. Bancroft, a Port Huron businessman of many talents, built the first part of the Grand Trunk Western's Port Huron–Chicago main line. Between 1869 and 1871 he built the part from his home city to Flint.

Willard Library, Battle Creek.

William Lyman Bancroft

Born 12 August 1825, Martinsburg, N.Y.; died 1 May 1901, Hot Springs, Ark.

Bancroft's family came to Michigan when he was seven and then came to Port Huron in 1844 after a two-year stay in Milwaukee. During his working life he was a newspaper editor and owner, attorney, judge, banker, lumberman, the first mayor of Port Huron, postmaster, and collector of customs.

Bancroft was one of the investors in the proposed Port Huron & Lake Michigan Railroad in 1847. As its president he bought a competing franchise, stimulated some local financing, and finally managed to get a line built from Port Huron to Flint between 1869 and 1871. In 1873 he formed the Chicago & Lake Huron to take over the Port Huron company and the Peninsular Railway, which owned a line from Lansing to Valparaiso, Indiana. Before the merger the PH&LM went into receivership, and Bancroft acted as the road's receiver until 1878. During 1876 he superintended the construction of the Chicago & Northeastern between Flint and Lansing, then integrated its operations into the Chicago & Lake Huron.

Bancroft retired from his railroad in 1878. After twenty years of failing eyesight he could no longer keep up his business interests. He wintered in Florida and kept up his writing and his political activities as a staunch Democrat. In 1888 President Grover Cleveland named Bancroft to be superintendent of the Railway Mail Service of the U.S. Post Office.

Between 1866 and 1870 Leonidas D. Dibble, a Battle Creek attorney, promoted and then built a line between Battle Creek and Lansing. Once bitten by the railroad "bug" he built another line between Battle Creek and Valparaiso, Indiana. This line provided his hometown with a second route to Chicago. Both lines he built became part of the Grand Trunk Western.

Willard Library, Battle Creek.

This 1876 schedule of the Chicago & Lake Huron is from *Appleton's Railroad Guide.* The link between Lansing and Flint that would connect its two parts was still a year away from completion. The through day train between Lansing and Valparaiso and the morning and afternoon trains between Port Huron and Flint were regular passenger trains, but the other trains appear to be mixed trains that handled freight cars as well as passengers.

Author's collection.

the company into receivership. In 1862 the PH&LM bought the PH&M. At the end of the Civil War the PH&LM came under the control of a group headed by the influential Port Huron businessman William L. Bancroft. He had moved to Port Huron in 1844, and had been a newspaperman, lawyer, banker, lumberman, and the town's first mayor, and had served terms in both the state legislature and in Congress. Thirty years after it was first proposed Bancroft was able to raise enough money to begin building the rail line. It was completed from Port Huron to Emmett in November 1869 and finished into Flint in December 1871.

It was no secret that the Grand Trunk Railway of Canada wanted to have a line across Michigan to reach Chicago and tap the fertile farmland of the American Midwest. In December 1866 a group of promoters, including several men from Jackson, formed the Grand Trunk Railway of Michigan. To improve the odds some of the same men formed the Grand Trunk Rail Road of Michigan in May 1868 to build from Ridgeway to Chicago on a more northern route through Lansing and St. Joseph. Then in July they consolidated the two Grand Trunk companies into a new company named the Michigan Air Line Railroad. The MAL at that time had a short line west from Ridgeway and by December 1869 was running trains between Ridgeway and Romeo.

In Battle Creek a group of area men headed by attorney Leonidas D. Dibble formed the Peninsular Railway in August 1865 to build a line between Lansing and Battle Creek. Apparently Dibble took a liking to being a railroad president since in October 1866, before work had

CHICAGO & LAKE HURON RAILWAY.
W. L. Bancroft, Receiver, Port Huron, Mich.

P.M.	A.M.	A.M.	M	L'VE] [ARR.	A.M.	P.M.	P.M.
4 15	10 25	7 20	0	..Port Huron..	9 55	3 25	7 05
6 83	1 55	10 00	46	.....Lapeer.....	7 45	11 10	4 47
7 50	3 10	10 55	66	.....Flint......	6 40	9 15	3 45
P.M.	P.M.	A.M.		ARR.] [L'VE	A.M.	A.M.	P.M.

WESTERN DIVISION.

A.M.	P.M.	A.M.	M	L'VE] [ARR.	P.M.	P.M.	P.M.
	7 85	9 10	0	....Lansing...	4 40	5 15	
	9 10	10 20	19	....Charlotte....	3 40	3 25	
6 00	11 05	11 35	45	..Battle Creek..	2 30	1 10	
8 50	P.M.	1 00	74	...Schoolcraft...	1 00	10 30	
1 15		3 23	120	..South Bend..	10 17	6 00	10 15
5 00		5 33	165	..Valparaiso..	8 07		6 30
P.M.		P.M.		ARR.] [L'VE	A.M.	A.M.	P.M.

started on the Lansing section, he and another group of men formed the Peninsular Railway Extension Company to build a line west from Battle Creek through Cass County to Indiana, and also formed a separate Indiana company to continue the road west. Construction began at Battle Creek in 1867 and crept toward Lansing slowly but by June 1870 was completed to Lansing. At the same time, the Extension road began building toward Indiana and completed its line to South Bend in the fall of 1872. The following year a related Indiana company built its line between South Bend and Valparaiso. Just west of Valparaiso it connected with the Pittsburgh, Fort Wayne & Chicago and began to operate its trains into Chicago.

The construction done by Bancroft and Dibble depleted their respective companies' treasuries completely, and both roads operated at a loss. Bancroft proposed that one management operate both roads, and he formed the Chicago & Lake Huron to do that. The two roads were separated by a gap extending from Flint to Lansing, but he began operating the two lines in 1873. The panic of 1873 immediately forced the two companies into receivership, and the court named Bancroft as receiver to reorganize its affairs.

SOURCES

Dunbar, Willis F. *All Aboard! A History of Railroads in Michigan*. Grand Rapids,
    Mich.: W. B. Eerdmans, 1969.

Ellis, Franklin. *History of Shiawassee and Clinton Counties*. Philadelphia: D. W.
    Ensign, 1880.

Hopper, A. B., and T. Kearney. *Canadian National Railways: Synoptical History . . . as
    of December 31, 1960*. Montreal: Canadian National Railways, 1962.

Meints, Graydon M. "Overwhelmed with Good Fortune." *Railroad History* No. 188
    (Spring 2003).

Stevens, G. R. *Canadian National Railways: Sixty Years of Trial and Error, 1836–1896*.
    2 vols. Toronto: Clark, Irwin, 1960, 1962.

The Railroad Boom: Commodore Vanderbilt Comes to Michigan

The completion of the Michigan Southern's subsidiary Northern Indiana into Chicago in 1852 brought no easy success with it. The Michigan Central proved to be a very tough competitor for through traffic. By the

Legrand Lockwood

Born 14 August 1820, Norwalk, Conn.; died 24 February 1872, New York City.

Lockwood became a Wall Street clerk at age eighteen and made it his life's work. "Commodore" Vanderbilt made him a director of a California steamship line that profited from the gold rush of 1849. By 1857 Lockwood had enough money to start his own stock brokerage house, becoming one of the country's first millionaires through his investments in steamships and railroads. In 1864 he began constructing his mansion, "Elmenworth," in Norwalk, a home that took four years and $2 million to build. He owned the street railway in front of his home and also the railroad along the Norwalk River in the rear.

In the early 1860s Lockwood teamed up with Henry Keep to buy control of the Michigan Southern & Northern Indiana. From this base they achieved a takeover of the New York Central Railroad in 1866. An enraged Commodore Vanderbilt bought into the road and soon gained control of it. Keep knew he was beaten and sold his stock to Vanderbilt. After Keep's departure from the NYC Lockwood managed to stay on good enough terms for his MS&NI to continue to handle Vanderbilt traffic. But he also began flirting with Jay Gould and his Erie Railroad. Vanderbilt reacted by buying more MS&NI stock. Lockwood tried to protect himself by merging two of his companies and followed this with more mergers, all of which culminated in May 1869 when he joined all of his roads into one company, the Lake Shore & Michigan Southern.

On 24 September 1869 Jay Gould, Daniel Drew, and James Fisk attempted a corner of the U.S. gold market. It failed on "Black Friday," and plummeting stock prices caught good brokers, and bad, in the maelstrom. Lockwood's brokerage firm failed, and desperate to raise money, he sold his control of the LS&MS to Commodore Vanderbilt. Vanderbilt even took a mortgage on Elmenworth.

Lockwood enjoyed his new home for only four years. He contracted pneumonia and died within ten days, at age fifty-two. The panic of 1873 completed the ruin of his family; his art and collectibles had to be sold. In 1876 his wife had to sell their home, which today is open as a public museum.

mid-1850s both roads had established eastern rail connections, making the competition still fiercer. Henry Keep and Legrand Lockwood, a pair of stock market operators, had put some money into the four roads running between Toledo and Buffalo. In 1859 they got control of the Michigan Southern & Northern Indiana and began improving the operations between Chicago and Buffalo to make their lines into a viable through route. East of Buffalo Keep and Lockwood had to depend on other railroads to deliver their traffic. One of these was the Jay Gould–controlled Erie Railroad, which they connected with at Dunkirk, New York. Gould had a reputation for being less than upright in his dealings, enough so that Keep and Lockwood very likely thought they should keep a prudent distance. The alternate road to New York was a combination route of the New York Central and "Commodore" Cornelius Vanderbilt's Hudson River Railroad. Vanderbilt already owned enough stock in the NYC to have a couple of his own directors on its board.

In 1866 Keep and Lockwood, with considerable financial help from William C. Fargo of Wells Fargo fame, bought enough NYC stock to

Cornelius "Commodore" Vanderbilt

Born 27 May 1794, Staten Island, N.Y.; died 4 January 1877, New York City.

Vanderbilt's nickname was an acknowledgment of his success on the water, first operating a ferry to Staten Island, later expanding into the important Hudson River shipping service, and eventually into sailing to Europe and to California during the 1849 gold rush. By exceptionally hard work, a willingness to take chances, and using tactics that completely disregarded the effects on any of his competitors or the public, he succeeded beyond all expectation. Near the end of the Civil War, at age seventy and worth nearly $30 million, Vanderbilt decided to retire from marine operations.

During the 1840s Vanderbilt made some modest investments in railroads around New York City. In 1863 he became president of the New York & Harlem and quickly turned it into a moneymaker. He then took control of the Hudson River Railroad, which had only one important connection, the New York Central, which operated from Albany to Buffalo. There was an uneasy cooperation between the two companies. After a dispute in January 1867 Vanderbilt abruptly cut off connections to the NYC, an act that quickly brought some owners of that road to his desk looking for his support. He agreed and within a year he owned the NYC, eventually consolidating it to become the New York Central & Hudson River.

In 1867 Vanderbilt decided to take control of the Erie Railroad, the only line into New York City he did not control. He faced Daniel Drew, James Fisk Jr., and Jay Gould in his attempt, three of the most dangerous and unprincipled men in railroading. Vanderbilt failed, but not without trying any means the courts and his bankbook would provide. In 1869, now seventy-five, he took over the Lake Shore & Michigan Southern, which he got at a bargain price from Henry Keep and Legrand Lockwood on "Black Friday" in September. Now that his railroad control extended into the Midwest, he began making investments in other railroads, some that might turn into competitors, such as the Michigan Central and the Canada Southern, and others that might provide profitable connections, such as the Big Four (Cleveland, Cincinnati, Chicago & St. Louis), the Chicago & North Western, and the Union Pacific.

Late in 1876 Vanderbilt's health began to fail; eventually he could not walk and moved only in his wheelchair. When death came on 4 January 1877 he was well into his eighty-third year and was by far the richest man in America. The second- and third-wealthiest men died within a year of him, and their combined estates did not match Vanderbilt's. In Michigan he personally owned more miles of railroad than did anyone else. His estate, estimated to be around $100 million, and the ownership of the railroads that made it up, went to his son William Henry and William Henry's four oldest sons, keeping all of it in his family.

Horace F. Clark may have been
Commodore Vanderbilt's son-in-law, but
he did bring reasonable management
skills to railroading. He served in the
U.S. House of Representatives, and was
president of the Lake Shore & Michigan
Southern and also of the Union Pacific.
His dreams of fortune, and questionable
business dealings, produced such a
debacle that, after his death, his wife was
left with nothing.

Collection of U.S. House of Representatives.

gain control for themselves and to unseat Vanderbilt's representatives. They soon learned that upsetting Vanderbilt was not profitable. Just after year's end, with the Hudson River frozen and the NYC now diverting traffic off the Hudson River boats and onto Vanderbilt's rails, he announced he would no longer connect his trains with the NYC's. Passengers had to cross the river at Albany on their own and buy separate tickets. Shippers had to find some way to move their freight between the two railroads. It did not take long for Fargo, Keep, and Lockwood to realize the size of their mistake. They acceded to Vanderbilt's terms, which included a personal cash bonus of $100,000, and he promptly reopened the connection between the two roads. But he was not finished.

"I bide my time," Vanderbilt is reputed to have said as he quietly bought up stock in the New York Central. At the next annual meeting he had a majority of the stock under his control, Fargo, Keep, and Lockwood were shoved aside, and Vanderbilt, his son and sons-in-law, and other associates took all of the seats for themselves. Henry Keep sold his stock to Vanderbilt and moved on to the presidency of the Chicago & North Western, which he held until his death in July 1869. In November 1869 Vanderbilt combined the three railroads he controlled into one new company, the New York Central & Hudson River.

Lockwood kept control of the roads west of Buffalo and managed to stay on friendly terms with the Vanderbilts, enough so that their two roads interchanged traffic smoothly at Buffalo. But Lockwood knew that he was in the sights of both Vanderbilt and Gould. Jay Gould was then casting covetous eyes on Chicago for his Erie Railroad and already had built his broad-gauge lines into both Cleveland and Cincinnati. Gould sounded out the Michigan Southern about installing a third rail so Erie six-foot-gauge trains could run from Toledo to Chicago. Commodore Vanderbilt had his own score to settle with Gould and so, to keep him from succeeding, began buying stock in Lockwood's Michigan Southern & Northern Indiana.

William Henry Vanderbilt and Horace F. Clark, Vanderbilt's son and son-in-law, respectively, were convinced of the importance of controlling the railroad between Buffalo and Chicago. Vanderbilt control would protect the family's interests as well as assure a friendly connection to the Chicago & North Western, which also was a beneficiary of Vanderbilt money. The Vanderbilts began to buy heavily, and it was obvious to Lockwood what was happening. In an attempt to delay the impending attack he combined all of his lines between

Erie and Toledo into a new company named the Lake Shore. Soon after he merged the Buffalo & Erie into the Lake Shore. On 6 April 1869 Lockwood combined his Lake Shore and his MS&NI into a new company, the Lake Shore & Michigan Southern. When officers and directors were elected for the new company, Elijah B. Phillips moved over from the MS&NI presidency to head the new company. At the time, Vanderbilt owned just enough stock in Lockwood's road to get Horace F. Clark in as a director.

During the summer of 1869 Lockwood began meeting with Jay Gould in an attempt to set up some sort of arrangement. Talk started of the Erie laying a third rail on its line to accommodate LS&MS trains rather than the earlier proposal to put in the third rail for the Erie to use between Toledo and Chicago. This must have seemed like a good idea to Lockwood because he and his investors began to strengthen their hold by buying more Lake Shore stock. Vanderbilt then started selling aggressively, driving the price down from $120 to $100 a share. At the same time, by mere coincidence, Jay Gould and Jim Fisk attempted to corner the gold market on Friday, 24 September 1869, a date that soon became much better known as "Black Friday." Their corner collapsed, resulting in a wild panic overrunning Wall Street. Lake Shore stock plummeted to $75 per share, and Lockwood and his brokerage firm watched as their other properties fell just as far just as fast. They unloaded stock as fast as they could to save themselves, and the obliging Vanderbilt bought it. By the end of September the Commodore had complete control of the Lake Shore & Michigan Southern. Lockwood resigned as the Vanderbilt men moved in. Although separate corporations, close ties and closely integrated service existed between the two Vanderbilt roads.

Well before the 1869 collapse Lockwood was improving the LS&MS's prospects by picking up some connecting roads, several of which were in Michigan. The first was an assemblage of companies that was first started in 1848 by a group of St. Joseph men, called the St. Joseph Valley Railroad, to build from St. Joseph to some point in St. Joseph County. In 1855 the group built a line from Constantine to Three Rivers and apparently took over operations of the Michigan Southern's White Pigeon–Constantine branch. Eventually SJV leased the latter segment from Lockwood in 1864. Another company, the Schoolcraft & Three Rivers, founded by Schoolcraft men, started to build between those two points immediately after the Civil War, with contractor Ransom Gardner completing the line in short order. Next Gardner went on to

LeGrand Lockwood assembled the Lake Shore & Michigan Southern in a desperate attempt to keep it out of the hands of Commodore Vanderbilt. Lockwood failed in a colossal way. Vanderbilt took over his railroad and then went so far as to take a mortgage on Lockwood's Norwalk, Connecticut, home, "Elm Hall."

The Vanderbilt family first came to Michigan, and they purchased the Lake Shore & Michigan Southern, in 1869. The map shows the growth of the LS&MS and its Michigan predecessors up to 1875, and the additions made after 1875.

KEY
— Lake Shore & Michigan Southern lines and lines built by subsidiaries in 1875
- - Added to LS&MS lines after 1875

build the line for the Kalamazoo & Schoolcraft between those two cities and completed that line in May 1867. On 14 August 1869 Lockwood brought the three short lines together when he formed the wholly owned Kalamazoo & White Pigeon.

Gardner then started on other ventures of his own. In 1867 he formed the Kalamazoo & Allegan to build a line between those two places, and in 1868, not long after construction started, he formed the Kalamazoo & Grand Rapids to continue the road from Allegan to Grand Rapids. Financial help came from James W. Converse, an old resident of Grand Rapids who had moved back to Boston and taken up banking and financing railroad construction. Some more help came from Grand Rapids citizens, who promised Gardner a bonus of $10,000 if he would get his road into the city by 1 March 1869. Gardner worked frantically on the Allegan road and at the same time tried to delay and impede the Grand Rapids & Indiana with court maneuvers and obstructions. On the deadline day he was able to run an engine with a flatcar into Grand Rapids, thereby earning his bonus. Both Lockwood and James F. Joy of the Michigan Central were interested in acquiring Gardner's road, now renamed the Kalamazoo, Allegan & Grand Rapids. In the end Lockwood won out and got a 999-year lease of the road.

Next Gardner turned his attention to the Northern Central Michigan, a line that was to straggle from Lansing, through Eaton Rapids, Albion, and Homer, to Amboy Township in Hillsdale County. Formed in 1866, the NCM bought the Amboy, Lansing & Traverse Bay's land grant south of Lansing early in 1867, but started no construction until Gardner signed up to build it. Lockwood apparently bought up all the line's stock from its owners at about the same time; with it he saw an opportunity to invade four Michigan Central markets and also get into the state's capital city. The line was completed by the end of 1872, but regular service apparently did not start until January 1873.

After the Vanderbilt takeover Horace F. Clark, the Commodore's son-in-law, became the new president of the Lake Shore in 1870. He was a competent enough executive but lived with dreams of glory. In 1872 Clark and Jay Gould and Augustus Schell, a Wall Street wheeler-dealer and Tammany politician who had succeeded Boss Tweed, decided to attempt to corner the stock of the Chicago & North Western. The corner was a wild success, and the three saw C&NW stock rise to $230 per share. Later that same year Clark was named president of the Union Pacific, a move that most certainly could help the traffic levels of the Lake Shore even if it did nothing for the Union Pacific. But Clark did extend further Vanderbilt influence over another important connecting road. The Union Pacific, the Chicago & North Western, and a predecessor of the Wabash all came to have Vanderbilt representatives on their boards.

Horace Clark died in the summer of 1873, leaving a wake of unsavory financial dealings and speculations that went as far as using the railroad's funds to tide him over. Earlier, in 1872, when Jay Gould was arrested for an attempt to defraud the Erie of $9 million, Clark posted his bail bond. After Clark's demise, Vanderbilt grabbed the Lake Shore by the neck, named himself president, canceled nearly every contract for new construction and improvements, and denounced his son-in-law's tactics. He brought in Amasa Stone Jr. as chief operating officer, and then went on his thrifty way.

New Hampshire–born James F. Joy came to Detroit in 1836 at the age of twenty-five to study law. During his eighty-five-year life he honed considerable legal skills, became deeply involved and a powerful force in state politics, guided the state's Republican Party, and gained formidable skills in railroad management, development, and financing.

Archives of Michigan.

SOURCES

Dunbar, Willis F. *All Aboard! A History of Railroads in Michigan*. Grand Rapids, Mich.: W. B. Eerdmans, 1969.

Durant, Samuel W. *History of Kalamazoo County, Michigan*. Philadelphia: Everts & Abbott, 1880.

Harlow, Alvin F. *The Road of the Century*. New York: Creative Age, 1947.

Hungerford, Edward. *Men of Erie*. New York: Random House, 1946.

Lane, Wheaton J. *Commodore Vanderbilt: An Epic of the Steam Age*. New York: Alfred A. Knopf, 1942.

The Railroad Boom: Joy's Railroads

James F. Joy is probably the most skilled railroad manager ever to come out of Michigan, and as close to a railroad baron as the state would ever produce. As a thirty-five-year-old attorney from Detroit he became involved in the state's sale of its internal improvements railroads and in the formation of the Michigan Central in 1846. He learned railroad operations from John W. Brooks, who was the MC's operating officer, and railroad finance from John Murray Forbes, who was the source of the road's financing. By the early 1850s Forbes, Joy, and Brooks were buying and building lines west of Chicago that were the genesis of the Chicago, Burlington & Quincy; Joy was president of several of these. When Brooks resigned the Michigan Central presidency in 1867, Joy took his place. In addition to his railroad skills Joy served a term in the Michigan legislature and was involved with the formation of the Republican Party in Jackson in 1854. Since coming to Michigan he had grown to be a powerful influence in all things political in the state, while only the equally powerful Senator Zachariah Chandler had a wider public reputation. One wag said that in Joy's day "Railroad" and "Republican" were spelled the same way.

The MC was both a pioneering and a successful company. Soon after it was built to Chicago in 1852 it leased a line to Joliet, Illinois, in 1854 to establish better connections with several western railroads. It adopted Morse's new telegraph to direct train movements in 1855 and in 1860 began operating sleeping cars that George M. Pullman manufactured in Detroit. Dining cars were another experiment, although they did not work out, and passengers had to go back to eating in depot restaurants. After the Civil War George H. Hammond built a refrigerated freight car to bring meat over the Central to his Detroit meat market.

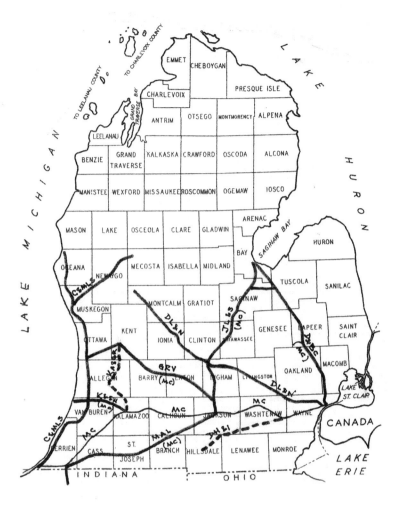

The Michigan lines that James F. Joy controlled or assisted between 1865 and 1875.

KEY

—— Original Michigan Central Detroit-Chicago main line in 1852

━━ Lines built with Joy's financial help
C&MLS: Chicago & Michigan Lake Shore
D&BC: Detroit & Bay City (acquired by the MC)
DL&N: Detroit, Lansing & Northern
GRV: Grand River Valley (acquired by the MC)
JL&S: Jackson, Lansing & Saginaw (acquired by the MC)
K&SH: Kalamazoo & South Haven (acquired by the MC)
MAL: Michigan Air Line (acquired by the MC)

- - Lines Joy failed to gain control
DH&I: Detroit, Hillsdale & Indiana
KA&GR: Kalamazoo, Allegan & Grand Rapids

President Joy understood that the railroad boom that developed after the Civil War could work to the advantage of the MC or be its undoing. Canny operator that he was, he gave financial support to some branch-line railroads that could provide traffic to the MC. Men from Jackson promoted three lines out of Jackson, one to Grand Rapids, one to Lansing–Saginaw–Bay City, and another to Niles and South Bend. Joy loaned money to build the three lines with the understanding that, when completed, they would be leased to the MC. In August 1870 he leased the Grand River Valley after it was completed to Grand Rapids, and in February 1871 the Michigan Air Line, which he saw completed to South Bend by the end of that year. In September 1871 he took a lease of the Jackson, Lansing & Saginaw, which was built into the north woods at Alger by the end of that year and by 1873 was as far north as Gaylord.

In July 1870 Joy obtained a lease of the nearly completed Kalamazoo & South Haven by guaranteeing the interest on the company's bonds.

In May 1871 a group of businessmen from along its proposed line incorporated the Detroit & Bay City. Originally it was planned to have three-foot narrow-gauge tracks, but that idea was scrapped in October in favor of standard gauge. The D&BC's owners turned to Joy for assistance, and in exchange for management control, the needed money was forthcoming. The first section was opened from Detroit as far as Oxford in October 1872, and the road was quickly completed to Bay City in July 1873. A number of the Michigan Central's New England financiers had seats on the D&BC board. Joy's joint management arrangement tied the two roads together until it was followed in March 1881 by a formal lease of the road.

The Kalamazoo, Allegan & Grand Rapids, completed in March 1869, also was a Joy target. Somehow he was outmaneuvered, and that road went instead to the Lake Shore & Michigan Southern. Another possible line for his support was the Detroit, Hillsdale & Indiana, formed in 1869 by Detroit businessman Christian H. Buhl and completed from Ypsilanti to Hillsdale by the end of 1871. Joy was one the road's directors until 1873 but was unable to add this road to his fold. It remained independent for a time, then began operating closely with the Fort Wayne & Jackson, so that eventually both of them went to the Lake Shore & Michigan Southern.

Managing the Michigan Central and several of the roads making up the Chicago, Burlington & Quincy was not enough to occupy Joy. He involved himself with other railroads as well, the first of which was the Detroit, Lansing & Lake Michigan. The Ionia & Lansing built the first part of that line in 1869. Before it was finished building it amended its corporate papers to allow it to build to Lake Michigan at Pentwater. At the same time, two other roads, the Detroit & Howell, formed in 1864, and the Howell & Lansing, formed in 1868, were trying to build their respective lines. The two roads merged in early 1870 to become the Detroit, Howell & Lansing, but it was a step that improved nothing. In early 1871 Joy and some of his New England friends incorporated the Detroit, Lansing & Lake Michigan, which in turn absorbed both the Ionia & Lansing and the Detroit, Howell & Lansing. By the end of 1871 the line was complete from West Detroit, where it connected with Joy's Michigan Central, to Howard City, where it connected with the Grand Rapids & Indiana for lumber traffic from northern Michigan. Joy became president of the new road and remained with it through 1878.

Westphalia, Hubbardston & Northern

The end of the Civil War brought a rush of enthusiasm for building railroads, and residents of many a small town thought their community had to have its own line to survive. Growth and prosperity could never come without a railroad. One such line was the Westphalia, Hubbardston & Northern, which was formed in August 1869. It was proposed to meander through the country from Hubbardston, through Matherton, Pewamo, and Westphalia, to a connection with the newly built Ionia & Lansing, probably in the vicinity of Eagle.

But, as with dozens of other such lines that were formed in the frothy years after the Civil War, it had difficulty raising money to build the line. The panic of 1873 put a final end to this nobly named effort.

On the west side of the state Alexander H. Morrison of St. Joseph incorporated the Chicago & Michigan Lake Shore in 1869 to build a line from St. Joseph to the Michigan Central at New Buffalo. The line was built quickly and began service early in 1870. Before its original line was completed Morrison bought the Lake Shore Railroad of Western Michigan with its rights to build from St. Joseph to the Muskegon River. He pushed north at a rapid pace so that by June 1871 the road was finished from St. Joseph, through Holland, to Muskegon. In 1870 Morrison also acquired the Grand Rapids & Lake Shore, which had rights to build from Grand Rapids, through Muskegon, to Manistee. He began pushing his road north from Muskegon, and by the beginning of 1872 the road was completed into Pentwater. At the same time, he picked up the line of the Grand Rapids & Holland then being built. Later in 1872 Morrison bought the Muskegon & Big Rapids and completed that line in July 1873 through White Cloud to Big Rapids. The first years were good ones, but the rapid pace of construction emptied the road's treasury, forcing Morrison to go hunting for money during the worst of the panic of 1873. He found Joy willing to help, but had to surrender control of his road to get the money. Joy stepped in as president in 1872 and brought his New England partners with him. Morrison stayed on as general manager but left his creation in 1873. George C. Kimball, also of St. Joseph, who replaced him, spent the next ten years with the road.

SOURCES

Dunbar, Willis F. *All Aboard! A History of Railroads in Michigan.* Grand Rapids,
    Mich.: W. B. Eerdmans, 1969.

Ellis, Franklin. *History of Berrien and Van Buren Counties*. Philadelphia: D. W. Ensign, 1880.

Harlow, Alvin F. *The Road of the Century*. New York: Creative Age, 1947

Ivey, Paul Wesley. *The Pere Marquette Railroad: An Historical Study of the Growth and Development of One of Michigan's Most Important Railway Systems*. Lansing: Michigan Historical Commission, 1919.

The Railroad Boom: The Canadian Dream

Since the late 1840s Canadian promoters had dreamed of a railroad that would shoot across southern Ontario directly between the Niagara and Detroit Rivers. Its primary function would be to haul U.S. freight on a short route from Michigan and the American Midwest to the East. It would compete against the Great Western, of course, but its shorter route was sure to make it a success. Nothing more came of the dream until the end of the Civil War. During the 1860s Isaac Buchanan went about touting the idea of the Great South Western Railway as just such a road. When he asked for money he met a stone wall. William A. Thomson built a short line between Fort Erie and Niagara-on-the-Lake in 1865, and he became filled with Buchanan's idea. In January 1868 Thomson used his advantage as a legislator to get a charter for the Erie & Niagara Extension Railway, which was to build from Fort Erie, through St. Thomas, to the Detroit River. Buchanan eventually fell in with Thomson, and they began working together to find the needed financing. British investors, already burned by other Canadian rail projects, were not interested. Most certainly there was no money in southern Ontario for an undertaking of this size. Among the Americans, James F. Joy was not interested, while Commodore Vanderbilt was satisfied with his modest investment in the Great Western and saw no need for another rail line.

By the end of 1869 the idea of a southern Ontario line suddenly blossomed, and the Ontario legislature talked about several lines for the route. In December 1869 Thomson and Buchanan renamed their road the Canada Southern Railway. To counteract this the Great Western Railway formed the Canada Air Line Railway to build a line from the Niagara River to connect to the GW's line near Glencoe, then continue over that road to Windsor.

The Canada Southern made its own case by emphasizing that it would be a route direct to Chicago and the American Midwest, where it

The owners of the Canada Southern had dreams of it becoming an important carrier between Niagara Falls and Chicago by building the shortest route. In the heady days after the Civil War the road was built across Ontario and into Michigan. The dream ran out of money in 1873 after the road had reached Fayette, Ohio.

KEY

—— Lines built by the Canada Southern and its U.S. subsidiaries

- - Line proposed to reach Chicago

could connect with the Chicago & North Western, the Rock Island, and other important carriers. Promoters raised some $2 million in May 1870, a quarter of it coming from Milton Courtright, an Erie, Pennsylvania, railroad contractor who had made real money building part of the Michigan Southern. Sidney Dillon was another investor; he had left railroad contracting, gone into railroad financing, and later became president of the Union Pacific. Also in were John F. Tracy, president of the Chicago & Rock Island; Daniel Drew, late of the Erie Railroad and responsible for many of its financial irregularities; and Benjamin F. Ham, treasurer of Crédit Mobilier, the infamous construction company that built the Union Pacific. Thomson and Buchanan were able to raise another $400,000 from municipalities along the route, and the province of Ontario put in $200,000 to help the road.

Construction began early in 1871 at Fort Erie. Late that year President Courtright announced that work was going well and the entire road should be completed across Ontario by the end of February 1873, as prescribed by its charter. By November 1872 the construction crews were laying three miles of track a day. By mid-December the line between Amherstburg and St. Thomas was finished, and in February 1873 the entire route to Fort Erie was completed.

Its extension to Chicago was a component vital to the success of the Canada Southern. It was necessary to develop traffic from U.S. sources to help find financing for this part. Early in 1872 the CS formed two companies to build a line between Detroit and Toledo, and these two merged in May 1872 to form the Toledo, Canada Southern & Detroit. Construction started at Toledo, with the road completed to Detroit in September 1873. The new road's tracks lay side by side with the Detroit branch of Vanderbilt's Lake Shore & Michigan Southern for miles and made direct connections with several roads in Toledo, the most important of which was with the Wabash. To garner business Courtright offered attractively low freight rates, which Vanderbilt not only met but undercut. Both roads hauled their Toledo business at a loss, a cost Vanderbilt could well afford but that Courtright could not.

The Toledo line was connected to the Ontario section of the Canada Southern by a branch line and a car ferry. The ferry operated between Gordon, just north of Amherstburg, and Stony Island on the east side of Grosse Ile; a rail line ran across Grosse Ile to Slocum Junction on the mainland, the jumping-off point for the Chicago line and the connection to the Toledo line. The ferry *Transfer* shuttled cars across the Detroit River on a regular basis, even through the severe winter ice problems.

The formation of the Canada Southern & Chicago in late 1870 was the first step toward Chicago; it was to build from the Detroit River to Hillsdale. Railroad contractor Ransom Gardner was among the founders of this road, and it appears that this was an independent effort on his part to provide the connection west of the river. This company did nothing, but in May 1871 the South Eastern Michigan was formed, again with Gardner among its incorporators. Two months later the Canada Southern merged the SEM with subsidiaries it had formed in 1871 in Indiana, Illinois, and Ohio to create a new company, the Chicago & Canada Southern Railway. Courtright started grading in Michigan, Ohio, and Indiana immediately, with rails laid on some of the line the next year. Regular service began in November 1873 on the finished section from Slocum Junction to Fayette, Ohio.

By the end of 1873 the Canada Southern was out of money. The building to Fayette and some grading farther west emptied the treasury. The panic of 1873 made fund-raising difficult. All building to Chicago was suspended for the winter of 1873–74. The next spring Courtright hired General John S. "Jack" Casement, who had built part of the Union Pacific, to take charge of the construction from Fayette to Chicago. But the company's financial situation did not improve, and Casement did no building. To make the best of a bad situation the CS decided to build an extension from Fayette to Butler, Indiana, where the road could connect with the Detroit, Eel River & Illinois, a part of the Wabash system. During the next year or two it did manage to grade some of a roadbed from Fayette as far as Wolcottville, Indiana, and also for the branch to Butler. But Courtright could do no more. Enough money could not be found to build even the thirty-five miles to Butler, and the extension that might have brought saving traffic to the road was never built.

In September 1873 the Canada Southern could no longer pay the interest due on its bonds, starting the road on a slide toward bankruptcy. It did avoid reaching this financial depth. In 1874 the CS arranged to use the suspension bridge at Niagara Falls to make it a more important link from the west to the Niagara frontier. Jay Gould then emerged as a potential suitor for the company. Gould had gained control of the Wabash and was warm to expand his empire in any direction. Another possible buyer was the Grand Trunk Railway of Canada, but nothing came of that. Only Cornelius Vanderbilt was left. He already owned some stock in the Great Western, which was controlled by British investors and which was the principal connection to the Michigan Central, and also he had been buying into the Michigan Central itself. Canada Southern stock was cheap, and Vanderbilt began buying it and the company's bonds at bargain prices. By 1874 he put control of the road in his pocket.

SOURCES

Currie, A. W. *The Grand Trunk Railroad of Canada*. Toronto: University of Toronto Press, 1957.

Harlow, Alvin F. *The Road of the Century*. New York: Creative Age, 1947.

Stevens, G. R. *Canadian National Railways: Sixty Years of Trial and Error, 1836–1896*. 2 vols. Toronto: Clark, Irwin, 1960, 1962.

Tennant, Robert D., Jr. *Canada Southern Country*. Erin, Ont.: Boston Mills Press, 1991.

The Railroad Boom: Other Lower Peninsula Roads

The post–Civil War economic boom brought enough money to Michigan to allow construction of a number of independent railroads. Although these did not remain independent in the long run, they were built without assistance from other major carriers.

Paw Paw was on the original route of the Detroit & St. Joseph and later also on the "Central" line of the state's railroads. When the Michigan Central was built in 1847, it bypassed the village by four miles. The best alternative of the early 1850s was a plank road from Paw Paw to Lawton, the nearest station on the MC. The plank road wore out quickly and was torn up in 1855. The Paw Paw Rail Road was organized in 1857 by a group of local businessmen to build a four-mile line from Paw Paw to the Michigan Central at Lawton. They did some grading but nothing more. The project was revived in 1866, and, with the help of a bond issue of $36,000 by Paw Paw Township, the road opened for business in October 1867. The road had a locomotive, named *Vulcan*, one passenger car, and one flatcar. A ticket from Paw Paw to Lawton cost 25 cents, a fare that the legislature allowed to be higher than was permitted for other railroads.

A more grandiose project was a company that eventually became the Mansfield, Coldwater & Lake Michigan, a line that planned to extend from Mansfield, Ohio, northwesterly to some port on Lake Michigan. The Pennsylvania Railroad came to see some value in the project and helped it a bit financially. Construction started at both ends, in Ohio toward Michigan and in Michigan east from, of all places, Allegan. By 1871 the Pennsylvania gained financial control of the Mansfield road. The Michigan section was completed in September 1871 from Allegan to Montieth, where the line connected with the Pennsylvania-controlled Grand Rapids & Indiana. Although some of the road was built in Ohio, all that the company ever built in Michigan was the segment from Allegan to Montieth. The GR&I operated this piece under contract for two years, then leased it in January 1874.

In 1868 and 1869 three short lines were formed to build rail lines from Allegan to Holland, from Holland to Ferrysburg, and from Muskegon to Ferrysburg. The middle road of these, the Michigan Lake Shore, was reorganized in September 1869 to consolidate all three roads and then amended its articles to allow it to build to Traverse City. From Allegan, the new company could provide the Lake Michigan access that

Mansfield, Coldwater & Lake Michigan

It was a moneymaking idea, at least on paper—a railroad line that would connect to the Pittsburgh, Fort Wayne & Chicago in mid-Ohio, then arc through northern Ohio and southern Michigan until it reached some place on the shore of Lake Michigan. The road would intersect every north-south line in Michigan, built or proposed, and they would feed it lumber traffic to haul to points east. In early 1870 the Ohio & Michigan was formed, and by the end of the year it was merged into a new and more ambitious company, the Mansfield, Coldwater & Lake Michigan.

The Pennsylvania Railroad saw merit in the project and arranged to finance and build the road. Construction started at Mansfield and at Allegan. The section between Allegan and Montieth, where it connected with the Pennsylvania-controlled Grand Rapids & Indiana, was completed in September 1871, and operated by the GR&I. By May 1873 the company started service on the section between Mansfield and Tiffin, Ohio, and had laid track on another forty-two miles from Tiffin to Weston, a hamlet west of Bowling Green. This latter segment was never put in service, and its rails were removed in 1873.

Apparently the Pennsylvania decided there was an advantage if it used the Mansfield road to improve its own route to Toledo. It built no more of the company with the mellifluous name, and after a reorganization in 1878 the name disappeared entirely.

the Mansfield, Coldwater & Lake Michigan wanted; any extension north would tap timberlands. The Muskegon & Ferrysburg built the northern piece first, completing that part in December 1869. This line was the first railroad into Muskegon, providing the city with a connection to the Detroit & Milwaukee, a distinct improvement over the seasonal transport available on Lake Michigan. The new Michigan Lake Shore was headed by Ransom Gardner, who started construction on the line in the spring of 1869 after his employees finished work on the Kalamazoo, Allegan & Grand Rapids. They worked quickly to complete the Allegan–Grand Haven part by the end of August 1870. While the Michigan Lake Shore was being built, the Detroit & Milwaukee must have thought it had to improve its location at Grand Haven. It built a swing bridge over the Grand River between Grand Haven and Ferrysburg, then laid its tracks into downtown Grand Haven. This allowed the Michigan Lake Shore to connect its Muskegon line at Ferrysburg to the southern part of its line at Grand Haven. It had to reimburse the D&M for a share of the use, expense, and maintenance of the bridge. Building its road cleaned out the MLS treasury, forcing the road into receivership in 1872. It languished there for six years, and was managed for part of that time by the Grand Rapids & Indiana and later by the Chicago & Michigan Lake Shore.

David P. Clay of Grand Rapids was the principal promoter of

Marshall & Coldwater

Some railroad dreams died hard. A line to connect Coldwater and Marshall was one of them. George Ingersoll and Charles P. Dibble and some others from Marshall brought it to life in 1870. The Marshall & Coldwater was to build its first section from Coldwater to Marshall, but at three different times in 1871 it changed its northern goal—first to the line of the Peninsular Railway (now the Grand Trunk Western) probably around Olivet, then to Muir, and finally to Elm Hall on the west edge of Gratiot County.

The financial panic of 1873 forced the company to rename itself as the Coldwater, Marshall & Mackinaw in 1874, and in 1876 it again changed its northern terminus, this time to Mt. Pleasant. But these changes brought it no more success. In 1884 the rights were bought by a group headed by Jacob A. Latcha, president of the Michigan & Ohio, which had just finished building the line from Dundee to Allegan through Marshall. The CM&M was renamed the Toledo, Marshall & Northern and planned now to build from Marshall to Elm Hall. Once again nothing happened.

In 1906 the CM&M was renamed the Toledo Michigan & Lake Huron. Nothing came of this last gasp effort, and Marshall's north-south railroad finally faded from sight.

the Grand Rapids, Newaygo & Lake Shore, a road formed in 1869 to build from Grand Rapids to Newaygo and then northwesterly to Lake Michigan. Money help came from both James W. Converse and Ransom Gardner. LS&MS president Horace Clark also bought some of the road's bonds to help the road. In 1870 the road started to build from a connection with Gardner's Kalamazoo, Allegan & Grand Rapids on Grand Rapids' west side, and was completed as far as Sparta in

Ohio & Lake Superior

Possibly the grandest proposal of the 1860s was the Ohio & Lake Superior Rail Road. It was formed by David L. LaTourette, a banker from Fenton, and several other Fenton businessmen in November 1865. It proposed to build 700 miles of line from Toledo, via Saginaw and the Straits of Mackinac, then shoot through the middle of the Upper Peninsula to Crow Wing, Minnesota. (Brainerd is located in Crow Wing County.) The line also planned to build branches to Detroit, Sault Ste. Marie, Marquette, Ontonagon, and Superior City, Wisconsin. At Brainerd, it might have planned to connect with the Northern Pacific to the West Coast. Apparently non-Fenton investors did not share LaTourette's enthusiasm for the undertaking, as nothing more was heard from the project.

In June 1866 LaTourette hatched another but more modest project, the Toledo, Ann Arbor & Saginaw Railroad. This road was to run from Toledo to either Saginaw or Flint, apparently through Fenton, but it fared no better than the Ohio & Lake Superior.

May 1872, to Newaygo in September, and finished to White Cloud in September 1875.

The Saginaw Valley & St. Louis was formed in May 1871 with Saginaw lumberman Ammi W. Wright and some of his friends as the principal promoters. The line was built rapidly and opened for public service on the first day of 1872. It extended from the Pine River in St. Louis to a connection with the Jackson, Lansing & Saginaw southwest of Saginaw at a place named Paines. It used JL&S rails to run its trains into Saginaw.

The Chicago, Saginaw & Canada was formed on Christmas Eve, 1872, by Edward L. Craw, a lumberman from Fruitport who brought in a group of investors from Rhode Island and Connecticut. He proposed

Chicago, Saginaw & Canada

Lumberman Edward L. Craw founded Crawville in 1868, and saw it renamed the next year as Fruitport. As a successful businessman in Saginaw he founded the Chicago, Saginaw & Canada Railroad in December 1872. He envisioned that the road would run from Grand Haven through Fruitport to St. Clair. Between Fruitport and St. Clair the road could go where opportunity arose. The panic of 1873 slowed progress, and it was 1875 before the first fifteen miles of line from Alma to Cedar Lake were built. That this section was out of a direct route was of no importance. It took another four years to build as far west as Lakeview.

By that time the company had gone into receivership, Craw was out of the company, Eastern money had taken over, and a new dynamo in the form of Civil War general Daniel E. Sickles was brought in as president. Even the general's persuasiveness and military reputation could not breathe new life into the road, much less make it profitable. In 1883 it was sold to another company and eventually became a part of the Pere Marquette system.

to build a 210-mile line from Grand Haven via Fruitport to St. Clair. To help raise money during the panic of 1873, Craw hired retired Civil War general Daniel E. Sickles as a promoter and president. His name apparently paid off, for in 1875 the road completed the first twenty miles of its line, from St. Louis west to the lumbering country at Cedar Lake. But before it completed this much of its line, even Sickles could not keep it out of financial difficulty, and the road dropped into receivership.

SOURCES

Baxter, Albert. *History of the City of Grand Rapids, Michigan.* New York: Munsell, 1891.

Brock, Thomas D. "Paw Paw versus the Railroads." *Michigan History* 39:2 (June 1955).

Dunbar, Willis F. *All Aboard! A History of Railroads in Michigan.* Grand Rapids, Mich.: W. B. Eerdmans, 1969.

Ivey, Paul Wesley. *The Pere Marquette Railroad: An Historical Study of the Growth and Development of One of Michigan's Most Important Railway Systems.* Lansing: Michigan Historical Commission, 1919.

Kleiman, Jeff. *The Rise and Fall of the CSCRR: A Short History of a Short-Lived Railroad.* Grand Rapids, Mich.: Friends of the Public Museum, 1992.

van Reken, Donald L. *The Railroads of Holland, Michigan.* Vol. 1, *The Nineteenth Century.* Holland, Mich.: author, 1997.

The Railroad Boom: The Upper Peninsula

The Marquette & State Line gained one of Michigan's Upper Peninsula land grants of 1857, with another to the Ontonagon & State Line. Men connected with the Chicago & North Western formed the Ontonagon road. The owners of the Iron Mountain organized the Marquette road and the Bay de Noquet & Marquette railroad, and they also obtained a land grant for a line between Marquette and Bay de Noquet. The one man involved in both the Marquette and Ontonagon lines was Charles T. Harvey, a figure important in the construction of the Soo locks. He became the agent for the St. Mary's Falls Ship Canal Company, which received the state's land grant to build the canal. It was very likely through Harvey's influence that both the Marquette & State Line and the Ontonagon & State Line, with their land grants, were taken over by the Chicago, St. Paul & Fond du Lac in March 1857, which in turn was bought by the Chicago & North Western in June 1859.

By 1862 the Chicago & North Western completed its line from Chicago, through Janesville and Fond du Lac, to Green Bay, Wisconsin, and began a line of ships between Green Bay and Escanaba, where they connected with the new Peninsula Railroad then being built to the iron mines in the Ishpeming-Negaunee area. After the end of the Civil War the C&NW began building a line between Green Bay and Escanaba to connect to its Peninsula road. The original plans located it along the Lake Michigan shoreline between Menominee and Escanaba, but this was changed after iron ore was discovered in 1866 in the vicinity of Iron Mountain in the Eastern Menominee Range. To allow better future access to this area the C&NW built due north from Menominee to Powers in 1871, and there made a turn to the east to Escanaba, which

Nearly all of the railroad construction in the Upper Peninsula between 1857 and 1874 was to reach iron and, to a lesser extent, copper mines. The iron ore usually moved to the nearest Great Lakes port, the copper to a stamping works. Note that not all branches to iron mines are shown.

it reached by the end of 1872. In 1877 Powers became the junction for a branch that was built west to Iron Mountain.

The Ely brothers and Lewis H. Morgan used their Bay de Noquet & Marquette company to take over the Iron Mountain's line between Marquette and Ishpeming, then built an extension from Ishpeming to the Winthrop Mine in 1862. This gave the company just twenty miles of road and made it eligible for the first section of the Marquette–Bay de Noquet land grant. The Elys sold the remainder of their land grant to the Chicago & North Western, either in an attempt to raise money or because fighting the financial muscle of the C&NW did not appeal to them. The Elys then bought out the owners of the Marquette & Ontonagon Railway and changed the road's name to the Marquette & Ontonagon Railroad. Soon after, the state allowed the transfer of the Marquette-Ontonagon land grant to the new owners. The M&O planned to build from Winthrop Junction to Ontonagon, going around the south side of Lake Michigamme, and by July 1865 extended its line to the eastern shore of that lake. Completing this twenty-mile segment entitled the company to another section of its grant lands.

Not much more happened until the Elys and Morgan bought the Houghton & Ontonagon in 1872 and merged it into their Marquette & Ontonagon to form the Marquette, Houghton & Ontonagon. Despite its name the new focus of the road was to reach Houghton rather than Ontonagon, and the H&O apparently had already started building this line before the merger. The MH&O built a branch line to the Republic

Mine in September 1872. By the end of the year the MH&O had pulled up its original line between Champion and Lake Michigamme and completed a new line between Champion and L'Anse. This extension used more money than the Upper Peninsula men were able to supply, forcing them to turn to New York City. There they found the needed funds, but to get the money control of the road passed out of the hands of the Elys and Morgan, and most Michigan men left the board of directors.

Copper mining did not require railroads to the extent that iron mining did. Raw ore moved by rail from the mine to the company's stamp mill, usually no more than twelve to twenty miles distant. Ships transported the refined ore from the stamp mill. The Hecla Mining Company formed the Hecla & Torch Lake Railroad, opening it for service in 1868 between the Hecla Mine near Calumet and the stamp mill near Lake Linden. The Mineral Range & L'Anse Bay Railroad was formed in 1871, was renamed the Mineral Range in 1872, and put the first part of its line between Hancock and Calumet in service in 1873. The line's two-mile grade climbing out of Hancock was more than 3.5 percent, the steepest hill in main-line operation in Michigan.

SOURCES

Boyum, Burton H. *The Saga of Iron Mining in Michigan's Upper Peninsula*. Marquette,
     Mich.: John M. Longyear, 1983.

Dunbar, Willis F. *All Aboard! A History of Railroads in Michigan*. Grand Rapids,
     Mich.: W. B. Eerdmans, 1969.

Hatcher, Harlan. *A Century of Iron and Men*. Indianapolis: Bobbs-Merrill, 1950.

Monette, Clarence J. *The Mineral Range Railroad*. Lake Linden, Mich.: author, 1993.

Stennett, William H. *Yesterday and Today: A History of the Chicago and North Western
     Railway System*. 3rd ed. Chicago: n.p., 1910.

The First Street Railways

At the end of the Civil War Michigan cities were growing in size and sprawling out from their centers. Dirt streets, deep in mud in wet weather, ice-covered in winter, and choking with dust in the summer, made city travel generally unpleasant and sometimes as difficult as that on the primitive roads in the country. The first improvement was a sort-of coach pulled by horses on a railroad track in the center of a

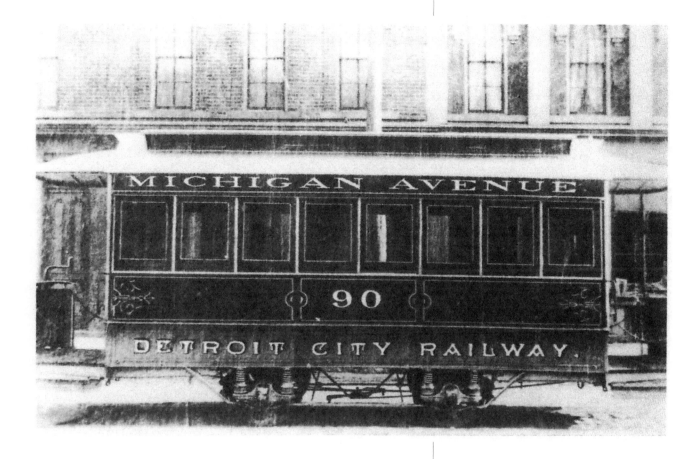

street that began in New York City in 1832. A similar "horse railway" ran in Boston by 1855 and one in Philadelphia by 1857. Detroit, with a population of 60,000 by 1860, was ready for this new modern form of transit. The Detroit City Railway was incorporated in May 1863. Within three years other street railway companies were formed in Saginaw, Grand Rapids, and Bay City, although not all of them started operations.

By November 1863 the Detroit City Railway had built four lines. On 4 August the first line began running on Jefferson from Third Street to Mt. Elliott. Soon after came lines on Woodward from Jefferson to Alexandrine; on Monroe, Randolph, and Gratiot from Woodward to Russell; and on Michigan from Woodward to Twelfth Street. These four lines totaled about six and a half miles of tracks. Extensions came not long after, pushing the Michigan line to Twenty-Fourth Street, the Gratiot line to Dequindre, and the Woodward line to Frederick. The Michigan and Gratiot cars operated down Woodward from Michigan to Jefferson. These routes tied together the downtown, the Michigan

The oldest street railway line in Detroit was that of the Detroit City Railway, which started service in 1863. This sixteen-foot car carried riders from Woodward Avenue, out Michigan, as far as Twenty-Fourth Street.

Jack E. Schramm, from DSR files.

Detroit's second horsecar company was the Fort Wayne & Elmwood. It started service in 1865, connecting a military post and Detroit's largest cemetery, from west to east of downtown.

Central Electric Railfans' Association, from Burton Historical Collection, Detroit Public Library.

Central depot, the Detroit & Milwaukee depot on both Brush Street and Gratiot, and the Michigan Southern depot on Woodward near Baltimore, and passed near the Elmwood and Mt. Elliott cemeteries. Jefferson Avenue cars ran every five to ten minutes from 6:00 A.M. to 10:00 P.M. At the end of the day's operations, the cars at first were left standing in the street. Eventually the company built a car barn near Third Street and stored the cars inside overnight.

The cars were small, only sixteen feet in length, with a platform with steps at each end to climb onto the car. A long bench on each side of the car seated about a dozen people, and several dozen more could stand in the center aisle. The cars were unheated in winter, although straw on the floor did offer a little warmth for the riders. A lantern hung at each end of the car provided light at night. A horse walking on a cinder path between the rails pulled the four-wheeled cars. The fare to ride was 5 cents or twenty-five tickets for $1. This new form of city transportation found riders immediately, but the owners learned that the demand did not translate into profits, even after they raised the fare to 6 cents. In 1866 the Detroit City owners leased the lines to George Hendrie and Thomas Cox. Hendrie and Cox were in the cartage and omnibus business, and the two thought they could make the operation profitable. Hendrie and Cox brought back the nickel fare and issued an additional $400,000 of stock to put the company's finances on a sounder footing.

In 1865 the Fort Street & Elmwood came on the Detroit scene. Most of the initial stock offering was snatched up within hours, and the company was profitable almost from the beginning. It began operating in September from Woodward Avenue west, and the next year it was running its entire line from Fort and Twenty-Fourth Streets to Elmwood and Crogan. In October 1868 a third company was started out Grand River Avenue. It built its own tracks on Woodward, parallel to the Detroit City's lines, and was extended gradually until in 1875 it reached Sixteenth Street. In September 1868 the Hamtramck Street Railway began operating a line on Jefferson Avenue from Mt. Elliott, where it connected with the Detroit City, to Burn, near Memorial Park.

In May 1873 another new Detroit company, with the ungainly name of Central Market, Cass Avenue & Third Street Railway, was organized. One of its founders was Thomas Cox, who had been George Hendrie's partner in the Detroit City Railway. By October this company was operating horsecars on Griswold from Larned, then via State, Cass, Ledyard, and Third out to Holden Road. The same year the Detroit & Grand Trunk Junction Street Railway began building its line from Randolph, out Congress, Seventh, and Baker, as far as Twenty-Second Street. In 1875 the company fell behind on paying for its construction, and the line was transferred to a new company, the Congress & Baker Street Railway. Both of these companies received their franchises over the veto of Detroit mayor Hugh Moffat.

The St. Aubin Street Railway began operating in 1874 from Gratiot and Russell north to the city limits. It ran its cars over the Detroit City tracks on Gratiot from Russell into the downtown, a step that represented the first real cooperation between companies in the city. In 1875 the company was renamed the Russell Street, St. Aubin Avenue and Detroit & Milwaukee Junction Street Railway Company.

To use city streets, companies had to get a franchise from the city. The city and the lines wrangled constantly over these franchises, while the problems of personnel, finance, and operating and maintaining cars and tracks were always there as well. Then came a far more serious problem. In October 1872 the "great epizootic," a respiratory disease for horses, struck Detroit. No cars ran for several days. One company borrowed a "dummy" engine, a small steam locomotive encased in a wooden shell to disguise its appearance in the hope that the altered shape would keep horses from being frightened by the mechanical monster. The Fort Wayne & Elmwood also borrowed a "dummy" from A. A. Wilder, a Detroit inventor, and ran it a few times as a replacement for its horses. After its trial Wilder's device disappeared into oblivion.

Michigan's first non-Detroit horsecar lines were built in Saginaw. At that time the community was two separate municipalities, East Saginaw on the east side of the river, and Saginaw City on the west. The earliest line, the East Saginaw City Railway, was formed in November 1863, which the next year completed a three-mile line extending from the Flint & Pere Marquette's Potter Street station south along Washington Avenue. In April 1864 the Saginaw Street Railway built a line that extended from the intersection of Genesee and Washington, over the river to Michigan, then south on Michigan and Hamilton to just south of Court Street on the west side of the river. There is some uncertainty about the exact date these two lines started operations, but the dates differ by no more than one year.

In May 1864 a local group of men tried but failed to form a street railway company in Grand Rapids. Five months later, in October 1864, George Jerome and E. H. Wilcox of Detroit, Thomas S. Sprague of Saginaw, and Daniel Owen of New York City obtained a franchise and formed the Grand Rapids Street Railway. In May 1865 they began operating their line down Fulton Street from Jefferson and out Monroe Avenue to Leonard Street, providing access to the "remote" Detroit & Milwaukee Railway's depot, which stood more than a mile and a half north of the city's downtown. In 1873 a line was built out Division Avenue from Monroe to the state fairgrounds at Hall Street. In 1875 another line was built to Reeds Lake, which usually ran cars only in the summer when the park was in operation. A "dummy" steam engine was used on this line rather than horses.

In late 1865 Thomas Alva Edison's brother Pitt and some other men from Port Huron formed the Port Huron & Gratiot Street Railway to build a line between downtown Port Huron and Fort Gratiot. At that time the Grand Trunk's depot for Port Huron was at Fort Gratiot, nearly a mile and a half north of the Black River. The horsecars replaced a small passenger boat that had provided the only public transportation between the fort and downtown. The horsecar line began operations in October 1866. In 1869 the line was extended on Military Street from the Black River to the Chicago & Lake Huron depot on Griswold just east of Military.

In 1873 the Grand Trunk began rebuilding its Fort Gratiot yard and removed some PH&G trackage. In retaliation the car line canceled the passes it had issued to Grand Trunk personnel. A deal was soon worked out that allowed the PH&G to lay its tracks through the yard to get to the Fort Gratiot depot once again. Presumably the passes were reissued. Also in 1873 a competing line was formed to build between Port Huron and Fort Gratiot. The City Railroad got its needed franchise, but when it tried to lay rails on Huron Street the older PH&G took it to court. After more than two years of injunctions, suits, and countersuits, the matter was finally resolved with the two companies merging into a new company, the Port Huron Railway.

SOURCES

Baxter, Albert. *History of the City of Grand Rapids, Michigan.* New York: Munsell, 1891.

Dunbar, Willis F. *All Aboard! A History of Railroads in Michigan.* Grand Rapids, Mich.: W. B. Eerdmans, 1969.

History of Saginaw County, Michigan. Chicago: Chas. C. Chapman, 1881.

Lee, Robert E. "The Streetcar Lines of Grand Rapids." *Michigan History* 46:1 (March 1962).

Schramm, Jack E., and William H. Henning. *Detroit's Street Railways.* Vol. 1, *City Lines 1863–1922.* Chicago: Central Electric Railfans' Association, 1978.

———. *When Eastern Michigan Rode the Rails, Book 2.* Glendale, Calif.: Interurban Press, 1986.

Zink, Maximillian A., and George Krambles, eds. *Electric Railways of Michigan, Bulletin 103.* Chicago: Central Electric Railfans' Association, 1959.

Into the Woods

In the earliest days of the Michigan Territory logging was done to clear land for agriculture and to provide material to build shelter. As the frame house began to replace the log cabin the need for lumber grew quickly, so much so that nearly every community had a sawmill. By the 1830s water-powered and steam-powered sawmills producing for local markets were a commonplace throughout Michigan. Much of the southern half of the Lower Peninsula was forested, while the northern half was covered densely and almost completely with pine and hardwoods. As Michigan logging increased, partly from the depletion of the Maine forests and partly from an increased demand in the Midwest, it needed larger amounts of capital and stronger entrepreneurs. A long list of such men included Charles Merrill of Bay City, Charles Mears of Oceana County, William Boardman of Traverse City, Nelson Ludington of Escanaba, and Henry H. Crapo of Flint, to name just a few. The 500 sawmills at work in 1840 doubled to 1,000 in 1860 that were sawing some 800 million board feet. This increase was supported by the reputation Michigan lumber gained after the first shipload was sent East via the Erie Canal in 1847.

By the start of the Civil War Saginaw had become a major sawmill town with at least thirty sawmills in operation. Saginaw and Bay City downriver benefited from the meandering tributaries of the Saginaw River, which reached into heavily timbered areas in Midland, Gladwin, and Clare Counties as well the areas south and southeast of Saginaw. After the Civil War the new national prosperity brought a greater demand for Michigan lumber. Chicago began to develop into an important market as well as a brokerage center, and several Lake Erie ports also grew. During the late 1860s railroads began to haul larger amounts of logs and lumber. The year 1870 found Michigan as the largest lumber producer in the nation.

The life of a lumberjack was a hard one. Five months of a year spent in the woods, logging trees twelve hours a day six days a week, was not for the weak or the timid but was in fact downright hazardous. A falling tree could cripple a man for life. When camp broke up the spring the jack caught the first train to Bay City or Saginaw or Cadillac to enjoy his long-awaited and hard-gained wealth. He anticipated the spree to come, so much so that when the train got to town nearly every window was broken out, seats damaged, and a number of brawling woodsmen disabled. Once off the trains he worked equal havoc on the town itself.

The woods themselves were equally hazardous to work in. Forest fires were a constant threat that might start from any spark. Dry conditions, piles of brush and dead branches, and high winds could create an inferno in an instant. The summer of 1871 was one such a season. Creeks were dry and swamps had dried out, adding to the crisis. On Sunday evening, 8 October 1871, the great Chicago fire broke out. Within two days nearly all of the city's wooden buildings and its downtown were gone. Fanned by high winds, embers jumped Lake Michigan to ignite new fires. The city of Holland was destroyed as was half of Manistee. Farms, homes, fields, and forests in Lake, Osceola, Isabella, Midland, Saginaw, Tuscola, Sanilac, and Huron Counties, a swath spanning the state, were laid waste. A surge in demand for Michigan pine followed in the devastating wake of the 1871 fires. The city of Chicago was rebuilt with it, and most Michigan homes were replaced with it. Elsewhere the demand for new homes of wood continued to grow.

By the year 1873 lumber and forest products made up 15 percent of all freight tonnage hauled by Michigan railroads, and was the third largest category of freight handled, with only agricultural products and merchandise-miscellaneous exceeding it. For some roads it was by far the most important commodity: 58 percent of all tonnage on the Flint & Pere Marquette was forest products; 64 percent on the Detroit, Lansing & Lake Michigan; 69 percent on the Chicago & Michigan Lake Shore; and a whopping 76 percent on the Grand Rapids & Indiana. On the minuscule Kalamazoo & South Haven, lumber made up 68 percent of its traffic.

The spring drive on the river was especially important for the towns of Manistee and Muskegon, which did not have much rail access to timberlands. For Saginaw and Bay City, the railroad at first supplemented the river drives, but by the 1870s the river's importance faded as it was replaced by the rails. After 1870 three railroads were pushing into the far north woods. The Jackson, Lansing & Saginaw, a subsidiary of the Michigan Central, began building north from Bay City in 1870. By August 1871 it was built to Standish and by year's end to Alger. In late 1873 it was running as far north as Gaylord. The Flint & Pere Marquette was completed through Saginaw to both Flint and Averill by 1870, then extended to Reed City by the end of 1871. These two roads ensured the preeminence of Saginaw as a mill town and as a shipping point for finished lumber. The Grand Rapids & Indiana was built primarily to move logs from the area north of Grand Rapids. It was operating to Paris in August 1870, to Cadillac by the end of 1871, to Fife Lake the following September, and completed into Petoskey in May 1874. Cadillac became a sawmill town, and the Grand Rapids furniture industry developed from the finished product coming down the GR&I. The growth in lumbering all over the Lower Peninsula, with the extending rail system that reached it, made the two million tons of forest products hauled the second most important tonnage category in 1875, 13 percent, while only agricultural products of all sorts exceeded it at 23 percent. Lumber comprised over 60 percent of the freight tonnage of the Chicago & Michigan Lake Shore; the Detroit & Bay City; the Detroit, Lansing & Lake Michigan; the Flint & Pere Marquette; and the Jackson, Lansing & Saginaw. For the Grand Rapids & Indiana, it made

By 1875 three railroads—the Jackson, Lansing & Saginaw; the Flint & Pere Marquette; and the Saginaw Valley & St. Louis—were feeding logs to the sawmills at Saginaw and Bay City. The Grand Rapids & Indiana moved them to Cadillac and Grand Rapids.

up 74 percent of all tonnage hauled. Moving only a tenth of the GR&I's traffic, the lumber tonnage on the Saginaw Valley & St. Louis was a whopping 79 percent of all freight hauled.

Lumber barons have been widely and loudly criticized for logging off Michigan in such short order. From today's perspective there is truth in the charge. It would probably have been prudent to plant new seedlings as the mature trees were harvested. However, in fairness to the lumbermen, they worked within the legal and ethical framework of the day. Each advanced his own money to produce a product for which he had no assurance there would be a market or an easy way to reach it. He might lose his investment overnight in a forest fire or sawmill fire. His ships developed Great Lakes shipping to maturity, but they could sink with a total loss. He brought men and then families that opened up remote areas that otherwise might never have been settled. He established new cities—among them Muskegon, Manistee, Saginaw,

Bay City, Alpena, and Cadillac—and a good many more smaller ones that evolved into important permanent communities. In most cases the money the lumberman made stayed where he lived. Much of it returned to communities in a wide variety of ways. The beneficence of Charles H. Hackley to the city of Muskegon may be the best-known example of the selflessness of civic concern, but it is far from the only case.

SOURCES

Holbrook, Stewart H. *Holy Old Mackinaw*. New York: Macmillan, 1938.

Quaife, Milo M., and Sidney Glazer. *Michigan: From Primitive Wilderness to Industrial Commonwealth*. New York: Prentice-Hall, 1948.

Railroad Regulation and the Railroad Commissioner

The first railroad charter granted by the Michigan Territory in 1830 contained some regulatory provisions, including taxation of some sort and a few not too onerous restrictions of the company's rights. In subsequent charters both the rights and the regulations were expanded so that the state gained some small measure of control, very often in the fares that could be charged passengers. Michigan's general railroad incorporation law, enacted in 1855, had provisions that regulated building and operating railroads, but with little enforcement mechanism. In 1857 the legislature created the Board of Control of Railroads, which did little and was abolished in 1865. From one point of view the weakness of both the railroad incorporation law and the board, as well as many of the earlier charters, was the lack of adequate means of enforcing any requirements.

By the early 1870s the Michigan legislature had growing concerns about rate abuses, about the general safety of passengers and employees, and about the general financial condition of the railroad companies. The Granger movement contributed, but it was only one of several forces pushing the lawmakers. Governor John J. Bagley, in his annual message to the legislature in 1873, stated that

> railroads are something more than mere private enterprises. They are not only a public convenience but a public necessity. By the law of necessity they must be made subservient to the public ends. The

Governor John J. Bagley picked Stephen S. Cobb of Kalamazoo to be Michigan's first commissioner of railroads. Cobb held the office from 1872 until 1877 and added to its importance. He acknowledged that he owed much of his success to what he learned from the dean of railroad commissioners, Charles Francis Adams Jr. of Massachusetts.

public are directly interested to see that these roads are constructed and operated honestly; that they are managed and operated alike for the benefit of their owners, creditors and the public, and with a view to the public convenience and interest.

The legislature concurred and early in 1873 established the office of commissioner of railroads. Michigan followed the lead of such states as Massachusetts, New York, Ohio, and Illinois, which already had created similar functionaries in attempts to regulate the worst abuses of a boisterous railroad industry. Governor Bagley named Kalamazoo businessman Stephen S. Cobb as the first commissioner.

A primary function of the commissioner was to inspect and make decisions about the safety of railroad operations. He was ordered to inspect track and, if found unsafe, could restrict its use until repairs were made. Passenger cars were required to have air brakes of a design approved by the commissioner. He could order a flagman to be stationed at road crossings as well as requiring that gates be put in at crossings with other railroads. He could inspect any company books or records and could require an annual report about the Michigan business of all railroads. Once his office was set up Cobb wrote to the railroad companies

that he has no wish, by means of hostile or unreasonable action, to inflict any injury whatever upon the great railroad interests of the State. Between these interests and those of the people at large, he considers no conflict necessary; and it seems to him that if they are thoroughly harmonized, the result cannot but benefit the State and the railroads together. No oppressive regulations, and no extraordinary exercise of power are contemplated by him; he simply, but firmly, intends to enforce the various provisions enacted and to be enacted by the law-making power with reference to railroad management without our borders.

Cobb knew he had to rely on cooperation from the railroads to do his work. Despite his reassuring words the railroads' responses to the required annual information report were, according to Cobb, "by no means perfect."

The information asked of the railroads was nearly identical to that asked by the Illinois commissioner and was, by today's standards, quite elementary. Yet it was an improvement over the haphazard information furnished the public by railroads, which most often gave out only what suited their purposes. Michigan law ordered forty-two specific pieces of information: names of officers; amounts of assets, liabilities, stock, and debt; value of the property; miles of track owned; miles operated by passenger and freight trains; number of passengers carried and earnings and expenses for this; number of tons of freight hauled and earnings and expenses for this; a breakdown of all operating expenses; the fares and rates charged for hauling passengers and freight; and some other miscellaneous questions. The commissioner was authorized to add to this list and very quickly did so. In his second annual report there are questions about accidents, personal injuries, and fatalities; about the amount of fencing along the railroad right-of-way; as well as more detailed information about the physical plant. The commissioner's annual reports for the years from 1872 through 1898 are a rich source of information about the state's railroads.

When it established the railroad commissioner the legislature also passed a new railroad incorporation law that added regulatory provisions as well as new detailed requirements for forming a railroad company. The law put particular emphasis on the financial requirements, on liabilities for nonperformance, and on the procedures for acquiring land for the railroad. Standards for highway crossings, maximum passenger fares, requirements applicable to the consolidation of two companies, rate of taxation, and procedures for handling baggage are only a few of the catalog of provisions included in the act. One paragraph explains which train has precedence when two trains arrive at a crossing at the same time. Conductors were charged with "the protection of the passengers . . . from the violent, abusive, profane, or indecent language or conduct of any passenger" and were given the powers of a sheriff to put offenders off the train. It was made a felony to sell fraudulent stock or debt. The railroad commissioner was charged with enforcing many of these requirements. But to do that he had to take his case to the state attorney general or a local prosecutor and ask him to enforce compliance. For all of this the commissioner was paid a salary of $4,000 per year plus expenses, and was allowed to have a clerk who was to be paid $1,000.

Neither of these important pieces of legislation gave the commissioner any jurisdiction over establishing freight rates. The principal complaint of the Patrons of Husbandry, or the Grange as it was commonly known, was that railroad freight rates were too high in general and were not applied equitably. The crux of their demand concerned what has become known as the "long and short haul clause," a situation

Charles Francis Adams Jr., a great-grandson of President John Adams, became an early and much respected railroad commissioner for the state of Massachusetts. Later he served six years as president of the Union Pacific Railroad, then retired to a career as historian and writer. Much of his writing argues for the need to reform railroad financing methods and corporate management.

in which a road charged more for a short-freight haul than for a longer haul. Such rates were a common practice of railroads of the time. Between points where there was railroad or steamship competition, the rails charged a lower competitive rate to retain business, and they offset this lower rate by charging higher rates to and from points where they had no competition. The railroads had no difficulty justifying this approach; their shippers disagreed vociferously.

Cobb's first annual report addressed the problem of freight rates with surprising good sense, at least from a railroad point of view, although hardly in language that the reformers wanted to hear. He wrote that the most common wrong was the difference in freight rates charged between points with competition and those without. Other states had attempted to remedy this condition in a variety of ways: by setting maximum rates per mile, by setting rates on a pro rata basis, by allowing earnings to determine rates, or by requiring roads to set "reasonable" rates. From a disadvantaged shipper's point of view, none of these worked effectively. Cobb then quoted the tart-tongued Massachusetts commission chairman, Charles Francis Adams Jr.:

> The passage of a statute law is the natural remedy to which every American has recourse in presence of any matter calling for reform. It is a species of popular political pill—a panacea good for all social disorders. As a general rule, the remedy is found to rather aggravate the disorder than to remove its cause; but faith is strong, and the nine failures out of ten trials do not in this case greatly shake it. An act of the Legislature is still our sovereign specific.

Adams closed by writing that "in this country alone one Congress and some forty State Legislatures turn out more or less statutes every year to the great benefit of the legal profession, but with results small enough so far as the end in view is concerned." After spending several pages discussing the alternatives available, Cobb concluded that even the most able managers and commissioners were "unable to contrive any general regulation which shall be equitable in all its parts."

Cobb warmed to the subject by pointing out that the legislature already had allowed Upper Peninsula railroads a different, and higher, passenger fare than allowed to Lower Peninsula lines. He brought out the need to consider ruling grades in each direction, the length of the haul in relation to the terminal expenses, and the competition from seasonal Great Lakes shipping. He believed that forcing lower rates between noncompetitive points could only be offset by increasing rates from points with competition, and this could drive business away from Michigan roads and to other lines and other forms of transport, all of which would not serve business generally or be of benefit. Further, the panic of 1873 was now causing a number of Michigan roads to operate at a loss. Cobb was upset that some Upper Peninsula carriers were diverting traffic through Wisconsin and Illinois, although no road had been built across the peninsula to establish connections with Lower Peninsula roads. But he saved his best argument for last by reminding readers that most of Michigan's railroads had not been built with Michigan capital and that arbitrarily lower rates might undermine profitability enough to reduce needed future investments in the state's carriers. In the final analysis Cobb thought that competition was the most effective means of holding freight rates low.

Cobb made every effort to be an effective commissioner. He certainly did have some sympathy with the railroads since a few years earlier he had been a director of the Kalamazoo & South Haven. He knew he had to rely on the voluntary cooperation of the railroads to furnish the information he needed; there was too much office work to allow for extensive verification in the field. He did meet with some success in his efforts to improve the cooperation of railroads with his office. Later annual reports were more complete and eventually became more detailed, although Cobb complained repeatedly about the excessive tardiness of some railroads in filing reports with his office. During his four years in office he gained a national reputation as an authority on railroad regulation. In 1877 William B. Williams succeeded Cobb and held the commissioner's office until 1883.

SOURCES

Barton, Richard H. "A History of Railroad Regulation in Michigan." Master's thesis, Michigan State University, 1948.

Dunbar, Willis F. *All Aboard! A History of Railroads in Michigan*. Grand Rapids, Mich.: W. B. Eerdmans, 1969.

Elliott, Frank N. *When the Railroad Was King*. Lansing: Michigan Historical Commission, 1966.

Michigan. *First Annual Report of the Commissioner of Railroads*. Lansing, Mich.: W. S. George, 1874.

Utley, Henry M., and Byron M. Cutcheon. *Michigan as a Province, Territory and State* . . . New York: Publishing Society of Michigan, 1906.

Westmeyer, Russell E. *Economics of Transportation*. Englewood Cliffs, N.J.: Prentice-Hall, 1952.

New Money and the Panic of 1873

At the end of the Civil War financiers had their pockets stuffed and were looking for profitable uses. Railroads soon came to the fore to use that money. Between the end of the war and the end of 1873 the national railroad network doubled in size to 70,000 miles. In Michigan, 2,300 miles were built, two-and-one-half times the trackage in use in 1865. Every Michigan city of size below Bay City and Ludington had rail service. Two lines penetrated farther north, one to Gaylord and another to Petoskey. Some roads had been built in the Upper Peninsula, although most of that mileage was concentrated in the iron-mining area west of Marquette.

As the railroad system grew after the war some Michigan communities were bypassed, and they wanted the rails pushed faster and given more aid. The state constitution barred the state from helping, and the federal government had distributed the land grants so that more could not be expected from that source. Enterprising legislators saw what some other states were doing and in 1863 began passing special acts authorizing municipalities, townships, and counties to issue bonds to assist railroad construction. State senator Henry H. Crapo, who was then building his Flint & Holly line, tried to get some sensible restrictions added to these bills but had little success. Twelve such acts passed in 1864 and another eight in 1865. When he became governor he signed several of these bills. In 1867 two Kalamazoo County townships issued bonds without waiting for state authorization. When enabling legislation came to him, Crapo sent it back with a strongly worded veto message. Both houses of the legislature overrode the veto. At another time Governor Crapo, still taking issue with such aid bills, vetoed fourteen of them in one day.

Most of the projects supported were in southern Michigan and were designed to provide a competitor for communities that already had one railroad. Still, many people were convinced that the only way their town could survive was to have a railroad built to it. The railroad aid that would provide a line remained very popular, and the bills started again when Governor Henry Baldwin took office in January 1869. That year the legislature enacted a general law that provided blanket authorization for all political bodies for such financial aid; Baldwin signed it. Townships began issuing bonds all out of proportion to their population or their taxing ability. By 1870 a total of $1,646,300 in aid had been sold and transferred to the railroads. The subject remained controversial and eventually wound up before the Michigan Supreme Court. Washtenaw County's Salem Township refused to deliver its bonds to the Detroit & Howell, so the railroad sued. In 1871, in *People v. Salem*, the court found the broad aid act unconstitutional. It followed up the next year in *Bay City v. The State Treasurer* by declaring that all the bonds issued under the 1869 law were invalid. Led by Chief Justice Thomas M. Cooley, the court held that the prohibition against support for internal improvements extended to all units of government. While other states' courts had found in favor of this kind of aid, that would not be the case in Michigan. The legislature attempted to amend the state constitution to reauthorize railroad aid, but the voters turned down the proposal in November 1872. The only recourse that now remained to bondholders was to sell the investment to an out-of-state owner, who could sue for payment in federal court. Some repayment might be obtained this way, but usually not the full invested amount.

Jay Cooke, a banker from Philadelphia, was in the forefront of the North's arrangements to finance the Civil War. In 1869 he took over management of the Northern Pacific Railroad, the first line to be built to the Pacific Northwest. As the Crédit Mobilier scandal of the Union Pacific Railroad grew in size, Congress became less than cooperative, financially speaking. This in turn strained Cooke's resources more and more as he attempted to keep construction going. The postwar eight-year boom got one of those periodic shocks to reality and came to an abrupt halt in September 1873 when Jay Cooke & Company closed for business.

The financial panic that followed blanketed the country and brought business almost to a complete halt. For railroads, too much money had been pumped into companies that would never be able to earn enough money to pay the interest on their debt, much less any dividends to the owners. Such financial stresses had caused panics in the past and did so again in 1873. In Michigan, only 100 miles of road were opened in 1874 and 1875, another 100 the next two years, and about 100 in 1878 and 1879. Six Michigan companies did not have enough income to cover their operating expenses, although most of these were short-distance carriers. More serious, four roads were unable to pay any of the interest due on their debt, and nine more could pay only a part. In

1875 twenty-one Michigan roads had operating expenses and interest that totaled more than their earnings for the year. Many of the smaller and marginal carriers were on this list, but they kept company with the likes of the larger Flint & Pere Marquette; Detroit, Lansing & Lake Michigan; Chicago & Michigan Lake Shore; Grand Rapids & Indiana; Detroit & Milwaukee; all of the leased roads of the Michigan Central; and both of Canada Southern subsidiaries in Michigan. The depression that followed the panic of 1873 reduced railroad revenues, yet the companies continued to borrow and push up their interest expenses.

SOURCES

Cochrane, Thomas C., and William Miller. *The Age of Enterprise*. Rev. ed. New York: Harper & Row, 1961.

Michigan. *First Annual Report of the Commissioner of Railroads*. Lansing, Mich.: W. S. George, 1874. (Reports the year 1872)

Michigan. *Fourth Annual Report of the Commissioner of Railroads*. Lansing, Mich.: W. S. George, 1876. (Reports the year 1875)

Michigan Railroad Commission. *Aids, Gifts, Grants and Donations to Railroads . . .* Lansing, Mich.: Wynkoop, Hallenbeck, Crawford, 1919.

Stover, John F. *American Railroads*. Chicago: University of Chicago Press, 1961.

Utley, Henry M., and Byron M. Cutcheon. *Michigan as a Province, Territory and State . . .* New York: Publishing Society of Michigan, 1906.

The Explosive Years, 1875–1897

The Gilded Age Begins

The booming prosperity that followed the end of the Civil War was brought to an abrupt stop by the financial panic of 1873. If one event has to be named as triggering the depression that followed, it was the collapse of the Philadelphia banking house of Jay Cooke on 18 September 1873. The effects rippled quickly through the country and soon grew into the most severe depression in the nation's history. The Civil War furnished new stimuli to the Industrial Revolution so that by the war's end the nation's industrialists, now wealthy from the war effort, were plowing money back into the economy. Old and new industries benefited, and the railroads were no exception. Domestic capital was matched by foreign inflows, especially from the Dutch, English, French, and Germans. The first transcontinental railroad, built by the Union Pacific and Central Pacific, was completed in 1869. By 1873 the nation's total rail mileage more than doubled from the 35,000 miles in 1865. Michigan's railroads grew from 931 to 3,253 miles in the same period.

The panic of 1873 rolled through the economy by severely restricting business expansion, with railroad construction particularly hard hit. Money for new businesses dried up. It took nearly all of the following four years to work the excesses out of the economy. During this period many companies reduced employee wages, causing a series of strikes and a never-before-witnessed level of industrial violence. The "Molly Maguires" in the Pennsylvania coalfields only hinted at the militancy labor was adopting. One result was a substantial growth in labor union membership. Corporate bankruptcies resulted in reorganizations that lightened the debt burden of many companies to such an extent they were made profitable. By the end of the decade confidence was reappearing, and once again money began to tiptoe into new ventures.

What followed was more spectacular than anything that had come before. There seemed to be no limit on the amount of money that poured

Growth of Michigan Population, Railroad Mileage, Traffic, Revenues, 1875–1895

	1875	1884	1890	1895
Population, Mich., thous.	1,334	1,853	2,094	2,242
Miles of road	3,347	5,120	6,809	7,609
Freight revenue, $thous.	17,233	18,712	22,533	18,979
Freight ton miles, thous.	1,231,022	2,027,473	2,991,458	2,483,915
Freight train miles, thous.	17,620*	39,961*	51,506*	13,854
Passenger revenue, $thous.	8,392	9,309	11,634	9,693
Passengers carried, thous.	6,751	9,150	12,411	10,108
Passenger miles, thous.	284,301	352,008	462,867	357,257
Passenger train miles, thous.	5,838	10,068	12,412	10,878

*Freight train miles for system, not Michigan only.

into businesses old and new. It came from the United States and from Europe. The European funds were accompanied by immigrant workers to man the growing economy. They poured through the ports into the terrible slums of all the large cities to find ready employment. Their work paid enough to allow the immigrant families to survive, but not much more. Only the pressure from a stream of still newer arrivals looking for work kept the labor force compliant to their bosses' demands.

Any sort of business conduct seemed legitimate, and most were legal. The 1880s brought out the full talents of such men as Andrew Carnegie, John D. Rockefeller, Jay Gould, William Henry Vanderbilt, James J. Hill, Cyrus McCormick, Philip D. Armour, Henry Clay Frick, and dozens more. These men, "robber barons" to some, used any device that might increase their profits. One newly favored tool was the "trust," a cartel of one or more owners of companies in a specific industry that created a monopoly. Oil, steel, tobacco, and other smaller fields came under the control of the trusts. The trusts may have improved the efficiency of businesses, provided employment, and improved distribution of the product. Every trust was created to achieve but one goal, and that goal was increased profits for the owners. It succeeded in this to a amount never before seen in human history. Money flooded in faster than it could be spent, and the wealthy eventually had to resort to giving it away for charitable ends. The noblest of Europe's kings and queens did not live as well as these American plutocrats.

The public thought they were largely excluded from these profits and yet were very much at the mercy of both the manufacturers and the railroads. There were close financial ties between the two groups and with the banks that provided capital to both. Interlocking directorates emphasized the close interreliance between them. The public also thought that businesses had such control of the state legislatures and judiciaries and of the Congress that the citizenry was excluded. Farmers formed the Patrons of Husbandry (the Grange) to correct their grievances against railroads and grain dealers. Labor unions grew still more aggressive in trying to alleviate the oppressive conditions of factory workers. All these efforts were met and challenged by corporate managements who marshaled the courts, police, and even the general government on their behalf. This suppression did nothing to mitigate the feelings of the public, and, in fact, our society continues to live to this day with the abrasions of a division between management and labor. Still, a not small segment of society did benefit from the increased production and profitability and moved into improved status, what today would be called the "upper middle class." These benefits included discretionary disposable income, leisure time, mobility, and an improved level of education.

SOURCES

Cochrane, Thomas C., and William Miller. *The Age of Enterprise*. Rev. ed. New York: Harper & Row, 1961.

Johnson, Paul. *A History of the American People*. New York: HarperCollins, 1997.

Morison, Samuel Eliot. *The Oxford History of the American People*. New York: Oxford University Press, 1965.

The Grangers and the Railroads

The Patrons of Husbandry was a movement that attempted to improve the social and economic conditions of the American farmer. Founded in 1869 not long after the end of the Civil War, its first Michigan chapter was established in 1872. The Grange, as it soon became known, grew quickly as the panic of 1873 spread; by October 1875 there were 609 chapters and 33,000 members in Michigan, with about 800,000 members nationally.

In its early years the Grange worked to improve daily life on the farm, to relieve some of the isolation and separateness that farmers endured, to encourage education, and to improve economic conditions. Women were admitted as equal members, an unusual step at the time that brought a social aspect to the Grange besides its reform agenda. The importance of economic reform, the need to relieve the farmer of the economic suffering he was experiencing, took on greater importance as the panic of 1873 took hold. As one response the Grange made a large-scale attempt to establish cooperatives. It founded grain elevators, warehouses, factories, stores, and even banks and fire and life insurance companies to benefit its members. The Grange organized marketing efforts that sold grain as far away as Europe.

The Grange's importance grew through a combination of influences. Farm prices had dropped from the inflated levels of the Civil War. Grain Belt states that straddled the Mississippi River experienced substantial increases in population as new farmers moved in, some in search of cheaper land and some simply to make a new start. Railroads expanded rapidly into these new agricultural territories, and the farmer was dependent on them from the start, both when buying supplies and equipment and when selling the grain he raised. The farmer thought he had supported the coming of the rails. He had purchased stock in new companies to assist in their construction, and often had seen his investment disappear through the double-dealings of their promoters. He had agreed to tax himself so his community could give aid to some railroad that demanded it to build to his town. Now these railroads were no longer owned locally but by men from New York and New England, absentee owners who had little concern for the farmer except the amount of revenue that could be extracted from him. Worse still, he assumed the railroads had corrupted state legislatures. The Crédit Mobilier scandal that came out of the construction of the Union Pacific provided the farmer ample support for his feelings. To the farmer looking for the largest villain nearest at hand, the railroads became the focus of his grievances. Regulating railroads, and more particularly the freight rates they charged, became an important political goal of the Grangers.

At first the Grangers succeeded. In 1871 Illinois passed legislation that fixed passenger fares and put limits on freight rates, and Minnesota later enacted a similar measure. In 1874 both Wisconsin and Iowa adopted laws that set maximum rates. As expected, the railroad companies aggressively opposed any form of rate regulation. They believed theirs was a privately owned business and that the government had no right to regulate it, any more than it regulated any other private business. Not until 1876, when the Supreme Court decided *Munn v. Illinois*, was it established that railroads were "engaged in a public employment affecting the public interest" and therefore were allowed to "charge only a reasonable sum" for their services. In the years following the Court expanded on this decision with others that firmly established the right of the states to regulate railroads. That part of interstate commerce that was conducted in a given state could be regulated by that state, at least until Congress took up the matter and enacted legislation regulating interstate commerce.

The Grange also encouraged state legislatures to establish railroad regulatory commissions. It was more successful in this, as many midwestern states established regulatory boards or commissioners by the end of the 1870s. Michigan was among the pioneering states; its first railroad commissioner took office in 1873.

What success the Grange enjoyed soon became undone. The railroads tied up rate regulation in the courts so completely that little was ever achieved to lower freight rates to the farmers' benefit. Some states' efforts proved to be so difficult to enforce or so counterproductive that several repealed their rate laws within just a few years. Legislatures proved themselves unsuited as the means to set rates; they learned there was no simple response to an exceedingly complex situation. Lawmakers soon passed off any responsibility by charging their railroad commissions with the duty of setting "just and fair" rates. Railroad influence over legislatures was little changed, and it would be several decades before free passes and financial palm-greasing were reined in. The state railroad commissions did remain, gaining influence and authority. Their ability to regulate a wide range of rail operations, in addition to rates, grew, and eventually replaced their information-gathering function.

In the recovery that followed the panic of 1877 and with the return of a more general prosperity, the militant influence of the Grange began to diminish. Membership began to shrink, and some financial difficulties cropped up due to poor management, all causing its political influence to wane. The Grange lives on to this day with its social functions now at the center of existence.

SOURCES

Cochrane, Thomas C., and William Miller. *The Age of Enterprise*. Rev. ed. New York: Harper & Row, 1961.

Elliott, Frank N. *When the Railroad Was King*. Lansing: Michigan Historical Commission, 1966.

Cornelius Vanderbilt—the "Commodore" (above)—used a combination of aggressive business tactics, stock manipulation, and shrewd management to build a family fortune. His son William Henry Vanderbilt (below) in less than a decade nearly doubled the family money.

Miller, George H. *Railroads and the Granger Laws*. Madison: University of Wisconsin Press, 1971.

Rubenstein, Bruce A., and Lawrence E. Ziewacz. *Michigan: A History of the Great Lakes State*. Arlington Heights, Ill.: Forum Press, 1981.

Stover, John F. *American Railroads*. Chicago: University of Chicago Press, 1961.

Westmeyer, Russell E. *Economics of Transportation*. Englewood Cliffs, N.J.: Prentice-Hall, 1952.

The Vanderbilt's Empire in Michigan

Financial panics provide opportunities, at least for men with money, and the panic of 1873 was no different. In Michigan railroading circles two such men were Cornelius Vanderbilt and his very capable son William Henry Vanderbilt. After the two took complete control of the Lake Shore & Michigan Southern in September 1869, William became more convinced that Chicago was to be the most important city in the American Midwest. The elder Vanderbilt took more persuading. He is reported to have said to William, "If we take hold of roads running all the way to Chicago, we might as well go on to San Francisco or even to China." To William, it was one thing to have favorable agreements with connecting roads and another to have outright control of them. The Commodore eventually changed his mind, although it took William and his brother-in-law Horace Clark to persuade him.

By 1873 the Vanderbilts owned some stock in the Great Western Railway in Canada as well as in the Michigan Central, largely because these seemed prudent investments. Although the Michigan Central was prosperous, the Canada Southern was not. In fact, the Commodore ignored the Canada Southern. In September 1873 the CS failed to make an interest payment on some of its bonds. Soon afterward came the Jay Cooke collapse, with the end result that the Canada Southern was bankrupt. The company managed to stay alive, and, despite two years of failed efforts to make any kind of financial arrangement with any potential owner, the road continued to operate and expand. It gained access to Niagara Falls, New York, which gave it some important eastern connections, and also got running rights into Hamilton, Ontario. Its search for a friendly buyer was fruitless. The Vanderbilts bought up CS stock and bonds at bargain-basement prices. In September 1877 it was announced that a financial arrangement had been made with Vanderbilt's New York Central & Hudson River. The Canada Southern

William Henry Vanderbilt

Born 8 May 1821, New Brunswick, N.J.; died 8 December 1885, New York City.

Vanderbilt grew up in the shadow of his domineering father, Cornelius "Commodore" Vanderbilt. His father put him in charge of a hard-luck farm that he made profitable. When he repeated this on a short railroad on Staten Island, his father decided that the son had some future in the railroad business. At age forty-three, in 1864, he was named vice president of his father's New York & Harlem Railroad. This was followed by more and greater involvement in the management and extension of the Vanderbilt railroads. One historian credits William Henry with persuading his father to invest in and later to acquire the Lake Shore & Michigan Southern, a purchase that extended the New York Central's line from Buffalo into Chicago.

When his father died in January 1877, William Henry had been prepared to assume the reins of his father's empire. To retain secure control in the family, the major share of Cornelius Vanderbilt's estate of nearly $100 million went to William Henry and four of his sons. During 1877 William Henry took over the presidencies of most of the Vanderbilt-owned companies and held them until 1883. In Michigan this included the Lake Shore & Michigan Southern and the Michigan Central. His primary goal was to preserve and increase the profits of his railroads through tight control over expenses, investments in better locomotives and equipment, and improvements of the physical plant. He bought important connecting roads, such as the Big Four (Cleveland, Cincinnati, Chicago & St. Louis), and competitors like the Nickel Plate (New York, Chicago & St. Louis).

William Henry Vanderbilt was a hands-on manager who found it almost impossible to delegate authority. Every detail passed over his desk, and everything had to have his personal approval. This approach wore at his less than robust health. The constant public and media criticism of his railroads and his family's wealth also took its toll. His blood pressure was high, he suffered a slight stroke, and he was losing the sight in one eye. He decided it was time to relieve the burden and arranged with J. Pierpont Morgan to sell a large block of his own New York Central stock. In May 1883, with the sale completed and with his two oldest sons groomed to continue control and policy management of the family roads, William Henry Vanderbilt resigned his presidencies and most of his directorships. He gave up driving his favorite trotting horse. He advised and counseled, but stayed in the background.

On 8 December 1885, while conferring with Baltimore & Ohio president Robert Garrett, he suddenly stopped talking, his face flushed a dark red, he fell to the floor, and he died almost immediately from a seizure.

His two oldest sons, Cornelius II and William K., became active in company management after receiving their inheritance from the Commodore. His son Frederick W. and sons-in-law Hamilton Twombly and William S. Webb held directorships. George W. Vanderbilt, William's youngest son, built Biltmore in Asheville, North Carolina.

now was a Vanderbilt road. Immediately new freight traffic began coming from the NYC&HR; William Henry Vanderbilt began to spend some money to upgrade the road.

The Vanderbilts also began to buy more heavily into the Michigan Central. The *Chicago Tribune* of 22 September 1875 editorialized that

Henry Brockholst Ledyard

Born 20 February 1844, Paris, France; died 25 May 1921, Detroit.

Ledyard graduated from West Point in 1865 and served in the U.S. Army for five years. In 1870 he became a clerk on the Chicago, Burlington & Quincy, which brought him to the attention of James F. Joy, who gave him increasingly responsible duties, then brought him to Detroit in 1874 as assistant general superintendent of the Michigan Central and a year later as general superintendent. William Henry Vanderbilt named him general manager of the MC in 1877 and president in 1883. He retired from active management in 1905 and served as chairman of the board until his death.

Ledyard's management of the MC was his obsession. His hand was in everything; no subject was too unimportant to come to his attention. The result was that he made a good railroad into a very good railroad. During his tenure the entire main line was double-tracked and some difficult grades moderated; better engines and equipment were acquired; passenger train service was improved; and new runs were instituted. The completion of the Detroit River Tunnel in 1910 and the plans for Detroit's Michigan Central Terminal were capstones of his remarkable career.

Henry B. Ledyard.

Reprinted from Clarence M. Burton, *The City of Detroit, 1701–1922* (Detroit, 1922), 4: facing 5.

"owing to the fact that Michigan Central had to pass its dividends during the past few years, its stock had depreciated and it was an easy matter for Vanderbilt to purchase a controlling interest." James F. Joy had his hands full as president of four important railroads: the Michigan Central; the Chicago, Burlington & Quincy; the Chicago & Michigan Lake Shore; and the Detroit, Lansing & Lake Michigan. The panic already persuaded him in 1873 to give up the presidency of the C&MLS. During 1873 Joy increased the MC debt from $7 to $11 million, using most of it for improvements and additions to the main line and for locomotives and cars to operate the entire system. Also, Joy took on interest guarantees on more than $7 million of debt for subsidiaries that the MC had leased in the early 1870s. Expenses rose faster than revenue during 1873, and Joy was forced to omit a dividend. Things did not improve during 1874, and in 1875 became still worse when freight revenues dropped nearly $1 million.

Vanderbilt knew an opportunity when he saw one. He began buying MC stock as its price dropped below its $100 par value, a serious event for a conservative company. At the same time, Joy had a falling out with John Murray Forbes. Forbes and his New England associates were the financial backbone of the Michigan Central and most of the other roads of which Joy was president. Forbes thought Joy mishandled some funds of the Chicago, Burlington & Quincy and that Joy misrepresented the events. Their close working relationship of thirty years was destroyed overnight. Forbes forced Joy out of the CB&Q presidency and took it himself. It may have been this mistrust of Joy that persuaded Forbes's fellow New Englanders to follow his lead and sell their MC stock to Vanderbilt.

As 1876 wound down it became apparent that the Vanderbilts were gaining influence at the MC. Commodore Vanderbilt died in January 1877, leaving the future of his railroads in the hands of son William Henry Vanderbilt. Vanderbilt agreed that Samuel Sloan would become the MC president at the June 1877 board meeting, just a year after he had been made vice president of the road. Joy was out. A year later, in June 1878, now owning a majority of the stock, William Henry Vanderbilt named himself president of the Michigan Central.

During Joy's tenure the Detroit River crossing to the Great Western remained a problem. He wanted to replace the cumbersome Windsor-Detroit ferry service. Early in the 1870s, with the help of the Great Western, he began tunneling under the river. His workmen found pockets of quicksand; two men were killed and more incapacitated by gases from the sulfur streams they uncovered. The tunneling stopped. Joy then tried for a bridge across the river. He obtained the permission of the appropriate Canadian authorities, but in Washington he found the Great Lakes shipping lobbyists ready for him. Eventually he gave up the whole effort.

With both the Canada Southern and the Michigan Central under his control Vanderbilt still had no convenient connection between the two roads. The CS Detroit River crossing at Grosse Ile had only a roundabout connection with the MC toward Chicago. One possibility was to build from Grosse Ile to Ypsilanti to connect the two, but that was never carried through. The idea of extending the CS to Chicago on its own route through Ohio and Indiana already was dead since much of the new line would closely duplicate his own Lake Shore & Michigan Southern line. By the end of 1882 the CS built a short-cut line between Welland and Niagara Falls to improve the running time to that important interchange point. It also completed a line between Essex, Ontario, and Windsor. With this, by using the Detroit River ferries that connected

In the early 1870s the Michigan Central established Jackson as a division headquarters. An important freight yard and shops complex were built to handle the three branch lines that connected with the main line there. In 1874 it opened this new depot to handle the press of business. This photograph, taken in the 1970s, shows how little the building had changed in 100 years. It has the honor of being Michigan's oldest structure in continuous use as a passenger station.

Sam Breck collection.

the MC to the Great Western, Vanderbilt had a second through route between the Niagara frontier and Chicago. At the end of 1882 Vanderbilt assigned operations of the Canada Southern to the Michigan Central and later formalized this with a lease.

With the CS lease came the fourteen-mile Michigan Midland & Canada, a line that extended from St. Clair to a connection with the Grand Trunk at Richmond, then called Ridgeway. Michigan Midland had built the line in 1873, and the Canada Southern's owners controlled it from the beginning. The little road played an outsized role in the CS's aims to build to Chicago. The CS owners built a line from St. Thomas to Courtright, Ontario, in 1873. From 1870 on they planned for this line to connect to the Michigan Midland and for that line to be extended to Chicago. As an alternative they considered buying the Michigan Air Line, which had started to build west from Ridgeway. The panic of 1873 destroyed all of these plans. The Vanderbilts got the Canada Southern, the Grand Trunk of Canada bought the Michigan Air Line in 1877, and the window of opportunity for the vision was closed.

Vanderbilt then added two more lines to his family of roads. A decade earlier, in September 1868, a group of Jackson men formed the Jackson, Fort Wayne & Cincinnati as well as an Indiana counterpart named the Fort Wayne, Jackson & Saginaw. Early in 1869 they merged the two, keeping the latter name. Between 1868 and 1870 they built its line from Jackson to Fort Wayne, Indiana. Relations with the Michigan Central were good enough that they used the MC station in Jackson and had a joint line with it out of Jackson.

The second road was the dream of Ypsilanti businessman Daniel L. Quirk, who envisioned building a connection between the Michigan Central from Detroit and railroads to the southwest in Indiana without going through Toledo. One valuable connection would be the Eel River road that was planned to be built between Butler and a connection with the Wabash at Logansport, Indiana. Early in 1869 Quirk formed the Detroit, Hillsdale & Indiana to build from Ypsilanti to the northeast corner of the state of Indiana. By November 1872 the line was built from Ypsilanti, through Hillsdale, to Bankers, where it connected with the Fort Wayne, Jackson & Saginaw. The Fort Wayne road provided a southern outlet for the Hillsdale road, and the two worked together in moving traffic. At Fort Wayne it had an important connection with the Fort Wayne, Muncie & Cincinnati (later part of the Nickel Plate road), which extended to Connersville and had solid connections to Cincinnati, Indianapolis, and Louisville. At Auburn, Indiana, the FWJ&S had an equally important connection with the Detroit, Eel River & Illinois. The Eel River road was opened between Butler and Peru, Indiana, in 1874; at Peru it connected with a predecessor of the Wabash Railroad and was able to reach St. Louis and Keokuk, Iowa, and, by another route, Peoria, Illinois. The Wabash leased the Eel River in 1877, and things must have looked promising.

The Detroit, Hillsdale & Indiana was built as the panic of 1873 closed, leading the company to a reorganization in 1875 as the Detroit, Hillsdale & South Western. Boston money came into the road, most of the local directors left, and Quirk replaced Christian H. Buhl as president. Late in 1879 the Fort Wayne road was reorganized as the Fort Wayne & Jackson, with New York City money taking over. Despite their different ownerships, the two roads continued to work together closely.

This rosy prospect changed completely early in 1880 when James F. Joy incorporated the Detroit, Butler & St. Louis. Joy saw this as an opportunity to bring Jay Gould's Wabash Railroad into Detroit, and as well embarrass the Vanderbilts for ousting him from the Michigan Central. Joy's line was to run from Detroit to Butler, Indiana, and there to connect with the Eel River road that the Wabash bought in 1879. When Joy's road was completed in August 1881, through service to the Wabash began via the Eel River. This took away traffic crucial to the FW&J and the DH&SW. There was only one place to which to turn. In September 1881 the Lake Shore & Michigan Southern leased the DH&SW, and followed this with a lease of the FW&J in August 1882.

The Detroit & Bay City, another of Joy's railroads, was reorganized early in 1881, and Vanderbilt used the Michigan Central's loans to it as an opportunity to lease the Bay City road for the rest of its corporate life.

SOURCES

Dunbar, Willis F. *All Aboard! A History of Railroads in Michigan*. Grand Rapids, Mich.: W. B. Eerdmans, 1969.

Harlow, Alvin F. *The Road of the Century*. New York: Creative Age, 1947.

Meints, Graydon M. *Michigan Railroads and Railroad Companies*. East Lansing: Michigan State University Press, 1992.

Swartz, William. "The Wabash Railroad." *Railroad History* No. 133 (Fall 1975).

Tennant, Robert D., Jr. *Canada Southern Country*. Erin, Ont.: Boston Mills Press, 1991.

Railroad Strikes

As the depression following the panic of 1873 worsened, railroad managers watched freight traffic fall off and profits drop. One traditional method of gaining business was to form a pool of companies and divide the revenues by some formula. Another was to undercut a competitor's rates in a rate war. In the attempt to maintain dividends one other tool brought into frequent use was to cut expenses. Managers squeezed down expenses, with employee pay, the largest single expense item, forced down as well. Throughout 1876 and into 1877 one road after another announced 10 percent pay cuts for employees, although usually exempting those who earned $1 a day or less.

Canadian enginemen struck the Grand Trunk of Canada the day after Christmas 1876 and stopped all traffic for four days. By the summer of 1877 the pay cuts were becoming widespread, and nerves were fraying. In mid-July the muttering turned to violence on the Baltimore & Ohio at Martinsburg, West Virginia. Passenger and mail trains were allowed to run, but the trainmen's union tied up all freight traffic. A few days later a riot erupted in Pittsburgh on the Pennsylvania Railroad, and the National Guard and some U.S. Army troops were called in to damp down the widespread fires, violence, and destruction. More than twenty people—military, railroadmen, idlers, and onlookers—lost their lives.

Michigan largely escaped the violence. On 1 July 1877 Vanderbilt cut pay 10 percent on the Canada Southern and the Michigan Central. He made preparations in Detroit to put down any disturbance, but quiet generally prevailed. Employees struck briefly at Jackson and St. Thomas, Ontario, but not much else happened. In October 1877 Michigan railroad commissioner William B. Williams tersely noted in his *Annual Report*:

> The present year has presented the unparalleled spectacle of a general system of strikes on the part of railroad employees, and of terrorism of entire communities unprecedented in the history of our country. Happily, Michigan, through the good sense and judgment of both railroad officers and men, and the forethought and prudence of the State Government, escaped the unseemly and terrible scenes presented in some of the sister States, of civil disorder, anarchy, and murder.

He made no mention of this condition in his next yearly report. The Michigan Central's *Annual Report* for 1877 remarked, almost in passing, that "with but very few exceptions the employees of the Company were its staunch friends, and remained at their posts discharging their duty. The trains and business of the Company were not interrupted for a single day."

By the end of July 1877 the strikes were over. By that time many roads had cut dividends, and a few were in receivership. Some roads rolled back the pay reductions while some others made changes in work rules that trainmen found particularly onerous. William Henry Vanderbilt distributed $100,000 among his workers for their "loyalty and faithfulness during the strike." In October he restored half of the wage cut and the rest of it in February 1880. As prosperity returned wages gradually were restored, leaving only a legacy of bitterness.

SOURCE

Bruce, Robert V. *1877: Year of Violence*. Indianapolis: Bobbs-Merrill, 1959.

The Lumbering Era Begins

The settlers of Michigan of the early 1830s introduced commercial lumbering on a small scale. Using small water-powered sawmills they logged small tracts of timber to sell close to the mill. In 1836 Charles Merrill, a transplant from Maine, bought a tract of standing timber on the St. Clair River and began logging it for shipment to the East. Isaac Stephenson came to the Wisconsin side of the Menominee River in 1845. As the forests of Maine were depleted logging men migrated in increased numbers. A few of them moved only to New York or Pennsylvania, but many others came west to Minnesota and Wisconsin and Michigan. They had heard stories about an abundance of timber, but what they found in Michigan staggered them: an entire state covered with millions of acres of timber of all sorts. In the southern part of the state they found hardwoods: beech, oak, hickory, sugar maple, and ash. Farther north were softwoods: hemlock, tamarack, cedar, spruce, and all kinds of pine. In all of this were three million acres of the Holy Grail—highly prized white pine of a quality and quantity found nowhere else in the United States.

By the 1850s lumbering was developing into a major Michigan industry. Nearly every river mouth along Lake Huron and Lake Michigan had a mill sawing logs that had been floated down the river. Charles Mears moved from Paw Paw to near Whitehall and established a sawmill in 1838, later built a second mill there, then gradually expanded his operations to other ports along the Lake Michigan shore. Three mills were operating on Muskegon Lake by 1840. George and John Ruddiman, Theodore Newell, Martin Ryerson, and Henry Knickerbocker all owned mills during the decade that followed. William M. Ferry built a mill at Pentwater in 1850. John Stronach built the first mill on Manistee Lake in 1841. In 1845 he added a steam sawmill, and in 1848 Roswell Canfield built his own mill. William and Horace Boardman began logging near Traverse City in 1847, and sold their operations to Hannah, Lay and Company in 1851. Daniel Wells Jr. and Jefferson Sinclair began a sawmill at Escanaba in 1846, and were joined by Nelson and Harrison Ludington in 1848.

Harvey Williams built the first sawmill at Saginaw in 1834; his nephews Ephraim S. and Gardner D. Williams ran it. In 1836 Albert Miller built a mill at Portsmouth in what is now Bay City. In the 1840s George Hazelton built some mills on the Flint River, as did Charles Merrill at Saginaw. In 1840 there were some 500 sawmills in Michigan,

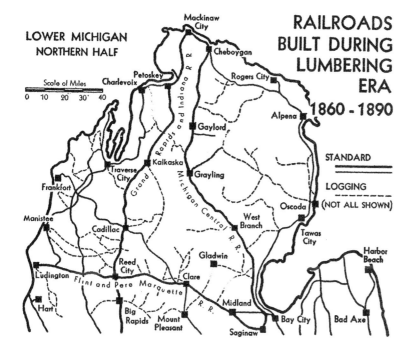

LOWER MICHIGAN
NORTHERN HALF

Scale of Miles
0   10   20   30   40

RAILROADS
BUILT DURING
LUMBERING
ERA
1860 - 1890

STANDARD

LOGGING
(NOT ALL SHOWN)

During the lumbering boom the railroads built a network of through lines and branches that reached every important timberland in the northern Lower Peninsula. Both the extensive use of railroads and the improvements in logging and sawing techniques contributed to the rapid decimation of Michigan's forests. This map is slightly modified from the original source.

Rolland H. Maybee, *Michigan's White Pine Era, 1840–1900* (Lansing, 1960), 42.

most of them supplying very local markets, but by 1860 the number doubled to nearly 1,000.

The secret of the Saginaw Valley spread quickly. The Saginaw River, with its major tributaries the Shiawassee, Tittabawassee, Pine, Chippewa, Tobacco, Bad, Cass, and Flint Rivers, drained an area of some 3,000 square miles covering parts of a dozen counties. The northern reaches of it had stands of white pine, often called "cork" pine for its buoyancy in rivers during the spring drive. With land available from the federal government at $1.25 per acre, the invasion started. The business exploded after the Civil War, from 100 million board feet sawed in 1860 to 250 million in 1865, nearly 600 million in 1870, over 800 million in 1880, and over one billion in 1882. Names familiar today amassed and sometimes lost fortunes. Aaron T. Bliss, Wellington R. Burt, C. K. Eddy and sons Arthur and Walter, Arthur Hill, Jesse Hoyt, William B. Mershon, and Ammi W. Wright are but a few of the best known.

The network of rivers and streams of the Saginaw Valley provided an easy way to move logs from the logging camp to the sawmill. Ice over a good snow in winter provided easy skidding from the cutting to the banking ground at the edge of a river. The spring thaw, helped at times by dams built by the lumbermen, provided fast-moving rivers to float the logs downstream. The seasonal but dangerous movement of logs from camp to mill was a fact of life that lumbermen lived with, but a lack of snow could cause a financial disaster. A season with little snow and the ensuing lack of high river water prompted lumbermen to try adapting railroads to their operations.

The earliest rail operations appear to have been cars pulled by horses to move logs a few miles from the logging site to the riverbank. There is evidence that several such roads were built to the Grand River near its mouth in Ottawa County. The best documented is a road built by the Blendon Lumber Company about 1857. A tract in the northeast corner of Blendon Township included 2,500 acres of timber first located by John Ball in 1836. It was not until 1855 that the owners were ready to log the stand. To get the logs to the Grand River they had to build a three-mile railroad that they completed early in 1857. Soon after they purchased a well-used locomotive, the *St. Joe*, from the Michigan Central and placed strap iron on top of its wooden rails. Ultimately the road extended eight miles and is reported to have been operated until 1870.

There is a report of a tram railway with wooden rails built near Tawas Bay along the Lake Huron shore in the summer of 1855. The Corlies & Thunder Bay Train Railway was formed in January 1864 to build a seven-mile line from Thunder Bay, at Alpena, northwesterly to the rapids of the Thunder River. John Trowbridge built the line in either 1864 or 1865, but operated it for only a few years.

In 1872 Van Etten, Campbell & Company built a fifteen-mile logging railway between the Lake Huron shore east of Pinconning and the logging settlement of Glencoe, apparently located near the southwest corner of Mount Forest Township, Bay County. It may have been built to overcome the lack of river transport between the camp and the mill. George and Hugh Campbell bought the road in 1874 and in March 1876 incorporated the Glencoe, Pinconning & Lake Shore to take it over. In 1877 the Campbells filed for bankruptcy; J. H. Plummer bought the railroad and renamed it the Pinconning Railroad. In 1880 it was sold again, this time to a group headed by Winfield S. Gerrish, and renamed the Saginaw Bay & Northwestern. In 1883 the SB&NW was leased to the Michigan Central, which built several more logging branches and eventually extended the main branch to Gladwin in 1887. When the Gladwin branch was abandoned in 1962 it was the last of the Michigan Central's many logging branches. In 1873 Van Etten, Kaiser & Company built a logging line between Pinconning and Kaiserville. No doubt logging companies built other lines, but these never became incorporated railroad companies.

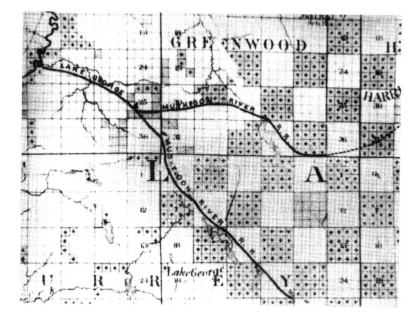

The Lake George & Muskegon River was a very early Michigan logging road and among the first to use steam locomotives rather than horses to move logs. Winfield Scott Gerrish's road hauled them year-round to the Muskegon River northwest of Temple in Clare County to feed the sawmills in Muskegon.

Rolland H. Maybee, *Michigan's White Pine Era, 1840–1900* (Lansing, 1960), 39.

The best known of the pioneering logging railroads was the Lake George & Muskegon River formed by Winfield Scott Gerrish in December 1876. In 1874 Gerrish and E. H. Hazelton had purchased a tract of timber in Lincoln Township, Clare County. The winters of 1874 and 1875 had produced little snow, and Gerrish's profits suffered for not being able to move logs. In the summer of 1876 he visited the Centennial Exposition in Philadelphia and there saw a small Baldwin locomotive on display. He began thinking about using a locomotive to move logs and convinced Hazelton to let him give it a try. He laid about eight miles of track from the Muskegon River, southwest of Temple, southeasterly into his timberlands. The Flint & Pere Marquette delivered his locomotive *Sampson* to Evart, and Gerrish built a flatboat to move it upstream to his railroad. Thirty logging cars were moved the same way. In January 1877 Gerrish began operating his railroad. The winter of 1876–77 was another mild one, and he was one of a very few loggers to move any amount of logs to the river. Not only did he move logs, but the railroad made a profit on its investment the first year. The next season Gerrish bought another locomotive and more cars, and extended his tracks. Gerrish died suddenly in May 1882 in Evart, and his railroad was sold to Hackley & Hume, which ran it as a private logging road for a few years and then abandoned it. James M. Ashley later used some of the LG&MR right-of-way to build his Toledo, Ann Arbor & North Michigan through the Lake George area in 1887–88.

Gerrish's railroad success story spread quickly. Dozens of other lumbermen soon built their own logging roads in Michigan and the Upper Midwest. Between 1877 and 1886 several dozen railroads were incorporated in Michigan to haul logs. In addition to these there were undocumented lines, probably numbering into the hundreds, which were built by the logging companies to move their own timber.

The railroad was just one of many technological improvements that lumbermen adopted. Improved saws, loading equipment, and vastly larger sawmills contributed much to the boom. The railroads made it possible to cut tracts farther from the rivers and in many cases not to use rivers at all. Railroads hauled more logs into Manistee than were floated down the Manistee River. The Michigan Central, the Pere Marquette's predecessors, and the Grand Rapids & Indiana all built branches into timberlands and hauled logs directly to the sawmills. Logging became a year-round business, and sawmills ran without a stop. Lumbermen were able to cut ten times more board feet than they could without the railroad. The lumberman with capital enough to build and equip a railroad, and able to weather the price vagaries of the lumber market itself, became wealthy beyond the imagination of the average person. Lumbering created more eighteenth-century millionaires than any other business in the state.

SOURCES

Bajema, Carl Jay. "The First Logging Railroads in the Great Lakes Region." *Forest & Conservation History* 35 (April 1991).

Bald, F. Clever. *Michigan in Four Centuries*. New York: Harper & Row, 1961.

Holbrook, Stewart H. *Holy Old Mackinaw*. New York: McMillan, 1938.

Keenan, Hudson. "America's First Successful Logging Railroad." *Michigan History* 44:3 (September 1960).

Maybee, Rolland H. *Michigan's White Pine Era, 1840–1900*. Lansing: Michigan Department of State, 1976.

Rector, William G. "Railroad Logging in the Lake States." *Michigan History* 36:4 (December 1952).

———. *Log Transportation in the Lake States Lumber Industry*. Glendale, Calif.: Arthur H. Clark, 1953.

Reimann, Lewis C. *When Pine Was King*. Ann Arbor, Mich.: Northwoods Publishers, 1952.

Rohe, Randall. "Tramways and Pole Railroads: An Episode in the Technological History of the Great Lakes Lumber Era." *Upper Midwest History* 5 (1985).

Iron Ore, Copper Ore, Profits

The demand for Michigan iron ore soared during the Civil War. The Marquette Range shipped 68,000 tons in 1859, then production jumped to 247,000 tons in 1864. After the end of hostilities shipments increased even more rapidly, to 565,000 tons in 1867, then to a high of 1,195,000 tons in 1873. The panic of 1873 held demand down for several years until 1877, when shipments began to increase once more. Until 1872 the ore moved from the Marquette Range over two routes: to Marquette over the Iron Mountain and its successors and over the Chicago & North Western to Escanaba.

There was little other growth in the Upper Peninsula rail network until 1872, when the Chicago & North Western completed its line between Green Bay, Wisconsin, and Escanaba. This tied its disconnected ore-hauling line to the rest of its system. It handled the usual freight and passenger traffic, but it appears that very little ore moved south of Escanaba. The mine owners were learning to save money by using ships as much as possible.

The Marquette & Ontonagon and the Houghton & Ontonagon merged in 1872 to form the Marquette, Houghton & Ontonagon Railroad. The M&O was a local concern that operated the Bay de Noquet & Marquette, which had bought the Iron Mountain in 1858. Its line extended from Marquette as far west as Lake Michigamme and served the Michigamme and Champion Mines as well as those in the Ishpeming-Negaunee area. The H&O was formed in 1870 by a group of Detroiters that included James F. Joy, Henry N. Walker, George Jerome, Charles H. Palmer, and soon-to-be governor John J. Bagley. When it was consolidated into the MH&O in 1872 it had money and ambitions but owned no railroad. The H&O management took over running the surviving MH&O. By the end of 1872 the MH&O extended its line from Michigamme, through Nestoria, to L'Anse. Ore from the Michigamme Mine began to move to L'Anse rather than to Marquette for lake shipment. The MH&O build a new branch to the Republic Mine, which had opened the year earlier.

During 1873 and 1874 both the C&NW and the MH&O built and abandoned a number of spurs to mines on the Marquette Range, but the panic of 1873 completely stopped new construction for nearly four years. At this time the eastern part of the Menominee Range came into production. Iron ore was discovered at Waucedah in 1866 and at

Iron Range & Huron Bay

It seemed like a great idea in 1890. Mines dotted the west end of the Marquette iron range all the way from Champion to Michigamme. The only way to move the ore out was over the Duluth, South Shore & Atlantic to its ore dock at Marquette, thirty miles or more away. The DSS&A ore dock at L'Anse was even farther removed. The Chicago, Milwaukee & St. Paul had been built into Champion only a few years earlier, and it tapped a number of mines at Republic but had no direct line to the ore docks.

Promoter Milo Davis saw the natural solution for what was sure to be a growing demand, the Iron Range & Huron Bay Railroad. In those heady days Davis had no problem finding enough money to build a line from Champion to Huron Bay. The Huron Mountains were sure to have iron ore that would provide more business. The Michigan Slate Company's quarry at Arvon was a bonus with the high-quality slate it produced. And the slate company already had a tram railroad from its quarry to the bay. The panic of 1893 put a damper on progress but not on Davis. He persisted, and by 1895 the thirty-four-mile line finally was finished. It had an impressive ore dock at Huron Bay, two locomotives, and twenty freight cars. As financing Davis had collected over $800,000 from stockholders and also borrowed a little more than $400,000, all of which was considerably more than the $500,000 Davis had originally projected as the cost to build the road.

The first through run was to be a test from Huron Bay to Champion. Employee Sam Beck recounted that "I was in the cab with the engineer and we had proceeded just a short distance up the grade when the roadbed gave way and we went into a ditch. From that moment on, the Iron Range and Huron Bay Railroad ceased to exist as a railroad"—which is just as well since farther up the line there was a deep cut through Canadian Shield granite at the head of the Slate River. The cut was on an 8 percent grade, a climb so steep that one engine could pull up only one empty car. Working a trainload of ore down the grade would have been absolutely perilous.

Eventually the road was dismantled. The 1896 report by the railroad commissioner carried a small print notation: "Road not finished, and was never operated." The engines were sold to the Algoma Central to run out of Sault Ste. Marie, Ontario. The rails were used on an interurban line near Detroit. The pine timbers used in the ore dock also went to Detroit. It is possible to drive over some of the Iron Range grade on the Huron Bay–Peshekee Grade Road.

the Quinnesec Mine in 1871. No substantial mining took place until a Chicago & North Western subsidiary, the Menominee River, was built from Powers to Quinnesec in 1877 and extended to Iron Mountain in 1880. The Vulcan Mine began shipping in 1877 and the Norway and the Cyclops in 1878.

The earliest copper country road was the Hecla & Torch Lake, a wholly owned subsidiary of the Calumet & Hecla Company, a company assembled by Quincy A. Shaw and run by his brother-in-law Alexander E. Agassiz. This four-foot-one-inch narrow-gauge line was formed in January 1868 and built that same year from the company mines at Red

Jacket and Calumet to its stamp mill near Lake Linden. It never hauled much besides its owner's freight and later discontinued its common carrier status. The second carrier in the area was the Mineral Range. At the time, the Keweenaw was closed to shipping during the winter. To remedy this Charles E. Holland and Jay A. Hubbell proposed to build the Mineral Range & L'Anse Bay in 1871 to provide rail service to copper country by connecting Calumet with the Marquette, Houghton & Ontonagon then being built to L'Anse. It was renamed the Mineral Range in October 1872 and completed a modest twelve miles from Hancock to Calumet in October 1873. By then Holland and Hubbell had decided to build toward Ontonagon rather than L'Anse. In December 1884 Joseph W. Clark and Albert S. Bigelow, two Boston men who owned the Osceola mine near Calumet, formed the competing Hancock & Calumet. They completed a line in 1885 from Hancock to Lake Linden and a branch to Calumet to serve their mine. Both the Mineral Range and the Hancock & Calumet

Alexander Emanuel Agassiz

Born 17 December 1837, Neuchâtel, Switzerland; died 27 March 1910, at sea.

No other man brought such intellectual, scientific, and financial talent to a railroad that was less than a dozen miles long. The son of naturalist Louis Agassiz, and living in a home visited by the best intellectual minds in New England, Alexander graduated from Harvard in 1855 with degrees in engineering and natural history. Probably in 1865 his brother-in-law Quincy A. Shaw persuaded him and some friends to buy controlling interest of the Calumet Mine from its discoverer, Edwin J. Hulbert. In March 1867 Agassiz moved to Calumet to take over management of his investment in both the Hecla and the Calumet Mines. His labors paid off in December 1869 when the Hecla paid its first dividend, followed the next year by one from the Calumet. In May 1871 Shaw merged several mines into the new Calumet & Hecla Mining Company; in August Agassiz became the company's president when Shaw retired.

In 1868 Agassiz built the Hecla & Torch Lake Railroad to haul copper ore from the mines around Calumet to stamping mills on Torch Lake near Lake Linden. Both Agassiz and Shaw were among the original founders of the rail line and remained as directors, Shaw until 1909 and Agassiz until 1910. Agassiz became the railroad's president in 1871 and remained that until his death.

Agassiz became a wealthy man from his Calumet & Hecla investment, and he donated $500,000 as an endowment to Harvard. As the mining company's operations became more stable and required less of his direct involvement, he returned to his favorite studies at Harvard, natural history and zoology, and published a number of books and papers on those subjects. He served a term as president of the National Academy of Sciences.

Agassiz died in the sinking of the S.S. *Adriatic*.

Charles A. Wright
Born 4 December 1854, Hartford, Conn.; died 17 May 1911, Hancock.

Wright moved to Hancock in 1873 at age eighteen to work in Edgar H. Towar's bank. In January 1881 he became secretary and treasurer of the Mineral Range Railroad. He sharpened his railroading skills, and became the road's general manager in 1885. New owners from New York City bought the Mineral Range and the competing Hancock & Calumet Railroad in 1886. Wright kept his job and also was made general manager of the Hancock & Calumet. In October 1888 Wright and other local businessmen organized the Northern Michigan Railroad, a line to connect the copper country with the Chicago, Milwaukee & St. Paul line to the south. Wright was made president of the proposed road, but the venture went nowhere for ten years.

In 1890 Wright organized and became president of the Superior Savings Bank. He resigned all his railroad positions in 1893 to take up a long-delayed study of the law. He continued his banking business, and after joining the bar he formed a second bank in Laurium. When William A. Paine formed the Copper Range Company in 1899, Wright persuaded him to use Northern Michigan's franchise for a new Copper Range Railroad. During that year Wright was in charge of building the Copper Range from Houghton to McKeever, and then returned solely to banking and some mining interests.

His mining interests brought him back to railroading in 1905 when he became president of the Keweenaw Central Railroad. He held that position until his death.

were built as narrow gauge, with only three feet between the rails, a practice that lasted until 1898. The Marquette, Houghton & Ontonagon extended its line from L'Anse to Houghton in July 1883 and established rail connections to the two copper country roads when they were built.

Also in 1885 Henry S. Ives and George H. Stayner, two stock market operators from New York City, bought the Mineral Range from Holland. The next year H. S. Ogden and Christopher Meyer joined them in buying the H&C. Now owning both roads they installed one management headed by Charles A. Wright to operate both narrow-gauge companies. In 1887 Thomas N. Cromwell, possibly the canniest of the group, joined his New York associates. In 1893 the Duluth, South Shore & Atlantic bought majority control of both the Mineral Range and the Hancock & Calumet and brought in its own management team to replace Wright.

More iron mines opened on the western Menominee Range, the most promising of which was Chapin Mine in Iron Mountain. It first produced in 1880; in 1900 it produced 1,101,000 tons of ore, the first Lake Superior underground mine to reach that mark. In 1882 the Crystal Falls, Fairbanks, and Great Western Mines were started near Crystal Falls; that same year the Iron River and Nanaimo Mines were opened near Iron River. A Chicago & North Western subsidiary, the Menominee River, built a line into Florence, Wisconsin, in 1880 to reach the Florence Mine, and by 1882 extended it into Crystal Falls and to Stambaugh. Another subsidiary, the Escanaba & Lake Superior, built from Narenta, west of Escanaba, to the Metropolitan Mine at Felch in 1882.

The first iron ore of the Gogebic Range, lying between Bessemer and Ironwood, came in 1884 and 1885 from the Ashland, Norrie, Aurora, and Pabst Mines just east of the Montreal River in Ironwood, as well as from several mines in Wisconsin. More mines opened in 1886, as did mines farther east in the Wakefield and Bessemer area. The first railroad to tap the Gogebic Range was the Milwaukee, Lake Shore & Western. It was formed in June 1872 as an outgrowth of a number of earlier Wisconsin lines. In 1874 new blood took over the company, with Frederick W. Rhinelander as its president and guiding spirit. By 1880 the MLS&W had built a line from Milwaukee, through Manitowoc, Sheboygan, and Appleton, to Wausau. From Wausau, Rhinelander had hopes of building to St. Paul, Minnesota. Timber became the magnet, and the Lake Shore began building north rather than west and was running to Rhinelander by 1882. From there it built a line due north into Michigan that was completed into Watersmeet in September 1883. Rhinelander decided to build from Watersmeet to Ashland, Wisconsin, to move the iron ore that the Gogebic Range was starting to produce. His line was completed to the Gogebic in 1884 and to Lake Superior at Ashland in 1885. At Ashland the road built the world's largest ore dock, with a reported capacity of one million tons per year. As soon as the dock was completed the road began hauling ore to Ashland for boat loading.

In 1887 another Chicago & North Western subsidiary, the Iron River, built from Stager, south of Crystal Falls, to Watersmeet, where it connected with the Lake Shore line to the Gogebic Range. The C&NW may have hoped to attract some of the Gogebic ore traffic to its Escanaba docks, but apparently very little actually moved in that direction. Another subsidiary, the Iron Range, began building west from Ishpeming to tap a number of iron mines; during 1888 it completed branches to the Michigamme, Republic, and Champion Mines. Ore traffic increased so much that the single-track line between Iron Mountain and Escanaba became overloaded by the number of ore trains from the Menominee Range and the trains of empty cars returning. The C&NW formed the Escanaba, Iron Mountain & Western in January 1890 to build a new line between Escanaba and Crystal Falls. By the end of the year it completed

The lure of iron ore encouraged these two men to extend their companies to the Upper Peninsula iron ranges. William Butler Ogden (above) founded the company that developed into the Chicago & North Western, the initial link between the Marquette Range and the port at Escanaba. Frederick W. Rhinelander (below) built the Milwaukee, Lake Shore & Western, the first road to reach the Gogebic Range in the western Upper Peninsula.

its line between Escanaba and Antoine yard just north of Iron Mountain. With this line the C&NW now had, in effect, a double-track line between Iron Mountain and the Escanaba ore docks. The line was built just in time to handle the increased ore traffic from new mines near Iron Mountain, the Crystal Falls area, and around Iron River. Another subsidiary, the Paint River, built an extension from Crystal Falls north to the Hemlock Mine near Amasa in 1891. In August 1893 the C&NW bought the Milwaukee, Lake Shore & Western. The Lake Shore appears to have been in good financial shape, but it did compete with the C&NW to some extent north of Milwaukee and did use C&NW tracks to the station in Milwaukee. The main impetus seems to have been that the C&NW wanted a stronger hold on the iron ore business and could gain it if it acquired the smaller Lake Shore road.

In June 1887 the Gogebic & Montreal River was built into the Gogebic Range to Bessemer; at Mellen, Wisconsin, it connected with the Wisconsin Central line into Ashland. The G&MR was formed in December 1883 just as the Gogebic Range began producing, although construction did not begin until late 1886. It built a yard and an ore dock at Ashland and was ready to handle ore by the summer of 1887. As the second road into the Gogebic, it got mostly leftovers and moved only a fraction of the traffic that the Lake Shore had. Even at those levels the second ore dock's capacity was stretched to its limit. The Gogebic line was leased to the Penokee Railroad when it was completed, and both were leased to the Wisconsin Central in May 1888. In 1890 there was some talk of a merger between the WC and the Northern Pacific. WC's lease of the Gogebic was transferred to the Northern Pacific as an extension of the NP line into Ashland from Duluth. The negotiations fell through; NP canceled its lease in September 1895, and the G&MR went back under WC operations.

SOURCES

Boyum, Burton H. *The Saga of Iron Mining in Michigan's Upper Peninsula*. Marquette, Mich.: John M. Longyear, 1983.

————. "Superior Copper and Iron." In *A Most Superior Land: Life in the Upper Peninsula of Michigan*. Lansing, Mich.: Two Peninsula Press, 1983.

Dunbar, Willis F. *All Aboard! A History of Railroads in Michigan*. Grand Rapids, Mich.: W. B. Eerdmans, 1969.

————. *Michigan: A History of the Wolverine State*. Grand Rapids, Mich.: W. B. Eerdmans, 1970.

Fuller, George N. *Michigan: A Centennial History*. 2 vols. Chicago: Lewis Publishing, 1939.

Gaertner, John. "The Gogebic Range." *SOO* 18:1 (Winter 1996), 18:2 (Spring 1996), 18:3 (Summer 1996), 18:4 (Fall 1996).

Hatcher, Harlan. *A Century of Iron and Men*. Indianapolis: Bobbs-Merrill, 1950.

Meints, Graydon M. *Michigan Railroads and Railroad Companies*. East Lansing: Michigan State University Press, 1992.

Detroit's First Big Industry

The explosive growth that took place in both Michigan's and the nation's railroad network brought Detroit its first major industry. Unlike most businesses, the railroads needed a wide variety of mechanical goods, chief among them being steam locomotives and both freight and passenger cars. Locomotives were first imported from Great Britain, with the incidental result that the standard gauge for tracks in the United States mirrored the English standard gauge. Most important among the very early American builders were the shops of Matthias Baldwin in Philadelphia, started in 1832; of Richard and William Norris, started around 1835; and of Rogers, Ketchum, and Grosvenor, started in 1837. A number of smaller works soon grew up along the East Coast from New England to the Middle Atlantic states. The complexity of fitting together the wide variety of parts hindered the widespread development of locomotive manufacturing, but rather kept it confined to a few specialized firms. In Michigan the Detroit Locomotive Works built a small number of engines in the 1850s for the Michigan Central, but the record of the company is quite sketchy. Several roads did use company shops to rebuild locomotives, most notably the Michigan Central at Jackson, and, to a lesser extent, the Grand Trunk Western at Battle Creek.

Two Michigan men contributed to the development of the steam locomotive. Benjamin Briscoe was hired by the Board of Internal Improvement as a machinist, and later promoted to superintendent of shops. In 1838 he devised an improved spark arrestor for smokestacks, but it appears that it was never widely adopted. In 1864 Elijah McCoy went to work on the Michigan Central as a locomotive fireman. The fourth son of a freed slave, he had a bent for engineering and began to devise an improved system to replace lubricating engines by hand. In 1872 he obtained his first patent for an automatic device, made improvements to it over the years, and obtained nine patents for them.

ABOVE: Throughout the middle of the nineteenth century the American-type locomotive—
four pilot wheels and four driving wheels—was
the most widely used to haul both passenger
and freight trains.

The American Railway: Its Construction, Development, Management, and
Appliances (New York, 1897), 111.

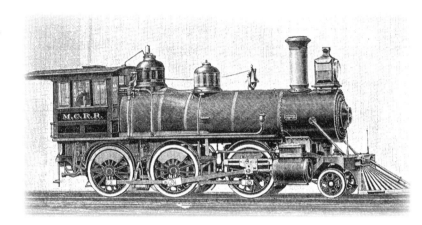

RIGHT: By the end of the Civil War the Mogul-
type locomotive had come into wide use.
Its third set of driving wheels gave it much
greater pulling power for freight trains than
the American-type.

The American Railway: Its Construction, Development, Management, and
Appliances, 123.

LEFT: Designers found that four wheels in the
front with six driving wheels made the ten-
wheeler into a faster locomotive that was able
to pull the heavier passenger trains that were
becoming more common.

The American Railway: Its Construction, Development, Management, and
Appliances, 123.

RIGHT: By the end of the nineteenth century
an even heavier-duty freight locomotive had
gained wide acceptance. The Consolidation-
type, with eight driving wheels, provided good
pulling power without adding very much more
weight on the rails.

The American Railway: Its Construction, Development, Management, and
Appliances, 124.

His devices were adopted widely by American railroads—which insisted on having "the real McCoy"—but in the end he gained little financial success from his efforts.

Although a few car-building shops appeared on the East Coast early on, most railroads built or contracted built their own cars. The state of Michigan built a few passenger and freight cars at Detroit around 1837 to use on its Central line. The Michigan Central established its own car shops at Detroit, with S. C. Case and later J. B. Sutherland as its master car builders. Case built, in Detroit in 1858, the first sleeping car used on the MC. Sutherland continued to improve on Case's designs, and built eight sleepers for the MC in 1860. By the early 1850s the Michigan Southern started its own shop at Adrian run by master car builder John Kirby. In about 1860 he built the *Elkhart* and *City of Toledo* as sleepers over the MS between Buffalo and Chicago. A further testament to Kirby's skill was the parlor cars *Garden City* and *Forest City*, which he built in Adrian in 1867. The cars cost an astronomical $17,500 each, but they were the first to introduce Chicago to the pleasures of parlor-car riding.

Henry A. Angell started a foundry in Adrian in 1853 that supplied car wheels to the MS shops, a company that about 1863 changed its name to the Adrian Car Company. A company named the Central Car and Manufacturing Company was reported in Jackson in 1871. It appears that, generally, the railroads ended their own freight car building as independent car builders appeared on the scene. Railroads did continue building passenger cars a little longer, but eventually ended this work as well. As specialized car builders developed the railroads used their shops only for rebuilding and car repairs. The New York Central continued shop work in Detroit and Jackson, as did the Grand Trunk Western at Port Huron and the Chesapeake & Ohio (née Pere Marquette) at Saginaw until the 1960s.

In 1853 Dr. George B. Russel started a car-building plant on Gratiot Avenue in Detroit. The Detroit & Pontiac order for twenty-five cars was his first. The company outgrew its original plant and built a new one just north of Lafayette Street at the Grand Trunk Western tracks. He reincorporated his company in 1868 as the Detroit Car and Manufacturing Company. Two wooden flatcars built by the company in 1875 for the Virginia & Truckee still survive. They are owned by Paramount Pictures but are not in operating condition.

About 1860 Edward C. Dean and George Eaton began their own new company to build freight cars in Detroit. Three years later John S. Newberry, a wealthy Detroit lawyer, joined the firm and renamed

Detroit doctor George B. Russel gave up his medical practice in 1853 and started a business building railroad cars. His pioneering company was continued by his sons and, under other names, lasted into the twentieth century building railroad equipment.

Cyclopedia of Michigan (New York, 1890), facing 74.

James McMillan, a man of wide and varied business talents and wealthy from lumbering and his investment in the Michigan Car Company, pushed the Detroit, Mackinac & Marquette across the eastern Upper Peninsula from Marquette to St. Ignace. He was U.S. senator from 1889 until his death in 1902.

Henry M. Utley and Byron M. Cutcheon, *Michigan as a Province, Territory, and State* (New York, 1906), 4:facing 168.

it the Michigan Car Company, then brought in his close friend James McMillan. The Civil War brought a boom in orders for freight cars, and the rebuilding of the nation's economy after the war brought still more demand. Adding to this was the growth of logging in Michigan and the newly developed use of railroads for logging in the woods and for moving logs to sawmills. McMillan ran the company so profitably that in 1873 it had to move to a new and much larger plant on Clark Avenue south of Michigan Avenue. On this site Newberry and McMillan also started the Detroit Car Wheel Company as a manufacturing subsidiary. By 1883 Michigan Car had turned out 48,731 cars. Also adjoining Michigan's factory was the Detroit Steel and Spring Works, with Newberry's son Truman H. as an investor. One Michigan Car employee in 1879 was fresh from the farm, a sixteen-year-old Henry Ford, but reportedly he did not work long for McMillan.

Michigan Central's master car builder J. B. Sutherland was granted the first patent for a refrigerated railroad car late in 1867, but there is little record of its use. Detroit meatpacker George H. Hammond, one of Michigan Car's early customers, wanted a better way to ship dressed beef to the East Coast. William Davis, another Detroiter, had devised a cooling system for railcars that Hammond began trying out around 1865. Hammond took delivery of his first refrigerated car in 1868, and it worked just well enough that he began to buy them in quantity. By 1885 Hammond had his own fleet of 600 cars, and by 1900 he had double that number. His success encouraged such Chicago meatpackers as Swift, Armour, and Cudahy to buy refrigerator cars, nearly all of which were owned by the packers themselves rather than by the railroads.

Thomas F. Griffin moved his car wheel foundry from Rochester, New York, to Detroit in 1870. Partnering with his son Thomas A., they formed the Griffin Car Wheel Company. The son later went his own way, opened his own wheelworks in Chicago, and eventually bought out his father but did keep the Detroit operation for a time.

George M. Pullman's first occupation was moving and lifting buildings in Chicago. In 1859, while busy in that field, he found time to tinker with the idea of a sleeping car, and persuaded the Chicago & Alton Railroad to rebuild two-day coaches to fit his vision. As his idea found success Pullman added more cars to his fleet, all of them built in railroad shops or by car manufacturers. He did buy a small manufacturing shop of his own near Chicago in 1863, but continued contracting out most of his work. In 1865 Pullman landed a contract to operate his cars on James F. Joy's Michigan Central. Joy already was running Case and Sutherland's sleeping cars, so Pullman offered to conduct a side-by-side comparison by running his cars at $2.00 fare per night against the MC's at $1.50. Pullman's cars won handily. With his business growing, he needed to add still more manufacturing capacity, a problem he solved in 1871 by buying Dr. Russel's Detroit Car and Manufacturing Company plant located between Monroe, Macomb, St. Aubin, and Dequindre Streets. After this purchase he began having fewer of his cars built in railroad company shops. Both Pullman's own private car, the *P. P. C.*, and Jay Gould's *Atalanta* were built in Detroit. The Detroit operation experienced losses during a depression in the mid-1870s, and may have contributed to Pullman's next move. In 1880 he began building a completely new car plant south of Chicago at a location that he modestly named Pullman. When completed in 1884 the new car shops reduced the need for the Detroit facility, which he

James McMillan

Born 12 May 1838, Hamilton, Ont.; died 10 August 1902, Manchester-by-the-Sea, Mass., buried Detroit.

McMillan came to Detroit in 1855 at age sixteen, and began clerking in a hardware store. Two years later his father arranged a position for him as purchasing agent for the Detroit & Milwaukee Railway. Next he took on a construction contract to build part of that road toward Grand Haven. In 1860 he married Mary Wetmore. With some money in his pocket and his wife's social status, McMillan began dealing in real estate.

In 1864 McMillan became involved with a faltering rail car building company, and with its founders and the wealthy John S. Newberry as partners, he founded the Michigan Car Company. The company had an immediate surge of business building freight cars for the Union army. Within ten years it became the largest manufacturer in Detroit and one of the largest railroad car manufacturers in the country.

In 1879, with his brother Hugh, Newberry, New York stock operator George I. Seney, and four other Detroiters, he founded, built, and became president of the Detroit, Mackinac & Marquette, which extended from St. Ignace to Marquette to link the Upper and Lower Peninsulas. In 1883 he became president of DM&M subsidiary Marquette & Western, and in 1886 of the connecting Marquette, Houghton & Ontonagon. He led the three roads into a merger in 1887 as the Duluth, South Shore & Atlantic and served as its president until 1889.

In 1889 the state legislature elected him U.S. senator, and he held that seat until his death. In Washington, McMillan soon gained a place on the Committee on the District of Columbia, and worked hard to improve the city's infrastructure. The most visionary of his undertakings was a master plan for future construction in the capital. In the spring of 1902 his son, grandson, and brother died. With his family in mourning at their summer home, McMillan died of a heart attack. He was buried in Elmwood Cemetery, and is still remembered in Washington by the McMillan Memorial Fountain in McMillan Park.

Frank J. Hecker (above) and Charles L. Freer (below) came to Detroit around 1880, formed the Peninsular Car Company, and built freight cars. They rode a rising tide of business that allowed them to be able to buy the competing Michigan Car Company in 1892. Wealthy men, they sold their company and other related companies to the American Car and Foundry Company in 1900.

Hecker: *Cyclopedia of Michigan* (New York, 1890), facing 86.

Freer: Courtesy of Freer Gallery of Art, Smithsonian Institution, Washington, D.C.

eventually closed in 1893. In 1902 the Detroit United Railways bought the idle Pullman works, and for a dozen years it served as the major Detroit shops for the company.

The success that Russel, Newberry and McMillan, and Pullman enjoyed made Detroit into the principal railcar manufacturing center in the United States. Success also brought them new competitors. In 1876 George H. and Walter S. Russel, two of Dr. George's sons, founded the Russel Wheel and Foundry, which specialized in making freight car wheels and castings. It grew to become a major manufacturer of cars to move logs just as Michigan lumbering was climbing to importance. The company kept its independence into the twentieth century, but sometime after 1908, and well after the end of lumbering in Michigan, it was renamed the Russell Car and Snow Plow Company and carried on for a few more years. In May 1879 Alexander DeLano incorporated the Detroit Steel and Spring Works to turn out springs for cars and locomotives.

In December 1879 Civil War colonel Frank J. Hecker and Charles L. Freer entered the Detroit car-building scene. Hecker was born on 9 July 1846 in Freedom Township, Washtenaw County, and Freer in 1856 in New York State. The two first met as officials of the Rondout & Oswego Railroad between 1870 and 1876. Although it appears neither brought much money to the venture, they climbed aboard the rising tide by incorporating the Peninsular Car Company, and were able to build a factory along the Detroit River between Walker and Adair Streets. In 1880 the two bought the Adrian Car Company, which they consolidated into Peninsular in 1884. The company benefited from the boom in national railroad operations, making both men quite wealthy in just a few years. In 1887 Peninsular built a new, larger factory north of Ferry Street a short distance south of Milwaukee Junction. It appears that Hecker's health began to deteriorate around 1888, causing him to leave the active management of Peninsular. Whether the impetus came from James McMillan or from Freer is not certain, but in December 1892 the two merged the Michigan Car Company and Peninsular Car Company to form the Michigan-Peninsular Car Company. As part of the merger they also absorbed the Detroit Car Wheel Company, the Detroit Pipe and Foundry Company, and the Baugh Steam Forge. By this time McMillan was a member of the U.S. Senate, remaining in the background as chairman of the board of the new company; Hecker became president, Freer and McMillan's son William C. its managing directors.

In March 1899 the newly formed American Car and Foundry

Company (ACF) bought the Michigan-Peninsular, and now, made quite wealthy, Hecker and Freer retired from management to pursue other interests. Hecker served in the Spanish-American War and a short term on the Panama Canal Commission. Freer became president of Parke, Davis and Company, but devoted most of his time to his very substantial art collection, which later went into the Freer Gallery of the Smithsonian Institution. Under the presidency of Adrian-born William K. Bixby, American Car and Foundry absorbed at least twelve other companies in short order to become the largest railcar builder in the United States. In 1902 ACF introduced the "progressive" procedure to car building in its Michigan-Peninsular plant in Detroit, a revolutionary production method in which the car was assembled by being moved through the factory on a railroad track from one work area to the next. In this system workers would perform specific assembly work on each car, then move it to the next work area. ACF introduced this "assembly line" technique a half-dozen years before Henry Ford refined it at his Highland Park factory to build the Model T. In 1909 it was still the largest company in Detroit. After World War I, demand dropped off; ACF ended railcar building in Detroit soon after by converting the plant to bus production. ACF ended all operations in Detroit in 1946. In the last half of the twentieth century two new car manufacturers appeared: Evans Products of Plymouth and Whitehead and Kales of River Rouge, both of which produced cars to move new automobiles.

Railroad car building became Detroit's largest nineteenth-century industry, and Detroit was the nation's largest supplier of railroad freight cars. At the time, the United States was awash in inventors and tinkers and mechanics, all of them sure they had some sort of improved device to use on railroad cars. The Michigan builders generally appeared content to let the railroads' master car builders choose the design of the cars and which devices they wanted to use on them. There is scant evidence of innovations that were developed by the car builders. Both the automatic coupler and the air brake came from outside the railroad industry, and their use ultimately was mandated by legislation. Most other features of car equipment came out of product development by independents. The builders built what the buyer wanted, and left the buyer to deal with any results of faulty design or equipment.

By 1890 the Michigan Car Company had 2,000 workmen, the Peninsular at least another 1,000, and other related companies another 1,500. By 1898 over 9,000 men worked in the car factories, the majority of them for Michigan-Peninsular, a number that continued under ACF

Manufacturing Floor of the Michigan Car Co. Before 1890

By 1890 James McMillan's Michigan Car Company had grown to be one of Detroit's largest employers, employing some 2,000 workmen. With other car builders—which included the Peninsular Car Company, the Russel Wheel and Foundry, and for a time the Pullman Company—Michigan Car made railroad car building the most important nineteenth-century industry in Detroit.

Burton Collection, Detroit Public Library.

until at least 1907. Railroad car building made fortunes for its owners, who in turn left a legacy for the city of Detroit in the Detroit Institute of Arts, hospitals, and a wide number of charitable organizations. The railroad car manufacturers provided a foundation for the later success of the automobile industry. The skilled labor force that the railroad car builders developed provided an important pool of workers who were an incentive for fledgling auto manufacturers to locate in Detroit.

SOURCES

Farmer, Silas. *History of Detroit and Wayne County and Early Michigan*. 3rd ed. Detroit: Silas Farmer, 1890. Reprint, Detroit: Gale Research, 1969.

Husband, Joseph. *The History of the Pullman Car*. New York: A. C. McClurg, 1917. Reprint, Grand Rapids: Black Letter Press, 1974.

Leyendecker, Liston E. *Palace Car Prince: A Biography of George Mortimer Pullman*. Niwot: University Press of Colorado, 1992.

Marshall, Albert P. *The "Real McCoy" of Ypsilanti*. Ypsilanti, Mich.: Marlan, 1989.

Peters, John Douglas, and Vincent G. Robinson. *Detroit: Freight Cars Before Automobiles*. Belleville, Mich.: Treasure Press, 2005.

Utley, Henry M., and Byron M. Cutcheon. *Michigan as a Province, Territory and State, the Twenty-Sixth Member of the Federal Union*. New York: Publishing Society of Michigan, 1906.

White, John H., Jr. *The American Railroad Passenger Car*. Baltimore: Johns Hopkins University Press, 1978.

———. *The American Railroad Freight Car: From the Wood-Car Era to the Coming of Steel*. Baltimore: Johns Hopkins University Press, 1993.

———. *American Locomotives: An Engineering History, 1830–1880*. Rev. ed. Baltimore: Johns Hopkins University Press, 1997.

The Grand Trunk Gets to Chicago

The Grand Trunk Railway of Canada was caught off guard by the prosperity that followed the Civil War. It owned a line from Portland, Maine, to Port Edward, Ontario—probably the longest railroad line in the world under one management. With its subsidiary road between Port Huron and Detroit and an agreement with the Michigan Central, it was able to gather traffic from Chicago and the American Midwest. During and after the Civil War freight traffic boomed, and the GT got

The Grand Trunk Railway was predominantly a Canadian road, but in the 1850s it understood that the American Midwest could be an important source of freight traffic and established a friendly connection with the Michigan Central to reach Chicago. After the Vanderbilt family gained control of the MC, the Grand Trunk moved aggressively, between 1878 and 1880, to neutralize the Vanderbilts and gain an independent line. This timetable map shows the U.S. system that Sir Henry Whatley Tyler assembled. A little later his system also acquired the Great Western Railway, which owned the Detroit–Grand Haven line.

Author's collection.

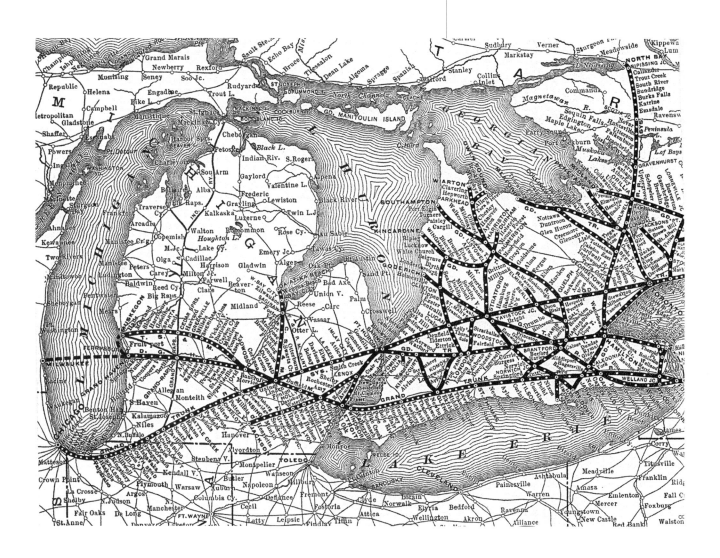

Sir Henry Whatley Tyler first came to Canada when the Grand Trunk's English directors wanted to find out what was going on with their investment. He stayed and eventually became president of the road. By 1880 he had outmaneuvered William Henry Vanderbilt and gained his own line into Chicago.

Railroad History, from Canadian National Railways files.

its share of it. But by the early 1870s the Grand Trunk knew it had to solve a number of very difficult problems. Although its traffic levels were satisfactory the company was not earning the profit it wanted; its board of directors in London was unhappy, to say the least. Its fiercest competitor was the Great Western, which had traffic arrangements with both the New York Central and the Michigan Central that put it on slightly sounder ground. Both lines were Canadian broad gauge—five feet six inches between the rails—rather than the standard gauge of four feet eight and one-half inches used in the United States. To handle to the growing amount of traffic moving from the Michigan Central at Windsor to its eastern connections at Buffalo, the Great Western laid a third rail between Windsor and the Niagara River to be able to handle cars of both gauges and eliminate transloading. In addition to the problem of gauges the Grand Trunk was desperately short of freight cars, and new ones were needed badly. Most of its rails were iron and needed to be replaced with modern steel ones. The wood-burning locomotives had to be replaced with coal-burning ones. President Richard Potter, in trouble with his board right from his appointment in 1869, worked as best he could to make over the railroad and was able to get some of the changes started. The panic of 1873 brought some reduction in traffic and also lower rates on that which remained. But Potter could not please his directors. To add to his problems, he appears to have had less than full support from his two principal subordinates, managing director Charles John Brydges and secretary-treasurer Joseph Hickson. The ever-touchy Brydges resigned in a huff in March 1874, and Hickson took his place; Lewis Seargeant was brought in from England as traffic manager. Nothing improved, and Potter finally was forced to resign in October 1876.

Sir Henry Whatley Tyler replaced Potter. Tyler, Hickson, and Seargeant hit it off immediately. Tyler made the plans and became the man out in the public while the other two worked at implementation, an arrangement that put the best talents of all to the Grand Trunk's advantage. Tyler had first visited the Grand Trunk in the summer of 1867 when the directors sent him to Canada to check on Potter's management of the road. Tyler's involvement grew, eventually to a seat on the board, then later as vice president.

When he took the presidency he faced problems aplenty. Potter's changeover from broad to standard gauge was nearly completed; the badly needed new locomotives and freight cars were arriving. The road had completed half of its project to replace the older iron rails

Sir Henry Whatley Tyler

Born 7 March 1837, London, England; died 30 January 1908, London, England.

Tyler began a term as chief inspector of railways for the Board of Trade in Britain in 1866 and later was knighted and became a member of Parliament.

In the summer of 1867 the Grand Trunk Railway's board of directors sent him to Canada to investigate the operations of the road, and he returned again in the winter of 1870–71. Eventually he was named to the road's board of directors and in 1875 was named the company's vice president. Tyler became president of the Grand Trunk Railway in October 1876. He brought the road successfully through the depressions that followed the panics of 1873 and 1877. He bought and built a new main line from Ontario to Chicago that was completed in February 1880, now operated as the Grand Trunk Western. He was able to merge the archrival Great Western Railway of Canada into his Grand Trunk in 1882; oversaw the acquisition of most of the Grand Trunk's branch lines in Michigan; built and added branches in Canada; and put the talents of his chief engineer, Joseph Hobson, to building the St. Clair River tunnel.

He held the presidency until 5 May 1895, when he resigned in a dispute with his board of directors. He refused to apply the drastic measures they wanted to institute to see the company through the depression that followed the panic of 1893.

with new steel ones. Money was needed for everything, it seemed, but the depression that followed the panic of 1873 continued to affect traffic and profits. The road's freight solicitors were more successful in getting freight tonnage at any price than at a price that would yield a profit. Competition from the Great Western continued to be a nagging problem. Finally, in the back of Tyler's mind was the long-held goal of the Grand Trunk's own line to Chicago. That soon grew to be the most important of his concerns.

In 1876 it was no secret that Cornelius Vanderbilt was buying stock in the Michigan Central, the Grand Trunk's outlet to Chicago, and in the Canada Southern, a new GT competitor. The older Vanderbilt died in January 1877, and by June his son William Henry Vanderbilt had decided to gain control of the MC. He had old friend Samuel Sloan named as MC president, a job Sloan held for one year until the younger Vanderbilt took it for himself in June 1878. Vanderbilt also gained complete control of the Canada Southern in 1877.

Tyler and Hickson knew that the Grand Trunk could continue to use the Michigan Central into Chicago only so long as William Henry Vanderbilt agreed. It was time for Tyler to make a defensive move. There

Lewis J. Seargeant, a transplanted Englishman, managed freight and passenger traffic business for Tyler.

Myles Pennington, *Railways and Other Ways* (Toronto, 1894), facing 154.

Olivet

Poor Olivet—a village in the southern part of Eaton County. It was settled in 1844, was home to a prestigious Congregational college, and altogether was a pleasant place to live. But Olivet had no railroad. When the Peninsular Railway (later to become the Grand Trunk Western) was built between Battle Creek and Lansing in 1870, it went through Bellevue and bypassed Olivet by several miles. That may have happened because not enough local money was forthcoming to persuade the promoters to jog the line over a bit to touch Olivet. But the Peninsular did establish an Olivet station, well out in the country, at a place also called Ainger.

After twenty years of this, Olivetians decided their community had to have a railroad right into town and formed the Olivet Railway in April 1890 to get it. Its purpose was straightforward: build 2.33 miles of railroad between Olivet and Olivet station. Some noble goals, however, are fated not to be attained. The Olivet Railway, a very short railroad with one of the shortest names in the books, was never built, and its potential customers had to continue using their wagons and carriages to reach the depot far out of town at Ainger.

were two possibilities: the Michigan Air Line Railroad and William L. Bancroft's Chicago & Lake Huron. William L. Bancroft formed the Chicago & Lake Huron in April 1873 to unite the Port Huron & Lake Michigan, which ran from Port Huron to Flint, and the Peninsular, which operated between Lansing and Valparaiso, Indiana. Bancroft planned to merge the two roads into his new company, but for some reason the C&LH only took over operations of the two disconnected pieces. To close the gap between Flint and Lansing a group headed by James M. Turner, a Lansing real estate dealer and former treasurer of the Ionia & Lansing, formed the Chicago & Northeastern in July 1874, with Bancroft subscribing to the largest block of stock. By January 1877 the road was completed, and Bancroft began running Lake Huron road trains over it. With Grand Trunk cooperation, the C&LH became part of the Great Eastern Fast Freight Line, a forwarding company that handled expedited freight car movements between Chicago and the East Coast. With a through line and a friendly connection with the Pittsburgh, Fort Wayne & Chicago from Valparaiso into Chicago, Bancroft's prospects were looking up despite the fact that the company was all but broke.

Tyler's other possibility was the Michigan Air Line Railroad, a little road that was running a short line between Ridgeway (now Richmond) and Romeo. After the western part of the MAL between Jackson and Niles was built in 1871 and leased to the MC, its owners lost interest in the disconnected part on the eastern end. They leased it to the St. Clair River, Pontiac & Jackson in 1872, a road that was soon renamed the St.

Clair & Chicago Air Line. That company went under, and the MAL let the Romeo section of its line be foreclosed on. A new company, the Michigan Air Line Railway, took it over in December 1875. Tyler thought that it would be better that the Grand Trunk buy the little line than to let it get into the hands of someone who might use it against him. In October 1877 Tyler bought the MAL with its rights for a line into Pontiac, rights that were soon changed to allow building to Jackson. The MAL was completed into Pontiac in October 1880. When it reached South Lyon it connected with the Toledo, Ann Arbor & Grant Trunk. This set up an improved Grand Trunk route to Toledo, a service that became well patronized.

In the depression that followed the panic of 1873, with traffic levels and profits reduced, several of the railroads in the eastern United States began cutting rates in an attempt to keep traffic at any price. Former president Potter had tried to get the Great Western to agree to stabilize rates. The Vanderbilts, owning a sizable block of GW stock, would not agree, and his proposal went nowhere. No one was completely innocent when the periodic rate-cutting orgies broke out; each road did it. Just before his death, Cornelius Vanderbilt and the Eastern roads reached a rate agreement but excluded the Grand Trunk from their deliberations; the Grand Trunk elected to set its own rates. In late 1877, after Vanderbilt's death, all the roads, including his own, agreed on a new program to stabilize rates. When William Henry Vanderbilt learned he had westbound cars moving empty he announced he would hold to all agreed rates except when he had empty cars to fill. Once again the whole arrangement collapsed.

Tyler was concerned about the Grand Trunk's relations with the Great Western. As the managing director of the GW between 1853 and 1862, Charles J. Brydges had used sheer personal will to whip the road into shape, all the while facing a constant shortage of money. When Brydges left the Grand Trunk in 1874 the Great Western hired him back as a special commissioner. Brydges quickly instituted a wide range of efficiencies, but in so doing managed to offend the GW's officers and directors. The panic of 1873 caught the GW with a physical plant and equipment supply greater than it needed. At the same time, the Canada Southern was building between Niagara Falls and the Detroit River, a route almost parallel to the GW. Tyler contacted GW officers several times in an attempt to work out some sort of amalgamation of the two companies, but each of his attempts brought GW objections. In the end Tyler could only bide his time, waiting for a better opportunity.

By the summer of 1878 the Grand Trunk had a new problem with William Vanderbilt. In a secret move Vanderbilt bought $1,200,000 in Chicago & Northeastern bonds from James M. Turner. When Michigan Central control was firmly in his hands, Vanderbilt acted. On 27 June 1878 he blockaded the C&NE and announced that the road would be operated separately from the Chicago & Lake Huron. When asked about his move his reply was, "We will treat the road fairly and avoid all collisions which will be detrimental." The C&LH's receiver, Charles B. Peck, was operating the C&NE, and he was caught completely unawares. Peck did manage to get Vanderbilt to agree to have the C&LH continue through passenger and local freight service. Through freight would be handled but charged for at local rates, a charge that killed that business entirely. The Great Eastern Fast Freight Line shut down completely. At the same time, Vanderbilt continued his "friendly spirit" and allowed the Grand Trunk freight traffic to move over the Michigan Central between Detroit and Chicago. Tyler realized that Vanderbilt might well say one thing and do another, but that whatever happened would be to Vanderbilt's advantage.

There were two problems to resolve about a line to Chicago. The first was to find a route, and the second was to find the money to pay for the project. The money came by a fortuitous accident; the Grand Trunk had an underused line east of Montreal that the Canadian government wanted to buy to use with another line it was building. In 1879 the deal closed for $1,500,000, with the specific provision that the funds be used for the Chicago extension and for double-tracking the Montreal-Toronto main line.

For the route into Chicago Tyler had at least six options, all of which involved avoiding Vanderbilt's Flint-Lansing line. First, buy the Chicago & Lake Huron; second, extend the Michigan Air Line from Rochester to Lansing and connect with the C&LH; third, obtain running rights on the Detroit, Lansing & Northern between Detroit and Lansing and there connect with the C&LH; fourth, extend the MAL from Rochester to Ann Arbor or Ypsilanti, connect with the Detroit, Hillsdale & Southwestern to Auburn, Indiana, and thence on the Wabash to Chicago; fifth, build from Detroit to Wayne Junction, use the Flint & Pere Marquette and connect to the Toledo & Ann Arbor and then to the Wabash to Chicago; or sixth, have the Wabash build to Detroit or the Grand Trunk build to Toledo. Tyler and Hickson started meeting with everyone and anyone who might be able to offer any possible route to Chicago. Time passed, but neither Tyler nor Hickson gave any clue as to what the Grand Trunk might do. In a show of activity the Michigan Air Line did start building west from Rochester. During the summer of 1878 Hickson quietly bought a small railroad in Chicago, the Chicago & State Line. That road owned a twenty-mile line from the west side of Chicago to Thornton, Illinois.

Things went along uneasily between Tyler and Vanderbilt for nearly a year, until June 1879. The Port Huron–Flint section of the Chicago & Lake Huron went up for foreclosure sale. There was one bid of $300,000 by the bondholders, and then silence. The hammer came down, the money was paid, and the bondholders turned the road over to the Grand Trunk. A similar auction in August for the Lansing-Indiana state line section was hammered down at another $300,000. In both cases the bondholders turned their roads over to Tyler. He then announced he would build his own line between Flint and Lansing, which would run through Owosso and tap the coalfields there for fuel for his locomotives. This left Vanderbilt with a short railroad that only connected with the MC at Lansing and had no other traffic. By September he knew he had lost the confrontation and offered Tyler his $1,200,000 of C&NE bonds for $600,000. Tyler thought the price a little high and countered with $450,000; the two settled at $540,000. Tyler now had the needed middle section of his road and in October picked up the Indiana section of the C&LH at auction for another $200,000. Then followed immediate arrangements to close the gap between Valparaiso and Thornton. Building began at a frantic rate, and the job was completed quickly. In early February 1880 Tyler realized his dream. The Grand Trunk began through service on its own line between Port Huron and Chicago. There were some minor legal hoops to get through, but the entire line was in place and operated as the Chicago & Grand Trunk Railway. Tyler also continued building the Michigan Air Line, and it was completed into Jackson in January 1884.

Relations between the Grand Trunk and the Great Western grew no better during this period. Discussions degenerated into an "I said, you said" dialogue with neither party completely innocent or wholly to blame. Both regaled the press with counteraccusations about who was at fault for the loss of revenues and who had acted in a business-like manner. In sum, while each tried to look blameless, each tried to outmaneuver the other. In the long run the Grand Trunk's through route between the eastern seaboard and Chicago, and the advantages that could be obtained from that, gave it the edge. The Great Western still depended heavily on its connections at both ends for its traffic. All

Soon after it was built into Grand Haven, the Detroit & Milwaukee arranged connecting steamship transport to Milwaukee. The Detroit, Grand Haven & Milwaukee promoted the delights and elegance of a trip on its *City of Milwaukee* in this early 1880s advertisement.

Sam Breck collection.

James M. Ashley, after ten stormy years in the U.S. House of Representatives and a year as territorial governor of Montana, retired to Toledo in 1872. He decided that, having no money, he would go into railroad building. He built a 300-mile railroad on borrowed money—in his phrase, "entirely on wind."

Collection of U.S. House of Representatives.

the while it had to try to keep in the good graces of the Vanderbilts, a thing not easily done.

The Great Western's board worked aggressively in its attempt to retain independence. In 1880 it struck a deal with a predecessor of Jay Gould's Wabash Railroad, which was building a line into Detroit, by making a special contract to handle freight between Windsor and the Niagara Frontier. The Wabash line was completed into Detroit in August 1881, and the GW began benefiting immediately. Early in 1882 the GW worked out an agreement with the Rome, Watertown & Ogdensburg, which had a line east from Suspension Bridge. With its connections this road could handle traffic almost to New York City. Rumors were going around that the Canadian Pacific was thinking about building a line from Toronto to Windsor. But it all was a case of too little too late.

Tyler came to realize that there was no satisfying the GW board, which found some fault in or objected to any proposal for cooperation that he put on the table. Tyler decided to go around the board and deal directly with some of the major stockholders, a group more receptive to the idea or at least willing to listen. Part of their interest came from having to tolerate too little in dividends while watching the board and its friends get their income. The Great Western's president, Francis Grey, was furious at the turn of events that Tyler engineered. He finally did allow that some sort of lease to the Grand Trunk might be worked out. The stockholders ultimately prevailed, Grey resigned, the Canadian government passed the enabling legislation, and in August 1882 the Great Western was merged into the Grand Trunk Railway of Canada. Accompanying the Great Western was its affiliated Detroit & Milwaukee with its line between Detroit and Grand Haven.

In addition to the Great Western and Detroit & Milwaukee acquisition, Tyler picked up two other properties in Michigan. In 1887–88 the Toledo, Saginaw & Muskegon built a line between Ashley and Muskegon. James M. Ashley of the Toledo, Ann Arbor & North Michigan, and Ammi W. Wright, the Saginaw lumberman, were two important promoters of this road. Tyler saw no need for the weak Detroit & Milwaukee to have a competitor paralleling it fifteen miles to the north. In 1888 he bought the road as well as connecting running rights over Ashley's road between Owosso and Ashley. A second line, the Toledo, Saginaw & Mackinaw, built a line from Durand to Bay City

Ashley's railroad looks far more impressive on this timetable map printed by the company in 1894. The Wisconsin line was not his but that of a valuable connection that he linked to using his Lake Michigan rail car ferries.

Author's collection.

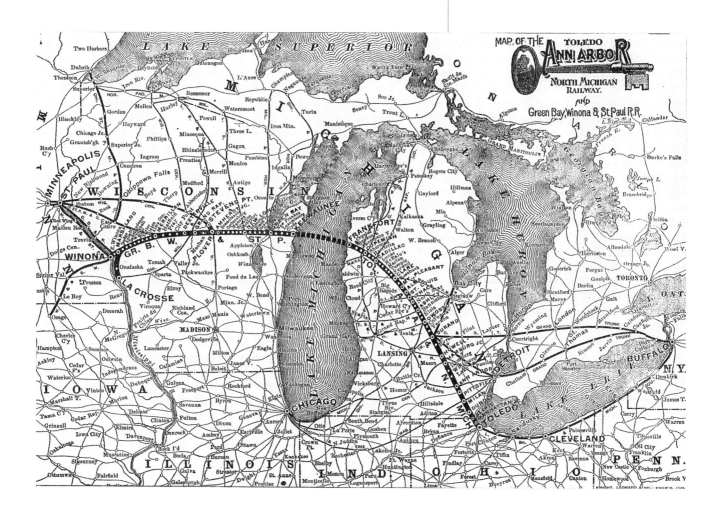

James M. Ashley

Born 24 November 1822, near Pittsburgh; died 16 September 1896, Toledo, Ohio.

Ashley moved to Toledo in 1851 and in 1858 was elected to the U.S. House of Representatives. Out of his strong antislavery feelings he introduced unsuccessful legislation to emancipate the slaves. He had an active role in the formation of the Montana Territory and was rewarded for it in 1868 when President Andrew Johnson appointed him the first territorial governor. In 1869 he resigned that post and returned to Toledo.

In 1877 Ashley bought the partly graded route of the Toledo, Ann Arbor & Northern at foreclosure sale. During the next eleven years he built the Toledo, Ann Arbor & North Michigan Railway from Toledo, through Ann Arbor, Owosso, Mt. Pleasant, and Cadillac, to Frankfort. Ashley and his two sons, James Jr. and Henry W., built the 300-mile line entirely with borrowed funds on land that they got as a gift or for free railroad passes. When a landowner would not sell, they built anyway and settled the matter later, usually in court. Although Ashley was president and owned controlling interest of the railroad, he also acted as independent construction contractor, making another profit from building his own railroad.

In November 1892 Ashley put the first of two car ferries on Lake Michigan and started the first cross-lake service of its type, able to move an entire train of railroad cars between Frankfort and Wisconsin ports. In 1895 the TAA&NM went into receivership. Ashley was forced off the railroad he had built and died a year later.

between 1888 and 1890. Ashley also operated it for a couple of years until its owners went looking for a more promising arrangement. In 1890 they reorganized the company as the Cincinnati, Saginaw & Mackinaw and separated themselves from Ashley. They offered the road to Tyler if he would guarantee the interest on the road's bonds. Tyler was hesitant but finally agreed to a ten-year lease of the road. Eventually the Grand Trunk bought the road.

The St. Clair River crossing between Port Huron and Sarnia remained the one bottleneck in the Grand Trunk's line from Chicago. Since 1859 the Grand Trunk operated ferries to move railcars across the river, a method that was reasonably satisfactory. But there were some delays that were unacceptable to shippers of perishable goods. A tunnel was talked about the early on, and in 1883 more detailed plans were drawn up. In 1886 Tyler presented the idea to his shareholders, who eventually approved the project. Digging began from each side in January 1889, and work moved ahead at about ten feet per day. The boring was completed 30 August 1890, and the first revenue train moved through the tunnel in September. Within a year 750 cars were moving through the tunnel daily, which had a capacity of 2,000 cars per day.

SOURCES

Currie, A. W. *The Grand Trunk Railroad of Canada.* Toronto: University of Toronto
    Press, 1957.

Hopper, A. B., and T. Kearney. *Canadian National Railways: Synoptical History . . . as
    of December 31, 1960.* Montreal: Canadian National Railways, 1962.

Meints, Graydon M. "Overwhelmed with Good Fortune." *Railroad History* No. 188
    (Spring 2003).

Stevens, G. R. *Canadian National Railways: Sixty Years of Trial and Error, 1836–1896.* 2
    vols. Toronto: Clark, Irwin, 1960.

James M. Ashley Builds the Ann Arbor

As early as 1845 the citizens of Ann Arbor were talking about the need
for a railroad running between Ann Arbor and Toledo. The feeling was
that the Michigan Central already had such a monopoly on freight
traffic that it was charging rates as high as it wished. A competing rail
line would force the MC to lower its charges. Nothing came of this
talk until the end of the Civil War, when in October 1869 a group of
Ann Arbor, Howell, and Dundee businessmen formed the Toledo, Ann
Arbor & Northern Railroad. It was to be a line 100 miles long extending
from the Ohio state line near Toledo, through Ann Arbor, to Owosso.
Owosso may have been picked because there it connected with the
Detroit & Milwaukee. The city of Ann Arbor voted $100,000 in bonds to
aid the company, and Ann Arbor Township added another $10,000. By
the end of 1873 the company acquired a right-of-way and graded about
thirty-eight miles of road south of Ann Arbor. The panic of 1873 dried up
money, and all work stopped. The company went into bankruptcy, and
its assets were sold to one of the contractors that was building the line.

In June 1877 James M. Ashley bought the property for $25,000.
Ashley had been a congressman from Toledo and for one year the
territorial governor of Montana. The governor reportedly said, "I got
out of a job in politics, came back to Toledo, and, having no business
to get back into and very little money, I decided to build a railroad."
Working with him were his equally ambitious sons James Jr. and Henry
W., nicknamed "Harry."

During the summer of 1877 Ashley went to Ann Arbor to raise
money to build his railroad. A fortuitous strike in July threatened to
close down the Michigan Central and apparently brought Ashley success.
In November 1877 he filed incorporation papers for the Toledo & Ann

Arbor Railroad and the following January 1878 signed a personal contract with his railroad to build its line. By May he completed track laying between Ann Arbor and Alexis on Toledo's north side. Also that May Ashley bought the Toledo & State Line from the Pennsylvania Railroad, a short road that allowed his line to get into downtown Toledo.

On 21 June 1878 the first freight train operated into Ann Arbor. Regularly scheduled passenger train service began a few days later, kicked off by the customary special trains carrying dignitaries who made the customary speeches at the customary dinners and also celebrated the customary number of alcoholic toasts.

To extend his line north Ashley then formed the Toledo, Ann Arbor & North Eastern to build thirty-three miles from Ann Arbor to Pontiac. Work started on this section in October 1879. The extension must have been an attempt to develop more traffic than Ann Arbor was providing. A dozen miles north of Ann Arbor, at South Lyon, was the Detroit, Lansing & Northern, which extended from Detroit, through Lansing and Ionia, to Howard City, where it connected with the Grand Rapids & Indiana to northern Michigan. A little farther on, at Wixom, was the Flint & Pere Marquette line, which extended to Saginaw and northwesterly into timber country. At Pontiac the line could connect with the western end of the projected Michigan Air Line Railway, then controlled by the Grand Trunk Railway of Canada. Also at Pontiac was the Detroit–Grand Haven line of the Detroit, Grand Haven & Milwaukee. Of these four lines only the F&PM had access to Toledo, and that was by using the tracks of the Lake Shore & Michigan Southern between Monroe and Toledo. Ashley may have figured that his new company could get the Toledo-bound traffic from the D&LN and the MAL at the least, and possibly some from the others.

With construction toward Pontiac under way Ashley consolidated the Ann Arbor and the North Eastern into a new company, the Toledo, Ann Arbor & Grand Trunk, in October 1880. Its line was opened to regular service from Ann Arbor as far as South Lyon in August 1881.

By this time the situation had changed. By September 1879 the Grand Trunk of Canada obtained control of most of the parts needed for its own route between Port Huron and Chicago. Its Michigan Air Line into Pontiac was no longer needed for this goal, but it continued to feed some freight traffic to Ashley to haul to Toledo. To make the best of it Ashley formed another railroad, the Toledo & Saginaw Bay Railway, to build a 120-mile line from Pontiac to Caseville. At Pontiac he also would be able to connect with the proposed Pontiac, Oxford

& Port Austin, which also planned a line north from Pontiac into the Thumb region. But in early September a massive forest fire swept over the Thumb. Gone in one day was the lumber that could bring profits to Ashley, and with that the appeal of a line into the Thumb. To make the best of a bad situation Ashley sold his grade and franchise between South Lyon and Pontiac to the MAL for $45,000. The MAL moved quickly and had its line between Pontiac and South Lyon in operation in October 1883. The outcome was somewhat different than Ashley had originally planned, but his goal was realized for the most part. At South Lyon he had connections with both the Detroit, Lansing & Northern and the Michigan Air Line. Ashley appears to have discarded the Toledo & Saginaw Bay project, although the Pontiac, Oxford & Port Austin did soon after build to Caseville rather than to Port Austin. Connecting with the MAL was a success when the Grand Trunk set up a through service to Toledo.

In August 1882 Ashley tinkered with the TAA&GT's incorporation papers to allow a line from Toledo, via South Lyon, to Durand. There he could connect with the Grand Trunk's Chicago–Port Huron main line as well as with the Detroit, Grand Haven & Milwaukee at the crossing of the two roads.

Lumbering country remained attractive to Ashley. Looking for an easy way to extend his road north, he came upon the Owosso & North Western. A group of Owosso men had organized the Owosso & Big Rapids Railroad in June 1869 to build an 81-mile line between those towns. In December 1871 the company, headed by Thomas D. Dewey of Owosso, changed its name to the Owosso & North Western, and changed its purpose now to be a 150-mile line from Owosso to Frankfort via Alma. The company never raised much money, but it had been able to assemble a right-of-way and grade some of its line between Owosso and St. Louis. Ashley saw possibilities in the unused grade, and in October 1882 he incorporated the Toledo, Ann Arbor & North Michigan to operate a line from St. Louis, via Alma, Ithaca, and Owosso, to his line near South Lyon. Ashley bought the Owosso road's grade in 1883 for $180,000 and in September 1883 personally contracted with his North Michigan to build the line from Owosso to St. Louis. From St. Louis Ashley thought he might build through Mt. Pleasant and Lake City on his way to Frankfort. The Owosso–St. Louis line was put in operation in early August 1884. The first public mention of a terminus on Lake Michigan came with Ashley's purchase of the O&NW, but it is uncertain when he first developed the idea of building to the lake. If it was his intention with his initial involvement in the Ann Arbor, he never made a formal indication of it in any of the corporations that he formed. Until the TAA&GT articles were amended in August 1882 and the North Michigan was formed in October, Ashley's intention appears to have been to build northeast or north from Ann Arbor, not northwest. What seems more likely is that he formed his plans as opportunity presented. It was not until 1888, with the formation of the Toledo, Ann Arbor & Lake Michigan, that Ashley formally named any Lake Michigan town as his road's terminus. It does seem reasonable, however, to conclude that Ashley had decided on a Lake Michigan goal at some time in 1883, since the TAA&GT's annual report of that year carried a map showing a line projected to Frankfort. Opportunist and innovator that he was, Ashley probably had seen the lake transfer service of the Pere Marquette at Ludington. But neither the Pere Marquette, which had reached Ludington in 1874, nor the Grand Trunk, which had been built into Grand Haven in 1858, had advanced beyond the break-bulk method of cross-lake shipping. He was also familiar with the car ferry services across the Detroit and St. Clair Rivers, which moved freight and passenger cars. But just when the flash of inspiration occurred—to ferry loaded freight cars across Lake Michigan—is unknown. The Mackinac Transportation Company ordered its first railcar ferry in 1887 for use at the Straits of Mackinac. This may have been the inspiration. It was not until 1890, when the line to Lake Michigan was well advanced, that Ashley first asked for plans for a translake railcar ferry.

Ashley's next challenge was to bridge the gap between the ends of his two lines at South Lyon and Owosso. In May 1884 he merged the North Michigan and his Grand Trunk into a new North Michigan company; its articles provided for a line between Toledo and St. Louis. Construction to close the gap very likely began that same year. In 1885 Ashley completed a line between Durand and Hamburg Junction, as Lakeland was first known, and obtained running rights over the Michigan Air Line between South Lyon and Hamburg Junction. Also he got running rights between Durand and Owosso on the Detroit, Grand Haven & Milwaukee. These two rights tied Ashley's lines together, so he could operate trains between Toledo and St. Louis. In October 1886 Ashley finished his own line between Durand and just west of Owosso Junction, and also in 1886 built a short piece from Leland, north of Ann Arbor on the line to South Lyon, to a connection with the MAL at a point just east of Hamburg on that road. This provided Ashley with a more direct route between Toledo and St. Louis.

The LAMP Road

By 1869 Lansing was connected to the outside world by rail lines coming in from Owosso and from Jackson, and others were planned from Detroit, Hillsdale, and Battle Creek. Not to be left out, the communities of St. Johns, Alma, and Mt. Pleasant, all north of Lansing, wanted to build a railroad from their city to Lansing. In 1869 men formed the Lansing, St. Johns & Mackinac to build it, and in 1871 some of the same men formed the Lansing & St. Johns to try again.

James M. Ashley talked about extending his railroad somewhere into the area, but nothing came of it until his Toledo, Ann Arbor & North Michigan bought the grade of the Owosso & North Western and built a line into St. Louis in 1884. That spurred both Alma and Mt. Pleasant residents to action. They formed the Lansing, Alma, Mt. Pleasant & Northern (the "LAMP" Road) to fulfill their dream of a line to the state capital. Lansing businessmen were not very excited about the idea, and after two years of trying to raise money the LAMP was sold to Ashley. He built it from Alma to Mt. Pleasant in 1886.

One final effort to build to Lansing was made in 1888 with the formation of the Lansing, Saint Johns & Northern, but nothing ever came of that road.

In 1886 Ashley also was busy making plans to extend his road north from St. Louis. He first considered building directly north from St. Louis and angling northwest to reach Mt. Pleasant. But this route bypassed Alma completely, and Ashley overlooked the wishes of Alma's leading citizen, Ammi W. Wright. Lumberman Wright favored a railroad that ran north from Alma, not from St. Louis, and Wright had considerably more money than Ashley. Wright also had been part of a group promoting a railroad from Lansing, through Alma, north to some place as opportunity presented itself. This line had been talked about since the end of the Civil War, but there had been more rhetorical than financial support coming from the businessmen of Lansing. Wright had money enough to build the line on his own, but he chose to let others help out.

As Ashley pushed his rails into St. Louis, Wright decided to act. In February 1884 he formed the Lansing, Alma, Mt. Pleasant & Northern Railroad, the "LAMP," to build a sixty-eight-mile line from Lansing to Mt. Pleasant. Wright began building north from Alma and completed about twelve miles of railroad during 1885. By December 1885 Wright and Ashley apparently had struck a deal. Ashley agreed to buy the LAMP from Wright and also would build a connection between St. Louis and Alma that would connect the LAMP to his own line. With this move Ashley would acquire a partly built line and its financing, and at the same time remove a possible competitor. Wright, for his part, would get his wished-for line extending north from Alma and the timber traffic into Alma that it would provide. It appears that Ashley never made any attempt to use the LAMP franchise rights south of Alma.

In March 1886 Ashley bought the LAMP for $122,530. In May 1886 he renamed it the Toledo, Ann Arbor & Mt. Pleasant Railway, and finished the line into Mt. Pleasant in July 1886. Ashley bought an abandoned grade of the Chicago, Saginaw & Canada between Alma and St. Louis and used it to build a connecting line between these two cities and link his two sections together.

As Ashley was laying rails into Mt. Pleasant in the early months of 1886 he also was planning for the extension of his company to the north. In June 1886 he incorporated the Toledo, Ann Arbor & Cadillac Railway to build a sixty-three-mile line between Mt. Pleasant and Cadillac. Surveying this route, he found the abandoned grade of the Lake George & Muskegon River, Winfield Scott Gerrish's pioneering logging railroad, and built his line on part of it in the Lake George area. The line between Mt. Pleasant and Cadillac was completed in 1888, apparently early in the year. Next Ashley turned to completing his railroad to Lake Michigan. In March 1888 he formed the Toledo, Ann Arbor & Lake Michigan Railway to build a sixty-mile line from Cadillac to Frankfort. Track laying must have started immediately since the line was finished as far as Harrietta by the end of 1888.

Ashley did express some interest in running into Manistee over the tracks of the Manistee & Northeastern, but nothing ever came of that idea. Ultimately Ashley chose Frankfort for two reasons. The Frankfort harbor has been described as an "extremely snug harbor, offering excellent protection against storms." The citizens of Frankfort knew the value of their harbor, and some local businessmen formed their own railroad company, the Frankfort & South Eastern Railroad, in November 1885 to make use of it. It was to be a narrow-gauge line, and the inland terminal was not definitely decided. In November 1887 the F&SE's incorporation articles were amended to change the line to a standard gauge one, and later it set Copemish as its eastern terminus. The F&SE completed its line on 25 November 1889 and intersected the Chicago & West Michigan, which was far along in building its line between Grand Rapids and Traverse City. Ashley's Lake Michigan completed its line to Copemish on 17 November 1889, and established a working relationship with the Frankfort road. In May 1892 Ashley bought the Frankfort & South Eastern outright and merged it into his North Michigan.

Completing the railroad from Toledo to Frankfort was a monumental achievement. James Ashley and his two sons had been able to "push a railroad three hundred miles into new undeveloped territory with inadequate money, 'on wind' as Jim Ashley, Junior, put it." It had been built, during the early years at least, without any definite objective but as opportunity provided. Ashley got rights-of-way in the cheapest way he could, and if he could not he would put down rails anyway and settle later with the owners in court. The line was built very cheaply and almost entirely with borrowed money. The earnings of the road paid the interest charges, kept Ashley's credit in good stead, and allowed him to borrow more for more construction. The chief engineer of the Ann Arbor, Henry E. Riggs, commented on the conditions he found on the line when he wrote his recollections of the first inspection trip he made in 1890, when Ashley had hired him and not long after the line had been completed.

> My first trip . . . convinced me that I was on a "jerkwater" railroad. It was a single-track line, laid with 56-pound rail on ties that were 90% hemlock with no ballast anywhere on the line except over a few "sinkholes" where cinder ballast had been used, probably not over two or three miles in all. The bridges were all of wood, the great majority small pile or timber trestles. . . .
>
> The equipment at the beginning of 1890 was nothing to brag about, but during the year considerable new passenger equipment was purchased, including two parlor cars. The Company had, at the end of 1890, thirty-six locomotives in pretty good condition, but light, and twenty-four passenger train cars and 1,073 freight train cars, most of which were old and shabby.

With his rail line completed between Toledo and Lake Michigan, Ashley turned his attention to the cross-lake car ferry service. In 1890 Ashley placed his order for two specially designed railcar ferries. To hold the market intact for his new service he began operating the steamer *Osceola* from Elberta to Kewaunee, Wisconsin, in early 1892. Although transloading was needed at both ports, the service was planned to last only until the car ferries were received. The first of the ferries, appropriately but simply named *Ann Arbor No. 1*, made its first revenue trip from Frankfort on 24 November 1892.

In March 1893 Ashley could not pay the interest due on his road's bonds. Every dollar Ashley had raised or borrowed had been used to build and equip the railroad and to buy the Lake Michigan car ferries. A strike began on 7 March 1893 and was soon followed by the financial panic of 1893. The two events brought the company down. Wellington R. Burt was appointed receiver of the company; in March 1894 James M. Ashley resigned the presidency of the railroad he had created and built.

Burt was "one of Michigan's typical lumber barons, wealthy, hard headed, and perfectly willing to spend money for a much better kind of construction and maintenance than that to which the Ann Arbor had ever been accustomed." Ruling grades in several places were reduced. The line between Durand and Oak Grove was relocated to a completely new route. The section between Howell and Chilson was moved out of the swamp to higher ground. In 1894 the section between Lake George and Temple was rebuilt on a better alignment. Late in 1893 or early in 1894 the company acquired land for a new passenger terminal in Toledo that fronted on Cherry Street immediately north of the Wheeling & Lake Erie station. Passenger trains began operating into the Cherry Street station in the summer of 1896. With the completion of this new station the Ann Arbor obtained a new and, for the first time, permanent general headquarters building. Between 1894 and 1896 it built a new line between Ann Arbor and Lakeland, replacing the old roundabout route through Leland. In the fall of 1895 the Ann Arbor began negotiating with the Detroit, Grand Rapids & Western for an exchange of property. The Ann Arbor acquired the Alma-Ithaca branch of the DGR&W, the DGR&W acquired some Ann Arbor tracks in St. Louis, and the two companies agreed to build a new line through downtown Alma, much of it along the right-of-way originally used by the LAMP. In the period from April 1893 to July 1897 Burt spent $1,227,183 to upgrade the roadway and buildings and buy new equipment. This sum was about one-fifth the amount that Ashley had spent to construct and equip the entire railroad. By the end of the receivership Burt had upgraded Ashley's road into a "real" railroad line.

The Lake Michigan car ferry service was as successful as Ashley had envisioned. Receiver Burt expanded the service to more west-shore ports, and this brought additional freight traffic to the Ann Arbor. These annual increases in traffic pointed out the inadequacies of the physical plant as Ashley had originally built it. Burt's changes in line, some of which Ashley had planned for before 1893, improved the plant and allowed it absorb the increased business without difficulty.

A new company, the Ann Arbor Railroad Company, was formed on 20 September 1895. Receiver Burt operated the reorganized company

until the end of October. The new corporation began operations on
1 November.

SOURCES

Ceasar, Ford Stevens. *The Lamp Road*. Lansing, Mich.: Wellman, 1983.

Dunbar, Willis F. *All Aboard! A History of Railroads in Michigan*. Grand Rapids,
    Mich.: W. B. Eerdmans, 1969.

Frederickson, Arthur C., and Lucy F. Frederickson. *Early History of the Ann Arbor
    Carferries*. Frankfort, Mich.: Patriot Publishing, 1949.

Hilton, George W. *The Great Lakes Car Ferries*. Berkeley, Calif.: Howell-North, 1962.

Meints, Graydon M. *Michigan Railroads and Railroad Companies*. East Lansing:
    Michigan State University Press, 1992.

Riggs, Henry E. *The Ann Arbor Railroad Fifty Years Ago*. Toledo, Ohio: Ann Arbor
    RR, 1947. Reprint, Ann Arbor, 1991.

U.S. Interstate Commerce Commission. *Valuation Docket No. 127*. Washington, D.C.:
    Interstate Commerce Commission, 1924.

Rails to Northern Michigan

By 1875 settlers were moving into the northern half of Michigan's
Lower Peninsula. When the panic of 1873 stopped railroad construction,
only three lines had built into this part of the state. The Flint & Pere
Marquette ran from Saginaw to Ludington across the base of the area.
Two other roads ran north, the Michigan Central and the Grand Rapids
& Indiana. There were few permanent settlements away from the rail
lines, with none of them numbering more than a hundred souls. The
harbors at Tawas City, AuSable, Harrisville, Alpena, Cheboygan, Petoskey,
Traverse City, Manistee, Ludington, and Pentwater had small communities that built up around mills that sawed logs that were then floated
down rivers. As the effects of the panics of 1873 and 1877 ebbed away
and a demand for lumber rekindled, the enthusiasm for more railroads
also returned. Although the northern half of the Lower Peninsula of
Michigan was the center of the logging industry, there was little else in
the region to attract settlers or businesses or railroads.

In 1870 the Flint & Pere Marquette began building west from Averill.
It stalled at Reed City for more than a year, until 1873, but the next year
finished its line across the state on the land-grant route from Flint to
Ludington. With the road came such communities as Reed City, Baldwin,

Walhalla, and Scottville. The line breathed life into such lumbering sites as Clare, Farwell, and Hersey, and brought new prosperity to the port of Ludington.

In 1871 the Jackson, Lansing & Saginaw, now controlled by the Michigan Central, began building north from Bay City. At the end of the year the road reached Alger, and by the summer of 1873 it was completed to the vicinity of Gaylord. Standish, West Branch, Roscommon, Grayling, Frederic, and Gaylord all had their beginnings with the coming of the railroad. On the west side of the peninsula the Grand Rapids & Indiana, being built by its financial backer, the Continental Improvement Company, was completed to Paris in 1870, to Cadillac in 1871, to Fife Lake in 1872, and to Petoskey in 1874. The branch owned by the Traverse City Railroad was built to that city in 1872. There had been settlements at Petoskey and Traverse City in the late 1830s, and at Big Rapids and Paris in the 1850s, but that was about all. The communities of Howard City, Morley, Stanwood, Reed City, Leroy, Tustin, Cadillac, Manton, Fife Lake, Kalkaska, Mancelona, Alba, Elmira, Boyne Falls, and Kingsley were developed as the rails were laid down.

In 1875 a group of Methodists came north looking for a place to establish a denominational Chautauqua—a summer educational program. After inspecting several sites they chose land just north of Petoskey fronting on Little Traverse Bay. The following year the Bay View Assembly started its programs. In the 1870s Bay View was a remote place. The Grand Rapids & Indiana agreed to extend its tracks for another mile to the grounds. To carry riders a used horsecar was bought from the Kalamazoo street railway and brought to Petoskey. The horse pulled the car up the slight grade from Bay View to Petoskey; on the return trip down grade the horse enjoyed a ride on the vestibule.

By 1879 the dream of building the Detroit, Mackinac & Marquette to connect the Marquette iron-mining region with St. Ignace was becoming a reality. The Michigan Central built only a little more than sixty miles to the Straits of Mackinac at Mackinaw City to connect to it. (The MC had to build from Gaylord, but the GR&I had to build only the thirty-five miles from Bay View to reach the Straits.) The Michigan Central started first and was completed to the Straits in December 1881. The first station north of Gaylord on the new section was named to honor the MC's president, William Henry Vanderbilt. The line brought good access to Mullet and Burt Lakes and to Indian River and Cheboygan. Resorts were opened along the shoreline at Topinabee and Birchwood. It was not until early 1881 that the GR&I decided to build a line to Mackinaw City, which branched off its just-completed Harbor Springs branch.

The DM&M line from Marquette into St. Ignace also was finished in December 1881. The Grand Rapids & Indiana arrived in Mackinaw City in July 1882. Tying together the three roads on two peninsulas at the Straits of Mackinac proved difficult. The roads considered a bridge, but that was thought to be too challenging and too expensive. The MC, GR&I, and DM&M established the Mackinac Transportation Company in October 1881 to operate a railcar ferry between St. Ignace and Mackinaw City. The company started up immediately, first using the barge *Betsy*, which carried four railcars and was towed most often by the *Algomah*, a break-bulk steamer owned by the MTC. When the straits were frozen solid, passengers and baggage were sledded across the ice. The *Betsy*'s performance forced the MTC to order a car ferry. Frank E. Kirby of Detroit, with help from the *Algomah*'s captain, Louis R. Boynton, designed the first ferry, the *St. Ignace*. It went into service in April 1888. The *St. Ignace* had a capacity of only ten railcars, and the volume of traffic soon demanded a ferry with greater capacity. The *Sainte Marie* was received in June 1893; the *St. Ignace* underwent some rebuilding and was then returned to service. By 1910 the demands of traffic were so great that the MTC decided to order another new car ferry and retire the older two. The *Chief Wawatam*, received in October 1911, could carry twenty-six railcars and became the mainstay of the MTC. The *Sainte Marie* was sold and converted to a barge and the *St. Ignace* kept only to supplement the *Chief*. In 1927 the *Sainte Marie*'s engines were put in a new car ferry also named *Sainte Marie*, and the *St. Ignace* was sold. By the 1950s the *Sainte Marie* was used only as a backup ship and for ice-breaking service until it was sold in October 1961.

In addition to the Straits' railcar and passenger ferry service, the Michigan Central, the Grand Rapids & Indiana, and the Detroit & Cleveland Navigation joined forces in an unusual venture. Since the early 1800s Mackinac Island had been developing into an exclusive summer resort of unusual appeal. George T. Arnold came up from Saugatuck and began a Mackinac Island ferry service in 1881 after the railroads were built. The Detroit & Cleveland Navigation Company began sailing from Detroit to Mackinac Island in 1882, and the next year it launched the *City of Mackinac*, which could make the trip in only thirty hours. All three companies were trying to promote tourist travel and in 1886 decided to build a new and impressive resort hotel. They bought land from Francis B. Stockbridge of Kalamazoo, who had dreamed and planned a like grand undertaking, but who could not pursue it after he was appointed to the U.S. Senate. During the winter of 1886 lumber was hauled across the ice to the island, and the following spring other supplies were shipped in. In July 1887 the fabulous structure was finished, and the landmark Grand Hotel opened for business. The hotel claimed that Cornelius Vanderbilt (not the Commodore but his son) and Chauncey M. Depew were present, although the hotel may have been somewhat overenthusiastic in describing the inaugural event. The three-party ownership continued until 1904, when they sold half of their stock to the hotel's manager. In 1910 they sold the other half and were finally, and happily, out of the hotel business. As a financial undertaking the hotel was a disappointment to its owners.

Both the Michigan Central and the Grand Rapids & Indiana built and bought a few branches to garner lumber traffic. In 1883 the MC leased the Saginaw Bay & Northwestern, which had bought the Pinconning Railroad in 1880. During the next fifteen years the MC built and abandoned lumbering spurs off this line and eventually pushed it into Gladwin in 1887. In 1892 the MC formed the Grayling, Twin Lakes & Northeastern, which built a branch from Grayling to Lewiston and then built several spurs from that main branch. The Grand Rapids & Indiana also built a few lumbering branches. The longest was proposed in 1885 to reach the sawmills at Manistee but ultimately was built only to Luther and Carey.

Along the Lake Huron shore other lumbering roads were starting up. Russell A. Alger built one out of Alcona, and Charles D. Hale another out of Tawas City. To raise more capital Hale brought in C. H. Prescott of Bay City in 1878, and they started building the Lake Huron & Southwestern. The winter of 1878 was an unprofitable one, so Prescott bought out Hale. In 1880 he renamed the railroad as the Tawas & Bay County. In 1881 Russell A. Alger and Martin S. Smith of Detroit formed the Bay City & Alpena Railroad to build a line between those two cities. In 1882 Alger and Smith bought the Tawas & Bay County and the next year renamed the entire project the Detroit, Bay City & Alpena. By the end of 1883 Alger had extended their road west to a junction with the Michigan Central at a station appropriately named Alger, and also had the road extended north as far as AuSable. Two passenger trains each way began running, which connected with Michigan Central trains running to Saginaw and Detroit.

In September 1886 Alger, using some of his own lumbering road tracks and building some, extended the DBC&A into Alpena. Over the

Russell Alexander Alger

Born 27 February 1836, Lafayette Twp., Medina Co., Ohio; died 24 January 1907, Washington, D.C., buried Detroit.

Alger was raised by his uncle after both of his parents died when he was eleven years old. He worked the farm until he was eighteen, then attended Richfield Academy, taught school for a while, then studied law and was admitted to the bar in 1859. He moved to Grand Rapids that year and began dabbling in the lumber business. In 1861 he married Annette Henry, and with her had nine children.

In August 1861 Alger enlisted in the volunteer cavalry as a private and shortly became captain of the Second Michigan Cavalry and was later promoted in other cavalry regiments. He fought in numerous battles and was twice wounded. He resigned in 1864, later earning a brevet promotion to major general.

Once back in Detroit he returned to the lumber business, and soon began a successful partnership with Martin S. Smith as Alger, Smith & Company. The two began their timbering operations in northern Alcona County, and by 1878 the two built the thirteen-mile Black River Railroad for logging out of Black River. As their lumbering expanded along the Lake Huron shoreline, they formed the Bay City & Alpena Railroad in 1881 to provide year-round access to the Saginaw sawmills. In 1882 the two bought the Tawas & Bay County Railroad and extended it to a connection with the Michigan Central at Alger. In 1883 the two, leagued with a number of their wealthy Detroit neighbors, renamed their railroad the Detroit, Bay City & Alpena, with Alger as the road's president. By 1886 Alger extended the road from Tawas City to Alpena.

Now a multimillionaire, and with the best years of lumbering now passing, Alger decided to enter politics. He became the Republican Party candidate for governor in 1884, won the four-man race, and served just one two-year term. In 1889 he was elected commander in chief of the Grand Army of the Republic, strongly urging improved pensions for Civil War soldiers. Alger continued as president of the DBC&A through 1893, then founded the Alpena & Northern as a lumbering extension into Montmorency County and remained its president until it was merged into the DBC&A.

Alger was put forward as a presidential candidate in 1892, but he declined the nomination. In 1896 he campaigned strenuously for William McKinley, and served as secretary of war from 1897 to 1899. He resigned under criticism for several contracts he awarded during the Spanish-American War. Late in 1902 Governor Aaron T. Bliss appointed Alger as U.S. senator to succeed the late James McMillan, and despite his deteriorating health Alger held the office until his death.

next decade the company built and then abandoned hundreds of miles of lumbering branches in Alcona and Iosco Counties. During 1885–86 Alger served a term as governor of Michigan, then returned to his lumbering business. By 1893 the timber was beginning to play out in this area; Alger and Smith took their money and let the DBC&A go into receivership. Receiver Don M. Dickinson brought in James D. Hawks of Detroit, who had spent twenty years as assistant engineer on the Lake

Shore & Michigan Southern and then as chief engineer on the Michigan Central, and named him general manager. When New York City money bought the road in 1894 after the receivership, they renamed it the Detroit & Mackinac, wisely kept Hawks on as general manager, and in 1896 named him president. Hawks went after new freight business aggressively and promoted the route for passenger and tourist travel. At the same time, the D&M's owners announced that the road would be extended to Bay City, a move that would allow connections with more lines than just the Michigan Central. The extension was completed in September 1896, and it shortened the trip for the two daily passenger trains with connections to Detroit. The D&M also bought the Alpena & Northern, a road that Alger and Smith had formed in 1893 to build from Alpena to Mackinaw City. When Hawks bought it in 1895 its line was a long arc from Alpena into the woods in Montmorency County.

Another east-shore lumbering road was the Au Sable & Northwestern, which started as a logging road. J. E. Potts built two narrow-gauge lines out of McKinley in Ogemaw County in the late 1880s. Gradually he extended his branches, and about 1891 built to the Lake Huron port of Au Sable. Financial difficulties forced Potts to sell his land, sawmill, and railroad to Henry M. Loud in 1891. Loud and his sons built and abandoned lumbering branches as they needed to, but did operate one lone passenger train that made a round trip each day out of Au Sable to Comins.

On the west side of the state Petoskey developed into the most important of all the summer resort areas. In 1882 the Grand Rapids & Indiana built a branch to Harbor Springs, and the entire distance from Petoskey quickly became a continuous row of summer cottages and resorts. Midwestern notables called Wequetonsing, Roaring Brook, and Harbor Point their summer home. Church association campgrounds at Bay View and Wequetonsing drew crowds. The GR&I ran trains almost hourly between Petoskey and Harbor Springs and made several accommodation runs daily to Alanson and to Walloon Lake. Oden took its name from William Oden Hughart, the president of the GR&I. The railroad accompanied all of this with an extensive advertising program as well as an annual booklet that described the area in enticing detail.

In the 1890s the GR&I ran three trains each way between Grand Rapids and Mackinaw City, and a fourth as far north as Cadillac. For summer travelers it began the *Northland Express*, which ran through from Cincinnati to Mackinaw City, and hauled sleeping cars from Cincinnati, Louisville, Indianapolis, St. Louis, and Chicago. A connecting service to

Detroit, Charlevoix & Escanaba

In March 1887 a group of men from Charlevoix and Kalkaska believed that their cities should have a rail line to connect to the Michigan Central at Grayling. To build it they formed the Detroit, Charlevoix & Escanaba. Later in the year they modified the route to include a line from Charlevoix to the Straits of Mackinac. Today it is impossible to determine any reasonable need for the road. Possibly the promoters thought their road could be a shortcut between the Marquette iron range and Lake Erie ports. Using ships between Escanaba and Charlevoix and rail to Detroit and on to the steel mills would reduce the distance below that of the rail line via the Straits of Mackinac or of the all-water route from Marquette via the Soo Locks.

Alas, this idea did not succeed, and the DC&E came to nothing.

Chicago was operated over the Grand Trunk Western via Vicksburg for a short time, then changed over to the Michigan Central from Kalamazoo.

The Chicago & West Michigan bought the Chicago & Michigan Lake Shore and its line from New Buffalo to Pentwater in 1878. In 1881 the C&WM changed its proposed northern terminus to Manistee, but nothing ever came of an extension north from Pentwater. In July 1881 it bought the Grand Rapids, Newaygo & Lake Shore, which owned a line from Grand Rapids to White Cloud. The Newaygo's route entered more heavily timbered territory than the West Michigan's, so White Cloud became the jumping-off point for the C&WM's route north into still more timber country.

By 1883 the C&WM extended its line as far as Baldwin to a connection with the Flint & Pere Marquette, and in 1890 completed it to Traverse City. In early 1891 the C&WM formed a construction subsidiary, the Chicago & North Michigan, to build an extension from Leland on Lake Michigan, through Traverse City, to the Straits of Mackinac. Work got under way immediately, with the line from Traverse City through Charlevoix to Bay View finished in July 1892. The C&WM also built a number of short branches into timberlands and also built branches to Elk Rapids and Ironton to reach iron smelters. Once completed the C&WM began operating its overnight summertime *Resort Special* between Chicago, Traverse City, Charlevoix, Petoskey, and Bay View. The train had a connecting leg that reached Detroit. The comfort of sleeping cars brought summer travelers to the Charlevoix Inn and Chicago and Belvedere resorts at Charlevoix and the shoreline of Torch Lake.

The C&WM also leased the newly built Grand Rapids, Kalkaska & Southeastern, a road that ran southeast from Rapid City through

Kalkaska and ended in the now forgotten community of Stratford. There was some rumor about extending it south from Stratford to Leota, where it could connect with a branch off the Flint & Pere Marquette's Saginaw-Ludington line to create a new Detroit–northern Michigan route. Nothing ever came of this will-o'-the-wisp, and the Kalkaska road continued on for years losing money for its owner.

The Manistee & Northeastern was one lumbering road that developed into a commercial carrier. Owners Edward Buckley and William Douglas built it to haul logs to their sawmill in Manistee. Although it would have been simpler to build the road as a private lumbering road, that status would have made it more difficult to get the needed route in the city of Manistee. The first section of line was finished in November 1888 northeast from Manistee thirty-two miles to Nessen City. By 1890 it built several short branches and extended the main line to Lake Ann. The next year the road was extended to Traverse City, but the extension meandered through more timberlands to feed the owners' Manistee sawmills. The M&NE ran two passenger trains each way between Manistee and Traverse City, taking two and a half hours for the trip over the seventy-mile roundabout route. Lumber traffic was by far the most important commodity and continued to move principally to Manistee.

SOURCES

Barnett, Le Roy. "Detroit, Mackinac & Marquette." *SOO* 12:4 (October 1990), 13:1 (January 1991).

Burgtorf, Frances D. *Chief Wawatam: The Story of a Hand-Bomber*. Cheboygan, Mich.: author, 1976.

Dunbar, Willis F. *All Aboard! A History of Railroads in Michigan*. Grand Rapids, Mich.: W. B. Eerdmans, 1969.

Hilton, George W. *The Great Lakes Car Ferries*. Berkeley, Calif.: Howell-North, 1962.

Inglis, James G. *Northern Michigan Handbook for Traveler's, 1898*. Petoskey, Mich.: George E. Sprang, 1898. Reprint, Grand Rapids, Mich.: Black Letter Press, 1974.

Ivey, Paul Wesley. *The Pere Marquette Railroad: An Historical Study of the Growth and Development of One of Michigan's Most Important Railway Systems*. Lansing: Michigan Historical Commission, 1919. Reprint, Grand Rapids: Black Letter Press, 1970.

Michigan Railroad Commission. *Aids, Gifts, Grants and Donations to Railroads . . .* Lansing, Mich.: Wynkoop, Hallenbeck, Crawford, 1919.

Stroup, Donald. "Boom to Bankruptcy: The Story of the Manistee and

Northeastern Railroad." Master's thesis, Western Michigan University, 1965.
(Also published in abridged form as *The Life and Death of a Railroad, The
Manistee and Northeastern* [Lansing: Michigan Historical Commission, 1964])

Thornton, W. Neil. *High Iron along the Huron Shore.* Tawas City, Mich.: Printer's
Devil Press, 1982.

Wakefield, Lawrence, and Lucille Wakefield. *Sail and Rail: A Narrative History of
Transportation in Western Michigan.* Grand Rapids: W. B. Eerdmans, 1980.
Reprint, Holt, Mich.: Thunder Bay Press, 1996.

Wakeman, George L. "My Story of the Detroit and Mackinac Railway."
Unpublished manuscript, Michigan Historical Collections, University of
Michigan, Ann Arbor.

Rails across the Upper Peninsula, Part 2

In the early 1870s several Upper Peninsula newspapers and the *Detroit
Free Press* began promoting the idea of a railroad from the Straits of
Mackinac into the heart of the Upper Peninsula at Marquette. The
argument was that the dominant Chicago & North Western diverted
business toward Wisconsin and Chicago and away from the Lower
Peninsula. A through rail line, with a car ferry or bridge or tunnel
across the Straits of Mackinac, would allow ore to move year-round
through the Lower Peninsula. The legislature favored the idea and
asked Congress for a grant of federal land to help the project along. In
December 1872 the Marquette, Sault Ste. Marie & Mackinac Railroad was

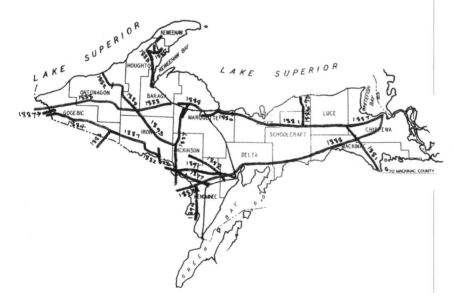

Upper Peninsula rail lines built between
1875 and 1895. Note that not all branches
to iron and copper mines are shown.

KEY

—— Upper Peninsula lines built before
1875

■■■ New lines built between 1875 and
1895

formed to build a 200-mile line from Marquette to the St. Marys River with a branch to the Straits of Mackinac. All of the founders were from Marquette: Peter White, an early settler, banker, and insurance agent; Sidney Adams, a real estate dealer; Daniel H. Ball, an attorney; Seymour Brownell, the manager of the Marquette Brown Stone quarry; Samuel P. Ely, who completed the Iron Mountain railroad and now managed several iron mines; Jay C. Morse, who was involved with several iron mines; James Pickands, a dealer in mining supplies who later founded Pickands, Mather & Company; and Frederick P. and William L. Wetmore, both of whom were merchants and involved with mining. The state awarded it a grant of ten sections of state swampland per mile of road but required a $10,000 bond and a guarantee that the road would be completed between St. Ignace and Marquette by the last day of 1875. As the company began to organize it ran into financial problems. The panic of 1873 slowed progress, which forced the company to ask for extensions of time to build. The state not only obliged the road but also increased the land grant to sixteen sections of land per mile, and agreed to award the land as each twenty-mile segment was completed. There can be no doubt that such generosity was politically motivated; the legislature considered a rail link between the two peninsulas to be of great importance.

By mid-1875 no tracks had been laid, so the state began talking with another group that was interested in building the line. Nothing came out of this, and the state went back to pinning its hopes on the original company. Another year slipped by with no construction, and then another. By August 1879 the state was ready to cancel its contracts with the Marquette company. Within days a new company, the Detroit, Mackinac & Marquette, was formed to build the line. Its founders all were well-to-do Detroiters: George Hendrie, Waldo M. Johnson, James McMillan, Elijah W. Meddaugh, William K. Muir, John S. Newberry, and Francis Palms. In September William B. Moran was added to the group. The state eagerly signed a contract with this company to build the road but stipulated that it must be completed by the end of 1881. Before the first rail was put down the promoters began attempting to sell some of the grant land on conditional sales agreements. Construction got under way at Marquette in January 1880. By July the first twenty miles of road were completed from Marquette to Glenwood, a point now known as Onota, and the road received title to the first 128,000 acres of grant land. It began aggressive efforts to sell the grant land to raise money to continue building.

By the summer of 1881 the DM&M again was running short of cash. It was forced to sell a $4,500,000 bond issue in New York to continue construction. A fire destroyed 15,000 ties, and these had to be replaced. Workmen continued in short supply despite a 25-cent-a-day pay increase. Rain forced men to work waist deep in the Tahquamenon swamp to keep the road going. By November it was certain that the road could be completed by the deadline, and the company set an official completion date of 9 December. The road was opened for traffic on 19 December, and the next day Governor David H. Jerome, his staff, and the road's directors left St. Ignace on an inspection trip. Within weeks the road received rights to over one million acres of state land.

The company planned to haul ore from the Marquette Range to St. Ignace, a port that had a longer shipping season than either Marquette or Escanaba. The DM&M built an ore dock to make use of this advantage and ordered 800 ore cars. The road also built a second dock that allowed railcars to be loaded on the Mackinac Transportation Company's new ferry service across the straits to Mackinaw City. The steamer *Algomah*, pulling the barge *Betsy*, could move four cars at a time between ports.

To gain its own share of the ore traffic President James McMillan organized the Marquette & Western in October 1883. By the end of 1884 the M&W completed a line from Marquette to the Winthrop Mine west of Ishpeming. That line also built an ore dock in Marquette. The ore traffic through St. Ignace never materialized in the hoped-for volume. In both 1882 and 1883 net income failed to cover the interest on the road's debt. Through some financial juggling and creative bookkeeping the road managed to stay afloat, but in October 1884 it had to default on a bond interest payment. In another attempt to bolster the road's fortunes President McMillan, his brother Hugh McMillan, and the rest of the board formed the Ishpeming, L'Anse & Ontonagon in January 1885 to extend west from the M&W line. Nothing ever came of that project, nor did anything come of the Wisconsin, Sault Ste. Marie & Mackinac, which they formed in September 1886 to build to Ironwood. To raise cash McMillan leased the M&W line to the Marquette, Houghton & Ontonagon in May 1885. As part of the bargain the McMillan brothers joined the MH&O board. But they could not save the DM&M, and it was sold at foreclosure in September 1886. Hugh McMillan, the only bidder, bought it at a price well under the $13 million reported cost of construction.

In December 1886 the McMillans, having made one profit on the construction of the road, now bought it back at a reduced price. With a group that included New York railroad speculators Calvin S. Brice and George I. Seney, along with Columbus R. Cummings of Chicago, the McMillans formed the Duluth, South Shore & Atlantic Railway. Brice and Seney had been the brains behind the New York, Chicago & St. Louis—the Nickel Plate Road—which was formed early in 1881. By the end of 1882 they had built a line between Chicago and Buffalo that ran for miles next to Vanderbilt's Lake Shore & Michigan Southern. They built the Nickel Plate solely to sell it to someone, and they cared little who bought it. William Henry Vanderbilt was one candidate; Jay Gould and his Erie Railroad were another; even the Pennsylvania was a remote possibility. By the end of 1882 Vanderbilt had the Nickel Plate. Brice, Seney, and Cummings pocketed their profits and took up with the McMillans and the MH&O in 1886 in a new financial foray.

They formed the DSS&A out of the lines of the reorganized Detroit, Mackinac & Marquette and the rights of the Wisconsin, Sault Ste. Marie & Mackinac. In early 1887 the DSS&A leased the Marquette, Houghton & Ontonagon, and in so doing also regained control of the Marquette & Western. The DSS&A completed a branch into Sault Ste. Marie in October 1887. In December 1882 the DSS&A completed its line between Nestoria and Superior, Wisconsin. In 1890 it bought up the Marquette, Houghton & Ontonagon, which owned lines from Marquette through the Marquette iron range and had one long branch to L'Anse and Houghton. The principal traffic potential along the new line was lumber; it tapped a small piece of the Gogebic iron range by a short branch to Bessemer and bypassed the port city of Ashland completely.

In the years in which the DSS&A was assembled, a second line was built across the Upper Peninsula. The idea of a Twin Cities–Sault Ste. Marie direct route had been talked about since the early 1880s. Flour miller John S. Pillsbury persuaded a number of friends to join the project and formed the Menominee & Sault Ste. Marie in April 1885 to build the Michigan section of the line. The Minneapolis, Sault Ste. Marie & Atlantic was organized in March 1887, after construction was well under way, to merge the M&SSM and a non-Detroit company. When the line was opened on 1 January 1888 its owners claimed it had been built entirely with private and mostly English capital, with no land grant, and with only enough stock issued to cover the cost of construction. In June 1888 the MSSM&A and several other non-Michigan roads were merged into a new company, the Minneapolis, St. Paul & Sault Ste. Marie, a name soon made colloquial as the Soo Line.

The financial structures of the two Upper Peninsula roads reflected the approach of their respective owners and could not be more

William Henry Canniff

Born 22 October 1847, Litchfield, Mich.; died 17 September 1925, Cleveland.

Canniff began railroading at the age of fifteen as a night watchman at the Michigan Southern & Northern Indiana station at Osseo. He learned telegraphy and two years later was made station agent at Trenton, then later at Otis, Indiana. Between those two jobs he applied to the Union Pacific as a telegrapher and was sent to Big Springs, Nebraska. Canniff recalled that "I didn't care to have a rifle across my knees while sending messages, nor to carry a revolver in one hand while unloading freight with the other." He returned to the Lake Shore & Michigan Southern as road master of track in 1872. In November 1880 he became the division superintendent at Hillsdale and in November 1889 was promoted to assistant general superintendent at Cleveland. He held that position until March 1896, when he was again promoted, this time to general manager.

In May 1898 the Vanderbilts moved Canniff to the presidency of the New York, Chicago & St. Louis—the Nickel Plate—which they owned. At that time the Vanderbilts gave their roads' presidents considerable leeway in managing their roads' profits. "Paddy" Canniff concentrated on fast-running through freight trains, an approach that paid off. The road's operating ratio dropped, its profits grew, and it paid dividends. He encouraged the formation of an association of veteran employees, the first on any U.S. railroad. Nearly seventy years old, Canniff retired from railroading in July 1916, when the Vanderbilts sold the Nickel Plate to the Van Sweringen brothers.

different. Michigan's railroad commissioner, in his annual report for 1888, stated that the Soo Line had built 787 miles at a cost of $39 million, with outstanding capital of $42 million. The cost works out to $49,000 per mile and the capital to $54,500 per mile. McMillan's DSS&A had 390 miles, cost a reported $28.6 million to build, and was capitalized at $32.5 million. The gives a cost per mile of $73,500 and capital per mile of $83,500. Brice and Seney's proclivities to "water" stock seem to have carried up to the Upper Peninsula. Also, when the commissioner made his inspection trips, he complimented the Soo Line but made several critical remarks about the quality of the DSS&A.

It is very likely that Brice, Cummings, and Seney bought into the DSS&A only for another round of profits from a quick sale. Cummings and Seney were gone from the company by 1890. In 1886–88 one possible buyer was the Wisconsin Central. It probably saw little promise in connecting to the Canadian Pacific at the Soo and already had a connection with the Michigan Central at Chicago. The Northern Pacific had close working ties with the WC, and there was even some talk of merger, but probably had even less reason to want to move freight to Sault Ste. Marie. There was a rumor that the Vanderbilts might try to extend their influence by buying it, but that appears to have died quickly. The Canadian Pacific was building a branch into Sault Ste. Marie, and would become the natural eastern outlet for both the DSS&A and the Soo Line. At the same time, the Grand Trunk Railway of Canada was talking about building into the Soo. For both Canadian roads any route above Lake Superior was through an absolute wilderness and subject to harsh extremes of weather. A route south of the lake had many advantages. When the Grand Trunk's surveyors showed up, the CP took immediate steps to secure its advantage. With the Soo Line and the DSS&A, it built a jointly owned international rail bridge over the St. Marys River. This marked the beginning of a close cooperation between the two Michigan roads and the CP. To solidify its edge over the Grand Trunk the CP then began buying into the two American roads, so that by 1888 it owned a controlling interest in both of them. In 1888 three Canadians came on the board of the DSS&A, one of them William C. Van Horne, the guiding spirit behind the growth of the CP. In 1890 Van Horne also came onto the Soo Line's board, completing the CP's controlling interest in both Michigan lines.

The last railroad to be built from Wisconsin into the Upper Peninsula was the Milwaukee & Northern Railway, a Wisconsin company that was formed in February 1870. By 1873 it had built from Milwaukee as far as Green Bay and had a branch to Menasha. Soon after completion the M&N was leased to the Wisconsin Central to give that road access to Milwaukee. This arrangement did not solve the problems first raised by the panic of 1873; the M&N defaulted on its mortgage and in June 1880 was reorganized as the Milwaukee & Northern Railroad. The WC lease of the M&N was canceled in 1882 since the WC was by then planning to build its own line from the Fox River valley to Milwaukee.

Between 1882 and 1886 the Wisconsin & Michigan Railroad built a line that extended from Green Bay north to the state line at the Menominee River just south of Iron Mountain. When building was starting the W&M agreed to sell the M&N its line when completed. The sale to the M&N took place in January 1887. A month earlier the M&N bought the line that its subsidiary, the Menominee Branch, had built from Stiles Junction, Wisconsin, to Menominee. In December 1886 the M&N filed new incorporation papers in Michigan to acknowledge the purchase of the W&M, the Menominee Branch, and another road, the Republic Branch. The Republic Branch was formed by the owners of the M&N to build from Iron Mountain to a connection with the Marquette, Houghton & Ontonagon at Champion. This part of the line was opened for service in November 1887. The M&N now had access to a number of mines in the Iron Mountain area—most important, the Quinnesec and Chapin—and to the Republic and Champion Mines farther north.

In June 1890 the M&N bought the Ontonagon & Brule River. That road was formed in September 1880 to build an eighty-mile line from Ontonagon to the Wisconsin state line. It had a state land grant, one that had been transferred from the Ontonagon & State Line, which never used it. In August 1882 the O&BR completed the required twenty miles of road, from Ontonagon to Mass, and was awarded the first section of the land grant. At Mass it tapped several copper mines located in the vicinity of Greenland. The road did no more building until 1888, when the M&N began work again. The extension to Sidnaw was completed in October 1889. To connect this disconnected O&BR segment to its own line the M&N obtained running rights over the Duluth, South Shore & Atlantic between Champion and Sidnaw. In September 1890 the Chicago, Milwaukee & St. Paul obtained control of the M&N. By 1892 the M&N started building its own line between Sidnaw and Channing, probably encouraged to do this by the discovery of iron ore in the area around Amasa. This section of line was opened in January 1893, and the Champion-Sidnaw running rights were discontinued. In June 1893 the Chicago, Milwaukee & St. Paul Railway bought the Milwaukee & Northern.

SOURCES

Barnett, LeRoy. "Detroit, Mackinac & Marquette." *SOO* 12:4 (October 1990), 13:1 (January 1991).

Dunbar, Willis F. *All Aboard! A History of Railroads in Michigan.* Grand Rapids, Mich.: W. B. Eerdmans, 1969.

Durocher, Aurele A. "The Duluth, South Shore and Atlantic Railway Company." *(Railway & Locomotive Historical Society) Bulletin No. 111* (October 1964).

Gaertner, John. *The Duluth, South Shore & Atlantic Railway: A History of the Lake Superior District's Pioneer Iron Ore Hauler.* Bloomington: Indiana University Press, 2009.

Michigan Railroad Commission. *Aids, Gifts, Grants and Donations to Railroads . . .* Lansing, Mich.: Wynkoop, Hallenbeck, Crawford, 1919.

Specht, Ray. "Milwaukee, Lake Shore & Western." *(Railway & Locomotive Historical Society) Bulletin No. 121* (October 1969).

———. "The Milwaukee & Northern." *(Railway & Locomotive Historical Society) Bulletin No. 121* (October 1969).

Water Everywhere: Tunnels, Bridges, and Car Ferries, Part 1

The Great Lakes surrounding the two peninsulas posed a challenge for railroads to get into Michigan. The earliest cross-water operation anywhere on the Great Lakes was in 1853 by the Buffalo & Lake Huron between Buffalo and Fort Erie on the Niagara River. At first this was a break-bulk service, with freight unloaded from railcars into the boat on one side, then loaded back into other railcars on the other side. By 1858 this was replaced by the railcar ferry *International*, which moved railcars across the river.

The Great Western Railway began train service between Niagara Falls and Windsor in January 1854, making itself a connecting rail link between eastern roads at the Niagara River and the Michigan Central at Detroit. It put three break-bulk ferries in service between Detroit and Windsor. Not long after completion it gained the use of the suspension bridge over the Niagara River and had no need for a car ferry there. Canadian roads were built to a different track gauge than was used in the United States, and it soon became obvious that this was an obstacle to the Great Western's ability to handle traffic. During 1866 the Great Western installed a third rail on some of its Ontario lines, allowing it to move the standard-gauge cars used in the United States. On 1 January 1867 it began a Detroit River car ferry service between Windsor and Detroit with the side-wheeler *Great Western*. At 220 feet it was the largest metal ship on the Great Lakes and could carry twelve cars on a trip. It continued crossing the river at Detroit until December 1923, when it was sold for barge service.

In 1859 the Grand Trunk Railway began a car ferry between Point Edward and Fort Gratiot across the St. Clair River, when it opened its line from Fort Gratiot to Detroit. This was a swing ferry, anchored to a post near the Michigan shore, with the river's current moving the ferry in both directions. This ferry handled only standard-gauge freight cars; all other freight was transshipped. By 1872 the Grand Trunk decided to replace the swing ferry with a new *International*. The hull was built in England, shipped in sections to Fort Erie, and assembled there. When it went into service at Sarnia in August, it was the first ship not a side-wheeler to be built for car ferry service. In 1875 the larger *Huron* joined the *International* in the St. Clair River service. Business was so good that a second slip was built on each side to speed their movements.

Given the short distance of both of these crossings and the relatively rapid currents, together with the volume of river traffic that caused an occasional collision, it was only natural that the railroad studied alternative means of crossing. In 1871 James F. Joy formed the Detroit River Railroad Tunnel Company, which was to dig from both the Michigan Central and the Grand Trunk depots in Detroit to Windsor. Another tunnel project was discussed in 1877, but Joy turned it down, possibly because the road's profits were not good enough at the time or possibly because of the Vanderbilt influence on the Michigan Central. Not much later the Vanderbilts announced they were going to replace the Grosse Ile–Amherstburg, Ontario, ferry with a tunnel. Some work started in 1880, but nothing more came of it. New proposals for a Detroit River bridge or tunnel surfaced periodically, but each disappeared almost as quickly as it appeared.

In 1882 the Grand Trunk acquired the Great Western Railway and its car ferries. Dissatisfied with several of the wooden ferries, the GT decided to put an iron hull on the *Michigan*, and had Detroiter Frank E. Kirby redesign it into a new ferry. The result was the *Lansdowne*, which went into service in November 1884. The St. Clair River ferry service of the Grand Trunk ended in 1891 with the completion of the St. Clair River

The first rail ferry across the St. Clair River was a swing ferry, anchored to a chain and propelled by the river current. It was replaced in 1872 by the *International*, the first three-track ferry on the lakes. It was sold in 1898 and eventually went to the Pere Marquette Railway. It ferried rail cars across the St. Clair River until 1934.

Reprinted, by permission, from George W. Hilton, *Great Lakes Car Ferries* (Berkeley, Calif., 1962), 21.

The side-wheeler *Great Western* replaced the Detroit River break-bulk ferries in 1867. When built it was the largest iron ship on the Great lakes—220 feet in length. It was converted to a barge in 1923.

Reprinted, by permission, from George W. Hilton, *Great Lakes Car Ferries* (Berkeley, Calif., 1962), 10.

tunnel. The *Lansdowne,* together with the *Huron,* was also reassigned from Port Huron, and the *Great Western* handled all the Detroit River traffic of both the Grand Trunk and the Wabash until 1923.

Before the Canada Southern Railway was integrated with the Michigan Central, it maintained its own car ferry service to cross the Detroit River between Grosse Ile and Gordon, Ontario, near Amherstburg. Two ferries handled traffic, but bad luck, heavy ice, mechanical difficulties, and eventually a disadvantage in rail routes brought it to an end. The Michigan Central had traffic arrangements with the Great Western and did not have to operate a ferry service at Detroit. This changed in 1883 when the Vanderbilts built the Canada Southern into Windsor to connect directly with the Michigan Central. The *Transfer* and *Transport* came up from Grosse Ile, and Vanderbilt built a third ferry, the *Michigan Central.* In January 1905 a fourth ferry, the *Detroit,* joined the fleet. But the heavy increase in freight business after 1900, more than the delays in service caused by winter ice, brought an end to the ferry service. After MC trains began running through the Detroit

River tunnel in late 1910, the ferries were sold. All except the *Michigan Central* went to the Wabash Railway, which used them to start its own Detroit River ferry service.

The service between the Lower and Upper Peninsulas at the Straits of Mackinac by the car ferries of the Mackinac Transportation Company already has been covered. There was talk from time to time of the railroads building a bridge to St. Ignace, either from Mackinaw City or by crossing Bois Blanc Island from Cheboygan. Nothing ever came of any of this talk. The other rail crossing into the Upper Peninsula was at Sault Ste. Marie. The Duluth, South Shore & Atlantic, the Soo Line, and the Canadian Pacific cooperated in 1888 to build an international bridge, which was owned by the three roads jointly.

With the completion of the Grand Trunk Railway's line to Chicago in 1880 the car ferries across the St. Clair River developed into something of a bottleneck in handling the new rush of traffic. Delays occurred, and shippers of perishable goods complained loudly. A tunnel had been talked about years earlier, so Sir Henry Whatley Tyler brought out the old plans, and new detailed plans were drawn up in 1883. Chief engineer Joseph Hobson found an ideal crossing with a

Michigan's only international railroad bridge crosses the St. Marys River at Sault Ste. Marie. Owned by the three roads that operated into the two Soos, and opened in 1888, the span of nearly half a mile was built in part by the Detroit Bridge and Iron Works and in part by a Canadian company. Little changed in appearance for more than a century, the bridge remains an important rail link between the two countries.

Department of the Interior, Heritage Conservation and Recreation Service, Historic American Engineering Record, *The Upper Peninsula of Michigan* (Washington, D.C., 1978), 201.

good rock foundation. In 1884 Tyler incorporated the St. Clair Tunnel Company and in 1886, despite the naysayers, presented the idea to his shareholders, who approved the project. Digging began at both Sarnia and Port Huron in January 1889, using tunneling shields of the sort used for Hudson and Thames river tunnels. The work crews were Grand Trunk employees since the road had been unable to find any contractor willing to take on the project. Digging an average of ten feet per day, work went on twenty-four hours a day. As the crew in the shield dug out the rock a second crew fitted cast-iron plates to the tunnel wall and waterproofed them. To slow sand and water seepage the crews had to work in dense air pressure. Those working in the shield had to be relieved every thirty minutes. Both the digging shield and using compressed air were innovations Hobson brought to the project. So, too, were the electric arc lights for illumination and the telephone for communications. For working in such cold, wet, and dangerous conditions workmen were paid an extra dollar per day. Surprisingly there was not a fatality during the work. Boring was completed on 30 August 1890; the first revenue train went through in September. Passenger trains began using the tunnel regularly in December. The tunnel had a capacity of 2,000 cars per day, and 750 a day were moving through it within a year of its opening. Its total cost was $2,700,000, of which the Canadian government contributed about 15 percent. The tunnel was considered an engineering marvel and was reported widely by both the professional and the public press.

Steam locomotives pulled trains through the tunnel. Despite an extensive ventilation system, three crewmen were asphyxiated by locomotive fumes in 1897 when they tried to recover the rear of their train that had become uncoupled. In 1904 a similar event caused more deaths. As a result of the 1897 deaths the Grand Trunk began to study the use of electric locomotives and in 1904 decided to make the change. Nine miles of track had electric wire hung, the tunnel walls were cleaned and painted white, additional lighting was installed, and electric engines began running in February 1908.

The Toledo, Ann Arbor & North Michigan Railway pioneered the use of cross-lake car ferries. Although railroad car ferries had been used to cross the Detroit and St. Clair Rivers for four decades, the much longer crossing by car ferry at the Straits of Mackinac did not begin until 1882. It is not clear just when the Ann Arbor's president, James M. Ashley, came to the decision that ferries also could carry railroad cars across the open waters of Lake Michigan. The first of his ferries, *Ann Arbor No. 1,*

The first of the railroad car ferries to cross Lake Michigan was *Ann Arbor No. 1.* It first sailed from Frankfort in November 1892. *No. 2* followed it into service the next year and *No. 3.* in 1898. *No. 1* burned to the water in 1910 at Manitowoc and was converted to a barge.

Reprinted from Michigan, *Twenty-Fifth Annual Report of the Commissioner of Railroads.*

The first of the Flint & Pere Marquette's Lake Michigan car ferries was aptly named *Pere Marquette.* Launched in 1896, it was the first of fourteen ships that made up the largest fleet of Lake Michigan ferries. *Pere Marquette* sailed for nearly forty years, until it was scrapped in 1935 at Manitowoc.

Reprinted from Michigan, *Twenty-Fifth Annual Report of the Commissioner of Railroads.*

began sailing in November 1892, and was joined by *Ann Arbor No. 2* in January 1893, both of them sailing to Kewaunee, Wisconsin. In 1894 the road cut back the number of sailings to Kewaunee and began three a week to Menominee. Trips to Gladstone were started in the summer of 1895 and made a call at Escanaba en route. In 1896 a route to Manitowoc was begun. Four routes stretched the fleet quite thin; when business began to pick up after the depression of the mid-1890s, there was a pressing need for more ferries. *Ann Arbor No. 3* was built at Cleveland in 1898 to meet the demand.

The Flint & Pere Marquette closely watched the development of car ferries at the Straits of Mackinac and on the Ann Arbor. After 1874 it accumulated a fleet of five break-bulk steamers that sailed from Ludington to several Wisconsin ports. It was not until December 1895 that the F&PM hired Robert Logan, a well-known Cleveland naval architect, to design the first Lake Michigan all-steel car ferry. *Pere Marquette* was launched at Bay City, first sent to Milwaukee for public tours, and then began regular sailings from Ludington in February 1897. Freight business boomed. The Pere Marquette's original intention was to use both car ferries and break-bulk ships, but the increased ferry loadings brought a change of mind.

This was soon augmented by a separate service of the Flint & Pere Marquette from Ludington to Wisconsin and by the Grand Trunk from Grand Haven. Car ferries carrying freight cars and entire passenger trains began crossing the Detroit River between Detroit and Windsor in 1854 and the St. Clair River in 1859 from Fort Gratiot and later Port Huron to both Port Edward and Sarnia.

SOURCES

Anderson, Jim, and Dwayne Anderson. "Unseen Wonder of the World: The St. Clair Railroad Tunnel." *Chronicle* 19:2 (Summer 1983).

Dunbar, Willis F. *All Aboard! A History of Railroads in Michigan.* Grand Rapids, Mich.: W. B. Eerdmans, 1969.

Frederickson, Arthur C., and Lucy F. Frederickson. *Early History of the Ann Arbor Carferries.* Frankfort, Mich.: Patriot Publishing, 1949.

Harlow, Alvin F. *The Road of the Century.* New York: Creative Age, 1947.

Hilton, George W. *The Great Lakes Car Ferries.* Berkeley, Calif.: Howell-North, 1962.

Stevens, G. R. *Canadian National Railways: Sixty Years of Trial and Error, 1836–1896.* 2 vols. Toronto: Clark, Irwin, 1960.

God's Time or Railroad Time

On Michigan's earliest railroads train schedules were of little concern. Local residents knew when trains were going to run and fitted their arrangements to that. If one missed today's train, one simply waited until tomorrow. An Erie & Kalamazoo notice in 1837 notified the public that the railroad was in operation with a steam locomotive from Toledo to Adrian, but the company did not think it worthwhile to mention when its trains ran. The state's Southern road advertised in July 1842 that its "Cars leave Monroe daily for Adrian, Sundays excepted, at 8

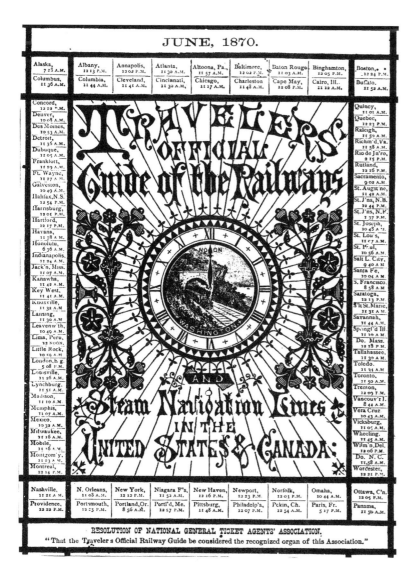

Before standard time was devised, every community had its own local time based on the sun. The cover of this book of train schedules compares local times throughout the country with noon at Washington, D.C. Michigan Central trains ran on Detroit time. The Michigan Southern used Chicago time until the line was merged into the Lake Shore & Michigan Southern, when it began using Cleveland time.

Author's collection.

o'clock A.M. and leave Adrian for Monroe at 2 o'clock P.M. Running time 2½ hours." No times were given for intermediate stations or for arrival at the destination. This casual approach continued even throughout the Civil War, when most generals issued orders to move at dawn or at first light.

As rail lines became longer and trains became more numerous, operations demanded more precise timekeeping. A designation by only the hour or even quarter hour was totally inadequate; minutes became imperative. Since there was only one track to handle trains in both directions, it was critical to know with some certainty when an opposing train was due so the track could be cleared at the proper time. Also, the same time had to apply over the entire line. For the Michigan Central, the immediate problem was that when its trains got to Chicago, the time there was different: 11:00 A.M. by the MC clock in Detroit was only 10:38 Chicago local time. The MC decreed all of its trains would operate based on time read from the clock in its station at Detroit. The MC's eastern connection, the Great Western, operated by time based on Hamilton, Ontario.

The MC's arch-competitor, the Michigan Southern, ran its trains by Chicago time. As it began to integrate with the Lake Shore it used three different times between Buffalo and Chicago. From Buffalo to Erie it used Buffalo time; from Erie to Toledo it used Columbus time, which was seventeen minutes slower than Buffalo; and from Toledo and Chicago it used Chicago time, eighteen minutes slower than Columbus or thirty-five minutes slower than Buffalo. Even after its merger as the Lake Shore & Michigan Southern it continued to use the three different times. The New York Central route east of Buffalo used New York City time. When it was noon in New York City, it was only 11:45 in Buffalo, 11:28 in Columbus, and 11:10 in Chicago.

It did not stop there. The Jackson, Lansing & Saginaw used Jackson as its time base. The Flint & Pere Marquette ran its trains by East Saginaw time; it used the Detroit & Milwaukee as a connection into Detroit from Holly, and the D&M ran its trains by Detroit time. According to one study there were at least twenty-seven local times in use in Michigan, twenty-three in Indiana, and twenty-seven in Illinois.

It was not until the early 1860s that railroads began using the telegraph to send daily time signals to all offices to adjust clocks system-wide. Until then, once a train was out on the road there was no way to check watches with the headquarters clock. The solution was to require each conductor and engineman to compare watches and

185

MICHIGAN CENTRAL RAILROAD.

James F. Joy, President, Detroit, Mich.
H. E. Sargent, Gen. Supt., Chicago, Ill.
C. H. Hurd, Asst. Gen. Supt., Detroit, Mich.
C. D. Whitcomb, Gen. Tkt Agt, Detroit, Mich.

A. S. Sweet, Jr., Master Mechanic.
J. B. Sutherland, Mast. Car Builder, Detroit.
C. E. Noble, Gen. Eastern Agent, 349 Broadway, New York.

H. C. Wentworth, Gen. Passenger Agent, Chicago, Ill.
Jas. Newell, Purchasing Agnet, Detroit, Mich.

Schedule in effect May 8, 1870.

Westward Bound Trains—New York & Boston to Chicago.

STATIONS.	Mls	Mail	Fast Exs.	Atlc Exs.	Pac. Exs.	Acc		
		P. M.	A. M.	A. M.	P. M.			
Lve. **New York** ...		11 00	10 30	11 00	7 00			
		P. M.	A. M.	A. M.	P. M.			
„ **Boston**		9 00	5 00	8 30	3 00			
		A. M.	P. M.	P. M.	A. M.			
„ **Albany**		7 20	3 00	4 50	12 55			
		P. M.	A. M.	A. M.	P. M.			
„ **Susp. Bridge**		9 50	12 20	6 40	12 40			
		A. M.	A. M.	P. M.	P. M.	P. M.		
„ **Detroit** [1]	0	6 50	7 30	5 45	10 10	4 35		
„ G.T.Junction [2]	3	7 05	7 45	6 00	10 25	4 50		
„ Dearborn	10	7 25	....	....	....	5 08		
„ Inksters	14	7 33	....	....	....	5 16		
„ Wayne	18	7 45	....	6 33	....	5 28		
„ Secords	23	8 00	....	6 51	....	5 41		
„ Denton's	25	8 05	....	....	....	5 45		
„ Ypsilanti	30	8 33	8 28	7 10	11 20	6 00		
„ Geddes	34	8 42	....	....	....	6 10		
„ Ann Arbor	38	8 57	8 43	7 35	11 40	6 24		
„ Foster's	41	9 04	....	....	....	6 35		
„ Delhi	43	9 10	....	....	....	6 42		
„ Scio	45	9 15	....	....	....	6 47		
„ Dexter	47	9 25	....	8 00	....	6 55	Kalamazoo Accommodation.	
„ Chelsea	55	9 45	....	8 20	....	P. M.		
„ Francisco	62	10 02	....	8 37	....			
„ Grass Lake	66	10 15	....	8 50	....			
„ Leoni	69	10 22	....	8 56	....			
„ Michigan Cent	72	10 30	....	9 03	A. M.			
„ Jackson [3]	76	10 45	9 45	9 20	1 05			
„ Trumbull's	81	10 58	....	9 34	....			
„ Sandstone	82	....	....	....	....			
„ Parma	87	11 13	....	9 48	....			
„ Concord	90	11 20	....	9 55	....			
„ Bath Mills	92	11 27	....	10 02	....			
„ Albion	96	11 37	10 14	10 12	1 48			
„ Marengo	101	11 50	....	10 25	....			
„ Marshall	108	12 25	10 35	10 45	2 18			
„ Ceresco	113	12 38	....	10 58	....			
„ White's	115	12 42	....	....	....			
„ Battle Creek .	121	1 00	10 57	11 20	2 48	Dexter Accommodation.		
„ Bedford	126	....	....	....	....			
„ Augusta	130	1 23	....	11 42	....			
„ Galesburg	135	1 35	....	11 52	....			
„ Comstock	140	1 43	....	12 00	....		A. M.	
„ Kalamazoo [4] ..	144	2 00	11 37	12 15	3 35		5 45	
„ Ostemo	149	2 15	....	....	....		6 00	
„ Mattawan	156	2 30	....	....	....		6 15	
„ Lawton	160	2 40	....	12 53	....		6 25	
„ White Oaks ...	162	2 51	....	....	....		6 30	
„ Decatur	168	3 07	....	1 15	....		6 45	
„ Tietsort's	172	3 20	....	....	....		6 57	
„ Dowagiac	179	3 35	....	1 43	....		7 12	
„ Pokagon	185	3 50	P. M.	....	....		7 25	
„ **Niles**	191	4 10	1 10	2 25	5 25		7 55	
„ Buchanan	197	4 27	....	....	....		8 10	
„ Dayton	202	4 37	1 30	....	....		8 23	
„ Galien	205	4 45	....	....	....		8 32	
„ Avery's	209	4 55	....	....	....		8 42	
„ Three Oaks ...	211	5 00	....	....	....		8 47	
„ New Buffalo ..	218	5 17	....	....	....		9 05	
„ Corymbo	223	5 27	....	....	....	P. M.	9 15	
„ Michigan City [5]	228	5 43	2 15	4 00	6 43	7 18	9 32	
„ Furnessville ...	234	5 58	....	....	....	....	9 50	
„ Porter	240	6 13	....	....	....	8 00	10 05	
„ Lake [6]	249	6 35	2 50	....	7 30	....	10 25	
„ Tolleston	255	6 50	....	....	....	....	10 40	
„ Gibson's	261	7 00	....	....	....	8 40	10 53	
„ Calumet	270	7 20	3 25	5 45	8 15	9 07	11 15	
Arr. **Chicago** [7]	284	8 05	4 00	6 30	9 00	9 20	12 00	
		P. M.	P. M.	A. M.	A. M.	P. M.	N'ON	

Eastward Bound Trains—Chicago to New York, Boston, &c.

STATIONS.	Mls	Mail	Fast Exs.	Eve Exs.	Ngt Exs.	Exs.	Acc	
		A. M.	A. M.	P. M.	P. M.	A. M.	P. M.	
Lve. **Chicago** [7] ...	0	5 00	11 00	5 15	9 00	9 00	4 30	
„ Calumet	14	5 45	....	5 58	9 43	9 43	5 10	
„ Gibson's	23	6 03	....	....	....	10 03	5 30	
„ Tolleston	29	6 13	....	....	....	10 15	5 40	
„ Lake [6]	35	6 28	12 13	6 35	10 27	10 27	5 55	
„ Porter	44	6 45	....	....	....	10 47	6 13	
„ Furnessville ..	50	6 58	....	....	....	11 00	6 23	
„ **Michigan City** [5]	56	7 20	12 50	7 23	11 10	11 20	6 43	
„ Corymbo	61	7 30	....	....	....	11 30	6 53	
„ New Buffalo ..	66	7 43	....	....	....	11 40	7 05	
„ Three Oaks ...	73	8 00	....	....	....	A. M.	7 20	
„ Avery's	75	8 05	....	....	....		7 25	
„ Galien	79	8 15	....	....	....		7 35	
„ Dayton	82	8 23	....	....	....		7 43	
„ Buchanan	87	8 35	....	....	A. M.		7 53	
„ **Niles**	93	8 55	2 07	8 50	12 27	St. Joseph and Cincinnati Express.	8 22	
„ Pokagon	99	9 10	....	....	....		8 36	
„ Dowagiac	105	9 25	....	....	....		8 50	
„ Tietsorts'	112	9 38	....	....	....		9 04	
„ Decatur	116	9 52	....	....	....		9 18	
„ White Oaks ...	122	10 03	....	....	....		9 30	
„ Lawton	124	10 10	....	....	....		9 37	
„ Mattawan	128	10 20	....	....	....		9 47	
„ Ostemo	135	10 33	....	....	....		10 02	
„ Kalamazoo [4] ..	140	10 50	3 28	10 35	2 05		10 15	
„ Comstock	144	11 03	....	....	....		P. M.	
„ Galesburg	149	11 17	....	10 55	....			
„ Augusta	154	11 28	....	....	....			
„ Bedford	158	....	....	....	....			
„ **Battle Creek** ..	163	11 53	4 04	11 20	2 48			
„ White's	169	12 05	....	....	....			
„ Ceresco	171	12 10	....	....	....			
„ Marshall	176	12 45	4 30	11 57	3 22			
„ Marengo	183	1 00	....	A. M.	....			
„ Albion	188	1 15	....	12 20	3 47			
„ Bath Mills	192	1 23	....	....	....			
„ Concord	194	1 30	....	....	....			
„ Parma	197	1 40	....	....	4 08			
„ Sandstone	202	....	....	....	....	Acc.		
„ Trumbull's	203	1 52	....	....	....	A. M.		
„ Jackson [3]	208	2 10	5 25	1 05	....	4 50		Cincinnati Express and Kalamazoo Accommodation, running daily to Michigan City, and daily, except Sunday, to Kalamazoo.
„ Michigan Cent	212	2 20	....	....	4 45	5 00		
„ Leoni	215	2 28	....	....	4 52	5 08		
„ Grass Lake	218	2 38	....	....	5 00	5 20		
„ Francisco	222	2 50	....	....	5 10	5 32		
„ Chelsea	229	3 07	....	....	5 25	5 50		
„ Dexter	237	3 25	....	....	5 40	6 10		
„ Scio	239	3 32	....	....	....	6 17		
„ Delhi	241	3 37	....	....	....	6 21		
„ Foster's	243	3 43	....	....	....	6 27		
„ Ann Arbor	246	3 55	6 24	2 20	6 00	6 45		
„ Geddes	250	4 05	....	....	....	6 55		
„ Ypsilanti	254	4 20	6 42	2 40	6 20	7 10		
„ Denton's	259	4 30	....	....	....	7 22		
„ Secord's	261	4 33	....	....	....	7 27		
„ Wayne	266	4 48	....	....	....	7 45		
„ Inkster's	270	4 58	....	....	....	7 59		
„ Dearborn	274	5 08	....	....	....	8 19		
„ G.T.Junction [2]	281	5 25	7 20	3 30	7 15	8 25		
Arr. **Detroit** [1]	284	5 40	7 35	3 45	7 30	8 40		
		P. M.	P. M.	A. M.	A. M.	A. M.		
Arr. **Susp. Bridge**	514	3 20	4 40	2 25	6 00			
		A. M.	A. M.	P. M.	P. M.			
„ **Albany**	818	3 00	3 00	1 50	5 30			
		P. M.	P. M.	A. M.	A. M.			
„ **Boston**	1018	11 50	11 50	11 00	3 30			
		P. M.	P. M.	A. M.	P. M.			
„ **New York**	961	7 00	7 00	7 00	11 00			
		P. M.	P. M.	A. M.	A. M.			

NOTES on RUNNING OF TRAINS.

Pacific Express leaving Detroit 10 10 p.m., runs daily in connection with the 7 00 p.m. train from New York.

Evening Express leaves Detroit daily, except Sundays, 5 45 p.m.; on Saturday this train will run only to Jackson, making all the stops, and on Sunday morning from Michigan City.

Special Fast Chicago Express and Mail West run daily, except Sundays.

Dexter Accommodation, West, leaves Detroit daily, except Saturdays and Sundays.

N. B.—A train leaves Michigan City Sunday a.m., 4 05 a.m., arriving at Chicago 6 30 a.m.

EASTWARD BOUND TRAINS.

Dexter Accommodation daily, except Sundays from Dexter to Detroit; on Mondays only from Jackson.

Mail and Special Fast New York Express leave Chicago daily, except Sunday, 5 and 11 a.m.

Atlantic Express leaves Chicago daily 5 15 p.m., in connect'n with through trains to New York and Boston.

Night Express leaves Chicago daily, except Saturdays and Sundays, 9 00 p.m., and stops at signal stations between Jackson and Dexter.

☞ Special Drawing-Room and Palace Sleeping Cars are run through between New York and Chicago daily, on the 7 00 p.m. train from New York and the 5 15 p.m. train from Chicago.

CONNECTIONS.

[1] At Detroit with Great Western Railway of Canada for Suspension Bridge, Niagara Falls, Buffalo, Rochester, Utica, Syracuse, Albany, Boston and New York.

[2] At Grand Trunk Junction with Grand Trunk Railway for Montrea , Quebec, Portland, and other points on Grand Trunk Railway; also via Montreal or Portland to Boston. Close connection is also made by the Grand Trunk Railway to Buffalo with passenger trains on the New York Central and Erie Railways.

[3] At Jackson with trains on the Jackson, Lansing & Saginaw Railroad, for Lansing, Owosso, Saginaw and Winona; also with Grand River Valley R.R., for Eaton Rapids, Charlotte, Vermontville, Hastings, &c.

[4] At Kalamazoo wtih trains on the St. Joseph Valley Railway for White Pigeon and intermediate stations.

[4] At Kalamazoo with Kalamazoo, Allegan and Grand Rapids Railway for Cooper, Silver Creek, Plainwell, Otsego, Watson and Allegan.

[5] At Michigan City with trains on Northern Division of Louisville, New Albany and Chicago Railway, running via Lafayette to Indianapolis, Louisville and Cincinnati.

[6] At Lake with Branch to Joliet, forming the short cut off for freight between St. Louis and Detroit.

[7] At Chicago with Chicago & North-Western Railway for Milwaukee, Green Bay, Madison, Rockford, Freeport, Clinton, Boone, Council Bluffs, Omaha, &c.

[7] With Illinois Central Railroad for Cairo and all points South; also for St. Louis, via Effingham.

[7] With Chicago and Alton Railroad for Joliet, Bloomington, Springfield, Alton, St. Louis, and all points West in connection with the North Missouri and Pacific Railways; also for Southern cities, via St. Louis and Iron Mountain Railroad, or Memphis and St. Louis, Packet Co.

[7] With Chicago, Rock Island and Pacific Railroad for La Salle, Rock Island, Davenport, Wilton, Iowa City, Des Moines, Council Bluffs Omaha, &c.

[7] With Chicago, Burlington and Quincy Railroad for Mendota, Galesburg, Burlington, Peoria, Quincy, and all Western cities via Hannibal and St. Joseph Ratlroad.

The *Fast Express* dashed over the Michigan Central between Detroit and Chicago in just eight hours thirty minutes in this May 1870 schedule in the *Traveler's Official Guide*. Connections could be made at Jackson with trains to Bay City and Hastings, but not to Grand Rapids. From Kalamazoo one could transfer to White Pigeon and Allegan.

Author's collection.

MICHIGAN CENTRAL RAILROAD "The Niagara Falls Route."

Going East.										MAIN LINE—CHICAGO AND DETROIT.		Going West.						

12	8	4	18	34 & 14	6	20	2	16	Mls. fr. Chic'o	STATIONS. June 18, 1893. Central Standard Time.	11	3	5	13 & 15	17	1	19	9	7
Detroit Night Expr. Daily.	At'ntic Expr. Daily.	N.Y'k and Chicago Limited Daily.	Niag'ra Falls & Buffalo Special. Daily.	Kal'zoo and Gr. Rps Exp. Ex. Sun	N.Y. and Eastern Expr. Daily.	North Shore Limited Daily.	Detroit Day Expr. Except Sunday	Mail Ex. Sund.			Mail Ex. Sund.	Chicago Day Expr. Except Sunday	Chgo. and W'st'n Exp. Daily	Chicago Accom. Except Sunday.	Chgo. Spec'l Daily	N.Y'k and Chicago Limited Daily.	North Shore Limitd Daily	Pacific Expr. Daily.	Chgo. Night Expr Daily
*9.50	*7.30	*5.30	*8.40	†4.15	*3.10	*11.30	†9.00	†7.05		Lv....CHICAGO....Ar.	7 35	4.10	9.10	1.25	11.15	9.45	4.30	7.55	6 50
9.53	7.33	5.33	8.43	4.18	3.13	11.33	9.03	7.08	3	....22d Street....	7.32	4.07	9.07	1.22	11.12	9.42	4.27	7.52	6.47
9.59	7.39	5.39	8.49	4.24	3.19	11.39	9.09	7.14	4	....39th Street....	7.26	4.01	9.01	1.16	11.06	9.36	4.21	7.46	6.41
10.06	7.46	5.46	8.56	4.31	3.26	11.46	9.16	7.21	7	....Hyde Park....	7.19	3.54	8.54	1.09	10.59	9.29	4.14	7.39	6.34
10.30	8.10	6.05	9.20	4.55	3.50	12.10	9.40	7.45	15	....Kensington....	6 55	3.30	8.30	12.45	10.35	9.05	3.50	7.15	6.10
10.42				5.05			9.52	7.59	22	....Hammond....	6.40	3.18		12.33	10.22			6.58	5.53
10.56								8.15	30	....Tolleston....	6.22								5.33
11.06				5.25			10.07	8.28	37	....Lake....	6.09			12.36	9.58			6.12	5.21
								8.35	40	....Christman's....	6.02								5.12
11.21				5.38			10.33	8.45	46	....Porter....	5.50	2.37						5.52	5.00
								8 53	50	....Furnessville....	5.42								4.52
11.40	9.20	7.08	10.22	5.55	4.57	1.10	10.55	9.10	58	Ar. { Mich. } Lv.	5 25	2.18	7.05	11.36	9.25	8.05	2.45	5.35	4.25
11.43	9.25	7.11	10.25	5.58	5.00	1.12	11.00	9.15		Lv. { City } Ar.	5.20	2.15	7.00	11.33	9.22	8.03	2.42	5.30	4.30
								9.20	59	....Michigan City Y'd..	5.15								
	9.42						11.20	9.37	68	....New Buffalo....	4.53	1.56		11.18	9.03				4.10
	9.53			6.25			11.31	9.50	75	....Three Oaks....	6.38				8.49				3.53
	10.02			6.34			11.40	10.02	80	....Galien....	4.28				8.38				3.37
	10.07							10.08	83	....Dayton....	4.22			10.54					3.28
	10.14			6.46			11.53	10.17	88	....Buchanan....	4.13				8.25				3.17
12.40	10.25	8.00	11.20	6.58	5.55	2.05	12.06	10.30	94	Ar. { Niles.. } Lv.	4 06	1.10	6.00	10.38	8.13	7.19	1.48	4.10	3.00
11.43	10.30	8.05	11.25	7.02	6.00	2.08	12.25	10.35		Lv. { } Ar.	3.55	12.50	6.00	10.35	8.10	7.08	1.45	4.05	2.55
								10 47	101	....Pokagon....	3.42				7.59				
1.05	10.47			7.22			12.55	10.58	107	....Dowagiac....	3.32	12.27			7.51				2.22
								11.08	113	....Glenwood....	3.20			10.05					
1.27				7.41			1.27	11.17	115	....Decatur....	3.12				7.35				1.58
1.40	11.12			7.53			1.40	11.32	126	....Lawton....	2.58	11.55		9.44	7.24				1.40
								11.44	130	....Mattawan....	2.37			9.38					
								12.07	136	....Ostemo....	2.25			9.28					
2.07	11.35	9.07	12.32	8.20	7.05	3.21	2.08	12.20	142	Ar. { Kalamazoo } Lv.	2.08	11.26	4.48	9.20	7.00	6.03	12.39	2.37	1.10
2.07	11.38		12.32	†7.00	7.05		2.08	12.35		Lv. { } Ar.	2.02	11.26	4.48	9.50	7.00		12.35	2.37	1.05
				7.08				12 42	146	....Comstock....	1.51			9.41					
				7.18				12.58	151	....Galesburg....	1.43	11.11	a..	9.33					12.47
	11.51			7.98				1.03	155	....Augusta....	1.35	11.08		9.26					12.30
	11.57			7.48				1.20	165	....Battle Creek....	1.20	10.45	4.17	9.03	6.25	5 32	12.00	1.45	12.10
2.45	12.10	9.38	1.10		7.40	3.57	2.48	1.22	166	....Nichols....	1.13			9.00					
				8.03				1.32	171	....Wheatfield....	1258								
				8.07				1.35	173	....Ceresco....	1254			8.47					
3.10	12.32			8.17	8.00		3.13	1.45	178	....Marshall....	12.43	10.23	3 55	8.38	6.05			1.40	11.40
				8.28				1.58	184	....Marengo....	12.30			8.25					
3.31	12.58			8.38	6.15		3.36	2.07	190	....Albion....	12.20	10.03	3.33	8.15	5.47			12.36	11.21
								2.14	193	....Bath Mills....	12.12								
				8.55				2.25	199	....Parma....	12.02			7.53					11.05
				9.05				2.37	206	....Trumbull's....	1150			7.43					
4.10	1.35	10.45	2.15	9.15	8.47	5.05	4.25	2.50	210	Ar. { Jackson.. } Lv.	11.40	9.28	3.10	7.33	5.15	4.28	10.48	12.00	10.45
4.15	2.25	10.48	2.18	9.40	8.52	5.08	4 36	3.10		Lv. { } Ar.	11.20	9.25	3.07	7.13	5.10	4.25	10 45	11.55	10.39
								3.15	211	....Jackson Junction....	11.15								10.35
								3.20	214	....Michigan Centre..	11.07								10.25
								3.27	217	....Leoni....	11.00								10.16
4.38				10.00			‡4.47	3.32	220	....Grass Lake....	10.52			6.55					10.07
								3.39	224	....Francisco....	10.42								9.58
5.02				10.22			‡5.02	3.52	231	....Chelsea....	10.23			6.38					9.42
5.18	3.25			10.35			‡5.12	4.05	238	....Dexter....	10 05			6.26					9.27
								4.10	241	....Scio....	9.48								
	3.39							4 15	243	....Delhi....	9 45								9.18
5.40	3.50	11.40	3.10	10.53	9.45	6 08	5.30	4.27	248	....Ann Arbor....	9.34	8.19	2.14	5.15	4.14		9.45	10.32	9.05
	4.03							4.36	252	....Geddes....	9.25			6.21					8.55
6.00	4.17			11.07	9.57		5.47	4.45	256	....Ypsilanti....	9.18	8.05	2.00	5.53	4.02	3.22		10.15	8.45
6.17								4.56	261	....Denton's....	9.08			5 45					8.36
6.32	4.38			11.23			6.07	5.10	268	....Wayne Junction....	8.55			5.30				9.53	8.22
								5.15		....County House..	8.48								
6.40								5.21	272	....Inkster....	8.46								8.15
6.48								5.30	275	....Dearborn....	8.40			5.23					8.10
7.02								5.47	282	....Junction Yard....	8.28								
7.05	5.10			11.50			6.35	5.50	283	....West Detroit....	8.25	7.25		5.10				9 30	7.55
7.15	5 20	12.35	4.15	12.01	10.45	7.15	6.45	6.00	286	Ar....Detroit....Lv.	8 15	†7.15	*1.15	*3.15		*2.35	*8.45	*9 10	†7.45
*9.35	*5.35	*12.45	*4.25		*10 55	*7.25				Lv....Detroit....Ar.		6.50	*1.05	4.10	2.05	2 25	*8.35	*8.50	
4.16	1.36	6.52	11.00		5.35				514	Ar Niagara Falls, N.Y..		11.28	6.28		3.33			12.55	
5.00	2.20	7.40	11.50		6.25	2.05			536	Ar ..BUFFALO...Lv.		*10.45	5.45	*9.00	*7.45	2.20		12.10	
7.00	6.30	7.30	+10.30		8.50	2.40				...NEW YORK...		†10.30	*6.00	*8.00	*8.30	*10.00		9.15	
10.50	10.50	11.45	§6.15		11.45	4.45				Ar...BOSTON...Lv.		†8.30	†4.20					*2.00	*7.15

* Daily.   † Except Sunday.   § Except Monday.   x Except Saturday. | Stops on signal only.   ‡ Stops only to let off passengers.   S Stops on Sunday.

TRAINS Nos. 1, 4, 19 and 20 are Limited Trains, upon which an extra fare is charged and limited tickets required.

FREIGHT TRAIN No. 51, carrying passengers *only with Freight Train Permits.* as follows: Leave (except Sundays) Kalamazoo 3.56, Ostemo 4.13, Mattawan 4.33, Lawton, 4.50, Decatur, 5.30, Glenwood, 5.47, Dowagiac 6.20, Pokagon, 6.37, ar. Niles 6.50 p. m.

No. 52 Eastward, leave Niles (except Sundays) 6.00 a.m.; Pokagon, 6.25; Dowagiac, 6.50; Glenwood, 7.10; Decatur, 7.35; Lawton, 8.15; Mattawan, 8.30; Ostemo, 8.48; Kalamazoo, 9.15; Comstock, 9.35; Galesburg, 9.53; Augusta, 10.10; Battle Creek, 12.00 n.; Wheatfield, 12.55; Marshall, 1.50; Marengo, 2.30; Albion, 3.44; Parma, 4.20; Trumbull's, 5.08; arriving Jackson 5.20 p. m.

TRAINS Nos. 8 and 13 will stop at West Niles, Corymbo and Avery's on signal and to let off passengers.

TRAINS Nos. 7, 11, 16 and 12 will make regular stops at Sheldon's and Foster's.   **Nos. 7 and 12,** will stop regularly at Wiard's.

Jackson and Detroit Accom. No. 22, leaves Jackson, +6.45; Jackson Jct., 6.50; Michigan Centre, 6.55; Leoni, 7.02; Grass Lake, 7.07; Francisco, 7.13; Chelsea, 7.24; Dexter, 7.35; Scio, 7.3; Delhi, 7.42; Ann Arbor, 7.51; Geddes, 7.58; Ypsilanti, 8.08; and arr. Detroit, 9.15 a. m., stopping at intermediate stations.

a No. 2 stops at Galesburg to let off passengers from Kalamazoo.

For **Grand Rapids Express Trains,** via Chicago & West Michigan Railway, see page 16.

The Columbian Exposition opened on Chicago's lakefront in 1893, attracting riders to every railroad that ran to Chicago. Many roads ran several sections of some trains to handle the crowds. Special excursion fares attracted still more riders. The regular service on this June 1893 Michigan Central schedule has almost double the number of trains run in 1870. Some trains made the run to Chicago in a few minutes under eight hours. No other Michigan route had this number of trains on it.

Author's collection.

CHICAGO & GRAND TRUNK RAILWAY.

Joseph Hickson, President, Montreal. Que.
W. J. Spicer, General Manager, Detroit, Mich.
G. B. Reeve, Traffic Manager, Chicago, Ill.
W. H. Pettibone, Superintendent, Battle Creek, Mich.

6*	4†	2†	Mls	Tk't fare	Dec. 30, 1883. Lve. Arr.	1	3	5
P. M.	A. M.	....	...	....	MONTREAL......	....	P. M. 8 00	A. M. 8 00
11 30	9 00							
P. M.	P. M.						A. M.	P. M.
12 15	11 00	....	...	....	TORONTO	....	8 10	7 10
P. M.	A. M.						A. M.	P. M.
1 05	1 10	....			SUSP. BRIDGE..	...	8 05	3 15
P. M.	A. M.	A. M.				P. M.	A. M.	A. M.
8 00	7 50	6 35	0	00	PT. HURON...8883	10 40	1 26	7 50
8 10	8 00	6 45	4	.10	GR'ND TR'K C'N6	10 30	1 16	7 40
....	....	7 17	18	.55	Emmet........300	9 59	....	....
9 05	....	7 35	27	.80	Capac........544	9 40	....	....
9 30	9 12	7 50	34	1.00	Imlay City..1005	9 25	....	6 53
...	...	8 15	46	1.40	Lapeer......2911	8 58	12 07	6 35
		8 45	57	1.70	Davison.....163	8 34	....	....
10 10	9 55	9 07	66	1.95	FLINT.......8418	8 15	11 35	6 00
4 30	6 50	..		....	DETROIT......	9 50		11 45
10 45	10 30	9 45	82	2.45	Durand.......196	7 25	11 06	5 23
11 50	11 32	11 00	115	3.45	LANSING....8326	6 01	10 15	4 15
...	...	11 27	127	3.80	Potterville..471	5 35	....	....
12 22	12 06	11 40	134	4.00	CHARLOTTE.2910	5 24		3 37
....	....	11 55	141	4.25	Olivet 520	5 05	....	....
....	....	12 10	146	4.40	Bellevue 628	4 55	....	....
1 23	1 25	12 40	160	4.80	BATTLE CR'K 7000	4 20	8 55	2 35
...	...	no'n	170	5.10	Climax......268	3 50	....	....
2 17	2 10	....	183	5.50	VICKSBURG ..785	3 22	8 10	1 46
2 28	2 20	....	189	5.65	SCHOOLCR'FT951	3 08	....	1 36
...	2 45		199	6.00	Marcellus ...604	2 45	....	1 16
3 19	3 09	....	213	6.40	CASSOPOLIS. 912	2 16	7 21	12 51
4 00	...		231	6.95	MISHAWAKA.2640	1 37		12 17
4 08	3 50		235	7.05	SOU. BEND.13279	1 30	6 44	12 10
5 52	5 25	..	280	8.40	Valparaiso..4461	11 50	5 25	10 40
8 10	7 45	..	335	9.60	CHICAGO ..503304	*9 10	*3 21	8 30
A. M.	P. M.				Arr. Lve.	A. M.	P. M.	P.*M

Train lvs. Pt. Huron †4 10 pm., arr. Battle Creek
10 20 pm. Ret., lve. Battle Creek 4.35 am., arr. Pt.
Huron 10 40 am. Lve. Battle Creek †6.00 am. arr.
Chicago 12 30 noon. Lve. Valparaiso †6 20, §7.40 am.,
arr. Chicago 8 40, 10.00 am. Ret., lve. Chicago §1.15,
†5.20 pm., arr. Valparaiso 3 40, 7 45 pm.

DETROIT & MILWAUKEE RAILWAY.

C. C. Trowbridge, Receiver. Alfred White, Gen.
Pass. & Fr'ht Agt., Detroit, Mich. [Nov. 21.

P.M.	P.M.	A.M.	L'VE]	[ARR.	A.M.	P.M.	A.M.
11 15	5 30	10 55	0	....Detroit....	11 25	6 00	6 30
12 35	6 35	12 20	26	....Pontiac....	10 20	4 47	5 05
1 35	7 30	1 15	47	....Holly	9 35	4 00	3 40
1 50	7 40	1 25	50	....Fenton	9 20	3 50	3 10
3 00	8 50	2 35	75	...Corunna....	8 00	2 35	1 45
3 10	9 00	2 45	78	....Owosso....	7 50	2 25	1 35
4 10	10 00	3 58	93	..St. Johns..	6 55	1 10	12 20
5 10		5 05	124	....Ionia......		11 53	11 08
5 40		5 38	140	...Lowell.....		11 18	10 33
6 30		6 21	158	Grand Rapids.		10 40	9,50
7 40		7 32	180	....Nunica....		9 30	8 30
8 10		8 00	189	Grand Haven 1		9 00	8 00
A.M.	P.M.	P.M.	ARR.]	[L'VE	A.M.	A.M.	P.M.

1 Steamers to Milwaukee, and points on Lake Michigan.

FLINT & PERE MARQUETTE RAILWAY.

S. Keeler, Supt., E. Saginaw, Mich. [Dec. 19.

P.M.	P.M.	A.M.	M.	L'VE]	[ARR.	P.M.	P.M.	A.M.
8 20	12 15		0	...Toledo...	4 50	9 10	9 15	
9 15	1 10		25	....Monroe....	3 50	8 10	7 55	
10 20	1 10	8 00		lv..Detroit..ar	8 45	6 25	7 00	
11 30	2 10	8 50	51	....Wayne 1...	2 50	5 50	5 45	
12 00	2 30	9 09	58	...Plymouth...	2 34	5 18	4 55	
2 45	4 00	11 06	91	....Holly	1 15	4 00	2 20	
4 00	4 40	11 06	108	....Flint 2...	12 20	3 20	12 20	
6 25	6 00	12 30	142	E. Saginaw.	11 00	2 00	9 45	
7 13	6 40	1 00	155	..Bay City..	10 20	1 30	8 40	
A.M.	P.M.	A.M.	ARR.]	[L'VE	P.M.	P.M.	A.M.	
7 45		3 00	142	.East Saginaw.	10 55		8 00	
8 53		4 10	162	....Midland....	9 50		6 52	
11 11	P.M.	6 30	203	....Lake....	7 40		4 38	
12 20	2 25	7 50	232	....Reed City...	6 30		8 20	
	5 00	12 00	278	..Ludington..	4 00		11 30	
P.M.	P.M.	NIHT	ARR.]	[L'VE	A.M.		A.M.	

1 Con. with Mich. Cen. R.R.   2 Branch to Otter Lake (19 mls.)
Extra Train leaves Detroit 5 00 p.m., arriving at
Bay City 10 05 p.m. Leave Bay City at 7 00 a.m.,
arriving at Detroit 12 15 p.m.

GRAND RAPIDS & INDIANA RAILWAY,

Operating Cincin., Richmond & Ft. Wayne R. R.
H. D. Wallen, Jr., Supt., Grand Rapids, Mich.

	A.M.	L'VE]	[ARR.	M.		P.M.	
	4 50	..Petoskey...	424		9,30		
P.M.	7 25	..Mancelona..	384	A.M.	7 10		
3 10	7 50	Traverse City	378	11 45	6 30		
A.M. 5 05	9 07	....Walton....	352	10 00	5 05 P.M.		
5 15	10 45	..Clam Lake..	331		4 05 10 00		
6 51	P.M. 12 23	..Reed City..	301	A.M.	2 16 8 24		
7 27	3 27 1 05	..Big Rapids..	290	11 45	1 40 7 48		
8 36	5 10 2 24	.Howard City..	268	10 05	12 20 6 89		
10 30	8 PM 4 15 ar	Grand } lv	284	7 AM 10 00	4 45		
11 10	7 AM 4 35 lv	Rapids } ar		9¼PM 9 45	2 10		
1 25	9 38 7 15	..Kalamazoo..	185	7 35 7 30	11 45		
P.M.	11 16 8 49	...Sturgis...	149	5 40 5 42	9 48		
	12 36 10 06	.Kendallville..	119	4 23 4 23	8 25		
	2 20 11 50	..Fort Wayne.	92	3 05 3 00	7 00		
	5 21 3 31	..Winchester..	24	11 49 11 28	A.M.		
	6 32 5 07	..Richmond..	0	10 40 10 10			
	9 40 8 35	..Cincinnati...		7 30 7 00			
	P.M. A.M.	ARR.]	[L'VE	A.M.	P.M.		

(Dec. 26.)

ABOVE, LEFT: This 1883 timetable for the recently completed Chicago & Grand Trunk is so compact that seven more trains are mentioned below the schedules. A thirteen-hour trip between Detroit and Chicago probably was not much competition for the Michigan Central.

Author's collection.

ABOVE, RIGHT: The service on three of Michigan's roads as they appeared in an 1876 *Appleton's Railroad Guide*. These are "condensed" tables that show only the important cities and not all local stops. Note that the Grand Rapids & Indiana extended only to Petoskey, and the trip from Grand Rapids took nearly twelve hours. Cadillac was still called Clam Lake. The Flint & Pere Marquette's trains reached Detroit by running on Michigan Central tracks between Wayne and Detroit.

Author's collection.

Detroit, Lansing and Northern Railroad.

LOCAL TIME TABLE—In Effect October 5th, 1884.

Trains run Daily, Sunday excepted. | **MAIN LINE.** | Central Standard Time.

Going West—Read Down. / Going East—Read Up.

Exp. No. 9.	Exp. No. 5.	Exp. No. 1.	Distance	STATIONS.	Exp. No. 2.	Exp. No. 6.	Exp. No. 10.
5.00 P. M.	9.35 A. M.	6.15 A. M.	0	Lv......Detroit......Ar	11.50 A. M.	3.30 P. M.	9.00 P. M.
5.10 "	9.45 "	6.25 "	3	"......Springwells...... "	11.40 "	3.20 "	8.50 "
*5.20 "	9.57 "	*6.35 "	8	"......Greenfield...... "	*11.30 "	3.09 "	‡8.48 "
5.35 "	10.12 "	6.49 "	14	"......Beech...... "	11.18 "	2.56 "	8.25 "
*5.39 "	*10.16 "	......	16	"......Elm...... "	*11.14 "	*2.45 "	......
5.46 "	10.23 "	6.56 "	19	"......Stark...... "	11.58 "	2.40 "	8.15 "
5.55 "	10.31 "	7.04 "	23	"......Plymouth...... "	11.00 "	2.32 "	8.07 "
5.57 "	10.23 "	*7.05 "	......	"......F. & P. M. Crossing...... "	10.58 "	2.30 "	8.05 "
*6.10 "	10.46 "	*7.17 "	29	"......Salem...... "	10.46 "	2.17 "	*7.51 "
6.22 "	11.01 "	7.28 "	34	"......South Lyon...... "	10.34 "	2.07 "	7.40 "
*6.29 "	11.08 "	*7.34 "	38	"......Green Oak...... "	*10.26 "	1.59 "	*7.32 "
6.42 "	11.20 "	7.45 "	43	"......Brighton...... "	10.15 "	1.49 "	7.20 "
7.01 "	11.39 "	8.02 "	52	"......Howell...... "	9.57 "	1.31 "	7.01 "
7.26 "	11.55 A. M.	8.15 "	60	"......Fowlerville...... "	9.40 "	1.14 "	6.42 "
7.34 "	12.14 P. M.	8.30 "	65	"......Webberville...... "	9.26 "	1.00 "	6.25 "
7.47 "	12.26 "	8.42 "	71	"......Williamston...... "	9.15 "	12.48 "	6.16 "
*7.56 "	12.38 "	*8.50 "	75	"......Meridian...... "	9.07 "	12.38 "	*6.06 "
*8.04 "	12.47 "	*8.58 "	79	"......Okemos...... "	8.58 "	12.29 "	*5.58 "
8.11 "	12.55 "	9.05 "	82	"......Trowbridge...... "	8.51 "	12.22 "	5.51 "
8.20 "	1.05 "	9.10 "	85	Ar }......Lansing......{ Lv	8.45 "	12.15 P. M.	5.46 "
	1.25 "			Lv } { Ar		11.55 A. M.	5.25 "
8.32 "	1.33 "	9.20 "	86	"......North Lansing...... "	8.35 "	11.50 "	5.20 "
*8.43 "	1.45 "	*9.31 "	92	"......Delta...... "	*8.22 "	*11.38 "	*5.09 "
......	*1.49 "	......	94	"......Ingersoll's...... "	......	*11.34 "	......
8.55 "	1.56 "	9.41 "	97	"......Grand Ledge...... "	8.12 "	11.28 "	4.59 "
*9.04 "	2.05 "	*9.50 "	101	"......Eagle...... "	*8.01 "	11.19 "	*4.50 "
9.20 "	2.21 "	10.04 "	109	"......Portland...... "	7.46 "	11.04 "	4.35 "
*9.31 "	2.32 "	*10.14 "	114	"......Collins...... "	*7.35 "	10.54 "	*4.24 "
9.38 "	2.39 "	10.21 "	117	"......Lyons...... "	7.28 "	10.47 "	4.17 "
9.50 "	2.50 "	10.35 "	123	Ar }......Ionia......{ Lv	7.15 "	10.35 "	4.05 "
9.55 "	3.05 "			Lv } { Ar		10.20 "	4.00 "
10.07 "	3.17 "	10.45 "	127	"......Stanton Junction...... "	7.00 "	10.10 "	3.48 "
*10.16 "	3.27 "	10.55 "	131	"......Orleans...... "	6.52 "	10.00 "	*3.39 "
*10.22 "	3.33 "	*11.01 "	134	"......Chadwick's...... "	*6.46 "	9.54 "	3.33 "
10.28 "	3.38 "	11.05 "	136	"......†Kiddville...... "	6.41 "	9.49 "	3.28 "
10.40 P. M.	3.50 "	11.18 "	142	"......Greenville...... "	6.30 A. M.	9.39 "	3.16 "
......	4.03 "	11.30 "	147	"......Gowen...... "	......	9.26 "	3.03 "
......	4.15 "	11.42 "	152	"......Trufant's...... "	......	9.14 "	2.53 "
......	4.20 "	11.46 "	155	"......Maple Valley...... "	......	9.09 "	*2.49 "
......	4.25 "	*11.51 A. M.	156	"......Coral...... "	......	9.04 "	2.44 "
......	4.35 P. M.	12.00 Noon.	161	Ar......Howard City......Lv	......	8.55 A. M.	2.35 P. M.

Exp. No. 7.	Exp. No. 3.			**STANTON BRANCH.**		Exp. No. 4.	Exp. No. 8.
......	3.10 P. M.	7.35 A. M.	123	Lv......Ionia......Ar	......	10.10 A. M.	3.35 P. M.
......	3.22 "	7.46 "	127	"......Stanton Junction...... "	......	9.57 "	3.17 "
......	3.31 "	*7.56 "	131	"......Wood's Corners...... "	......	9.48 "	*3.06 "
......	3.37 "	*8.02 "	134	"......Shiloh...... "	......	9.42 "	3.00 "
......	3.44 "	*8.09 "	137	"......Fenwick...... "	......	9.34 "	2.53 "
......	3.56 "	8.22 "	141	"......Sheridan...... "	......	9.21 "	2.42 "
......	*3.58 "	*8.24 "	......	"......Wagar's...... "	......	*9.17 "	*2.38 "
......	......	......	......	"......Fish Creek Branch...... "	......	......	......
......	4.05 "	8.32 "	145	"......Colby...... "	......	9.10 "	2.32 "
......	4.12 "	8.39 "	147	"......Stanton...... "	......	9.05 "	2.26 "
......	*4.15 "	*8.43 "	149	"......Wood's Mill...... "	......	*8.57 "	*2.20 "
......	......	......	......	"......Slaght's Track...... "	......	......	......
......	4.22 "	8.51 "	151	"......McBride's...... "	......	8.51 "	2.15 "
......	*4.26 "	......	......	"......Nelson...... "	......	......	*2.10 "
......	......	*8.57 "	155	"......Graffville...... "	......	‡8.43 "	*2.08 "
......	4.35 "	9.04 "	154	"......Edmore...... "	......	8.40 "	2.05 "
......	4.42 "	9.13 "	159	"......Wyman...... "	......	8.29 "	1.53 "
......	......	......	160	"......Remick's...... "	......	......	......
......	4.55 "	9.28 "	165	"......Blanchard...... "	......	8.15 "	1.40 "
......	5.03 "	9.37 "	167	"......Millbrook...... "	......	8.07 "	1.31 "
......	*5.12 "	*9.48 "	171	"......Remus...... "	......	7.56 "	*1.21 "
......	5.25 "	10.01 "	176	"......Mecosta...... "	......	7.43 "	1.09 "
......	5.42 "	10.20 "	182	"......Rodney...... "	......	7.25 "	12.51 "
......	......	......	188	"......Marshfield...... "	......	......	......
......	6.05 P. M.	10.46 A. M.	190	Ar......Big Rapids......Lv	......	7.00 A. M.	12.30 P. M.

GOING EAST.				**SAGINAW DIVISION.**			**GOING WEST.**
......	3.55 P. M.	9.40 A. M.	0	Lv......Lakeview......Ar	......	9.20 A. M.	2.45 P. M.
......	4.35 "	10.20 "	12	"......Edmore...... "	......	8.40 "	2.05 "
......	4.44 "	10.29 "	15	"......Cedar Lake...... "	......	8.28 "	1.53 "
......	4.52 "	10.37 "	19	"......Vestaburg...... "	......	8.20 "	1.45 "
......	5.02 "	10.47 "	24	"......Riverdale...... "	......	8.11 "	1.36 "
......	5.25 "	11.10 "	32	"......Alma...... "	......	7.50 "	1.15 "
......	5.35 P. M.	11.20 A. M.	35	Ar......St. Louis......Lv	......	7.40 A. M.	1.05 P. M.

GOING EAST.				**SAGINAW VALLEY & ST. LOUIS R. R.**			**GOING WEST.**
6.05 A. M.	......	12.20 P. M.	0	Lv......Ithaca......Ar	6.25 P. M.	......	11.30 A. M.
6.25 "	......	12.40 "	7	"......Alma...... "	6.05 "	......	11.10 "
6.35 "	......	12.50 "	10	"......St. Louis...... "	5.55 "	......	11.00 "
6.51 "	......	1.06 "	17	"......Breckenridge...... "	5.39 "	......	10.44 "
7.22 "	......	1.37 "	29	"......Hemlock...... "	5.09 "	......	10.14 "
7.45 "	......	2.00 "	39	"......Paines...... "	4.45 "	......	9.50 "
8.00 "	......	2.15 "	43	"......Saginaw City...... "	4.30 "	......	9.35 "
8.15 A. M.	......	2.30 P. M.	45	"......East Saginaw......Lv	4.15 P. M.	......	9.20 A. M.

GOING NORTH.				**GRAND RAPIDS & INDIANA R. R.**			**GOING SOUTH.**
8.47 A. M.	10.36 P. M.	12.10 P. M.	161	Lv......Howard City......Ar	6.08 P. M.	3.47 A. M.	2.29 P. M.
9.04 "	10.52 "	12.26 "	168	"......Morley...... "	5.51 "	3.33 "	2.13 "
9.43 "	11.28 "	1.05 "	183	"......Big Rapids...... "	5.12 "	7.56 "	1.34 "
10.00 "	11.42 "	1.21 "	189	"......Paris...... "	4.56 "	7.43 "	1.21 "
10.17 "	11.59 "	1.40 "	196	"......Reed City...... "	4.39 "	7.26 "	1.05 P. M.
11.25 A. M.	1.05 A. M.	3.10 "	225	Ar }......Cadillac......{ Lv	3.3 P. M.	6.00 "	11.35 A. M.
......	1.20 "	3.20 "		Lv } { Ar		5.40 "	11.25 "
......	2.11 "	4.12 "	246	"......Walton...... "	......	4.34 A. M.	10.35 A. M.
......	......	5.45 P. M.	272	Ar......Traverse City......Lv	......	......	9.00 A. M.
......	2.25 A. M.	4.33 "	251	"......Fife Lake...... "	......	4.22 A. M.	10.14 A. M.
......	3.10 "	5.09 "	265	"......Kalkaska...... "	......	3.41 "	9.41 "
......	3.49 "	5.41 "	278	"......Mancelona...... "	......	3.05 "	9.12 "
......	4.48 "	6.41 "	302	"......Boyne Falls...... "	......	2.02 "	8.10 "
......	5.30 "	7.20 "	318	Ar......Petoskey...... "	......	1.20 "	7.30 "
......	5.32 "	7.42 "	319	"......Bay View...... "	......	1.18 A. M.	7.28 "
......	7.00 A. M.	9.10 P. M.	353	Ar......Mackinaw City......Lv	......	11.50 P. M.	7.01 "

GOING WEST.				**DETROIT, MACKINAC & MARQUETTE R. R.**			**GOING EAST.**
......	10.00 A. M.	......	357	Lv......St. Ignace......Ar	......	8.50 P. M.	......
......	12.20 P. M.	......	411	"......Newberry...... "	......	6.33 "	......
......	12.45 "	......	419	"......McMillan...... "	......	6.10 "	......
......	1.15 "	......	431	"......Seney...... "	......	5.40 "	......
......	2.55 "	......	464	"......Munising...... "	......	4.06 "	......
......	3.56 "	......	485	"......Onota...... "	......	3.17 "	......
......	4.50 P. M.	......	507	Ar......Marquette......Lv	......	2.30 P. M.	......

*Flag Stations. ‡Trains do not Stop. †Horse Car to and from Belding. Dining and Refreshment Rooms at Detroit and Lansing.

In 1884 this predecessor of one part of the Pere Marquette had not yet been built into Grand Rapids. Trains from Detroit and Lansing turned northwest at Grand Ledge to go through Ionia to Howard City and Big Rapids into the heart of the lumbering area.

Author's collection.

Jno. P. Sanborn, President, Pt. Huron, Mich.   H. McMorran, General Manager, Pt. Huron, Mich.
Fred. L. Wells, Sec. and Treas., Pt. Huron, Mich.   I. R. Wadsworth, S. & G.F. & P.A., Pt. Huron, Mich.

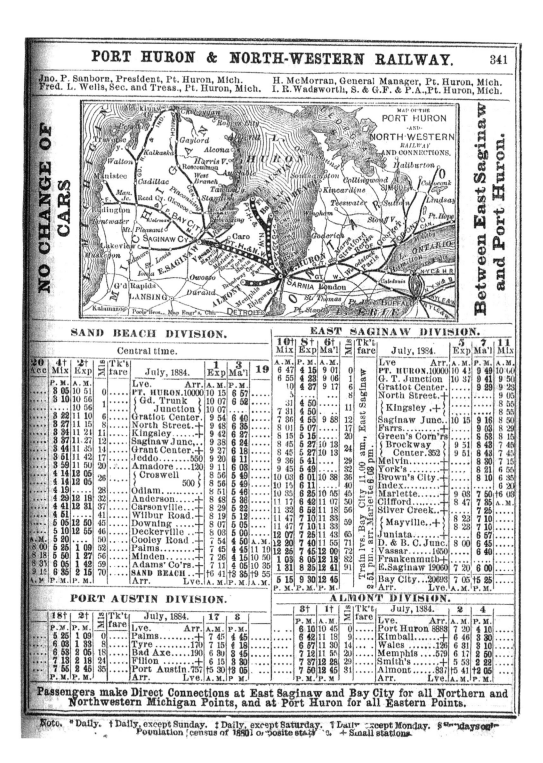

NO CHANGE OF CARS

Between East Saginaw and Port Huron.

SAND BEACH DIVISION.

Central time.

20 Acc	4† Mix	2† Exp	Mls	Tk't fare	July, 1884.	19	1 Exp	3 Ma'l
P. M.	A. M.				Lve. Arr.		A.M.	P.M.
3 05	10 51	0		PT. HURON.10000		10 15	6 57	
3 10	10 56	1		{ Gd. Trunk } Junction		10 07	6 52	
	10 56					10 07		
3 22	11 10	6		Gratiot Center.		9 54	6 40	
3 27	11 15	8		North Street.+		9 48	6 35	
3 34	11 21	11		Kingsley		9 42	6 27	
3 37	11 27	12		Saginaw Junc.		9 38	6 24	
3 44	11 35	14		Grant Center.+		9 27	6 18	
3 51	11 42	17		Jeddo....550		9 20	6 11	
3 59	11 50	20		Amadore....120		9 11	6 03	
4 14	12 05			{ Croswell }		8 56	5 49	
4 14	12 05	26		{ 500 }		8 56	5 49	
4 19		28		Odlam.		8 51	5 46	
4 29	12 18	32		Anderson....+		8 48	5 36	
4 41	12 31	37		Carsonville..+		8 29	5 22	
4 51		41		Wilbur Road.+		8 19	5 12	
5 05	12 50	45		Downing ....+		8 07	5 05	
5 10	12 55	46		Deckerville .+		8 03	5 00	
A.M. 5 20		50		Cooley Road .+	A.M.	7 54	4 50	
8 00	5 25	1 09	52		Palms	7 45	4 45	11 10
8 18	5 50	1 27	56		Minden....+	7 26	4 15	10 50
8 35	6 05	1 42	59		Adams' Co'rs.+	7 11	4 05	10 35
9 15	6 35	2 15	70		SAND BEACH...+	†6 41	†3 35	†9 55
A.M.	P.M.	P.M.			Arr. Lve.	A.M.	P.M.	A.M.

EAST SAGINAW DIVISION.

10† Mix	8† Exp	6† Ma'l	Mls	Tk't fare	July, 1884.	5 Exp	7 Ma'l	11 Mix
A. M.	P. M.	A.M.			Lve. Arr.	A. M.	P.M.	A.M.
6 47	4 15	9 01	0		PT. HURON.10000	10 45	9 49	10 00
6 55	4 23	9 06	1		G. T. Junction	10 37	9 41	9 50
	4 37	9 17	6		Gratiot Center.		9 29	9 28
			8		North Street.+			9 05
7 31	4 50		11		{ Kingsley .+ }			8 55
7 36	4 55	9 38	12		Saginaw Junc..	10 15	9 16	8 50
8 01	5 07		17		Farrs.......+		9 03	8 29
8 15	5 15		20		Green's Corn'rs		8 53	8 15
8 45	5 27	10 13	24		{ Brockway } Center. 352	9 51	8 43	7 46
8 45	5 27	10 13				9 51	8 43	7 45
9 36	5 41		29		Melvin........+		8 30	7 15
9 45	5 49		32		York's........+		8 21	6 55
10 03	6 01	10 38	36		Brown's City.+		8 10	6 35
10 15	6 11		40		Index.........+			6 20
10 35	6 25	10 55	45		Marlette......+	9 08	7 50	†6 03
11 17	6 42	11 07	50		Clifford......+	8 47	7 35	A.M.
11 32	6 52	11 18	56		Silver Creek..+		7 25	
11 47	7 10	11 33	59		{ Mayville..+ }	8 23	7 10	
11 47	7 10	11 33				8 28	7 10	
12 07	7 25	11 43	65		Juniata......+		6 57	
12 20	7 40	11 55	71		D. & B. C. Junc.	8 00	6 45	
12 25	7 45	12 00	72		Vassar....1650		6 40	
1 03	8 05	12 18	82		Frankenmuth+			
1 31	8 25	12 41	91		E.Saginaw 19060	7 20	6 00	
5 15	9 30	12 45			Bay City...20693	7 05	†5 25	
P. M.	P. M.	P. M.			Arr. Lve.	A.M.	P.M.	

(column note: Central time. Train lvs. Bay City 11.00 am., arr. Marlette 6.08 pm. Train lvs. Bay City 11.00 am., arr. Marlette 2.51 pm.)

PORT AUSTIN DIVISION.

18†	2†	Mls	Tk't fare	July, 1884.	17	8
P.M.	P.M.			Lve. Arr.	A.M.	P.M.
5 25	1 09	0		Palms........+	7 45	4 45
6 03	1 33	8		Tyre.......170	7 15	4 18
6 53	2 05	18		Bad Axe....190	6 30	3 45
7 13	2 18	24		Filion........+	6 15	3 30
7 55	2 45	35		Port Austin.757	†5 30	†3 05
P.M.	P.M.			Arr. Lve.	A.M.	P.M.

ALMONT DIVISION.

3†	1†	Mls	Tk't fare	July, 1884.	2	4
P.M.	A.M.			Lve. Arr.	A. M.	P.M.
6 10	10 45	0		Port Huron 8883	7 20	4 10
6 42	11 18	9		Kimball.....+	6 46	3 30
6 57	11 30	14		Wales.....126	6 31	3 10
7 12	11 55	20		Memphis....579	6 17	2 50
7 37	12 28	29		Smith's.....+	5 53	2 22
7 50	12 45	31		Almont.....887	†5 41	†2 05
P.M.	P.M.			Arr. Lve.	A. M.	P.M.

Passengers make Direct Connections at East Saginaw and Bay City for all Northern and Northwestern Michigan Points, and at Port Huron for all Eastern Points.

Note. * Daily. † Daily, except Sunday. ‡ Daily, except Saturday. ¶ Daily except Monday. § Sundays on'y.
Population [census of 1880] opposite stations. + Small stations.

The Port Huron & Northwestern was Michigan's longest narrow-gauge railroad, with its headquarters in Port Huron. In a sparsely populated area, the road offered quite good but not very speedy service. The ninety-one-mile run from Port Huron to Saginaw took nearly four hours, and three-and-a-half hours to get from Port Huron to Port Austin, then still called Sand Beach.

Author's collection.

The Michigan Central stopped its premier *North Shore Limited* to pose for this photograph in the early 1890s. The westbound New York–Chicago train carried no coach-class passengers and cost an extra fare to ride. The companion eastbound run was more democratic, with no extra fare and with coaches.

Michigan Commissioner of Railroads, *Twenty-First Annual Report for 1893* (Lansing, 1894), frontispiece.

for the outgoing crew to compare with the incoming. If the crew had reasonably good watches, they should have fairly accurate time and be able make their run without problems. Company rules continued this sensible requirement well into the twentieth century.

In the early 1870s a movement started that would establish standard time zones in the United States, but each zone used the time of a major city. By 1881 William Frederick Allen, a staffer of *The Official Guide of the Railways and Steam Navigation Lines*, began work on a different and more reasonable plan for standard time for a railway trade group, the General Time Convention. Allen provided for four time zones for the United States based on the 75th, 90th, 105th, and 120th meridians—approximately those of Philadelphia, Memphis, Denver, and Fresno, respectively. The simplicity of Allen's proposal was that each time zone was exactly one hour different from the adjoining zones. The railroads adopted Allen's plan in October 1883 and set noon Sunday, 18 November, as the date to put it into effect.

Newspaper editors generally liked the plan. There were others, some clergymen among them, who objected to any time but the local sun time that shone over their pulpits. These same men already were displeased with the railroads violating the Sabbath by running trains on Sunday. But Allen's plan did go in effect, at least so far as the railroads were concerned. What the community might do was not the railroad's concern. As noon that Sunday neared, trains stopped, and all watches were reset. Some trains had to wait until the time caught up with their schedule, and others hurried to catch up.

Being much nearer to Chicago than to New York, Michigan was placed in the Central time zone. It was not until the fall of 1936 that the Lower Peninsula moved to the Eastern time zone. Railroads in the Upper Peninsula continue to run on Central time although most counties have changed to Eastern time. Only the four counties adjoining Wisconsin—Gogebic, Iron, Dickinson, and Menominee—now remain on Central time.

SOURCES

Corliss, Carlton J. *The Day of Two Noons*. Washington, D.C.: Association of
    American Railroads, 1941.

Holbrook, Stewart H. *The Story of American Railroads*. New York: Crown, 1947.

The Railroads Standardize

The adoption of standard time was the most visible change that railroads were undertaking. Changes in their equipment and procedures were less noticeable but probably of greater importance. The American Civil War spurred the need for many of them; some came from a desire for greater efficiency and profits; and a few were forced by public outcry and the resulting legislative response.

Until the 1860s railroads pretty much picked a track gauge (the distance between the rails) that suited them or allowed them a good connection to another company. There was no need for standardization since a company's cars never left its owner's rails. During the Civil War it was necessary to move freight quickly over several roads. Different gauges impeded their ability to work as a network. But by the end of the war still less than 50 percent of U.S. railroad mileage was of standard gauge, four feet eight and one-half inches between the rails. The change to standard gauge continued in the North during the next two decades. The principal holdout was the Pennsylvania Railroad, which retained four feet nine inches as its track gauge. By 1880 most southern lines were five-foot gauge, but this was changed over in 1886 to the gauge of the Pennsylvania Railroad with which many of them connected. To facilitate movements between the different gauges a "compromise" car, one with a wider wheel tread, was developed, but it quickly proved to be dangerous and was soon discontinued. Cars with wheels that could be shifted vertically along the axle were tried, but they were no safer. Nearly all the remaining U.S. lines were changed to standard gauge by the early 1890s.

Most Michigan lines were built to standard gauge. The pioneer Erie & Kalamazoo was built to the "Ohio" gauge of four feet ten inches, but was changed over in 1848 when its owners prepared to sell it to the Michigan Southern. Mining and lumbering railroads used a wide variety of gauges, ranging from two feet six inches up to standard gauge; this posed little problem since the owner's cars were never moved onto another road. A number of three-foot narrow-gauge lines were built in Michigan in the 1870s as part of an enthusiasm called "narrow-gauge fever." The Toledo & South Haven, the Port Huron & Northwestern, the AuSable & Northwestern, the Mason & Oceana, and the Mineral Range and its subsidiary, the Hancock & Calumet, were among them. The "fever" died soon, as the lower cost of building the line was lost in the inability to interchange cars with other roads. Most of them were converted to standard gauge by about 1890 and all of them by 1900.

As the standard-gauge network grew the need for cars to move from one road to another became obvious. In 1873 the first steps were taken to establish standards for freight cars. Eventually coupler heights, floor sills, ladders, and brakes came to be of uniform design and located in uniform places. Rules for interchange of cars between roads were put in place to provide a system for the return of cars, for the expenses of car repairs, and for car rentals to be paid to the car's owner.

Tracks themselves began to show inadequacies in both the rails and the bridges. T-shaped rails, the standard design by the Civil War, were of iron, and had a shorter life as traffic loads increased. The Bessemer steel-making process was perfected in 1856, and in 1863 the Pennsylvania Railroad made an early test installation of steel rails. Detroiter Eber Brock Ward's North Chicago steel mill was one of the first to produce rolled steel rails. They were much less prone to fissures and had a life that was seven to eight times longer than iron. By 1890, 80 percent of

Toledo & South Haven

When rails are less than four feet eight-and-a-half inches apart the line is called "narrow gauge." The narrow gauge idea developed a considerable following in the 1870s and 1880s as a means of building a new road at a reasonable cost—a kind of poor man's rail empire. Money would be raised to build the first section of the line, and, when completed, its success would encourage investors to finance the next section of the road. One such project was the Toledo & South Haven to be built with a three-foot gauge. The first section formed was the Bangor & South Haven Division in 1876 by a group of South Haven men. Next came the Van Buren Division, with Franklin B. Adams of Lawton and John W. Free of Paw Paw as the principals. Last was the St. Joseph County Division, formed in December by a group from Centreville. In 1877 Adams and Free built a line from Paw Paw to Lawrence and later extended it to Hartford.

In 1886 Adams combined the three parts into the Toledo & South Haven, and in 1877 the T&SH bought the Paw Paw Railroad (which ran from Paw Paw to Lawton) and also completed the line to South Haven in 1887. The Paw Paw was changed over from standard to narrow gauge. With the acquisition of the Paw Paw the T&SH gained the talents of John Ihling, who continued as superintendent of the new company. Local ownership ended in 1887, and, after many years of struggle, the company went into receivership in 1890. In 1898 the Toledo & South Haven was changed to standard gauge, the last road in the Lower Peninsula to make the changeover, and the dream of a narrow-gauge empire came to an end. The line changed hands and names several more times before it finally became a part of the Pere Marquette system in 1903.

all U.S. main tracks had steel rails, and by 1910 iron rails had were a thing of the past.

The use of steel rails made it possible to run heavier freight trains at higher speeds. This caused the lightweight wooden and iron Howe truss bridges to became the weakest part of the track structure. New bridge designs increased load limits, but not until several horrific accidents between 1867 and 1887 were bridges redesigned and upgraded to completely safe standards.

Locomotives were improved to increase their speed and hauling capacity. The American-type 4-4-0 arrangement (four pilot wheels, four driving wheels, none under the cab) hauled both passenger and the light freight trains in the early years. During the Civil War the ten-wheeler (4-6-0) and the heavier-duty Mogul (2-6-0) for freight service followed it. The still heavier Consolidation (2-8-0) was introduced in 1867, and it became the standard freight engine. When a much larger firebox was devised, wheels were needed under the engine cab, and applied first to the Columbia type (2-4-2) in 1892, the Atlantic (4-4-2) in 1895, and the Pacific (4-6-2) by 1900. More adequate engine brakes were developed.

Freight cars grew in size and capacity so that by 1910 they were car-
rying as much as forty tons per car, four times the load carried in 1865.
Specialized cars were developed to carry livestock, refrigerated goods,
oil, and coal. Passenger cars slowly gained specialized improvements.
The enclosed vestibule between cars made it safer to walk between cars.
Sleeping and dining cars were introduced around the end of the Civil
War. In 1881 steam heat from the locomotive for the first time replaced
coal stoves for heat in cars, and by the late 1880s electric lighting was
in limited use.

Michigan never became a locomotive-manufacturing state despite
the maintenance facilities most roads had there. The number of car-
building companies developed into a major industry in Detroit. James
McMillan's Michigan Car Company and Detroit Car Wheel Company,
established in 1865, Frank J. Hecker's Peninsular Car Company in 1879,
and George H. Russel's Russel Wheel and Foundry in 1876 were all major
car and car-part producers. George M. Pullman's first factory was in
Detroit, and he built some of his first sleeping cars there.

Railroad signaling, protecting opposing trains from one another and
following trains from the one ahead, was made possible by the introduction of electric track circuit in 1871 and was in use on the Michigan
Central by the 1880s. The mechanical interlocking, with a grid of levers
and blocking devices that allowed only one clear route at a time, was
devised in the early 1870s. It ended the need for trains to stop at crossings
of other railroads. Michigan's first mechanical interlocking was installed
in November 1884 at Wasepi, a remote crossing near Centreville where
the Michigan Central's Air Line crossed the Grand Rapids & Indiana.
The next year the second was put in at Osceola, just south of Calumet,
at the crossing of the Mineral Range and Hancock & Calumet.

Together these improvements allowed the railroads to increase
substantially the number of cars hauled, train speeds, and tonnage
of freight handled, and to do so without increasing the number of
employees needed to operate a train. Two problems remained that
affected train operations more severely as trains became longer. Cars
were coupled together by an iron link inserted in a slot at the end of
each car and held in each car's slot by an iron pin. This method was
so primitive and dangerous that a brakeman's years of service could
be measured by the number of missing fingers on his hand. For many
years it was the largest cause of injuries to employees. Eli Janney first
patented an automatic coupler in 1868 and by 1873 had improved it
further. A few years later the Pennsylvania Railroad tested it, found

The most dangerous job on the railroad was that of the brakeman in the snow and sleet of winter. He had to walk from car roof to car roof to turn each hand brake to stop a train. Lorenzo Coffin worked all his life to eliminate this deadly menace, which took more railroaders' lives than any other.

Author's collection.

it of merit, and began to install it on some of its cars. It was not until 1882 that the Master Car-Builders Association adopted Janney's device as a national standard. Adopting a standard was easy, but installation of the automatic coupler was slow and grudging.

Stopping a moving train was even more dangerous than the coupling procedure. Brakes on locomotives were of some help in stopping a freight train, but brakemen always had to climb to the tops of freight cars and, using a club, turn a car's brake wheel, and then continue from one car to the next and repeat the act until the train was stopped. The dark of night made this duty more hazardous, and winter snow and ice made it absolutely perilous. Falling from the top of a car was a constant threat, and death often followed such a fall. In 1869 George Westinghouse first patented an air brake and during the following years made further improvements to it. He was able to convince a few roads

Eli Janney invented an automatic car coupling device that eventually was made the universal standard. This advertisement shows the dangerous link-and-pin coupling used until the Railroad Safety Appliance Act was passed in March 1893 and the Janney coupler that replaced it.

to install it on a few passenger trains, but that was all the acceptance he could muster for his revolutionary device.

Lorenzo Coffin, a farmer from Iowa, knew well the gruesome outcome of the link-and-pin couplers and hand brakes. In 1874 he began a personal crusade to end the mayhem. Traveling, speaking, writing, pamphleteering, lobbying, and using any means that would get anyone in authority to listen became Coffin's life. Railroad officials were impervious to Coffin's badgering until he was named Iowa's railroad commissioner in 1883. From his new pulpit he continued his efforts, even appearing at trade meetings as an uninvited guest. In 1886 and 1887 he managed to get the Master Car-Builders Association to make a thorough test of Westinghouse's air-brake system. This third trial worked perfectly. But the cost to the railroads to install automatic couplers and air brakes on all cars was much greater than the cost of several hundred trainmen losing their lives each year. Nothing happened until March 1893, when Congress passed and President Harrison signed the Railroad Safety Appliance Act—Coffin's pet legislation—mandating automatic couplers and air brakes on all lines in the United States. The accident rate to employees plummeted as these devices were installed and the railroads found it possible to run faster and longer trains under safer conditions.

SOURCES

Holbrook, Stewart H. *The Story of American Railroads*. New York: Crown, 1947.

Marshall, Albert P. *The "Real McCoy" of Ypsilanti*. Ypsilanti, Mich.: Marlan, 1989.

Michigan Railroad Commission. *Aids, Gifts, Grants and Donations to Railroads . . .*
      Lansing, Mich.: Wynkoop, Hallenbeck, Crawford, 1919.

Stover, John F. *American Railroads*. Chicago: University of Chicago Press, 1961.

Taylor, George R., and Irene D. Neu. *The American Railroad Network, 1861–1890*.
      Cambridge, Mass.: Harvard University Press, 1956.

White, John H., Jr. *The American Railroad Freight Car: From the Wood-Car Era to the
      Coming of Steel*. Baltimore: Johns Hopkins University Press, 1993.

Riding the Trains

At the end of the Civil War riding a passenger train may have been for convenience or out of necessity, but it most certainly was not a pleasure. The sleeping car was a novelty introduced around 1858 by inventors George M. Pullman and J. Webster Wagner. But sleeping cars ran on only a few main routes. The progressive Michigan Central built one in its company shops in 1860, but its success is unclear and its fate is uncertain. In 1867 Pullman put several of his cars on Michigan Central trains, charging 50 cents more than the MC had for its own sleepers, possibly indicating the character of the MC's efforts. But these few sleeping cars were the only exception to the standard day coach in which nearly all passengers had to ride. The day coach may have been an improvement over the stagecoach, but that is faint praise. Coaches had hard, straight-back seats with a light covering of plush. They were lit by oil lamps hung from the ceiling, with open windows providing the only circulating fresh air. Open windows also allowed in smoke, soot, cinders, dust, and dirt. The cars were built of wood, and in the fortunately infrequent wreck they became an inferno and ultimately a crematorium. Then, too, there was the ever-present cigar smoke from male travelers; it would be a few more years before women would be provided a separate no-smoking car. For meals, most travelers brought a picnic basket of food. Others dashed into depot restaurants that provided barely palatable food that had to be wolfed down in a twenty-minute station stop.

Train speeds were not especially fast. The Michigan Central on its premier Detroit-Chicago route ran at a top speed of about forty miles per hour. In 1869 the fastest train of the five through runs made ten stops and took ten hours and thirty minutes for the trip, an average speed of twenty-seven miles per hour. The Chicago-Kalamazoo accommodation took six hours to make the 140-mile trip—a little over twenty-three miles per hour.

Following the depression of the 1870s the MC made a new and substantial commitment to passenger train service. During the 1880s it built new stations in its major cities. In 1882–84 timetables the *Fast New York Express* made the Chicago-Detroit run in seven hours and forty-five minutes, averaging nearly thirty-seven miles an hour. The other runs were, however, no faster than fifteen years earlier. When MC trains changed over from the Great Western to the Canada Southern between Windsor and Niagara Falls, it speeded up runs across Ontario. Main line amenities did improve; some through trains carried a smoking car and had both first- and second-class coaches. Several day runs featured a dining car, and overnight runs offered sleeping cars. Also, there were Chicago–Bay City, Detroit–Bay City, Detroit–Mackinaw City, and Detroit–Grand Rapids Wagner sleepers. There was a Wagner parlor car between Bay City and Mackinaw City, possibly run to support the MC's investment in the Grand Hotel on Mackinac Island. Most of these enhanced features did not reach daytime branch-line trains; most had only day coaches. MC branch train service included four each way between Jackson and Grand Rapids and between Detroit and Toledo, and four between Detroit and Bay City, two of which went through to Mackinaw City; the Jackson-Saginaw branch had three. Other MC branches usually had two runs each way. All branch-line trains were locals, stopping every five to ten miles, and averaged about twenty-five miles per hour over their run.

The Columbian Exposition opened in Chicago in May 1893, and the Michigan Central carried passengers to a station at the entrance to the fairgrounds. At seven hours and five minutes the *New York and Chicago Limited* was the fastest Chicago-Detroit run; its westbound counterpart took only five minutes more. Passengers paid an extra fare to ride this train. Between Chicago and Detroit the MC ran five express and two local trains, plus a Kalamazoo-Chicago local and a Kalamazoo-Detroit local. The Michigan Central advertised its main line to the East extensively, highlighting "new and sumptuous Wagner vestibuled sleeping cars, buffet and library cars, dining cars," and twenty-five-hour running times to New York. A Detroit–Mackinaw City–Marquette–Houghton sleeping car was put on. Three through trains ran between Chicago and Grand Rapids, via Kalamazoo and the Grand Rapids & Indiana. The overnight run had sleepers for Grand Rapids and Muskegon. A summertime sleeping car to Mackinaw City was featured. One Detroit–Jackson–Grand Rapids run had a summertime sleeper that went on to Petoskey. But for all the top-line features provided, the branch-line train service changed very little. Most trains still plodded along at the 1880s speeds, stopping at every station.

In 1892 the Michigan Central found it had new competition for its Detroit-Chicago traffic. The Wabash, St. Louis & Pacific completed a line into Chicago and inaugurated through service. Daytime and overnight through express trains were put on along with one express and one local run that involved a change of trains in Montpelier, Ohio. Usual running time of the through trains was a few minutes over eight hours, matching that of the Michigan Central.

The Lake Shore & Michigan Southern became the Michigan Central's principal Chicago–East Coast competitor when it completed its Toledo-Elkhart direct "Air Line" in 1858. That line was built to higher standards than its original "Old Road" line, which meandered through Adrian, Hillsdale, and Sturgis. In 1872 the LS&MS ran two New York–Chicago through trains via the Air Line, and two via the Old Road, which stopped at most stations. It was not until the Columbian Exposition in 1893 that the LS&MS upgraded its service. In cooperation with the New York Central & Hudson River it ran the *Exposition Flyer* on a twenty-hour schedule between New York and Chicago over the Air Line, fast running in those days. No coach passengers were allowed—first-class riders only. Its makeup included sleeping cars, a buffet library and smoking car, and a dining car at mealtimes. In 1894 it was joined by the *World's Fair Special* on a twenty-four-hour westbound schedule from New York to Chicago via the Air Line. Old Road service remained at two local trains and two that made only six or seven stops. On other branches the rule was two trains each way daily except Sundays.

The Grand Trunk was the third major system in Michigan. After the Port Huron–Chicago line was assembled in 1883 it began running two through trains, which made a dozen or so stops, and one local train between Port Huron and Chicago. The fastest run was eight hours by one eastbound train; the remainder took ten hours. East of the Niagara River the timetable listed six connecting roads to New York City and Boston. It also featured a Pullman sleeping car between Chicago and Saginaw–Bay City using the Flint & Pere Marquette north of Flint. The GT subsidiary Detroit, Grand Haven & Milwaukee ran four trains each way between Detroit, Grand Rapids, and Grand Haven. Most runs took eight hours. By 1894 the Chicago service was expanded to three eastbound and four westbound through runs that made ten or eleven stops, and two local runs each way. Usual running time was about nine hours for all but the locals, which took nearly thirteen hours. The *Limited Express*, a through train to New York that ran over the Lehigh Valley east of Buffalo, made its run in twenty-eight hours. Most of the other runs took thirty-two to thirty-four hours. The Wabash Railroad used Grand Trunk rails across Ontario and provided sharp competition, with one Chicago–New York run taking only twenty-nine hours and the two others thirty-two hours. Detroit–Grand Haven service was unchanged. Four trains were scheduled each way between Port Huron and Detroit, three between Durand and Bay City, two between Jackson and Ridgeway, and one local and one "mixed" train—a run that hauled both passenger and freight cars—between Owosso and Muskegon on the line through Ashley and Greenville.

The Grand Rapids & Indiana was built as far as Petoskey in 1874. From Grand Rapids south to Fort Wayne the road ran three local trains, and two north to Cadillac. One of the Cadillac trains went on to Petoskey and had a connection to Traverse City. In 1884 all trains still were locals stopping at every station, but there were now three runs from Grand Rapids to Cadillac, two of which went through to Mackinaw City, and two connecting runs to Traverse City. In the summer there were four round-trips from Petoskey to Harbor Springs. By 1893 Grand Rapids–Cadillac runs were expanded to four locals, and Cadillac–Mackinaw City and Traverse City service increased to three round-trips a day. Two through runs from Grand Rapids to Kalamazoo, then over the Michigan Central to Chicago, were added to the schedule. The Muskegon Branch had four round-trips from Grand Rapids.

In the 1860s the Flint & Pere Marquette ran two trains each way between Saginaw and Detroit, using the Detroit, Grand Haven & Milwaukee tracks south of Holly. By 1884 service had been increased to four trains each way between Detroit and Bay City, using Michigan Central tracks from Detroit to Wayne. Two runs connected at Saginaw with trains to Ludington. The trip from Ludington to Detroit took eleven hours. Eight round-trips ran from Saginaw to Bay City; express runs made the thirteen-mile trip in thirty minutes, locals took forty-five. The Detroit, Lansing & Northern, then completed into Grand Rapids, ran three trains a day between Detroit and Grand Rapids. At four to five hours for the trip, it offered the fastest service of any of the three lines running between those cities. Connecting at Grand Ledge, three trains a day ran to Howard City and two to Big Rapids. Its partner, the Chicago & West Michigan, ran three trains a day between Chicago and Grand Rapids, using Michigan Central tracks west of New Buffalo. One of these was an express train that made the trip in five hours and twenty minutes and carried a Wagner buffet parlor car. The overnight run had a Wagner sleeping car. All trains had a connection at Holland to Grand Haven and Muskegon, and there were two additional shuttles between Grand Rapids and Holland. North of Grand Rapids the C&WM ran two trains to Traverse City, with one of them going through to Petoskey. It also ran two shuttle trains between Charlevoix and Petoskey.

Passenger service in the Upper Peninsula, through the mid-1880s, usually was one train a day, but many short branches did without passenger runs. By 1895 service was much improved. The Chicago & North Western, the north-south mainstay, ran three trains from Wisconsin to Escanaba, two of which operated through to Ishpeming. These two were supplemented by two mixed trains between Escanaba and Republic. Three runs a day went to Iron Mountain and Crystal Falls, two of which also went on to Watersmeet. The Milwaukee, Lake Shore & Western ran one through train between Milwaukee and Ashland via Watersmeet and Ironwood. This was supplemented by four additional runs between Wakefield and Hurley, Wisconsin, to carry miners to and from work. The Duluth, South Shore & Atlantic ran two through trains between Duluth and St. Ignace. With stops at every station, they took from eighteen to twenty hours for the trip. One carried an overnight sleeper between Detroit and Marquette and the other between Duluth and Sault Ste. Marie. The Soo Line ran only one overnight train between St. Paul and the Soo, using twenty hours for the run.

Overall the railroads provided reasonably adequate passenger service throughout Michigan. With the greatest concentration of population and riders, southern Michigan had the best service. The Michigan Central and the Wabash vied for Chicago–Detroit and Chicago–Buffalo travelers, with the Lake Shore & Michigan Southern and the Grand Trunk also in the latter field. Three roads competed between Detroit and Grand Rapids and between Detroit and Saginaw–Bay City, two between Grand Rapids and Chicago. Service throughout the northern half of the Lower Peninsula was adequate, but to Petoskey and the Straits of Mackinac it was surprisingly good.

The growth of Michigan's railroad network and its train service largely mirrored the growth of the state itself. Railroad mileage more than doubled between 1875 and 1890, from 3,347 to 6,809 miles, and further increased to 7,609 miles in 1895. Freight traffic, measured by tons carried one mile, rose 143 percent from 1875 to 1890, but, of greater concern, freight revenues on that traffic rose only 30 percent over fifteen years. By 1895, after the panic of 1893 had taken hold, freight traffic dropped off by one-fifth, although revenues did not drop by that much. The result was that by 1895 Michigan railroads were carrying more than twice as much freight as in 1875, but that was producing only 10 percent more revenue. This outcome lent support to the argument that competition provided a better restraint on railroad charges than did government regulation, although it still did not please those who demanded still greater reductions in corporate profits.

The picture for the railroad's passenger business was worse. From 1875 to 1890 the state's population increased 56 percent and the number of passengers riding trains jumped 83 percent, showing the popularity of the increasingly available new form of transport. Also, the state's populace rode more; trips per person per year were up from 4.5 in 1875 to 5.9 in 1890. To carry these riders the railroads ran more than double the number of trains. The net effect was that each train carried fewer passengers. Passenger miles, which is the sum of the number of passengers riding one mile, rose by only 63 percent, showing that passengers were making shorter trips. To make it worse, total passenger revenues rose by only 32 percent. In sum, the 56 percent population increase between 1875 and 1890 and the 63 percent ridership increase are roughly equal, but revenues increased by only half as much. It got worse by 1895. The number of passengers dropped by 2.3 million (18 percent); passenger miles dropped 23 percent from 1890, down nearly to the level of 1884. Revenues also dropped, but by not quite as much, and were barely above 1884 revenues.

The net result, without question, is that over this twenty-year period rail passenger travel did not increase as fast as the overall population. Worse still, revenue growth lagged the growth in ridership by two-thirds. No ratio measure improved during the period. It would be interesting to know the costs of operating the passenger service, but since the railroad commissioner did not ask for that figure, any estimate would be very rough. However, it is possible to conclude from this that the investment in new stations and equipment and the cost of increased numbers of trains both worked against improving profits. There may have been a general public and regulatory feeling that the railroads were obliged to provide a better than adequate passenger service, but one can see why the railroad companies might have been less than enthusiastic about doing so. A cynical view might take it that the railroads tolerated passenger traffic as a way to quiet a potential public outcry.

SOURCES

Grand Trunk Railway, public timetables, various dates.

Harlow, Alvin F. *The Road of the Century*. New York: Creative Age, 1947.

Holbrook, Stewart H. *The Story of American Railroads*. New York: Crown, 1947.

Lake Shore & Michigan Southern Railway, public timetables, various dates.

Michigan. *Fourth Annual Report of the Commissioner of Railroads*. Lansing, Mich.: W. S. George, 1876. (Covers the year 1875)

Michigan. *Thirteenth Annual Report of the Commissioner of Railroads*. Lansing, Mich.: W. S. George, 1885. (Covers the year 1884)

Michigan. *Nineteenth Annual Report of the Commissioner of Railroads*. Lansing, Mich.: Robert Smith, 1891. (Covers the year 1890)

Michigan. *Twenty-Fourth Annual Report of the Commissioner of Railroads*. Lansing, Mich.: Robert Smith, 1896. (Covers the year 1895)

Michigan Central Railroad, public timetables, various dates.

The Official Guide of the Railways. New York: National Railway Publication, various dates.

Travelers Official Guide of the Railways. New York: National Railway Publication, June 1893.

Wreck, Part 1

"WRECK!" No word in railroading is more fearsome. Death of passengers, death of employees, and destruction of property conjure up awful images to every railroader. Michigan has not escaped these awful tragedies. There have been accidents of all sorts almost from the beginning: derailed cars, derailed engines, sideswiped cars, collapsed bridges, and fires to property. Nearly two decades passed before any Michigan road experienced a serious wreck.

The earliest major wreck in the United States in which more than a dozen died was that of two Michigan roads that occurred at Grand Crossing south of Chicago. On Monday night, 25 April 1853, less than a year after both roads had been built into Chicago, a Michigan Central mixed emigrant and freight train beat a Michigan Southern train to the crossing. The Southern train rammed the middle of the Central train. At that time neither road required its trains to stop before using the crossing, and, in fact, both encouraged their enginemen to be aggressive as they approached it. The collision killed eighteen people outright, and some forty more were taken to Chicago hospitals. Soon after both roads began stopping their trains before going over the crossing. A half a century later the two roads agreed that a bridge should replace the ground-level crossing.

On the morning of Friday, 29 August 1873, a westbound Detroit & Milwaukee express train stopped a mile east of Muir when its locomotive lost a driving wheel. The flagman went back to protect the rear of the train, but did not go back far enough. A following freight train, coming down grade, saw the flagman and tried to stop, but reversing its wheels and its brakemen applying hand brakes could not stop it in time. It rammed the rear of the passenger train, killing four immigrants from Iceland and injuring eleven other Icelanders and three others. A coroner's jury found the flagman criminally guilty and all of the crew of the freight train criminally negligent in some manner. On the following 15 September, a Detroit & Milwaukee passenger train ran over a cow two miles west of Lowell; several cars derailed, killing two passengers instantly. Two more died later, and fourteen were injured. The D&M's bad luck continued on 30 June 1875 when a westbound passenger train left Holly without orders against an eastbound passenger. The two collided, with only four passengers and four employees injured.

The state's most serious wreck, to that time, happened near Jackson in the early hours of Friday, 10 October 1879. A switch engine pulled nine cars and its caboose from the north side onto the main track about one-half mile west of Dettman Road, and was just starting to back into the yards on the south side. Number 2, the westbound *Pacific Express*, running almost thirty minutes late, rounded the curve east of Dettman Road at a speed of twenty-five miles per hour. Because of the fog its engineman could not see the switch engine or switch lights until too late. Apparently the switch engine had started to back up when its crew saw the other train and jumped off their engine to save themselves. At 1:10 A.M. the passenger train collided head-on with the switch engine. Both engines derailed, as did the first three cars of the passenger train. The next car carried second-class passengers from the Great Western Railway and was telescoped by the following car; most of the deaths occurred in these two cars. The engineman and fireman of the passenger train were killed instantly. Thirteen passengers were killed in the wreck, and twenty-five were injured.

The Jackson yardmaster was found criminally negligent for not for authorizing the switcher's move without first learning how late the passenger train was running. The switch engine crew was censured for being on the main track when they knew a passenger train was due. The coroner's jury found that added safeguards and danger signals were needed in light of the high speeds at which trains were operated. Michigan Central officers and the railroad commissioner both agreed with the jury, but neither could identify a system that would provide this sort of protection.

The worst year was 1893. On Friday, 13 October, the Michigan Central was handling nearly a dozen special trains west to the Columbian Exposition at Chicago. A special had stopped at the Jackson station for its passengers to have breakfast. As it was preparing to move out at 9:10 A.M., a following special came up behind it at somewhere between eighteen and thirty miles per hour and could not stop. The second engineman claimed that his air brakes failed. He rammed the rear coach, which then telescoped into the car ahead. Husbands standing on the platform for a smoke saw their wives killed. Fourteen people died instantly, and a staggering seventy people were injured.

One week later, on 20 October, the Chicago & Grand Trunk was handling a special headed east from Chicago. The special had train orders to meet Number 9, the westbound *Pacific Express*, at the Battle Creek station. The special's engine crew disobeyed orders and left the station. Running at about thirty miles per hour, they met the *Pacific Express* head-on at Nichols Yard on the east side of Battle Creek. The second and third day coaches on the westbound telescoped, and the result was twenty-eight people dead, most of them burned beyond recognition at the scene, and another twenty-six left injured. The engine crews of both trains escaped injury, apparently by jumping before the collision. This became the worst wreck in the sixty years of Michigan railroading.

Wrecks of this era proved to be particularly deadly. The number of passenger trains was increasing. The trains were handling more passenger cars, and they were moving at higher speeds. Nearly all cars were made of wood, and only a very few had steel undercarriages. Many cars were heated by coal stoves and lit with either kerosene lamps or Pintch gaslights. A wreck often caused one car to telescope into another. Flame and flammable material came together to cause an immediate inferno. The 29 December 1876 disaster at Ashtabula, Ohio, was a horrific example of what could happen. A Lake Shore & Michigan Southern bridge collapsed as a passenger train rolled over it. The train dove into a ravine and caught fire. Eighty-three people died on the scene, mostly due to the fire, and nine more died later; sixty-seven were injured, and only eight people were not injured. Two weeks later the Lake Shore's chief engineer, Charles Collins, shot himself. After an investigation the coroner blamed managing director Amasa Stone Jr., who had designed and ordered the bridge built to his specifications. Stone became a pariah in Cleveland, finally committing suicide in 1883.

The Railroad Way of Life

In the three decades before 1900 the railroad became an integral part of American life. The railroad brought fundamental changes in Michigan's way of life, just as it did throughout the nation. New rail lines developed new communities, one every half-dozen miles or so; they brought growth to isolated hamlets; and they made cities out of villages. A look at the founding dates in Walter Romig's *Michigan Place Names* shows how important the arrival of the railroad was to most communities.

Many place names were decided by the railroads. Vanderbilt was named after the Michigan Central's president; other presidents also honored were Ashley, Hawks, Alger, and Ingalls. Directors and a host of ranked officials were memorialized in such places as Muir, Devereaux, Elwell, Mulliken, Merrill, Wakelee, Kendall, Woodbury, Agnew, Farwell, Sears, and Shelby(ville). Junctions were common, as in Grand Junction,

Milwaukee Junction (in Detroit), and Soo Junction. The Soo Line honored the statesman Gladstone and poets twice in Rudyard and Kipling, all to acknowledge British investment. The Chicago & North Western used mythology in Dryads, Faunus, Comus, and Hylus in Menominee County; trees in Elmwood, Basswood, Beechwood, Birch Creek, Pine Ridge, and Maple Ridge; and things British in Kew, Cunard, and Brampton. Almost every promoter involved in the Detroit, Mackinac & Marquette got a station: Driggs, Hendrie, McMillan, Moran, Newberry, Palms, Seney, and Allen(ville). Sometimes the downtown of the community was laid out in alignment with the railroad: Decatur, Dowagiac, Chelsea, New Buffalo, Ionia, and Midland are some of them. At least a hundred towns have a Railroad Street or Railroad Avenue, a Depot Street or Station Street, even though in some cases the tracks and station are long gone. A Grand Trunk Street remains in Battle Creek and a Pere Marquette Drive in Lansing. For the traction interest, there are several Interurban Streets in the state.

Every town had a railroad station, the *depot*. It became a center of social contact for the town because it was the place at which people arrived and departed when they traveled. Mixed into this importance was a fascination for things new and mechanical and even exciting. The entire family came to the depot to meet a visiting relative. The newspaper reporter came down to see who was traveling and to catch up on local gossip. The village loafers gathered to settle the affairs of the world and to talk about affairs in town. Young boys came to hear the mysterious telegraph or to admire a favorite engineman or just to watch a train go through. Young girls came, with appropriate caution, because the boys were there. There was little that happened in town that did not involve the depot in some way.

The station was the office of the railroad's local representative, the station agent. He worked a twelve-hour day, six days a week, and was subject to call the rest of the time. The agent was responsible for the company's affairs in that community. That meant handling freight, mail, telegrams, and express; selling tickets and handling baggage; collecting freight charges; watching the money and balancing the books for the office; handling signals and train orders for trains; taking care of legal affairs, leases, and agreements; notifying headquarters of anything that affected the company; dealing with every problem that came along; and answering the public's questions. Those were his railroad duties; he might also be a justice of the peace or a village councilman or play in the community brass band. In the very smallest stations he was a lone sentry; in slightly larger ones he might have a clerk as a helper. Still larger stations might have separate ticket clerks, telegraph operators, freight clerks, and freight warehouse men. If the town had two railroads crossing or had a population of, say, 5,000, then the depot was open twenty-four hours a day, seven days a week.

The agent had to have mastered the mysterious Morse telegraph. He could understand the baffling staccato of clicks that were letters, which he formed into words and sentences. Railroad business was important; he had to be skilled and accurate. In the days before the telephone and the radio, the telegraph provided instantaneous contact with the outside world, the next station, or the nation's capital. The agent knew before everyone else when someone important died, what the up-to-the-minute baseball game score was, when war or peace was declared, what famous person might be on a train due to pass through, who won the boxing match, and what the weather forecast was. He could chat as easily with a man a hundred miles down the line as with someone on the depot platform. His skill brought with it the responsibility of handling messages for railroad business and also Western Union telegrams. A sender could compose a ten-word day message (extra words cost additional), and it would be delivered almost anywhere in the nation, incredibly, within an hour or two. Night letters were cheaper, could be up to fifty words, and would be delivered the next morning.

When the railroad came it brought the outside world with it to the depot. The rails went not just to the next station but led eventually to major cities. Each line joined others to make up systems, and these connected to form a nationwide network. By the early 1870s it was possible to travel from any major Michigan city to any other. Connecting railroads at Detroit, Toledo, Fort Wayne, and Chicago allowed travel to any other large city in the United States and Canada. The lines built in Michigan in the two decades beginning in 1875 brought rails into nearly every community of any size in the state. Travel became possible at unheard of speeds. A stagecoach ride of three days from Detroit to Chicago was replaced by 1852 with an eleven-hour train ride on the Michigan Central, which by 1890 was reduced to seven or eight hours.

Railroads published timetables and distributed them to inform the public and advertise themselves. Many stations were stocked with a supply of colorful timetables from other connecting railroads, which could be given to the public. But for the agent's use the *Travelers Official Railway Guide of the United States and Canada* was a thousand-page compendium of the timetables of all railroads. It began publication in

June 1868, appeared monthly until the 1970s, and is still published today. There were other guides, such as *Appleton's Railway Guide*, which was the best known and older. But the former outlasted its competition, and evolved through several publishers and name changes, until it became *The Official Guide of the Railways*, or most commonly just "The Official Guide." The knowledgeable traveler in Michigan could buy the *Michigan Railway Guide*. First published by John R. Wood in January 1880, it continued under several names until the 1930s. A *Michigan Electric Railway Guide* was published for the interurbans in the 1910s.

The arrival of the passenger train brought improved mail service. The horseback rider and the stagecoach could not compete in speed and dependability. In 1862 the post office experimented with sorting letters in a special car on a moving train. The experiment worked, and the idea was adopted on a few other lines. In 1871 the post office created a separate department, the Railway Mail Service, to expand the service nationwide. Eventually most trains had a Railway Post Office (RPO), a specially designed car in which clerks sorted letters and caught mail pouches of letters from cranes at trackside and threw off pouches without stopping the train. The train and the RPO speeded up mail service and improved the entire operation of the post office.

The train also created a new kind of shipping service, the express company. In the 1830s a few enterprising individuals began to carry other people's packages, mail, and valuables from one city to another by train. The idea originated in New England, caught on, and the concept expanded. Within two decades Adams Express, American Express, and eventually Wells Fargo were formed. American Express handled business on the Michigan Central, the Chicago & North Western, the Detroit, Lansing & Northern, and the Chicago, Milwaukee & St. Paul; U.S. Express served on the Grand Rapids & Indiana; and both U.S. Express and American Express were on the Lake Shore & Michigan Southern. The business generally prospered, to such an extent that the post office barred it from handling first-class letters and in 1913 established a parcel post service to compete. For small town Michigan, the express service brought small goods shipments from Sears-Roebuck and Montgomery Ward, fruit shipments from relatives in Florida, and valuables for the bank.

While the colorful passenger train was important to the townspeople, it was the humble freight train that brought profits to the railroad. Any kind of shipment too large to handle by express came by freight train. The "peddler" car in local freights was stopped at the freight house dock to unload a variety of merchandise that was undreamed of before the rails came. Every small town had a lumberyard and coal yard, and both commodities came by train. Usually there was also a grain elevator that received farm supplies and equipment, and shipped out grain. Most important, any town with a railroad could become a manufacturing center. Goods made of wood from nearby hardwood forests were produced in nearly every community. In northern Michigan during the last three decades of the nineteenth century, logging and lumbering were the primary source of freight business. Small towns in southern Michigan had furniture factories, paper mills, iron foundries, pickle works, stockyards, flour mills, food processors, buggy and wagon makers, clothing mills, and a host more. All of this was made possible by the train, which brought in the raw materials needed and moved the final product to market.

SOURCES

Holbrook, Stewart H. *The Story of American Railroads*. New York: Crown, 1947.

Massie, Larry. "Depot Dreams and Jerkwater Schemes." *Michigan History* 77:6 (November–December 1993).

Michigan Railway Guide, June 1909. Detroit: John R. Wood, 1909.

Romig, Walter. *Michigan Place Names*. Grosse Pointe, Mich.: author, n.d.

The Grand Railway Station, Part 1

Early railroad stations in Michigan were much like those in the rest of the nation—primitive, dirty, cheerless, and comfortless. These utilitarian structures usually were made of wood, the cheapest and most accessible building material available. By the end of the Civil War only a very few new and better stations had been built. When the Grand Trunk Railway of Canada built its line between Port Huron and Detroit in 1858–59 it erected substantial brick stations at Fort Gratiot, Fraser, Richmond, Smiths Creek, New Haven, and Mt. Clemens. Of these, the Mt. Clemens and Fort Gratiot stations remain in place, while the Smiths Creek structure has been moved to Greenfield Village. These three are the oldest railroad passenger stations in Michigan.

When the Michigan Central took over three branch lines out of Jackson in the early 1870s, Jackson developed into an important transfer point. To handle the growing traffic demands the MC replaced its older depot in 1874 with an Italianate brick station that included a wide platform overhang supported by columns. This station is used today by Amtrak and is the oldest station in continuous passenger traffic use in Michigan. That same year the Grand Rapids & Indiana built a smaller station of similar style in Kalamazoo to replace one that had been destroyed by fire; this station still stands but not in railroad use. In 1870 the Detroit, Grand Haven & Milwaukee (now Grand Trunk Western) built a new Grand Haven station when it built its line into downtown. The building now serves as a museum.

Between 1876 and 1881, after the industry recovered from the panics of 1873 and 1877, passenger traveling increased sharply. Numbers of passengers and passenger miles (passengers carried one mile) rose; with a few adjustments for non-Michigan traffic, both increased by 38 percent. The Michigan Central's passenger revenue grew 70 percent, the Lake Shore & Michigan Southern's 13 percent, and the Flint & Pere Marquette's 80 percent. Numbers of passengers increased from 7.6 million to just over 10 million, and passenger miles from 361 million to 497 million. This press of new travelers led state railroad commissioner William B. Williams to remark in his report for the year 1881 that most stations in the state were "respectable" but that "in some instances the station-houses are not only very inadequate to the requirements of the business of the towns where located, but of a character not at all creditable to the corporations by whom they are owned." He had words of praise for the Flint & Pere Marquette, which in 1882 built a new station in Saginaw on Potter Street, and for the Michigan Central, which announced it would build a new one in Detroit to replace the original Third Street depot built in the late 1840s. With business profits flowing but public criticism rising, the railroads took a long look at what to do. The commissioner's report for 1884 was more critical. He wrote that "at some places however it appeared . . . to me that the passenger houses were not of sufficient capacity and construction to comfortably accommodate the public, nor of a character, architecturally speaking, to compare favorably with other public structures at the important places where located." He identified the Michigan Central stations at Ann Arbor, Battle Creek, and Kalamazoo; the Lake Shore & Michigan Southern at Kalamazoo; the Chicago & Grand Trunk at Lansing; and the Detroit, Grand Haven & Milwaukee station at Ionia as particularly unsuitable. This time the railroads took the public relations side of things and planned to build some new passenger terminals, particularly in larger cities.

Detroit grew so rapidly that the Michigan Central had to build a new—and far more impressive—passenger station on Third Street. Opened in 1883, it was used only until 1896, when it was replaced by a new and still larger station.

Silas Farmer, *History of Detroit and Wayne County and Early Michigan* (Detroit, 1890), 900.

In 1883 the MC completed a new Detroit terminal at Third and Jefferson. This mammoth red brick Richardsonian Romanesque building, with a 157-foot-tall clock tower, lasted until the 1960s, when it was razed to make room for Joe Louis Arena and an expressway. Other new MC stations followed: at Ann Arbor in 1886 designed by Frederick H. Spier, at Kalamazoo in 1887 designed by Cyrus L. W. Eidlitz, at Battle Creek in 1888 designed by Rogers & MacFarlane, at Bay City East Side and Saginaw

Opened in January 1893, Detroit's Fort Street Union Depot was a Victorian monument to transportation. It was home to the Wabash, the Canadian Pacific, and two predecessors of the Pere Marquette. In the 1920s the Pennsylvania Railroad also began to use it. With the coming of Amtrak in 1971, it lost all of its trains. Deserted and vandalized for three years, it was razed in 1974.

Michigan Commissioner of Railroads, *Twenty-First Annual Report for 1893* (Lansing, 1894), facing xxiii.

ABOVE: Showing the palmy days of resort travel by train, this photograph of the Chicago & West Michigan station at Charlevoix was taken not long after it opened in 1893. The tracks and the landscaping now are long gone, but the station, later painted white by the Pere Marquette, remains impressive in private use.

Michigan Commissioner of Railroads, *Twenty-Fifth Annual Report for 1897* (Lansing, 1898), between xlii and xliii.

BELOW: After three years in building, the Chicago & West Michigan opened this Richardsonian Romanesque station in Muskegon in 1895. In its early years it served as Muskegon's union station for three railroads, but by the 1930s only Pere Marquette trains stopped.

Postcard view, Sam Breck collection.

This Lake Shore & Michigan Southern station at Sturgis was replicated in a number of towns along the line between Buffalo and Chicago. Built in 1896, and now completely restored for civic use, the station is open to the public.

Sam Breck collection.

Genesee Avenue in 1890, and at Niles in 1891 designed by Spier & Rohns. The Bay City and Saginaw stations now are gone, but the others remain. All of them were monuments to Henry Hobson Richardson and the commercial architectural style he made popular. Each was unique but used red brick trimmed with red sandstone, was characterized by a turret or clock tower, and usually had an arched entryway.

In 1887 the MC built a fieldstone structure at Grass Lake also designed by Spier and Rohns, and others in 1889 at Standish and 1890 at Lawton. The three survive, although the Grass Lake depot was heavily damaged by fire and the interior and roof replaced. The brick 1893 depot at Columbiaville was the gift of a local millionaire. The 1880 wooden depot at Chelsea, replete with all its gingerbread, and the 1880 board-and-batten depot at Augusta are extant today, with the latter now moved to the village park. On MC branches, the 1882 depots at Grayling and Mackinaw City, with board-and-batten siding and a second story with hotel rooms for the public, still stand, but they are of a size that shows only modest traffic expectations.

With a much smaller passenger business the Lake Shore & Michigan Southern did not face the demands that the Michigan Central did. However, it did build a new brick station in Hillsdale in 1881. The Coldwater station built later in the decade is of the same design.

The Flint & Pere Marquette built its Potter Street station in Saginaw in 1882. Designed by Bradford Lee Gilbert of New York, this

Richardsonian Romanesque two-and-a-half-story red brick building, with a variety of bays, chimneys, and dormers accenting a central four-story square tower, is one of the largest passenger stations remaining in Michigan. It is currently unused after being damaged by arson. Within a year the F&PM also built a new but smaller station in Flint.

On the west side of the state, the Chicago & West Michigan completed its line into Petoskey in 1892 and built a brick station for the resort city on the shore of Little Traverse Bay. In 1895 the C&WM built a new union station in Muskegon, which also was used by the Grand Rapids & Indiana. Designed by Grand Rapids architect Arthur W. Rush, this Richardsonian structure was of red brick and red sandstone with a massive two-story tower over an arched entranceway, offset with a small turret. Both William Jennings Bryan and Harry Truman spoke at the Muskegon depot while campaigning for the presidency.

The Ann Arbor railroad (then named the Toledo, Ann Arbor & North Michigan) built several impressive stations as it extended its line north from Toledo to Frankfort between 1878 and 1889. In 1889 the road built a new wood-framed depot in Ann Arbor, but it was not an imposing one. In 1886 the brick depot in Howell was built. The line's station at Cadillac was built sometime after 1890. This two-story brick passenger station with its adjoining baggage building is probably the most impressive depot built in Michigan by the Ann Arbor.

The Upper Peninsula's most impressive station of this period was at Sault Ste. Marie. Built about 1890 for the joint use of the Soo Line and the Duluth, South Shore & Atlantic, this finished cut red sandstone structure had a two-story center section and two one-story wings. Both tenants were not heavy passenger carriers and built very few impressive depots. The structure has been razed. The Copper Range built its most impressive Houghton station in 1899. This two-story brick structure, with Jacobsville sandstone corners and decoration, served as both passenger station and general offices of the railroad. The DSS&A masonry depot at Houghton, built about 1890, is now unused.

The Chicago & North Western built a number of pleasing brick stations during this period: at Iron Mountain in 1889, at Bessemer about 1890, and at Ironwood about 1895. The Chicago, Milwaukee & St. Paul depot in Menominee, built in 1885, is one of the very few examples remaining of wooden stations of this era built for cities.

This era of showiness was the railroads' attempt to use some profits to put on a good municipal face. But it did little to mitigate the criticism that came from the Grange and other civic-minded organizations, and did nothing to reduce the demands for governmental regulation. But it did provide an opportunity to develop a body of architectural styles that gave new grace to the corporate facade as well as new building techniques that found wide application in other commercial uses.

SOURCES

Eckert, Kathryn Bishop. *Buildings of Michigan*. New York: Oxford University Press, 1993.

Grant, H. Roger, and Charles W. Bohi. *The Country Railroad Station in America*. Sioux Falls, S.Dak.: Center of Western Studies, 1988.

Potter, Janet Greenstein. *Great American Railroad Stations*. New York: John Wiley & Sons, 1996.

Uhelski, John M., and Robert M. Uhelski. *An Inventory of the Railroad Depots in the State of Michigan*. Crete, Neb.: Railroad Station Historical Society, 1979.

U.S. Department of the Interior, Heritage Conservation and Recreation Service, Historic American Engineering Record. *The Upper Peninsula of Michigan: An Inventory of Historic Engineering and Industrial Sites*, by Charles K. Hyde and Diane B. Abbott. Washington: U.S. Department of the Interior, 1978.

U.S. Department of the Interior, National Park Service, Historic American Engineering Record. *The Lower Peninsula of Michigan: An Inventory of Historic Engineering and Industrial Sites*, by Charles K. Hyde and Diane B. Abbott. Washington, D.C.: U.S. Department of the Interior, 1976.

Working on the Railroad

On the first run of the *Adrian*, the first engine on the Erie & Kalamazoo in the summer of 1837, the engineman and fireman worked on a platform behind the boiler and made their run completely exposed to the elements. From that day to this trains run at all times of the day and night, every day of the year, in every kind of weather. Railroading today still is demanding, dangerous, dirty, tiring, wearing work.

When the Michigan commissioner of railroads office was created in 1873 the legislature made the safety of the public and employees an important concern. For the year 1872 the commissioner reported 146 accidents that involved twenty-nine passengers and forty-three others, many of whom were trespassers. Employees accounted for half of all accidents—seventy-four in all. Of passengers, twenty-seven were injured, and only two were killed; of the others, nineteen were injured, and twenty-four were killed. The hard-hit railroaders had thirty-six injuries and thirty-eight deaths. The single worst cause was the link-and-pin used in coupling cars by which eleven died and thirteen more were injured. Nine more workers died in falling from a train; five died and nine were injured in derailments.

By 1879 Michigan railroad track miles had increased by 30 percent over 1872, but train operations were up by nearly 50 percent. Accidents doubled over 1872 to a total of 300. The number killed rose from sixty-four to eighty-eight in seven years, while the number of injuries leaped from 82 to 212. Of the eleven million passengers carried, forty-seven were injured and only seventeen died. The wreck of the Michigan Central's *Pacific Express* at Jackson caused thirteen deaths and twenty-five injuries. Of nearly 15,000 employees in the state, 28 were killed and 122 injured. Once again coupling cars was the worst cause, resulting in five deaths and sixty injuries. Eight died and twelve were injured in falling from trains, with derailments causing three deaths and five injuries.

For railroad men, the three hazards taking the largest toll were coupling cars with a link-and-pin coupler, falling from a train as a result of brakemen having to work hand brakes on the tops of cars, and having a foot caught in the frog of a track switch. Railroad managers rather callously attributed most of the workers' deaths to a lack of caution by employees, which had some element of truth. The commissioner concurred in this position, at least in the case of coupling cars. There were unreported effects of working on icy car roofs, of working in snow and sleet and ice storms, of working in the black darkness of night, and of working train runs for sixteen, twenty-four, thirty, and thirty-six hours at one stretch. Twenty of twenty-eight employee deaths and 99 of 122 injuries were charged by the employer as "employee lack of caution." The general corporate attitude was that unless the company directly caused an injury or fatality, the employee was at fault. The company hired men who were expected to be competent and able to perform their duties under any conditions at any time. If an employee was injured or died, that was a fact of life he faced when he took the job.

Railroad workers acted on several fronts to try to improve their lot. The development and adoption of the automatic coupler and the air brake were pressed forward by both government and individuals, and have been covered in greater detail above. Working conditions describe a wide variety of nontechnological problems: hours on duty, hours of rest between assignments, arbitrary hiring and discharge practices, wages,

In this modest home of Jared C. "Yankee" Thompson, at 633 West Hanover in Marshall, a meeting of twelve Michigan Central enginemen held in April 1863 led to the formation of the Brotherhood of the Footboard—the nation's first railroad labor organization. The Brotherhood of Locomotive Engineers has commemorated the founding with an impressive monument on East Michigan Avenue.

Marshall Historical Society.

preferential promotions and demotions, discipline for rules infractions, and inadequate training are among the major problems. Capricious supervisors fired men at any time for any reason. Managers used wage cuts routinely to keep expenses under control. These circumstances were not unique to railroads and existed in most of American industry. Only well-organized unions in a few small businesses were able to lean against such a prevailing wind.

Unions came early to the railroad business. The pioneering effort was the formation of the Brotherhood of the Footboard—a group of locomotive enginemen working on the Michigan Central. It was organized at the home of Jared C. "Yankee" Thompson in Marshall in April 1863 and later was renamed the Brotherhood of Locomotive Engineers (BLE). Thompson's home still stands at 633 West Hanover Street. A fraternal and insurance benefit organization, it insured enginemen who were considered by insurance companies to be in too hazardous an occupation to be issued life insurance. At first the brotherhood attempted to enhance the status of engineers by working in cooperation with railroad managers. It was not until later that it took up working conditions and wages and then went against management to gain improvements.

Before the 1870s Marshall was the changing point for train and engine crews on the Michigan Central's Detroit-Chicago main line. The MC had hired Alanson S. Sweet as superintendent of motive power

No one man pushed and agitated more for the railroad labor movement than Eugene V. Debs. Distinguished in appearance in 1897 at the age of forty-two, this portrait belies his radical and militant work for railroadmen throughout the country.

based on his reputation as a cost cutter. He altered job assignments in such a way that caused pay reductions. Some of the men protested, and Sweet fired a number of them. To drive home his authority Sweet also laid off some senior firemen and hired untrained replacements with whom, in turn, the experienced engineers refused to run trains. The enginemen also agreed among themselves that if Sweet fired any one of them, the others would quit. Their approach spread to other crew on the MC. A committee of them went to Sweet, who at first refused to see them, but then he relented and eventually agreed to many of their demands.

The early success of the BLE encouraged the formation of other brotherhoods: the Order of Railway Conductors in 1868, the Switchmen's Union of North America in 1870, the Brotherhood of Locomotive Firemen in 1873, the Brotherhood of Railroad Trainmen in 1883, the Order of Railroad Telegraphers in 1886, the Brotherhood of Railway Carmen in 1888, and the Brotherhood of Railway Clerks in 1899. Each of these was organized by the men in a specific railroad craft. In the earliest years they were largely fraternal and also provided insurance for railroad men. Each stressed training and professional standards in an attempt to improve the pay and gain employment stability for their members. The brotherhoods demonstrated considerable support for management and had little enthusiasm for strikes, an attitude that put the railroad brotherhoods at odds with most of the American labor movement as it developed.

One of those pushing for much more union activity was the editor of *Locomotive Firemen's Magazine*, Eugene V. Debs. Despite widespread opposition the firemen and enginemen took some joint actions and did gain some successes. Three of the train service brotherhoods tried forming a coalition, but the enginemen refused to join. Debs kept at it until, in June 1893, he started the American Railway Union (ARU).

It was to lobby for living wages and proper working conditions, with its membership open to any white male railroad employee. By the end of the year 125 locals were started. In 1894 the ARU led its first strike against the Great Northern Railway. With the public and businessmen behind it the ARU won most of its demands in just eighteen days. Next came a strike against the Pullman Company, which built and operated most of the sleeping cars on American railroads. This action affected most of the major rail lines in the country and generated a vigorous reaction. The companies finally persuaded the federal government to intervene. In July federal troops were ordered to Chicago, so that by

midmonth ARU leaders were in jail. Without support from nonrailroad unions, the Pullman strike was broken. The strike also fatally injured the ARU itself.

The Great Northern strike and the Pullman strike demonstrated to both the craft-oriented brotherhoods and the trade union movement that unified action was critical in making any gains for the rail worker. No amalgamation among the brotherhoods came from this, nor was another broad union of the ARU sort created, although more cooperation did develop. Most important, these strikes led the brotherhoods to the realization that their future was in working aggressively on behalf of their membership. The days of outright support and cooperation with rail management ended, replaced by a new undercurrent of animosity between the employees and their brotherhoods vis-á-vis railroad officials and managers.

This spirit of distrust pervaded the air as the nineteenth century turned into the twentieth. One has only to read Walter F. McCaleb's

A small-town depot in America was indeed a most democratic place. In this 1888 engraving women and men, affluent and not, assembled with dogs, employees, watchers, and the village idlers.

The American Railway: Its Construction, Development, Management, and Appliances.

Brotherhood of Railroad Trainmen to find the hostility on every page. Like the drone of a bagpipe, one can hear it when a workman puts pen to paper or when workers talk among themselves. Ordinary railroaders have written but little, but the reminiscences encouraged by editor Freeman H. Hubbard and published in the 1920s and 1930s in *Railroad Magazine* show the contempt for railroad officials held by most of the men. A conversation today with a group of rail workers will soon elicit the same response as that of a hundred years ago. One has only to read Linda Niemann's *Railroad Voices* to hear those echoes today.

On the other hand, corporate management a century ago had one goal—to preserve the level of dividends on what many critics believed was an inflated issue of company capital stock. Laissez-faire capitalism held a workman alone responsible his fate; his sufferings were of little concern to the owners. As professional managers took the place of actual owners in running the railroad, they were judged by how well they maintained profits and dividends. The largest variable expense was, and still is, employee wages, and pay was almost always the first to be cut if profits began to drop. That pay did or did not match the cost of living was of no concern. This management tactic was closed off during World War I as the brotherhoods gained new work rules and pay schedules that soon were well entrenched. Employee furloughs and maintenance deferrals became the new courses of action. Yet it was the worker who was affected most directly. Companies changed the department name from "labor relations" to "human resources" in more recent years, but this has done nothing to alter or reduce the friction between workers and managers.

SOURCES

Brotherhood of Locomotive Engineers. Official history Internet page, http://www. ble.org/pr/history/.

Foner, Philip S. *History of the Labor Movement in the United States*. Vol. 2. New York: International Publishers, 1947.

Ginger, Ray. *The Bending Cross: A Biography of Eugene Victor Debs*. New Brunswick, N.J.: Rutgers University Press, 1949.

McCaleb, Walter F. *Brotherhood of Railroad Trainmen . . .* New York: Albert & Charles Boni, 1936.

Neimann, Linda, and Lina Bertucci. *Railroad Voices*. Stanford, Calif.: Stanford University Press, 1998.

Railroad Magazine, various issues.

Building the Pere Marquette's Predecessors

James F. Joy resigned the presidency of the Chicago & Michigan Lake Shore in 1874, of the Michigan Central in 1876, and of the Detroit, Lansing & Northern in 1878. During his years as president Joy had seen them develop into strong carriers. Many of the working relationships he developed with connecting roads continue to this day. The C&MLS continued its close ties with the MC and ran its trains over MC rails into Chicago until 1903, when the Pere Marquette finally assembled its own route. The DL&N used MC tracks from West Detroit to the MC's Detroit station until 1893 and still uses them through Lansing.

Nathaniel Thayer of Boston followed Joy as president of the Chicago & Michigan Lake Shore. In November 1876, as a result of several years of rapid expansion, the company was forced into receivership and emerged two years later as the Chicago & West Michigan. In April 1881 the company changed its northern terminus to Manistee, although it never did build a line beyond Pentwater. Three months later the C&WM absorbed the Grand Haven, which had a line from Allegan to Muskegon; the Grand Rapids, Newaygo & Lake Shore, which ran from Grand Rapids to White Cloud; and the Indiana & Michigan, which built a line from New Buffalo to LaCrosse, Indiana, during 1882. Although the LaCrosse branch was only thirty-six miles long, it provided the West Michigan with important connections. It crossed every east-west line in northern Indiana, seven in all. At LaCrosse it connected with the Monon, the Chesapeake & Ohio, and the Pennsylvania, all coming from the Ohio River, and with the Chicago & Eastern Illinois from the booming southern Indiana coalfields. (The C&EI line became the Chicago, Attica & Southern in 1922.) The West Michigan granted the C&EI trackage rights on its line to New Buffalo. After the merger the C&WM abandoned its parallel line between Holland and Fruitport in favor of the Grand Haven's line through that city.

The boom in lumbering persuaded Thayer to amend the company's articles in 1889 to allow a branch from Baldwin to Mackinaw City. In 1891 the West Michigan formed the Chicago & North Michigan to build that extension. In July 1892 the line was finished through Traverse City, Charlevoix, and Petoskey, to Bay View. It never did reach Mackinaw City, but it did build a half-dozen branches into timber grounds and in 1892 a branch from Williamsburg to Elk Rapids. As the lumber traffic played out in the 1880s and 1890s there was little other freight to replace it, and the road found that its earnings barely covered expenses and interest on the company's debt. With the coming of the panic of 1893 the West Michigan began showing net losses.

The Detroit, Lansing & Northern was formed in December 1876 to reorganize the Detroit, Lansing & Lake Michigan after it went through a receivership. Bostonian Alpheus Hardy took Joy's place as president in 1878. Hardy already had joined the board of the Chicago & Michigan Lake Shore after Joy's departure in 1874. C&MLS president Nathaniel Thayer came on the DL&N board in 1874. Charles Francis Adams Jr., H. Hollis Hunnewell, Charles Merriam, George O. Shattuck, and Nathaniel Thayer Jr., all Bostonians, served on the boards of both roads. Several of them had served earlier with Joy on the board of the Michigan Central. The reorganized DL&N had a line from West Detroit through Lansing and Ionia to Howard City, a branch line from Ionia to Stanton, and a short branch into Belding. In 1878 and 1879 the DL&N extended its Ionia-Stanton line north through Edmore to Blanchard. In 1880 this line reached Big Rapids, where it connected with the Grand Rapids & Indiana and the Chicago & West Michigan.

In 1879 the DL&N bought control of the Saginaw Valley & St. Louis. That road had been built by Alma lumberman Ammi W. Wright and began operations between Saginaw and St. Louis in 1873. Its principal freight was lumber, and it was a moneymaker from the first. The DL&N's owners also formed the Saginaw & Grand Rapids in 1879 to extend their SV&SL from St. Louis to Alma. At Alma, the S&GR connected with the ambitiously named Chicago, Saginaw & Canada. This little road had been able to build twenty miles of line from St. Louis to Cedar Lake in 1875 before it went into receivership. By 1879 the CS&C's receiver built it west another sixteen miles to Lakeview.

In 1883 the CS&C was reorganized and sold to a new DL&N subsidiary, the Saginaw & Western. By 1886 the S&W extended west from Lakeview to Howard City and there made a connection with the Grand Rapids & Indiana. The DL&N began through passenger service between Saginaw and Grand Rapids over this route. The DL&N also began operating the Ithaca & Alma between those points in 1882 and ran it until 1897, when it sold the line to the Ann Arbor Railroad.

The owners of the DL&N and the Chicago & West Michigan saw merit in creating a new east-west route across Michigan with a better link between their two roads. This called for a short-cut connection between Grand Rapids and Grand Ledge. They formed the Grand Rapids, Lansing & Detroit to build this line, and by August 1888 the link was completed. Three passenger trains each way were put on between Detroit and Grand Rapids. These connected with Chicago trains, although no trains ran through nor were cars operated through. A branch was built to the amusement park at Reeds Lake in Grand Rapids. A final improvement to passenger service was made in 1893 when trains quit the Michigan Central station in Detroit and switched to the new Fort Street station. A new line to Delray was built to reach the station. This gave freight trains a route through southwestern Detroit and better access to the downriver area, the Wabash Railroad, and the Wabash's ferry service across the Detroit River.

The DL&N remained profitable until 1888, then lost money every year after. Declining lumber traffic was one reason, but other tonnage declined as well. The improved connection of 1888 with the Chicago & West Michigan proved of little benefit to the DL&N. The panic of 1893 made things worse, and the road finally went into the hands of a receiver in 1896.

In 1878 Port Huron businessmen Silas Ballentine, James Beard, Charles F. and Edmund B. Harrington, Henry Howard, John P. and Peter B. Sanborn, and Frederick L. Wells formed the Port Huron & Northwestern. It was built to bring the agricultural produce of the Thumb area to Port Huron and expected no significant lumber traffic. Howard was named the first president and was succeeded by John P. Sanborn in 1883. To improve its financial prospects its owners planned to build the road to a three-foot narrow gauge to reduce its construction costs. In 1879 the first part was put in service from Port Huron to Croswell, and by September 1880 the line was finished into Harbor Beach. By that time it had a second line under way, which was completed from Port Huron to Saginaw in February 1882. The road got some help from the Flint & Pere Marquette, which offered it the unused grade of the East Saginaw & St. Clair, permission to build along its tracks from Hoyt to its East Saginaw station, and the full use of that station. By the end of 1882 Howard built a line from Palms through Bad Axe to Port Austin and also owned a subsidiary's line from Port Huron to Almont. When completed the company owned 215 miles of road and was Michigan's longest narrow-gauge railroad. The company was marginally profitable, with the Saginaw–Port Huron section contributing enough to offset the losses from the other branches. The Flint & Pere Marquette saw potential in the PH&NW and in April 1889 bought it for $2.3 million; it allocated an additional $1.2 million to convert the tracks to standard gauge. The changeover between Saginaw and Yale was made in 1889, and in 1891 a new standard gauge route between Yale and Port Huron eliminated its difficult Black River crossing. In 1898 the Port Huron–Port Austin line gauge was changed as was the Harbor Beach branch in 1899.

The Saginaw, Tuscola & Huron was a second line running into the Thumb. It was formed by a combination of Saginaw businessmen and investors in the Flint & Pere Marquette. Between 1882 and July 1886, with the support of the F&PM, it built a three-foot narrow-gauge line out of Saginaw to Bad Axe. The need to transship freight at Saginaw reduced the road's profitability until it was converted to standard gauge in 1891. Despite their close ties the F&PM did not acquire the ST&H until 1900, when both roads were combined into the new Pere Marquette company.

The Flint & Pere Marquette completed its line across Michigan from Monroe to Ludington in 1874. No sooner was it finished than the business depression brought on by the panic of 1873 reduced income sharply. It was not until 1879 that the picture improved sufficiently to allow more expansion. Two wholly owned subsidiaries added to the company's mileage. In 1879 the Saginaw & Mt. Pleasant built a line from Coleman to Mt. Pleasant and the Saginaw & Clare County began a branch from Clare, which was completed into Harrison in 1880. For some reason the Mt. Pleasant road was built as a three-foot narrow-gauge line, but it was converted to standard gauge in 1884. By that time the F&PM had accumulated a loss of $2.2 million, and management decided that the road should go through a "friendly" receivership, with general manager Henry C. Potter as receiver. The ownership of the road did not change during the receivership, but in 1882 William W. Crapo replaced the late Jesse Hoyt as president. Crapo was the son of Governor Henry H. Crapo, who had built the Flint & Holly in 1863. William joined the F&PM board of directors after his father's death in 1869, developed his railroading skills, and became a vice president in 1876.

In 1881 the wholly owned Manistee Railroad built from Walhalla to Manistee to give the F&PM access to that important saw-milling port. There were some miscellaneous branches built into lumbering areas during the 1880s, reflecting Crapo's conservative approach to the business, but in the 1890s a more aggressive building program was undertaken. Throughout the 1880s and 1890s the F&PM built and abandoned at least 100 miles of logging branches, most of them in Clare County, in an attempt to keep lumber flowing into Saginaw. Eventually the lumber was gone and by 1900 so were most of the logging branches.

The Fort Street Union Depot Company was organized in 1890 under the joint control of the F&PM, the Detroit, Lansing & Northern, the

Three different companies merged to form the Pere Marquette system in 1900.

KEY

BUILT OR OWNED

1875 AND LATER		BEFORE 1874
▄▄▄▄	Flint & Pere Marquette	▬▬▬
▄ ▄ ▄	Chicago & West Michigan	▬ ▬
+ + + +	Detroit, Lansing & Northern and successor	+ + +

Wabash, and the Canadian Pacific to build and operate a new union railroad station for Detroit. The F&PM worked with the Detroit, Lansing & Northern to build a new line from Oak to Delray to reach the new station; that line was finished in January 1893, and the station opened the same month. The F&PM stopped using the Michigan Central from Wayne to reach Detroit, as did the DL&N from West Detroit. In 1893 the F&PM formed the Monroe & Toledo Railway to build an extension to give it direct access to connecting railroads in Toledo in hopes of improving freight revenues, and opened the line to business in November 1896.

The Lake Michigan port Ludington was the site of another important step. As early as 1875 the F&PM hired the ship *John Sherman* to carry freight from the railroad at Ludington to a railroad at Sheboygan, Wisconsin. This was a break-bulk operation in which freight had to be reloaded from railcar to ship at one port and from to ship to car at the other. In 1876 the F&PM hired several ships from the Goodrich Line, and sailings began to several Wisconsin ports. By 1880 sailings started to Milwaukee, and this developed into the most important route. In 1883 the F&PM ended its charter of Goodrich ships and bought two ships for its service. The competition from other lake shipping companies for freight business was intense, and the railroad apparently could not make through rates at a level to assure a profit. During the late 1880s the F&PM had three more ships built to handle rail business. Grain shipments moving eastbound developed into the most important traffic, and the ships were designed to handle grain in bulk.

Railcar ferry service began at the Straits of Mackinac in 1882. In 1892 James M. Ashley's railroad began car ferry operations out of Frankfort, and the *Sainte Marie* was delivered to the straits in 1893. President Crapo and General Manager Henry C. Potter watched this development closely and decided to adopt it for the Ludington-Manitowoc service, its shortest cross-lake route. They arranged with the Wisconsin Central for a ferry slip on the west shore of Lake Michigan and in 1896 contracted with Cleveland naval architect Robert Logan to build a steel railroad car ferry. In December 1896 the *Pere Marquette* was launched at Bay City and made its first Lake Michigan voyage on the night of 16 February 1897 to Manitowoc, carrying twenty-two freight cars and new F&PM general manager Stanford T. Crapo's private car.

The ferry service helped keep the F&PM in the black. Lumber traffic began to drop sharply by 1890, and there was no lack of competition for other kinds of freight. The ferries brought grain and flour traffic that the railroad would not have been able to get any other way. The increased freight tonnage, passengers, and revenue that came through the ferry service and new routes more than offset the other reductions. The extension of the line to Toledo also made a substantial contribution. The F&PM continued to show profits throughout the panic of 1893 and afterward.

SOURCES

Frederickson, Arthur C., and Lucy F. Frederickson. *Pictorial History of the C&O Train and Auto Ferries*. Rev. ed. Ludington, Mich.: Lakeside, 1955.

Hilton, George W. *The Great Lakes Car Ferries*. Berkeley, Calif.: Howell-North, 1962.

————. *American Narrow Gauge Railroads.* Stanford, Calif.: Stanford University
Press, 1990.

Ivey, Paul Wesley. *The Pere Marquette Railroad: An Historical Study of the Growth
and Development of One of Michigan's Most Important Railway Systems.* Lansing:
Michigan Historical Commission, 1919. Reprint, Grand Rapids, Mich.: Black
Letter Press, 1970.

Kirkpatrick, Frank A. "The Saginaw, Tuscola & Huron: An Early Railroad of the
Thumb Peninsula." *Michigan History* 52:2 (Summer 1968).

Meints, Graydon M. *Michigan Railroads and Railroad Companies.* East Lansing:
Michigan State University Press, 1992.

Michigan Railroad Commission. *Aids, Gifts, Grants and Donations to Railroads . . .*
Lansing, Mich.: Wynkoop, Hallenbeck, Crawford, 1919.

Simons, Richard S., and Francis H. Parker. *Railroads of Indiana.* Bloomington:
Indiana University Press, 1997.

Street Railways, Part 2

The largest and strongest of the street railway companies in Detroit
was the Detroit City Railway, managed by George Hendrie. In 1875 it
bought the Russell Street company and gradually abandoned parts of it
until it was completely gone by 1878. Some of the tracks removed were
used to put a double track on Michigan Avenue. In 1876 Hendrie and
his associates bought the Detroit City company, which brought that
road into local ownership. In 1876 the Central Market company began
extending on Larned east of Woodward. Hendrie objected to the city to
the extension, and the mayor agreed. Work stopped, and the next year
the Central Market went into receivership. It changed its name to the
Cass Avenue Railway, but that change did it no good. Hendrie bought
the company, and the Detroit City now ran five lines.

In 1876 the Congress & Baker company wanted to extend its line
eastward from Woodward Avenue, but it ran into the same difficulties
at city hall. There was talk of an extension west from Twenty-Second
Street, but the company could find no financial assistance and had to
give up the idea. Eventually its owners gave up their struggles with city
hall and in June 1882 sold the line to the Detroit City company. The
horsecar lines in Detroit built modest extensions during the late 1870s.

The financial panics of 1873 and 1877 slowed the growth of the
street railways in Michigan, but as the effects ebbed the money began
to flow once again. More extensions were built in Detroit to reach

As Detroit grew in size, so, too, did the number of horsecars—and the number of horses to pull them. The care and feeding of those horses, with their attendant refuse, was not only a major expense but also a considerable sanitation problem.

Jack E. Schramm, from DSR files.

more "suburban" areas. There was additional growth in the lines in Grand Rapids and Saginaw and new interest developed in other cities. Muskegon received its first horsecar line in 1882. Battle Creek had one the next year, and Kalamazoo had a line in 1885. Both Jackson and Lansing received horsecars in 1886. A line connecting Benton Harbor with St. Joseph was built in the late 1880s. Mt. Clemens obtained its first line in 1890.

Despite their growth, the horsecar lines faced substantial difficulties. Companies needed to maintain large stables of horses to pull cars. In 1886 the forty-three miles of line operated in Detroit required 155 cars, 1,470 horses, and 607 men to operate. A company needed from six to ten horses to pull each car. The horses were subject to a variety of illnesses, had a useful life of only about four years, and brought little at resale. They moved at a uniform slow speed of about four to five miles per hour. They required a special crew to keep them stabled, fed, watered, and in good health. So long as the terrain was quite flat, they could work satisfactorily, but they could not pull cars up much of a grade.

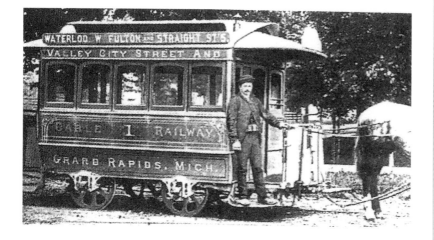

It was the late 1880s when this Grand Rapids horsecar posed for this photo. The horse and car were retired in the early 1890s when all the lines in the city were changed over to electric operation.

When Grand Rapids wanted to establish a car line on Lyon Street from Monroe, the hill was determined to be too steep for horse-pulled cars to surmount. The promoters of the line adopted something new—introduced only nine years earlier in San Francisco—the cable car. Cars were pulled by a continuously moving steel cable that was guided between the rails just below the surface of the street. In 1885 the Valley City Street Cable Railway started operating, and despite occasional mechanical malfunctions, it did provide service. As the company extended its lines farther out it used horsecars as well as its cable operations. When the city council granted the Valley City franchise, it included a line on Monroe Street, where its competitor, The Street Railway Company of Grand Rapids, already was operating. The Street Railway took the matter to court but eventually lost and had to tolerate its competitor's rails. In 1886 the Street Railway acquired three connecting lines: Division Street, Reeds Lake, and one on the west side. The Valley City soon developed financial problems. Some of its lines competed against the Street Railway's, and others were lightly patronized. More important, the cable mechanical system proved quite expensive. It had cost too much to install and cost substantially more than expected to maintain. In 1890 the Valley City and the Street Railway merged and in 1891 became the Consolidated Street Railway. The company now operated all of the street railway lines in Grand Rapids except those of two recently formed companies, the North Park Street Railway and the South Grand Rapids Street Railway.

The prosperity that returned in the early 1880s brought demands by many cities that lines be extended farther into the suburbs. Fortune smiled with a new form of power, electricity. In 1880 Thomas Alva

Edison built an electric locomotive but never tried to find a practical use for it. In 1883 Leo Daft and Charles VanDepoele, two inventors working independently, both demonstrated a streetcar that moved by electricity. Daft's system used a low-voltage exposed third rail to deliver electricity to the car. The danger of this approach was eventually reduced by placing the power in a slotted rail between the two running rails. Daft later devised a four-wheeled device that the streetcar pulled along on two overhead wires. Daft called his device a "troller," from which we can reasonably assume that "trolley" was the people's pronunciation. VanDepoele used a single overhead wire and a wheel, mounted on a pole extending from the roof of the car that pressed against the wire to draw current. VanDepoele's design had simplicity in its favor, but the chain drive he used to connect the electric motor to the car axle was unsatisfactory.

Frank J. Sprague may properly be called the father of the electric streetcar. His experiments, while in the U.S. Navy and later with Thomas Edison, solved VanDepoele's motor problems and those of Daft's current pickup. In 1887 Richmond, Virginia, ordered a Sprague system, and when it opened in 1888 it was a great success.

In September 1886 the Detroit Electric Railway began running cars on Vernor between Twenty-Fourth Street and the west city limits using VanDepoele's electric system. The company may have chosen him from a familiarity with the installation he made in Windsor, Ontario, some months earlier. In Port Huron the horsecar line was reorganized as the Port Huron Electric Railway, and it installed VanDepoele's electric system. This was the first use of electricity on a street railway in Michigan outside of Detroit. Unfortunately, VanDepoele's equipment did not work as well as expected, and it took a good deal of tinkering and adjusting to get it to operate to some degree of satisfaction. The company had a first when it devised a way to transmit power to the Black River swing bridge; it also had to install an underwater cable to transmit power to the lines across the river.

Horsecar companies in other Michigan cities began to see the immense advantages of electricity over horse power, especially as Sprague built and refined his systems, and these companies began to convert to electric operations in the early 1890s. By 1895 the changeover of Michigan street railways was complete, and the horses were retired.

George Hendrie's Detroit City Railway continued to be the largest of Detroit's street railways. As prosperity returned Hendrie bought the Hamtramck Street company in 1881, and integrated this extension of his

George Hendrie

Born 9 February 1834, Glasgow, Scotland; died 20 December 1913, Detroit.

Hendrie left Scotland for Canada in 1859, where he operated a cartage business, until prospects appeared brighter and he moved to Detroit and another cartage business. In 1866 he leased and operated the Detroit City Railway, a horsecar line, and ten years later bought the company. From that time on he founded several other important horsecar lines. In 1890 he formed the Detroit Street Railway to take over and electrify the Detroit City Railway. In 1893 he sold off his street railway investments, but found a new fascination in the new electric interurban business. He formed several small roads on the north side of Detroit, which eventually became part of the Detroit United Railways. From 1904 until 1911 he was president of the Grand Rapids, Holland & Chicago interurban line, his last active involvement in electric railways.

In 1879 he joined with James McMillan and other Detroiters to form the Detroit, Mackinaw & Marquette, a company that built a line between St. Ignace and Marquette in 1881. He continued as a director of the road until its sale to the Duluth, South Shore & Atlantic in 1886. Between 1908 and 1914 he was a director of the Traverse City, Leelanau & Manistique.

In an addition to his rails, Hendrie's interests included the Detroit Savings Bank, the Detroit Taxi Cab Company, and the Detroit & Cleveland Navigation and Boat Company.

Jefferson Avenue line. In 1882 he acquired the Cass Avenue and Congress & Baker companies. This left only two independent companies, the financially weak Grand River and the Fort Wayne & Elmwood, the latter of which was newly renamed from the extended Fort Street & Elmwood company.

The late 1880s brought several new companies that extended farther into the suburbs of Detroit. In 1886 the Highland Park Railway and the Detroit Electric were formed, and in 1887 the East Detroit & Grosse Pointe and the Hamtramck & Grosse Pointe were founded. All but the Hamtramck companies had charter provisions to use electricity. Real estate developer Frank Snow was one of the prime movers behind the Highland Park and the East Detroit lines. George Hendrie and James McMillan were founders of the Hamtramck Street company, which was planned as an easterly extension of the Detroit City's Jefferson Avenue line. The company used a Healy motor, a steam-powered "dummy" engine, partly out of necessity since the road had rights to handle freight and also carried U.S. mail.

Hendrie became convinced of the need to convert the Detroit City's horsecar lines to electric power, and in November 1890 he formed the

Hazen S. Pingree, the owner of the largest shoe factory in the Midwest, became Detroit's mayor in January 1890. He soon began a personal war with the owners of the Detroit City Railway about inadequate service, too high fares, and too small payments to the city for franchises. When Pingree became governor in January 1897, he tried to stay on as mayor at the same time. The Michigan Supreme Court forced him to choose just one office, but the war he began with the railroads continued long after he went to Lansing.

Henry M. Utley and Byron M. Cutcheon, *Michigan as a Province, Territory, and State* (New York, 1906), 4:facing 226.

Detroit Street Railway, a new company with a capitalization to cover the changeover as well as some other needed improvements. When he applied to city hall for a transfer of the Detroit City's franchises to his new company, Hendrie ran into a political buzz saw.

In the November 1889 election the Republicans made an all-out effort to wrench city hall away from the Democratic Party. As candidate for mayor they ran Hazen S. Pingree, an owner of the Pingree & Smith shoe company, reputedly the largest shoe manufacturer west of the Hudson River. James McMillan, the head of everything Republican, thought Pingree would be a safe member of the "club" to put into the mayor's office. McMillan was completely wrong.

In his inaugural address to Common Council in January 1890 Pingree announced that Detroit's cedar block street paving should be replaced by asphalt or stone, that land held on speculation should be taxed at the same rate as improved property, and that the city should own its own electric light plant, and to these he added other complaints and projects. He reserved special ammunition for George Hendrie, informing him that the city deserved better street railway transportation and that in the future franchises would be awarded only to the highest bidder. Pingree believed the Detroit City's franchise was worth between $5 and $6 million, well below the company's valuation, and that it should set its fares to earn a satisfactory return on this figure. There was no doubt in the mayor's mind that 3 cents, not 5 cents or 6 cents, was a fare that would provide an adequate return. Moreover, Pingree knew the street railways paid a grand total of $12,000 in taxes to the city in 1890. To the mayor, the citizens were being overcharged in fares, and the city underpaid in taxes and for franchises. When Hendrie's franchise request got to his desk the mayor returned it unsigned. Pingree said the line's current franchise was due to expire in 1892, and Hendrie might well prepare himself to cut a much different deal with the city than the ones he had gotten in the past. Common Council upheld the mayor 18-0, and the franchise expiration date affair wound up in court.

Later that year Hendrie's employees went on strike when the company announced its plans to cut wages when hours were reduced. The mayor proclaimed that the employees were in the right and that the company should settle with them immediately. Don M. Dickinson, President Cleveland's future postmaster general, is said to have led a mob that rolled a streetcar down the tracks and into the Detroit River. Hendrie caved in and settled.

In November 1890 Hendrie transferred his Detroit City company

John Burritt Mulliken

Born 30 May 1837, Campbell, N.Y.; died November 1892, Detroit.

Mulliken was raised in Crete, Illinois, and at age fifteen moved to Maumee, Ohio, where first he clerked for his uncle, then worked two years for James M. Ashley. Back in Illinois he worked for the post office, and then for the Illinois Central Railroad. In 1856 he joined the Galena & Chicago Union in Chicago, later serving as its agent at Rockford and Belvedere, Illinois. He became a general agent for the Chicago & North Western at Winona, Minnesota, and in October 1874 was promoted to division superintendent at Escanaba.

Mulliken moved to the Detroit, Lansing & Lake Michigan (later renamed Detroit, Lansing & Northern) in May 1875 as general superintendent at Detroit and became its general manager in May 1877. In June 1879 the Saginaw Valley & St. Louis was added to his duties; he became its general manager and in July 1884 its president. At that time he was given added responsibility as vice president and general manager of the Chicago & West Michigan. In 1887–88 he supervised construction of a new line between Grand Ledge and Grand Rapids. One community along this new line was founded in 1888 and named Mulliken in his honor.

He resigned from the railroad in March 1890 because of his health, and became a commissioner on Detroit's board of public works. The next year he was one of the organizers of the Detroit Citizens' Street Railway and served a short time as its first manager.

to his new Detroit Street Railway. In August 1891 a different group of businessmen formed the Detroit Citizens' Street Railway. With a capitalization of $4 million it planned to buy both the Detroit Street Railway and the Grand River line. Of its first board of directors only John B. Mulliken and Hoyt Post were from Detroit. Hendries sold his Detroit Street to the Detroit Citizens' in September 1891, and soon thereafter the Citizens' bought the Grand River company. George Hendrie was tiring of the never-ending battles with city hall. Dealings never had been completely smooth, but his companies usually fared quite well. With Pingree as mayor, he faced an implacable opponent.

In May 1893 the U.S. Circuit Court handed down its decision about the street railway franchise extension date. It went against Hendrie. He appealed the decision to the U.S. Court of Appeals, which promptly reversed the circuit court and held that the franchises were valid until 1909. The Michigan Supreme Court refused to hear the matter at all. Mayor Pingree was furious at this outcome. Despite negotiations between the Citizens' general manager, James D. Hawks, and Common Council, no settlement could be reached acceptable to the mayor. For Pingree, the only solution was a new street railway to take on Hendries and one that would charge only a 3-cent fare. It took some time to find anyone interested in financing the venture, but eventually Pingree managed to interest Albert, Charles L., and Greene Pack of Detroit and Henry A. Everett of Cleveland. The Packs had made their money in lumbering in the Oscoda and Alpena regions; Everett owned a number of local telephone companies in Ohio and also had investments in several street railway companies in Canada.

About 1893 Hendries and the other owners sold the Citizens' to a New York–based group of owners. At its head was Richard T. Wilson, a New York City investment broker. One of Wilson's associates was Tom L. Johnson, who thought he had to remain a silent partner until his term in Congress expired, at which time he became president of the company. General Manager Hawks several years earlier had come to the Citizens' from the Michigan Central, and now was preparing to assume the presidency of the Detroit, Bay City & Alpena. In a stroke of great fortune Wilson hired Jere C. Hutchins, who was in line to become a top officer of the Louisville & Nashville. Hutchins arrived in Detroit in November 1894. During 1895 the Citizens' began to electrify its streetcar lines, and by November Hutchins finished the project.

At this same time Pingree's new Detroit Railway was starting to build some lines. Since the Citizens' had rights over most of the major city streets, the Detroit had to build on others. In July 1896 service began on the first line, and by May 1896 Pingree's system was fairly well completed. His dream of a 3-cent fare line (actually 3⅛> cents) was a reality. Late in 1895 the Citizens' raised its fare from six rides for 25 cents to a flat 5 cents, and Pingree's lines got more riders out of that.

There was a fair amount of contact between the two companies when they had to work out operating facilities and joint trackage. Pingree became suspicious that Wilson and Johnson, with their ample financing, had designs on the Detroit Railway. Through their necessary contacts Hutchins and Albert Pack became fairly good friends. Johnson's fare increase hurt ridership and revenues, so he dropped fares back to the level of the competition. This reduction did not restore enough revenue, so he went back to the six rides for 25 cents fare.

In July 1896 Pack and Everett, now joined by Everett's Cleveland associate Edward W. Moore, formed the Detroit Electric Railway. A need to raise more capital was the reason given, but Pingree rightly thought the change was suspect. He did not know that Pack had approached Hutchins about Wilson and Johnson's Citizens' company taking over the Detroit Railway. Pingree's suspicious grew when Pack closed his

power-generating plant and began to buy electricity from the Citizens'
company. Hutchins relayed Pack's proposal to Wilson, and it was agreed
to. The mayor was furious when he found out that his dream company
had been leased to the hated Citizens' company. At this same time the
Citizens' leased the Detroit Suburban Railway, a company that over
time had acquired five different routes outside the Detroit city limits.

SOURCES

Baxter, Albert. *History of the City of Grand Rapids, Michigan*. New York: Munsell,
    1891.

Dunbar, Willis F. *All Aboard! A History of Railroads in Michigan*. Grand Rapids,
    Mich.: W. B. Eerdmans, 1969.

History of Saginaw County, Michigan. Chicago: Chas. C. Chapman, 1881.

Hutchins, Jere C. *Jere C. Hutchins: A Personal Story*. Detroit: author, 1938.

Lee, Robert E. "The Streetcar Lines of Grand Rapids" *Michigan History* 46:1 (March
    1962).

Schramm, Jack E., and William H. Henning. *Detroit's Street Railways*. Vol. 1, *City
    Lines 1863–1922*. Chicago: Central Electric Railfans' Association, 1978.

———. *When Eastern Michigan Rode the Rails, Book 2*. Glendale, Calif.: Interurban
    Press, 1986.

Zink, Maximillian A., and George Krambles, eds. *Electric Railways of Michigan,
    Bulletin 103*. Chicago: Central Electric Railfans Association, 1959.

Birth of the Interurban

Ypsilanti wanted a street railway only because its sister city, Ann Arbor,
had one. As a promoter of street railways Charles D. Haines was the
man that Ypsilanti needed. A native of Kinderhook, New York, Haines
looked over 1890 Ypsilanti and thought that it was too small to support
its own line, but he had another idea. He suggested the organizers build
a line to connect Ypsilanti with the street railway line in Ann Arbor,
eight miles away. Haines claimed the line would carry 500 riders a day
at a 10-cent fare. Its competitor, the Michigan Central, carried only forty
passengers a day between the two cities, charging 25 cents to do so.

Haines hired a contractor from New York State to build the line. It
cost $45,000 to build from downtown Ypsilanti and along Packard Road
to the Ann Arbor city limits. This amount included a Porter "dummy"
engine—an engine enclosed to appear like a passenger car and painted

cardinal red—and two passenger cars painted canary yellow. Most of the money came from a mortgage loan of $40,000. The road asked permission to operate over the street railway into downtown Ann Arbor, but some residents objected to a steam engine on city streets. The company had to settle with transferring its passengers to the street railway at the city limits.

It took about three months to build the line. The first official run was on 3 January 1891 and carried invited dignitaries and newspapermen from both cities. President Junius E. Beal recounted that the riders

> went out on the electric car to the Ann Arbor city limits where transfers were made to the steam motor. Fortunately, it did not jump the track on that excursion trip and it only set fire to one barn. But that was soon put out and the party was safely landed in Ypsilanti. Not wishing to run any more risks they were all returned home on the Michigan Central night train, declaring the road a success because no one was killed or even maimed for life.

Regular service began on 9 January, with a train running every ninety minutes. The line was an immediate success. Ridership soared to as high as 600 people a day. It probably helped that Ann Arbor's University of Michigan had 5,000 male students and relatively few females, while Ypsilanti had the Normal school—the teacher training school—with 1,000 female students and few males. Also, farmers along the line could buy a coupon book for seventeen rides for $1. Beal recalled that because it ran through farm country,

> horses, cows and chickens were occasionally offered up as sacrifices. Whether they were sometimes very old and driven on the track purposely or not by the owner, the road never had a suit, but always settled for the live stock. This kept the good will of the farmers and they would turn out in the night or storm to help boost the motor back on the track.

Ann Arbor newspaperman Beal was president and general manager of the tiny line, Ypsilanti mayor Henry Glover was vice president, Joseph Jacobs was secretary, and Ypsilanti businessman Daniel L. Quirk was treasurer. Haines's interest was in building the road, not in owning it, and soon after it was opened he sold his $45,000 in stock to Glover. During the spring thaw of 1891 the owners found that Haines had built

ABOVE: The "Ypsi-Ann" used a steam engine hidden inside in a passenger coach. This design was supposed not to frighten horses when it ran on city streets. The engine-car became known as a "dummy," and the road that used them was called "the dummy line." This car was replaced by an electric one in 1896.

C. T. Stoner collection, Bentley Historical Library, University of Michigan.

LEFT: An enterprising Ann Arbor merchant issued this very early timetable of the "Ypsi-Ann" service. Cars ran between Ypsilanti and the city limits of Ann Arbor, where riders had to transfer to city horsecars. Residents wanted no part of the steam-powered "dummy" on city streets.

Jack E. Schramm collection.

one section of the line on frozen ground, and they had to rebuild that part. It took another loan of $20,000 to get the road into proper operating shape. In January 1891 Glover bought the Ann Arbor street railway system and merged it into the "Ypsi-Ann." The two companies continued to be operated separately, and the "dummy" trains still ran only to the Ann Arbor city limits.

In 1896 Glover and Beal decided that the two companies should be merged. A new line, the Ann Arbor & Ypsilanti Electric Railway, took over. The "dummy" engine was beginning to show its age and would have to be replaced. By the end of year the "Ypsi-Ann" had overhead electric wires in place, and the "dummy" was retired. This allowed the cars from Ypsilanti to run into downtown Ann Arbor. Operating expenses totaled $60 a day, and receipts often topped $100. The "Ypsi-Ann" entered history as a pioneer, and service continued over the route until the end of the interurban era.

SOURCES

Beal, Junius E. "The Beginnings of Interurbans." *Michigan Pioneer & Historical Collections* 35 (1907). Lansing, Mich.: Wynkoop, Hallenbeck, Crawford, 1907.

Dunbar, William F. *All Aboard! A History of Railroads in Michigan*. Grand Rapids, Mich.: W. B. Eerdmans, 1969.

Schramm, Jack E., William H. Henning, and Richard R. Andrews. *When Eastern Michigan Rode the Rails, Book 3*. Glendale, Calif.: Interurban Press, 1988.

The Golden Years, 1897–1920

The Twentieth Century Opens

Despite the severity of the short depression following the panic of 1895, the ebullience that preceded it could not be kept down for long and in fact soon reasserted itself. President Grover Cleveland, a Democrat with law-and-order attitudes who helped to break the Pullman strike in 1894, was blamed for the financial panic. The voters replaced him in 1896 with Republican William McKinley. Prosperity returned, thanks in part to the Spanish-American War and in part because industries began to renew their aggressive development of foreign markets. In September 1901, less than a year into his second term, Cleveland was assassinated while attending the Pan-American Exposition at Buffalo, New York.

Vice President Theodore Roosevelt replaced McKinley. Roosevelt also was thought to have a generally conservative attitude toward business, but at the same time political leaders knew he did hold some new and individualistic views as to how business should conduct itself. Because of these opinions he was "kicked upstairs" to become McKinley's vice president, this done in an attempt to retain his political value yet to quiet him after seeing his "reformist" attitudes as governor of New York. An intelligent man, very well read and a writer, and wealthy as well, his insight into the evolution of American business over the preceding half century as well as the changes in American society had made him into a markedly different politician. He had read the muckrakers—Ida Tarbell, Upton Sinclair, and others—and was prepared to force American business to accept new responsibilities and standards for its conduct.

Roosevelt was particularly irritated at one form of business conduct. Beginning after the Civil War a group of companies in a particular field of business would make "pooling" agreements between themselves to divide a market, guarantee prices and standards, and use any means available to stabilize and maximize profits. As the American railroad network approached maturity in the 1890s, corporate management also underwent a change. The days of the buccaneer were over; the old no-holds-barred techniques no longer produced the gains they once did. Stability of profits with a steady stream of revenue that covered interest charges became the new goal, with enough left over to pay ample dividends to the owners. Railroad owners turned increasingly to professional managers, men who knew how to pump up income and squeeze costs and who would hold to agreements to protect the dividends. One form these agreements took was to use pooling, as used by other industries. In 1897 the Supreme Court used the Sherman Anti-Trust Act of 1890 to strike down one pooling agreement, the Trans-Missouri Traffic Association. The decision put this entire approach in jeopardy and exposed the participants to prosecution.

Businesses then adopted consolidations and mergers as the means of protecting themselves, but these formed new and still larger companies. John D. Rockefeller's Standard Oil and J. P. Morgan's U.S. Steel were the two largest; hundred of companies in dozens of other lesser industries formed similar combinations. Both the Pennsylvania Railroad and the Vanderbilts' New York Central continued to add completed roads to their systems. In fact, some railroad magnates went a long step further and began to assemble coast-to-coast empires. With ample funds from J. P. Morgan and some other banking houses, and with the bankers adequately protecting themselves with seats on the various boards of directors, the railroadmen plunged ahead. In 1906 seven groups had divided up and were in control of two-thirds of the rail mileage of the United States: the Vanderbilt family (New York Central roads and Chicago & North Western); the Pennsylvania Railroad (which included the Baltimore & Ohio and Chesapeake & Ohio); J. P. Morgan (the Erie, the Southern, and other roads in the south); Jay Gould and his son George (Missouri Pacific, Wabash, Texas & Pacific, and others); William H. Moore (Rock Island and other midwestern roads); James J. Hill (Great Northern, Northern Pacific, and Burlington); or Edward H. Harriman (Union Pacific, Southern Pacific, Illinois Central). A few of these managers were men of considerable ability in management, gave their roads a good physical plant and equipment, and provided a quality of service that could earn good profits. In the end Gould and Moore left such sorry legacies that it took their properties decades to recover after they were gone. Harriman and Morgan ownerships produced some good and some disastrous results. Some of the less important roads made their way into other smaller combinations with varying results.

In Michigan, Frederick H. Prince's control of the Pere Marquette became as shameful a spectacle as could be found.

In 1902 President Roosevelt decided to apply his "reform" standards against the Northern Securities Company, a holding company formed by James J. Hill and J. P. Morgan to own the Great Northern and Northern Pacific roads. The Supreme Court found that Northern Securities constituted a "restraint of trade" by deciding in the government's favor, as it also did some years later when it considered the Union Pacific's ownership of the Southern Pacific. Despite the predictable protest from wealthy businessmen and political contributors, Roosevelt held on to wide support among the voters and in 1904 won a second term by a wider margin than had McKinley in 1900. This encouraged Roosevelt to try for enhanced powers to regulate interstate commerce and apply it to the railroads in particular. He was only partially successful, and it was left to his successor, William H. Taft, to carry on Roosevelt's policies in 1909. Taft had some further success in getting new regulations passed, legislation that had eluded his predecessor. Despite this the 1912 election replaced the Republican Taft with Democrat Woodrow Wilson, and the voters bypassed as well Theodore Roosevelt who ran as an independent. Wilson further strengthened federal government control over businesses generally and railroads particularly. Wilson was in office when the United States eventually entered World War I in 1917 and gave strong support for federal control of the railroads during the war.

SOURCES

Cochrane, Thomas C., and William Miller. *The Age of Enterprise*. Rev. ed. New York: Harper & Row, 1961.

Johnson, Paul. *A History of the American People*. New York: HarperCollins, 1997.

Morison, Samuel Eliot. *The Oxford History of the American People*. New York: Oxford University Press, 1965.

Completing the Network

The twenty-year railroad-building spree in Michigan was nearly done by 1895. By that year only a few more lines remained to be built to complete Michigan's railroad network. The railroad commissioner reported that Michigan had 7,609 miles of railroad line at the end of 1895. This grew by another 20 percent by 1909 to an all-time high of 9,059 miles. After that nearly every year saw abandonments more than offsetting new construction. By 1920 Michigan's rail mileage had dropped to 8,734, a loss of 325 miles. The national rail system continued to expand until 1916, to a total of 254,037 miles, a growth that continued for so long largely due to construction in the western states. Only 1,200 miles were abandoned nationally by the end of 1920.

The major carriers in Michigan—the New York Central and its Michigan Central subsidiary, the Grand Rapids & Indiana, the Pere Marquette, and the Grand Trunk Western—were substantially complete in covering the Lower Peninsula. They did build and abandon lumbering branches, particularly in the northern Lower Peninsula, but this caused little net change in mileage. The longest nonlumbering branch built after 1900 was eighteen miles built by the Grand Trunk Western in 1913, from Cass City to Bad Axe.

Smaller carriers did build some additional lines. In 1895 the Lima Northern, the oldest predecessor of the Detroit, Toledo & Ironton, began building a line north from Lima, Ohio, to a connection with the Wabash Railroad at Seneca, southwest of Adrian, completing it in 1896. To improve its prospects it decided to have its own line into Detroit. The company changed its name to the Detroit & Lima Northern in 1897, and that year built an extension from Adrian to Tecumseh and got running rights over the Wabash between Seneca and Adrian. In 1898 it built a line from Delray, on the southwest side of Detroit, to a point just south of Trenton called Chandler. To close the gap between Tecumseh and Chandler it bought, in 1897, part of an unused Lake Shore & Michigan Southern line from Chandler southwest to Dundee. This was a part of the line built by the Chicago & Canada Southern from Grosse Ile to Fayette, Ohio, when it was attempting to build to Chicago. The purchase of this section and running rights between Tecumseh and Dundee over the Detroit, Toledo & Milwaukee gave the D&LN a through but rather roundabout line between Detroit and Lima, Ohio. Doing all of this was such a financial strain that the road went into receivership the next year. In 1901 it was reorganized as the Detroit Southern, and it built its own line between Seneca and Adrian and ended its running rights over the Wabash. Detroit Southern also bought the line of the Ohio Southern between Lima and Springfield, Ohio, as a southern extension and then began planning for a further extension to reach the Ohio River. Then the DS went through receivership in 1905 and emerged as the Detroit, Toledo & Ironton, with new owners who named Eugene Zimmerman of Toledo as president. Zimmerman also bought control of the Ann Arbor

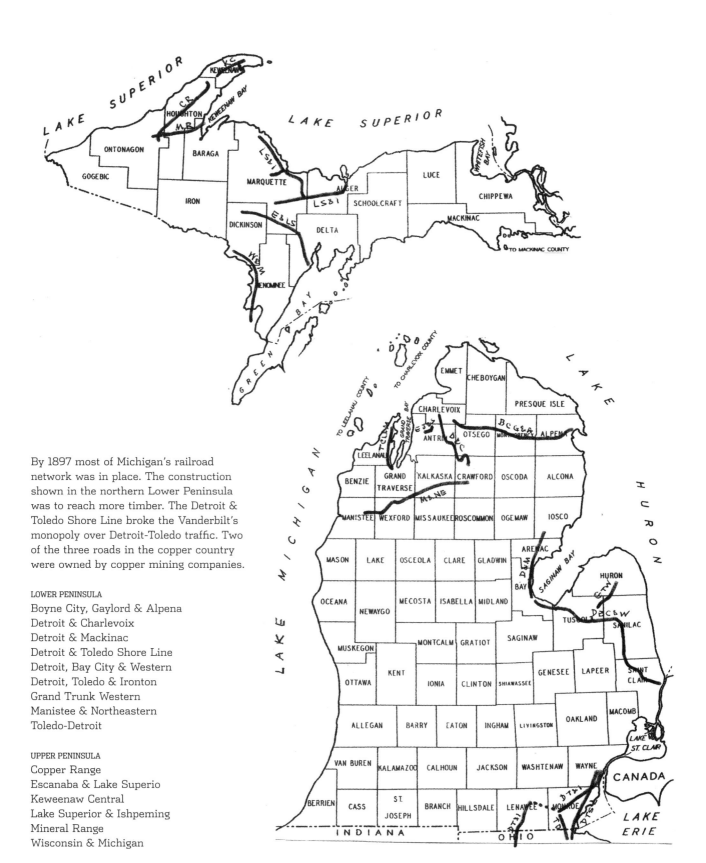

By 1897 most of Michigan's railroad network was in place. The construction shown in the northern Lower Peninsula was to reach more timber. The Detroit & Toledo Shore Line broke the Vanderbilt's monopoly over Detroit-Toledo traffic. Two of the three roads in the copper country were owned by copper mining companies.

LOWER PENINSULA
Boyne City, Gaylord & Alpena
Detroit & Charlevoix
Detroit & Mackinac
Detroit & Toledo Shore Line
Detroit, Bay City & Western
Detroit, Toledo & Ironton
Grand Trunk Western
Manistee & Northeastern
Toledo-Detroit

UPPER PENINSULA
Copper Range
Escanaba & Lake Superio
Keweenaw Central
Lake Superior & Ishpeming
Mineral Range
Wisconsin & Michigan

Railroad, in the hope that it would provide an added source of freight traffic and probably to provide the DT&I with access to Toledo. The traffic hopes soon faded; the DT&I sold the Ann Arbor in 1910 and was reorganized from yet another receivership. It emerged from this now called the Detroit, Toledo & Ironton Railroad, instead of Railway. The DT&I found that access to Toledo, which the Ann Arbor had provided, was a benefit worth having. It was able to gain its own access in 1916 when it leased the Toledo-Detroit Railroad. The Toledo-Detroit had been dreamed of for a dozen years under other names as an interurban line from Toledo to either Ann Arbor or Jackson. Between 1913 and 1915 the T-D built a line from Toledo as far as Petersburg, where it connected with the DT&I, which promptly took it over.

In southeastern Michigan the Detroit & Toledo Shore Line was completed between Detroit and Toledo in 1903. The road began in 1898 when a group of Toledo men formed the Pleasant Bay Railway, planning to build a line from Toledo to Otter Creek south of Monroe. In March 1899 they renamed it the Detroit & Toledo Shore Line. In April 1901 the company sold its partially completed line out of Toledo to Henry A. Everett and Edward W. Moore, the interurban promoters from Cleveland. The new owners continued building, intending to make it an interurban line rather than a steam railroad. By early 1902 the road was almost complete between Toledo and Trenton when Everett and Moore ran into financial problems, forcing them to put the partially completed D&TSL up for sale. In July 1903 they sold the D&TSL to the joint ownership of the Grand Trunk Western and the Toledo, St. Louis & Western, with each road owning 50 percent of the Shore Line. With it the GTW gained direct access to Toledo, and the Clover Leaf, as the TSL&W was nicknamed, obtained an important traffic outlet to Detroit and Canada. The new owners completed the line to River Rouge in September 1903.

By the end of the 1898 some farmers in Michigan's Thumb region had started to grow an important new crop, sugar beets. Refiners built plants in Bay City and Caro to process the beet crop. In 1907 the Handy brothers of Bay City formed the Detroit, Bay City & Western Railroad to connect two plants they owned; the road began operations in October 1910. During the next six years the road was gradually extended across the Thumb to Sandusky and then down into Port Huron, ninety-eight miles from Bay City. In 1916 the Handys bought the Port Huron Southern, an industrial line running south from Port Huron, most likely in an attempt to reach Detroit. In 1917 they formed the Port Huron & Detroit to build to Marine City, and that line was finished in August 1918.

Detroit, Caro & Sandusky

Michigan's first factory to refine beets into sugar was built in Bay City in 1898 by the Michigan Sugar Company. With aggressive support from the state of Michigan, farmers across the Thumb area began growing sugar beets. The Handy brothers—Thomas L., George W., and Frank S., all of Bay City—earlier had formed and sold the Huron & Western as a coal-hauling line, and then had owned the Pontiac, Oxford & Northern, which they sold to the Grand Trunk Western. With their profits they formed the Detroit, Bay City & Western Railroad in May 1907, to take advantage of the boom in sugar production. Despite the road's grandiose name, its incorporation papers called for a line that was to extend from Bay City to Caro. The line was opened in 1910, and the Handys promptly filed papers to extend their line to Wilmot. In the next few years there were more extensions, and ultimately the road built into Port Huron in October 1916. It made a brave showing running two passenger trains each way between Bay City and Port Huron as well as a mid-day round trip from Bay City to Caro.

Once completed the Handys wanted to sell their line, but they could find no takers. So they expanded by buying the Port Huron Southern, a short industrial road at Port Huron, and then forming the Port Huron & Detroit, which they built to Marine City by 1918. Financial success eluded the DBC&W, which slid into receivership in 1922 and was sold in May 1925 to new owners as the Detroit, Caro & Sandusky Railway. As part of the reorganization the tracks between Roseburg and Port Huron were removed. Sugar beet processing became concentrated in Caro, and when the Akron coal mine closed in 1924 no need remained for the Bay City–Caro section. The two Port Huron roads were sold to a new owner. Things grew worse as beet-producing acreage was halved by 1929 brought about by a drop in the price of sugar as well as a shortage of farm labor. In 1937 six more miles of line were abandoned, and in 1948 another eleven miles went. Trucks continued to move more and more of the beet traffic; the remaining thirty-one miles of track between Caro and Sandusky were taken up in 1953.

North of Bay City the Detroit & Mackinac came out of the 1894 reorganization of the Detroit, Bay City & Alpena with a new president, James D. Hawks, fresh from a job with the Michigan Central. In 1895 Hawks bought the Alpena & Northern, a lumber hauler that stretched in a broad curve from Alpena fifty-four miles to Montmorency County. The A&N was started in 1893 by Russell A. Alger, who then was also the president of the DBC&A. In September 1896 Hawks completed a main-line extension from National City to Bay City. There the D&M connected with three railroads and no longer had to rely on its sole indirect connection with the Michigan Central at Alger, which was abandoned the same year. As lumber diminished in importance as a freight commodity, the D&M became an all-purpose carrier from Alpena south along the Lake Huron shoreline. As part of this change it built a new main line along Lake Huron between Tawas City and Black River and in 1901 abandoned part of its more difficult original route through

James Dudley Hawks

Born 13 October 1847, Buffalo, N.Y.; died 21 September 1921, Detroit.

In 1870 Hawks joined the Lake Shore & Michigan Southern as an assistant engineer. In 1881 he moved to the New York, West Shore & Buffalo as superintendent of construction of a road that was to compete head-on with Vanderbilt's New York Central. When that road was completed, and before the Vanderbilt family took it over, Hawks moved to Detroit as chief engineer for the Michigan Central. In the early 1890s he became general manager of the Detroit Citizens' Street Railway until Russell A. Alger, then president of the Detroit, Bay City & Alpena, persuaded him to take the general manager position with that road. Alger soon was named secretary of war by President McKinley, and Hawks took over the road's presidency. By building extensions to Bay City and Cheboygan, he changed the line from a lumber road to an important intercity carrier, and changed the road's name to Detroit & Mackinac. In 1912 Hawks was replaced as president by Henry K. McHarg, who had bought control of the D&M in

James D. Hawks.

Reprinted from Clarence M. Burton, *The City of Detroit, 1701–1922* (Detroit, 1922), 4:facing 54.

1902, but Hawks was made vice president and remained the general manager. In May 1920, now age seventy-two, he resigned his place with the D&M.

During the early 1900s, while holding the D&M presidency, Hawks went into partnership with Samuel F. Angus in promoting several electric lines, the largest of which became the Detroit, Jackson & Chicago between Detroit and Jackson. Between 1902 and 1905 he also was president of the Grand Rapids, Grand Haven & Muskegon interurban line.

Lincoln. In 1906–7 it tapped the calcite quarry at Alabaster and formed the Erie & Michigan Railway & Navigation Company to run that branch line. In 1912 Hawks leased the sixty-three-mile lumber-carrying AuSable & Northwestern from the Loud brothers, and in 1914 bought the feeder road outright.

Over more than a twenty-year span lumberman David Ward of Detroit accumulated an immense tract of high-quality timber northwest of Grayling, and built a logging railroad to tap it. After Ward's death in 1900 his trustees worked to settle his estate promptly by building a major sawmill complex at Deward and forming the Detroit & Charlevoix to operate the rail lines. The D&C main line extended from the Michigan Central at Frederic through Alba to East Jordan supported by a constantly changing maze of branches into the woods. Deward became the ultimate company town for its 800 residents, who were provided with a company store, schoolhouse, church, community hall, and no saloons. In 1907 the Michigan Central gained control of the D&C, and later merged it. By 1912 the lumber had been cut, the sawmill was dismantled, and the railroad was left to a slim existence that continued until 1932. South of the Ward tract the Manistee & Northeastern extended its River branch from Kaleva into Grayling in 1909–10 in an effort to reach new timberlands, adding fifty-four miles to its road. Also in search of new timber, the White family renamed their Boyne City & Southeastern as the Boyne City, Gaylord & Alpena and extended the main line to Gaylord in 1905, on a route north of the Ward lands. After 1914 the Whites extended it still farther east, first to Atlanta and, in 1918, to Alpena, and built a few logging branches as well.

Also in the northern Lower Peninsula, the East Jordan & Southern was formed in 1901 to convert the East Jordan Lumber Company's logging road into a public carrier. In October it completed building a connection to the Pere Marquette at Bellaire, eighteen miles distant from East Jordan. William P. Porter was the road's first president and held that office into the 1930s. In Leelanau County, in 1902 the Manistee & Northeastern extended its branch from Cedar City to Provemont on the shore of Lake Leelanau. While this branch was being built Leelanau County received a second line, the Traverse City, Leelanau & Manistique.

Ephraim Shay

Born 17 July 1839, Huron County, Ohio; died 19 April 1916, Harbor Springs.

Shay came to Ionia County in 1864 as a lumberman and in 1872 moved to the Cadillac area. By 1880 Shay had designed and manufactured a gear-driven locomotive, far different from the common piston-driven steam engine. It immediately became popular for use on logging railroads and became widely known as the "Shay" locomotive. He continued to develop and improve his locomotive over the next several decades. His engine design revolutionized lumbering as an industry. This important form of motive power was ideal for use on the difficult terrains encountered on logging and lumbering railroads, and year-round logging became a reality. Of the more than 2,700 built, a small number of Shay locomotives continue in use today.

In 1888 Shay moved to Harbor Springs and continued his "inventing." In 1900 he built the Harbor Springs Railroad, known locally as the "Hemlock Central," and continued logging operations in a modest way until 1912, when he abandoned his railroad. Shay's home, the "Hexagon," still stands in Harbor Springs. An 1898 Shay locomotive is on stationary display in City Park, Cadillac.

This ambitious little company planned to build from Traverse City to Northport and operate a railroad and passenger car ferry from Northport to Manistique. At first the rail line and its ferry had the financial backing of the Grand Rapids & Indiana, as did the Manistique, Marquette & Northern (later to become the Manistique & Lake Superior), which it connected to in the Upper Peninsula. The railroad was completed in June 1903, and its car ferry put in service in October. Almost immediately the railroad developed financial problems and went into receivership. The road's car ferry service ended in 1908, with the ferry sold to the Grand Trunk Western for its Muskegon-Milwaukee service. The road continued to lurch along as an independent until 1919, when it was sold to the Leelanau Transit Company. Its new owners promptly leased the line to the Manistee & Northeastern.

In the central Upper Peninsula, lumberman Isaac Stephenson of Marinette, Wisconsin, built the Escanaba & Lake Superior. Its main line was completed in December 1900 from Wells, a suburb just north of Escanaba, to Channing, where it connected with the Milwaukee Road. The road had some financial support from the Milwaukee, which gained running rights on the line to reach Escanaba. This arrangement allowed the Milwaukee to move iron ore from several mines it reached on the Menominee Range to Channing, then over the E&LS to Great Lakes ore boats at Escanaba. In 1902 the E&LS built a branch from Northland to Kates Lake and, with other spurs that it built later, tapped an extensive timber area to feed the mills at Wells.

Not far away the first part of the Wisconsin & Michigan was completed in 1894. It began life as a lumber carrier under John Bagley, a Chicago lumberman, and John N. Faithorn, a Chicago railroadman. First they bought the Ingalls, White River & Northern, which ran into timberlands along the Menominee River in western Menominee County. They tore up part of the line and built a new line from a junction with the Milwaukee Road at Bagley Junction, Wisconsin, to a connection with the Soo Line at Faithorn Junction. In 1895 it was extended into Peshtigo, Wisconsin. The company then set up the Lake Michigan Car Ferry Transportation Company to haul lumber from Peshtigo to Chicago. It also arranged for trackage rights over the Milwaukee Road to reach Menominee and the Ann Arbor car ferries. To boost its lumber traffic it built a thirty-one-mile Western division into Wisconsin from Everett in 1904 and 1905. As part of this undertaking the road built a resort hotel on Miscauno Island. In 1905 the road built an extension toward Iron Mountain and tapped several iron mines in the Menominee Range.

This new traffic moved to Peshtigo and then down Lake Michigan by car ferry to the Illinois Steel Company at South Chicago. Service into Peshtigo ended in 1918, when that part of the main line was abandoned. Eventually the Miscauno Island hotel was sold, and in 1919 the Western division was abandoned. Throughout its life the W&M remained a marginal carrier, and it lost money more easily than it made a profit. Its car ferry service ended in 1910 and with that went the Lake Michigan iron ore movement. In 1918 the extension into Peshtigo was abandoned, and by that year service to Iron Mountain had already been reduced. But the plucky road clung to life.

The Lake Superior & Ishpeming Railroad grew out of three separate and disconnected roads: an earlier LS&I, the Marquette & Southeastern, and the Munising Railway. The oldest was the LS&I, which was formed by the owners of the Cleveland Cliffs Iron Company (CCI) in 1893 to move its ore to its own Lake Superior dock. The business recession slowed construction slightly, delaying the opening of the line between the mines at Ishpeming and the road's ore docks at Presque Isle just north of Marquette until August 1896. Other mine owners built the Munising Railway in 1896 and 1897 from the mine area around Little Lake to the Lake Superior harbor at Munising. To provide timbers needed in its mines the CCI planned to build twenty-five-mile branches northeast and southeast from Munising. The CCI bought the Munising in 1899 and the next year formed the Marquette & Southeastern to build from the LS&I at Presque Isle, along the Marquette waterfront, to Manistique and also to make a connection with the line of the Munising. It built as far as Lawson in 1902, connected with the Munising–Little Lake line, and went no farther. In 1905 it added a branch from Marquette to Big Bay. In 1911 Cleveland Cliffs merged the Munising and the M&SE into a new company, the Munising, Marquette & Southeastern. Although by this time the Munising had extended from Little Lake to the Gwinn Mine and moved some iron ore from the mines in that vicinity, most of the MM&SE's traffic was wood products used by the mining company. Although the LS&I was kept separate from the MM&SE, the CCI ownership was apparent. The two had identical management teams, and their schedules appeared together in the *Official Guide*.

The copper country in Houghton and Keweenaw Counties received two new railroads. The Copper Range Company, which was formed in 1899, was a latecomer to the area and first bought up a number of older copper mines. Next it bought and developed several mines south of Houghton in the South Range, and built stamp mills on the

Lake Superior shore at Redridge, Edgemere, and Freda. The final act was to build the Copper Range Railroad, first to tie these together, then to connect the entire complex to the outside world. By the end of 1899 it had built the forty-one miles from Houghton to McKeever, where it connected with the Milwaukee Road. In 1903 it built north from Houghton to Calumet, using the Mineral Range's bridge over the Portage Lake Ship Canal. The copper company acted in a typically paternalistic fashion, providing a wide variety of social services to employees and supporting many community functions. The company established Freda Park as a recreational facility and ran special trains for its employees to enjoy a Sunday outing. In 1917 it leased the Mohawk Mining Company's railroad, which the Mineral Range had been operating, and began hauling ore from its mines around Calumet to a stamp mill at Gay.

The Mineral Range remained a web of lines to copper mines and stamp mills in the area between Hancock and Calumet, growing and waning over the years. Its largest single piece of construction after the 1890s was in 1900 when it built a thirty-five-mile line south of Houghton, extending west from Keweenaw Bay to Riddle Junction to reach the Copper Range Railroad and tap several copper mines in the Greenland and Adventure Mine area.

In 1905 the Keweenaw Copper Company formed the Keweenaw Central Railroad. It took over the Lac La Belle & Calumet, which then extended from Mohawk to Phoenix, changed it to standard gauge, extended it to Mandan, and built a branch to Lac La Belle. Each day it ran a passenger train from Calumet to the Phoenix Mine and back, but on Wednesdays, Saturdays, and Sundays the train went on to Mandan. The line always was low traffic and not very profitable. The KC got permission in 1918 to abandon its line between Phoenix and Mandan as well as the branch to Lac La Belle; the remainder was sold to the Mineral Range, which operated it for only five years, then sold it to the Calumet & Hecla Company, which used it as a private ore road. The KC held the distinction of being the farthest north carrier in Michigan.

SOURCES

Burton, Robert E. "Car Ferry from Northport: Broken Link to the Upper Peninsula." *Michigan History* 51:1 (Spring 1967).

Dunbar, Willis F. *All Aboard! A History of Railroads in Michigan.* Grand Rapids, Mich.: W. B. Eerdmans, 1969.

———. *Michigan: A History of the Wolverine State*. Grand Rapids, Mich.: W. B. Eerdmans, 1970.

Leech, C. A. "Deward: A Lumberman's Ghost Town." *Michigan History* 28:1 (Spring 1944).

McLeod, Richard. "History of the Wisconsin and Michigan Railway." *(Railway & Locomotive Historical Society) Bulletin* No. 118 (April 1968).

Michigan Railroad Commission. *Aids, Gifts, Grants and Donations to Railroads . . .* Lansing, Mich.: Wynkoop, Hallenbeck, Crawford, 1919.

Monette, Clarence J. *The Copper Range Railroad*. Lake Linden, Mich.: author, 1989.

———. *The Mineral Range Railroad*. Lake Linden, Mich.: author, 1993.

Pletz, William C. "The Railroad That Went No Place." *Inside Track* 10:5 (November–December 1979), 11:1 (January–February 1980).

Rehor, John A. *The Nickel Plate Story*. Milwaukee: Kalmbach, 1965.

Trostel, Scott D. *Detroit, Toledo and Iron Railroad: Henry Ford's Railroad*. Fletcher, Ohio: Cam-Tech Publishing, 1988.

Riding the Train

Where there was water, there were steamships to ride. Even small rivers and lakes had them. The Atlantic seaboard, the Mississippi and Ohio Rivers, and the Great Lakes were well supplied with them, and they had great appeal as a leisurely mode of travel. Steamships, however, were not always completely safe since boilers had a disturbing proclivity to explode, an event followed by a loss of passengers. Also, stagecoaches still ran, and for travelers on horseback or by buggy there were some miles of graveled and macadamized roads. But for most travelers the train had become not only the best way to go, but often there was no alternative.

By 1900 the railroad network reached into nearly every corner of the nation and to every city of any importance. Yellowstone was created as the first national park in 1872 and was followed by Mackinac Island and Yosemite—all made more accessible by the train. Florida's west coast already had become a popular winter resort with Henry B. Plant's trains bringing in winter tourists. Henry M. Flagler began to develop Florida's east coast by building his own railroad to bring in northern vacationers with their money. Cities large and small promoted their cultural, civic, and historic attractions. None of these would have attained any measure of success if they were not made easy to reach by passenger train service. Between 1870 and 1890 national passenger train travel more than doubled. The best measure is passenger miles, the sum of the length of all trips by all passengers. These tripled between 1890 and 1916 to reach thirty-five billion passenger miles, an all-time record. This well outpaced the nation's population growth. After the end of World War I, in 1920, travel jumped by a third above the 1916 level, to another all-time record of forty-seven billion passenger miles.

For most people the passenger train *was* the railroad, and they judged a company by the quality of its trains and its depots. As the year rolled into the twentieth century it was, as we can view it in hindsight, the beginning of the golden age of rail travel. The end of the five-year depression that followed the panic of 1893 released a pent-up demand for travel. New travel opportunities—fairs, parks, excursions—developed, and many people now had the money and the time for them. Major events of any sort in Michigan prompted special fares and, sometimes, special trains. The annual meetings of the Pioneer and Historical Society of Michigan, state political conventions, and Grand Army of the Republic (GAR) gatherings were only a few of many such events. World fairs and expositions, church events, and tours to Niagara Falls all brought riders. Summers in northern Michigan with travel to the resorts at Charlevoix, Petoskey, Cheboygan, and Mackinac Island grew in popularity as soon as the railroad was built into town. A particularly healthy sort of travel brought travelers to the mineral springs, to "take the waters," at Mount Clemens or Alma, or one of several other smaller such resorts. Dr. John Harvey Kellogg's sanitarium brought patients from every state to Battle Creek.

In 1900 the Michigan Central was running two local and three express trains between Detroit and Chicago but had dropped three other express trains. By 1905 two of the express trains were restored. The usual timing was seven hours thirty minutes for the Detroit-Chicago trip. By 1916 service was increased to ten trains each way between Detroit and Chicago, with only two of them making all local stops. The fastest was the eastbound *Michigan Central Limited*, which made the run in six hours twenty minutes, while the *Wolverine* used six hours thirty minutes in both directions. Passengers on both trains paid an extra fare to ride, and no coaches were carried on the *Michigan Central Limited*. The *Detroiter* was added to the schedule as an all-sleeping car, extra-fare train running from Detroit to New York City in fourteen hours twenty minutes, the fastest service of all. Among the unnamed branch-line trains the overnight Detroit–Mackinaw City run was slightly faster than twenty years earlier but only because it made fewer stops. It carried sleepers

GRAND RAPIDS & INDIANA RY.

GRAND RAPIDS, PETOSKEY, MACKINAW

P.M	P.M	P.M	A.M			Lv Sept 27 1908 Ar	A.M	A.M	P.M	P.M	
†10 50	†6 10	†2 25	D7 20	....	234	...Grand Rapids....	6 35	10 50	4 50	9 50	.....
10 56	6 16	2 31	7 26		235	...Bridge Street....	6 28	10 43	4 43	9 43	....
.....	6 24	2 39	7 34		237	...Fuller......	6 20	10 35	4 35	9 35	
.....	6 30		7 40		239	..Comstock Park...	6 15	10 30			
.....	6 40	*2 53	7 50		244	...Belmont.....	*6 06	10 21	4 20	*9 20	
.....	*6 45		*7 55		246	...Childsdale....		*10 14	*4 14		
11 27	6 50	3 02	8 00		248	...Rockford.....	5 57	10 11	4 10	9 10	
.....	*6 55		*8 05		251	...Edgerton.....	*5 51	*10 01	*4 04		
11 42	7 07	3 17	8 15		255	..Cedar Springs...	5 42	9 53	3 55	8 54	
*11 51	7 18	3 27	8 25		260	...Sand Lake....	5 32	9 42	3 43	8 44	
.....	7 23	3 31	8 30		262	...Pierson......	5 27	9 36	3 38	8 38	
12 10	7 34	3 45	8 43		268	..Howard City....	5 16	9 25	3 25	8 28	
‡12 23	7 48	3 59	8 56		274	...Morley......	*5 02	9 09	3 07	8 14	
.....	*7 55		*9 03		278	...Borland		*9 03	*2 59		
*12 36	8 05	4 12	9 10		281	...Stanwood.....	*4 49	8 55	2 53	7 58	
12 55	8 25	4 31	9 28		290	...Big Rapids....	4 32	8 35	2 35	7 40	
.....	8 28	4 34	9 32		291	.Upper Big Rapids.		8 29	2 30		
.....	8 38	4 43	9 42		295	...Paris......		8 20	2 21	7 25	
1 28	8 58	5 03	10 02		303	...Reed City....	4 06	8 03	2 05	7 08	
.....	*9 07		*10 11		307	...Orono......		*7 52	*1 53		
.....	9 12	5 17	10 16		310	...Ashton.....		7 47	1 48	6 52	
.....	9 23	5 28	10 27		315	...Le Roy.....		7 35	1 36	6 40	
*2 01	9 34	5 39	10 38		320	...Tustin.....	*3 33	7 25	1 25	6 30	
.....	*9 42	*5 47	*10 46		323	..Osceola Junc...		*7 17	*1 17		
.....	*9 50		*10 52		326	...Hobart.....		*7 10	*1 12		
2 25	10 00	‖6 05	‖11 05		332 Ar	..Cadillac.. Lv	3 10	†7 00	1 00	6 05	
2 35	P.M	6 25	11 25		332 Lv	..Cadillac.. Ar	3 05	A.M	‖12 40	‖5 45	
3 05		6 50	11 56		344	...Manton.....	2 34		12 07	5 17	
.....		7 10	12 20		353	..Walton Junc...			11 50	5 00	
.....		†8 10	D1 25		379 Ar	.Traverse City..Lv			D10 45	†3 55	
.....			†6 30		408 Ar	...Northport...Lv			†8 00		
*3 31		7 21	12 30		358	...Fife Lake....	*2 06		11 36	4 47	
*3 42		7 33	12 43		363	..So. Boardman...	*1 53		11 23	4 36	
.....		*7 39	*12 49		367	...Crofton.....			*11 16	*4 30	
4 01		7 52	12 59		372	...Kalkaska....	1 37		11 05	4 20	
.....		*8 01	*1 10		376	...Leetsville....			*10 53	*4 06	
.....		*8 09	*1 20		381	...Westwood....			*10 43	*3 57	
4 30		8 18	1 27		385	..Mancelona....	1 08		10 35	3 50	
.....		*8 22	*1 34		388	...Wetzel.....			*10 31	*3 43	
*4 44		8 31	1 43		392	...Alba......	*12 54		10 22	3 38	
*5 02		8 50	2 01		400	...Elmira.....	*12 39		10 03	3 23	
5 22		9 10	2 20		409	..Boyne Falls....	12 14		9 39	2 59	
*5 39		9 27	2 37		417	...Clarion.....	11 56		9 21	2 41	
6 00		9 45	3 00		425 Ar	..Petoskey..Lv	11 40		9 05	2 25	
.....					426	...Bay View.... Ar					
7 55			4 25		433	.Harbor Springs..	5 35		8 20	12 01	
.....					428	..Wa-ya-ga-mug..					
*6 12		*9 56	*3 13		430	...Conway.....	*11 22		*8 47	*12 03	
*6 18		*10 02	3 18		432	...Oden......	*11 16		8 42	1 57	
6 23		10 07	3 25		435	...Alanson.....	11 10		8 35	1 50	
*6 31		*10 16	3 33		438	...Brutus.....	*11 02		8 27	1 42	
6 41		10 25	3 43		443	...Pellston.....	10 53		8 18	1 33	
*6 48		*10 30	*3 50		446	...Van......	*10 45		*8 09	*1 25	
6 57		10 38	3 58		448	...Levering....	10 38		8 03	1 18	
7 07		*10 48	4 08		451	..Carp Lake....	*10 27		7 52	1 07	
7 25		11 05	4 25		460	..Mackinaw City..	‡10 10		D7 35	†12 50	
.....						..Mackinac Isld by Str.					
A.M		P.M				Ar ... Lv	P.M		A.M	P.M	

CADILLAC, LAKE CITY

	P.M	P.M	A.M		Lv ... Ar	A.M	P.M	P.M	
.....	†3 35	†12 05	†6 45	0	...Cadillac....	11 00	3 00	5 55	....
.....	3 45	12 30	7 00	4	.Missaukee Junc..	10 45	2 45	5 45	....
.....	4 00	12 50	*7 20	8	.Round Lake Jc..	*10 30	2 25	5 30	....
.....	4 10	1 05		12	...Jennings....		†2 10	4 15	....
.....	4 25			8	.Round Lake Jc..				....
.....	4 30		7 25	10	...Wagner....	10 25		5 25	....
.....			*7 37	13	.Missaukee Park.	*10 12			....
.....	4 55		7 50	16	...Lake City....	†10 00		†5 00	....
	P.M	P.M	A.M		Ar ... Lv	A.M	P.M	P.M	

WALTON, TRAVERSE CITY

	P.M	P.M	A.M		Lv ... Ar	A.M	P.M	
.....	†7 10	D12 25		0	..Walton Junc...	D11 45	4 55	....
.....	*7 17	*12 32		3	...Holmes.....	*11 38	*4 48	....
.....	7 25	12 40		6	..Summit City...	11 30	4 40	....
.....				8	..Westminster...			....
.....	7 33	12 48		9	...Kingsley....	11 21	4 31	....
.....	7 42	12 57		13	...Mayfield....	11 13	4 23	....
.....	*7 52	*1 07		17	...Slights.....	*11 03	*4 13	....
.....	*7 57	*1 12		19	...Keystone....	*10 58	*4 08	....
.....	8 10	1 25		26	..Traverse City..	D10 45	†3 55	....
	P.M	P.M	A.M		Ar ... Lv	A.M	P.M	

TRAV. CITY LEELANAU & MANISTIQUE

	A.M		P.M	
Lv ..Traverse City.. Ar	9 15		5 15	
..Hatch's Crossing..	8 55		5 33	
...Bingham......	8 46		5 43	
..Sutton's Bay....	8 28		6 00	
...Omena......	8 13		6 17	
Ar ...Northport... Lv	8 00		6 30	

The Grand Rapids & Indiana offered the largest amount of service to northern Michigan resorts. This September 1908 schedule from the *Michigan Railway Guide* is impressive for the number of trains in the off-season.

DETROIT DIVISION

DETROIT TO BUFFALO AND CHICAGO

Miles.	STATIONS.	Det. & Cleve. Day Ex 325	Det. & Cleve. Exp. 321	Chic. & Cin. Exp. 319	Sunday Train 335	Sunday Trains 343	Clev. & Pitts. Ex. 323
		AM	PM	PM	PM	Note PM	PM
..	Lv DETROIT	* 7.02	* 2.45	† 5.20	§ 6.00	§ 6.30	* 9.00
2	Gratiot Avenue	7.11	2.54	5.29	6.09	6.39	9.09
3	D. & M. Junc.						
5	Woodward Ave	7.20	3.03	5.40	6.18	6.48	9.18
11	Delray		f 3.16	f 5.54			f 9.31
14	Ecorse			f 5.57			
17	Wyandotte	x 7.41		f 6.00			f 9.39
20	Sibley			f 6.06			
21	Trenton			f 6.09			
28	Rockwood			f 6.17			
33	Newport			f 6.23			
40	Ar MONROE	8.09	3.52	6.35		7.45	f10.06
		PM		AM		AM	
285	Ar CHICAGO	a 5.55		7.00		7.00	
40	Lv MONROE	8.09	3.52	6.35			f10.06
45	LaSalle						
50	Vienna			f 6.47			
58	West Toledo			f 7.00			
60	Wagon Works	8.35	4.20	7.05	7.30		10.31
65	Ar TOLEDO	8.45	4.30	7.15	7.40		10.40
		AM	PM	PM	PM		PM
					PM		PM
..	Lv TOLEDO	8.52	4.45	7.45	7.45		10 50
178	Ar CLEVELAND	11.25	7.30	10.15	10.15		1.30
273	Ar ERIE	1.44	9.51	12.48	12.48		3.47
361	Ar BUFFALO	3.55	11.59	3.15	3.15		6.05
	ArPITTSBURGH(P.&L.E.R.R.)	4.45					6.30
		PM	PM	AM	AM		AM

SLEEPING CAR—Detroit to Pittsburgh on No. 323.
PARLOR CARS—Detroit to Cleveland on Nos. 325, 321, 319 and 335.

a—Via Toledo.

BUFFALO AND CHICAGO TO DETROIT

Miles.	STATIONS.	Clev. & Detroit Ex. 322	Det. Exp. 324	Sunday Train 344	Sunday Train 320	Clev. & Det. Day Ex. 350	Cleve. & Detroit Ex. 352	Sunday Train 354
		PM	AM	Note AM	Note AM	AM	PM	PM
	LvPITTSBURGH(P &L.E.R.R.)	*10.30				* 7.15	†12.35	§12.35
..	Lv BUFFALO	* 6.15	* 3.30			* 6.30	†12.28	§12.28
88	Lv ERIE	8.13	5.14			8.31	2.23	2.23
183	Lv CLEVELAND	10.45	7.35		§ 7.45	12.45	4.40	4.40
296	Ar TOLEDO	1.25	10.00		10.40	3.40	7.05	7.05
		AM	AM			PM	PM	PM
0	Lv TOLEDO	* 5.15	†10.30		§10.45	* 3.50	† 7.30	§ 9.45
5	Wagon Works	5.23	10.38		10.55	4.00	f 7.40	9.55
7	West Toledo		f10.41					
15	Vienna		f10.51					
20	LaSalle							
25	Ar MONROE	5.46	11.02		11.21	4.30	f 8.06	10.18
			AM			AM		
..	Lv CHICAGO		† 3.00			† 9.00		
..	Lv MONROE	5.46	†11.02	§ 9.50	11.21	* 4.30	f 8.06	10.18
32	Newport		f11.13					
37	Rockwood		f11.19					
44	Trenton		f11.26					
45	Sibley		f11.28					
48	Wyandotte		f11.31					x 1046
51	Ecorse							
54	Delray	f 6.23	f11.39					
60	Woodward Avenue	6.35	11.51	10.45	12.14	5.22	8.55	11.07
62	D. & M. Junction		f11.55					
63	Gratiot Avenue	6.46	12.01	10.56	12.26	5.31		11.16
65	Ar DETROIT	6.55	12.10	11.05	12.25	5.40	9.15	11.25
		AM	PM	AM		PM	PM	PM

SPEEPING CAR—Pittsburgh to Detroit on No. 322.
PARLOR CARS—Cleveland to Detroit on trains Nos. 320, 324, 350, 352 and 354.

MONROE BRANCH—DETROIT, MONROE AND CHICAGO

Sunday Train 343	Det. & Chic. Exp. 347	Det. & Chi. Exp. 345	Miles.	STATIONS.	Sunday Train 344	Chic. & Det. Exp. 348	Chic. & Det. Exp. 342
PM	PM	AM			AM	PM	PM
§ 6.30	† 5.20	† 7.02	...	Lv .... DETROIT .... Ar	11.05	12.10	5.40
§ 7.50	† 6.40	†10.55	40	Lv .... Monroe .... Ar	9.45	10.35	4.25
f 8.02	f 6.52	f11.07	46	Strasburg	f 9 30	f10.23	f 4.10
8.07	6.57	11.12	50	Ida	9.25	10.17	4.03
f 8.12	f 7.02	f11.16	53	Federman	f 9.17	f10.12	f 3.58
8.18	7.08	11.22	57	Petersburg	9.11	10.05	3.50
8.25	7.15	11.29	61	Deerfield	9.05	9.58	3.42
f 8.31	f 7.21	f11.35	64	Sisson	f 9.00	f 9.50	f 3.35
f 8.36	f 7.26	f11.40	67	Wellsville	f 8.55	f 9.46	f 3.30
8.45	7.35	11.50	70	Lenawee Junction	8.50	9.38	3.25
8.55	7.45	12.01	74	Ar .... Adrian Lv	§ 8.25	† 9.30	† 2.50
PM	PM	PM			AM	AM	PM
7.00	7.00	9.00		Ar .... CHICAGO Lv	§ 3.00	† 3.00	† 9.00
AM	AM	PM			AM	AM	AM

* Daily. † Daily except Sunday. § Sundays only.

x Stops Sundays, June 11 to Sept. 10, inclusive. f Stops to discharge and on signal to receive passengers

NOTE.—This train in service each Sunday June 11 to Sept. 10, inclusive.

DETROIT DIVISION

FAYETTE BRANCH

328	326	Mls.	STATIONS.	329	327
PM	AM			AM	PM
† 5.25	† 8.32	0	Lv .... ADRIAN .... Ar	8.32	3.30
5.33	8.45	4	Ar .... Lenawee Junction .... Ar	8.20	2.55
5.43	8.50	...	Ar .... Grosvenor Lv	8.11	2.45
5.50	9.00	8	Lv .... Grosvenor .... Ar	8.00	2.45
5.57	9.28	13	Ogden	7.49	2.05
6.04	9.48	16	Jasper	7.42	1.45
6.15	10.08	19	Weston	7.35	1.25
6.22	10.40	26	Morenci	7.23	12.55
f 6.2.	f10.55	30	Ritters	f 7.16	f12.32
6.40	11.10	33	Ar .... FAYETTE Lv	† 7.10	†12.20
PM	AM			AM	PM

Way Freight No. 326 starts from Grosvenor. Main Line train No. 48 should be taken at Adrian to connect.

Train No. 329 connects at Grosvenor with Main Line train No. 45 for Adrian.

JACKSON BRANCH

313 Note	311	331	309	315	Mls.	STATIONS.	316	312	314	318	310 Note
	PM	AM	AM			Mich. Cent. R. R.	PM	PM	PM		
	* 5.20	*11.10	† 7.25			Lv..... Grand Rapids ..... Ar	1 00	5.10	10.30		
	7.15	1.45	10.20			Ar....... JACKSON Lv	10.30	2.40	7.3		
AM	PM	PM	AM	AM			AM	PM	PM	PM	PM
§ 7.15	* 8.10	† 2.05	†10.30	† 6.05	0	Lv....... JACKSON .... Ar	10.15	2.33	7.20	9.45	10.05
f 7.26	f 8.21			f 6.14	6	Eldred	f10.00			f 9.30	f 9.50
7.30	8.27	2.20	10.48	6.21	10	Napoleon	9.54	2.08	6.57	9.23	9.43
7.37	8.32	2.27	10.55	6.28	14	Norvell	9.48	2.01	6.50	9.17	9.37
7.49	8.42	2.39	11.07	6.40	21	Manchester	9.35	1.51	6.37	9.07	9.27
f 7.55	f 8.47		f11 13	f 6.47	25	River Raisin	f 9.29		f 6.29	f 9.00	f 9.22
8.01	8.54	2.52	11.20	6.53	29	Clinton	9.19	1.38	6.23	8.54	9.17
8.09	9.03	3.01	11.29	7.03	33	Tecumseh	9.09	1.30	6.15	8.42	9.08
8.11	9 05	3.03	11.31	7.05	34	Tecumseh Jct.	9 05	1.28	6.12	8.37	9.05
f 8.16	f 9.09			f 7.14	38	Sutton	f 9.00			f 8.34	f 9.00
f 8.22	f 9.14			f 7.20	40	Raisin Centre	f 8.53			f 8.29	f 8.54
8.30	9.20	3.20	11.50	7.25	42	Ar.... Lenawee Junc..... Lv	8.50	1.14	5.55	8.25	8.50
8.54			12.01	7.33	47	Ar....... ADRIAN Lv	* 8.32	† 1.00	† 5.25	† 8.10	§ 8 30
AM	PM	PM	PM	AM			AM	PM	PM	PM	PM
			AM	7.51	...	Lv....... ADRIAN .... Ar					
	9.20	3.20	11.50		...	Lv.... Lenawee Junc.... Ar	8.45	1.12	5.55	8.21	8.45
	10.05	4.15	12.30	8.40	71	Ar....... Toledo Lv	7.50	12.30	5.10	7.25	7.50
	1.30	7.30	4.10	11.25	184	Ar....... Cleveland Lv	4.25	7 35	12.45	4.40	4.40
	3.47	9.51	6.17	1.44	279	Ar....... Erie Lv	12.21	5.14	8.31	2.23	2.23
	6.05	11.59	8.20	3.55	367	Ar....... BUFFALO Lv	*10.20	† 3.30	† 6.30	†12.28	§12.28
	AM	PM	PM	PM			PM	AM	AM	PM	PM
AM				AM			AM			PM	PM
8.51				8.32	...	Lv....... Adrian .... Ar	7.51			1.55	1.55
3.45				3.45	257	Ar....... CHICAGO Lv	* 3.00			† 9.00	§ 9.00
PM				PM			AM			AM	AM

DUNDEE BRANCH

D. T. & I. 1	421	419 Note	427	425	429	Mls.	STATIONS.	422	428	430	434	420 Note	D. T. & I. 2
AM	PM	AM	PM	AM	AM			PM	PM	PM	PM	PM	PM
	†2.20	§8.00	†5.10	†7.50		0	Lv.... Toledo.... Ar	12.30			10.05	9.15	
		8.05				3	Air Line Jct.	c			c	9.08	
		8.22				11	...Sylvania..	c			c	8.48	
		8 31				16	Ottawa Lake	c			c	8.38	
		8.40				21	.....Riga.....	c			c	8.30	
	f2.52	8.47	5.42	f8.31		22	..Blissfield..	11f58			c	8.25	
		8.53	5.47			25	..Grosvenor.	c			c	8.18	
		8.57				27	...Palmyra...	c			c	8.14	
		9.02		8.45		29	ArLenawee Jct.Lv	11.50				8.10	
	†3.30	8.35	5.25	8.10	†6.10	...	Lv... Adrian ...Ar	11.10		5.25	8.40	8.55	
	3.40	9.02	5.55	8.20	6.25	...	LvLenawee Jct.Ar	11.00		5.10	8.20	8.10	
								AM		PM		PM	
†1005			†1.45			0	Lv... Dundee....Ar		1.30				4.50
f1016			1.57			4	.....Rea.....		1.18				f4.38
f102.			2.15			9	...Britton....		1.00				f4.26
1033			2.2.			11	..Ridgeway..		12.45				f4.20
1045			2.40			16	ArTecumseh Jct.Lv		12.30				†4.10
										PM		PM	
	4.02	9.22	6.20	9.10	7.30	38	LvTecumseh Jct.Ar	10.43	11.15	3.50	8.00	7.50	
	4.16	9.33	6.31	9.23	7.50	44	....Tipton....	10.29	11.01	3.00	7.46	7.38	
	4.23	9.39	6.37	9.30	f8.02	47	..Pentecost..	10.22	11.54	f2.40	7.40	7.32	
	4.32	9.48	6.46	9.40	8.25	51	....Onsted ...	10.15	10.46	2.25	7.33	7.24	
	4.45	9.58	6.56	9.51	f8.43	56	Devils Lake.	10.04	10.34	f1.45	7.23	7.12	
	4.52	10.03	7.01	9.59	9.00	58	.Addison Jct.	9.59	10.29	1.35	7.18	7.05	
	4.55	10.07	7.05	10 05	9.56	59	...Addison...	9.56	10†25	1.20	†7.15	§7.00	
	f5.07					65	....Baker....	f9.44					
	5.11				10.30	66	...Jerome....	9.41		12.45			
	5.18				10.45	69	... Moscow...	9.34		12.30			
	5.29				11.20	74	...Hanover..	9.24		12.05			
	5.40				11.40	78	.Wheelerton.	9.14		11.40			
	f5.50					83	.. Grover....	f9.04					
	6.02				12.20	87	Ar... Homer ...	†8.55		11†10			
PM	PM	AM	PM	AM	PM			AM	AM	AM	PM		PM
	PM						Mich. Cent. R. R.	AM					
	6.02					...	Lv...Homer...Ar	8.55					
	6.12					92	Lv...Eckford...Ar	8.45					
	6.25					99	Ar..Marshall...Lv	8.28					
	6.58					113	Battle Creek	8.00					
	7.27					126	..Yorkville ..	7.33					
	8.35					155	Ar...Allegan ..Lv	†6.30					
	PM							AM					

*Daily. † Daily except Sunday. § Sunday only.
f—Stops to discharge and on signal to receive passengers.
c—Stops to discharge passengers.

GRAND RAPIDS BRANCH

GRAND RAPIDS TO BUFFALO AND CHICAGO

Mls.	STATIONS.	515 Note	527 Note	523 Note	543 Note
		AM	AM	PM	PM
0	Lv GRAND RAPIDS	† 6.15	§ 7.15	† 1.30	* 5.50
2	Eagle Mills	......	f 7.19	......	f 5.55
6	Wentworth	......	f 7.28	f 1.41	f 6.03
12	Byron Center	6.30	7.39	1.54	6.13
15	Herps	6.34	f 7.44	......	f 6.18
18	Dorr	6.39	7.50	2.05	6.23
22	Hilliards	6.45	7.57	2.11	6.30
26	Hopkins	6.51	8.06	2.21	6.38
...	Miner Lake	f 6.57	f 8.14	f 2.28	f 6.46
33	Allegan	7.06	8.24	2.36	6.55
39	Abronia	f 7.15	f 8 36	......	f 7.05
43	Otsego	7.25	8.44	2.55	7.14
46	Plainwell	7.33	8.52	3.03	7.23
49	Argenta	f 7.38	f 8.56	......	f 7.30
53	Cooper	f 7.44	f 9.01	......	f 7.35
58	Kalamazoo	8.10	9.23	3.30	7.50
65	Portage	f 8.20	f 9 33	f 3.40	f 8.05
71	Schoolcraft	8.33	9.43	3 55	8.26
75	Flowerfield	f 8.40	f 9.59	4.00	x 8.34
79	Moorepark	8.49	10.06	4.10	8.42
83	Three Rivers	8.58	10.15	4.20	8.52
88	Florence	f 9.06	f10.22	......	f 9.00
91	Constantine	9.13	10.31	4.38	9.08
95	Ar White Pigeon	9.20	10.45	4.55	9.25
...	Lv White Pigeon	9.20	10.45	4.55	9.25
100	Ar Vistula	9.35	10.54	5.06	9.35
106	Bristol	9.42	11.03	5.16	9.45
114	Ar Elkhart	10.00	11.20	5.35	10.10
		AM	AM	PM	PM
...	Lv Elkhart	10.10	12.55	6.00	10.30
215	Ar CHICAGO	12.50	3.45	9.00	1.20
		PM	PM	PM	AM
		AM	AM	PM	
...	Lv White Pigeon	......	11.50	6.50	......
...	Lv Elkhart	10.50	......	......	11.45
219	Ar TOLEDO	1.40	2.45	10.45	3.30
332	Ar CLEVELAND	4.10	5.45	1.30	6.40
425	Ar ERIE	6.17	9.51	3.47	9.39
515	Ar BUFFALO	8.20	11.59	6.05	11.45

BUFFALO AND CHICAGO TO GRAND RAPIDS

Mls.	STATIONS.	532 Note	504 Note	516 Note	528 Note	
		PM	PM	AM		
...	Lv BUFFALO	* 7.30	†10.20	† 6.30	§ 6.30	......
88	Lv ERIE	9.24	12.21	8.31	8.31	......
183	Lv CLEVELAND	11.45	4.25	10 55	10.55	......
296	Lv TOLEDO	2.20	7.20	2.20	2.15	......
...	Ar Elkhart	5.20	......	......	5.55	......
420	Ar White Pigeon	......	11.40	5.22	......	......
		AM	AM	PM	PM	
...	Lv CHICAGO	* 3.00	† 8.25	† 1.40	§ 3.00	......
101	Ar Elkhart	5.20	10.45	4.15	6.00	......
		AM	AM	PM	PM	
...	Lv Elkhart	* 6.00	†11.10	† 4.45	§ 6.35	......
109	Bristol	f 6.13	......	v 4.58	6.48	......
115	Vistula	f 6.20	......	v 5.06	6.54	......
120	Ar White Pigeon	6.30	11.38	5.22	7.05	......
0	Lv WHITE PIGEON	6.30	11.50	5.22	7.05	......
4	Constantine	6.42	11.57	5.35	7.14	......
7	Florence	f 6.49	......	f 5.42	f 7.21	......
11	Three Rivers	6.59	12.13	5.51	7.31	......
16	Moorepark	7.09	12.23	6.02	7.41	......
20	Flowerfield	f 7.17	......	f 6.09	f 7.48	......
23	Schoolcraft	7.23	12.39	6.17	7.55	......
30	Portage	f 7.33	......	f 6.30	f 8.05	......
36	Kalamazoo	7.45	1.15	6.55	8.25	......
42	Cooper	f 8.04	......	f 7.08	f 8.47	......
45	Argenta	f 8.10	......	f 7.15	f 8.52	......
48	Plainwell	8.16	1.40	7.23	8.58	......
52	Otsego	8.25	1.47	7.31	9.06	......
56	Abronia	f 8.36	......	f 7.41	f 9 14	......
62	Allegan	8.50	2.06	7.54	9.26	......
...	Miner Lake	f 8.58	......	f 8.03	f 9.33	......
69	Hopkins	9.09	2.21	8.13	9.41	......
73	Hilliards	9.18	2.30	8.22	9.50	......
76	Dorr	9.26	2.39	8.30	9 57	......
...	Herps	9.33	......	f 8.37	f10.04	......
83	Byron Center	9.40	2.52	8.45	10.10	......
88	Wentworth	f 9.52	f 3.06	f 8.59	f10.21	......
92	Eagle Mills	f10.05	......	f 9.10	f10.30	......
95	Ar GRAND RAPIDS	10.10	3.20	9.15	10.35	......
		AM	PM	PM	PM	

NOTE—Tickets issued from Toledo, Ohio, and points east thereof to Otsego, Mich., and points north, will be accepted either via the Old Road Division and White Pigeon direct or via the Air Line Division and Elkhart.

In like manner tickets issued from Otsego, Mich., and points north thereof, to Toledo, Ohio, and points beyond, will be accepted either via White Pigeon and the Old Road Division or via Elkhart and the Air Line Division.

Passengers from Toledo or stations east, destined to Plainwell, Mich., Bristol, Ind., or intermediate stations, and passengers from these stations to Toledo, and beyond, may if desired, secure tickets reading via Elkhart and Air Line Division at slightly higher fares than apply via White Pigeon and Old Road Division.

GOSHEN AND MICHIGAN BRANCH

		556	512	Mls.	STATIONS.	503	557		
		PM	AM			PM	PM		
......	......	† 5.00	† 7.10		Lv....Battle Creek (M. C. R. R)....Ar	12.40	6.40	......	......
......	......	† 6.20	† 9.35	0	Lv....FINDLEY....Ar	10.10	5.25	......	......
......	......	6.35	9.50	7	Sturgis	9.50	5.10	......	......
......	......	f 6.44	f10.40	13	Twin Lakes	f 9.07	f 4.50	......	......
......	......	f 6.49	f10.50	16	Seyberts	f 9.01	f 4.43	......	......
......	......	6.57	11.15	20	Shipeshwana	8.51	4.35	......	......
......	......	f 7.02	f11.20	22	Pashan	f 8.43	f 4.28	......	......
......	......	f 7.05	f11.26	23	Oak	f 8.40	f 4.24	......	......
......	......	7.10	11.50	27	Middlebury	8.30	4.18	......	......
......	......	f 7.15	f11.55	30	Burns	f 8.15	f 4.11	......	......
......	......	f 7.19	f12.01	32	Williams	f 8.10	f 4.07	......	......
......	......	7.30	12.20	36	Ar....GOSHEN....Lv	† 8.00	† 4.00	......	......

*Daily. †Daily except Sunday. §Sundays only. f Stops to discharge and on signal to receive passengers. x Stop Sundays.

LANSING DIVISION

LANSING BRANCH

450 Note	444	442	446 Note	Mls.	STATIONS.	445	455	453 Note
§ 5.00PM	† 3.55PM	† 9.10AM	§ 6.15AM	0	Lv ..NORTH LANSING... Ar	10.15AM	4.55PM	9.55PM
5.10	4.10	9.25	6.30	1	LANSING	10.05	4.45	9.45
f 5.19	f 4.19	f 9.35	f 6.39	5	Packard	f 9.50	f 4.32	f 9.32
5.25	4.26	9.43	6.45	8	Dimondale	9.43	4.26	9.26
f 5.31	f 4.34	f 9.50	f 6.51	12	Kingsland	f 9.35	f 4.18	f 9.19
5.43	4.46	10.02	7.03	18	Eaton Rapids	9.26	4.09	9.09
5.53	4.56	10.12	7.13	23	Charlesworth	f 9.14	f 3.56	8.55
6.01	5.04	10.20	7.21	27	Springport	9.08	3.49	8.48
6.09	5.12	10.28	7.29	31	Devereux	8.59	3.39	8.38
6.21	5.24	10.38	7.41	39	Albion	8.49	3.28	8.28
f 6.28	f 5 32	f10.46	f 7.48	43	Condit	f 8.38	f 3.18	f 8.17
6.34	5 39	10.55	7.56	46	Homer	8.31	3.11	8.10
6.47	5.51	11.08	8.11	53	Litchfield	8.11	2.58	7.57
7.05	6.10	11.25	8.24	61	Ar.......Jonesville.......Lv	7.55	2.45	7.45
7.15PM	6.20PM	11.35AM	8.35AM	65	Ar.......HILLSDALE.......Lv	* 7.45AM	† 2.35PM	§ 7.35PM
10.15PM	9.41PM	12.02PM	9.57AM	......	Lv.......Hillsdale.......Ar	7.06AM	1.11PM	......
7.00AM	7.00AM	5.55PM	3.46PM	235	Ar.......CHICAGO.......Lv	* 3.00AM	† 9.00AM	......
8.40PM	8.40PM	1.11PM	......	......	Lv.......Hillsdale.......Ar	9.41PM	12.02PM	......
10.45	10.45	2.45	......	131	Ar.......Toledo.......Lv	7.25	10.10	......
1.30	1.30	5.45	......	244	Ar.......Cleveland.......Lv	4.40	7.35	......
3.47	3.47	9.51	......	339	Ar.......Erie.......Lv	2 23	5.14	......
6.05AM	6.05AM	11.59PM	......	427	Ar.......Buffalo.......Lv	*12.28PM	† 3.30AM	......

FT. WAYNE BRANCH

414	412 Note	418 Note	410	452	456	Mls	STATIONS.	461	457	411 Note	459
PM		PM	AM	AM	AM			AM	PM	PM	PM
† 5.25	......	§ 7.15	†11.45	§ 7.20	† 6.50	0	Lv.......JACKSON.......Ar	9 15	3.05	......	8.35
f 5.41	......	f 7.32	......	f 7.36	f 7.07	6	Wilsons	f 8.55	f 2.45	......	......
5.48	......	7.41	12.08	7.45	7.14	11	Horton	8.45	2.35	......	8.04
5.53	......	7.54	12.13	7.50	7.20	14	Hanover	8.38	2.28	......	7.54
f 5.57	......	f 7.57	......	f 7.53	f 7.24	16	Stony Point	f 8.33	f 2.23	......	f 7.50
6.03	......	8.02	12.23	7.59	7.29	19	Mosherville	8.28	2.18	......	7.47
6.18	......	8.14	12.37	8.10	7.45	25	Jonesville	8.17	2.07	......	7.38
6.23	......	8.16	12.41	8.13	7.53	...	Ft. Wayne Junction	8.13	2.03	......	7.33
6.35	......	8.25	12.50	8.23	8.05	29	Ar.......Hillsdale.......Lv	* 8.05	† 1.55	......	* 7.25
9.41	......	10.15	3.52	9.45	9.44	...	Lv.......Hillsdale.......Ar	7.06	1.11	......	......
7.00	......	7.00	9.00	3.45	3.45	...	Ar.......CHICAGO.......Lv	* 3.00	† 9.00	......	......
AM			AM	AM	AM			PM		PM	AM
......	......	......	† 9.00	§ 3.00	† 3.00	...	Lv.......CHICAGO.......Ar	3.45	......	5.55	7.00
......	......	......	1.11	7.06	7 06	...	Ar.......Hillsdale.......Lv	9.44	......	12.02	9.41
† 6.30	......	......	†3.30	......	......	...	Lv.......Buffalo.......Ar	7.25	11.59	11.59	6.05
8 31	......	......	5.14	......	......	...	Lv.......Erie.......Ar	5 09	9.51	......	3.47
10.55	......	......	7.35	......	......	...	Lv.......Cleveland.......Ar	† 1.50	7.30	5.45	1.30
2.20	......	......	10.10	......	......	...	Lv.......Toledo.......Ar	9.50	4.05	2.45	10.45
3.52	......	......	12.02	......	......	...	Ar.......Hillsdale.......Lv	7.37	1.55	1.11	8.40
PM	PM		PM		AM			AM	PM	AM	PM
† 6.40	§ 5.25	§ 8.45	† 1.15	§ 8.37	† 8.05	29	Lv.......Hillsdale.......Ar	7.35	1.45	10.10	7.25
f 6.50	f 5.35	f 8.54	1.30	f 8.46	8.15	34	Bankers	f 7.20	1.30	f 9.55	7.09
7.05	5.45	9.04	1 38	8.55	8.25	39	Reading	7 11	1.21	9.45	7.00
7.15	5.54	9.14	1.47	9.04	8.34	44	Montgomery	7.01	1 11	9.35	6.48
7 24	6 02	9.21	1.55	9.11	8.42	48	Ray	6.53	1.04	9.27	6.41
7.33	6.10	9.29	2.03	9.20	8.50	52	Fremont	6.45	12.57	9.20	6.34
7.46	6.22	9.41	2.15	9.32	9.04	60	Angola	6.33	12.45	9.07	6.22
7.56	6.34	9.50	2.24	9.42	9.15	64	Pleasant Lake	6.22	12 35	8.57	6.12
8.02	f 6.40	f 9.56	2.30	f 9.48	9.21	67	Steubenville	6.12	12.27	f 8.51	6.04
f 8.05	f 6.43	......	2.32	f 9.50	9.25	68	Summit	......	12.25	f 8.49	6.02
8.15	6.54	10.08	2.42	10.00	9.40	73	Ar.......Waterloo.......Lv	6.00	12.15	8.39	5.52
† 1.40	§ 1.40	......	†10.30	......	......	...	Lv.......CHICAGO.......Ar	11.43	......	......	......
5.43	5.43	......	2.47	......	......	...	Ar.......Waterloo.......Lv	7.19	......	......	......
† 6.30	§ 6.30	......	......	‡10.15	......	...	Lv.......BUFFALO.......Ar	7.25	11.59	......	3.15
8.31	8.31	......	......	12.11	......	...	Lv.......Erie.......Ar	5.09	9.51	......	12.48
10.55	10.55	......	......	2.40	......	...	Lv.......Cleveland.......Ar	† 1.50	7.30	......	10.15
2.15	2.15	......	......	5.15	† 7.15	...	Lv.......Toledo.......Ar	10.05	3.25	......	7.40
4.24	4.22	......	......	7.19	9.45	...	Ar.......Waterloo.......Lv	7.48	1.00	......	5.43
8.15	6.54	10.08	2.50	10.00	9.50	...	Waterloo	6.00	12.15	8.39	5.35
8.25	7.04	10.18	3.00	10.10	10.00	78	Auburn	5.50	12.04	8.29	5.23
8.28	7.08	10.21	3.03	10.13	10.03	79	Auburn Junction	5.48	12.01	8.25	5.19
f 8.34	f 7.14	......	f 3.09	f10.19	f10.09	83	St. Johns	......	f11.54	f 8.19	f 5.11
f 8 38	f 7.17	......	3.13	f10.23	f10.13	85	New Era	......	f11.51	f 8.16	5.07
......	......	......	......	......	......	89	Stoners	......	......	......	......
......	......	......	......	......	f10.21	91	Huntertown	......	......	......	f 4.59
......	......	......	......	......	f10.24	93	Carroll's Crossing	......	......	......	f 4.56
......	f 7.33	......	f 3.30	......	f10.28	95	Academie	......	......	f 8.03	f 4.53
9.05	7.45	10.55	3.45	10.50	10.40	100	Ar.......FT. WAYNE.......Lv	* 5.20	†11.30	§ 7.55	* 4.45
PM	PM	PM	PM	AM	AM			AM	AM	AM	PM

YPSILANTI BRANCH

	454	448	Mls.	STATIONS.	443	447	
......	† 9.00AM	* 3.00AM	......	Lv.......CHICAGO.......Ar	5.55PM	7.00AM	......
......	1.11PM	7.06AM	......	Ar.......Hillsdale.......Lv	12.02PM	9.41PM	......
......	† 2.45PM	* 7.50AM	0	Lv.......HILLSDALE.......Ar	10.55AM	8.37PM	......
......	3.00	8.05	7	North Adams	10.41	8.22	......
......	3.09	8.14	12	Jerome	10.31	8.12	......
......	3.16	8.21	16	Somerset Center	10.22	8.03	......
......	3.20	8.25	18	Somerset	10.17	f 8.00	......
......	3.26	8.31	20	Woodstock	10.11	7.55	......
......	3.37	8.42	25	Brooklyn	10.01	6.46	......
......	f 3.48	f 8.54	31	Watkins	f 9.50	f 7.35	......
......	3.59	9.08	37	Manchester	9.40	7.24	......
......	4.17	9.27	44	Bridgewater	9.03	7.05	......
......	4.23	9.38	50	Saline	8.54	6.54	......
......	4.36	f 9.46	54	Pittsfield Junction	8.47	f 6.46	......
......	4.50PM	10.00AM	61	Ar.......YPSILANTI.......Lv	† 8.35AM	* 6.30PM	......
......	5.55PM	10.45AM	......	Ar.......Detroit (M. C. R. R.).......Lv	† 7.30AM	* 5.45PM	......

*Daily. †Daily ex. Sun. §Sun. only. ‡Saturday only. f—Stops to discharge and on signal to receive passengers.

This sampling from the Lake Shore & Michigan Southern timetable of 11 June 1911 shows the exceptional level of local service provided only a few years before the onset of World War I.

Author's collection.

The Ann Arbor Railroad bought five McKeen motor cars to improve its passenger business without having to use a full train crew. Put in service in 1911 between Toledo and Cadillac, they supplemented steam trains to offer three and four trains a day each way over much of the line. The cars were less than a mechanical success and ran only until 1925.

Sam Breck collection.

from Detroit to both Mackinaw City and Sault Ste. Marie. The day train to Mackinaw had a parlor car and a café coach. Jackson–Grand Rapids service was increased by one trip to five trains, but the fastest running time still stood at a little over two hours thirty minutes. Most ran through to Detroit and handed off Detroit cars to main-line trains. The overnight run had a Detroit–Grand Rapids sleeping car; another run handled a Grand Rapids–Pittsburgh sleeper (which was handed off to a New York Central branch run at Jackson) and a Muskegon-Buffalo sleeper. Chicago–Grand Rapids service via Kalamazoo and the Grand Rapids & Indiana had through day and overnight trains; two other runs with through cars made close connections. In the summer the day run had a Chicago-Cadillac parlor car; another run carried Chicago–Harbor Springs and Chicago–Mackinaw City sleepers.

The Lake Shore & Michigan Southern service changed only gradually. The New York Central, which owned the LS&MS, inaugurated the *20th Century Limited* on 15 June 1902, a five-car train that cost an extra fare to travel on a twenty-hour schedule between New York City and

ANN ARBOR R. R.
TOLEDO, ANN ARBOR, OWOSSO, CADILLAC, FRANKFORT

107	11	53	13	51	Oct 3 1920		54	52	12	14	106
PM	PM	PM	AM	AM			PM	PM	AM	PM	PM
s5 00	15 00	t3 00	10t00	D7 00	0	Lv Cherry St. Ar	1 05	6 30	9 00	4 00	12 05
*5 15	5 16		10 19	8	9	.. Temperance ..		8	8 31	3 28	11*42
*5 19	5 24		10 24	8	11	.. Samaria ..		8	8 26	3 20	11*38
*5 29	*5 40		10 35	8	17	... Lulu		8	8 13	*3 02	11*28
*6 32	5 50		10 39	8	19	.. Federman ..		8	8 07	2 57	11*24
5 43	6 00	3 46	10 48	7 39	22	.. Dundee ..	12 17	5 43	7 57	2 48	11 15
5 53	6 10		10 59	8	27	.. Azalia ..		8	7 47	2 36	11*05
6 03	6 21	3 58	11 14	7 55	31	.. Milan ..	12 01	5 22	7 31	2 26	10 56
*6 16	*5 35		11*32		37	.. Urania ..			*7 18	*2 12	10*46
*6 23	*5 42		11*40		41	.. Pittsfield ..			*7 10	*2 05	10*40
	7 00					Ar	Lv 11 30	4 50	t7 00	1 55	10 30
Sun	PM				45	.. Ann Arbor ..			AM		Sun
6 40		4 32	11 56	8 30	51	Lv Ar Osmer				*1 39	
*6 54			12*18		57	Whitmore Lake	11 06	4 16		1 25	10 00
7 07		5 00	12 30	8 52	59	.. Hamburg ..	10 59	4 08		1 18	9 54
7 13		5 07	12 37	8 59	62	.. Lakeland ..	10 52	4 01		1 10	9 48
7 20		5 14	12 44	9 05	67	.. Chilson ..	10*43	N		1 00	*9 38
*7 32		*5 25	*00	N	72	.. Annpere ..				12*47	
7 48		5 43	1 15	9 29	74	.. Howell ..	10 31	3 36		12 42	9 23
*8 01		5 57	1 29	*9 42	80	.. Oak Grove ..	10 18	*3 22		12 29	9 11
*8 10		6 06	1 38	*9 50	85	.. Cohoctah ..	10 09	*3 13		12 20	9 02
8 19		6 17	1 47	10 00	89	.. Byron ..	10 00	3 03		12 10	8 54
		II6 30			96	Ar Lv Durand	9 45	2 47		11 52	8 42
8 35		6 45	2 00	10 25		.. Vernon ..	9 20				
8 49		6 53	2 09	10 35	99	.. Vernon ..	9 11	2 36		11 41	8 33
8 57		7 04	2 25	10 46	104	.. Corunna ..	9 00	2 25		11 27	8 24
9 10		7 15	2 40	10 54		Ar Lv	8 50	2 15		11†15	8 15
	15		PM		107	.. Owosso ..			16	AM	
	AM					Lv Ar			PM	PM 18	
9 15	D7 20	7 25	t3 00	11 05		Owosso	8 40	2 05	12 01	7 00	8 10
9 20	7 25	7 29	3 05	11 10	108	.. Owosso Junc ..	8 35	2 00	11 50	6 55	8 03
*9 35	7 48	*7 45	3 20		116	.. Carland ..	*8 17		11 30	*6 34	*7 48
9 45	8 07	7 54	3 31	11 42	120	.. Elsie ..	8 07	1 34	11 15	6 22	7 37
*9 54	8 15	8 02	3 40		124	.. Bannister ..	7 58		11 06	6 12	7 27
10 04	8 24	8 10	3 61	12 01	128	.. Ashley ..	7 49	1 17	10 54	6 02	7 17
10*17	8 37	8 23	4 05		134	.. North Star ..	7 35		10 40	5 47	7 04
10 28	8 47	8 34	4 16	12 25	138	.. Ithaca ..	7 25	12 54	10 31	5 36	6 54
10 45	9 02	8 55	4 34	12 48	145	.. Alma ..	7 05	12 30	10 15	5 21	6 39
10*55	9 12	*9 10	*4 44		150	.. Forest Hill ..	*6 49		10 06	5 10	*6 28
11 08	9 24	9 24	4 57	1 12	156	.. Shepherd ..	6 36	11 54	9 53	4 57	6 17
11 40	9 38	9 56	5 20	1 35	164	.. Mt. Pleasant ..	†6 20	11 34	9 26	4 31	s6 00
PM	9 58	PM	5 37	1 49	171	.. Rosebush ..	AM	11 16	9 15	4 16	AM
Sun	10 32		6 00	2 07	179	.. Clare ..		10 58	8 59	3 53	Sun
	10 46		6 10	2 17	184	.. Farwell ..		10 46	8 45	3 41	
	10*58		*6 22		189	.. Summit ..			*8 35	*3 31	
	11*10		*6 36		194	.. Lake George ..			*8 24	*3 19	
	11*17		*6 43		198	.. Clarence ..			*8 17	*3 12	
	11 23		6 49		201	.. Temple ..			8 11	3 04	
	11*29		*6 55		204	.. Pennocks ..			*8 05	*2 56	
	11 42		7 10	3 10	209	.. Marion ..		9 58	7 54	2 42	
	11 51		7 21		213	.. Park Lake ..			7 45	2 32	
	11 59		7 31	3 28	217	.. McBain ..		9 40	7 39	2 25	
	12 08		7 41		221	.. Lucas ..			7 31	2 16	
	12 25		8 00	4 00		Ar Lv		9 15	t7 15	D2 00	
	PM		PM		227	.. Cadillac ..		AM	PM		
				4 05		Lv Ar		9 10			
				*4 28	236	.. Millersville ..		*8 47			
				4 34	238	.. Boon ..		8 42			
				4 47	245	.. Harrietta ..		8 26			
				*4 57	249	.. Yuma ..		*8 14			
				5 09	254	.. Mesick ..		8 03			
					258	.. Bagnall ..					
				5 24	264	.. Harlan ..		7 47			
				*5 30	265	.. Pomona ..					
				5 37	268	.. Copemish ..		7 35			
				5 49	271	.. Thompsonville ..		7 24			
				*6 05	278	.. Homestead ..		*7 08			
				6 15	283	.. Beulah ..		6 55			
				6 40	292	.. Frankfort ..		D6 30			
				PM		Ar Lv		AM			

11 13 15 17 are Motor Cars
12 14 16 18 are Motor Cars

51 will stop at all stations No. of Owosso Junc. to let off passengers from all stations So. of Corunna and to take passengers for stations No. of Millersville.
52 will stop at all stations No of Mt. Pleasant to take passengers for Durand and South
54 will stop at all stations So. of Ann Arbor to let off passengers from stations North of Owosso Jc. and on Sunday will stop on signal at all stations Mt. Pleasant to Toledo.
N will stop to let off or take passengers from or to Toledo
S stops on signal Sunday

This schedule from the March 1921 *Michigan Railway Guide* shows the extent to which the Ann Arbor's McKeen motor cars supplemented the steam train service provided by numbers 51–54. The service changed little between 1911 and 1925.

Author's collection.

LAKE SUPERIOR & ISHPEMING RY.
MUNISING RAILWAY
MARQUETTE & SOUTH EASTERN RY.

PM	AM	PM	PM	PM	PM	AM	Mi	Lv May 30 1909 Ar	AM	PM	PM	PM	AM	PM
s6 00	s8 00	†8 00	†4 45	†3 45	12†55	†6 50	0	...Munising...	9 45	2 00	4 20	7 30	10 50	8 25
*6 10	*8 10	*8 15	.....	*3 55	*1 06	*6 59	4	...Hallston...	*9 31	*1 48	4 03	*7 20	*10 39	*8 14
*6 13	*8 13	*8 21	*4 58	*3 58	*1 10	*7 02	5	...Merriam...	*9 27	*1 43	3 58	*7 17	*10 36	*8 11
.....	.....	8 50	.....	4 00	1 12	.....	6	.Munising Junc.	.....	†1 40	.....	.....	.....	.....
		AM		PM	PM		9	Ar .Stillman. Lv	9 15		3 30	7 09	10 28	8 03
6 21	8 22	.....	5 10	.....	.....	7 10	9	Lv .Stillman. Ar			3 10			
*6 34	*8 35	.....	*5 24			*7 22	14	..Dixon..	*8 54		2 50	*6 57	*10 14	*7 49
*6 37	*8 38	.....	*5 28			*7 25	16	..Calciferous..	*8 50		2 45	*6 54	*10 11	*7 46
6 44	8 43	.....	5 35			7 30	18	...Chatham...	8 42		2 35	6 49	10 06	7 41
*6 50	*8 48	.....	*5 43			*7 35	20	...Eben...	*8 35		2 10	*6 44	*10 00	*7 35
6 58	8 55	.....	5 53			7 43	23	...Rumely...	8 25		1 45	6 37	9 53	7 28
*7 03	*9 01	.....	*6 00			*7 48	25	...Dorsey...	*8 18		1 31	*6 32	*9 48	*7 22
7 12	9 10	.....	6 10			7 58	28	Ar .Lawson. Lv	8 10		1 20	6 25	9 41	7 15
7 15	9 45	.....	6 30			8 10		Lv .Lawson. Ar	7 58			6 10	9 05	7 00
7 25	9 55	.....	6 45			8 20	32	..Carlshend..	7 46		12 55	5 55	8 55	6 50
7 40		.....	7 05	PM	AM	8 37	38	Ar .Little Lake. Lv	7 30	PM 12†25		5 25	8 40	6 35
7 52	10 10	.....	7 52	†3 40	10†05			Lv .Little Lake. Ar	6 35	9 35	2 55			
8 05	10 25	.....	*8 05	*4 00	10 24	*8 55		...Gwinn...	6 20	9 15	2 35	4 58	8 25	6 20
8 10	10 30	.....	8 10	4 05	10 30	9 00	45	...Princeton...	†6 15	†9 10	†2 30	†4 50	s8 20	s6 15

PM	AM	PM	PM	PM	PM	AM	Mi	Lv ... Ar	AM	AM	PM	PM	PM	AM	PM
s7 15	s9 10	.....	†6 20	.....	.....	†8 10	28	...Lawson...	8 00			6 15	9 41	7 13	
*7 23	*9 18	.....	*6 28			*8 18	31	...Selma...	*7 47			*6 07	*9 33	*7 05	
7 30	9 27	.....	6 35			8 25	34	...Skandia...	7 39			5 59	9 27	6 58	
*7 34	*9 31	.....	*6 39			*8 29	36	..New Dalton..	*7 34			*5 55	9 23	6 54	
7 38	9 35	.....	6 42			8 33	37	...Yalmer...	7 30			5 51	9 20	6 50	
7 47	*9 43	.....	*6 50			*8 42	41	..Green Garden..	*7 21			*5 42	*9 12	*6 41	
7 50	9 45	.....	*6 52			8 45	42	...Mangum...	7 18			5 40	9 10	6 39	
8 03	9 58	.....	7 03			8 57	47	...Harvey...	7 04			5 27	8 58	6 27	
8 15	10 10	.....	7 15			9 10	52	Ar .Marquette. Lv	†6 50			5 15	8 45	6 15	
8 25	10 15	.....		PM	s3 50	9 20		Lv .Marquette. Ar		AM	2 20	5 05	8 35	6 05	
						9 32		...West Yard...				4 53			
*8 53	*10 44	.....		*4 34		*9 48	62	...Dead River...		*1 56		*4 38	*8 11	*5 37	
*9 00	*10 51	.....		*4 41		*9 55	65	...Eagle Mills...		*1 49		*4 31	*8 04	*5 30	
9 11	11 02	.....		4 52		10 06	70	...Negaunee...		1 38		4 20	7 54	5 19	
9 20	11 10	.....		5 00		10 15	73	...Ishpeming...		s1 30		†4 10	s7 45	s5 05	

STILLMAN, CUSINO

AM	AM	Mi	Lv ... Ar	PM	AM
.....	†7 00		...Marquette...	7 15	.....
.....	7 00	0	...Munising...	3 40	.....
		4	...Hallston...		
		5	.Merriam...		
†10 25	9 15	9	Lv .Stillman. Ar	3 05	
10 37	9 30	11	...Coalwood...	2 30	11 30
10 50	9 40	13	...Roscoe...	2 15	11 17
	10 25	22	...Hartho...	2 05	†11 05
	10 35	24	...Chapman...	12 55	
	10 45	26	...Masters...	12 45	
	11 05	31	...Leroux...	12 30	
	11 15	32	...Cusino...	12 12	†12 05
AM			Ar ... Lv	PM	

MUNISING, BIG BAY

AM	AM	Mi	Lv ... Ar	PM	PM
.....	†6 50		...Munising...	1 55	7 20
s8 50	9 15	0	...Marquette...	*1 40	*7 05
*9 02	*9 27	4	...West Yard...	*1 22	*6 52
*9 16	*9 43	9	.Pickerel Lake.	*1 10	*6 41
*9 26	*9 55	12	...Buckroe...	1 00	6 32
.....	10 05	15	Ar ..Birch.. Lv	12 27	
9 37	10 35		Lv ..Birch.. Ar		
*9 50	*10 51	20	...Powell...	*12 11	*6 17
*9 53	*10 55	22	...Antlers...	*12 07	*6 14
*10 04	*11 06	25	...Ransom...	*11 56	*6 05
10 10	11 20	27	...Big Bay...	†11 50	s6 00
AM	AM		Ar ... Lv	AM	PM

These three roads, all owned by Cleveland Cliffs Iron Company, were not yet merged into one company when this 1909 *Michigan Railway Guide* schedule was issued. An "s" next to the first train time means the train ran Sundays only, a dagger (†) that it ran daily except Sundays. An asterisk means the train stopped only if flagged—a flag stop. The oldest of the lines shown had been built only twelve years earlier.

Author's collection.

Chicago. This sort of service did not carry over to the Michigan branch lines. The six runs in 1895 on the Toledo–Elkhart Old Road through Hillsdale were reduced to five by 1902, with more of them making all local stops. When the LS&MS was merged into the New York Central at the beginning of 1915, Old Road service was further reduced to four trains, three of which were locals. Old Road trains were put into a separate schedule, with no indication that the trains ran beyond Toledo or Elkhart or made connections to do so. Service on other branches fared only somewhat better. Toledo-Detroit trains were increased from three to four by 1905 and to five by 1907. (The Michigan Central also ran four a day on its own line.) Jackson-Toledo service was increased from two a day in 1895 to three by 1902 and four by 1909. The Elkhart–Grand Rapids and the Jackson–Fort Wayne services were increased from two to three trips by 1910.

In 1896 the Grand Trunk cut off two of its Chicago–Port Huron runs, leaving only three each way, but branch-line service remained little changed. By 1904 main-line service was back up to the 1896 levels, and one more local had been added. A new eastbound train from Chicago went by way of Detroit, presumably to provide direct service to Mt. Clemens and its health spas. By 1916 one through trip was discontinued, and by 1918 another was gone, as was the run via Detroit. On the branches only the Detroit–Grand Rapids service changed to any extent: the four trains of 1895 were reduced to three by 1902, back up to four by 1909, and down to two in 1918. One of the 1909 runs was a morning eastbound and afternoon westbound express that ran between Grand Haven and Detroit in four and a half hours, with close connections at Grand Haven and with overnight steamships to Chicago and Milwaukee. This service was ended by 1918. All other branch lines had strictly local service.

The Pere Marquette followed the merger of its three components in 1900 with improvements in service. The Chicago–Grand Rapids service was increased to five trips by 1902, one of which was the summers-only service between Chicago and Petoskey. Of the remaining four, one was an overnighter, and the others made nearly all stops. One day train made the run in five hours, but the others took at least six. One run made close connections with a Grand Rapids–Bay City express run to offer a Chicago–Bay City service. Three trains a day ran from Grand Rapids to Traverse City, two of which went on to Petoskey. The Detroit–Grand Rapids service stayed at three trips, most of which made connections at Grand Ledge with trains to Ionia, Howard City, and Big Rapids. Four trains a day ran from Bay City to Detroit, three of which also went on from Plymouth to Toledo. Two trains a day ran from Saginaw to Ludington and a third from Saginaw to Harrison. Most branch lines had two locals a day each way, but Port Huron–Saginaw and the Manistee branch had three. With the 1902 completion of its Saginaw–Edmore–Grand Rapids route, it put on two trains a day and ended service via Howard City and the Grand Rapids & Indiana. One unique service, which lasted only a year or two, was a Detroit–Grand Rapids run that went on to Ottawa Beach at Holland and connected with a steamship to Milwaukee. The new Saginaw–Grand Rapids trains were coordinated with this train. By 1912 the PM started a new Detroit-Toledo service using the Wabash between Detroit and Romulus, and three runs a day from Detroit to Cincinnati, via the Cincinnati, Hamilton & Dayton, were scheduled. Very likely reflecting the PM's second receivership within a decade, overall service changed very little between 1912 and 1915, but with a fifth Chicago–Grand Rapids daytime run added.

Throughout the rest of the Lower Peninsula passenger train service changed very little in the first two decades of the twentieth century. About 1910 the Ann Arbor supplemented its Toledo-Frankfort and Toledo-Cadillac passenger trains with a number of runs served by motor cars. The stepped-up service included at least four trips a day each way over all of the line south of Cadillac, and three between Cadillac and Frankfort. The motor cars stopped at road crossings every mile or two along their runs.

The Chicago & North Western continued to provide the most extensive service into the Upper Peninsula. By 1908 it added a third Menominee-Escanaba run to supplement the two Chicago-Ishpeming runs. The overnight *Iron and Copper Country Express* hauled sleeping cars from Chicago to Escanaba, Sault Ste. Marie, and Marquette. The *Iron Range Express* was a similar run between Chicago and Iron River. There were no substantive changes after that. About 1910 the Chicago, Milwaukee & St. Paul added to its two Chicago-Champion runs a third that ran between Chicago and Ontonagon. In 1914 its branch to Iron River was completed, and three round-trips a day were put on to connect with trains at Channing. Duluth, South Shore & Atlantic service changed little throughout the period. The mainstay was an overnight Duluth–Sault Ste. Marie run with one leg joining it at Nestoria from Calumet and another separating at Soo Junction for St. Ignace. Additionally, it provided a daytime run from St. Ignace and Sault Ste. Marie to

Calumet, and a round-trip run mornings from Marquette to Calumet with an afternoon return. There was no change in the Soo Line service between the Twin Cities and Sault Ste. Marie, with the *Montreal and Boston Express* handling cars from Minneapolis to Montreal and Boston.

Despite the abundance of service available during the Golden Age, what the rider rode in was far from the best. The affluent could afford to ride in Pullman sleeping cars and sit on plush seats in parlor cars and eat served meals in the dining cars. They had to pay an additional accommodation fare, and an extra fare to ride some trains, but they could ride in comfort. Ordinary riders rode in wooden coaches, many of them built not long after the Civil War. They may have had electric lights and steam heat, but open windows provided the air-conditioning. Seats had just enough fabric to hide the wood and metal they were made of. For meals, some families carried a picnic basket, while others choked down bad food in depot restaurants during twenty-minute meal stops. By 1912 a few roads started to advertise their electric lighting or their steel cars, but most roads made no mention of either because they were far from universally used.

The electric interurban and the private automobile brought new competition to the railroads. While railroad branch lines saw ridership drop, overall traffic levels changed little. While branch and local trains may have had fewer riders, they also handled U.S. mail and express, so they stayed as long as those revenues continued. The Michigan Central did add some faster trains, mostly on its main line, but it was the exception. The Pere Marquette made very few changes, while the Grand Trunk reduced service. Very few routes showed enough growth in traffic to warrant any additional service. Management believed that added trains were not needed, nor would they contribute to profits. Branch-line riders found the automobile to be especially alluring, a trend that became clear after the end of World War I. The private car was such a convenience that the slow local passenger train could not compete against it.

SOURCES

Chicago & North Western Railway, public timetables, various dates.

Grand Trunk Railway, public timetables, various dates.

Lake Shore & Michigan Southern Railway, public timetables, various dates.

Michigan Central Railroad, public timetables, various dates.

Michigan Railway Guide, various dates.

The Official Guide of the Railways. New York: National Railway Publication, August
   1902, August 1912, June 1916.

Pere Marquette Railroad, public timetables, various dates.

Travelers Official Guide of the Railway and Steam Navigation Lines. Reprint of June
   1893 issue.

A Summer Up North

The Grand Rapids & Indiana was built into northern Michigan to haul out the lumber. It found some potential in tourist travel when it built into Petoskey in 1874. By that time the Little Traverse Bay area already was developing as a summer resort area. Great Lakes steamers brought resorters from Chicago and Milwaukee to Harbor Springs, Petoskey, Charlevoix, and Mackinac Island. A small boat sailed regularly between Harbor Springs and Petoskey, calling at resorts en route. In 1875 the Methodist Church established the Bay View Association as a summer religious Chautauqua just north of the end of the GR&I tracks at Petoskey.

In 1875 the GR&I published its first edition of *A Guide to the Haunts of the "Little Fishes," the "Speckled Brook Trout" and the Beautiful "American Grayling" and Many Other Kinds of the Finny Tribe in the Land of Northern Michigan*. The guide included a directory of summer resorts and inns for the "invalid and the pleasure seeker." The guide reappeared annually under a variety of names; it became *Michigan in Summer* in 1903 and kept that name until the final issue in 1917. The GR&I reinforced its early appeal to fishermen by using "The Fishing Line" as its corporate slogan and a logo depiction of an oversized speckled trout leaping from the waters. The road's *Where to Go Fishing* was published almost annually until 1917. The company also widely promoted the Ottawa Indian pageant *Hiawatha*, which was performed each summer at Wa-ya-ga-mung near Conway.

In February 1882 the Bay View, Little Traverse & Mackinac, a Grand Rapids & Indiana subsidiary, began operating between Bay View and Harbor Springs to serve the string of resorts that were developing along the shoreline of Little Traverse Bay. At the same time, another GR&I subsidiary, the Grand Rapids, Indiana & Mackinac, began building north, completing its line to Mackinaw City on 3 July 1882, just seven months after the Michigan Central and the Detroit, Mackinac & Marquette arrived at the straits. The GR&I formed a partnership with the Michigan

Central and the Detroit & Cleveland Steam Navigation Company in 1886 to build and operate the Grand Hotel on Mackinac Island.

About 1898 the GR&I established the *Northland Limited* as its premiere overnight summer train between Cincinnati and Mackinaw City. Leaving Cincinnati between six and seven in the evening, it picked up sleeping cars along the way that connecting trains brought from St. Louis, Louisville, Indianapolis, Columbus, and Chicago. It arrived in Petoskey about 7 A.M., made a side trip to Harbor Springs, then backed up to the main line to continue on to Mackinaw City for an arrival around noon. For a brief time a separate train was operated from Chicago to Mackinaw City using the Grand Trunk Western between Vicksburg and Chicago. After only a few years this latter train was replaced by the *North Michigan Resorter* on a route that used the Michigan Central between Kalamazoo and Chicago. During World War I the U.S. Railway Administration renamed the summer train simply the *Northland*.

In addition to its through summer train and three other Grand Rapids–Mackinaw City trains each day, the GR&I developed an impressive local service for the resorts near Little Traverse Bay. The most heavily

The Grand Rapids & Indiana's premier summer train, the *Northland Limited*, heads south along Little Traverse Bay, just north of Bay View.

Cleland B. Wyllie collection.

Chicago to Grand Rapids and Northern Michigan

Via Kalamazoo and Pennsylvania System

Table 5

36	44	42	22	2	Michigan Central	47	41	43	15
AM	PM	PM	AM	AM		AM	PM	PM	PM
*12.05	*5.10	*12.01	*8.47	†6.40	Lv....Chicago.....Ar	7.20	12.15	5.00	7.30
12.14	5.18	12.08	8.55	6.48	"......43d Street....."	7.10	12.05	4.51	7.21
12.18	5.21	12.11	8.58	6.51	".....53d Street....."	7.06	12.01	4.48	7.18
12.21	5.24	12.14	9.01	6.54	".....63d Street....."	7.02	11.57	4.45	7.15
g12.40	5.40	12.30		7.10	"...Kensington....."	h6.45		4.30	
12.53	g5.51	12.40	g9.26	7.21	"....Hammond....."	6.26	11.27	4.16	
g1.08	g6.06	12.52		7.40	".....Gary......"	6.02	11.11	4.01	
				7.50	"....East Gary....."				
				8.08	"......Porter....."	h5.37			
1.45	6.39	1.23	10.11	8.35	"..Michigan City..."	5.17	10.35	3.25	5.46
				8.53	"...New Buffalo..."	h4.58			
		1.49		9.04	"...Three Oaks...."	h4.47		3.00	
				9.20	".....Galien....."	h4.37	10.03	2.53	
		2.05		9.38	"....Buchanan....."	h4.26		2.43	
2.45	7.30	2.15	10.57	10.03	".....Niles......"	4.10	9.42	2.29	4.53
				10.15	"....Pokagon....."				
	7.47	2.32	11.13	10.25	"....Dowagiac....."	h3.53	9.23	2.13	
		f2.43		10.44	"....Decatur....."			f1.58	
		f2.52		10.56	".....Lawton....."	h3.29		1.49	
				11.04	"....Mattawan....."				
3.55	8.33	3.15	11.58	11.29	Ar....Kalamazoo....Lv	3.05	*8.33	*1.25	*3.51

1	17-3	17	15-9	11	Penna. System	6	18	14	10	8
AM	PM	PM	PM	PM		PM	AM	AM	PM	PM
*5.05	*8.40	*8.40	*3.25	*12.15	Lv....Kalamazoo....Ar	a7.30	2.50	8.20	1.20	a3.40
	b8.57	b8.57	f3.43	12.35	"....Plainwell....Lv			8.00	j1.00	3.11
			f3.55		"......Martin......"					f2.55
				f1.00	"....Shelbyville...."			f7.42		2.50
				f1.10	"....Wayland....."			f7.30		2.39
6.30	10.05	10.05	4.50	1.45	Ar...Grand Rapids...Lv	*5.50	*1.20	†6.50	*12.01	1.55
AM	PM	PM	PM	PM		PM	PM	AM	AM	PM
*7.15			*5.20	*5.20	Lv...Grand Rapids..Ar	*4.55	11.00		10.50	
8.45			6.45	6.45	Ar....Muskegon....Lv	*3.25	9.40		*9.30	
AM	PM	PM	PM	PM		PM	PM	AM	AM	PM
*7.00	†10.55	*10.30	6.00	†2.10	Lv...Grand Rapids..Ar	4.45	1.15	‖6.25	10.45	
7.37	11.35		6.36	2.42	Ar....Rockford....Lv	4.04			10.06	
7.53	11.53		6.50	2.58	"..Cedar Springs..."	3.43			9.51	
8.05	¶12.05		7.00	3.10	"...Sand Lake....."	3.30			9.40	
8.25	12.25		7.20	3.30	"...Howard City...."	3.13			9.23	
8.39			7.33	3.41	".....Morley......"	2.57			9.04	
8.53			7.51	3.53	"....Stanwood....."	2.43			8.53	
9.18	1.10	12.15	8.15	4.15	"....Big Rapids...."	2.25	e11.25	4.35	8.30	
9.48	1.40		8.44	4.42	"...Reed City....."	1.53		4.09	8.01	
10.14			9.10	5.06	"....Le Roy......"	1.22			7.35	
10.24			9.20	5.16	"....Tustin......"	1.13			7.22	
‖10.55	2.40	1.30	9.45	5.45	Ar....Cadillac....Lv	12.50	10.10	3.20	7.00	
11.15	2.55	1.40	PM	6.05	Lv....Cadillac....Ar	12.30	10.05	3.12	AM	
†1.40					Ar....Lake City....Lv	10.20	1.50			
11.45	3.32			6.36	Ar....Manton....Lv	11.55		2.36		
12.05				6.52	Ar...Walton Junc...Lv	11.35				
*1.15				†7.55	Ar...Traverse City..Lv	10.20	3.45			
*12.40				7.16	Ar..South Boardman..Lv	10.58				
1.00	4.29			7.30	"....Kalkaska....."	10.41		1.38		
1.25	4.57			7.55	"...Mancelona....."	10.15	e8.22	†1.07		
1.40				8.10	".....Alba......"	10.02				
1.59	c5.31			f8.26	".....Elmira......"	9.46	e7.56			
2.20	5.50			8.45	Ar....Boyne Falls..Lv	9.18	e7.39	12.06		
4.10	9.50				Ar Boyne City(B C G&A)Lv	8.30				
*2.39	6.07	b4.35		f9.03	Ar....Clarion....Lv	9.00	e7.16	e11.50		
3.05	6.25	5.05		9.25	Ar....Petoskey....Lv	8.45	7.00	11.35		
3.05	6.35	5.05		9.25	Lv....Petoskey....Ar	8.45	7.00	11.35		
3.08	6.38	5.08		9.28	Ar...Bay View....Lv	8.34	6.51	11.26		
f3.27	6.47	6.47		f9.57	Ar.Menonaqua Beach.Lv	7.27	6.32	10.27		
3.35	6.55	6.55		10.05	"..Wequetonsing..."	7.20	6.25	10.20		
3.40	7.00	7.00		10.10	"..Harbor Springs.."	7.15	6.20	10.15		
3.17	8.38	b5.17		f9.37	Ar....Conway....Lv	8.25	6.00	11.18		
3.23	8.44	b5.23		9.42	"......Oden......"	8.20	5.54	11.13		
3.30	8.51	b5.29		9.48	"....Alanson....."	8.15	5.48	11.07		
3.38	8.59			f9.56	"....Brutus......"	8.08	5.41			
3.47	9.08	b5.48		10.06	"....Pellston....."	8.00	5.33	10.53		
4.02	9.20	b6.00		10.21	"....Levering....."	7.48	5.23	10.40		
4.25	¶9.45	6.30		10.50	"..Mackinaw City..."	7.25	*5.00	10.15		
5.35	11.50	8.45			"..Mackinac Island.."		*4.00	7.15		
9.45		1.05			Ar.Sault Ste. Marie..Lv		†6.50	4.50		
PM	AM	PM		PM	(D. S. S. & A.)	AM	AM	PM		

*Daily. †Daily except Sunday. ‖Meals.
§Sunday only. ‡Daily except Saturday. ¶Daily except Monday.

a Penna. System Train does not run into M. C. R. R. Station.
b Stops to discharge passengers from Michigan Central points beyond Kalamazoo.
c Stops to discharge passengers from Grand Rapids or beyond.
d Stops only to discharge passengers.
e Stops on signal for passengers for Grand Rapids and beyond.
f Stops on signal.
g Stops on signal for passengers for points on Penna. System beyond Kalamazoo.
h Stops to discharge passengers from points on Penna. System beyond Kalamazoo
j Stops to receive passengers for points on Michigan Central beyond Kalamazoo.

For equipment, see pages 11 and 12.

Between Chicago and Grand Rapids-Northern Michigan—Table 5
(Via M. C. R. R.-Penna. System.)

No. 22 Daily.

Parlor Car.................Chicago to Kalamazoo.
Dining Car..............Chicago to Kalamazoo.
Coach...................Chicago to Grand Rapids.

No. 42 Daily.

Parlor Car.................Chicago to Grand Rapids.
Cafe Coach...............Chicago to Grand Rapids.
Coaches...................Chicago to Grand Rapids.

No. 44 Daily.

Sleeping Cars.............Chicago to Mackinaw City—12 Sec. D. R., Daily. (From Grand Rapids in Penn. Sys. No. 17).
 Chicago to Petoskey-Harbor Springs—10 Sec., 2 D. R., Daily. (From Grand Rapids Penn. Sys. No. 3 week days and No. 17, Sundays).
 St. Louis to Petoskey Harbor-Springs—10 Sec., D. R., 2 Comp. via I. C. R. R. No. 20 daily until July 16, inc., and Tuesdays, Thursdays and Saturdays until August 25 then daily until September 21. In Penn. Sys. No. 3 week days from Grand Rapids and No. 17 Sundays.

Parlor Car.................Chicago to Grand Rapids.
Dining Car...............Chicago to Grand Rapids.
Coaches..................Chicago to Grand Rapids and Mackinaw City

No. 36 Daily.

Sleeping Cars.............Chicago to Grand Rapids—12 Sec., D. R.
 Chicago to Grand Rapids—16 Sec.
 Sleeping cars ready for occupancy at 10.35 p.m.
Coaches..................Chicago to Grand Rapids.

No. 41 Except Sunday.

Coach......................Grand Rapids to Chicago

No. 43 Daily.

Parlor Cars.................Grand Rapids to Chicago.
Cafe Coach...............Grand Rapids to Chicago.
Coaches...................Grand Rapids to Chicago.

No. 47 Daily.

Sleeping Cars.............*Grand Rapids to Chicago—12 Sec., D. R.
 *Grand Rapids to Chicago—16 Sec.
 Kalamazoo to Chicago—12 Sec., D. R. (No. 11, Detroit to Kalamazoo, Sundays No. 109-21).
 Mackinaw City to Chicago—12 Sec. D. R., Daily.
 Harbor Springs-Petoskey to Chicago—10 Sec., 2 D.R., Daily.
 Harbor Springs-Petoskey to St. Louis—10 Sec., D. R., 2 Comp., via I. C. R. R. No. 19, daily June 25 to July 17, then Wednesdays, Fridays and Sundays from Harbor Springs until August 26, and daily until September 22.
 * Sleeping cars ready for occupancy at 10.00 p.m.
Coaches...................Mackinaw City and Grand Rapids to Chicago.

trafficked was the Petoskey–Harbor Springs route. The little trains made eleven stops en route, including at Menonaqua Beach, Roaring Brook, and Wequetonsing, and several in Bay View and Petoskey. At times the service was run as often as one train every hour. One set of equipment made three runs a day between Petoskey and Walloon Lake and two round-trips to Oden. Later the Oden leg was extended to run to Alanson. Indiana Point on Crooked Lake, Oden, the large passenger station on Bay Street in Petoskey, and the smaller one in Harbor Springs are solitary reminders of the importance of the GR&I in the development of summer resort travel.

The Michigan Central's line to Mackinaw City was an extension of a line built from Bay City to tap timberlands. Begun in the early 1870s, it was completed to Gaylord by July 1873. Built through a nearly unpopulated region, its coming led to the founding of West Branch, Grayling, and Gaylord. The construction of the Detroit, Mackinac & Marquette between St. Ignace and Marquette in 1880 and 1881 prodded the MC to extend its road from Gaylord to the Straits of Mackinac. The new line ran mostly through forestlands, but did skirt along the west shore of Mullett Lake and touched the village of Cheboygan. The road reached Mackinaw City on 18 December 1881. The company tried to promote development along Mullett Lake as resorts sprang up at Indian River, Topinabee, Long Point, and Birchwood on the lakeshore. The MC's appeal lay in its quick route from Detroit and the East to Mackinac Island and the Upper Peninsula. The MC promoted its advantage with its 1882

THIS PAGE AND OPPOSITE: The Michigan
Central carried Detroiters to the resorts
along Mullett Lake, Burt Lake, and the
Lake Huron shoreline. This 1923 schedule
has two trains overnight between Detroit
and Mackinaw City—an exception to
the usual service. Trains 207 and 210
carried sleeping cars between Mackinaw
City and Columbus, Pittsburgh, and
Cincinnati. Trains 202 and 209 handled
Detroit-Mackinaw, Jackson-Mackinaw, and
Detroit—Sault Ste. Marie sleepers.

Author's collection.

Mackinaw City and Upper Peninsular Points to Bay City, Saginaw, Detroit, Jackson and Chicago

Via Detroit–Bay City Mackinaw Branch

Table 18

4	4			6	Mls.	STATIONS	45	19	9		9
PM	PM			AM			AM	AM	PM		PM
*12.30	*12.30			*10.00		Lv....Chicago....Ar	† 6.30	* 8.00	† 2.50		† 2.50
† 5.18	† 5.18			* 4.25		"....Jackson.... "	† 7.50	* 2.00	† 9.30		† 9.30
† 8.15	† 8.15			* 7.00		Ar..Saginaw, Gen. Ave.Ar	† 4.05	*10.28	† 6.01		† 6.01
† 8.45	† 8.45			* 7.35		Ar....Bay City....Lv	† 3.30	*10.00	† 5.30		† 5.30
207	**209**		**203**				**206**	**206**	**210**		**202**
*10.00	* 9.10		* 8.20		0.0	LvDetroit(East. Time)Ar	10.30	10.30	7.40		8.45
* 9.00	* 8.10		* 7.20		0.0	"..Detroit (Cent. T.). "	† 9.30	† 9.30	† 6.40		* 7.45
*12.20	*11.42		*10.30		105.8	Ar Saginaw, Gen. Ave.Lv	† 5.53	† 5.53	* 2.55		* 4.35
*12.46	*12.11		*11.00		118.9	" Bay City (W. Side) "	† 5.24	† 5.24	2.30		* 4.10
*12.50	*12.15		*11.05		119.6	Ar....Bay City....Lv	† 5.20	† 5.20	2.25		* 4.05
AM	AM	PM	AM	AM			PM	PM	AM	AM	AM
207	**209**	**89**	**203**	**157 Mix**			**158 Mix**	**206**	**210**	**88**	**202**
* 1.00	12.25	† 2.40	†11.10	† 8.35	0.0	Lv....Bay City....Ar	3.30	5.10	2.20	10.00	3.55
.....	12.45	.....	.....	8.40	0.7	"Bay City (W. Side) "	3.24	5.05	2.15	f 9.55	3.50
.....	.....	f 2.50	.....	8.50	2.7	"....Wenona.... "	3.15	.....	.....	f 9.48	.....
.....	.....	3.00	.....	9.11	4.8	"...Kawkawlin... "	3.00	.....	.....	9.43	.....
.....	.....	3.11	.....	9.32	10.8	"....Linwood.... "	2.48	.....	.....	9.32	.....
.....	.....	f 3.21	.....	f 9.41	15.2	"...State Road... "	f 2.37	.....	.....	f 9.18	.....
.....	1.08	3.30	11.45	9.50	18.9	"...Pinconning... "	2.22	4.26	1.45	† 9.10	3.13
.....	.....	PM	.....	f10.02	23.7	"....Worth.... "	f 2.05	.....	AM	.....	.....
.....	1.25	.....	11.57	10.12	27.7	"...Standish... "	1.52	4.10	1.25	.....	2.55
.....	.....	.....	.....	10.26	32.4	"...Sterling... "	1.38	4.02	.....	.....	.....
.....	.....	.....	.....	10.42	40.7	"....Alger.... "	1.13	.....	.....	.....	.....
.....	.....	.....	.....	f10.54	44.8	"..Greenwood.. "	f 1.03	.....	.....	.....	.....
.....	.....	.....	.....	f11.01	47.9	"...Loranger... "	f12.55	.....	.....	.....	.....
2.52	2.15	.....	12.38	11.15	52.7	"..West Branch.. "	12.38	3.28	12.30	.....	2.15
.....	.....	.....	.....	f11.42	60.9	"..Beaver Lake.. "	f12.04	.....	.....	.....	.....
.....	f 2.43	.....	.....	11.53	64.5	"...St. Helen... "	11.53	.....	.....	.....	.....
.....	.....	.....	.....	f12.04	69.3	"....Geels.... "	f11.44	.....	.....	.....	.....
.....	.....	.....	.....	f12.10	71.8	"....Moore.... "	f11.37	.....	.....	.....	.....
a 3.39	3.05	.....	1.20	12.24	77.1	"..Roscommon.. "	11.25	2.54	11.45	.....	1.31
.....	.....	.....	.....	f12.38	83.7	"....Cheney.... "	f11.12	.....	.....	.....	.....
4.05	3.28	.....	1.45	1.00	92.4	Ar } ...Grayling... { Lv	10.40	2.25	11.15	.....	1.07
4.10	3.38	.....	1.50	2.20		Lv } { Ar	10.15	2.20	11.05	.....	1.02
.....	f 3.53	.....	2.05	2.43	101.0	"....Frederic.... "	9.54	2.05	e10.49	.....	.....
.....	f 4.06	.....	.....	f 3.02	109.0	"....Waters.... "	9.34	.....	.....	.....	.....
a 4.48	g 4.11	.....	g 2.21	3.10	111.7	"..Otsego Lake.. "	9.26	e 1.46	e10.32	.....	.....
.....	g 4.14	.....	g 2.24	f 3.15	113.6	"..Arbutus Beach.. "	9.20	.....	f10.29	.....	.....
a 4.55	g 4.18	.....	g 2.26	f 3.19	115.1	"...Oak Grove... "	9.18	.....	f10.27	.....	.....
5.05	4.26	.....	2.32	3.28	119.2	"....Gaylord.... "	9.07	1.32	10.20	.....	12.17
.....	4.40	.....	2.47	3.45	127.7	"...Vanderbilt... "	8.37	1.12	9.58	.....	11.55
5.37	4.59	.....	3.06	4.10	138.3	"...Wolverine... "	8.05	12.47	9.32	.....	11.29
a 6.00	5.21	.....	3.22	4.32	148.4	"..Indian River.. "	7.34	12.26	9.18	.....	dj1111
.....	.....	.....	.....	f 4.40	151.7	"..Grand View.. "	f 7.24	.....	.....	.....	.....
a 6.12	5.33	.....	3.31	4.45	153.9	"...Topinabee... "	7.20	12.16	9.03	.....	dj1101
.....	f 5.42	.....	g 3.37	f 4.52	157.5	"...Long Point... "	7.12	12.11	e 8.58	.....	.....
a 6.27	b 5.47	.....	g 3.42	f 4.58	159.1	"...Birchwood... "	7.06	e12.08	e 8.55	.....	.....
a 6.30	5.51	.....	g 3.45	5.02	160.4	"..Mullet Lake.. "	7.00	12.05	8.52	.....	dj1050
6.43	6.04	.....	3.55	5.20	166.3	"...Cheboygan... "	6.43	11.54	8.40	.....	10.39
.....	f 6.14	.....	.....	f 5.37	173.0	"..Point Nip-i-gon.. "	f 6.25	.....	f 8.28	.....	.....
.....	.....	.....	.....	f 5.48	176.6	"...Freedom... "	f 6.19	.....	.....	.....	.....
7.10	6.30	.....	4.25	6.00	182.3	Lv..Mackinaw City..Lv	† 5.50	†11.30	8.10	.....	*10.15
* 8.45	* 8 45	.....	5.35	.....		Ar..Mackinac Island..Lv	.....	10.15	* 7.15	.....	* 7.15
AM	AM		PM	PM			AM	AM	PM		PM
.....	* 7.30		† 4.40	.....		VIA D. S. S. & A. Lv..Mackinaw City..Ar	.....	†11.15	.....		* 9.55
.....	9.00		6.10	.....		Ar...St. Ignace...Lv	.....	10.10	.....		8.25
.....	10.40		7.20	.....		Ar...Trout Lake...Lv	.....	† 9.04	.....		* 7.20
.....	1.05		9.45	.....		Ar..Sault Ste. Marie..Lv	.....	† 6.50	.....		* 4.50
.....	3.30		11.30	.....		Ar...Marquette...Lv	.....	5.15	.....		2.30
.....	4.45		12.25	.....		"...Negaunee... "	.....	4.35	.....		1.40
.....	5.00		12.35	.....		"..Ishpeming.. "	.....	4.25	.....		1.30
.....	8.15		5.40	.....		"..Houghton.. "	.....	11.00	.....		10.15
.....	8.30		5.55	.....		"..Hancock.. "	.....	10.45	.....		10.05
.....	9.05		6.30	.....		"..Calumet.. "	.....	10.10	.....		9.30
.....	PM		1.35	.....		"..Nestoria.. "	.....	3.25	.....		AM
.....	.....		6.56	.....		"...Bibon... "	.....	10.00	.....		.....
.....	.....		7.52	.....		"..Iron River.. "	.....	8.50	.....		.....
.....	.....		9.35	.....		"..Superior.. "	.....	6.45	.....		.....
.....	.....		10.15	.....		Ar...Duluth...Lv	.....	* 6.10	.....		.....
.....	PM		PM			VIA M. ST. P. & S. S. M. Lv...Trout Lake...Ar	.....	AM	.....		PM
.....	† 2.35		* 7.25	.....		Lv...Trout Lake...Ar	.....	9.05	.....		3.45
.....	4.45		8.55	.....		Ar...Manistique...Lv	.....	7.00	.....		10.45
.....	6.30		10.15	.....		"..Gladstone.. "	.....	5.50	.....		† 6.15
.....	.....		9.30	.....		"...St. Paul... "	.....	7.00	.....		.....
.....	.....		10.15	.....		Ar..Minneapolis..Lv	.....	* 6.20	.....		.....
.....	PM		AM				.....	PM	.....		AM

All a.m. time is given in light figures; all p.m. time in heavy figures.
*Daily. †Daily, except Sunday. ‡Daily, except Saturday. ¶Except Monday.
  a Stops to discharge passengers from points beyond Detroit.
  b Stops to let off passengers from Detroit and beyond.
  c Freight trains carrying passengers do not run Sundays, nor holidays. Permits to use
freight trains are required of passengers which may be secured from ticket agents.
  d Stops to let off passengers from points beyond St. Ignace.
  e Stops on signal to receive passengers for Bay City and south thereof.
  f Stops on signal.
  g Stops to let off passengers from Bay City and points south.
  j Stops on signal to pick up passengers for Bay City, Saginaw and points south of Saginaw
on Bay City-Rives Jct. Branch.
  k Monday, Wednesday and Friday only.

Between Detroit, and Saginaw, Bay City, Mackinaw City and Upper Peninsula Points—Tables 15-18

No. 203   Daily, Detroit to Bay City and Except Sunday,
Bay City to Mackinaw City.

Sleeping Car....................	New York to Saginaw-Bay City. (From No. 17).
Parlor Car....................	Detroit to Mackinaw City, Sundays Detroit to Bay City only.
Cafe Coach....................	Detroit to Mackinaw City except Sunday.
Coaches....................	Detroit to Mackinaw City, Sunday to Bay City.

No. 205   Except Sunday.

Parlor Car....................	Detroit to Saginaw and Bay City.
Cafe Coach....................	Detroit to Saginaw and Bay City.
Coaches....................	Detroit to Saginaw and Bay City.

No. 207   Daily

Sleeping Cars....................	Detroit to Mackinaw City—12 Sec. D. R.
	Columbus-Toledo to Mackinaw City—12 Sec. D. R., except Sunday via O. C. No. 3. (From Toledo-M. C. 310).
	Cincinnati to Mackinaw City via Big Four No. 10—12 Sec., D. R. (From Toledo No. 310).
	Pittsburgh to Mackinaw City Tuesday, Thursday and Saturday—12 Sec., D. R., P. & L. E., N. Y. C. No. 85. (From Toledo No. 306).
Coaches....................	Detroit to Mackinaw City.

No. 209   Daily.

Sleeping Cars....................	Detroit to Sault Ste. Marie—16 Sec. via D. S. S. & A. Ry.
	Detroit to Mackinaw City—12 Sec. D. R.
	Jackson to Mackinaw City—12 Sec. D. R. (No. 77, from Jackson). On Sunday Night—Monday morning car runs from Bay City only.
Coaches....................	Detroit to Mackinaw City.

No. 202   Daily.

Sleeping Cars....................	Sault Ste. Marie to Detroit—16 Sec. via D. S. S. & A. Ry.
	Mackinaw City to Detroit—12 Sec., D. R.
	Mackinaw City to Jackson—12 Sec., D. R. (No. 72, from Bay City). Car leaving Mackinaw City Saturday Night, runs to Bay City only.
Coaches....................	Mackinaw City to Detroit.

No. 206   Except Sunday.

Parlor Car....................	Mackinaw City to Detroit.
Cafe Coach....................	Mackinaw City to Detroit.
Coaches....................	Mackinaw City to Detroit.

No. 208   Daily.

Sleeping Car....................	Bay City and Saginaw to New York—12 Sec., D. R (No. 22-8 Detroit to New York).
Parlor Car....................	Bay City and Saginaw to Detroit.
Cafe Coach....................	Bay City and Saginaw to Detroit.
Coaches....................	Bay City and Saginaw to Detroit.

No. 210   Daily.

Sleeping Cars....................	Mackinaw City to Detroit—12 Sec., D. R.
	Mackinaw City to Toledo-Columbus except Saturday—12 Sec., D. R. (From Detroit No. 301-O. C. No. 6).
	Mackinaw City to Cincinnati via Big Four No. 1—12 Sec., D. R. (From Detroit No. 301).
	Mackinaw City to Pittsburgh, Wednesday, Friday and Sunday—12 Sec., D. R., from Detroit, N. Y. C. No. 1-52, P. & L. E. No. 26.
Coaches....................	Mackinaw City to Detroit.

brochure, *Mackinac Island, the Wave-washed Paradise of the Unsalted Seas.* The MC was in the partnership that built the Grand Hotel.

The MC began overnight train service between Detroit and Mackinaw City soon after the line was completed. During the summer season the train's lone Detroit–Mackinaw City sleeping car was supplemented by, in different years, a Cincinnati–Mackinaw City sleeper and a Detroit–Sault Ste. Marie sleeper. A daytime Detroit–Mackinaw City run complemented the night train service. It carried a parlor car and at times a Detroit-Houghton sleeper. Despite its efforts the MC's line never became as important a summer carrier as was the GR&I. The cutover forest land that the line ran through appealed far more to hunters and fishermen than to summer resorters. Except along Mullett Lake, resorts never were built in the numbers that appeared along the GR&I.

The day train north of Bay City became a casualty of the Great Depression. After World War II the night train carried additional sleepers in the summer; in 1946 the Detroit–Sault Ste. Marie sleeper was reinstated. The next summer there were two Detroit–Mackinaw City sleepers and one between Columbus and Mackinaw City. The triweekly Detroit-Alpena sleeper returned on a year-round basis. A new train, the *Michigan Timberliner,* began service in the summer of 1947, making a Friday evening trip from Detroit to Mackinaw City, and returning Sunday evening. But the effort did not pay off; the extra sleeping cars were gone by the summer of 1949. The night train continued as long as its mail contract provided revenues to offset the small numbers of passengers but was replaced in 1959 by a single-unit railcar running on a daytime schedule. The *Timberliner* made its last trip south on 3 September 1962, with the daytime railcar discontinued soon after.

The Pere Marquette and its predecessor, the Chicago & West Michigan, was the third major player in Michigan summer travel. By the end of 1890 the PM was built as far Traverse City and by July 1892 to Bay View, where it connected with the Grand Rapids & Indiana. Charlevoix had experienced a decade of growth as a summer resort community, so the PM gave it special emphasis in the road's promotional literature. The C&WM began publishing an annual booklet entitled *Tours* in the 1890s, while Grand Rapids & Indiana publications also covered the area. The PM began operating its own summers-only *Resort Special* between Chicago and Bay View. Some years it also ran a Toledo–Detroit–Grand Rapids leg to that train. It carried Pullman cars to Bay View from as far away as St. Louis and Cincinnati.

The summer train was not run during World War II; when it returned in 1946 it ran six days a week from Chicago and three days a week from Detroit. It carried four sleepers from Chicago and two from Detroit, all but two of which went through to Bay View. In 1948 the PM cut the train back to three trips a week from Chicago; in 1949 the train began terminating at Petoskey instead of Bay View; and in 1952 it dropped the Detroit section entirely. In 1953 the *Resort Special* began making only a single trip each week, leaving Chicago on Friday evening and Petoskey on Sunday evening. In 1956 the Chesapeake & Ohio (which had acquired the Pere Marquette) abandoned part of the Grand Rapids–Petoskey line and began using a longer line via Manistee. The end of the *Resort Special* came with its farewell run from Petoskey on 2 September 1957. For a few years in the 1920s the Pere Marquette operated a summer shuttle between Bay View and the Belvedere resort at Charlevoix, but this service did not survive the Great Depression.

The Detroit & Mackinac's route along the Lake Huron shoreline never developed an extensive summer tourist traffic. Through overnight sleeping cars and daytime coaches between Detroit and Alpena were run, using the Michigan Central and at times the Pere Marquette south of Bay City. Regular service to Lake Huron shoreline points was adequate, but no enhanced amenities were offered for summertime passenger riders. The Ann Arbor's only entry was in the 1920s when it handled a Chicago sleeping car from the Pere Marquette at Thompsonville and hauled it to Frankfort twice a week.

Summers in the Upper Peninsula brought no special train service. Both the Chicago & North Western and the Milwaukee Road promoted

1939 Schedule
THE RESORT SPECIAL
Beginning June 19th
FROM CHICAGO AND DETROIT

NORTHBOUND		CENTRAL STANDARD TIME Shown at Chicago, 63rd Street and South Chicago EASTERN STANDARD TIME at all other points	SOUTHBOUND	
Detroit Section	Chicago Section		Chicago Section	Detroit Section
Monday Wednes. Friday	Daily except Sunday		Daily except Saturday	Tuesday Thursday Sunday also Sept. 4
	7:15 PM	Lv. Chicago.............Ar.	7:20 AM	
	7:37 PM	Lv. 63rd Street..........Ar.	6:50 AM	
	8:01 PM	Lv. South Chicago ....Ar.	6:27 AM	
	a11:57 PM	Lv. Holland..............	....	
	12:35 AM	Ar. Grand Rapids..........Lv.	3:40 AM	
9:00 PM		Lv. Detroit.............Ar.		7:30 AM
10:54 PM		Lv. Lansing.............Lv.		5:18 AM
12:20 AM		Ar. Grand Rapids..........Lv.		3:45 AM
1:01 AM	1:01 AM	Lv. Grand Rapids..........Ar.	3:15 AM	3:15 AM
b3:20 AM	b3:20 AM	Ar. Baldwin.............Lv.	12:59 AM	12:59 AM
4:18 AM	4:18 AM	Ar. Kaleva ....Lv.	12:03 AM	12:03 AM
4:36 AM	4:36 AM	Ar. Thompsonville ....Lv.	11:47 PM	11:47 PM
b4:58 AM	b4:58 AM	Ar. Interlochen ....Lv.	b11:25 PM	b11:25 PM
5:25 AM	5:25 AM	Ar. Traverse City ....Lv.	11:00 PM	11:00 PM
6:19 AM	6:19 AM	Ar. Alden ....Lv.	10:07 PM	10:07 PM
6:36 AM	6:36 AM	Ar. Bellaire............Lv.	9:51 PM	9:51 PM
b6:47 AM	b6:47 AM	Ar. Central Lake.........Lv.	b9:39 PM	b9:39 PM
b6:57 AM	b6:57 AM	Ar. Ellsworth...........Lv.	b9:28 PM	b9:28 PM
e7:12 AM	e7:12 AM	Ar. Belvedere...........	....	
7:20 AM	7:20 AM	Ar. Charlevoix..........Lv.	9:10 PM	9:10 PM
7:55 AM	7:55 AM	Ar. Petoskey...........Lv.	8:35 PM	8:35 PM
8:00 AM	8:00 AM	Ar. Bay View...........Lv.	8:30 PM	8:30 PM

a—Stops to let off passengers from Chicago.
b—Stops to take or leave passengers for or from Grand Rapids or beyond.
e—Stops to let off passengers only; baggage should be checked to Charlevoix.

Regular Season

Northbound Monday, June 19, to Friday, September 8; Southbound Tuesday, June 20, to Sunday, September 10.

Pre-Season

Runs between Chicago and Bay View will be made as follows:
Northbound leaving Chicago 7:15 P.M for Bay View.
   Friday, June 9.
   Friday, June 16.
Arrive Bay View 8:00 AM.
Southbound leaving Bay View 4:10 PM, Traverse City, 6:15 PM for Chicago.
   Sunday, June 11.
   Sunday, June 18.
Arrive Chicago 5:30 AM.

Post-Season

Runs will be made as follows:
Northbound leaving Chicago 4:00 PM for Bay View on Tuesday and Friday, September 12 and 15, arriving Traverse City 5:25 AM, Bay View 8:00 AM.
Southbound leaving Bay View 8:30 PM, Traverse City 11:00 PM for Chicago on Wednesday and Sunday, September 13 and 17.

Northbound leaving Detroit 5:10 P. M., Friday September 15. Southbound leaves Resorts on same schedule as Chicago Section, on Sunday, September 17.

For Further Information, Address:
F. A. YOUNG, General Passenger Agent.
General Motors Building, Detroit, Michigan.

TRAVEL PERE MARQUETTE ... ECONOMICAL AND CONVENIENT

DIRECT TO THE HEART OF
Michigan
HOLIDAYLAND

THE RESORT SPECIAL

PERE MARQUETTE
RAILWAY

The Pere Marquette issued a color flyer to announce the 1939 season of the *Resort Special.* It enticed riders with a special round-trip fare from Chicago to Petoskey of just $15.10.

north woods vacationing in print and in their timetables, but it appears most travelers went from Chicago to Wisconsin, and only a most adventuresome few journeyed on to Michigan.

SOURCES

Dunbar, Willis F. *All Aboard! A History of Railroads in Michigan*. Grand Rapids, Mich.: W. B. Eerdmans, 1969.

Grand Rapids & Indiana Railway, public timetables, various years.

Michigan Central Railroad, public timetables, various years.

New York Central Railroad, public timetables, various years.

The Official Guide of the Railways. New York: National Railway Publication, various dates.

Pennsylvania Railroad, public timetables, various years.

Pere Marquette Railroad/Railway, public timetables, various years.

The Vanderbilts Expand and Improve

The Vanderbilts, starting with the father Cornelius and continuing with his son William Henry, picked up railroads at a frantic pace during the last half of the nineteenth century. Their approach was to get control of any road that might become a competitor and thereby prevent financial damage to their properties. By 1890 the Vanderbilts had acquired control of the Cleveland, Cincinnati, Chicago & St. Louis, a major road in Ohio, Indiana, and Illinois commonly called the Big Four. With it the Vanderbilts gained the exceptional talents of Melville E. Ingalls. Ingalls had been president of predecessors of the Big Four since 1873, aggressively expanding at any opportunity. When the Big Four was formed in 1889, he was the logical choice to become its president. By that time Ingalls had developed a good working relationship with the Chesapeake & Ohio, so much so that when the Vanderbilts gained control of that road they saw to it that Ingalls was made its president as well. Using the considerable latitude that the Vanderbilts allowed him, he made the Big Four into a major profit source and developed the C&O as well.

In 1890 the Big Four owned one line into Michigan. By the end of 1882 the Cincinnati, Wabash & Michigan had assembled a line between Anderson, Indiana, and Benton Harbor. In 1891 Ingalls extended the line's service into Louisville. The CW&M became known as the Michigan Division, with Ovid W. Lamport as its superintendent from 1880 until

1891. From his office in Wabash, Indiana, he ran trains by the rule book and solved executive problems based on teachings and examples gleaned from the ever-present Bible on his desk.

A later Ingalls addition was a road that began in 1883 as the Cincinnati, Jackson & Mackinaw, which in turn was a merger of the Ohio-based Cincinnati, VanWert & Michigan and Michigan's unbuilt Jackson & Ohio. In 1887, before it built any lines in Michigan, the CJ&M bought the Michigan & Ohio. The M&O was a hard-luck line that had started life as the grandly conceived Mansfield, Coldwater & Lake Michigan. With some help from the Pennsylvania Railroad, the Mansfield had been able to build a dozen miles from Allegan east and some more in Ohio, all in the early 1870s, before it fell into bankruptcy. It was reorganized, and then reorganized again in 1883 as the Michigan & Ohio. It finished building its line between Dundee and Allegan in November 1883. The new M&O was owned by George I. Seney, Calvin S. Brice, and Dan P. Eels, a trio flush with the profits gained from unloading the Nickel Plate road on William Henry Vanderbilt. The M&O obtained trackage rights over the Ann Arbor between Dundee and Toledo and led a precarious short life until Seney and his friends sold it to the CJ&M in 1887.

The CJ&M line, which extended from a short distance north of Cincinnati up to Addison Junction to a connection with the M&O's Dundee-Allegan line, finished building its line in 1889. Accomplishing this forced the company back into receivership. It was not until January 1892 before it was reorganized as a new CJ&M. Success was short-lived, however, and it went back in receivership again in December 1894. Calvin S. Brice returned to the road in 1895 and took over its presidency. He split off the Dundee-Allegan line to a company that became the Detroit, Milwaukee & Toledo, and put the Cincinnati–Addison Junction line into a newly formed Cincinnati Northern. Next Brice added to the CN the Jackson–Addison Junction line that the Jackson & Cincinnati had built in 1896. Brice left the CN in 1899, and that same year it leased the DT&M. The lease lasted only until 1902, when the Big Four gained control of the CN. The Vanderbilts took the DT&M off the Big Four's hands, then divided the DT&M stock, half to the Michigan Central and half to the Lake Shore. It may be that when Brice bought the CJ&M in 1895 his sole intent was to create another road he could sell to someone. If so, he succeeded in selling the Vanderbilts another road that had little more than nuisance value.

In 1905 the Michigan Central and Lake Shore together built, then owned, the Lansing Manufacturers to reach new automobile factories

At age twenty-seven, Melville E. Ingalls had built a reputation in corporate law when he moved to Cincinnati from Massachusetts in 1870 to manage a small railroad. He never left the Queen City. In 1888 he became president of the Chesapeake & Ohio and in 1889 of the Big Four system. In 1904, a year before his retirement, the landmark Ingalls Building was opened in downtown Cincinnati and stands today in recognition of his work on behalf of his adopted home.

on the north and west side of Lansing. In 1906 the MC bought control of the Chicago, Kalamazoo & Saginaw, a road that straggled northeast from Kalamazoo but which had more value for the industries it served in Kalamazoo. The move may well have been partly a defensive one, for it did prevent Frederick H. Prince of the Pere Marquette from buying the road and using it to shorten his Chicago-Detroit route. Soon after 1910 the Detroit Terminal began to build an industrial belt line around Detroit. The Grand Trunk Western owned 50 percent of the road, the Michigan Central 25 percent, and the Lake Shore 25 percent.

After owning the Lake Shore & Michigan Southern for some forty years, the Vanderbilt family decided around 1910 it was time to simplify its corporate structure. The two mainstay properties were the New York Central & Hudson River, which owned the main line from Buffalo to New York City, and the Lake Shore & Michigan Southern between Buffalo and Chicago. Both companies owned a number of subsidiaries, some wholly owned and others by a stock majority, and also leased other roads and had joint ownerships of still others. The proposal was for a share-for-share exchange of Hudson River stock; Lake Shore shareholders would get 3.05 shares of the new company for each of their shares. But in such an undertaking all sorts of legal problems can arise. Several of the roads had issued bonds that required bondholder approval of any merger; those owners had to be persuaded. There were several minor owners of LS&MS stock who opposed the merger in the hope of being persuaded with a sweetened offer of more money. Four years of work went into getting everyone to agree. On 22 December 1914 the new New York Central Railroad emerged, with its corporate life to begin officially on the first day of 1915. Into it went the NYC&HR and several of its subsidiaries: the Geneva, Corning & Southern in New York and Pennsylvania, and the Terminal Railway of Buffalo; the Lake Shore & Michigan Southern and the lines it owned: the Dunkirk, Allegheny Valley & Pittsburg, the Detroit, Monroe & Toledo, the Northern Central Michigan between Jonesville and Lansing, the Kalamazoo & White Pigeon, and the Detroit & Chicago (the former Chicago & Canada Southern), the Swan Creek Railway of Toledo, and the Chicago, Indiana & Southern, which owned two lines in Indiana. Along with these outright mergers the NYC accepted the transfer of a number of leases of other Michigan lines: the Erie & Kalamazoo; the Kalamazoo, Allegan & Grand Rapids; the Fort Wayne & Jackson; the Detroit, Hillsdale & South Western; and the Sturgis, Goshen & St. Louis.

Around this same time the Vanderbilts tried to get some corporate simplification of the Michigan Central. James F. Joy leased several roads in the 1870s and operated them as an integral part of the MC system, so that by the twentieth century they had little more than a legal existence. In September 1916 the MC amalgamated the Grand River Valley; the Detroit & Charlevoix; the Kalamazoo & South Haven; the Bay City & Battle Creek; the Detroit & Bay City; the Jackson, Lansing & Saginaw; Toledo, the Canada Southern & Detroit; and the Detroit, Delray & Dearborn. In December it merged the Detroit Belt Line. This left the MC with only four leased lines: the Joliet & Northern Indiana in Illinois and Indiana; the Canada Southern in Ontario; and two financially weak roads, the Battle Creek & Sturgis and the St. Joseph, South Bend & Southern from St. Joseph to South Bend. The Canada Southern in turn owned three roads in Michigan: the Canada Southern Bridge Company on Grosse Ile, the Detroit River Tunnel Company under the river in Detroit, and the St. Clair & Western from St. Clair to Richmond.

SOURCES

Harlow, Alvin F. *The Road of the Century*. New York: Creative Age, 1947.

Meints, Graydon M. *Michigan Railroads and Railroad Companies*. East Lansing: Michigan State University Press, 1992.

Michigan Railroad Commission. *Aids, Gifts, Grants and Donations to Railroads . . .* Lansing, Mich.: Wynkoop, Hallenbeck, Crawford, 1919.

The Pere Marquette: New Owners, New Directions

The second largest system in Michigan, the Pere Marquette, was in a much more difficult situation than the very profitable Vanderbilt roads. When the newly formed Pere Marquette Railroad began business at the opening of 1900, its founders hoped that it would be stronger than the three companies that went to make it up. All three—the Flint & Pere Marquette; the Detroit, Grand Rapids & Western; and the Chicago & West Michigan—were built after the Civil War and had early success mostly hauling lumber to sawmills. By the 1890s lumber traffic was in sharp decline, and new traffic to replace it was slow to develop. All three companies were managed fairly conservatively, a reflection of the substantial amounts of New England money that had been invested in them over the years. There was so much overlap of ownership that the Chicago & West Michigan and the Detroit, Lansing & Northern (a predecessor of the Detroit, Grand Rapids & Western) had identical managements and boards of directors. The panics of 1893 and 1897 brought home the fundamental weakness that all three carriers had in common, a difficulty in meeting interest payments on their bonds. Hardest hit was the Detroit, Lansing & Northern, which had its income so reduced that it could no longer pay the interest on its bonds. This forced the road into receivership in 1896, and it was reorganized as the Detroit, Grand Rapids & Western. The West Michigan also failed to earn its interest charges but had built up a profit surplus large enough to be able to continue to pay the charges. The Flint & Pere Marquette was the most fortunate. It had built an extension from Monroe to Toledo in November 1896, which brought new traffic from its good connections, producing added income enough to provide profits. Its innovative railcar ferry service from Ludington to Wisconsin added still more. The idea for a merger probably originated with F&PM president William W. Crapo, its manager for more than thirty years. He talked with Charles W. Heald, president of both the DGR&W and the C&WM, and the two agreed that their three roads combined had a better chance of making a go of it than they did separately. The merger agreement was signed late in 1899, providing for a new Pere Marquette Railroad to begin life on 1 January 1900.

The capital structure, its stocks and bonds, played a critical role in the life of the new Pere Marquette for two decades. The road was capitalized with $16,000,000 in common stock and $12,000,000 in 4 percent preferred stock. On top of this the company remained obligated for $25,286,000 in bonds of various sorts issued by numerous predecessor companies that were now part of the PM. To all of this another $3,500,000 was added for bonds issued at the time of the merger for various purposes. There were also some equipment trust certificates carried over that were paid off soon after the merger. Looked at another way, the PM operated 1,556 miles of railroad, and had stock issued in the amount of $16,709 per mile of road and bonds in the amount of $18,547 per mile. Neither of these latter two figures is particularly high when compared to many other Michigan carriers of like importance. But for a company with a less than a good earnings record over the preceding decade, they probably were higher than they should have been.

The problem the Pere Marquette faced, as had the predecessor lines, was the amount of interest it had to pay annually. The company had a total of about $1,481,000 in interest due each year on the bonds issued, and this amount had to be paid out of net operating profit. If bond

Jeremiah W. Boynton

Born 17 September 1837, Jackson County, Mich.; died 30 March 1912, Grand Rapids.

Boynton moved to Grand Rapids in 1847 and two years later started up a furniture business. In 1875 he became the manager of the Grand Rapids & Reeds Lake Street Railway and built the road to an amusement park. In 1878 he formed the West Side Street Railway of Grand Rapids, and was its president and general manager. He extended his interests in 1884 when he was one of organizers of the Kalamazoo Street Railway.

In 1886 Boynton and several others from Grand Rapids formed the Alaska Railway to build a line from Grand Rapids to Lansing; in 1887 they formed the Lowell & Hastings, and the City Street Railway of Grand Rapids in 1888. Of all of these, only the Lowell & Hastings was built, but that happened after Boynton left the road. In 1888 the same group also formed his most ambitious project, the Central Michigan Railroad. This road was to build a line from Rogers City to Indiana south of Coldwater. Boynton kept this dream alive for nearly twenty years, although the road was never built. In 1906 the Central Michigan's rights were sold to a new Boynton creation, the Grand Rapids Electric. This company had been founded in 1903 to build a line from Grand Rapids to some place on Lake Huron. After buying the Central Michigan rights the GRE changed its goal and planned to build its main line from Grand Haven through Grand Rapids to Gladwin and a branch from the main line through Battle Creek to a point south of Hillsdale.

The dream that Boynton kept alive for so long was never realized.

interest was paid and a net profit remained, there was an obligation for $532,250 in dividends on the preferred stock. In all, the road owed a total of just over $2,000,000 to bondholders and preferred stock owners before any dividend could be paid on the common stock. In 1899 the three component companies had a combined net income of $1,545,000.

President Crapo and General Manager Heald continued to manage the new company in the same conservative manner they always had. In January 1900 the PM acquired control of two other companies: the smallish Grand Rapids, Belding & Saginaw, which had bought the Lowell & Hastings a year earlier to own a line between Freeport and Belding, and the Saginaw, Tuscola & Huron, which owned a line between Saginaw and Bad Axe. The PM also took over operating the Grand Rapids, Kalkaska & Southeastern. To strengthen the financial structure of the new company the PM arranged, in January 1901, for a new consolidated mortgage bond issue up to $50,000,000. Of this the company had to hold back enough to refinance all of the existing outstanding bonds as they matured, a total of $26,650,000 at that time. The remainder of the bonds were to be used only to add to or improve the road itself. During

William W. Crapo

Born 16 May 1830, Dartmouth, Mass.; died 28 February 1926, New Bedford, Mass.

After Crapo graduated from Yale University in 1852 he took up the study of law. His father, Governor Henry H. Crapo, died in 1869 in Flint, and William came to Michigan to administer his father's estate. In 1872 he became a director of the Flint & Pere Marquette, in 1876 a vice president, and in 1882 its president. The company grew from 200 to over 600 miles of line during his administration. He also began the road's extensive car ferry service from Ludington to a number of Wisconsin ports.

In an attempt to strengthen his company he proposed mergers with two other railroads, the Detroit, Lansing & Northern and the Chicago & West Michigan, both of which had some New England money in their financing. Out of these discussions came the Pere Marquette Railroad, formed in November 1899 and which began business in January 1900. Crapo was named president of the new company and remained with it until he resigned in late 1902. When the PM entered receivership in 1904, Crapo was brought back as receiver. By the end of 1907 he had done what he could to return the PM to financial health and left the company for the last time.

William W. Crapo had been with the Flint & Pere Marquette for thirty years when, in 1900, he took the presidency of the newly created Pere Marquette Railroad. He resigned in late 1902 over differences with Frederick H. Prince, but was brought back in 1904 when the road went into receivership.

Bay State Monthly, 3:facing 309.

1901 and 1902 the road issued $4,600,000 of these bonds, with most of the money put into new equipment and various road improvements.

In 1902 the state of Michigan changed the way that it taxed railroads. Through 1901 the railroads were taxed on gross Michigan income, with the rate varying based on the amount of income per mile of road. This reliance on income alone produced wildly varying amounts of tax revenues. To stabilize as well as to increase tax revenues, beginning in 1902 the state's tax became based on the value of the company's property. The PM's tax bill almost doubled, from $255,000 in 1901 to $482,000 in 1902. Several railroads challenged the new tax in court. Crapo and Heald held to their goal of pushing the PM into better operating shape. There were profits each year, a small surplus accumulated from net earnings, and dividends were paid on the preferred stock. The prosperity that followed the end of the panic of 1897 began working to the PM's benefit.

Frederick H. Prince, a banker and director of the PM since its 1900 formation, and some of his friends accumulated a block of 110,000 shares of PM stock by late 1902. Now owning two-thirds of the issued stock, the group had control of the company. Prince had his own ideas about what the Pere Marquette should be doing, plans that were substantially different from those of the conservative Crapo and Heald. Crapo and Heald abruptly resigned; Prince seated a new board of directors and took charge of the PM at the beginning of 1903.

Crapo and Heald had been working to reestablish the PM's financial health by rebuilding and upgrading it in its present territory. Prince wanted to remake the company by expanding it into a Chicago-Buffalo bridge line. At that time the PM handled freight to and from the West at two places, at New Buffalo from the Michigan Central and from other southern and western connections on the LaCrosse branch, and from the cross–Lake Michigan railcar ferries into Ludington that brought freight from western roads through Wisconsin ports. The PM handed this traffic to eastern connections at Detroit, Toledo, and Port Huron. But the greater proportion of PM freight either originated or terminated at PM stations, with only a smaller share carried through overhead from one end of the line to the other.

To remake the PM Prince planned to extend it from New Buffalo into Chicago, where he could make direct connections with western railroads, and also to extend it from either Port Huron or Detroit eastward to Buffalo or Niagara Falls to connect with lines to the East Coast. Money would be no problem. There were $20 million of PM bonds in the vaults unsold, and certainly he could arrange to increase capitalization to provide for still more that could be sold. In January 1903 Prince bought the Lake Erie & Detroit River from the Walker family (of Hiram Walker distillery fame) for its Walkerville–St. Thomas, Ontario, line and its branch that extended to Sarnia, opposite Port Huron. This cost some $3 million in new PM bonds, and the PM also had to assume the responsibility for interest payments on $3 million of LE&DR bonds. With this deal came the LE&DR's lease of the London & Port Stanley, which was to run until 1914. Late in 1903 Prince arranged for running rights over the New York Central–owned Canada Southern from St. Thomas to both Niagara Falls and Black Rock. In July 1904 the PM obtained more running rights from the New York Central so it could reach terminal facilities at Niagara Falls. Later in 1904 Prince obtained rights to operate over the International Bridge from Black Rock directly into Buffalo. To shorten his Sarnia–St. Thomas roundabout route Prince negotiated another agreement with the Canada Southern to run over its line between Courtright and St. Thomas. This shortcut was never used, and eventually the agreement was canceled. Between Port Huron and

Frederick H. Prince took over the Pere Marquette Railroad in 1902 with dreams of making it into a major midwestern carrier with a route from Chicago to Buffalo. He and his associates were able to extend the road while in the meantime emptying its treasury.

National Cyclopedia of American Biography (New York: 1900–1909), 10:222.

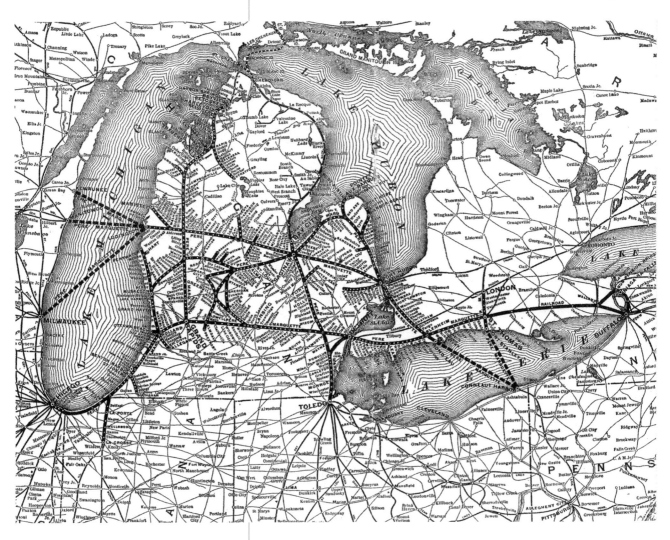

The Prince syndicate enlarged the Pere Marquette out of Michigan to reach both Chicago and Buffalo, as shown on this 1909 timetable map. His trains used running rights on other railroads to reach both terminals, but he gained a competitive advantage as a "bridge" carrier between Chicago and East Coast lines at Buffalo.

Sarnia and between Detroit and Walkerville the PM began operating railcar ferries.

The extension from New Buffalo into Chicago was more difficult to complete since there were no existing lines to take over. Prince decided to build an entirely new line and in February 1903 incorporated the Pere Marquette of Indiana to build it. It had rights to construct a line from New Buffalo to Hammond, Indiana. Work started immediately, so that by 15 December the line was built as far west as Porter, Indiana. It had cost Prince more than $1.1 million to build to Porter; building into Chicago from that point would be considerably more expensive, even by Prince's standards. The territory through which he would have to build already had innumerable lines that he would have to squeeze between or cross. It might have been possible to get running rights over the U.S.

Steel–owned Elgin, Joliet & Eastern, but this never developed. He was able to negotiate running rights over the New York Central (then the Lake Shore & Michigan Southern) to Pine, Indiana, and over the Chicago Terminal Transfer Railroad from Pine into Chicago. PM trains were running into Chicago before the end of the year. The Transfer's tracks proved to be so congested with freight traffic that the PM's passenger trains experienced considerable delays. In June 1904 Prince negotiated a new arrangement with the Pennsylvania and the Chicago & Alton for an alternate route for PM passenger trains. In the end Prince had achieved his Chicago-Buffalo line, at a cost of more than $4 million, plus rental charges, and plus mileage charges for each train run. In addition, he had to depend on the favor of the New York Central at both ends to move his trains.

Prince's Chicago-Detroit route was the longest at 336 miles in length, contrasted with the Wabash line at 267 miles, the Michigan Central at 283, the Lake Shore via Toledo at 291, and the Grand Trunk Western at 321. In an effort to shorten this Prince bought a package of three short money-losing roads from Frederick W. Steele in April 1903: the three-mile Benton Harbor, Coloma & Paw Paw Lake, which ran from Coloma to Paw Paw Lake; the twenty-six-mile Milwaukee, Benton Harbor & Columbus, extending from Benton Harbor to Buchanan; and the thirty-four-mile South Haven & Eastern, extending from South Haven to Lawton. The Benton Harbor–Buchanan line might have some possibilities if it were to be extended to South Bend, Indiana, something that would never come to pass. The South Haven & Eastern line was what Prince really wanted. It crossed his main line at Hartford, where his trains would turn onto the branch toward Lawton. From the line's east end at Lawton he would build an extension into Kalamazoo and make a connection with the Chicago, Kalamazoo & Saginaw line from Kalamazoo to its junction with the PM at Woodbury, between Grand Rapids and Lansing. This route between Hartford and Woodbury through Kalamazoo would be about twenty miles shorter than his present line via Grand Rapids. As a bonus he would have access to Kalamazoo's industries.

In the sunny days at the beginning of 1903, Prince was sure he could do with the PM all that he wanted to. The railroad was showing a profit, was paying all the interest on its debt, and had almost $20 million worth of unissued bonds to finance still more expansion. The economy was growing, and the money market was favorable for his expansions. But to continue to sell bonds at a favorable price Prince had to keep the PM looking as good as possible, at least on paper. He had increased the road's mileage and that growth improved the appearance of the company. Prince issued PM bonds to buy the stock of the roads purchased. Any other expense that he could throw into the cost of road account he did, and that further increased that asset. When bonds were sold at a discount from par, when the cash received was less than the face value of bonds, the difference was added to the cost of road account, rather than deducting it from profit and loss as a cost of doing business. This was a usual practice of the day, since the cost of selling bonds to buy lines was considered an additional part of the cost of the lines. The PM's bonds were sold through deals made by associates of Prince, which then was not considered a conflict of interest. Also, it appears that Prince made some contracts for services and purchases that directly profited him and his associates. He reduced any expense he could find, particularly maintenance of tracks, to drive up profits. He formed the Eastern Equipment Company, and that subsidiary issued about $5.5 million in notes to buy rolling stock and car ferries. Any revenue of any sort was put into current income. Finally, to put the best possible face on the PM, he began paying dividends on the common stock. It did not matter that he had to use short-term borrowings to pay them. Dividends made the company look profitable.

All of this might have succeeded, and the PM prospered accordingly, except that revenues began to drop following the business panic of 1903. It appears that Prince and his associates saw events turning against them if they continued on. On 4 July 1904 Prince and twenty-eight other individuals and companies formed a syndicate, a group that agreed to work together to profit from their mutual activities. The syndicate planned to continue to use the PM to their personal advantage. The first deal forced the PM to buy the Chicago, Cincinnati & Louisville Railroad. The CC&L was a 254-mile road from Cincinnati to Griffith, Indiana, and connected with the PM at LaCrosse, Indiana. It was on the verge of bankruptcy because of years of operating losses and was of no conceivable value to the PM. But a member of the syndicate handled the deal for some friends of Prince. The PM issued some $4 million in bonds to buy the CC&L stock and to make some improvements to the road. As a reward to Prince and the other holders of their block of PM stock, the syndicate bought the block for $125 per share, giving Prince a profit of $40 per share for owning the stock for less than two years. Prince was paid in bonds and notes of the Cincinnati, Hamilton & Dayton, which the syndicate also controlled. In exchange, on 1 March 1905 the PM was leased to the CH&D. The hope was that the traffic interchanged between the two roads would strengthen both. The opposite developed when other connecting lines reduced their traffic to and from both roads, with the end result that, rather than gaining, both roads lost traffic moving through Toledo.

By the beginning of 1905 the syndicate had used nearly all of the $50 million in PM bonds authorized at the 1900 incorporation. It was no great problem to go back to the market for an entirely new $60 million bond authorization that gave the syndicate another $10 million to work with. On 1 January $6 million was issued at a 12.5 percent discount, but the record is murky as to what the money was used for. In June 1905 the syndicate arranged for the PM to buy control of another of their roads, the Toledo Railway & Terminal Company, a belt line and terminal railroad in Toledo. The PM, and for that matter the CH&D, had no need for additional terminal facilities in Toledo, but the syndicate saw the sale as an opportunity to further enrich itself. At first the line was rented for a fixed charge with a guarantee of the interest on $3.5 million in Toledo company bonds. Soon after, the PM issued $1.6 million in bonds and bought all the capital stock of the Toledo. The syndicate benefited again as the PM incurred another substantial expense for a second railroad that was operating at a loss. The Toledo stock was sold to a broker for $41 per share, who sold it to the CH&D for $42 per share, which then forced the PM to buy it at $47 per share. Two other syndicate members represented the American Car & Foundry Company and U.S. Express. The former received car orders from both the PM and the CH&D; the latter gained a contract to operate its services on the PM.

By October 1905 the financial situation of the both the PM and the CH&D had reached the point where there was no more money to be extracted from them. Bonds had been issued to the limit, and the interest expense of the debt was so high it could not be paid. Prince and the syndicate had increased total debt in less than two years by $23.5 million, from $31.4 million to $54.9 million. The property was in poorer physical shape than when it was acquired. Prince and the syndicate decided it was time to get out.

What followed in October 1905 has been explained in two widely different versions. The upshot is that the syndicate engaged J. P. Morgan and Company to sell the CH&D and the PM. Whether Morgan went to the Erie Railroad, as the Erie stated, or the Erie came to Morgan, as he testified, cannot now be known with certainty. In any event the Erie agreed to buy control of the CH&D and its wholly owned PM at $160 per share, paying Morgan a 3.5 percent commission for his efforts. The Erie soon found out its mistake. A closer look at the books showed that its purchase was making very little profit, was unable to pay the interest on its debt, and would have fallen into bankruptcy if the Erie had not taken it. For this opportunity it had paid $160 a share. The Erie rushed back to Morgan shouting "foul," and Morgan, having made his commission, eventually agreed to buy back the CH&D stock at the sale price. Morgan had no interest in investing his own money in the insolvent road but rather wanted someone to take it off his hands. On 5 December 1905 the CH&D and the PM went into receivership.

William W. Crapo returned as the receiver for the PM, and Judson Harmon, a man of equal stature, was named receiver for the CH&D. In many railroad receiverships the company's financial affairs are reorganized by writing down the amount of debt to a level that the road's earnings can pay the interest and by exchanging that debt for new common or preferred stock in the company. Morgan had no wish to have his ownership interest diluted and opposed every effort to restructure the company on such terms. Crapo was able to get the purchase of the Chicago, Cincinnati & Louisville canceled, although the PM had to pay $400,000 in damages to the CH&D to get out of it. To satisfy its own preferred stockholders the CH&D had to issue more than $9 million in notes to buy them out. When it was over the Prince syndicate was completely in the clear, its profits were intact, and it was completely out of its railroad investment.

The PM fared better with the Toledo Railway & Terminal transaction. It was awarded just over $1.3 million for its losses, this to be paid in CH&D mortgage bonds. The road was reorganized as the Toledo Terminal Railroad; five other railroads bought a 60 percent interest in the line, and the CH&D and he PM each took a 20 percent ownership. The CH&D's lease of the PM was canceled for the inability of the latter to fulfill the terms of the lease, although the CH&D continued to own the controlling block of PM stock. When the receivership ended in December 1907, the Pere Marquette's future was hardly any brighter. Little existing debt had come off the books of the road while $5 million in new debt was added, some additional preferred stock was issued, and nearly $5 million of losses were zeroed out and added to the cost of road and equipment accounts. In sum, the weak balance sheet found at the beginning of the receivership remained in place at the end, and was in fact somewhat further weakened.

For the next twenty-one months the Pere Marquette limped along. Revenues from passenger operations did not increase as hoped because

Michigan passed a 2-cents-per-mile fare law. This legislation required railroads to sell passenger tickets for no more than 2 cents per mile. This reduced the PM's income by between $400,000 and $700,000 per year. Also in 1906 the U.S. Supreme Court decided that Michigan's railroad tax based on the value of property was constitutional. The Pere Marquette then had to find $1.2 million to pay past-due taxes. Penalties continued to accrue on any that the receiver did not pay during his administration. A final piece of ill luck came with the return of prosperity following the panic of 1907. Costs of goods and supplies purchased began to rise faster than revenues, and new wage agreements with employees further added to increased costs. The PM's poor credit reputation also affected its ability to sell new bonds; it had to sell one block at a 25 percent discount.

In August 1909 the Cincinnati, Hamilton & Dayton was reorganized when J. P. Morgan found a willing buyer for that company, the Baltimore & Ohio Railroad. Although the PM had modest profits in 1909 and 1910, the year ending 30 June 1911 showed a loss of $1.8 million. More than half of this was due to wage increases to employees and changes in work rules that required more men for certain kinds of work. Interest on the road's debt also increased since new bonds had been issued to buy some equipment and to do some maintenance that had been deferred earlier. No one, including the B&O and J. P. Morgan, was willing to lend the PM more money. The B&O concluded that the PM was not a desirable property to own but did keep the CH&D for its fit into its plans. The B&O had the CH&D put its 110,000 PM shares up for sale in early 1911. The purchaser was J. P. Morgan and Company.

Morgan bought the PM stock at $23 per share, probably as a speculation and intending to sell it at some profit to any buyer that might be found. Morgan soon learned that the PM needed some $8 million to meet maturing bonds and to pay the interest on debt; there was no accumulated profit from which to pay this. Morgan agreed to loan the $8 million but demanded the security of $16 million in PM mortgage bonds. This money was quickly used up, and early in 1912 more new funds were needed; $5 million in debentures was due for refunding in July. Morgan chose to spend no more of his money and in April 1912 allowed the PM to go into receivership once again.

Four-and-a-half years of negotiations were needed to work out the second reorganization plan. Although common stock was increased to $45.2 million, the company's debt was reduced by $43 million to $36 million. This reduced interest charges by nearly $2.5 million per year and made it an amount the PM could handle better. The PM's total capitalization, stock and debt, was reduced by $8 million. Some $23.6 million in preferred stock was issued, the dividends of which had to be paid only if earned, but were cumulative against future earnings. When the second receivership ended in April 1917 the PM had somewhat better prospects than it had seen in nearly two decades.

SOURCES

Dunbar, Willis F. *All Aboard! A History of Railroads in Michigan*. Grand Rapids, Mich.: W. B. Eerdmans, 1969.

Ivey, Paul Wesley. *The Pere Marquette Railroad: An Historical Study of the Growth and Development of One of Michigan's Most Important Railway Systems*. Lansing, Mich.: Michigan Historical Commission, 1919. Reprint, Grand Rapids, Mich.: Black Letter Press, 1970.

Rehor, John A. *The Nickel Plate Story*. Milwaukee: Kalmbach, 1965.

U.S. Interstate Commerce Commission. *Finance Docket No. 6833*. Washington, D.C., 1917.

The Government Takes Over

During 1914 and 1915, while war was threatening to spill out of Europe after the assassination of Archduke Franz Ferdinand, it was business as usual in the United States. Most Americans cared little about the ominous developments in Europe and certainly had no wish to get into this entanglement. Nor did President Woodrow Wilson have any desire to get the United States into it either, despite strident calls to do so coming from Theodore Roosevelt and others. The neutrality Wilson worked so hard at maintaining allowed the United States to ship supplies to both sides in the first years of the conflict. This was a particularly popular policy with midwesterners who spoke and worked against entering the war itself but were happy to open their weekly pay envelopes.

The sudden surge in business in 1915, induced by European buyers for all sorts of U.S. products, began to lift the economy out of its five-year depression. This slump had been especially hard on the railroads. They had been unable to make any sizable investments in new equipment or locomotives, both of which were sorely needed, nor had they been able to keep up maintenance. A few Michigan lines that were not strong to begin with, such as the Wabash, the Pere Marquette, the

Wisconsin & Michigan, and the Boyne City, Gaylord & Alpena, were in the hands of receivers, as were a good many more outside of Michigan. The war-induced prosperity began to squeeze the nation's railroads from several sides. Freight traffic was increasing because of war production, and it had to be moved on an aging physical plant. Materials costs rose while requests for rate increases to cover them fell on unsympathetic ears at the Interstate Commerce Commission (ICC). The railroads held wages down in an attempt to control costs, a move that encouraged railroad men to leave for higher-paying jobs in war industries. Early in 1916 the four operating brotherhoods (enginemen, firemen, conductors, and brakemen) demanded that their ten-hour work day be reduced to eight hours. President Wilson tried to mediate, but railroad management rejected his attempt. A strike was called for 1 September, a step that pushed Congress into passing legislation for an eight-hour day, to take effect in January 1917. The railroad presidents refused to obey the new law, resulting in another strike call by the brotherhoods. The Supreme Court upheld the law's constitutionality, leaving the railroads with no choice but to accept.

In March 1917 President Wilson declared the United States at war with Germany. In an attempt to cope with the increasing demands on their facilities, the companies created the Railroads' War Board in April 1917, this to implement their resolve to operate their lines as "a continental railway system." This meant they would try to subordinate their personal corporate interests in favor of the nation's war effort. They established pools to relieve the shortage of freight cars, worked with shippers to load more freight in cars, and tried to reduce some duplicating passenger trains. This valiant attempt was not very successful. Too many years of intense competition could not be gotten over; adding continuing shortages of capital, labor, and equipment made a difficult task nearly impossible. In December 1917 a bad winter set in to make things still worse. A year earlier Congress had given the president authority to take over any transportation system if the war effort required it, although the federal government had not operated a railroad system of any size since the Civil War. Now conditions seemed to demand that step. The day after Christmas President Wilson announced that government operation of the railroads would begin at noon, Friday, 28 December. Wilson named his son-in-law William G. McAdoo, who was then the secretary of the treasury, as director general of United States Railway Administration (USRA) and gave him authority to do whatever needed to be done. McAdoo kept the managements

In 1917 President Woodrow Wilson named his son-in-law William G. McAdoo to take charge of the federal government's management of the nation's railroads. With finance and some engineering in his background, and three years as secretary of the treasury, he was a dapper, hardworking, conscientious public official.

The *Independent*, 93.

Walker D. Hines came to the United States Railroad Administration as assistant director general under William McAdoo, and replaced him as director general in 1919. He came to Washington, D.C., with impressive legal credentials from the Louisville & Nashville and the Atchison, Topeka & Santa Fe. Later he returned to railroading to serve as a director of the Colorado & Southern and the Chicago, Burlington & Quincy.

Library of Congress, Prints & Photographic Division, LC-USZ62-42645.

of most companies in place, then strengthened the moves first taken by the Railroads' War Board. To meet the brotherhoods' demands for wage increases, McAdoo appointed a commission to study the issue. Eventually, the commission found that the cost of living had risen much faster than railroaders' pay, and McAdoo recommended a sliding scale of increases made retroactive to the first of the year. The lowest-paid employees received a 40 percent raise, the highest-paid one of 16 percent. In exchange, the operating brotherhoods had to relinquish some of their pet wage differentials. This pushed up labor costs by 50 percent from 1917 to 1918. Although McAdoo took no pay for his USRA duties, he paid each member of the executive staff as much as $25,000 per year, and regional directors up to $50,000 per year, sums well above President Wilson's salary.

To meet the rising costs for everything used by the railroads the USRA did not have to go to the ICC for rate increases; it simply raised them as it wished. A sizable increase was made in 1918, averaging 28 percent for freight charges; passenger fares also were increased. McAdoo pumped money into new locomotives and freight cars and also did some much needed track rehabilitation. Under the USRA, the government agreed to pay the railroads a rental based on a net income formula, as well as for any damage or loss of property, while the railroads were charged for any improvements the USRA made. The final bill for twenty-six months of government operation came in at about $1 billion, of which some $200 million was for claims for loss and damage to railroad assets. This total cost is but a small fraction of the ultimate cost of preparing for and conducting the war.

The government's takeover worked a severe hardship on a few of the state's smallest carriers. Under the December 1917 order all railroads were taken over. This included the Manistee & Northeastern and resulted in its employees receiving the April 1918 wage increase ordered by USRA. Two months later McAdoo announced that the M&NE would be released from USRA control. The M&NE management thought it could not pay the increased wages and stay in business without the federal guarantees, but it could not convince its employees to give up the pay raises. The road went into receivership at the end of 1918.

The armistice in Europe came on the eleventh hour of the eleventh day of the eleventh month of 1918. President Wilson asked Congress to consider returning the railroads to their owners. When he retired at the end of the war, William McAdoo recommended the railroads be kept under government control for another five years. The four largest brotherhoods wanted the government to buy the roads outright. The Plumb Plan the four unions developed had wide support in the labor movement but almost none among the public at large. At the beginning of March 1920 the railroads were returned to private control, again returned to the tender oversight of the ICC. Now again on their own, the railroads had to deal as best they could with rapidly dropping traffic levels, a little-changed rate structure, a deteriorated physical plant, and the higher wages and changed working conditions given its employees by the federal government.

With the exception of the hardships inflicted on the small roads, not much changed on Michigan railroads during the war. They met the demands of the war effort put on them and handled freight and passengers efficiently. Color disappeared from public timetables and the "USRA" legend appeared on the cover, but there was little change in passenger train service itself. The war effort took about 135,000 men out of Michigan's population of about three million, 9 percent of the males. The railroads were affected probably somewhat more, given the military enlistments as well as the transfers to other industries. New traffic developed from a new army base at Camp Custer west of Battle Creek and from an aviator training school at Selfridge Field near Mt. Clemens. Camp Custer originated a large number of troop trains as soldiers' training was completed and they were sent off to combat. The National Guard camp at Grayling was pressed into service. The railroad tunnels at Detroit and Port Huron were guarded closely to prevent entry by saboteurs intent on damaging wartime production facilities.

One remembrance of the war was made when the Pennsylvania Railroad established a new overnight Detroit–New York train and named it the *Red Arrow* in honor of Michigan's Thirty-Second Infantry Division.

The Pennsylvania Railroad did not put much money in its advertising budget, but it did include this modest promotion in its April 1929 timetable for its Detroit–New York *Red Arrow*.

Author's collection.

SOURCES

McAdoo, William G. *Crowded Years*. New York: Houghton Mifflin, 1931.

Morison, Samuel Eliot. *The Oxford History of the American People*. New York: Oxford University Press, 1965.

Stover, John F. *American Railroads*. Chicago: University of Chicago Press, 1961.

Westmeyer, Russell E. *Economics of Transportation*. Englewood Cliffs, N.J.: Prentice-Hall, 1952.

"When U.S. Took Over the Railroads." *Railroad Magazine* 24:5 (October 1938).

Water Everywhere: Tunnels, Bridges, and Car Ferries, Part 2

The Lake Michigan service was the most extensive of all rail ferry operations in North America. It involved more companies and had longer routes. Weather was always a consideration since a fierce storm could come up in any season. Winter brought the most difficult season, with ice on the lake and in the harbors. Pack ice was always a severe problem at the Straits of Mackinac, and the *Sainte Marie* and *Chief Wawatam* built up remarkable records for reliability in crossing in the worst of weather. Hardly a winter passed that did not bring a call for one of them to rescue another ship trapped in the ice. Grounding was not infrequent as a ship approached port, while getting lost in heavy fog was especially perilous in the days before radar.

The heavy seas that might be encountered on a lake crossing demanded a new method of securing the freight cars. The Ann Arbor developed a system of screw jacks to lift one side of the car slightly with chains to fasten it down on the other side, used wheel clamps to hold car wheels, then set the air brakes and sometimes hand brakes on the cars as well. These measures worked well and were adopted throughout the Great Lakes ferry service. After several cars rolled off the end of the car deck, sea gates were installed.

Although no ship was exempt from accidents some seemed almost to attract them. *Ann Arbor No. 1* had a series of mishaps during its career, which ended when it caught fire at Manitowoc in March 1911. *Ann Arbor No. 4* capsized in May 1909 at Manistique while being loaded with cars of iron ore. *Ann Arbor No. 6* proved over time to be a poor icebreaker and demonstrated this on its first trip from the shipyard during January 1917. It was a severe winter, and it became fast in the ice in the Detroit River, in the St. Clair River, and again at St. Helena Island west of St. Ignace. The crew worked the ship free from St. Helena, and it made for Mackinaw City to repair some damage and take on more coal. It started out again and had to return again after more damage to its screws. It was towed to St. Ignace for repairs and finally started out once again, in fairer weather, for Frankfort.

Possibly the worst fated of the Pere Marquette ferries was *Pere Marquette 16*. It had groundings, collisions, and miscellaneous accidents in numbers sufficient for the entire fleet. The travails of the Lake Michigan ferries, the sudden storms, the ice holding them fast, the thick fog or blinding snow that took them off course, and much more have been chronicled in many places and form a tribute to the sturdiness of the men who went to the inland sea and were a fascinating part of Michigan railroading.

The business recovery following the depression of 1905 brought a new surge of traffic to the railroad car ferries. For the 1906 summer season the Ann Arbor Railroad was forced to lease two Pere Marquette ferries, and also ordered *Ann Arbor No. 4*, which was added to the fleet in December 1906. In March 1911 *Ann Arbor No. 1* burned to the waterline at Manitowoc and was a total loss. Its replacement was already being built at Toledo; when *Ann Arbor No. 5* was delivered in January 1911 it set new records. Of all the Great Lakes ferries it was the longest at 360 feet, the heaviest at 2,988 tons, and the most powerful at 3,000 horsepower. It had the greatest capacity at thirty railcars and was the best icebreaker. It was the first car ferry to be fitted with a sea gate, a innovation that prevented water coming in over the open stern to swamp the car deck that was so successful that the line retrofitted the road's other ferries with them. In 1912 *No. 2* was sold, and *No. 5* became the mainstay of the Ann Arbor fleet.

PM carloadings were about 27,000 in 1900 and jumped to about 75,000 in 1904. The road needed new car ferries and placed orders for a total of four. *Pere Marquette 17* was launched at Cleveland in 1901, *Pere Marquette 18* in 1902, and *Pere Marquette 19* and *Pere Marquette 20* the following year. As these came into service the break-bulk steamers were sold, with one of them sailing for a few years for a competitor, the Pere Marquette Line Steamers, between Milwaukee and Holland's Ottawa Beach. The complement of six ferries provided adequate capacity for the PM's routes from Ludington to Kewaunee, Manitowoc, and Milwaukee.

The Grand Trunk Railway's subsidiary, the Detroit, Grand Haven & Milwaukee, and its predecessors began operating a break-bulk service between Grand Haven and Milwaukee in 1858. Part of the time the road used chartered or contract vessels and part of the time its own railroad-owned steamers. It was not until 1903 that the railroad ordered its first car ferry, *Grand Haven*. It added a second ship in 1908 when it bought *Manistique Marquette & Northern 1* from the defunct Northport-Manistique service. It was renamed *Milwaukee* and with *Grand Haven* provided Milwaukee–Grand Haven service into the 1920s.

There were several other short-lived Lake Michigan car ferry services about this time. The Detroit, Grand Rapids & Western leased a Lake Erie car ferry in late 1897 and began sailing from Muskegon to Milwaukee. The road obtained trackage rights over the closely related Chicago & West Michigan from Grand Rapids to a dock at Port Sherman, just west of Muskegon. A year or so later the ship was renamed *Muskegon*, and in late 1900 it was transferred to Ludington following the formation of the Pere Marquette system. It was renamed *Pere Marquette 16* and continued a checkered career until it was laid up in 1907 and sold in 1917.

Two other services also linked the Lower and Upper Peninsulas. One was the service to Manistique. The Ann Arbor operated from Frankfort to connect to the Manistique, Marquette & Northern (later the Manistique & Lake Superior). Most often the service was one round-trip a day. The Manistique road extended from Manistique northwest into an extensive forest area and hauled out logs as well as iron ore from the Marquette Range, turning them over to the Ann Arbor Railroad's car ferry for cross-lake handling from Manistique. The Ann Arbor's car ferry operation handled such an amount of traffic that the Grand Rapids & Indiana planned to offer a similar service. It appears that Daniel W. Kaufman, a Manistique lumberman, and Richard R. Metheany, secretary of the GR&I, believed there was promise in a route that linked the Manistique road directly to the GR&I. A Traverse City to Manistique line, at 105 miles, was promising, but by sailing from Northport, at the tip of the Leelanau Peninsula, the run would be cut to only 75 miles. Metheany and Kaufman formed the Traverse City, Leelanau & Manistique in November 1901 to build the needed line from Traverse City to Northport, then arranged for a Grand Rapids firm to build the line and for the GR&I to operate it when it was completed. In June 1903 the road was completed, and the car ferry *Manistique, Marquette and Northern No. 1* began sailing in October. In 1904 the Pere Marquette obtained control of the Manistique road and changed the ferry's southern terminus from Northport to Ludington, a port twice the distance from Manistique. After eighteen months of red ink the Pere Marquette gave up, and the ferry resumed sailing out of Northport. In January 1908 the ferry sank at Manistique, and while it was being repaired the line had to charter an Ann Arbor ferry to keep the service running. Try as they might, the GR&I and the Manistique road's successor could not make the service profitable, the losses driving both the Manistique road and the Leelanau road into receivership. Late in 1908 the ferry was sold to the Grand Trunk Western, renamed *Milwaukee*, and put in the Grand Haven–Milwaukee service.

If ever a ship had a jinx, it was *Pere Marquette 16*. This engraving shows it around 1899 with its original name, *Muskegon*, sailing for an earlier owner between Muskegon and Milwaukee. Renamed in 1901 and with Ludington as its new home port, its lack of power continued its run of bad luck until it was laid up in 1907.

Pictorial History of the C&O Train and Auto Ferries.

The Grand Trunk Western's ill-fated car ferry the *Milwaukee*. Built in 1903 as the *Manistique Marquette & Northern 1* to sail between Northport and Manistique, it was sold to the Grand Trunk in 1908. Renamed the *Milwaukee*, it and its sister ship *Grand Haven* sailed between the two ports for twenty years. In October 1929 the *Milwaukee* foundered after leaving its namesake port to become the worst loss in Great Lakes car ferry history.

Reprinted, by permission, from George W. Hilton, *Great Lakes Car Ferries* (Berkeley, Calif., 1962), 178.

The *S. M. Fischer* was built 1896 for Lake Michigan Car Ferry Transportation to tow barges between Peshtigo, Wisconsin, and South Chicago and for a while between Peshtigo and Benton Harbor hauling coal from the Big Four line. But most of the freight it hauled came from the Wisconsin & Michigan Railroad, a service that ended in 1909.

Reprinted, by permission, from George W. Hilton, *Great Lakes Car Ferries* (Berkeley, Calif., 1962), 197.

Possibly the most unusual rail ferry operation was that of the Lake Michigan Car Ferry Transportation Company. Formed in 1893 and beginning service in 1895, the ferry was an extension of the Wisconsin & Michigan Railroad, a line running from Peshtigo, Wisconsin, to the Menominee iron range. Rather than car ferries as were used on the Ann Arbor and Pere Marquette, the W&M's owner, John N. Faithorn, instead chose to use two tugboats and four barges. When received in 1895, each barge could carry twenty-eight cars on open decks. The first service sailed between Peshtigo and South Chicago, Illinois. Lumber products from the W&M were the principal traffic; only a small amount of northbound freight developed. A trickle of iron ore began to move south in 1903, but no substantial volume ever developed.

In June 1897 Faithorn made an agreement with the Big Four Road (Cleveland, Cincinnati, Chicago & St. Louis) to provide ferry service between Benton Harbor and Manitowoc. From Benton Harbor the Big Four line ran due south to Louisville, Kentucky, and the hope was to develop coal traffic from Kentucky to Wisconsin via the ferries. But traffic in any amount never developed. Just a handful of ferry trips were made in 1897, then closed down during the winter of 1897–98, and never resumed. Two barges were lost in September 1900 and were not replaced. In 1906 another barge was lost, forcing the company to go to the Pere Marquette to charter *Pere Marquette 16*. Accidents of all sorts continued to plague that ship, and in November 1907 it was severely damaged in a storm. The W&M could not afford to repair it and simply towed it back to Ludington, where the Pere Marquette took it out of service.

Michigan Central president Henry B. Ledyard viewed the Grand Trunk's St. Clair River tunnel with envy. In the early 1900s he persuaded the New York headquarters to try once more to dig a Detroit River tunnel. To handle all the traffic between Chicago and the East Coast the New York Central main line used four tracks east of Buffalo. There was too much traffic to handle all of it on the two-track line through Cleveland and Toledo, so the Michigan Central route had to be upgraded. The entire route was double-tracked, some grades were reduced by line relocations, automatic block signals were installed, and the Air Line between Niles and Jackson was upgraded to handle more freight trains. Two bores were dug between Detroit and Windsor, which allowed one track for eastward and one for westward normal operations. When completed, a third rail was laid to provide power for the electric locomotives that were used. Two new yards were built

Comparison of Detroit River and St. Clair River Tunnels

Tunnel	GT–St. Clair	MC–Detroit
Number of bores	One	Two
Tunnel length	6,026 feet	8,376 feet
U.S. portion	0.50 mile	0.68 mile
Canada portion	0.64 mile	0.89 mile
U.S. approach	0.47 mile	0.48 mile
Canada approach	0.60 mile	0.72 mile
Total tunnel and approach	2.21 miles	2.77 miles

to help freight movements as well as a new coach yard for passenger equipment. The new tunnel elevation made it impractical to continue using the Third Street depot, so a new and more much impressive passenger station and office tower were built as part of the project. The tunnel was built with metal tubing pressed into a layer of concrete three to five feet thick, then coated with a two-foot-thick layer of concrete. Tunnel construction began in 1906 and was completed on 1 July 1910. The first train went through it late that same month, regular freight operations began in September, and all operations changed over in October. The new passenger station was first used in December 1913 after a fire at the Third Street station forced a premature changeover.

Comparisons between the Detroit River and St. Clair River tunnels are inevitable.

SOURCES

Burgtorf, Frances D. *Chief Wawatam: The Story of a Hand-Bomber*. Cheboygan, Mich.: author, 1976.

Burton, Robert E. "Car Ferry from Northport: Broken Link to the Upper Peninsula." *Michigan History* 51:1 (Spring 1967).

Cousins, G. R., and Paul Maximuke. "The Station That Looks Like a Hotel." *Trains*, August 1978.

———. "The Ceremony Was 61 Years Too Late." *Trains*, September 1978.

Hilton, George W. *The Great Lakes Car Ferries*. Berkeley, Calif.: Howell-North, 1962.

Zimmerman, Karl. *Lake Michigan's Railroad Car Ferries*. Andover, N.J.: Andover Junction Publications, 1993.

The Grand Railway Station, Part 2

By 1895 only one great railroad station remained to be built in Michigan. Grand Rapids needed a new union station, and under the aegis of the Pennsylvania Railroad a new one was planned. Daniel H. Burnham designed a block-long, two-story brick Greek temple–style building with a four-column portico entrance at the middle of the structure. The large waiting room was flanked by ticket windows on the south and a dining room and offices on the north. At the south end of the building were facilities for handling baggage, U.S. mail, and express. All had easy access to the tracks, which were sheltered by a train shed—the only one in Michigan outside of Detroit. Opened in 1900, the structure bore a marked resemblance to the Burnham-designed Pennsylvania Railroad station built at Richmond, Indiana, that same year. On Ionia Avenue north of the station the Grand Rapids & Indiana and Pennsylvania Railroad maintained a separate building for their offices. The union station and office building stood for barely fifty years until they were razed to make room for an expressway ramp. In 1911 the GR&I built a small-town station at Kalkaska and one at Pellston around 1915.

During the first two decades of the twentieth century the Grand Trunk Western embarked on a program that provided new stations in most of the large cities on its lines. In 1902 it opened a new station for Lansing. Designed by Spier and Rohns, built of red brick with limestone trim and a tile roof, the outstanding feature of this smallish building is a square two-story tower fit for a medieval castle. In 1905 two more Spier and Rohns–designed stations were completed, and they could not have been more dissimilar. The 1905 union station at Durand replaced an earlier one that burned; the new two-and-one-half-story brick building, with its tile roof and upstairs division offices, was much larger than a community its size called for. The wide platform overhangs allowed large numbers of riders easy movement as they transferred between trains. The Battle Creek station is much more ornate and possibly the most impressive of all Grand Trunk stations. Also of red brick, with Spanish tiles and a Moorish influence, it housed expansive passenger facilities, and its second floor held division offices. These stations were followed by more modest ones in 1908 at Pontiac, in 1909 at Ionia, in 1910 at Flint, in 1915 at Owosso, and in about 1921 at St. Johns. Most of these structures remain today. In 1906 the Grand Trunk built an impressive station for Grand Rapids on Michigan Street just east of the

In the early 1900s the Michigan Central built a series of stations of this design in Michigan and Indiana. The station at Dowagiac has been restored as an intermodal center with daily stops by Amtrak trains.

Sam Breck collection.

Michigan has had relatively few stone stations, but some of them still survive. This Manistee & Northeastern structure at Suttons Bay, built around 1903, now houses professional offices.

Sam Breck collection.

Built in 1902, this Detroit & Mackinac station at Harrisville is one of the few of cut-stone construction in Michigan. Today the weeds are gone, the stone is cleaned, and, with a new roof, it looks ready for a passenger to walk in to buy a ticket.

David Beauregard photo, Sam Breck collection.

This Grand Trunk Western station in Battle Creek is likely the road's most impressive in Michigan. Designed by Spier and Rohns and completed in 1906, the building housed a depot restaurant and, on the second floor, the road's division offices. Now beautifully restored for public offices, only the towers have been changed since this late-1920s photograph.

Willard Library, Battle Creek.

The depot at Trout Lake is very likely the most photographed railroad building in the Upper Peninsula. Built in 1907 it served both the Soo Line and the Duluth, South Shore & Atlantic. This 1975 view shows a building that is little changed from its original appearance.

Sam Breck collection.

Grand Rapids Union Station opened late in 1900 to handle trains of all lines entering the Furniture City, except the Grand Trunk Western. It lived less than sixty years, then was razed to make way for an expressway ramp.

Kenneth Nagel collection in Sam Breck collection.

Grand River. This brick-and-stone building was marked by a six-story watchtower at its southwest corner. It was replaced by a new and more compact station on Plainfield Avenue in 1949 and was torn down a few years later. In 1927 the Grand Trunk built a new station in Flint on the new main line that bypassed the heart of downtown. An earlier station near the city center was disassembled, stone by stone, and moved to Muskegon to serve as the Peck Street station for both the Grand Trunk and the Pennsylvania.

The Michigan Central built new branch-line and small-city depots in Dowagiac and Charlotte in 1902; New Buffalo in 1903; Nashville in 1904; Middleville, Lapeer, and Cassopolis in 1906; Galien in 1913; and Hastings in 1922. Many of these were brick and ashlar, and quite similar in style. The Dowagiac station still has railroad use; the stations at Owosso, New Buffalo, and Cassopolis have since been demolished. In 1902 the MC built a new station on Michigan Avenue in Lansing designed by Spier and Rohns. It has many of the features of the smaller stations mentioned above but on a larger scale since it was used jointly with the Pere Marquette. The "witch's hat" roof over the telegrapher's office is an unusual feature for Michigan Central depots. About 1900 the New York Central and Michigan Central built new freight houses in many large Michigan cities. Most of these were razed by the 1970s, but Hillsdale, Lansing, Albion, Ypsilanti, and Grand Rapids have some of the few that remain.

Detroit became home to Michigan's most impressive rail terminal, a new MC station, somewhat by accident. Digging started on a Detroit River tunnel in 1906. There was opposition to building the tunnel, particularly from shipping interests, although it would seem that the car ferries crossing the river would have been a greater threat. Digging was finished in 1909 to at last bring reality of the dreams of James F. Joy and Henry B. Ledyard. The tunnel's route made continued use of the Third Street station impractical. The architectural firm of Warren and Wetmore, fresh from working on the New York Central's Grand Central Terminal in New York City, was brought in to design an ambitiously grand new Detroit station. The public entered the completed structure through a two-story entrance hall and waiting room, which held shops, restaurants, a drugstore, a newsstand, restrooms, and personal grooming facilities. Immediately behind this was a sixteen-story office tower for railroad offices. The ceiling of the grand concourse, leading to the tracks, was five stories high with a domed ceiling. The station approach was on Vernor Highway just off Michigan Avenue, through the newly laid out Roosevelt Park. The depot streetcar line ran to an eastside entrance door. The station opened to the public on 26 December 1913, eight days ahead of schedule because of a fire at the Third Street station.

The Pere Marquette and Grand Trunk Western built a joint passenger-freight station at South Lyon in 1909. This wooden structure, with its "witch's hat" roof feature, was moved and has been preserved. Another of the few remaining "witch's hat" depots is an older one at Lake Odessa, now also moved off-site. The Pere Marquette built a new one-story brick-and-stucco station at St. Joseph in 1914, with a platform overhang supported by columns, reminiscent of the MC's Jackson depot, although on a smaller scale. It followed this after World War I with new brick passenger stations at Holland, Grand Haven, Bangor, and Traverse City as well as one stone depot at Fowlerville. Ludington received a new brick station in 1931, one of the last built in Michigan. The Detroit & Mackinac replaced its Alpena station with a new one on Tenth Avenue in 1911. Designed by Spier and Rohns, the brick building on its stone foundation seems almost too large a structure for this city and was only recently demolished.

The Upper Peninsula received a few major new stations in the twentieth century. About 1910 the Mineral Range, which was owned by the Duluth, South Shore & Atlantic, built a new station at Calumet. This followed new DSS&A stations in Marquette in 1902 and Newberry in 1907. The most photographed depot in the Upper Peninsula was built in 1907, a wooden structure at the crossing of two railroads at Trout Lake. In 1910 the DSS&A, with the Chicago & North Western, built a union station in Negaunee to replace their separate stations. About the same year the Chicago, Milwaukee & St. Paul built its new station at Iron Mountain.

No major stations were built in Michigan after World War I. The few that were put up were smaller ones, most of them to replace ones that had been destroyed by fire or accident. By 1930, as a result of the Depression and the growth of competing forms of transport, most major city stations were larger than needed. New stations, especially large ones, could not be justified in the light of these changed conditions.

SOURCES

Cousins, G. R., and Paul Maximuke. "The Ceremony Was 61 Years Too Late." *Trains*, September 1978.

———. "The Station That Looks Like a Hotel." *Trains*, August 1978.

Dunbar. Willis F. *All Aboard! A History of Railroads in Michigan*. Grand Rapids, Mich.: W. B. Eerdmans, 1969.

Eckert, Kathryn Bishop. *Buildings of Michigan*. New York: Oxford University Press, 1993.

Potter, Janet Greenstein. *Great American Railroad Stations*. New York: John Wiley & Sons, 1996.

Uhelski, John M., and Robert M. Uhelski. *An Inventory of the Railroad Depots in the State of Michigan*. Crete, Neb.: Railroad Station Historical Society, 1979.

U.S. Department of the Interior, National Park Service, Historic American Engineering Record. *The Lower Peninsula of Michigan: An Inventory of Historic Engineering and Industrial Sites*, by Charles K. Hyde and Diane B. Abbott. Washington, D.C.: U.S. Department of the Interior, 1976.

Woodford, Frank R., and Arthur M. Woodford. *All Our Yesterdays*. Detroit: Wayne State University Press, 1969.

Detroit United Railway

City streetcar lines grew into an important business in the late 1890s. As routes extended and more people rode, the companies also developed a need for considerably more capital. This brought with it new investors, men from financial centers with ample funds at their disposal. In Detroit at the beginning of 1896 two companies were maneuvering for control of the street railway business. Richard T. Wilson of New York City and Tom L. Johnson owned the older Detroit Citizens' Street Railway. Wilson had recently hired Jere C. Hutchins to manage operations. Two Cleveland entrepreneurs, Henry A. Everett and Edward W. Moore, with Albert Pack, owned Mayor Hazen Pingree's creation, the Detroit Railway. In July 1896 Pack, Everett, and Moore formed the Detroit Electric Railway to take over the Detroit Railway, claiming a new company was needed to raise more capital for further improvements, particularly to convert to electric operations. Mayor Pingree objected loudly, declaiming that the sale was not permitted under the terms of the company's franchises. Despite the mayor's loud protestations, the Detroit Electric absorbed its predecessor within a few weeks.

The goodwill that had developed from meetings between Hutchins and Pack began to pay off, at least for the Citizens' Street Railway. Pack asked Hutchins to take over management of the Detroit Electric and its 3-cent lines. In January the Citizens leased its competitor and then controlled all of the important street railway routes in Detroit. Soon

Henry A. Everett was only thirty-four years old when he and his partner, Edward W. Moore, formed the Detroit United Railway in December 1900. By that time the two already had complete control of the transit system in Cleveland and had many other investments in telephone and traction companies throughout the Midwest and in Canada.

Progressive Men of Northern Ohio (Cleveland, 1906), 171.

Edward W. Moore was Everett's close associate in the Detroit United Railway and most other investments. Just two years older than Everett, he maintained a career in Cleveland banking as well as being heavily involved in their multitude of traction and telephone enterprises.

Reprinted from *Men of Ohio in Nineteen Hundred* (Cleveland, 1901), 30.

ABOVE: This map shows the extensive Detroit United Railway interurban system at its height. After this map was printed in the June 1909 *Michigan Railway Guide*, one extension was built from Romeo, through Almont, to Imlay City, completed in 1914 and 1915. The DUR had an important connection west and north from Jackson and several in all directions from Toledo.

Author's collection.

OPPOSITE: These schedules for the Detroit United Railway appeared in the June 1909 *Michigan Railway Guide*.

Author's collection.

DETROIT UNITED RAILWAY. 129

Eastern Stan. Time

Port Huron Division.

M	June 29 1915	Lim		Lim	AM	AM	AM	AM	AM		PM	PM	
0	Detroit lv	8.15	every two hours there after until	8.15	....	....	....	6.00	....	and every 2 hours there-after until	7.00	9.00	....
5	Leesville	....		....	....	....	....	....	....		....	....	....
21	Mt. Clemens......	9 17		9.17	....	....	6.17	7.17	....		8.17	10.17	....
32	New Baltimore..	9.38		9.38	....	....	6.50	7.50	....		8.50	10 49	....
35	Anchorville	9.43		9.43	....	....	6.56	7.56	....		8.56	10.54	..
37	Meyers	....		....	Car leaves Detroit for Mt. Clemens 6.30 AM and every hour thereafter until 6.30 PM, also 10.00 11.00PM								
40	Falkerts......	....		....									
43	M. C. Jct.........	....		....									
37	Fair Haven.......	....		....	....	....	7.01	8.01	....	and every 2 hours ...thereafter until..	9.01	11.01	....
43	Pearl Beach	....		....	....	....	7.14	8.14	....		9.14	11.14	....
47	Algonac	....		....	....	....	7.23	8.23	..		9 23	11.23	....
50	Roberts Landing.	....		....	....	....	7.27	8.29	....		9 29	11.29	....
54	Marine City......	10.05		1005	†6.33	....	7.43	8.43	....		9.43	11.42	....
61	Oakland Hotel...	...		....	....	....	....	....	....		....	....	....
62	St. Clair..........	10.22		1022	6.57	....	8.10	9.10	.. ..		10.10	12.04	....
63	Somerville Hotel.	....		....	....	....	....	....	....		....	....	....
67	Marysville	10.31		1031	7.13	....	8.24	9.24	....		10.24	12.13	....
74	Port Huron W.R. ar	10 40		1040	7.30	....	8.40	9.40	....		10.40	12.30	....

M		Lim		Lim	AM	AM	AM	AM	AM		PM	PM	PM
0	Port Huron W.R. lv	7.35	.... every 2 hours thereafter until....	7 33	....	....	6.10	7.10	8.10	every 2 hours thereafter until	8.10	9.30	11.00
7	Marysville	7.48		7.48	....	....	6.32	7.32	8.32		8.32	9.45	11.22
11	Somerville Hotel.	...		....	....	....	....	....	....		....	....	....
12	St. Clair..........	7.58		7.58	....	....	6.47	7.47	8 47		8 47	9.55	11.36
13	Oakland Hotel...	....		....	....	....	....	....	....		....	....	....
20	Marine City	8 14		8.14	....	6.12	7.12	8.12	9.12		9.12	10.15	11.55
21	M. C. Jct..... Short Line	....		....	Cars leave Mt. Clemens 5.04, 5.24, 5.54, 6.39 7.10AM and hourly until 5.10PM								
24	Falkerts......	....		....									
27	Meyers	....		....									
24	Robert's Landing	....		....	....	6.25	7.25	8.25	9.25	every hour thereafter until		9.25	10.25
27	Algonac	....		....	....	6.33	7.33	8.33	9.33			9.33	10.32
31	Pearl Beach......	....		....	....	6.41	7.41	8.41	9.41			9.41	10.40
37	Fair Haven.......	....		....	....	6.55	7.55	8.55	9 55			....	10 53
39	Anchorville	8.37		8.37	....	7.01	8.01	9.01	10.01			10.01	10.59
42	New Baltimore..	8.42		8.42	....	7.07	8.07	9.07	10.07			10.07	11.04
53	Mt. Clemens......	9 03		9.03	....	7.39	8.39	9.39	10.39			10.39	11.27
69	Leesville.....	.		....	....	....	....	....	..			....	....
74	Detroit.........ar	10 00		10.00	....	8.55	9.55	10.55	11.55			10.55	....

Pontiac Division.

Sept 21, 1915	AM		PM		PM	PM	PM	PM	PM		PM	PM	PM	PM	AM	
Detroit lv	5.50	every 20 min. until	3.30	15 min. to	5.30	5.50	6.10	6.50	7.30	every 30 min. until	9.30	1030	1100	11.30	1200	....
Royal Oak.	6.45		4 25		6.25	6.45	7.00	7 40	8.20		1020	1120	1150	12.30	1250	....
Birmingham......	6.58		4.38		6.38	6.58	7.13	7.53	8.35		1033	1135	1205	12.33	1.03	....
Pontiac..... ....ar	7.25		5 05		7.05	7.25	7.40	8.20	9.00		1100	1200	1230	1.05	...	....

	AM	AM	AM		PM		PM	PM	PM	PM	
Pontiac..........lv	5.52	6.12	6.52	...every 20 min. until...	5.32	every 30 min. until	9.02	1002	1032	1132	....
Birmingham......	6.17	6.37	7.17		5.57		9.22	1022	1052	1152	....
Royal Oak......	6.30	6.50	7 30		6.10		9 37	1037	1107	1207	....
Detroit..........ar	7.20	7 45	8.25		7 05		1030	1130	1200	1 00	....

DETROIT UNITED RAILWAY. 131

Central Standard Time

Flint Division.

M	Sept 21, 1915	Lim.		Lim.	AM	AM	AM		North	PM	PM		PM
0	Detroit W. R. ..lv	6 20	.... Limiteds every two hours until	6.20	....	....	7.00	....	Cars lv every 2 hours thereafter fo Flint until	7.00	9.00	....	10.30
13	Royal Oak........	7.12		7 12	....	....	7.55	....		7.55	9.50	....	11.20
27	Rochester	7.36		7.36	6.08	6.14	8.33	....		8.31	10.25	....	11.55
28	Lake Orion Jct...	7.40		7.40	6.13	6.25	8.37	....		8.37	10.30	....	12.00
37	Orion	7.56		7.56	....	6.44	8.57	....		8.57	10.50	....	12.20
40	Oxford	8.04		8.04	....	6.53	9.09	....		9 09	10.55	....	12.28
50	Ortonville	8.18		8.18	...	7.13	9.33	....		9.31	11.20	....	12s45
56	Goodrich....	....		....	....	7.25	9.46	....		9.43	11.30	....	12s58
68	Flint,............ar	8.50		8.50	....	7.59	10.20	....		10 18	12.00	....	12s56
..	Saginaw.	10 10		1010	....	....	....	....		....	....	....	1.19
..	Bay City...	10 50		1050	....	....	....	....		....	....	....	.

M														
0	Detroit W.R. ...lv	4.20	6 20	....	...	....	....	6 00	8.00	..every 2 hrs until..	6.00	8.00	9.00	10 30
13	Royal Oak	5 12	7.12	....	...	....	....	6.55	8.55		6 55	8.55	9.52	11.20
27	Rochester	5.36	7 36	....	...	....	6 05	7.31	9.31		7 31	9.31	10.25	11.55
28	Lake Orion Jct ..	5 40	7.40	....	...	....	6.18	7.40	9.40		7 40	9.36	10 30	12.06
39	Romeo..........ar	6.00	8 00	....	...	....	6.40	8.10	10 10		8 10	10.00	11.55	12.35
48	Almont	6.21	8 21	....	...	....	7.05	8 35	10.35		8 35	10 25	...	12.57
56	Imlay City	6.40	8.40	....	...	....	7.30	9.00	11 00		9 00	10.50	...	1.28

M		Lim	Lim		Lim	AM	AM	AM	South	PM	PM	PM	PM	AM
0	Bay City..........	5.15	7.30	every two hours until	5.30	....	....	....	Cars leave for Oxford and Detroit every two hours until.......	....	...	....	...	....
10	Saginaw	5.55	8.10		6.10	....	....	....		....	....	....	....	....
12	Flint lv	7.00	9.28		7.28	....	....	6.28		4.28	6.28	9.00	1030	....
18	Goodrich.........	*7.25	*9.53		7.53	....	....	7.01		5.01	7.03	9.30	1100	....
28	Ortonville	7.33	10.01		8.01	....	....	7.18		5.18	7.13	9.40	1110	....
31	Oxford	7.46	10.15		8.15	....	5.41	7.40		5.40	7.41	10.02	1131	....
40	Orion............	7.53	10.23		8.23	....	5.53	7 52		5.52	7.53	10.10	1140	....
41	Lake Orion Jct.ar	8.08	10.37		8.37	....	6.13	8.13		6.13	8 13	10.30	1200	....
45	Rochester.........	8 10	10.40		8 40	5.16	6.16	8.16		6.16	8.16	10.33	1203	....
55	Royal Oak.......	8.36	11.03		9.03	5.55	6.55	8.55		6.55	8.55	11.10	....	....
68	Detroit.........ar	9.20	11.50		9.50	6.50	7.50	9.50		7.50	9.50	12.00	....	....

Imlay City	5.20	8 10	9.10	....	....	....	...	6.50	9.50	..every 2 hrs until..	7.50	9.10	11.10
Almont	5.45	8.28	9 28	....	....	....	....	7 15	10 15		8.15	9.35	11.35
Romeo..........lv	6.09	8.49	9.49	....	....	....	....	7.40	10.40		8.40	10.00	12 08
Lake Orion Jct ..	6.38	9 08	10.08	....	....	....	....	8.10	11.10		9.10	10.30	12.30
Rochester	6.40	9.10	10.10	....	....	....	....	8 16	11.16		9.16	10 33	12.33
Royal Oak.	7.03	9 36	10.36	....	....		....	8.55	11.55		9.55	11.10	....
Detroit W. R...ar	7.50	10.20	11.20	....	....	....	....	9 50	12.50		10.50	12 00	....

Wyandotte and Trenton Division.

M	May 25 1915	AM		PM		PM	PM	PM	PM	PM	PM	PM	PM	PM	
0	Detroit W.R. lv	5.00	every 30 minutes until	2.00	every 20 min. until	5.00	5.33	6 03	6 35	7.05	7 35	8.35	9.35	10 35	...
5	River Rouge.	5.23		2.33		5.33	6 03	6.33	7.03	7 33	8.03	9.03	10 03	11 02	....
12	Wyandotte...	6.03		3.03		6.03	6.53	7.08	7.35	8.05	8.35	9.35	10.35	11 35	....
14	Sibley.........	...				....	....	....				....		11.42	....
16	Trenton ar	6.13		3.23		6.13	6.48	7.18	7 50	8 20	8.50	9.50	10.50	11 50	....

M		AM	AM	AM		AM		PM		PM	PM	PM		PM			PM
0	Trenton.....lv	4.10	4.40	5.03	....	6.18	every 30 min. until	1.48	every 20 min. until	5.48	6.20	6.46	every 30 min. until	8.20	every hour until	..	11.20
2	Sibley.........	4.20	....	....	....	....		....		5.53	6.27	6.55		8.27		...	11.27
4	Wyandotte	4 37	5.05	5 24	...	6.00		2.09		6.00	6.48	7.12		8.42			11.42
	River Rouge	4.58	5 24	5.45	....	6.30		2 30		6.33	7.05	7.35		9.05		....	12.05
		5.33	6.03	6 18	....	7.03		3 03		7 03	7 35	8 05		9 35			

Car leaves Trenton at 11.20 PM, connects with night car at Clark Ave.

130 DETROIT, JACKSON & CHICAGO.

M	Eastern Standard Time	LIMITEDS				AM	AM	AM		PM	PM	PM	PM	PM	PM	PM
0	Detroit, W.R...lv	7.00	every 2 hours thereafter until	....	7.00	....	....	7.30	Cars leave for Jackson every 2 hours there-after until	5.30	6.30	8.00	9.00	1000	1100	....
10	Dearborn.........	7.49		....	7.49	....	....	8.2		6.27	7.27	8.57	9.57	1057	1154	....
18	Wayne	8.02		...	8.02	....	....	8 48		6.43	7.43	9 13	1013	1118	1209	....
30	Ypsilanti.........	8.26		....	8.26	5.52	7.18	9.18		7.18	8.22	9 45	1045	1150	1243	....
59	Ann Arbor.......	8.48		...	8.48	6.12	7.50	9 50		7.50	8.55	1020	.115	1 20	1.10	...
50	Lima Center......	....		....	....	6 34	8.14	1014		8.14	....	1043	....	1244		....
53	Chelsea.........	9.10		....	9.10	6.45	8.24	1024		8 24	....	1053	....	255	....	....
60	Grass Lake.......	9.27		....	9.27	7.06	8.50	1050		8.50	....	1120	....	1.20	....	....
65	Jackson, W.R...Ar	9.55		....	9.55	7.35	9.20	1120		9.20	....	1150	....	1.50	....	....
68	Battle Creek......	10.28		....	....	....	....	....		....	....	....	....	....	....	....
71	Kalamazoo........	11.28		....	....	....	....	....		....	....	....	....	....	....	....
76	Lansing..........	. .		....	1045	....	....	....		....	....	....	....	....	....	....

M	Sept 21, 1915	LIMITEDS				AM	AM	AM		PM	PM			PM	
0	Lansing.........lv	5 40	..	every 2 hours thereafter until	....	....	....	....	Cars leave for Detroit every 2 hours thereafter until.....	.	....	....	....	....	....
5	Kalamazo lv	....	6.35		4.25	....	....	....		....	....	....	....	....	....
8	Battle Creek......	....	7.30		5.30	....	....	....			....	....	....	....	.
11	Jackson, W.R...lv	8.05	1005		8.05	....	....	7.35		7.35	9 30	..	...	12.00	....
16	Grass Lake......	8.28	1028		8.28	....	....	8.06		8.06	9.56	.	...	12.30	
23	Chelsea..........	8.45	1045		8.45	....	....	8 30		8 30	10.15	..	....	12.5	
26	Lima Center......	....	....		....	....	....	8.39		8.39	10.24	....	....	1 01	....
37	Ann Arbor...	9.10	1110		9.10	5.35	6.40	8.59		9.59	10.46	....		1.30	....
46	Ypsilanti.........	9.33	1133		9.33	6.00	7.10	9.35		9 34	11.15	....		1.58	....
58	Wayne.....	9.56	1156		9.56	6 36	7 43	1013		10.14	11.55	....		....	....
66	Dearborn.........	1007	1207		1009	6.58	8 05	1034		10.34	12.15	....		.	....
76	Detroit, W.R....ar	1055	1255		1055	7.55	9 00	1130		11.30	1.00	.			

Connection at Jackson for Albion, Marshall, Battle Creek and Kalamazoo.

Express cars leave Detroit for Ann Arbor at 8:0 AM and every two hours thereafter until 6:00 PM. Leave Ann Arbor at 8:10 AM and every two hours thereafter until 6:10 PM.

SALINE BRANCH

Cars lv. Ypsilanti for Saline at 7:00, 8:45 AM and every 2 hours thereafter until 6.45 PM.; cars also leave Ypsilanti at 8:30, 10:50, 11:50 PM. and 12.50 AM.

Cars lv. Saline for Ypsilanti 7:35, 7:45 AM. and every two hours thereafter until 7:45 PM.; cars also lv. Saline for Ypsilanti at 9. 0 PM, 12:15 and 1:15 AM.

PLYMOUTH AND NORTHVILLE BRANCH

Cars leave Detroit for Westwood Otto Inn, Wayne, Plymouth and Northville at 5:30 6:30 AM and every hour thereafter until 5:30 PM, also at 7:30, 9 and 11 PM.

On Sundays first car one hour later from Detroit.

Orchard Lake Division.

M	Sept 21. 1915	AM	AM		Going North	PM	
0	Detroit..........	....	....	6.05	.... and every hour thereafter until	11.05	
13	Redford	....	....	6.57		11.57	
18	Farmington Jct...	....	6.06	7.09		12.09	
19	Farmington	....	6.09	7.12		12.12	....
27	Northville.......ar	...	6.28	7.31		12.31	
18	Farmington Jct.lv	†5.39	6.09	7.09		12.09	....
28	Orchard Lake....	6 05	6.35	7.35		12.35	.
34	Pontiac	6.21	6.51	7.51		12.51	

M		AM	AM	Going South	PM	PM	AM	
0	Pontiac..........lv	....	6.11	.... and every hour thereafter until	10.11	11.11	12.11	. ..
6	Orchard Lake....	.. .	6.31		10 31	11 31	12.31	....
16	Farmington Jct.ar	.....	6.59		10 59	11.59	12 59	.
0	Northville lv	6.05	6 35		10.33	11.36	12.35	..
8	Farmington	6.58	6.58		10 53	11.53	12.53	....
9	Farmington Jct.ar	6.29	6.59		10 59	11 59	12.59	..
14	Redford lv	6.40	7.10		11 10	...	...	....
27	Detroit	7.35	8.05		12 05			.

DETROIT, MONROE & TOLEDO SHORT LINE.

Central Time	Express				LOCALS								
Sept 26 1915	AM		PM	....	AM	A.M		PM	PM	P.M	....		
Detroit...... Lv	6.55	.every two hours until .	6 55		5.40	7 55	every two hours thereafter until	7.55	8.55	9.55	....	....	....
Woodmere......	....		....	....	...			....	....		....	....	....
Ecorse	....		....	....	6 21	8.41		8 41	9.39	10 39	....	....	....
Wyandotte.....	7.39		7.39	....	6.25	8.45		8 45	9.42	10 42	....	....	....
Sibley	7.44		7.44	....	6 30	8.50		8.50	9.48	10 48	....	....	....
Trenton	7.47		7.47	....	6.35	8.54		8.54	9 52	10 52	....	....	....
Rockwood.....	7.58		7.58	....	6 40	9.04		9.08	10.00	11 00	....	....	....
Newport.......	8.05		8.05	....	6.50	9 16		9.18	10.12	11 10	....	....	....
Stony Creek...	8.08		8.08	....	6 56	9.22		9 22	10.14	11 14	....	....	....
Monroe	8.20		8.20	....	7.12	9.39		9 37	10.27	11 29	....	....	....
Erie...........	8.41		8.41	...	7 35	1002		10 02	10.52	....	....	....	....
Toledo.........	9.15		9.15	....	8.20	1045		10.45	11.30	..	....	....	....
Arrive	AM		PM		AM	AM		PM	PM	PM	...		

	Express					LOCALS								
Leave	AM	A.M.		PM		A.M.	AM			P.M	P.M	PM	PM	P.M
Toledo	7.15	9.15	....every two hours until....	7.15	....	....	6.05	....	every two hours thereafter until	6 05	8 30	9 15	1000	1130
Erie	7.50	9.46		7.46	...	...	6 41	....		6 41	9.09	9.50	1037	1203
Monroe.........	8.20	10.05		8 05	....	6 00	7 07	....		7.07	9.35	10.13	1100	1220
Stony Creek ...	8.34	10.18		8.18		6.10	7 20	....		7 20	9.45		1110	....
Newport	8.38	10.23		8 23	....	6.14	7 25	....		7 25	9.50	.. .	1115	....
Rockwood	8.46	10.31		8 32	....	6.23	7 36	....		7 36	10.01	....	1126	....
Trenton	8.53	10.40		8 40	..	6.35	7 46	....		7 45	10.11	.	1133	....
Sibley.........	8.55	10.42		8.42	...	6.37	7.49	....		7.49	10 14	....	1 35	....
Wyandotte	9.02	10.49		8.49	....	6.45	7.58	....		7.58	10 23	....	1142	....
Ecorse	....	....		....	....	6.48	8 02	....		8.02	10.27	. .	1145	....
Woodmere	....	....		....	....	....	....	....					....	....
Detroit.........	9.40	11.30		9 30	....	7.35	8.50	...		8.50	11.15		1220	....
Arrive	A.M.	AM		PM		AM	AM			PM	PM	PM	AM	AM

Limited Trains Between Detroit, Toledo and Cleveland.

Central Standard Time

PM	PM	PM	PM	AM	AM	AM	Leave / Arrive	AM	PM	PM	PM	PM	PM	PM
7.25	5.25	3.25	1.25	11.25	9.25	7.25	....Detroit ...	10.00	12.00	2.00	4.00	6.00	8.00	1000
8.39	6.39	4.39	2.39	12.39	10.39	8.40	....Monroe...	8.45	10.45	12.45	2.45	4.45	6.45	8.45
9.30	7.30	5.30	3.30	1.30	11.30	9.30	Ar ..Toledo.. Lv	8.00	10.00	12.00	2.00	4.00	6.00	8.00
.....	7.30	5.30	3.30	1.30	11.30	9.30	Lv ..Toledo.. Ar	.....	10.00	12.00	2.00	4.00	6.00	8.00
.....	8.40	6.40	4.40	2.40	12.40	10.40	....Fremont..	.....	8.40	10.40	12.40	2.40	4.40	6 40
.....	.....	7.30	5.30	3.30	1.30	11.30	...Sandusky..	.....	7.45	9.45	11.45	1.45	3.45	5.45
.....	9.45	7.45	5.45	3.45	1.45	11.45	...Norwalk...	.....	7.40	9.40	11.40	1.40	3.40	5.40
.....	10.50	8 50	6.50	4.50	2.50	12.50	....Lorain	.....	6.30	8.32	10.32	12.32	2.32	4.32
.....	11.50	9.50	7.50	5 50	3.50	1.50	..Cleveland..	.....	5.00	7.30	9.3	11.30	1.30	3.30
PM	PM	PM	PM	PM	PM	PM	Arrive / Leave	AM	AM	AM	AM	AM	PM	PM

Jere Chamberlain Hutchins

Born 13 October 1851, Concordia County, La.; died ?, Detroit.

Hutchins started railroading as a timekeeper for construction crews and taught himself engineering while on the job. His reputation grew, and in 1894 he was invited to Detroit to meet Richard T. Wilson, owner of the Detroit Citizens' Street Railway. Wilson offered him the position of vice president and manager of the company that owned all of Detroit's street railways. When Henry A. Everett and Edward W. Moore formed the Detroit United Railways to take over and further develop the interurban system out of Detroit, Hutchins was made vice president and general manager. Hutchins's hand was in everything the DUR undertook. In making it a model property, he gained a national reputation for his management skills. Within a few years he was named the DUR's president. He conducted years of negotiations with city hall about municipal ownership of the street railways and earned the respect of all the parties involved. In May 1916 he announced that the workload was too heavy and that he had to retire.

Hutchins has the unique distinction of being one of a very few Michigan railroad men to write his own memoirs—*Jere C. Hutchins: A Personal Story.*

after the Citizens also got control of the last independent line, the Detroit, Fort Wayne & Belle Isle, the new name recently adopted by the Fort Wayne & Elmwood.

Hazen Pingree moved to the governor's office in 1897. Despite his best efforts to continue as mayor of Detroit at the same time, the courts forced him to give up one of the two chairs. He preferred being governor, but his departure for Lansing did not reduce the demand for municipal ownership of the city's streetcar lines. His legacy was that it remained a contentious issue in city politics for the next two decades. Tom Johnson must have tired of the constant battles with city hall, for apparently he began to see some wisdom in municipal ownership. He had Hutchins continue to meet with local officials and the governor. To negotiate a sale a three-man commission was named early in 1899 made up of Pingree, Detroit attorney Elliott G. Stevenson, and Charles Schmidt, who soon resigned and was replaced by Hutchins. The sticking point between the two parties was setting the value of the street railway system. Finally both sides agreed on $16,578,563, and the proposal went to the city council. The Citizens said it was willing to sell for $15,273,000 if the city paid cash, but the full value would be the price if payment were in city bonds.

In early July the Michigan Supreme Court declared the state law that allowed the city to purchase and operate the street railway system unconstitutional. To keep things moving the city supported forming the Detroit Municipal Railway in July 1899. It was to buy the Citizens to consummate the sale and would hold it until the state constitution could be amended. Detroit Citizens' Street Railway president Wilson lost patience over the delays in dealing with the city. He announced that he was breaking off negotiations with the commission and at the same time bumped up the sale price to an even $17 million.

Another buyer came forward that began vying against the city's purchase. Henry A. Everett and Edward W. Moore, two of the original owners of Mayor Pingree's Detroit Electric in 1896, were now ready to buy. The two Clevelanders had worked together for a decade on telephone and electric railway projects in Ohio and in Canada, and they were buying almost any electric railway they could find. Apparently, they hoped to duplicate in Detroit what they had done in Cleveland—to control of all of the electric railways and streetcar lines in the city. Wilson was ready to sell out simply because he was tired of the continual pressure of managing his investments. Wilson's major partner, Tom Johnson, now wealthy from other ventures, also was eager to leave the business world and reenter political life.

On 28 December 1900 Everett and Moore formed the Detroit United Railway to buy the four Detroit street railway companies. Assured he would not have to be involved in direct management, Wilson did stay with the company. Tom Johnson left the venture after Wilson made some personal settlement with him. Jere Hutchins also was an original investor in the Detroit part of the Everett-Moore syndicate. The DUR immediately bought the Detroit Electric, the Detroit Suburban, the Detroit Citizens' Street Railway, and the Detroit, Fort Wayne & Belle Isle.

Everett and Moore intended to have complete control of all of the traction lines in the area and began buying suburban and interurban roads as well. Wilson was not interested in these but had concentrated only on city lines. Everett and Moore's first suburban purchase was the Wyandotte & Detroit River. This small road, formed in 1892 and built from Detroit to as far as Trenton by 1893, was the first interurban line in Michigan built to operate with electric power. Everett and Moore came to Hutchins and offered to sell the road to Hutchins personally. Hutchins contacted his bosses, got their approval, and Hutchins and his aide Alex B. duPont bought the line in November 1898. After the DUR was formed the two sold their line to Everett and Moore in February 1901.

In May 1901 the DUR bought the Detroit & Northwestern. This company was an 1899 merger of two earlier roads—the Pontiac & Sylvan Lake, which was built between those two points in 1895, and the Grand River Electric, which was built in 1898 out Grand River Avenue as far as Farmington. The D&NW built a connection between Farmington Junction and Sylvan Lake and extended from Farmington to Northville in 1900.

The next month Everett and Moore added the Detroit & Pontiac to their company. In January 1895 real estate developer Frank E. Snow, with George Hendrie, had formed the Oakland Railway to build a line from Six Mile Road to Pontiac. Despite problems assembling the necessary municipal franchises Snow got his line built as far as Birmingham by 1896. Getting into Pontiac from Birmingham was considerably more difficult. In the city of Pontiac there was no end of conflicts with the Pontiac & Sylvan Lake franchise; the city itself was less than helpful. Snow had to cross the Detroit, Grand Haven & Milwaukee (now Grand Trunk Western) on the south edge of Pontiac, and it refused to allow any crossing at all. A bridge over the railroad was talked about, but it would be an expensive extra. Finally Snow was able, when the DGH&M crews were distracted, to put in a prepared section of track for the crossing, and, once in, there was no undoing the deed. When the DUR offered to purchase the road Hendrie had no problem selling it for a quick profit.

In August the Detroit & Flint was added to the system. The earliest predecessor of this road was the Detroit & Lake Orion, which was formed in March 1899 to build from Detroit to Lake Orion via Pontiac and Rochester. The Pontiac city fathers demanded it use routes of their choosing. The line's promoters—John Winter, who owned the Grand Rapids, Holland & Lake Michigan; Dr. Oliver Lau of Lake Orion; and Frank Andrews, an electric line promoter—balked at this demand. They decided to bypass Pontiac and organized a new company, the Detroit, Rochester, Romeo & Lake Orion, to have the route they needed. Within a few months construction was under way from Royal Oak north to Rochester. By October 1899 cars were running from Royal Oak, through Rochester, to Romeo, and were using Detroit & Pontiac tracks to reach the city of Detroit. Work then began on the section between Rochester and Oxford and was completed by the summer of 1900. When Everett and Moore bought the Detroit & Pontiac they turned their sights to the Rochester road. Andrews did not want to sell. The men from Cleveland simply formed another company to build a line from Pontiac to Flint

Cornelius John Reilly

Born 26 May 1848, Walworth Co., Wis.; died 21 April 1913, Detroit.

Reilly grew up in Racine, Wisconsin, moved to Detroit, and began practicing law there in 1870. In 1875 he was elected circuit court judge, and while seated was named receiver of the Cass Avenue Railway and oversaw its sale to George Hendrie. Within a few years he returned to private practice for more income, but later returned to the bench.

During the 1890s, while still a judge, Reilly became involved in promoting an electric railway to Mt. Clemens, in 1894 formed the Rapid Railway to build a line from Detroit to Port Huron, and was president of the road and several other roads that built parts of the line. In 1902, after Detroit United Railways took over the Rapid, he turned his attention to the Toledo & Monroe, which built some of the line of the Detroit, Monroe & Toledo Short Line.

After the DM&TSL was completed and leased to the DUR in 1906, Reilly and his son undertook building the Chicago & Southern Traction from Chicago to Kankakee, Illinois, as a part of a projected Chicago–St. Louis road. This last venture went into receivership in October 1911, and just two months later his son died. Reilly's health then began to fail, and he died after a bout with pneumonia.

that would ignore Andrews's road. Then they reminded Andrews that they owned his connecting route into Detroit, and he would have to deal with them to get into Detroit over any tracks. This persuaded Andrews to sell. Later in August Everett and Moore bought the Sandwich, Windsor & Amherstburg, the company that owned the city lines in Windsor, Ontario, along with suburban routes to Walkerville and Tecumseh, to Essex and Leamington, and to Amherstburg.

What Everett and Moore could not buy outright they tried to control. They were able to gain control of two other electric lines operating out of Detroit. One was a line between Detroit and Port Huron. This route had started with the Rapid Railway, formed early in 1894 by Judge Cornelius J. Reilly. Reilly had to bring Charles M. Swift and his financiering capabilities into the picture. In July 1895 the road was completed between the Detroit city limits and Mt. Clemens, and later that year it began operating into downtown Detroit on Gratiot Avenue. At the beginning of 1898 Reilly announced his expansion plans—he formed the Rapid Railroad to build to Port Huron from some point on the Rapid Railway's route. Reilly planned for his route to bypass Mt. Clemens and to run along the lakeshore. Senator James McMillan of Detroit, railroad promoter, lumberman, and shipping line owner, disapproved of this route and was able to delay the start-up.

While Reilly was promoting his project the Detroit, Lake Shore & Mt. Clemens arose as a new competitor. Frederick T. Ranney formed this company in July 1896 to build from the end of the Jefferson Avenue streetcar line in Detroit, out Jefferson through the Grosse Pointes to Mt. Clemens. Ranney met with no end of wrangling with the residents of Grosse Pointe, who enjoyed the sedate clop of horses' hooves and wanted no electric cars passing their estates. Ranney needed money to build, and he persuaded Merrill B. Mills, who had recently sold his Pontiac & Sylvan Lake to the Detroit & Northwestern, to join him and take the presidency. This tactic allowed the road to begin through service between downtown Detroit and Mt. Clemens at the end of September 1898.

Once into Mt. Clemens, the Swift-Reilly and Mills-Ranney combines had to deal with getting through Mt. Clemens. A short horsecar line had been built there in 1890, extended a bit when the line was electrified in 1893, and eventually sold to John B. Dyar. Dyar had his own plans for a Detroit–Port Huron line, but he met financial difficulties that forced him in 1897 and 1898 to sell off his investments. It appears that Ranney and Mills thought they had won out, for they issued DLS&MC bonds that included the city trackage as security. Swift and Reilly took the matter to court, and eventually won over Ranney and Mills. Combined with a three-month interruption in service onto Detroit city lines, that decision forced out Ranney and Mills. Swift and Reilly formed the Detroit & Lake St. Clair in March 1900, then the next day bought the Detroit, Lake Shore & Mt. Clemens. At about the same time the two were able to gain control of the city street lines in Mt. Clemens.

Next Swift and Reilly turned to completing their line to Port Huron. In March 1899 they formed the Detroit, Mt. Clemens & Marine City and put their Mt. Clemens city lines into that company. At the same time, a group of Port Huron men who owned the city electric line there, and headed by William L. Jenks, formed the Port Huron, St. Clair & Marine City to build in the same territory. By the end of 1899 Swift was able to pick up the bankrupt Detroit & River St. Clair, which its owners and later its receiver had been able to build between Chesterfield and Algonac.

Swift and Jenks then managed to come to terms. Jenks reluctantly agreed to an arrangement that called for the formation of a holding company, the Detroit & Port Huron Shore Line. All of the assets of both men's roads—the Rapid Railroad; the Rapid Railway; the Detroit, Mt. Clemens & Marine City; the Port Huron, St. Clair & Marine City; and the City Electric Railway of Port Huron—went under the umbrella of the Shore Line in July 1900. With these financial details out of the way construction to finish the line went quickly. The segment between Mt. Clemens and Chesterfield was built first. When the line between Algonac and Port Huron was finished, service over the entire route started in August 1900, with cars running through Algonac. A cutoff line between New Baltimore and Marine City was built not long after, with the fastest through cars running over it. The advertising to the public called it the Rapid Railway System, although that was not its legal name.

Everett and Moore were interested in buying the Shore Line, but Swift was never able to find a deal that he liked. Because of Everett and Moore's mounting financial problems Swift in the end had to content himself with the DUR operating the line under an agreement. The details of the arrangement are not completely clear, but the DUR did start operating the Rapid Railway System in July 1901.

All that remained for Everett and Moore to do was to link their lines in Michigan to theirs in Ohio by closing the fifty-mile gap between Detroit and Toledo. They owned the Lake Shore Electric, a first-rate line between Cleveland and Toledo, which they planned to use east of Toledo as the link to the rest of their system. As early as 1893, well before Everett and Moore came on the scene, such a line named the Toledo, Monroe & Detroit Electric Railway had been proposed. Nothing happened, and the idea lay dormant until Peter N. Jacobsen and W. C. Johnson became interested in it. They formed the Toledo & Monroe Railway in March 1898 and soon began building, completing the line in April 1901. Another line, this one a steam railroad named the Detroit & Toledo Shore Line, was formed in March 1899. Everett and Moore bought it in April 1901 after only a little work had been done on it. Soon after they also gained control of the Toledo & Monroe. They pushed work on the Shore Line north from Monroe, and by the end of December 1901 the line was finished as far as Trenton. Everett and Moore began operations by using the T&M from Toledo to Monroe, the Shore Line to Trenton, and their Wyandotte & Detroit River line into Detroit. They also continued work on the Shore Line between Toledo and Monroe because of its better route.

Fortune turned against Everett and Moore when, by the end of 1901, they were facing serious financial difficulties. They had acquired all the lines in the Detroit area, paying good prices and assuming the debts of the former owners. At the same time, they were involved in a good many other projects in Ohio and Ontario with their expanding electric lines empire. They also were developing their telephone interests in the face of stiff competition developing from the Bell telephone system. With so many projects under way, they stretched their resources thin. One of their construction subsidiaries went bankrupt when Everett and Moore could not meet some of its obligations. Banks in Cleveland stepped in and took over a number of their properties, a strain that caused one bank to fail as a result. Everett and Moore eventually lost control of the Cleveland Electric Railway and had to sell off a profitable Chicago line and another in Ohio that was under construction. To keep as much as they could they sold the Detroit & Toledo Shore Line in July 1903 to a pair of buyers, the Grand Trunk Western and the Toledo, St. Louis & Western. These two roads eventually completed it as a steam railroad. But the sale of the Shore Line severed Everett and Moore's Detroit-Toledo line, and through service ended for a time. The two men did manage to keep control of all their Detroit properties as well as their crown jewel, the Lake Shore Electric. They raised money by selling blocks of stocks, which brought in a group of Canadian investors who developed into important partners of Everett and Moore.

In December 1902 a group of investors who were involved in the interurban lines between Detroit and Port Huron, including Cornelius J. Reilly and Matthew Slush, formed the Detroit, Monroe & Toledo Short Line to build a new electric line in Everett and Moore's territory. Reilly bought the Toledo & Monroe to use as the southern leg, then began building from Monroe to a connection with the DUR's Fort Street city route in Detroit. In May 1904 through service began between Detroit and Toledo. Everett and Moore bought control of the DM&TSL in March 1906, integrated it into the rest of their system, and established a speedy through service between Detroit and Cleveland.

One other line into Detroit eluded Everett and Moore ownership. In some ways the Detroit, Jackson & Chicago's line from Detroit through Ann Arbor to Jackson was the most important since it connected Detroit to central and western Michigan. As the name indicates, it held the possibility of some day reaching Chicago. James D. Hawks, who at the time was president of the Detroit & Mackinac and was a former general manager of the Detroit Citizens' Street Railway, and Samuel F. Angus became interested in building electric interurbans in the late 1890s. The two formed the Detroit, Ypsilanti & Ann Arbor in November 1897 to build west from Detroit. It was soon completed to Dearborn, and reached Ypsilanti the following June. They had a spate of difficulty with the citizens of Wayne, who did not want electric cars disturbing the serenity of what is now Michigan Avenue. An alternate route proposed through a residential neighborhood brought even more objections. Finally Michigan Avenue was agreed on, and the road was built. Hawks and Angus also picked up the "Ypsi-Ann," the Ann Arbor & Ypsilanti Electric, to get rights through Ypsilanti and into Ann Arbor. With their profits from the sale, Henry P. Glover and Robert W. Hemphill, the Ypsi-Ann's former owners, incorporated the Ypsilanti & Saline in April 1899 to build an electric line between those cities. Hawks also was one of the incorporators of that road, which was completed in short order in September 1899.

Early in 1901 Hawks and Angus formed a new company, the Detroit, Ypsilanti, Ann Arbor & Jackson, to build the extension from Ann Arbor to Jackson. In March they merged the Detroit, Ypsilanti & Ann Arbor and the Ypsilanti & Saline into this new company. They obtained franchises to build along Jackson Road as far as Chelsea and along the Michigan Central tracks from Chelsea into Jackson. They began building at Ann Arbor. As they were starting up William A. Boland and James B. Foote, the brother of William A. Foote, formed two companies to build a line between Jackson and Detroit. Foote's suburban line out to Grass Lake and Wolf Lake was used as the western section to provide access into Jackson. Construction started toward Ann Arbor but went more slowly, as Foote appears to have been more concerned with having a well-built line rather than one quickly built, an approach opposite to that used by Hawks and Angus.

In Ann Arbor both companies had to cross the Ann Arbor Railroad just west of the downtown. Both roads wanted to use Huron Street into the city. The Ann Arbor Railroad refused to allow a grade-level crossing, insisted on a bridged crossing, and kept an engine and cars there to block any attempt to install the proposed crossing. Hawks and Angus built tracks up to the railroad but could not get across. Boland and Foote also tried to negotiate a crossing for themselves but had no more luck than Hawks and Angus. Eventually the Michigan railroad commissioner, making a rare exception, authorized a grade crossing until some other solution could be found. Hawks and Angus quickly laid their crossing, completing their line from Ann Arbor to Jackson in April 1902. Foote and Boland continued to build east from Jackson, eventually completing their line as far as Dexter. There they stopped, still having no entrance into Ann Arbor. In 1904 Foote and Boland conceded the battle, settled up with Hawks and Angus, and abandoned most of their line between Grass Lake and Dexter.

About this time the Foote and Boland parted company. While Foote lost interest in building east of Jackson, Boland saw his dream of a Detroit-Chicago interurban line begin to fade. He clung to it long enough to buy the little Detroit, Plymouth & Northville line, which he hoped he could use as an entrance into Detroit. That company had built a line from Wayne, where it had connections into Detroit, to Plymouth in February 1899, and to Northville the following November. Boland thought its franchises could be useful and bought the company in July 1901; he then acquired additional franchises east toward Detroit. In March 1906 Boland formed a new company, the Jackson, Ann Arbor & Detroit. He merged the Northville road into it, but it was now too late. The DJ&C was solidly in place with ample service, so Boland found it difficult to raise money for his competing parallel line.

Early in 1907 officers of the Detroit United formed the Detroit, Jackson & Chicago Railway to buy the Detroit, Ypsilanti, Ann Arbor & Jackson from Hawks and Angus. In February they bought that road and in July bought Boland's Jackson, Ann Arbor & Detroit. Although the DUR owned controlling interest in the DJ&C, for some reason Everett and Moore never merged the company into the DUR. Rather, they were contented with a lease while operating the line as an integral part of their system.

The DUR offered quality interurban service, one that was a vast improvement over the local service offered by the steam railroads. Every major road that fanned out from downtown Detroit had DUR service: East Jefferson, Gratiot, Woodward, Grand River, Michigan, and West Fort. In 1909 local cars ran every thirty minutes from downtown Detroit on a ninety-minute trip to Pontiac. A local car ran every hour to Northville and connected to Pontiac via Orchard Lake. There was a car every hour to Mt. Clemens via the Shore Line through the Grosse Pointes. There were four limiteds a day using the cutoff line to Port Huron making the trip in two hours fifteen minutes; local cars ran every hour. A car ran every thirty minutes on the seventy-five-minute trip to Wyandotte and Trenton. The Toledo service was four limiteds on a two-hour schedule and locals every hour. Three limiteds ran to Flint and were supplemented by a local every two hours. At Flint they connected with cars to Saginaw. Four limiteds ran to Jackson on a two-hour running time supplemented by a local every two hours. In addition there was a Detroit–Ann Arbor local car between each through car so that there was hourly local service between Detroit and Ann Arbor. Also, cars ran each hour from Detroit, via Wayne, to Plymouth and Northville. A car ran every two hours between Ypsilanti and Saline.

By 1915 the DUR service had improved more. Limiteds ran every two hours to both Port Huron and Flint, and from Flint through to Bay City. On the Detroit-Toledo line a limited ran every two hours and operated through to Cleveland, an express run that stopped only at major stations ran every two hours, and this was supplemented by a local leaving every two hours. Limiteds ran through every two hours on the Detroit–Ann Arbor–Jackson–Battle Creek–Kalamazoo run, and these were supplemented by express and local runs between Detroit and Ann Arbor. Local cars ran between Detroit and Imlay City every two hours. Although the number of trains run increased, running times for all these services changed very little between 1909 and 1915.

City streetcar service in Detroit was another matter. Mayor Pingree had planted deep the seeds of dissatisfaction about private ownership of the city's street railways. Nearly two decades passed before a mayor came onto the political scene who was able to wrestle a solution from the morass. On the DUR side the very capable Jere C. Hutchins was able to maintain private ownership and reasonable profitability while negotiating with a succession of mayors and aldermen and city commit-tees. The DUR's property was evaluated several times between 1900 and 1920, but a number that was satisfactory to both the city and the DUR proved elusive. Tom Johnson, former Detroit Citizens' Street Railway president and now the mayor of Cleveland, came back to Detroit to help Mayor William B. Thompson work out a solution by using Johnson's experience in attaining municipal ownership in Cleveland. The effort came to nothing. The city began to refuse to renew DUR franchises for some of the city lines when they expired. This forced the DUR to resort to day-to-day rentals to continue operations on them, but provided no incentive for it to do more than absolutely vital maintenance. Finally in February 1915 the city and the DUR agreed on a $24,900,000 sale price. The *Detroit News* raised vociferous objections, and the agreement died. All this changed when James Couzens, running on a platform loudly in support of municipal ownership, was elected mayor in 1918.

SOURCES

Hague, Wilbur E., and Kirk F. Hise. *The Detroit, Monroe & Toledo Short Line Railway.* Forty Fort, Pa.: Harold E. Cox, 1986.

Hilton, George W., and John F. Due. *The Electric Interurban Railways in America.* Stanford, Calif.: Stanford University Press, 1960.

Hutchins, Jere C. *Jere C. Hutchins: A Personal Story.* Detroit: author, 1938.

Michigan Pathfinder Guide, December 1915. Detroit: Pathfinder, 1915.

Michigan Railway Guide, June 1909. Detroit: John R. Wood, 1909.

O'Geran, Graeme. *A History of the Detroit Street Railways.* Detroit: Conover Press, 1931.

Schramm, Jack E., and William H. Henning. *Detroit's Street Railways.* Vol. 1, *City Lines 1863–1922.* Chicago: Central Electric Railfans' Association, 1978.

———. *When Eastern Michigan Rode the Rails, Book 2.* Glendale, Calif.: Interurban Press, 1986.

Schramm, Jack E., William H. Henning, and Richard R. Andrews. *When Eastern Michigan Rode the Rails, Book 1.* Glendale, Calif.: Interurban Press, 1984.

———. *When Eastern Michigan Rode the Rails, Book 3.* Glendale, Calif.: Interurban Press, 1988.

———. *When Eastern Michigan Rode the Rails, Book 4.* Polo, Ill.: Transportation Trails, 1994.

Michigan United Railways

The enthusiasm for electric interurbans was not restricted to Detroit but quickly spread throughout Michigan. Eager promoters formed dozens of companies to build lines all over southern Michigan, as well as some throughout northern Michigan and the Upper Peninsula. Any community of more than 2,000 or 3,000 residents might have an interurban. No route was too impractical. Capital was found for some of the best of the routes, but a lack of money killed off most of them. The Detroit United Railways expanded to cover the Detroit area, and the Michigan United Railways a decade later developed into the largest non-Detroit interurban system.

The first interurban line built outside southeast Michigan was a line between Bay City and Saginaw. Three Detroiters, William A. Jackson, John M. Nicol, and Frank E. Snow, formed the Union Street Railway of Saginaw in 1893 to buy up the city lines, and in 1894 formed the Riverside Park Railway to reach an amusement park they built in the Saginaw suburbs. Later in 1894 Snow headed another group that had formed the Saginaw Consolidated Street Railway, although the record is unclear what it may have consolidated. In March 1895 the three men formed the InterUrban Railway, which completed its road in 1896 between the south end of the city lines in Bay City and the Saginaw city lines on the west side of the Saginaw River near Zilwaukee. In 1899 a new company, the Saginaw Valley Traction, was formed, with Saginaw lumberman George B. Morley as one of its promoters. This

Western Michigan University, Regional History Collection, A. Rodney Lenderink collection.

new company bought up both Saginaw street railway companies and leased the InterUrban Railway.

In western Michigan Major Loren N. Downs formed the Michigan Traction Company at the end of 1896 to build an electric line between Kalamazoo and Battle Creek. It took him some time to raise the needed funds; he started construction in 1899, and by August 1900 his line was finished. Downs's company owned the city streetcar lines in both cities and used them to reach both city centers. The first car from Battle Creek in June 1900 ran only as far as Galesburg because the spindly bridge over the Michigan Central just east of that village was not yet finished. By August the Galesburg bridge was done, as was the company's short branch line to Gull Lake from Gull Lake Junction, just east of Augusta. The road was an immediate success and ran a car every hour that would stop anywhere if flagged down by a rider.

A third early segment of the Michigan United was the Jackson & Suburban Traction. Detroit attorney James B. Corliss owned the money-losing Jackson city streetcar company and was looking for a buyer. In September 1900 William A. Boland, a New York City electric railway financier and Jackson native, outbid James D. Hawks and Samuel

The first part of the Michigan United system was built by Loren Downs's Michigan Traction between Battle Creek and Kalamazoo. The largest obstacle to overcome was crossing the Michigan Central tracks. Both the MC and the commissioner of railroads gave thumbs-down to a conventional grade-level crossing. Downs was forced to build this bridge just east of Galesburg. The road to the left of the bridge is now state highway M-96.

William A. Foote is best remembered for his pioneering work in generating electricity. In 1900 he owned a few smallish electric companies, then partnered in building an interurban line from Jackson to Battle Creek to have a steady customer for his power. In 1910 he was one of the organizers of Commonwealth Power Railway & Light Company, with Consumers Power Company and several interurban lines as its principal assets.

Consumers Energy.

Michigan United Traction was outstate Michigan's largest interurban. This much-condensed schedule of October 1915 from the *Pathfinder Railway Guide* shows the extensive service it provided. The trains of the Michigan Central took three to four hours to make the Detroit-Kalamazoo run compared to the DUR-MUT through limiteds' running time of five hours thirty minutes.

Author's collection.

132 MICHIGAN UNITED TRACTION CO.
Limited Trains Between Kalamazoo, Jackson and Detroit.

PM	PM		AM	AM	Oct. 1, 1915	AM	PM			
4 00	2.00		6 00	...	Leave..Detroit.Arrive	1155	1.55		9 55	.
7.00	5 00		9.00	7.00	.....Jackson.....	9.00	11.00		7.00	9.51
7.23	5.23		9 23	7.22	.....Parma......	8.89	10.84		6 89	9.22
7.87	5.37	and every tw	9.87	7.35	.....Albion......	8.26	10 19	and every tw	6 19	9 05
7.58	5.58	hours thereaft	9.58	7.57	.....Marshall.....	8.04	9.58	hours thereaft	5.58	8 43
8.25	6.28	until.......	1028	8.25	ar ..Battle Creek.. ar	7.86	9.30	until.......	5 30	8.16
8.28	6.28		1028	8.28	lv	7.36	9.30		5 30	8.15
8.54	6.54		1054	8.54	.....Augusta.....	7.12	9 02		5 02	7.47
9.08	7.03		1103	9.03	.....Galesburg....	7.03	8.53		4.58	7.86
9 28	7 28		1128	9.28	Arr. Kalamazoo Lv	6.85	8 25		4 25	7.05

Jackson, Battle Creek and Kalamazoo.

Oct 1 19.5	AM	AM	A.M	AM	AM		PM	PM	PM	PM	PM	PM
Jackson........	....	....	....	†5.30	7.30	and every two hours thereafte until	1.25	3 25	5.80	8.00	10.00	11 00
Parma.........	....	....	....	6 00	8.05		2.03	4 00	6.07	8 34	10 04	11.34
Albion........	....	....	†5.25	p6 22	8.28		2.23	4.21	6.30	8.57	10 23	11.53
Marshall.......	....	....	5.58	7.00	9.00		3.53	4 53	7.02	9 27	10.37	....
Battle Creek ..	†5.15	p5.40	p6.31	7.38	9.38		3 36	5.33	7.40	10 06	11.25	....
Gull Lake Jct	5.39	6.05	7.00	8.07	10.09	and every two hours thereafte until	4.09	5 50	8.08	....	11.53	....
Augusta......	5.42	6.08	7.03	8.10	10.12		4 12	6 12	8.11	....	11 56	....
Galesburg	5.54	6.14	7.18	8.22	10.28		4 24	6.27	8.23	....	12 06	....
Comstock	6.06	6.34	7.32	8.35	10.35		4 35	6.40	8.31	....	12 16	....
Kalamazoo..ar	6.30	6.56	7.55	9.00	11.00		5.00	7.00	9.00	....	12.35	....

	AM	AM	AM		PM	PM	PM	PM	PM
Kalamazoo..lv	....	....	†5.15	7.05	and every two hours thereafte until	5.05	6.00	7 55	9.35	11.00
Comstock	....	....	5.82	7.27		5.30	6.24	8.19	9.59	11 21
Galesburg	....	....	5.41	7.42		5 43	6 39	8.33	10 12	11 32
Augusta	....	....	5.52	7.56		5.57	6 52	8 47	10.24	11.42
Gull Lake Jct	....	....	5.56	7.59		6.01	6.56	8.51	10.27	11.45
Battle Creek	....	....	†5 10	p6.30	8 30	and every two hours thereafter until	6.30	7.30	9 22	10.55	12 20
Marshall......	....	....	5.40	7.09	9.09		7.10	....	10.03	11.34	....
Albion........	....	....	†5.29	6.06	7.43	9.43		7.46	....	10.93	12.01	....
Parma........	....	....	5.47	6.26	8.04	10.05		8.09	....	....	12.18	....
Jackson....ar	....	....	6.15	6.56	8.38	10 38		8.45	....	....	12.45	....

Jackson and Grass Lake.

PM	PM		AM	AM		AM	AM		PM	PM	
11.00	9.00	and eve.yhou	6.00	†5.10	lv...Jackson ...ar.	5.59	7.28	and everyhou	8.58	10.23	12 20
11.22	9.22	and half the	6.22	5 3h	Michigan Center	†5 85	7.07	and half the	8.33	10.08	12.00
11.44	9.44	reafter until	6.44	....	ar...Grass Lake..lv	...	6.45	reafter until	8.15	9.45	11.45

Lansing and St. Johns.

PM	PM	PM	PM		AM	AM	AM	Oct. 1 1915	AM	AM		PM	PM	AM
10 50	8 25	6.00	3 40	and every two hours until	9.40	8.00	6†00	lv.....Lansing.....ar	7.56	1·02	and every two hours until	8 02	10 07	12 30
11.15	8.46	6.28	4.39		10.06	8.25	6.25	.....Dewitt.....	7.27	9.35		.35	9.40	12.07
					....	....	....	...Merle Beach...	....	....		....	....	....
11.38	9.10	6.55	4 35		10.30	8.50	6.50	ar...St. Johns..lv	7†00	9.10		7.10	9.15	11 45

Lansing and Owosso.

PM	PM	PM	PM		AM	M	Leave Arrive	AM		PM	PM	AM
11.00	9.30	7.35	6 20	Leave Lansing every two hours thereafter until	6.20	0	...Lansing....	7 30	Leave Owosso ev'y two hours thereafter until	9 30	10 30	12.15
11.17	9.41	7.52	6.38		6.38	4	..East Lansing..	7.14		9 14	10 16	12.02
11 27	9.57	8.03	6.50		6.50	8	.....Haslett....	7.01		9 01	10 06	11.52
11.39	10.11	8.18	7.06		7.06	14	...Shaftsburg..	6.47		8 47	9 53	11.39
11.47	10 18	8.25	7.13		7.13	19	.....Perry.....	6.88		8 38	9 44	11.30
11.53	10 23	8 30	7.18		7.18	21	.....Morrice....	6.33		8 30	9 39	11 28
12.15	10.45	8 54	7 45		7.45	32	Ar...Owosso Lv	6.05		8 05	9 15	11.00

Jackson and Lansing Branch.

Oct. 1, 1915	LIMITEDS					L O C A L S						
	AM		PM	PM	PM	AM	AM	AM		PM	PM	PM
Jackson........L.	7.05	every two hours until	5.05	7.05	†5.05	6 00	8.00	every two hours until	6 00	9.20	11.00	....
Rives Jct......	7.28		5.28	7.28	5.28	6.25	8.28		6.28	9.48	11.29	....
Leslie........ ..	7.38		5.38	7.38	5.38	6.37	8.41		6 41	9 58	11.38	....
Eden........	7.44		5.44	7.44	5.44	6.48	8.52		6.52	10 05	11.46	....
Mason	7.51		5.51	7.51	5.51	6.59	9.01		7 01	10.14	11.53	....
Holt........	8.03		6.03	8.03	6.00	7.14	9.15		7.12	10 24	12 02	....
Lansing........Ar.	8.21		6.21	8.21	6.19	7.40	9.38		7.34	10 45	12.20	....
	AM				AM	AM	AM		PM	PM	PM	
Lansing ......Lv.	7.30	every two hours until		7 30	5.40	†6.10	p8.05	every two hours until	p8 05	9 30	11·00	....
Holt...............	7.54			7.59	6.00	6 34	8.38		8.29	9.54	11.23	....
Mason	8.05			8.05	6.10	6.47	8.42		8.42	10.06	11.34	....
Eden..	8.09			8.09	6.14	6.53	8.47		8.47	10.09	11.38	....
Leslie.............	8.18			8.18	6.24	7.07	9.01		9 01	10.18	11.47	....
Rives Jct..........	8.28			8.28	6.38	7.19	9.18		9 18	10.22	11.5	....
Jackson........Ar	8.50			8.50	6.58	7.53	9.47		9 47	10.50	12 26	....

F. Angus for the line and merged it into another road he owned, the Jackson & Suburban Traction. Boland began to extend the road east to Grass Lake and built a short spur line to the summer resort at Wolf Lake, both of which were completed within nine months. But in the back of his mind Boland had more ambitious plans for an electric railway that would extend from Jackson east to Detroit and west to Chicago, and he formed the Detroit & Chicago Traction Company in February 1901 for that purpose. His first step was to make ready to build from Jackson to Ann Arbor. He brought in William A. Foote, who owned the Jackson Electric Light Company, to provide additional financing. Problems arose for the two when the Hawks-Angus line was completed between Ann Arbor and Detroit early in 1902, and was preparing to build to Jackson. As was described in the account of the Detroit, Jackson & Chicago, Boland and Foote eventually withdrew from the contest, and sold their rights and franchises east of Grass Lake to Hawks and Angus. Boland then began working with Hawks and Angus on lines out of Detroit.

With building toward Ann Arbor under way Boland and the Footes formed three construction companies to build a road from Jackson to Battle Creek. This line was the piece needed to complete a route between Detroit and Kalamazoo. Construction began in 1901, and the entire line was put in service in the summer of 1903. Once completed, through cars began to run between Detroit and Kalamazoo.

Another early little piece of the MUR was a road organized in April 1900 as the Lansing, St. Johns & St. Louis. The idea for a railroad from Lansing to St. Johns, St. Louis, Mt. Pleasant, and somewhere farther north had been around for twenty years, but nothing had ever developed, mostly from a lack of investors with sufficient funds. The incorporators of the St. Johns road were able to bring in John E. Mills of Port Huron and Bion J. Arnold, a Chicago traction promoter and a pioneer in the application of electricity to interurbans. The two bought control of the company and announced that they would build it and then convert it into an electric line. Arnold claimed he was in the process of developing a new type of electric motor for the road's cars. Delays in making a workable motor forced the two to start operations in February 1902 between Lansing and St. Johns with a steam locomotive pulling trains. Arnold could not make his innovative ideas about the use of alternating current work well. At Mills's insistence a more conventional direct-current electric system was installed in late 1903 to replace steam operations. A December 1903 fire in the road's Lansing car barns destroyed Arnold's experimental cars and motors, ending his attempts to use alternating current on the line. In 1904 control of the company passed to Myron W. Mills, also of Port Huron, after the death of his brother John E. and his father, Nelson.

William A. Foote, the Jackson electric company owner, was more fascinated with making electricity than with electric railways. He had bought his first electric generating company in about 1886 in Jackson, then bought another in Battle Creek. From then on Foote, with his brother James B. as engineer, continued to expand their electric company holdings as fast as their scant financing would allow. William understood the use of falling water to generate electricity, but pondered the problem of how to transmit it over a distance without the energy being dissipated. By 1896, while the two brothers were looking at the Kalamazoo River between Plainwell and Allegan, William decided to build a dam southeast of Allegan and transmit the power almost twenty-five miles to Kalamazoo, an unheard-of distance; James applied his talents to solving the problem of dissipation. The Trowbridge Dam began producing an astounding 22,000 volts in 1899, sending much of it to two of Foote's better customers, the Kalamazoo street railway and Colonel Downs's Kalamazoo–Battle Creek electric interurban line then being built. The Foote brothers' innovations in long-distance transmission revolutionized the electric energy business.

After the completion of the Battle Creek line and after they ended their attempt to build to Detroit, William A. Foote and William A. Boland went their separate ways. Foote decided he wanted to concentrate on the power business and met to strike a deal with Myron W. Mills of the Lansing–St. Johns interurban. Mills brought in Port Huron attorney George E. Moore and Lansing businessman James R. Elliott; the three incorporated the Michigan United Railways in March 1906. Mills first transferred his own St. Johns line to the MUR. Next he bought Foote's Jackson–Battle Creek line and Downs's Michigan United Traction line between Battle Creek and Kalamazoo. He also bought the city streetcar lines in Kalamazoo, Battle Creek, and Jackson. Hawks and Angus owned the city street railway in Lansing, which Mills also bought. As a final step he organized the Lansing & Jackson to build a line between those two cities, then added it to the MUR. In 1907 Mills acquired control of Jackson Consolidated Traction. Under his ownership the Jackson company was run by a committee that allowed the owners of the Detroit-Jackson line a say in its operations. The Lansing-Jackson line was not completed until September 1909. Mills had to build an expensive overpass at Rives Junction to get over the Michigan Central's branch to Grand Rapids. The

William Augustine Foote

Born 9 June 1854, Adrian; died 12 April 1915, Jackson.

Foote followed his father into the flour milling business in Adrian. His mill failed, but he was so fascinated by the electricity used to power the mill that he decided to try generating it. His first attempt did not work well, but in 1886 he tried again in Jackson with a street-lighting project. This led to the formation of the Jackson Electric Light Works, the first of what became a succession of power-generating companies. W. A.'s genius was as an entrepreneur with an ability to raise money; his brother James B. brought exceptional technical and engineering skills that could accomplish his brother's expectations. The two expanded into Albion, then Battle Creek and Kalamazoo. In 1899 the brothers built the Trowbridge dam near Allegan and transmitted power twenty-five miles to Kalamazoo—the first successful attempt at long-distance transmission. The growth that followed led Foote to merge his numerous companies in 1904 into one, the Commonwealth Power Company. Later growth led in 1910 to the formation of a new holding company, the Consumers Power Company, and the Commonwealth Power Railway and Light as another holding company to own holding companies.

W. A. first became involved with electric rail operations while serving as receiver of the Jackson Street Railway, an important customer of his power company. Next he was involved in building a Jackson–Ann Arbor interurban, then a Jackson–Battle Creek line. About 1903 Foote sold his interest in the rail lines and dedicated himself to his utility companies. When Commonwealth Power Railway and Light was formed in 1910, Foote returned to the field to buy up the interurban roads that were important users of his electricity. By his death Commonwealth was operating about 250 miles of intercity lines as well as street railways in seven Michigan cities.

city of Mason proved difficult to deal with. It wanted the line to come downtown on city streets, something Mills wanted to avoid because it would involve crossing the Michigan Central's tracks twice. When it was built the interurban ran just west of the MC line through Mason.

With his system now complete Myron Mills began to look to new fields. In January 1910 his attorney, George E. Moore, incorporated the Lansing & Northeastern, which was to build a line from Lansing through Owosso to both Flint and Saginaw. Work started promptly, and in July 1911 the line was finished between Lansing and Owosso. At about this time Mills bought the Owosso-Corunna streetcar line and added it to his lines.

In 1910 William A. Foote made the first move that would affect the future of Mills's interurban company. In March Foote formed Consumers Power Company as a holding company for utility companies. Next, working with Anton G. Hodenpyl and Henry D. Walbridge, both from Bay City and involved in electric and streetcar companies, the three formed Commonwealth Power Railway and Light as a holding company to own holding companies. Money for the entire venture came from E. W. Clark & Company of Philadelphia, an old-line banking firm with which Foote earlier had dealings. Commonwealth took over all of Foote's electric companies, those owned by Hodenpyl and Walbridge, and a number of other smaller utility companies that these men controlled.

Streetcar and interurban lines became important customers for Commonwealth's electricity. With a substantial share of the electric and natural gas business now under its control, and with adequate financial strength, Foote decided Commonwealth should reenter the interurban railway business by buying some of its important customers. At that time the interurban companies were more profitable than were the electric utilities. Mills's interurban lines spread across Commonwealth's service area, which made him a most likely prospect. Apparently Foote was unable to persuade Mills to sell out to him. Commonwealth began buying up all the Michigan United Railways stock it could find. Armed with Clark's ample checkbook, it was no contest. After enough stock moved into Commonwealth's hands, Mills had no choice but to agree to lease his Michigan United Railways to the utility company. Commonwealth formed another holding company, the Michigan United Traction, in December 1911, transferred the control of Mills's roads to it, then leased those roads to it in April 1912.

In one of his last independent acts Mills leased the smallish Kalamazoo, Lake Shore & Chicago. Samuel J. Dunkley of Kalamazoo had dreams of an interurban line from Kalamazoo to the Lake Michigan ports of South Haven, Benton Harbor, and Saugatuck, and started to drum up public interest in 1901. Nothing much happened until 1906, when Dunkley bought a recently abandoned grade of the Michigan Central between Kalamazoo and Mattawan and then built into Paw Paw and started operations. The Pere Marquette owned an unprofitable South Haven–Lawton line, which it agreed to lease to Dunkley in 1907. With very little effort he now his railroad. Dunkley planned on freight car interchange with the Michigan Central at Kalamazoo. The MC refused to allow the interchange, which severely affected the KLS&C's anticipated revenues and delayed converting it to electric operations. To Mills, the line had potential. With electrification and a connection to the interurban line in Kalamazoo it would be possible to have interurban service between Detroit and Lake Michigan steamers at South Haven. In June 1911 Mills leased the KLS&C to his Michigan United Railways.

But before Mills could do anything with the line Commonwealth took over Mills's company. It kept the KLS&C under lease, ran the road for five years, pronounced it a failure, then finally let the lease expire in 1916.

In 1900 Anton Hodenpyl and Henry Walbridge of Bay City, and Clarence M. Clark of the E. W. Clark & Company of Philadelphia, formed the Grand Rapids Railway to consolidate all of that city's streetcar lines. This was the first taste of this business for the Bay City men and was a natural supplement to their electricity business. In 1903 the three organized the Saginaw–Bay City Railway & Light Company as a holding company into which they put their stock of Bay City Traction, the InterUrban Railway, and the Saginaw Valley Traction. Early in 1910 the three roads were merged into one company, the Saginaw–Bay City Railway, which was wholly owned by the holding company. When the three men and Foote formed Commonwealth Power Railway & Light in 1910, the Saginaw–Bay City holding company became one of its properties, as did the Saginaw & Flint.

Also in the Saginaw area a company had been formed in 1898 to build a line between Saginaw and Flint, but it failed. In 1903 the Detroit, Flint & Saginaw was organized to cover the same route, and it began running cars between Saginaw and Frankenmuth in 1904. Profits eluded the road, and in 1908 it was sold at foreclosure. Isaac Applebaum of Detroit, president of the DF&S, formed a new Saginaw & Flint to buy his own bankrupt road. With financial help, apparently from Hodenpyl and Walbridge, it completed its line into Flint in March 1909. Now completed, it connected with the Detroit United line from Flint into Detroit and began running through cars between Saginaw and Detroit.

In August 1912 Foote formed the Michigan & Chicago Railway, which at first was to own a new line to be built between Kalamazoo and Grand Rapids. Later he added a Battle Creek–Allegan line to the charter and then a line from Kalamazoo to Benton Harbor with a branch from Paw Paw to South Haven. Subsequent changes added still more branches to Otsego and Gull Lake and a line from Owosso to Bay City. In April 1914 Foote built a new line from the south side of Bay City to the northeast side of Saginaw. This line lay entirely east of the Saginaw River, avoided an expensive bridge, and stepped up the speed of through runs from Detroit. In September 1913 Foote bought from the Michigan Central a part of the line of the Detroit, Toledo & Milwaukee between Allegan and the west side of Battle Creek. This line was to feed passengers to the Kalamazoo–Grand Rapids line he was building. The Grand Rapids line was put in service in May 1915, as was the electrified

Battle Creek–Allegan line. The Grand Rapids line was built to the highest construction standards of any interurban route in Michigan, allowing seventy-minute runs on the fifty-mile route.

By this time Foote, his partners, and Commonwealth owned and controlled so many companies that it became difficult to figure out legal ownerships. To simplify affairs Foote renamed the Michigan & Chicago company as the Michigan Railway Company in March 1914, and began to use it as a holding company for all of Commonwealth's interurban and street railway properties. The Michigan Railway already owned outright the Grand Rapids–Kalamazoo and Battle Creek–Allegan lines, and immediately acquired the Saginaw–Bay City Railway (which was transferred from the Saginaw–Bay City Railway & Light) and the Saginaw & Flint. When the new Bay City–Saginaw line was completed in April 1914 it was put into the Michigan Railway. In January 1916 the leases of all of Mills's former Michigan United Railways lines, then under lease to Michigan United Traction, were assigned to the Michigan Railway.

Two final moves brought Commonwealth's interurban properties to their apex. In January 1916 the Michigan Railway leased the Grand Rapids–Saugatuck line of the Grand Rapids, Holland & Chicago. This brought Michigan Railway up to 341 miles of intercity line and five city operations, the high-water mark of the Michigan Railway. If the trackage of the city streetcar lines is included, the total comes to about 450 miles of line. By this time the driving spirit behind the expansion was gone; William A. Foote died in April 1915. In May 1916 Michigan allowed the lease of the Kalamazoo, Lake Shore & Chicago to expire; the property went back to its owners for whatever fate awaited it. Without the KLS&C the hope to reach Lake Michigan and ultimately Chicago through Lake Michigan steamships was gone. The approach of World War I ended the growth of Commonwealth's electric interurban system.

SOURCES

Bush, George. *Future Builders*. New York: McGraw-Hill, 1973.

Ceasar. *The Great Northern Ghost*. Lansing, Mich.: Wellman, 1980.

Lenderink, A. Rodney. "The Electric Interurban Railway in Kalamazoo County." *Michigan History* 43:1 (March 1959).

Schramm, Jack E., William H. Henning, and Richard R. Andrews. *When Eastern Michigan Rode the Rails, Book 1*. Glendale, Calif.: Interurban Press, 1984.

———. *When Eastern Michigan Rode the Rails, Book 3*. Glendale, Calif.: Interurban Press, 1988.

Zink, Maximillian A., and George Krambles, eds. *Electric Railways of Michigan, Bulletin 103*. Chicago: Central Electric Railfans' Association, 1959.

Other Electric Lines

The successes of the street railway's conversion from horse-power to electricity and of the earliest interurban roads stimulated promoters to dream up new projects throughout Michigan. Most of these early ventures came to nothing. Some roads were quite local, such as the 1894 Traverse City, Peninsular & Old Mission Electric; the 1898 Long Lake, Durand & Corunna Electric; and the 1899 Petoskey, Harbor Springs & Shore. Others were much bolder. In 1894 the Toledo, Monroe & Detroit Electric was formed, in 1895 the Saginaw & Bay City Rapid Transit, and in 1898 the Lansing, Dexter & Ann Arbor. In 1899 the Grand Rapids & Kalamazoo Electric, the Jackson & Adrian Electric, and the Port Huron & Port Austin Electric were formed. Again, nothing came of any of these proposed lines.

Three early electric lines were built in the Upper Peninsula. All were relatively short and more resembled city streetcar lines than intercity interurbans. In late 1891 the Escanaba Electric Street Railway was formed and the next year completed a line from downtown Escanaba to the sawmills at Wells, a nearby suburban area. Several years later it was extended to Groos, six miles distant from Escanaba, and in 1911 to Gladstone. During its early years the company kept horses on standby in case the electricity failed. The Negaunee & Ishpeming Street Railway also was formed in 1891 and by 1893 had built a three-and-a-half-mile road between the two cities. At first it ran only during the summer, but the demand for winter service grew so much that eventually the company began year-round operations. At the western end of the peninsula the Twin City Railway began service about 1893. Its twelve-mile line extended from Bessemer through Ironwood to Hurley, Wisconsin. The city of Marquette received street railway service in 1891 when the Marquette City & Presque Isle was built. Its line extended from downtown to a suburban park at Presque Isle, with some city lines added later. Streetcar lines also sprang up in Sault Ste. Marie in 1888 and in Menominee in 1889. The Menominee company included an extensive operation in Marinette, Wisconsin, making it one of the few with interstate streetcar service. The company at the Soo eventually began a ferry service that crossed the St. Marys River to Sault Ste. Marie, and then owned a city line in that Canadian city.

Electric Lines

At its peak Michigan had just over 900 miles of intercity electric railways. Popularity begets enthusiasm, and Michigan had no shortage of entrepreneurs who wanted to build more such railways, in fact a good many more. No potential market went without at least one proposal. In 1899 eighteen street railway companies were incorporated, in 1900 fourteen, and in 1901 twenty-four. Ten were formed in 1903, but the numbers tapered off until, during the 1910s, an average of two a year were created. Additionally, a few companies were formed under the general railway incorporation law that proposed to run electric-powered railways. Of all of these, about half actually went into business and built or bought tracks, but a good many others were never again heard from.

In the eastern part of the state the Lansing, Dexter & Ann Arbor was proposed in 1897; the Jackson & Adrian and the Port Huron & Port Austin Electric in 1899; and the Michigan & Ohio Electric between Detroit and Dundee and the Toledo, Adrian & Jackson, both in 1900. In 1901 the Detroit, Howell, Lansing & Grand Rapids was proposed, as was the Detroit, Pontiac, Lapeer & Northern, to be built from Detroit to Bay City; in 1903 the Toledo & Michigan Electric was proposed, to be built from Adrian to Coldwater; and in 1904 the Ann Arbor Interurban that was to be built to Toledo.

On the west side of the state promoters tried to build the Kalamazoo & Lake Michigan in 1900 from Benton Harbor to Kalamazoo; the Michigan Electric in 1901 to build from St. Joseph to Michigan City; the South Haven & Lake Shore in 1901 to build along the coast from South Haven to Saugatuck; the West Michigan Traction in 1901 to build from Benton Harbor to Kalamazoo as well as branches to Dowagiac, Cassopolis, Decatur, Paw Paw, and Allegan (it was reorganized in 1905 as the West Michigan Railway and added terminals in Illinois and Wisconsin); the Michigan Central Traction in 1902 to build from Battle Creek to Lansing; the West Michigan Interurban in 1903, which planned to run from Grand Rapids through Muskegon to Hart; the Grand Rapids & South Michigan Traction in 1903 to build from Battle Creek to Grand Rapids; the Battle Creek & Coldwater Electric in 1904 for a line between Battle Creek and Coldwater; and the South Haven Traction in 1905, which hoped to build to both Saugatuck and Watervliet.

In June 1897 three Chicago men formed the Holland & Lake Michigan Railway. The idea had come up earlier, in 1890, when Holland businessmen proposed building the Holland South Shore Railway, but nothing came of those plans. The H&LM line was to provide a link between the railroad station in Holland and the Lake Michigan beaches at Macatawa, and certainly would be a substantial improvement over the dirt road through the sand as well as faster than the small steamships that provided the only connection at the time. By June 1898 the line was in service. Before completion its owners formed the Saugatuck, Douglas & Lake Shore to build from Holland to Saugatuck and Douglas. That line was completed to Saugatuck in the summer of 1899. It never built across the Kalamazoo River into Douglas but did provide omnibus service to the village. A bonus came when Luman Jenison, the founder

There were a few companies with grandiose names and modest goals. The Chicago, Kalamazoo & Eastern was to build from Kalamazoo to Paw Paw with a branch to Marcellus; the Michigan West Shore Traction, with its line from Grand Rapids to New Buffalo; the Trans-Michigan Street Railway, which proposed a line from Allegan to South Haven; the Tri-State Railways, which planned to build from Hillsdale to Adrian and Elkhart, with branches from Adrian to Jackson and Jonesville to Pioneer, Ohio; and the Ohio & Southern Michigan from Toledo, through Camden, to Jackson and Kalamazoo. Formed in Indiana, the Kalamazoo, Elkhart & South Bend planned to build from South Bend, through Elkhart, Constantine, Three Rivers, and Vicksburg, to Kalamazoo.

The resort country in northern Michigan was sure to benefit from a line between Petoskey and Harbor Springs. The first of several proposals was made in 1899, and two attempts were made to build out of Traverse City to the Old Mission peninsula and to Northport. In 1913 the Muskegon, Ludington & Manistee was to connect a string of resort areas. The Upper Peninsula also had a few unfulfilled proposals, among them the Calumet & Lac La Belle Traction & Power, the Delta Traction, the Menominee & Escanaba, the Soo-Snows, and the Marquette, Negaunee & Ishpeming Interurban, all of which were certain to fill some need.

For local riders, Michigan cities as small as Manistee had street railways. There were civic boosters who believed other communities also deserved them, and to get them street railway companies were formed in Ludington in 1889, in Cadillac in 1903, and in Traverse City in 1907.

There were a few for which it is hard to imagine any substantial demand. Such lines as the strangely named Albion, Charlotte, Northern proposed a line from Albion through Charlotte and Grand Ledge to Lansing; the Grosse Ile planned a five-mile line on that island; the Lake Shore was to run from Benton Harbor to both Baroda and Stevensville; and the Marshall & Northern would have a line from Tekonsha to Sunfield. Yet every one of these was a dream so tangible that investors and promoters put money, time, and effort into creating them.

of a village near Grandville, built Jenison Park as an amusement park along the line between Holland and Macatawa.

In February 1900 the Grand Rapids, Holland & Lake Michigan was formed to build from Grand Rapids to Holland. Benjamin S. Hanchett Jr., of Grand Rapids, was its principal promoter, and he brought in John Winter, Oliver H. Lau, and Frank C. Andrews, three Detroiters who were involved in other electric railways. The new company bought the Macatawa line and the branch to Saugatuck. A year passed before construction began, but when work did start the Grand Rapids–Holland line was built quickly and put in service in October 1901. Cars operated every two hours from both terminals. By the next year trains were being run every hour, and every half hour on weekends. In 1904 the company was renamed the Grand Rapids, Holland & Chicago. Winter,

Lau, and Andrews sold out, and only Hanchett remained of the original founders. One group of Detroiters was replaced by another, among them George and Strathearn Hendrie and Henry C. Potter, along with William H. Beach of Holland. In 1912 ownership changed again, this time to more local owners. The next year Commonwealth Power & Light, the holding company that owned Michigan United Railways, offered to buy the Holland line. No sale was agreed to, but at the beginning of 1916 the company was leased to the Michigan Railway to be operated as part of the Commonwealth's interurban holdings. It was linked to the rest of the Michigan Railway system when the Kalamazoo–Grand Rapids line was completed in 1915.

In March 1899 four Grand Rapids men formed the Grand Rapids, Grand Haven & Muskegon. In 1902 it completed its thirty-five-mile line from Grand Rapids to Muskegon and an eight-mile branch from near Fruitport into Grand Haven. It used city streetcar tracks to reach the city centers in Grand Rapids and Muskegon, and bought rights of the small Grand Haven Street Railway for entry into that city. The Grand Rapids men had to turn to James D. Hawks of Detroit for financial help to build their line. Out-of-town capital controlled the company thereafter, with Hawks serving as the road's first president. Hourly service was provided from Grand Rapids to both Muskegon and Grand Haven. In 1912 the United Light & Railways Company, which then operated several interurban lines in Iowa, bought control of the road.

Both the Holland and the Muskegon companies established close ties with Lake Michigan steamship companies, the Holland road with Graham & Morton Transportation to Chicago and the Muskegon road with Crosby Transportation from Muskegon to Milwaukee and Goodrich Transit from Grand Haven to Chicago. Cars of both companies ran onto steamship docks at Lake Michigan ports to provide their riders with a convenient transfer from rail to ship. Express and freight traffic moved from both lines to Lake Michigan ships en route to Chicago and Milwaukee. The relationship was an advantage that helped both roads stay in business longer than many others.

In southwestern Michigan the South Bend & Southern Michigan began operating an electric line between South Bend, Indiana, and Niles in 1903. The road was renamed the Southern Michigan when it completed its extension from Niles to St. Joseph in May 1906. Cars ran hourly from St. Joseph and South Bend, and additional service was provided between South Bend and the Notre Dame campus at St. Marys. Soon after it was completed, the road was taken over by

SOUTHERN MICHIGAN RAILWAY CO.

PM	PM	PM		AM	AM	M	Leave Arrive	AM	AM		PM		PM
11.00	9.00	7.30		6.30	....	0	...... St. Joseph	7.20	8.20		11.20	.....	9.20
11.13	9.13	7.43		6.43	....	4	..Royalton Heights..	7.04	8.04		11.04	.....	9.04
11.18	9 18	7.48		6.48	....	7	......Scotdale......	6.59	7.59		10.59	.....	8.59
		7.54		6.52	....	9	......Munich						
11.24	9.24	7.56		6.54	....	10	......Rockey's	6.54	7.54		10.54		8 54
11.27	9.27	7.57		6.57	....	11	...Twin Springs....	6.51	7.51		10.51		8 51
11.35	9 35	8.05		7.05	....	15	...Berrien Springs..	6.45	7.45		10.45		8 45
11.40	9.40	8 11		7.11	....	17	......Summit......	6.40	7.40		10.40		8 40
		8.18				20	.... Thompson's						
11.49	9 49	8.19		7.19	....	22	.... River Bluff	6.31	7.31		10.31		8.31
11.58	9 5?	8.28		7.25	....	24	......Niles......	6 2?	7.28		10.28		8 28
12.04	10.04	8.34		7.34		27	...Brandywine...	6.18	7.18		10.18		8 18
						28	......Bertrand......						
2.18	10 15	8 45		7.45		33	....St. Mary's	6.08	7 08		10.08		8.08
12 2?	10.25	8 57		7.57		35	.... South Bend ...	†6.00	7.00		10 00		8 00

(Vertical notes: "Lv St. J. every hour until"; "and every hour until"; "see note below")

ST. MARY'S LINE: Cars leave South Bend Station for Navarre Place, St. Mary's and Notre Dame, beginning at 6:45 a. m., and every thirty minutes thereafter, until 11:15 p. m., except Sundays. Sundays, 7:45 a. m. until 11:45 p. m. Cars leave St. Mary's and Notre Dame for South Bend, beginning at 6:30 a. m. and every thirty minutes thereafter until 11:00 p. m., except Sundays. Sundays, 7:30 a. m. until 11:00 p. m.

    Cars lv. Niles 5:58 a. m., ar. So. Bend 6:27 a. m., and hourly thereafter until 8:58, also at 9:28, 9:58 and 11:58 p. m., giving half hour service between Niles and So. Bend.

    Cars lv. So. Bend 6:30 a. m., ar. Niles 6:58 a. m. and hourly thereafter until 7:00 p. m., also lv. at 8:30, 9:00 and 11:00 p. m., giving half hour service between South Bend and Niles.

BENTON HARBOR & ST. JO. E. RY. CO.

	PM		AM	AM	Lv...EAU CLAIRE DIVISION..Ar	AM	AM		PM	AM
....	11.10	and every 1½	8.10	6.40	...Benton Harbor ...	7.50	9.20	and every 1½	10.50	12.2?
....	11.38	hours thereaf-	8.38	7.08	...King's Landing ...	7.22	8.52	hours thereaf-	10.22	11.52
....	12.00	ter until	9.00	7.30	......Eau Claire......	7.00	8.30	ter until	10.0?	11.3?
....	12.3?		9.30	8.00	Ar....Dowagiac...Lv	6.30	8.00		9.30	11.0?

Paw Paw Lake Div.

PM	PM	PM		AM	Leave Arrive	AM		PM	PM	AM
11.00	9 00	6 40	every hour	0.40	·Benton Harbor.	8.20		8.20	10.50	12.5?
11.20	9 20	7.00	and half the-	7.00	......Millburg......	8.00	every hour	8.00	10.30	12.30
11.35	9 35	7.15	reafter until..	7.15	......Coloma......	7.45	until	7.45	10.15	12.15
11.50	10.50	8.30		7.30	......Watervliet...	7.30		7.30	10.00	12.00

LEFT: This 1915 schedule shows the two electric lines that served far southwestern Michigan. The Southern Michigan was owned by the company that owned a Chicago-Goshen, Indiana, line, and benefited by serving the Notre Dame and St. Marys campuses. The Benton Harbor company grew out of the St. Joseph–Benton Harbor streetcar network. One popular destination was Eden Springs, home of the House of David amusement park. Both roads carried fresh fruit in season to the docks at Benton Harbor destined for Chicago markets.

Author's collection.

BELOW: Unique in Michigan was this now-removed three-level railroad bridge a few miles south of Niles. On top is the Southern Michigan's St. Joseph–South Bend line, below is the Michigan Central Niles–South Bend branch, and curving below is the Big Four's Benton Harbor–Elkhart line.

Central Electric Railfans' Association, from George Krambles collection.

134	TOLEDO & WESTERN R. R.														
W. R. Pierce, Supt., Sylvania.							A. C. Wegner, Traf. Mgr., Toledo.								
July 27, 1913	AM	AM	AM	AM	AM	AM	PM	PM	PM	PM	PM	PM	PM	PM	PM
0 Toledo......lv	6.30	7.80	8.15	9.30	10.80	11.30	12.30	1.20	2.30	3.30	4.30	5.30	6.30	8.39	9.30
4 West Toledo	6.52	7.55	8.45	9.55	10.55	11.55	12.55	1.55	2.55	3.55	4.55	5.55	6.55	8.55	9.55
14 Sylvania	7.16	8.18	9.18	10.18	11.18	12.20	1.18	2.18	3.18	4.20	5.18	6.25	7.18	9.18	10.18
16 Allen Jct....ar	7.30	8.30	9.30	10.30	11.30	12.30	1.30	2.30	3.30	4.33	5.30	6.40	7.30	9.30	10.27
16 Allen Jct....lv	7.30	....	9.30	10.30	11.30		1.30		3.30	4.33	5.30	....	7.30	....	10.27
24 Riga	7.47	....	9.47	10.49	11.48		1.48		3.48	4.53	5.47	....	7.47	....	10.47
26 Blissfield	7.55	....	9.55	10.55	11.55		1.55		3.55	5.05	5.54	....	7.55	....	10.55
31 Palmyra	8.07	....	10.08	11.10	12.08		2.08		4.10	4.18	6.08	....	8.08	....	11.08
37 Adrian.....ar	8.24	....	10.24	11.28	12.24		2.24		4.28	5.35	6.24	....	8.34	....	11.24
16 Allen Jct....lv	7†30	8.30	....	10.30	....	12.30	....	2.30	....	4.30	....	6.40	....	9.30	....
19 Berkey	7.39	8.38	....	10.38	....	12.38	....	2.38	....	4.39	....	6.50	....	9.39	....
23 Metamora	7.48	8.48	....	10.48	....	12.48	....	2.48	....	4.48	....	7.00	....	9.48	....
26 Whiteville	8.00	8.58	....	10.58	....	12.58	....	2.58	....	5.00	....	7.10	....	10.00	....
30 Seward	8.06	9.06	....	11.06	....	1.06	....	3.05	....	5.08	....	7.17	....	10.08	....
32 Lyons	8.13	9.10	....	11.10	....	1.10	....	3.10	....	5.13	....	7.22	....	10.13	....
39 Morenci	8.35	9.35	....	11.35	....	1.35	....	3.45	....	5.35	....	7.44	....	10.35	....
47 Fayette	8.55	9.55	....	11.55	....	1.55	....	3.55	....	5.55	....	8.04	....	10.55	....
52 Franklin	....	10.05	....	12.05	....		....	4.05	....	6.05	....	8.13	....		....
53 Alvordton	....	10.10	....	12.10	....		....	4.10	....	6.10	....	8.18	....		....
59 Pioneer	....	10.25	....	12.25	....		....	4.25	....	6.25	....	8.30	....		....
M		AM	AM	AM	AM	AM	PM	PM	PM	PM	PM	PM		PM	PM
0 Pioneer		6.30	....	....	10.35	....		2.25		4.40		8.35		....	
6 Alvordton		6.48	....	....	10.50	....		2.40		5.55		8.50		....	
8 Franklin		6.53	....	....	10.55	....		2.45		5.00		8.55		....	
12 Fayette	5.40	7.05	....	9.05	11.05	....	1.05	2.55	....	5.10	....	9.04			
20 Morenci	6.00	7.25	....	9.25	11.25	....	1.25	3.11	....	5.85	....	9.24			
28 Lyons	6.22	7.45	....	9.50	11.50	....	1.50	3.32	....	5.57	....	9.47			
30 Seward	6.27	7.50	....	9.54	11.54	....	1.54	3.36	....	6.02	....	9.52			
33 Whiteville	6.35	8.00	....	10.02	12.02	....	2.02	3.42	....	6.10	....	10.00			
37 Metamora	6.48	8.10	....	10.12	12.12	....	2.12	3.53	....	6.22	....	10.12			
40 Berkey	6.58	8.20	....	10.20	12.20	....	2.20	4.03	....	6.30	....	10.22			
43 Allen Jct...ar	7.05	8.30	....	10.30	12.30	....	2.30	4.11	....	6.40	....	10.30			
0 Adrian......lv	6.05	7.30	8.31	8.30	10.31	....	12.31	1.30	2.31	....	4.81	5.40	7.30	....	9.30
6 Palmyra	6.23	7.50	8.50	9.50	10.50	....	12.50	1.50	2.50	....	4.50	5.58	7.51	....	9.51
11 Blissfield	6.38	8.03	9.03	10.03	11.03	....	1.03	2.03	3.08	....	5.05	6.13	8.05	....	10.55
14 Riga	7.44	8.10	9.08	10.10	11.10	....	1.08	2.10	3.10	....	5.10	6.20	8.12	....	10.12
21 Allen Jct...ar	7.05	8.28	9.30	10.28	11.30	....	1.30	2.28	3.30	....	5.30	6.40	8.30	....	10.30
43 Allen Jct...lv	7.05	8.30	9.30	10.30	11.30	12.30	1.30	2.30	3.30	4.30	5.30	6.40	8.30	9.30	10.30
47 Sylvania	7.16	8.45	9.45	10.45	11.45	12.45	1.45	2.45	3.45	4.45	5.45	6.53	8.40	9.45	10.45
55 West Toledo	7.40	9.05	10.05	11.05	12.05	1.05	2.05	3.05	4.05	5.08	6.05	7.20	9.05	10.07	11.05
59 Toledo	8.15	9.30	10.30	11.30	12.30	1.30	2.30	3.30	4.30	5.40	6.30	7.45	9.30	10.30	11.30

The Toledo & Western hoped to be part of a Chicago-Toledo-Cleveland through route, but ran out of money too soon. It touched Michigan at Morenci, and had a branch to Adrian that used a part of the original Erie & Kalamazoo grade west of Palmyra. These schedules from the *Michigan Pathfinder Guide* of 1913 show cars every hour between Toledo and Adrian—far better than the competing New York Central service.

Author's collection.

James Murdock and Sons, who integrated the operations with the Chicago, South Bend & Northern Indiana they owned. That road had an interurban line in Indiana from Michigan City to Goshen and operated city cars in Michigan City, LaPorte, South Bend, Elkhart, and Goshen. In addition to its passenger service, the line hauled large amounts of fresh fruit in season for transfer to Graham & Morton ships at Benton Harbor.

The Benton Harbor–St. Joe Railway & Light Company operated the city streetcar lines in those two cities and a suburban route to the popular House of David amusement park. In 1906 it extended that line to Eau Claire and in 1911 to Dowagiac. In 1910 it built a line from Benton Harbor through Coloma to Watervliet. It also leased the tiny Benton Harbor, Coloma & Paw Paw Lake from the Pere Marquette, which enabled it to provide service to the resorts along the north shore of Paw Paw Lake. For a few years it made a connection there with a branch of the Kalamazoo, Lake Shore & Chicago, although little through traffic ever developed from this potential connection to Detroit. Both the Dowagiac and Coloma lines also handled an extensive fresh fruit traffic to the Benton Harbor docks for overnight movement to Chicago on Graham & Morton ships.

Two interurban lines running out of Toledo touched Michigan. The Toledo & Western was conceived in late 1899 to build from Toledo to Adrian and Morenci. Its founder, Toledo resident Frank E. Seagrave, hoped to extend the line west to connect with one of the lines building east through Indiana and thereby become a part of a Chicago–Toledo–East Coast route. Seagrave bought the unused right-of-way of the Toledo, Adrian & Jackson and by the end of 1901 was operating between Toledo and Adrian. During 1902 his road built a second line as far west as Fayette, Ohio, which touched into Michigan at Morenci, and he announced it would build an extension to the Indiana state line. By 1903 the road had extended as far as Pioneer, Ohio, but still held on to its plans to extend. In 1905 the T&W announced it would build a branch to Waterloo, Indiana, and extend its main line through Angola to Goshen, Indiana. The road also began grading a line from Adrian toward Hillsdale and Coldwater. The company's fall into bankruptcy in 1906, followed by its sale to Everett and Moore of the Detroit United, ended the attempts to expand the system. The next year the T&W bought the Adrian city streetcar line and could run into downtown on its own rails. In 1913 the road was again sold, this time to Henry L. Doherty, and then came under Cities Service Group control.

From its beginning freight traffic was important to the T&W. Seagrave built his line to handle both freight and passengers, and as it extended it gained an increasing volume of freight. It tapped a number of industries on the Adrian branch, and the Toledo-Morenci-Fayette-Pioneer route handled both stone and agricultural products. In most years freight provided more than a third of the company's total revenue, an unusually high percentage for an interurban road. The road had two interchanges with the Wabash Railroad, one of the few eastern railroads that looked kindly toward interurbans. The interchange at Adrian was particularly important, with a considerable volume moving out of Toledo to the Wabash. At Pioneer, it was barely a dozen miles from the east end of Indiana's St. Joseph Valley Railway, a road with very little financial strength. Despite high hopes the T&W was never to extend west to link with the SJV. Had the twelve-mile gap to the SJV been closed the Chicago-Toledo line would have been a reality. But neither the SJV nor the T&W had the resources to make the connection, and the hoped-for benefit ebbed away.

In 1897 the Toledo city lines began operating a line to Point Place,

ABOVE AND OPPOSITE: These two winter
scenes near Calumet show what the
Houghton County Traction faced every
winter that it operated in the copper
country.

Central Electric Railfans' Association, from Guy A. Richardson
collection.

north of the city. In 1905 another group formed the Ottawa Beach &
Southern to build an extension of this line to a resort they were establishing about eight miles north of the Ohio state line. In 1907 the line,
now renamed the Toledo, Ottawa Beach & Northern, was completed
with cars running into downtown Toledo. Everett and Moore, who
controlled the Toledo city lines, also obtained control of the Ottawa
Beach line. A unique feature of the Ottawa Beach line was its connection with three steam railroads—the Detroit & Toledo Shore Line, the
Michigan Central, and the Lake Shore & Michigan Southern—which
allowed trains of their cars to be moved directly to Toledo Beach. The
road was barely able to handle all its business in the summer months,
but after Labor Day two cars were ample for all of the traffic. About
1911 control of the city lines and the Ottawa Beach line was transferred
to Henry L. Doherty and the Cities Service Group.

　　Although it barely qualifies as an interurban the Manistee, Filer City

& East Lake began operating three routes out of Manistee in 1892: a city line to Filer City, and suburban routes to East Lake and Orchard Beach Park. The company was renamed the Northern Michigan Traction in 1905, the Manistee Light & Traction in 1907, and the Manistee Railway in 1912. But the sawmills and lumbering that had supported the company in its early years were gone by this time, with the road barely able to hang on. A collision with a Manistee & Northeastern train in 1917 at Peanut Junction on the north side of Manistee resulted in two deaths and a number of severe injuries. The company never recovered from the financial disaster, finally ending service in August 1921.

The most remote interurban in Michigan, if not the nation, was the Houghton County Street Railway, financed and operated by the Stone and Webster syndicate. This owner also operated several lines in Texas, as well as ones near Puget Sound and in Virginia. Located in the Keweenaw Peninsula, it was the farthest north road built east of the

Mississippi River. Its owners considered it such a local operation that it never bothered to publish its schedules in either the *Official Guide of the Railways* or in the *Michigan Railway Guide*. The major part of the line was opened in 1901, between Houghton and the Red Jacket and Wolverine Mines near Calumet, together with a branch from Calumet to Lake Linden and Hubbell. The majority of its riders were copper miners going to and from work. The road was renamed the Houghton County Traction in 1908 and extended north to Mohawk. Although all of the electric lines along the Lake Michigan shore faced problems with heavy snows, the Houghton County had the worst of it by far. Snowdrifts would hide not just the tracks but the electric overhead wire as well. To meet the challenge the road had small snowplows on both ends of all cars, three conventional wedge snowplows, and two rotary snowplows. Service was well maintained except during the very worst storms.

The last independent company to build an electric line was the Iron River, Stambaugh & Crystal Falls. Formed in 1914, it built a four-mile line from Iron River, through Stambaugh, to Gaastra. Money ran out quickly, and with no profits to keep the road going it was abandoned in 1921.

As first the horsecar and next the electric streetcar brought vast improvements in the movement of people in cities, the electric interurban brought an even greater benefit to residents of villages and rural areas. Most of the larger cities in the southern half of the Lower Peninsula eventually received service. The interurban's frequency of service combined with its low fares made travel not only easy but also affordable to a degree unknown by the preceding generation. The interurbans provided a service that the steam railroads were not interested in, leaving them without competition in their market. At the peak of the interurban era, in 1915, the Michigan Central ran twenty-five trains a day in both directions between Detroit and Ann Arbor; the DUR ran thirty-four. The Grand Trunk Western had nine trains between Detroit and Port Huron; the DUR had thirty-two. From Grand Rapids to Muskegon, the Grand Rapids & Indiana operated eight trains a day; the Grand Rapids, Grand Haven & Muskegon ran thirty-two. To Kalamazoo, the Grand Rapids & Indiana ran ten trains in both directions; the Michigan United ran forty-two. The Pere Marquette ran ten a day between Grand Rapids and Holland; the interurban had three times that number.

It became possible to work in the city center and live a considerable distance from it. Runs after supper allowed an evening at the theater in the city and an easy return home. Many city streetcar lines established amusement parks at the outskirts of the city, so far out that riding the streetcar was the only practical means of getting there. The Houghton County company established Electric Park midway between Hancock and Calumet; a horse and buggy on poor roads was the only other way to get to it. Kalamazoo had Oakwood Park, and Saginaw had Riverside Park; cars ran to Reeds Lake in Grand Rapids, Wenona Beach in Bay City, Lake Macatawa in Holland, and Mona Lake in Muskegon. A college campus was sure to have a car line. "Riding the cars" may at first have been a fad, but soon it became a necessity. Nothing else was as convenient for getting to shopping or social and cultural events, or for visiting relatives in towns 50 or 100 miles distant. The electric interurban introduced "mobility" to the nation, and the nation adopted the idea enthusiastically.

Electric lines also were profitable. Usually they were not built to high standards. Electricity, equipment, and personnel were inexpensive. Every revenue dollar not spent for operating expenses went into profit, and many of the major roads had an enviable reputation for profitability. The drive for profits meant that little money was put aside for future projects or even for the routine maintenance projects that would be needed. Such profitability also attracted other promoters to the field, and encouraged construction of marginal lines that had less potential to succeed. But by 1920 the interurban picture was as good as it was ever going to become.

SOURCES

Galloway, Joseph A. *Interurban Trails*. Toledo: Eastern Ohio Chapter, National
    Railway Historical Society, n.d.

Hilton, George W., and John F. Due. *The Electric Interurban Railways in America*.
    Stanford, Calif.: Stanford University Press, 1960.

Schramm, Jack E., William H. Henning, and Richard R. Andrews. *When Eastern
    Michigan Rode the Rails, Book 3*. Glendale, Calif.: Interurban Press, 1988.

Sell, Bob, and Jim Findlay. *The Teeter & Wobble*. Blissfield, Mich.: authors, 1993.

van Reken, Donald L. *The Interurban Era in Holland, Michigan*. Holland, Mich.:
    author, 1981.

Zink, Maximillian A., and George Krambles, eds. *Electric Railways of Michigan,
    Bulletin 103*. Chicago: Central Electric Railfans' Association, 1959.

———. *Electric Railways of Indiana, Bulletin 104*. Chicago: Central Electric Railfans'
    Association, 1960

"Wreck!" Part 2

Michigan's first serious wreck of the twentieth century occurred on Wednesday, 15 August 1900. The southbound Mackinaw City–Grand Rapids night passenger train of the Grand Rapids & Indiana usually went on the siding at Sand Lake for the northbound premier summer special *Northland Express*. On this morning the southbound was running late. To keep the summer train on schedule, the train dispatcher issued an order changing the meeting place between them to Maple Hill, two miles south of Howard City. At the last minute the dispatcher issued another order changing the meeting point again, this time farther south to Pierson. The telegrapher at Comstock Park apparently had been asleep when the *Northland* passed his station and soon learned he could not deliver the order. This created a condition that is called a "lap order," a conflict in train orders in which the first train is instructed in one order to meet the second at a point that is beyond where the second train is instructed in another order to meet the first. At 6:00 A.M. the two trains, running at full speed in an exceptionally heavy fog, met head-on one-half mile north of Pierson. Seven people were killed; five crewmen and nine passengers were injured. The *Northland Express* was running with eighteen cars and the southbound with eleven; it was the unoccupied cars at the head-end of both trains that absorbed most of the impact and kept the number of casualties as low as they were.

On 27 November 1901 the Wabash experienced a head-on collision near Seneca that left twenty-three persons dead. In the late afternoon of Thanksgiving eve westbound New York–Chicago passenger train Number 13 was running hours late. A local run, Number 3, followed it out of Detroit. Coming east was the premier train of the Wabash, Number 4—the *Continental Limited*—headed from Chicago to New York and Boston. By a little after 6 P.M. all three trains had one train order that instructed Number 4 and Number 13 to meet at Seneca and then for Number 4 and Number 3 to meet four and one-half miles farther east at Sand Creek. On that clear dark evening on the dead straight track the enginemen of both Number 4 and Number 13 could see each other's headlights as they rolled. But engineman Strong of Number 4 in some way misread his order and thought he was to meet Number 13 not at Seneca but at Sand Creek. As the train raced past the Seneca depot brakeman Dittman realized what was happening and applied the emergency brakes. It was too late. Before the *Continental* could stop it went head-on into the westbound passenger train. The engines were derailed and severely damaged; the wooden day coach on the *Continental* disintegrated, causing eight deaths. It was worse on the westbound. The second and third cars were immigrant day coaches made of wood; they collapsed together and caught fire. All of the fatalities were in these cars. The first rescue train, with doctors and nurses from Adrian, was at the site within an hour; a second from Detroit arrived two hours later. The railroad managed to put together a train that carried many injured riders to the company's hospital at Peru, Indiana, 130 miles away but the closest on a direct route.

The fire that burned for hours trapped the immigrant riders in the cars. The railroad reported a total of three crewmen and eighteen passengers dead, of which six were identified as immigrants. Another twelve were severely injured. Yet the conductor of Number 13 reported the two immigrant cars had at least 50 riders in them; other observers reported numbers as high as 100. No matter the number, few of the immigrants were accounted for after the wreck. What happened to them was never recorded accurately or reported reliably. How many died at Seneca will never be known.

Around four o'clock in the early morning of Friday, 7 August 1903, the first section of the Wallace circus train, moving from Charlotte to Lapeer, was stopped a short distance west of Durand by a flagman from a livestock train ahead. A flagman started back to protect the rear of the circus train. Before he got far enough the second section, running fast, came up. The brakes on the second section could not stop the train in time, and it plowed into the rear of the first section. At the rear of the first section were a caboose and two sleeping cars carrying workers and roustabouts. Twenty-three of them died instantly or very soon after, and about forty more were injured. The engine crew of the second section jumped before the impact and lived. That same section carried most of the menagerie, and three camels, an elephant, and a dog were killed. The animals were buried at the site, about 1,500 feet west of the South Oak Street crossing. The second section's engineman testified to the coroner's jury that his air brakes failed completely, but the jury concluded he could have prevented the collision if he had watched his air gauge.

On a snowy evening the day after Christmas, 1903, two Pere Marquette passenger trains were running late. The train dispatcher issued an order to both trains changing their usual meeting siding from Oakdale Park near Grand Rapids to Fox siding, two miles east of

ABOVE: On Thanksgiving eve, 1901, the Wabash Railroad's *Continental Limited* and a local train collided head-on at full speed between the little towns of Sand Creek and Seneca. The death toll was 21 people by the railroad's report, but observers at the scene claimed at least 50 to 100 people died.

Lenawee County Historical Museum.

RIGHT: A blizzard caused one passenger train to miss receiving a train order that changed the place it was to meet another passenger train. On 26 December 1903 the two trains, running at least at sixty miles per hour, collided head-on just west of East Paris station, southeast of Grand Rapids. Twenty-one passengers and employees died in the wreck, and another forty people were injured. The tall object is the boiler of one of the locomotives.

John W. Rothwell collection.

Two views of Michigan's worst train wreck. A Pere Marquette employee excursion train from Ionia collided with a work train at Salem, a short distance west of Plymouth. Thirty-three people were killed and more than 100 injured in the 20 July 1907 wreck.

Pere Marquette Historical Society collection.

East Paris, the best meeting point causing the least delay to both trains. The eastbound train got the order at Grand Rapids, but the westbound train passed Alto before it could be delivered there. The dispatcher then sent the order to McCords, and the telegrapher displayed a stop signal for the westbound train. The engine crew did not obey the red signal and did not receive the revised order. This created another "lap order" condition. Running at sixty miles per hour in a heavy snowstorm, the two passenger trains collided head-on near East Paris. Nineteen people died almost instantly, two more died later, and about forty more were injured in the wreck. The signalman at McCords claimed that the wind had blown out the oil lamp in his signal, which contributed to the train not seeing the signal. The engineman of the westbound miraculously survived the wreck, cleared his name in a subsequent trial, but later left his family and disappeared, apparently still feeling guilty.

On Saturday morning, 20 July 1907, a trainload of Pere Marquette workers and their families, about 800 in all, were riding an excursion train from Ionia to Detroit for a day outing. A work train west of Plymouth misread its orders and was standing on the main track instead getting out of the way onto a siding. The special was running at fifty miles per hour when it collided with the work train just east of Salem. The force of impact spun the work train's engine around. Three coaches derailed, two more telescoped into each other, while four stayed on the rails. Thirty-three people died in the wreck, and 101 were injured. The Salem wreck remains the worst in Michigan railroad history and a hoodoo hangs over it. The names "Pere Marquette" and "Salem, Michigan," both have thirteen letters; the names of the PM's general manager, general superintendent, chief train dispatcher, division superintendent, train master, and road master all have thirteen letters.

Probably Michigan's worst forest fire in the twentieth century swept through Presque Isle County in October 1908. The communities of Metz and Posen were burned to the ground. Some residents were able to board a Detroit & Mackinac logging train trying for an escape to safety. The fire overtook and surrounded the train. Thirteen riders and two crew members died in the inferno.

In the early hours of 22 June 1918 the Michigan Central conductor stopped the westbound second section of the Hagenbeck-Wallace circus train just east of Ivanhoe, Indiana, because he smelled a hot journal. On that clear night it was followed by an empty troop train. Moving at usual speed the train first passed a yellow caution signal, then a red stop signal, but still kept coming toward the circus train. The flagman's frantic signals were ignored, and the troop train plowed into the rear cars of the circus train. The wreck burst into flames, bringing riders and animals to an agonizing death. Nearby residents gave what help they could. No one could find water to put out the fires. Special trains rushed doctors and nurses from Gary and from Hammond. The circus manager totaled up 68 people dead in the wreck and another 127 sent to the hospital. The engineman on the troop train lived, and testified that he had had no sleep for twenty-fours before the wreck; he had dozed through two cautionary signals and the flagman's lantern.

Wrecks and accidents continue to the present day. All-metal cars with electric lights and steam heat replaced the old ones, improved signal systems were developed, and broken rails are a rarity thanks to much improved manufacturing and inspection techniques.

SOURCES

Dickens, Laurie C. *Wreck on the Wabash*. Blissfield, Mich.: Made For Ewe, 2001.

Holbrook, Stewart H. *The Story of American Railroads*. New York: Crown, 1947.

Michigan Commissioner of Railroads. *Annual Reports*, various years.

Million, Art. "Wreck at East Paris." *Pere Marquette Rails* No. 14. (2002).

Riddering, Don. "The Great Salem Wreck." *(Salem Area Historical Society) Historical Monograph* 1 (May 1987).

Good Roads

It was the bicycle that turned the first wheel on the road to the demise of the passenger train. Bicycling became a national craze around 1900, and "wheels," as bicycles were then called, sold in the millions. This fad for travel sprang out of a new enthusiasm for mobility that the electric interurban contributed so much to. Bicyclists formed clubs and then followed with a national organization named the League of American Wheelmen, with Michigander Horatio S. Earle as its president. Abysmal dirt roads made this pleasant recreation so extraordinarily difficult that bicyclists began demanding that the government furnish them with better roads to enhance their hobby. A few decades earlier the Grange had urged similar road improvements, although unsuccessfully. There had been such advocates earlier, when, in 1901, Earle, who was also a state senator, put forth a resolution calling for a committee on ways to improve highways. Michigan's constitution included roads among

This view of Michigan Avenue west of Battle Creek shows why the interurban gained immediate popular acceptance as a substitute for having to travel on Michigan roads.

Willard Library, Battle Creek.

internal improvements, and therefore the state had no authority to do anything. Earle got a constitutional amendment to exempt "public wagon roads," with the voters in every county approving it in 1905. Governor Fred M. Warner appointed Earle, the bicyclist, as the first commissioner of the newly created state highway department.

To provide some funding to improve roads, driver licenses and car registration became a requirement, with the fees collected dedicated to road improvements that benefited both bicycle and auto owners. The state also began paying bonuses of up to $1,000 a mile to townships and counties for building roads that met new higher state standards. Some localities jumped at the opportunity, while others made little use of it. The highway department still lacked authority to build or even to maintain roads; it could only advise road districts, collect statistics, and give out money. The improvements to roads that did appear supported two other important social changes. One was the movement already under way that encouraged the consolidation of one-room schools, and the second was the post office's newly inaugurated rural free delivery.

As the state experimented with different methods of road building, its roads gradually began to improve in quality. In 1909 the nation's first stretch of concrete highway was put down on Woodward Avenue between Six Mile and Seven Mile Roads north of Detroit. In 1911 Wayne County road commission president Edward N. Hines painted the first centerline in an effort to reduce accidents. In 1913 the state laid out a network of 3,000 miles of state trunk line highways and established the "M" prefix for the system. Roads that were part of this system and built to certain standards earned double bonuses from the state. The federal government began to provide some money in 1916 for construction of roads that were to be part of the "U.S." highway system. In 1920 the nation's first overhead three-color, four-direction traffic signal was put up in Detroit, using color lens provided by the Michigan Central Railroad.

Although bicycles started the push for road improvements, it was the automobile that made them urgent. Between the 1893 vehicle of Charles and Frank Duryea and Henry Ford's in 1896, the world was put on the road to a completely new form of transport. Early on it may have been imperfect and may have been difficult to operate, but time soon made the automobile a highly prized personal vehicle. Detroit and Michigan became the center of automobile manufacturing. As the quality of the product went up and the price came down, and as roads were improved, automobile use skyrocketed. In 1905 there were only about 3,000 cars registered in Michigan, a number that jumped to 60,000 in 1913, and exploded to 326,000 in 1919.

Henry Ford's first Model T out of Highland Park in 1908, the $5-a-day wage, the inventive genius of the automotive pioneers, and much more are an exciting saga that has been told often. To the railroads, the horseless carriage and the internal combustion engine first seemed little more than toys, and certainly not any sort of threat. Hauling parts and completed vehicles was a new source of freight revenue. At the worst the railroads lost a few local passengers. The short-distance trips made easier by the auto duplicated the service of the interurbans and the electric roads, which suffered mortal injury from the new vehicle and the state's support of it.

SOURCES

Dunbar, Willis F. *Michigan: A History of the Wolverine State*. Grand Rapids, Mich.:
    W. B. Eerdmans, 1970.

Fuller, George N. *Michigan: A Centennial History*. 2 vols. Chicago: Lewis Publishing, 1939.

Quaife, Milo M., and Sidney Glazer. *Michigan: From Primitive Wilderness to Industrial Commonwealth*. New York: Prentice-Hall, 1948.

The Roaring Twenties, the Depression, and World War II, 1920–1945

Between the Wars

The "Roaring Twenties" of the 1920s and the "Great Depression" of the 1930s aptly describe the two decades following World War I. That these twenty years changed American society completely is an understatement. The Eighteenth and Nineteenth Amendments to the Constitution, which, respectively, instituted prohibition and granted the vote to women, were two grand experiments to improve American society. In its trail Prohibition brought widespread smuggling, a new cottage industry to meet the increased demand for alcohol, a disregard for the law, and a guarantee of profits to organized crime. Universal suffrage had far more benign effects, although it was females that stereotyped the "flapper" era of the Roaring Twenties. It was the excitement of the age, women dressing and dancing more provocatively and drinking more openly, combined with the use of the now-very-popular automobile, that many claimed not only ruined the nation's moral character but also irretrievably damaged the image of the fair sex. World War I brought, as war usually does, wealth to those businesses that received war contracts. After the end of the war industrialists began to devote their accumulated profits to their businesses by improving efficiency and increasing production. Electricity was introduced to more homes, and it became more widely used in businesses as well. The automobile developed into a necessity rather than a plaything. The benefits of this increased economic activity did not work its way down very far. The national labor force was employed as much as it was only because of severe restrictions on immigration.

The railroads were returned to their owners in March 1920, and they were in sorry condition. In 1920, while operating revenues reached a new high, operating expenses climbed even faster and nearly eliminated net income. In 1921 freight traffic dropped by one-quarter and passenger travel by one-fifth. Revenues dropped by only 10 percent thanks to a

1920 rate increase, while expenses were cut by 20 percent. After 1921 freight business began a recovery that by 1925 brought the rails back to wartime levels of traffic, and this stayed relatively unchanged for the remainder of the decade. Passenger traffic seesawed throughout the 1920s, but began to decline in the last half of the decade.

The depression that began in 1929 was worse than anything before it in memory. A few lone voices had warned of excesses in the stock market, but new stock issues, rising prices, and increased loans from brokers characterized the market right up to the hour on "Black Thursday," 24 October, when prices began their precipitous drop. During the days that followed nearly everything economic and financial worked in tandem to make things worse. The plunge in the stock market made borrowing more difficult, and as investments disappeared, bank and insurance companies began to fail. Worldwide overproduction halved commodity prices and then halved them again. Production began to decline. Money disappeared into mattresses as still more banks failed.

During the Great Depression of the 1930s freight tonnage sagged to levels below those before World War I. From 1929 to 1932 railroad freight ton-miles dropped by nearly a half; freight revenues dropped by as much and passenger revenues by a bit more. This was followed by a slight improvement in the next few years, but again revenues dropped sharply in 1938. At the end of 1929 twenty-nine railroad companies were in receivership. Most were small roads, and none of them were in Michigan. By the end of 1932 the number had increased to fifty-five, and now included the Wabash and the Ann Arbor. When 1937 began ninety roads, with 71,000 miles of line, were in receivership. In Michigan, the list now included the Chicago & North Western; the Chicago, Milwaukee, St. Paul & Pacific; and the Copper Range. In 1937 the Duluth, South Shore & Atlantic joined the list, and was followed a year later by the Soo Line. Surprisingly, the Pere Marquette managed to evade receivership, but only because it was supported by the Chesapeake & Ohio, which controlled it.

By 1939 the railroads were hauling only two-thirds of the nation's freight, the smallest percentage since the railroads first appeared. As the Depression grew more severe, railroad revenues declined, and net income dropped faster. There were net losses in 1932 and 1938. For the year 1939 revenues were more than one-third lower than in 1929; expenses were reduced almost as much, but net income was only about 15 percent of the 1929 amount. The railroads, like the entire society, had never experienced anything of the duration and severity of this depression.

SOURCES

American Association of Railroads. *Railroad Transportation: A Statistical Record.* Washington, D.C.: American Association of Railroads, various years.

Meints, Graydon M. *Michigan Railroads and Railroad Companies.* East Lansing: Michigan State University Press, 1992.

Stover, John. *American Railroads.* Chicago: University of Chicago Press, 1961.

U.S. Interstate Commerce Commission. *Annual Reports.* Washington, D.C.: Government Printing Office, various years.

Westmeyer, Russell E. *Economics of Transportation.* Englewood Cliffs, N.J.: Prentice-Hall, 1952.

Henry Ford, Railroadman

In 1920 Henry Ford started production at his new River Rouge factory. It replaced his old Highland Park plant and began turning out the Model T in greater numbers than possible earlier. He also moved his corporate headquarters, but it went to a cleaner and quieter Dearborn. Work on the Rouge plant started in 1914, and it produced matériel for the war effort. In the plant Ford realized his dream of a completely integrated industrial complex, one in which wood and raw steel went in one end of the building and finished automobiles came out the other end. The Rouge River was made navigable for Great Lakes ships for them to reach the factory. Ford's Rouge plant was one facet of an innovative concept now called vertical integration—control over all of the products that went into his cars. He set about buying iron mines, timberlands, and Great Lakes ships. He grew soybeans and tried to find uses for them in automobile parts. When Ford was not able to own some part of the production process outright, he developed ties with its owner. His close friendship with tire supplier Harvey Firestone is one example of this approach. Ford built community factories and developed farms in southeastern Michigan to provide supplies and parts. In 1924 Ford bought up timberland along the Lake Superior shore in Marquette and Baraga Counties, and then built his own railroad to haul it to his sawmill and port at his company town of Pequaming. He developed Kingsford, just south of Iron Mountain, as a wood-processing and chemical works. For all his genius in the automotive and mechanical and industrial worlds, Ford gave the lie to his remark that "history is more or less bunk." He established the Henry Ford Museum and Greenfield Village in Dearborn in 1929 and filled both with an amazingly varied display of artifacts.

Henry Ford—with his wife, Clara, and son Edsel—bought the Detroit, Toledo & Ironton in 1920 as a family investment. He built a branch line that brought the road into his new Rouge complex. Ford brought his personal idiosyncrasies and innovations to the road, but few of them lasted very long after he sold the road in 1929.

From the collections of The Henry Ford, photographer George Ebling, ID# THF25072.

One other outgrowth was the railroad that Ford built to serve his Rouge complex. Both the Michigan Central and the Pere Marquette served the factory, but Ford wanted control over at least some of the service into it. In July 1920 Ford announced that he; his wife, Clara; and son Edsel had gained full control of the Detroit, Toledo & Ironton. It cost them $5 million to buy an insolvent road that had been valued at between $16 and $20 million. In its first twenty-five years the DT&I and its predecessors had been through several reorganizations from bankruptcy and a series of name changes. More than one reason has been given for the purchase, but once he owned it Ford made it clear that he would give his railroad a good deal of thought and attention.

The DT&I became a part of the Rouge production line. It hauled trainloads of coal from connections in southern Ohio to the plant in hopper cars that Ford owned, and which were timed to arrive just as they were needed. Carloads of completed automobiles moved south for interchange to one of the many roads that the DT&I intersected with over the length of Ohio. When the Rouge first opened, during World War I, the DT&I had to switch its cars to another road in Detroit for delivery to the Rouge. To integrate the best use of his DT&I with his factory Ford proposed to build a new road, the Detroit & Ironton. In October 1923 it completed a 13.6-mile line from just east of Flat Rock to the Rouge. Ford's freight now could move to and from the Rouge directly, eliminating the switching delays and associated costs.

Ford had some fully developed ideas about how to make a railroad a better and more efficient operation. Rewording his approach to his factories, these came down to "cut out the loafing of the men, the loafing of the engines, and loafing of the cars." In an interview in the November 1921 issue of *National Business* entitled "If I Ran the Railroads," he expanded his approach into four goals. First of all he proposed getting rid of "unproductive stockholders," people who owned stock and expected dividends on it but contributed nothing to the railroad. Ford thought it was the first duty of a railroad to provide service to the public, not to pay dividends to outside owners. On established roads stock should be bought back and debt retired, lifting the burden of borrowing money. Who should own the railroad? Obviously, those who worked on it—"proper hands" as Ford put it. The workers had the greatest incentive to make it a success and should be rewarded accordingly.

Second, Ford wanted to improve the design of equipment. He thought that cars were too heavy in relation to the load carried. One feature he wanted to improve was car trucks by replacing the fixed

axle with independently mounted wheels. Reducing car weight would allow changes in locomotives, rails, and ties. All of this would reduce costs to the railroads and, incidentally, would reduce the profits of steel, locomotive, and freight car manufacturers whom he believed were encouraging the extra weight.

Finally, Ford wanted to improve efficiency by improving service. In this way he believed he could obtain maximum productivity from employees in return for their pay, by keeping them fully occupied. He wrote that "we tolerate no idle men, idle cars or idle engines. Loaded cars or trains on side tracks are proof of inefficient operation. They can be made to keep moving." Delaying freight created a demand for more equipment, a cost that Ford thought to be an avoidable waste of money. Finally, Ford addressed surplus and inefficient employees. His first salvo was aimed at lawyers, a staff that a well-managed road did not need, except in the claims department. The railroad bookkeeping system was far too complicated, full of duplication and red tape. Finally,

Henry Ford dreamed of a railroad operated by electricity. He took the first step in 1926 when he began using electric locomotives between Flat Rock and his Rouge plant. The project went no further, and electric operations ended not long after he sold the road. The indestructible concrete arches for the overhead wires stand to this day.

E. B. Novak photo, Sam Breck collection.

he got rid of the employees who did not do a full day's work. He cut the DT&I workforce from 2,600 to 1,500 who still got all the work done. Ford put everyone on an eight-hour day, and increased wages, with a minimum wage set at $6 per day. This and subsequent pay increases to all men were made while the National Labor Board had authorized other U.S. railroads to reduce wages.

During his ownership Ford managed to get rid of its brotherhood labor contracts; every man worked on merit alone. There was no seniority, no working agreements, no smoking on duty, no alcohol on duty, no overtime, and no Sunday work except in exceptional cases. In exchange the pay was better than on other roads, and every man worked for eight full hours to get it. If a train went into a siding to wait for another one, the crew had other work to do while they waited. If a man's assigned work was completed in four hours, he spent the remaining four washing windows, painting, cleaning, or doing something that needed to be done. Ford had a broad definition of concern for the well-being of his workers. He had men out to remind the idlers that "Mr. Ford didn't give you that raise because he likes you." The investigators from Ford's Sociology Department visited every employee at home to develop a file about personal habits, financial condition—savings and debt—and everything else that might in some way affect the worker's performance. To say that this program was unpopular is an understatement, and it was dropped eventually because the evasions and cover-ups made it impossible to administer. Ford did provide quality rooming accommodations for over-the-road employees to use, and Ford-approved eating establishments were available. An array of medical and insurance benefits were provided that were not generally available to railroadmen on other lines. Committees constantly stressed the importance of safety to workers and the public. But the expectation about a day's work for a day's pay was never relaxed. The men stayed for the good wages and benefits.

The DT&I solicited freight business aggressively, and, while it did increase, 70 percent of the road's traffic still came from Ford himself. The sum of all the efforts at efficiency and new business did pay off as the road began to show a profit. Ford went after connecting railroads for better divisions of rates for interline traffic, and this helped too. At the same time, Ford decided to build a major improvement to the DT&I main line. He decided to replace the roundabout route through Tecumseh, Adrian, and Napoleon, Ohio, with a fifty-five-mile line on a more direct route. Construction started in 1924 and was completed in

November 1929. He also planned to make line changes in Ohio at Lima and Springfield, but these never were completed.

The most innovative improvement that Ford adopted was to use electric locomotives. Thomas Alva Edison was a fast friend of Ford, and Edison was a pioneer in the application of electric power to locomotives. Other railroads had adopted electric power, although most of these uses were either in mountainous terrain in the West or dense traffic areas in the East on the Pennsylvania and the New Haven railroads. No railroad used electricity to handle an average volume of traffic over a relatively flat terrain. Ford believed electric locomotives would be far more efficient than the steamers, and his Rouge plant generated ample alternating current power to supply the railroad. The locomotive he envisioned would draw current from an overhead wire, then use it to power a motor that would generate direct current power to operate the locomotive. He bought two specially designed engines and tested them during the last half of 1925. He put up precast concrete arches between the Rouge and Flat Rock, hung wires, and began regular operations at the start of 1926. Even before the installation was complete, Ford stated that he would eventually electrify the entire DT&I main line. As an additional part of this he dreamed of building an extension south and east from Ironton, Ohio, to a connection with the Virginian, a coal-hauling road that was completely electrified. Nothing ever came of the planned extension, and no electrification was done south of the Flat Rock yard.

By the end of 1928 Henry Ford had made up his mind to sell the DT&I and get out of the railroad business entirely. He had some negotiations with the Baltimore & Ohio, which was interested in getting into Detroit, but nothing materialized. Son Edsel Ford approached the Pennsylvania Railroad. The Pennsylvania formed Pennroad Corporation as a new holding company to get around the Clayton Antitrust Act, then offered Ford $36 million for his railroad. The deal was struck; in June 1929 Ford sold the DT&I to Pennroad. Henry Ford's cost was the $5 million original purchase and another $8 million he put into improvements and new equipment. The Pennsylvania bought a road that was making money, had a dedicated staff, and had a physical plant that was in exceptionally good condition. That Henry Ford nearly tripled his investment in nine years is testimony to the fact that he did something right when nearly every railroad expert said he was wrong.

The reason most often given for selling was that Ford grew tired of the Interstate Commerce Commission (ICC) constantly meddling in the affairs of *his* company. Government regulation never interfered with

President Cleveland appointed Thomas M. Cooley the first chairman of the Interstate Commerce Commission in 1887. Highly regarded as a legal scholar, he spent twenty years as justice and chief justice of the Michigan Supreme Court. Cooley Law School in Lansing and Cooley High School in Detroit were named in his honor.

automobile manufacturing. The ICC dictated his railroad's accounting rules, set practices that he thought were unnecessary, and seemed to want to control everything. It was reported that when the ICC, for whatever reason, ordered Ford's men to stop installing electric wires south of Flat Rock yard, it was the last interference with his railroad that he would tolerate. To his credit, Henry Ford demonstrated clearly what he could do with his own money if he "ran the railroad." Ford's innovations and practices were never widely adopted by any other railroad. The Great Depression that came after the sale and the ICC made any experimentation difficult. The railroad business seemed to be glad to be rid of Henry Ford the railroadman.

SOURCES

Lacey, Robert. *Ford, the Men and the Machine*. Boston: Little, Brown, 1986.

Pletz, William C. "The Railroad That Went No Place." *Inside Track* 10:5 (November–December 1979), 11:1 (January–February 1980).

Trostel, Scott D. *Henry Ford: When I Ran the Railroad*. Fletcher, Ohio: Cam-Tech Publishing, 1989.

The Government Regulates Everything

The railroads came out of World War I and government ownership in sorry shape. The demands of war left maintenance neglected or undone while equipment was used to the point that it wore out. The government charged the railroads full cost for any improvements and equipment purchases. On the other hand, the government made the final decision on how much it would pay for any damage or loss that it had caused, an amount the lines considered inadequate. To make it worse, the railroads were required to continue the pay schedules the government had awarded to workers as well as to live with the regulations from an ICC that seemed to become more intrusive each day.

In 1920 the railroads' problem was not about the amount of freight they hauled. All of the traffic was theirs except for the small fraction that moved in Great Lakes ships and river barges. If the United States continued to grow as an industrial success, the future of freight traffic and the railroads was bright. The immediate problem was how to restore profits. This called for decisions about how to stabilize and maximize those profits, how to do all of this with a physical plant and equipment that were badly run down and had to be rejuvenated, and finally how to find the money to pay for all that needed to be done. The roads went at this on several fronts. Tight management kept costs under control and squeezed them down still more. The railroads' largest single expense item was employee pay, which made up a little over 60 percent of all operating costs. This cost was kept level between 1920 and 1930 by cutting the workforce by about a quarter, to between 1.6 and 1.7 million men, despite granting several small pay increases. Employee payrolls did drop sharply between 1920 and 1921, but were up by about 5 percent by 1929 due to the selective wage increases. Other costs were reduced as much as possible.

The reductions in net income and profits that preceded World War I seriously affected how to pay for the needed improvements. Banks were wary, and money could be borrowed only at relatively high interest rates. President Wilson advocated the railroads should be given financial assistance to ease their transition back to private ownership, and the Transportation Act of 1920 (also called the Esch-Cummins Act) provided a six months' guarantee that was of some financial help. The federal government provided no other money, but did establish some short-term programs of support. The ICC authorized freight rate increases ranging from 25 to 40 percent, the first increases to respond to the sharply higher costs the railroads incurred during and after the war. At that same time, the Railroad Labor Board ordered pay increases averaging 22 percent for all workers. These increases in revenues, together with a substantial amount of new debt, provided the railroads enough funds to spend an average of $750 million each year during the 1920s, with about two-thirds of it going to track and facilities improvements and the other third to new engines and cars. In sum, the railroads did improve their financial position during the 1920s; the operating ratio of expenses to income dropped from 82 percent to 71 percent. No further help came from the federal government until 1933, when the Depression-induced Reconstruction Finance Corporation (RFC) was created to loan money to carriers that the ICC thought needed it.

The companies also made a convincing case to the Congress that one important means to preserve the railroads was to allow more rather than fewer consolidations. For two decades, even predating the Theodore Roosevelt administration, a general feeling was that mergers and "bigness" caused economic problems rather than solved them, and on this premise a large body of American antitrust legislation had built up. The Transportation Act of 1920 turned this on its head. The ICC asked

Harvard scholar and railroad expert William Z. Ripley to take on the task of designing consolidated systems for the country. Fifteen months later he recommended that the national rail network be reconstituted into nineteen regional carriers. In Michigan, the New York Central and its subsidiaries, the Chicago & North Western, the Pennsylvania, the Pere Marquette, and the Canadian-controlled Grand Trunk Western—were to remain separate. The Soo Line and the Duluth, South Shore & Atlantic were combined into one company. The small carriers were parceled out among the major systems. The recommended mergers had moderate Congressional approval, but still required approval from the ICC after it held hearings. Little came from this initial plan. Throughout the rest of the decade several other experts as well as railroad owners made other proposals for new alignments of the eastern railroads. But the ICC was not thrilled at the prospect of having to order mergers that the roads themselves did not want. The ICC hoped to be relieved of this responsibility, but Congress took no steps to accommodate it. After nine years, the ICC issued a final plan in 1929, but not much resulted from a decade of deliberations.

Congress granted the ICC still more powers, including jurisdiction over conflicts between interstate and intrastate rates and over divisions of rates between carriers. These gave it virtually complete control over freight rates and the ability to set maximum and minimum rates, as well as total control over all issues of securities (stocks or bonds), acquisitions of control, mergers, and construction and abandonment. The ICC was charged with setting rates that would allow carriers to earn a fair return on the value of their property. With complete control over rates the law assumed the ICC could assure a rate of return. The Ripley plan of mergers was designed to support this goal by making combinations of weak and strong roads, which would, as a group, be profitable. The Valuation Act of 1913 was to be used to calculate the value of the property, and that would determine a reasonable rate of return. Congress's biggest concern was not insufficient return, but that railroad earnings would be too large. To prevent this Congress set an arbitrary 5.5 percent return as "fair" for the first two years after passage, and authorized the ICC to determine a fair return after that. In an unusual arrangement this provision would apply to the sum of operations in a given territory or on a national basis, but not to individual roads. If an individual road failed to earn this fair return, it was its own fault, and there was to be no reimbursement from the government. But if any road's earnings exceeded 6 percent, the company had to return one-half of the excess over 6 percent to the federal government. The government would put this money in a fund that could be used to buy equipment and facilities that could be leased to needy roads. That this section of the act was full of pitfalls is an understatement; it generated so much controversy and litigation that it was largely ineffectual and was at last repealed in 1933.

Most remarkable in all of this was the blindness of the railroads, the government, and the regulators to the glaring truth that the railroads were beginning to lose their freight-hauling monopoly. During the 1920s, as the states expanded and improved the highway network, shipping by truck increased steadily. The same trend began to appear in passenger ridership; it was moving to automobiles and intercity buses. Although U.S. production increased in all industries throughout the decade, only about one-half of the increase, as measured by revenue ton-miles, went to the railroads. Despite the steady decline in traffic, the ICC held the railroads in check. Through its control of minimum and maximum rates, the ICC refused to allow the railroads to set competitive rates to retain traffic. Michigan made an attempt to begin regulating truckers in 1923, but in 1925 the U.S. Supreme Court held that the state statute was in error, leaving the business largely unregulated. It was not until 1935 that federal legislation was passed that gave the ICC jurisdiction over motor carriers, both trucks and buses.

Only a few changes occurred in the financial control of the state's rail lines. In May 1925 the Wabash Railway obtained control of the Ann Arbor Railroad. The Pennsylvania Railroad's holding company, the Pennsylvania Company, was formed in 1870 and owned many of the PRR's lines west of Pittsburgh. In 1929 the PRR formed the Pennroad Corporation as a second holding company to hold its investment in the Norfolk & Western. In June 1927 Henry Ford sold his Detroit, Toledo & Ironton, which the Pennsylvania added to the Pennroad. In 1928 the Pennsylvania acquired control of the Lehigh Valley and the Wabash, and put them into the Pennroad. With the Wabash came its control of the Ann Arbor, although the Pennsylvania allowed all of the roads to operate with a degree of independence. In January 1923 the Grand Trunk Railway of Canada was officially conveyed to the Canadian National Railways, a unit of the government of Canada, and the CN thereby acquired control of the Grand Trunk Western. In May 1928 the GTW was reincorporated to merge all of its subsidiaries except the Cincinnati, Saginaw & Mackinaw, which it continued to operate under a lease. The Chesapeake & Ohio bought control of the Pere Marquette in 1929. The Cleveland, Cincinnati, Chicago & St. Louis—the Big Four road—had controlled the Cincinnati Northern since 1902, and finally got around to a formal lease of the road in 1926. In February 1930 both the Big Four and the Michigan Central were leased to the New York Central after more than fifty years of nearly total ownership by the Vanderbilts. In 1938 the Big Four absorbed the Cincinnati Northern.

SOURCES

Stover, John F. *American Railroads*. Chicago: University of Chicago Press, 1961.

U.S. Interstate Commerce Commission. *Annual Reports*. Washington, D.C.: Government Printing Office, various years.

Westmeyer, Russell E. *Economics of Transportation*. Englewood Cliffs, N.J.: Prentice-Hall, 1952.

Rails Down; Rails Up

During the wild fluctuations of business and the nation's economy during the 1920s and 1930s, Michigan's railroad network changed relatively little. There was some reduction of mileage between 1919 and 1929, when about 600 miles of line were taken up, of which about 100 miles were Upper Peninsula logging and mining branches. More than half of the trackage abandoned was by the Escanaba & Lake Superior in the mid-1920s.

In the Lower Peninsula there were a few bits of construction. The most important was the decision by the Pennsylvania Railroad to build to Detroit. Its line had reached Toledo in 1873, and used a connecting service over the rather indirect Pere Marquette route into Detroit. By 1916 the Pennsylvania came to believe it had to tap the Detroit automobile factories with its own line. The world war put those plans on hold until 1920, at which time it began construction work. When the Detroit route was completed in 1922 it was made up of running rights over the Ann Arbor between Toledo and Alexis; over the Pere Marquette between Alexis and Carleton, a newly built line between Carleton and Ecorse Junction; and finally trackage rights on the Wabash and the Pere Marquette to reach Fort Street Union Station in downtown Detroit. It added to this in 1923 when it gained access to several industrial districts, some of it by construction and some by running rights on the PM and the Wabash tracks. Pere Marquette Toledo-Detroit passenger trains joined those of the Pennsylvania on this new route.

Lines abandoned between 1920 and 1945.
Note that not all short branches to mines
are shown.

KEY

— Lines abandoned between 1920 and
1945
— Lines remaining after 1945

The Pere Marquette in Pontiac

By 1920 the Pere Marquette served every major city in southern Michigan but two, Kalamazoo and Pontiac. In the early 1900s the Prince administration tried to buy up the Chicago, Kalamazoo & Saginaw in an effort gain access to Kalamazoo. The Michigan Central stepped in, bought the CK&S, and kept the PM out. In the early 1920s the PM cast a covetous eye on Pontiac. General Motors was by far the largest manufacturer there, as it had been since the company was founded, and planned more expansion in 1922. The PM was a major freight provider for GM in Saginaw and Flint. The only railroad then serving Pontiac was the Grand Trunk Western, which operated three different lines into the city. The PM filed a petition with the Interstate Commerce Commission to build a seventeen-mile branch from Wixom to Pontiac and a seven-mile belt line on the north and east sides of the city. The Grand Trunk objected vociferously to this invasion of its territory. The Interstate Commerce Commission (ICC) had had twenty years of dealings with the PM and its two bankruptcies. With an eye on the PM's balance sheet and an ear to the Grand Trunk's objections, the ICC decided in May 1923 against the PM's request. In 1931 the Grand Trunk built a belt line around Pontiac on much the same route that had been proposed by the PM.

The Pere Marquette built its 8-mile Flint Belt around the east side of Flint in 1923, which allowed its trains to bypass the downtown. In 1923 a Detroit, Toledo & Ironton subsidiary built a 13.6-mile branch from Flat Rock to the mammoth Rouge plant. The next year it began building a 55-mile cutoff from Durban, southwest of Maybee, to Malinta, Ohio. This provided a much improved and shorter route between Detroit and southern Ohio. When it was finished in 1927 the original main line through Adrian and Tecumseh was downgraded to branch-line status. These projects are covered in more detail in the section on Henry Ford's ownership of the DT&I. The Michigan Central built a new entry into Toledo from Vienna Junction on its Toledo-Detroit line and by it gained better access to the east side of Toledo and the roads entering that side of the city. To handle the increased Chicago-Detroit-East Coast freight traffic, it also built a new classification yard on the east side of Niles. It connected the yard to its Jackson–Three Rivers–Niles Air Line to allow through freight trains to move over that supplemental main line.

During the decade the Pere Marquette removed nearly 100 miles of line, including the Rapid City–Kalkaska line in 1921, and in the middle of the decade the Benton Harbor–Buchanan branch as well as the White Cloud–Big Rapids line. The Manistee & Northeastern took up all of its Platte River branch through Honor in 1924, and seventy-five miles of its River Branch between Kaleva and Grayling in 1925. The Detroit & Mackinac removed a number of lumbering branches as well as all fifty-five miles of the AuSable & Northwestern, which it had bought in 1914. The Michigan East & West, which came from a 1913 reorganization of the Manistee & Grand Rapids, abandoned all seventy-three miles of its line from Manistee to Marion in 1921. In the mid-1920s the hard-luck Detroit, Caro & Sandusky took up the twenty-eight miles of line between Caro and Bay City and twenty miles out of Port Huron to Roseburg. Throughout the decade the Michigan Central removed more than a hundred miles of lumbering spurs off its Mackinaw branch, leaving only a skeleton made up of the Gladwin, Twin Lakes, Bagley, and Haakwood branches. It also removed the short Grosse Ile branch in 1929, a remnant of the Canada Southern's dream of a line from Niagara Falls to Chicago.

During the 1930s Michigan lost another 600 miles of rail lines. The single largest abandonment was of the Detroit, Toledo & Milwaukee, a line that was jointly owned by the New York Central and the Michigan Central and which probably had never made a dollar of profit for any of its owners. About ninety miles of road between Dundee and Battle Creek were removed in 1932, although short pieces were kept in several cities. The MC also tore up the Bagley branch to Johannesburg in 1931, the St. Clair–Richmond line in 1932, the Twin Lakes branch to Lewiston in 1932, the Battle Creek–Sturgis route of the "Holy Land Flyer" in 1935, and the Haakwood branch in 1937. The East Jordan branch, the former Detroit & Charlevoix left over from the David Ward lumbering empire, was torn up from Frederic to East Jordan in 1932, although some logging branches at the west end were sold to the East Jordan & Southern. The Boyne City, Gaylord & Alpena took up eighty-seven miles of line between Alpena and Boyne Falls in 1935, a line that had been built less than twenty years earlier. The Detroit & Mackinac removed its thirty-one-mile Rose City branch in 1930. The Pere Marquette removed some small pieces of lines: the Ionia-Stanton section, the Elmdale-Freeport branch, and the ends of branches extending to Fostoria, Pentwater, and Grindstone City.

All of the Wisconsin & Michigan, extending from Bagley Junction, Wisconsin, to Iron Mountain, was taken up in 1938, after managing to live a precarious forty-four years. The Duluth, South Shore & Atlantic abandoned the Marquette & Western line between Marquette and Negaunee in 1930, a line that duplicated its own main line between those points. In the mid-1930s it abandoned seventy-nine miles of its main line through Wisconsin and began running over other roads to reach Superior and Duluth. In 1931 the Ontonagon Railroad abandoned all of its trackage, as did the Milwaukee Road its White Pine Mine branch.

The Chicago & North Western removed more than fifty miles of mining and lumbering spurs and branches.

Removing such lines provided savings to the railroads, savings that were badly needed to get through the Great Depression. On the other side, there were some scattered attempts to improve freight and passenger service in an attempt to increase business. But the reductions in marginal passenger train service played a more important part, as is described elsewhere, and freight train operations similarly were cut back. These service reductions allowed the railroads a further economy in discontinuing many small-town railroad stations. The Michigan Central alone closed up its depots at Onondaga, Morgan, Irving, Dutton, Bowen, Concord, Sherwood, Fabius, Vandalia, Dailey, Gobles, Kendall, Lacota, Eden, Holt, Bath, Bennington, Oakley, Thomas, Metamora, Hunters Creek, Linwood, Sterling, Alger, Otsego Lake, and Vanderbilt. The New York Central shuttered its stations at Riga, Palmyra, Cadmus, Klinger Lake, Ogden, Weston, Moore Park, Devereaux, Dimondale, Horton, Hanover, Mosherville, Bankers, Jerome, Somerset, Bridgewater, Norvell, and Napoleon. The Pere Marquette and other roads also closed dozens of depots that they considered no longer necessary. During the 1930s the Michigan Central downgraded its Niles–Three Rivers–Jackson Air Line and moved all through freight train movements to its double-track main line through Kalamazoo.

About 1925 the Grand Trunk Western took the first steps to change the Michigan port for its Lake Michigan car ferry service from Grand Haven to Muskegon. It struck a deal with the Pennsylvania Railroad that allowed it to run trains over part of that road's Muskegon branch. With the Pennsylvania, it established a jointly owned company to own and operate the car ferries. Grand Trunk Western ownership of the ferries became a problem in 1927 when another Great Lakes carrier challenged the operation as a violation of U.S. "cabotage" laws—a requirement that service between American ports could be only by American-owned companies. There was no disputing the fact that the GTW was owned by the Canadian government, but if the new ferry company were 75 percent owned by the Pennsylvania, U.S. law would be satisfied. Temporarily the Grand Trunk continued to operate the car ferries but stopped carrying any traffic that originated in either Milwaukee or Grand Haven to the other port. Freight cars were handled, but no passengers or automobiles were carried. The Pennsylvania found value in reaching the port of Milwaukee and finally agreed, in 1931, to own three-quarters of the car ferry company. The two roads eventually received all the needed permissions from the ICC and began operating in July 1933. Their application to sail to Manitowoc was eventually withdrawn because of the objections of the Ann Arbor Railroad. Congress later wrote a loophole into the legislation that permitted Grand Trunk Western, by itself, to operate the car ferry service. This allowed the Pennsylvania to drop out of the service at a later date. The changeover to Muskegon also allowed the GTW to downgrade its own line to Muskegon, via Greenville, and end through service on it.

SOURCES

Burgess, George H., and Miles C. Kennedy. *Centennial History of the Pennsylvania Railroad Company, 1846–1946*. Philadelphia: Pennsylvania Railroad, 1949.

Dunbar, Willis F. *All Aboard! A History of Railroads in Michigan*. Grand Rapids, Mich.: W. B. Eerdmans, 1969.

Hilton, George W. *The Great Lakes Car Ferries*. Berkeley, Calif.: Howell-North, 1962.

Pletz, William C. "The Railroad That Went No Place." *Inside Track* 10:5 (November–December 1979), 11:1 (January–February 1980).

U.S. Interstate Commerce Commission. *Finance Dockets*, various numbers. Washington, D.C.: Interstate Commerce Commission, various dates.

The Golden Years of Train Riding

Passenger train service changed dramatically in the two decades between the world wars. In 1920 most roads offered extensive branch-line and local train services. Two or three local trains, daily except Sundays, served many branches in southern Michigan. Michigan's electric interurban network was complete, with fast, convenient service and many more trains than the railroads operated. As automobile use increased, the demand for local trains dropped off and began a trend that soon brought the end of the interurban system in Michigan. The drop in travel during the Depression caused further reductions in what the railroads considered to be marginal services, most of which were local trains on lightly trafficked branches. The cost formulas of the ICC made clear that passenger trains were losing money, an accounting condition that first appeared in 1930. The local and branch trains that were kept on often were supported more by U.S. mail contracts than by passengers, a fact that distorted their importance to riders. Through trains probably came closer to covering their operating costs. Throughout the two decades the airlines, as an alternative means of longer-distance travel, remained inadequate. Many executives held to a hope that riders would leave their automobiles and return to the rails after the end of the Depression.

After the end of the World War I in 1919, the passenger train began its slow departure from the American scene. War-inflated ridership levels in 1920 dropped nearly 25 percent the next year, from forty-six to thirty-seven million passenger-miles (the number of passengers multiplied by the miles they traveled), and by 1930 ridership dropped by another quarter of that amount to twenty-six million. The low came in 1933, with levels down to just over sixteen million passenger-miles. The years that followed saw slow but steady increases until the number reached twenty-three million in 1940. The total number of riders, nationally, was another story; in 1940 they had dropped to less than half the 1920 number. There were fewer riders, but those remaining were traveling longer distances, reflecting the continuing attrition of the local passenger train. Over the same period passenger revenues mirrored ridership. From 1930 on, except for a few years during World War II, passenger train operations lost money every year.

The population of the Upper Peninsula changed little between 1920 and 1940; a sharp loss in Houghton County was more than offset by increases in others. The Chicago & North Western's overnight *Iron and Copper Country Express*, loaded with mail and express, still made the run in just over twelve hours. Its connection to Ironwood was cut back to Watersmeet and then to just Iron River; the Chicago–Iron River sleeping car was gone by 1937. Service on the Milwaukee Road changed little. In the mid-1920s it ended the through run via the Copper Range Railroad and with it the Chicago-Calumet sleeping car. The *Copper Country Limited*, operated by the DSS&A north of Champion, remained to provide a service to Calumet. In the late 1930s the Milwaukee Road replaced the Channing-Ontonagon mixed train with the *Chippewa*, a Chicago-Ontonagon day run on a ten-hour–thirty-minute schedule. The Milwaukee Road and Soo Line operated a Chicago–Sault Ste. Marie sleeper via Pembine. Over on the Soo Line the daytime round-trip Soo-Gladstone local was removed, leaving only the overnight Twin Cities–Soo overnight service.

The Duluth, South Shore & Atlantic ran nearly 3,300 train miles each day, anchored by an overnight train from Duluth to Sault Ste. Marie and St. Ignace and with a stub run between Calumet and Nestoria that provided overnight service to both ends of the road. A second run was offered over the entire main line and additional service out of Marquette to Michigamme and to Calumet. By the late 1920s service was cut back to an overnight Duluth-Marquette and a daylight Calumet–St. Ignace service, with one additional Marquette-Calumet round-trip. By the end of the Depression the DSS&A through trains to the Soo were ended. The Marquette-Calumet round-trip train was shortened to a Champion-Calumet to become the Calumet leg of the *Copper Country Limited*, with the Milwaukee Road handling it between Champion and Chicago. This reduced DSS&A service to barely a third of its 1920 level. Except for the *Copper Country* equipment and a lone Duluth-Marquette sleeping car, the amenities of twenty years earlier had disappeared. Gone were the observation cars, the dining and café cars, the Chicago-Marquette sleeper from the Chicago & North Western, and the year-round Upper Peninsula–Detroit sleeper via the Michigan Central.

In the Lower Peninsula in 1920 the Detroit & Mackinac had two through trains between Alpena and Bay City, and both of them handed off cars to the Michigan Central to continue through to Detroit. The day run had an observation parlor car between Detroit and Cheboygan; the night train carried a Detroit-Alpena sleeper. These runs were supplemented by a variety of mixed trains on the main and branch lines. By 1924 the day train was cut back to an Alpena–Bay City round-trip run, and about a year later the night train was cut back similarly. In 1930 a motor car was started that ran from Alpena to Rogers City, doubled back to Posen, went on to Cheboygan, then headed back straight through to Alpena. In the mid-1920s the East Jordan & Southern halved its passenger service by dropping one East Jordan–Bellaire round-trip. The Manistee & Northeastern ran two trains a day between Manistee and Traverse City, another between Manistee and Grayling, and one train that made a round-trip from Traverse City to Provemont in the morning and then to Northport in the afternoon. Early in the 1920s it discontinued one of its two Manistee–Traverse City runs. A few years later the Manistee-Grayling train was discontinued, and the Manistee–Traverse City run was made into a mixed train. This was supplemented by two round-trips each day from Manistee to Copemish to connect with Pere Marquette trains at Kaleva. In 1930 the through mixed train was discontinued, and the two runs out of Manistee were cut back to run only to Kaleva. The Ann Arbor's motor cars continued to supplement its through steam train service until the mid-1920s. When they were dropped the line was left with one through Toledo-Frankfort daytime run and one Mt. Pleasant–Toledo round-trip. An observation-parlor-café car ran through the 1920s and then was replaced by a parlor car for the first few years of the 1930s. The Toledo–Mt. Pleasant run ended in 1931, leaving only the day Toledo-Frankfort local.

Between 1920 and 1940 the Pere Marquette discontinued about 40 percent of its passenger service. By the end of World War I many marginal branches had lost their passenger trains or were reduced to mixed train service that handled both freight and passengers. By 1925 all trains in the Thumb area were gone except for one Port Huron–Bad Axe round-trip. Grand Rapids–Saginaw runs were cut back from three to one each way and Saginaw-Ludington runs from two to one. Muskegon-Pentwater and Muskegon–White Cloud–Big Rapids trains disappeared. Main-line service between Detroit and Grand Rapids was improved from three to four runs each way. By 1930 service was reduced somewhat more: only two trains a day ran into Bay City, Detroit-Saginaw runs were down to two a day, and branch runs into Elk Rapids and Bad Axe ended. There were further reductions during the 1930s. By 1940 service remained on only the Chicago–Grand Rapids and Muskegon, the Grand Rapids–Detroit, the Detroit–Bay City, the Detroit-Toledo, and the Grand Rapids–Petoskey principal lines. Despite the difficult financial times during the road's receivership and the 1930s depression, the PM service could be described as reasonably satisfactory. In the early 1920s it inaugurated the *Peninsular* as a six-hour overnight stroll between Detroit and Grand Rapids. About 1930 it was extended to run through to Muskegon by way of Holland, but this lasted only two years. In 1931 the Detroit–Grand Rapids leg was moved over to the Michigan Central, and the PM ran the part to Muskegon, an arrangement that lasted only until 1936. Throughout this entire period the PM operated its summers-only *Resort Special* between Chicago and Bay View six days a week, and a Detroit leg that ran three times a week in most years.

The Pennsylvania Railroad inaugurated passenger service into Detroit in 1922, running three trains a day. By 1926 service was up to four a day each way running through to Detroit. A new fast overnight train between Detroit and Washington, D.C., and New York, named the *Red Arrow* after Michigan's World War I Thirty-Second Infantry Division of the same name, was put on the schedule in 1926. The Baltimore & Ohio operated two or three trains a day into Detroit from Cincinnati over the Pere Marquette route. In 1930 it began an upgraded service between Detroit and Washington, D.C., on an overnight schedule, and renamed it the *Ambassador* in 1932. The Chesapeake & Ohio ran two trains a day between Columbus, Ohio, and Detroit, using the PM route between Toledo and Detroit. In 1930 it added the *Sportsman* to its Detroit

The Wabash and the Pennsylvania Railroads teamed up in 1941 to give the Michigan Central stiff competition in the Chicago-Detroit market as shown in this 1941 Wabash timetable ad. The four-hour–forty-five-minute trip was at an average speed of a fast sixty-two miles per hour and matched the MC's fastest trains.

Author's collection.

service, a train that ran overnight between Detroit and West Virginia and continued during daylight into Norfolk.

The Wabash Railway's presence in Detroit remained relatively modest. Its Detroit route connected Buffalo with both Chicago and St. Louis. In 1917 it ran three through trains from Buffalo, with the *Continental Limited* at the head of the fleet on a sixteen-hour schedule to Chicago. It also scheduled three runs a day from Detroit to St. Louis and three others to Chicago. After World War I these were reduced to two a day to Chicago and only one between Detroit and Buffalo. After the Pennsylvania Railroad gained control of the Wabash in 1928, more changes were forthcoming. In 1931 the two Chicago-Detroit trains via the Wabash's single-track northern Indiana route were dropped and were replaced by three runs using the Wabash from Detroit to Fort Wayne and the Pennsylvania between Fort Wayne and Chicago. Running on six-hour schedules, they were as fast as the Michigan Central's trains. At the same time, the three runs to St. Louis were cut back to two. This arrangement remained in effect through World War II. In the late 1930s train names began to reappear on the Wabash: the afternoon Detroit-Chicago run became the *Detroit Arrow* and the overnighter the *Mid-City Express*. By 1940 the Chicago-Detroit runs were speeded up to five hours westbound and four hours forty-five minutes eastbound, and the day trains departed earlier so the equipment could make a round-trip each day. The eastbound morning and westbound afternoon trains became the *Red Bird*.

The Grand Rapids & Indiana provided a surprisingly good passenger service in 1920, given its marginal financial situation and its dependence on the largesse of the Pennsylvania Railroad. South of Grand Rapids four trains a day ran to Fort Wayne, one of which was an overnight run to Cincinnati, and a fifth was an overnight run to Chicago using the Michigan Central west of Kalamazoo. Three trains were scheduled—on daytime, afternoon, and overnight runs—between Grand Rapids and Mackinaw City. Five trains ran between Grand Rapids and Muskegon and two between Walton Junction and Traverse City. At the end of World War I the GR&I added a daytime Grand Rapids–Chicago run and a fourth Grand Rapids–Cadillac train, but cut back Muskegon Branch service to three trains. By 1924 it dropped one Grand Rapids–Fort Wayne trip and cut back service north of Grand Rapids to two trains each way. During the mid-1930s it dropped one Grand Rapids–Chicago run and by 1938 discontinued all through Grand Rapids–Chicago trains. In 1938 it also reduced Grand Rapids–Mackinaw City service to one train a day and ended service on the Traverse City branch. The summers-only service was continued throughout the two decades, first as the *Northland* and later the *Northern Arrow*. In summer 1931 the *North Star* ran between Chicago and Mackinaw City for one season using Michigan Central tracks west of Kalamazoo.

Passenger service on the Grand Trunk Western main line was three through trains and one local train between Chicago and Port Huron, with a Battle Creek–Port Huron local complementing the service. In the mid-1920s a fourth through run, the *International Limited*, was added as an overnight Chicago-Toronto service. In 1926 it added a fifth train, the *Maple Leaf*, which left Chicago at 9:00 A.M. for a twenty-one-hour–thirty-minute run to Montreal. Although the Grand Trunk did offer a Chicago–Buffalo–New York City service, its strength was the Chicago-Toronto-Montreal market. In 1932 the road cut back its through service to three Chicago-Toronto-Montreal trains and also eliminated the main-line local runs. This remained the level of operations until the

Grand Trunk Western branch-line service usually was by a mixed train that handled both freight cars and passengers. One exception was between Detroit and Port Huron. In this 1939 pose, the crew of train 35, with "doodlebug" 15805, are preparing to leave Port Huron.

William J. Miller photo, Sam Breck collection.

1960s. The GTW's principal branch-line service was between Detroit and Grand Rapids. It ran three trains a day, with one of them going through to Grand Haven. In 1931 the Grand Trunk made arrangements with the Pennsylvania to begin running trains into Muskegon and moved its Lake Michigan car ferry operations there from Grand Haven. At first it ran one Detroit train to Muskegon each day and one to Grand Haven. In 1931 the GTW instituted a Pontiac-Detroit commuter train service, with five trains operated each way, supplementing the three that ran to Grand Rapids. In 1935 it dropped the through run to Grand Haven, added a second train to Muskegon, and put on a third train to Grand Rapids. This arrangement lasted until 1939, when the Detroit–Grand Rapids train was taken off. All other Grand Trunk branches had only one train a day except the Detroit–Port Huron service. This line had three runs a day, in 1925 was reduced to two a day, and in 1927 to just one. By 1930 nearly all other branch-line service was one run a day by mixed trains.

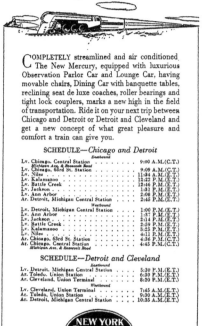

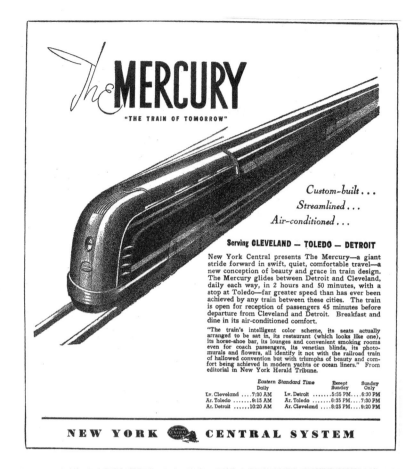

ABOVE, RIGHT: In 1936, during the depths of the Great Depression, the New York Central gave Michigan its first streamlined train, the *Mercury*. Using rebuilt equipment and a cowled locomotive, service between Cleveland and Detroit was never better.

Author's collection.

ABOVE: This 1941 timetable ad promotes the new service provided by the *Mercury* between Detroit and Chicago. A second set of cars enabled this improvement while keeping the original service to Cleveland.

Author's collection.

RIGHT: This is one of a brace of New York Central's streamlined locomotives that pulled the *Mercury* between Detroit and Chicago. It replaced the original cowled locomotive shown in the 1936 ad. This pose was taken in 1941 at Ann Arbor.

William J. Miller photo, Sam Breck collection.

The New York Central system, made up of its own lines and those of its wholly owned Michigan Central and Big Four—the Cleveland, Cincinnati, Chicago & St. Louis—was the major passenger train service provider in Michigan. The New York Central itself had a service between Detroit and Cleveland and Pittsburgh, with three or four through car services daily on this route, as well as two a day between Detroit and Columbus via its Toledo & Ohio Central route. The NYC's southern Michigan service was made up entirely of local trains on the Toledo–Hillsdale–Elkhart Old Road and the branches that intersected it. The Old Road saw four trains each way, the Jackson–Toledo and Jackson–Fort Wayne lines had three, and most other branches had two. From 3,500 miles run per day in 1920 service shrank to about 2,800 miles by 1928, and to 1,800 miles in 1931. By 1931 those three lines were down to two trains each way and the Jonesville-Lansing and Grand Rapids–Elkhart to one each way. Mixed trains handled the service on other branches. By 1933 daily train mileage was down to 1,200 and by 1937 to 700. In 1937 the Grand Rapids–Elkhart and Jackson-Toledo runs were ended and the Fort Wayne cut back to one Hillsdale–Fort Wayne round-trip.

In July 1936, during the depths of the Depression, the New York Central inaugurated a completely new train, the *Mercury*. Only two years earlier, in 1934, the Chicago, Burlington & Quincy introduced the first streamlined train, the *Zephyr*. That train was diesel-powered, but the NYC elected to have a steam engine suitably styled for its new train. Well-known industrial designer Henry Dreyfuss was recruited to design a streamlined train that was to make a daily round-trip from Cleveland to Detroit and back. In a money-saving move the NYC decided to have Dreyfuss rebuild older equipment rather than spend its money to buy all-new cars. On a two-hour–fifty-minute schedule, at an average speed of fifty-seven miles an hour, the train became an instant success. Its service was the best ever provided on the route. In 1938 the NYC expanded the *Mercury*'s service, as will be shown under the Michigan Central below. The *Mercury* also was the forerunner of the Big Four's *James Whitcomb Riley*, which began Cincinnati-Indianapolis-Chicago round-trips in 1941.

Big Four service into Michigan was limited. It ran one day through Benton Harbor–Louisville train and a local between Benton Harbor and Anderson, Indiana. By 1925 only the Anderson local remained, and all trains north of Elkhart ended in the early 1930s. The Cincinnati Northern, stretching from Jackson to Cincinnati, supported a day local between Jackson and Cincinnati and a second to Van Wert. About

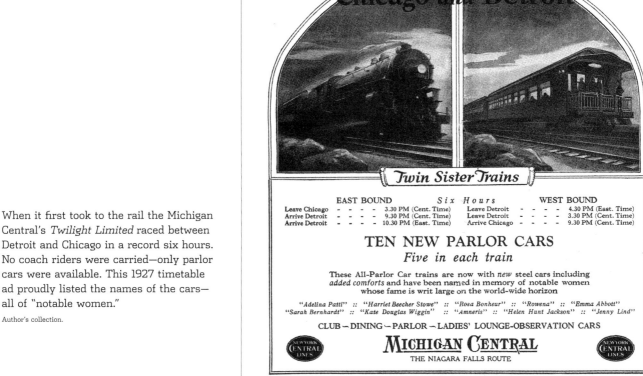

When it first took to the rail the Michigan Central's *Twilight Limited* raced between Detroit and Chicago in a record six hours. No coach riders were carried—only parlor cars were available. This 1927 timetable ad proudly listed the names of the cars— all of "notable women."

Author's collection.

1925 motor cars replaced the steam trains. By the late 1920s only the through local was running, and this was rearranged in about 1932 to be round-trip locals each way from Van Wert, Ohio, to the two ends of the road. In the mid-1930s the Van Wert–Jackson train came off, and only a few years later the Van Wert–Cincinnati service ended. The joint Big Four–Michigan Central's Detroit-Cincinnati service was a route of some importance. The norm was three runs a day to Cincinnati, with two of them handling through cars on connections to Indianapolis. Wintertime service usually expanded to four trains, the most famous of which was the *Royal Palm*, the premier Detroit-Florida train. Throughout these two decades this train ran on a "two nights and a day" schedule to Jacksonville. Opposite it was the "two days and a night" run of the *Ponce de Leon*. Both trains ran over the Southern Railway south of Cincinnati.

Niagara Falls De Luxe Special

A De Luxe Day Train Between

Chicago, Detroit and Buffalo

Via Niagara Falls

No Extra Charge for Individual De Luxe Seats

BRAND new cars—individual seats—beautifully finished interiors—carpeted aisles.

Latest type Michigan Central dining cars—
luncheon and dinner, a la carte.

Observation cars—carpeted—individual upholstered chairs.

Club-smoking car, with individual upholstered
chairs.

Train porter service. Lavatories with hot and
cold water.

Niagara Falls! The world's greatest moving
picture; train stops five minutes at Falls View.

Eastbound (Read Down)				Westbound (Read Up)
8.00 a.m. Lv.	Chicago	C.T. Ar.	8.30 p.m.
9.20 a.m. Lv.	Michigan City	" Lv.	7.07 p.m.
10.05 a.m. Lv.	Niles	" Lv.	6.22 p.m.
11.03 a.m. Lv.	Kalamazoo	" Lv.	5.25 p.m.
11.36 a.m. Lv.	Battle Creek	" Lv.	4.51 p.m.
12.30 p.m. Lv.	Jackson	" Lv.	4.00 p.m.
1.15 p.m. Lv.	Ann Arbor	" Lv.	3.15 p.m.
2.00 p.m. Ar.	Detroit	" Lv.	2.30 p.m.
3.05 p.m. Lv.	Detroit	E.T. Ar.	3.25 p.m.
3.20 p.m. Ar.	Windsor	" Lv.	3.10 p.m.
5.15 p.m. Ar.	St. Thomas	" Lv.	1.15 p.m.
7.23 p.m. Ar.	Falls View	" Lv.	11.03 a.m.
7.45 p.m. Ar.	Suspension Bridge	" Lv.	10.45 a.m.
7.53 p.m. Ar.	Niagara Falls, N. Y.	" Lv.	10.37 a.m.
8.30 p.m. Ar.	Buffalo	" Lv.	10.00 a.m.

MICHIGAN CENTRAL
The Niagara Falls Route

This 1929 Michigan Central timetable ad for the fast *Niagara Falls De Luxe Special* was not enough to save the train from the Great Depression.

Author's collection.

A Luxurious, Comfortable Lounge by day | *All ready for Your Night's Sleep*

Private Double Bedrooms on the Detroiter—

THE Detroiter is one of America's premier trains. In addition to valet service and an observation car, ladies lounge and bath, this train now has bedroom cars.

Also a commodious lounge car with current magazines, newspapers and stationery.

EASTWARD
Lv. Detroit - - - - 7.00 p. m.
Ar. New York - - - 9.27 a. m.

WESTWARD
Lv. New York - - - 6.30 p. m.
Ar. Detroit - - - - 8.45 a. m.

Dining Car open at 6.15 p. m. in Detroit, 6.00 p. m. in New York.

Tickets for occupancy of rooms between Detroit and New York by one person cost one and a quarter rail-road fares, plus double lower berth charge—or not greatly in excess of an ordinary section and materially less than a regular compartment, viz—

1¼ Rail Fares - - - - -	$30.90
Extra Fare - - - - -	3.00
Pullman Fare - - - - -	12.75
Total - - - -	$46.65

The rooms are equipped with upper berth and may be occupied by two persons at regular tariff rates.

MOTOR CITY SPECIAL

All-Pullman non-stop over-night sleeping car train of superior service including Single Bedroom Car between Chicago and Detroit.

Its Comfortable Lounge Car is a popular meeting place of business men from everywhere.

Valet Service for your Convenience

(Read down)			(Read up)
11.59 p.m.	Lv. Chicago	(Central Time)	Ar. 7.20 a.m.
6.50 a.m.	Ar. Detroit	(Central Time)	Lv. 11.30 p.m.
7.50 a.m.	Ar. Detroit	(Eastern Time)	Lv. 12.30 a.m.

Real Beds in Single Room Cars on the Motor City Special

These individual bedrooms were particularly designed for the occupancy of one person, but a door between each two rooms makes it possible to use them in suites of two.

The following tables show saving to the lone traveler who uses this car, the surcharge being included in the Pullman fares.

COMPARTMENT		SINGLE BEDROOM	
1¼ Rail Fares - -	$14.72	1¼ Rail Fares - -	$12.27
Pullman - - - -	10.50	Pullman - - - -	7.50
Total - - -	$25.22	Total - - -	$19.77

MICHIGAN CENTRAL
"The Niagara Falls Route."

This pair of timetable ads features two of the Michigan Central's trains. At the end of 1931, despite the Depression, both trains carried only sleeping car passengers.

Author's collection.

The Michigan Central itself operated about 12,000 passenger train-miles per day, as many per day as the Pere Marquette and the Grand Trunk Western combined. The mainstay service between Detroit and Chicago ran an average of ten trains each way during the 1920s. During 1922 and 1923 a peak service of eleven trains were run. The *Wolverine* ran on a twenty-four-hour schedule between Chicago and New York and the *Detroiter* between Detroit and New York overnight on a thirteen-hour–twenty-minute eastbound schedule. The *Michigan Central Limited* also had a twenty-four-hour run from Chicago to New York and ran via Niagara Falls. Between Detroit and Chicago the fastest running time was a little over six hours eastbound and seven hours westbound. The all-Pullman *Motor City Special* gave a leisurely eight-hour overnight ride with few intermediate stops. In 1926 the *Twilight Limited* was added to the Detroit-Chicago service, timed at six hours. With only parlor cars and charging an extra fare, it left Chicago at 3.00 P.M. and Detroit at 4.30 P.M. The latter was the latest westbound departure ever scheduled that did not operate overnight. In 1927 the MC added the *North Shore Limited* to its schedule on a twenty-one-hour run between Chicago and New York and in 1928 put on a Boston connection. The *Wolverine* was speeded up to a twenty-two-hour schedule and by 1930 was down to a twenty-hour run. All through the 1920s MC timetables advertised itself as "The Niagara Falls Route." The back cover of schedules touted the *Michigan Central Limited* and its successor, the *Trans-Atlantic Limited*. In 1929 it began the *Niagara Falls De Luxe Special* on a thirteen-hour–thirty-minute daytime run between Chicago and Buffalo. The *De Luxe* lasted only until 1931, then became a victim of the Depression.

During the 1930s the Michigan Central's Detroit-Chicago main line was unique: the two ends were major metropolitan areas and between them were a number of populous cities, several with major colleges. The MC issued a full-size timetable as if it were an independent road, and about 1930 began filling any white space it could find with half-page and full-page ads for its passenger trains. For a brief period in the early 1930s it showed schedules for some connecting air-line services out of Chicago and from Grand Rapids to Milwaukee. In 1931 the *Twilight Limited* began carrying coach passengers and dropped the extra fare charged to ride it, and in 1933 the *Wolverine* received the same changes. By 1933 Chicago-Detroit service was cut back to eight trains each way, and it stayed at this level until the beginning of World War II in 1941. But it did continue to upgrade the quality of its service. During the Chicago World's Fair in 1933 the MC renamed its *North Shore Limited* as the *Exposition Flyer*, although it went back to its former name in 1935. In 1933 it speeded up the *Twilight* to a five-hour–thirty-minute timing and speeded it more in 1935 to just five hours. In 1934 the MC began advertising that its major trains had air-conditioned cars. Before 1936 the entire New York Central system began experimenting with reduced round-trip ticket prices; in 1936 it reduced all coach fares to 2 cents a mile from over 3 cents.

Based on the success of the Cleveland-Detroit *Mercury*, the New York Central built a second set of streamlined equipment in 1938 for the train and extended its run to Chicago. Running on a four-hour–forty-five-minute time, it was the fastest train between Chicago and Detroit. At the same time, the MC speeded up the nonstreamlined *Twilight Limited* to an identical running time. Overall the MC main-line service was well designed to meet travelers' needs.

Throughout the 1920s the more important Michigan Central branch lines had little change in passenger service, but all others either lost all trains or were downgraded to mixed train service. The Detroit-Toledo run, no longer run independently but now integrated with the New York Central service out of Toledo after 1920, was the busiest at eleven trains each way by 1929. The Grand Rapids branch had, at different times, four or five trains each way, all of which made connections at Jackson with Detroit trains. The Detroit–Saginaw–Bay City and Jackson–Lansing–Saginaw–Bay City runs usually had four each way during the 1920s, although the Bay City–Mackinaw City service was cut back from three to two runs. During the 1930s the MC reduced all service north of its Detroit-Chicago main line. Grand Rapids runs dropped from five to three, Detroit–Bay City and Jackson–Bay City runs went from four to two, and the Mackinaw City run went to just one each way. Despite its importance as a link, the Detroit-Toledo service was reduced from eleven to seven runs each way. Overall, MC service in the United States dropped from about 12,000 train-miles per day in 1920 to just over 9,000 in 1931, and to just under 8,000 in 1939. Most of this reduction occurred in branch service, since the main line had about 6,000 miles per day in 1920 and just over 5,000 in 1939.

State legislators became so concerned at the number of passenger trains being removed that they passed legislation in 1941 to require a Public Service Commission hearing before the last trains on any line could be discontinued. Railroads could reduce the number of runs down to two a day each way without hearings, and seasonal passenger trains and short-term emergency reductions were exempted from the requirement. Few hearings were held during the war, but after 1946 the number did increase slowly.

As more and more passenger trains were dropped from the timetable, a new phenomenon developed, the "last run" train that marked the end of passenger service. Newspapers often reported the last run, and a few carried editorials regretting the end of an era, but one brought the report to new heights. Chet Shafer, in his "Three Rivers Doings" daily column in the *Chicago Journal of Commerce*, devoted two columns of purple prose to the last run through Three Rivers in December 1937. In advance of the day he reported that

> the High-Muckety-Mucks of the New York Central have capitulated— have complied with a request that the last passenger train to run through town, on Christmas Day, to wind up rail passenger traffic forever, will be equipped with an old-fashioned steam engine.
>
> On Christmas Day—in the graying dusk—an era will come to a close. But the sentimentalists here will have this satisfaction—they won't be compelled to list to the whamping and sputtering of the Diesel [a single-unit "doodlebug" that usually covered the run] that supplanted the locomotives on the L. S. & M. S. railroad fifteen years ago! This travesty—this flagrant insult to the nice proprieties—will remain in the roundhouse in Elkhart. And the epoch of railroad passenger transportation will, as a consequence, come to a close in keeping with traditions.

Shafer reported that NYC general manager J. L. McKee had instructed the engineer "to do plenty of whistling—and to wind out one long, mournful blast as a requiem."

A few days after Christmas Shafer recorded the event for posterity, and he claimed the entire town turned out for it. "The train came down out of the north with Christmas trees and red danger flares on the pilot—about a half-hour late. The conductor—Art VanGilder—collected a couple hundred cash fares from Moorepark and points north—at 10 cents each—and the New York Central Lines will be asked for a 10 per cent commission by the local promoters." He reported that "all scheduled speeches were drowned out by the local fire siren and the whistle of the locomotive—much to the crowd's appreciation." He concluded that "there were a lot of sentimentalists who turned out—mighty sorry to see her pull out—down over the railroad trestle—and disappear in the dark around the curve with a farewell blast of the whistle. Engineer

P. P. Perry—at the throttle of Engine 4322—marked the end of an epoch of passenger transportation—starting back in 1872."

SOURCES

American Association of Railroads. *Railroad Transportation: A Statistical Record.* Washington, D.C.: American Association of Railroads, various years.

Chicago & North Western Railway, public timetables, various dates.

Cook, Richard J., Sr. *New York Central's Mercury.* Lynchburg, Va.: TLC Publishing, 1991.

Duluth, South Shore & Atlantic Railway, public timetables, various dates.

Dunbar, Willis F. *All Aboard! A History of Railroads in Michigan.* Grand Rapids, Mich.: W. B. Eerdmans, 1969.

Grand Trunk Railway, public timetables, various dates.

Michigan Central Railroad, public timetables, various dates.

New York Central Railroad, public timetables, various dates.

The Official Guide of the Railways. New York: National Railway Publication, various dates.

Pennsylvania Railroad, public timetables, various dates.

Pere Marquette Railroad, public timetables, various dates.

Wabash Railway, public timetables, various dates.

The End of the Interurban

In the ten years between 1895 and 1905 the electric interurban transformed itself from a novelty to an important form of intercity transport. It rode that crest for two decades, then as quickly as it had appeared in Michigan it disappeared. Its life spanned barely forty years.

James Couzens took the Detroit mayor's office in 1919. A man wealthy from his early investment in the Ford Motor Company, he felt certain that a resolution could be found to the demand for municipal ownership of the city street car lines. The agitation had gone on for nearly twenty-five years, and, despite good-faith efforts on both sides, it was no closer to being settled than when Mayor Hazen Pingree first raised it before the turn of the century. The city tried to force the issue by continually hectoring Detroit United Railways with franchise demands. Couzens finally persuaded the city and the DUR to agree to a $31.5 million purchase price. The deal, along with a $24 million bond issue to finance it, was put to the voters. After heated debate the voters gave the proposal a simple majority in favor, but which fell short of the needed 60 percent approval. The next year, in 1920, Couzens put forward a plan for the city to build its own municipal system of about 100 miles of line, together with a $15 million bond issue. This squeaked by with 63 percent of the vote and the Department of Street Railways (DSR) began building some lines. The St. Jean–Charlevoix line was the first completed, in January 1921.

For the DUR, the DSR was transformed into a threat. Couzens brought the DUR back to the bargaining table, and finally, after considerable dickering, the DUR agreed to sell all of its remaining city lines for $19,850,000. This went to the voters, who again agreed in sufficient numbers. The city took ownership on 14 May 1922, but what it got for its money was nothing to be proud of. The years of wrangling, with the DUR's future neither clear nor certain, encouraged the company to put just enough money into its tracks and cars to keep them operating, but no more. The tracks and cars were completely run-down. Mayor Couzens, to his personal advantage, was appointed U.S. senator and was able to leave the mess to his successor.

After the DUR sold its city tracks it was allowed to use the DSR tracks to operate its trains into downtown Detroit, but the arrangement was not inexpensive—so much so that in 1924 the DUR stopped running its trains from Flint, Port Huron, and Toledo into downtown Detroit; passengers had to transfer at the city limits to a connecting DUR bus. Ridership continued to decline, forcing the DUR into receivership in 1925. That year it ended service on the Ypsilanti-Saline and Wayne-Northville branches. In 1927 the Farmington–Orchard Lake, Romeo–Imlay City, and Wyandotte branch services ended, as did the Plymouth-Northville run in 1928.

In August and September 1928 the DUR reorganized itself into two new companies, the Eastern Michigan–Toledo for its Toledo line and the Eastern Michigan for the remainder of its lines. The DUR left the Detroit, Jackson & Chicago out of the reorganization and canceled its lease of the road. That left that road to fend for itself, which it managed to do until September 1929, when it gave up the ghost and was abandoned. The Eastern Michigan ended service to Port Huron in May 1928, although Detroit's DSR maintained service as far as Mt. Clemens for a short time. The DSR also took over service to Wyandotte and Farmington to replace the DUR. In April 1931 all service north of Royal Oak, to Pontiac, Flint, and Romeo, ended. Through some legal maneuvering the city of Royal Oak managed to take control of the lines

Consolidated Time Table — ELECTRIC and DELUXE MOTOR COACH
DETROIT — JACKSON — BATTLE CREEK — KALAMAZOO — GRAND RAPIDS

WEST AND NORTH BOUND READ DOWN SUBJECT TO CHANGE WITHOUT NOTICE

STATIONS Central Standard Time
Lv. DETROIT Lv.
YPSILANTI
ANN ARBOR
Ar. JACKSON Ar.
Lv. JACKSON Lv.
PARMA
ALBION
MARSHALL
BATTLE CREEK
CAMP CUSTER
AUGUSTA
GALESBURG
Ar. KALAMAZOO Ar.
Lv. KALAMAZOO Lv.
PLAINWELL
MARTIN
SHELBYVILLE
BRADLEY
WAYLAND
MOLINE
Ar. GRAND RAPIDS Ar.

‡ Daily Except Sunday and Holidays between Grand Rapids and Kalamazoo.   * Daily Except Sundays between Kalamazoo and Jackson.

GRAND RAPIDS — KALAMAZOO — BATTLE CREEK — JACKSON — DETROIT

SOUTH AND EAST BOUND   READ DOWN

STATIONS Central Time
Lv. GRAND RAPIDS Lv.
MOLINE
WAYLAND
BRADLEY
SHELBYVILLE
MARTIN
PLAINWELL
Ar. KALAMAZOO Ar.
Lv. KALAMAZOO Lv.
GALESBURG
AUGUSTA
CAMP CUSTER
BATTLE CREEK
MARSHALL
ALBION
PARMA
Ar. JACKSON Ar.
Lv. JACKSON Lv.
ANN ARBOR
YPSILANTI
Ar. DETROIT Ar.

‡ Daily Except Sunday and Holidays—Grand Rapids to Kalamazoo.   * Daily Except Sunday—Kalamazoo to Jackson.

Consolidated Time Table — ELECTRIC AND DELUXE MOTOR COACH
JACKSON — LANSING — OWOSSO — ST. JOHNS

NORTH BOUND READ DOWN   SUBJECT TO CHANGE WITHOUT NOTICE

STATIONS Central Time
Lv. DETROIT Lv.
YPSILANTI
ANN ARBOR
Ar. JACKSON Ar.
Lv. JACKSON Lv.
RIVES JCT.
LESLIE
EDEN
MASON
HOLT
Ar. LANSING Ar.
Lv. LANSING Lv.
EAST LANSING
PINE LAKE
HASLETT
SHAFTSBURG
PERRY
MORRICE
Ar. OWOSSO Ar.
Lv. LANSING Lv.
FRANKLIN AVE.
DEWITT
Ar. ST. JOHNS Ar.

ST. JOHNS — OWOSSO — LANSING — JACKSON
SOUTH BOUND   READ DOWN

STATIONS Central Time
Lv. ST. JOHNS Lv.
DEWITT
FRANKLIN AVE.
Ar. LANSING Ar.
Lv. OWOSSO Lv.
MORRICE
PERRY
SHAFTSBURG
HASLETT
PINE LAKE
EAST LANSING
Ar. LANSING Ar.
Lv. LANSING Lv.
HOLT
MASON
EDEN
LESLIE
RIVES JCT.
Ar. JACKSON Ar.
Lv. JACKSON Lv.
ANN ARBOR
YPSILANTI
Ar. DETROIT Ar.

D Daily.   * Daily Except Sunday.   ‡ Does Not Run Sunday Jackson to Lansing.   † Sunday Only.   § Sat. & Sun. Only.

The end was only a year away when the Michigan Electric issued this August 1928 schedule. This successor of the Michigan United no longer ran any trains on its high-speed line between Kalamazoo and Grand Rapids. Between Kalamazoo and Jackson the company ran more buses than trains.

Author's collection.

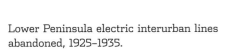

Lower Peninsula electric interurban lines
abandoned, 1925–1935.

KEY
━━━ Interurban lines abandoned.

in that city and contracted with the DSR to operate out Woodward
Avenue as far as Royal Oak. The Detroit-Toledo service was the last of
the major DUR services to end, with its final run in October 1932. Only
scattered DUR operations inside a few cities remained after 1930, which
soon were either abandoned or turned over to new owners to provide
municipal operation.

The experience of the Michigan Railway system, which took over
operations of Michigan United in 1919, was much like that of the DUR.
After the end of World War I it began showing losses largely because
of its high fixed charges, such as interest and taxes. Its newest and
highest-quality route, the high-speed third rail line between Grand
Rapids and Kalamazoo, produced disappointing revenues. The Battle
Creek–Allegan line that had been bought and electrified added nothing.

Detroit's Department of Street Railways (DSR) car 228 at Palmer Park. The DSR bought a total of 186 new cars between 1945 and 1949. These were known as PCC—President's Conference Committee—cars, the most modern built in the United States at the time. The cars had a short life in Detroit; 183 of the PCC cars were sold to Mexico City.

Thomas Dworman photo, Jack E. Schramm collection.

A handful of interurban cars had a second life—becoming a roadside diner. The Silver Diner at Parma and another at Martin were among the very few so fortunate.

Sam Breck collection.

System ridership dropped each passing year, forcing the company into receivership in October 1924. The Michigan's owner, Commonwealth Power and Light, had no desire to lose more money. In 1924 the lease of the Grand Rapids, Holland & Chicago was canceled and several other short branches discontinued. In August 1928 the Kalamazoo–Grand Rapids and Battle Creek–Allegan runs were ended, and in November the Jackson–Battle Creek–Kalamazoo service ceased. In 1929 the service from Jackson, through Lansing, to St. Johns and Owosso, ended, followed soon after by the remnants of the Bay City–Saginaw–Flint service and the branch to Frankenmuth. That same year all of the Michigan Railway's city lines were sold to new owners. Michigan's second largest interurban company disappeared even more quickly than had the Detroit United.

Small non-Detroit companies fared no better. The Grand Rapids, Holland & Chicago was not able to continue after the Michigan Railway system canceled its lease of the road. It ended service in November 1926, except for a short section through Grandville that was sold to the United Suburban Railway. The company was owned by some 700 area residents who bought the line between Grand Rapids and Jenison and managed to keep it going until June 1932, when the Grandville Avenue streetcar line was slated for abandonment by the city lines. Sidney L. Vaughan and Wilmot K. Morley, executive officers of the Grand Rapids, Grand Haven & Muskegon, bought that road in 1924 from the United Light and Power Company. It went into receivership in 1926 and ended operations in April 1928. The Benton Harbor–St. Joe Railway & Light ended operations on its two interurban lines to Watervliet and Dowagiac in 1928, after a controversy with the city of Benton Harbor. The company provided the city both electricity and streetcar service, but residents thought the traction part was subsidized by high electric rates. The company sold its city streetcar service, which was continued until 1935 as the Twin City Railway. The Toledo, Ottawa Beach & Northern ended service in 1927.

In the Upper Peninsula the first line to fail was its newest, the Iron River, Stambaugh & Crystal Falls, which stopped running in 1921. The Ishpeming-Negaunee line was abandoned in 1927. Three companies lasted until 1932, when the Escanaba Traction, the Ironwood & Bessemer, and the Houghton County Traction were torn up. The Houghton company went into receivership in 1921 as a result of the sharp decline in copper mining after World War I. Throughout its life it faced its annual battle with severe snowstorms and the perpetual stream of ship traffic on Portage Lake that caused delays in using the lift bridge between Hancock and Houghton. City streetcar lines in Menominee (and sister city Marinette, Wisconsin) lasted until 1928, ending service because it lost the use of the Menominee River bridge that connected the two cities. Sault Ste. Marie streetcars ran until 1931, but the company continued the city cars in Sault Ste. Marie, Ontario, until 1941. The last of Upper Peninsula services, the Marquette City & Presque Isle, ended all electric operations in April 1935. In its last months it divided the day's receipts as pay for its employees.

The Southern Michigan ended its passenger runs between South Bend, Indiana, Niles, and St. Joseph on 1 June 1934. This ended the era of interurban passenger transportation in the state of Michigan. A short piece of this line, between South Bend and St. Mary's College, stayed in operation until April 1936. Across the state the Toledo & Western was the last electric interurban to operate in Michigan. Faced with diminishing traffic it stopped its city streetcars in Adrian in 1924, terminating its trains at the Wabash station east of the city. It stopped running into downtown Toledo in 1925, and ended all of its passenger runs to Toledo-Morenci-Pioneer, Ohio, and Toledo-Adrian in July 1933. The revenue from its freight operations kept the T&W going as long as it did, but ultimately profits disappeared. The Toledo-Adrian freight service ended in June 1935. It sold off its Adrian-Blissfield line to the steam-operated Blissfield Railroad, a road that shut down in November 1936.

The city streetcar lines barely survived the interurbans. Muskegon city service ended in 1929, Port Huron cars stopped in 1930, and Saginaw service ended the next year. Battle Creek and Kalamazoo saw their last city cars in 1932, and Lansing its in 1933. In Grand Rapids a fire in 1924 destroyed part of its car fleet. General Manager Louis Delamarter let the riders decide which of three car builders should supply the replacements. Delamarter, who not above any public relations ploy, tried hard to keep his company going, but expenses continued to climb as ridership dropped. When the last car ran in August 1935 Grand Rapids became the largest city in the United States to have buses furnish all public transportation. Benton Harbor–St. Joseph cars also stopped in 1935, followed by Jackson and Flint in 1936.

This left only the city of Detroit's DSR, which abandoned line after line for the next twenty years. In Detroit the last car on Michigan Avenue ran in September 1955, on Gratiot Avenue in March 1956. With the end of service on the Woodward Avenue line in April 1956, all electric streetcar operations were gone in Michigan.

In the 1860s and 1870s the horsecar revolutionized travel within cities, allowing them to grow in area as they had not been able to up

400   Chapter Five

to that time. In the 1890s electricity was brought to them, and that allowed even greater expansion of municipalities with more reliable transport. Electric operations also made intercity movements possible. The development of the intercity electric interurban changed American society. If brought mobility, convenience, and affordability for local and short-distance travelers that was unprecedented. Casual and social travel became possible. An evening in the city at the theater became a possibility for those living thirty and more miles away from the city center. A Sunday excursion to a park or resort, often owned by the interurban line, became a popular form of relaxation.

The end came, first, from the competition from the newly popular automobile running on state-financed improved highways, as well as new competition from bus lines that ran on those same highways. Second, the roads took on debt to purchase equipment and build a line, incurring relatively high fixed interest charges that placed a burden that they never overcame. By the 1920s many the roads needed to improve their lines or buy better equipment. By then revenues were already in a decline, which made it difficult if not impossible to raise the money for the improvements. Third, most lines were built to low engineering standards, which made it difficult to achieve satisfactory running speeds outside of cities; in cities they used center-of-the-street city streetcar tracks at even lower running speeds. Last, the revenues that were declining were obtained largely from passengers; most lines had very modest freight traffic to supplement the declining passenger traffic. When passenger revenues evaporated there was nothing to replace them. But it was the automobile, more convenient and cheaper, that took away the passengers and forced the interurban from the scene.

SOURCES

Due, John F. "The Rise and Decline of the Midwest Interurban." *Railroad Magazine* 61:4 (September 1953).

Dunbar, Willis F. *Michigan: A History of the Wolverine State.* Grand Rapids, Mich.: W. B. Eerdmans, 1970.

Fuller, George N. *Michigan: A Centennial History.* 2 vols. Chicago: Lewis Publishing, 1939.

Hilton, George W., and John F. Due. *The Electric Interurban Railways in America.* Stanford, Calif.: Stanford University Press, 1960.

Zink, Maximillian A., George Krambles, eds. *Electric Railways of Michigan, Bulletin 103.* Chicago: Central Electric Railfans' Association, 1959.

"Wreck!" Part 3

The years between the world wars saw a very welcome reduction in the number of railroad wrecks as well as in the number of persons killed and injured. Several improvements brought this about. The wooden passenger cars had been largely replaced by steel ones, which did not collapse on impact or burst into flames from the potbellied stoves or the gas lighting inside. Out on the line, the signal systems were improved further to protect movements. The automatic block signal system, as it was used on double-track lines, prevented following trains from getting too close to the rear of a train ahead, which reduced rear-end collisions. On their single-track lines, some of the larger companies, most notably the New York Central system and the Pennsylvania, began the use of a manual block signal system, which prevented opposing and controlled following train movements between the two open stations at the end of each block. The manual block system provided a second overlay of safety precautions that supplemented train order operations. Most of the accidents that did occur were caused by a derailment often on faulty track, a low-speed collision caused by an employee misreading train orders, or a collision with a highway vehicle. Between 1920 and 1945 no wreck on a railroad resulted in more than three fatalities.

In July 1925 the Ann Arbor Railroad station agent at Farwell did not make enough copies of a train order and consequently did not deliver copies of it to a westbound passenger train. This order directed the passenger to go into the siding at Lake George to meet an eastbound freight train. The freight was on the main track at the water tank when the passenger came around the curve just east of the tank. The passenger engineman applied his brakes but could not stop in time. An employee on the freight engine died, and four others on the passenger train were injured. In November 1926 the Michigan Central experienced a collision that could have been more serious than the Lake George accident. A southbound freight train hauling sand left Lake Orion with its crew planning to go into the siding at Goodison to meet a northbound passenger train. The freight crew had barely sufficient time to run to Goodison, and not enough if they observed the speed limit and got onto the siding at least five minutes before the passenger was due, as the rules required. Apparently the train's brakes did not work properly as it prepared to stop for the Goodison siding. The train ran by the siding switch, finally stopping on the main track just north of the depot. The engineman said he planned to go into a second siding south of the depot, but found that track blocked by another freight train. While deciding what to do, the northbound passenger train came up. It rounded the depot curve at about forty miles per hour; the engineman saw the red manual block signal at the depot just ahead and made an emergency brake application. The passenger train's speed was too great to stop in time, and its engine collided with the freight's. The result was the death of a fireman and injuries to twenty passengers and sixteen others.

Trouble continued to dog the Michigan Central. In March 1931 the towerman at West Detroit was moving a Toledo-bound (southbound) passenger train around the wye track normally used by northbound trains. To prepare for the next movement, a northbound yard run, he had opened a switch from a yard track onto the wye track. Apparently he overlooked that this switch was set wrong for the passenger train. The passenger train came up to the switch at about ten miles per hour, saw that it was set for the yard; the engineman applied its brakes, but collided with the yard run. The result was slight damage to both locomotives, and one employee and forty passengers were injured. In February 1938 a severe electrical storm occurred between Trenton and Monroe, causing a loss of power to some automatic block signals and false "stop" indications to appear in others. After the storm an exceptionally thick fog covered the area. A southbound Michigan Central Detroit-Toledo passenger crept along because of the limited visibility, stopped at each signal as required by company rules, and then moved ahead at the mandated ten miles per hour. A following passenger train found the same conditions south of Trenton, but rolled at low speeds past each of the signals without stopping. About four miles north of Monroe it ran into the train ahead, which had stopped for a signal and had not protected its rear with a red fusee. The rear-end collision injured ten passengers and four employees.

In August 1942 a rare collision of two trains at a crossing occurred at Raisin Center. The signals at the crossing were controlled by a system that automatically operated the signals when a train approached. The first train to approach received "proceed" signals; a second train would have to wait for the first to cross before it received a "proceed" signal. A northbound New York Central freight was ambling across when a westbound Wabash passenger train neared. For whatever reason the Wabash engineman did not reduce speed when he passed a signal more than a mile east of the crossing that indicated the signal at the crossing was at "stop." At 1,800 feet from the crossing, and with the "stop" signal in plain view, the Wabash engineman applied the brakes. The train slowed, but ran into the freight train at thirty-five miles per hour. Both men on the Wabash engine were killed, and sixteen others were injured.

In June 1945 a head-on collision between a freight train and a passenger train took place on the Michigan Central at Eaton Rapids. A train order was issued for the westbound night passenger train and an eastbound freight train to meet at Eaton Rapids, with the freight train to take the siding. The passenger train stopped to do station work. For an unknown reason the freight train did not go onto the siding west of the depot but continued to proceed at speed on the main track. It was unclear whether the brakes on the freight train were applied before the collision, but the passenger train crew said the freight train was running at about forty miles per hour when it hit. The engineman and forward brakeman of the freight train died in the wreck, while fifty-four passengers and seven employees were injured.

Train derailments increased. In January 1929 a Pere Marquette freight train derailed as it operated over poor track near Fenwick. The train was running at between ten and fifteen miles per hour when the accident happened. The fireman and head brakeman died when the engine overturned, and the engineman was hospitalized. This section of the line was abandoned in 1933. In July 1929 an Ann Arbor westbound freight train derailed at a washout under the tracks a few miles east of Pomona. The engineman and fireman died when the engine went over on its side, and the brakeman was injured.

In May 1930 a Grand Trunk Western passenger train headed for Chicago was derailed at Belsay Yard east of Flint. The track going from one main track to the other is called a crossover, and apparently the east crossover switch was left open when track workers moved their work. The GTW was then installing an automatic block signal system that would have indicated to the approaching train that the switch was open. Trains may use crossovers at a speed of between ten and fifteen miles per hour. The passenger train was running at forty miles per hour or more when it came to the switch. The locomotive and seven of the train's ten cars derailed. The engineman and fireman died in the wreck, and twelve others were injured.

In September 1931 a Pere Marquette mixed train derailed. The accident took place as the train rounded the sharply curved connecting wye track at Edmore while running from Grand Rapids to Saginaw. Trains using this connection between the line to Grand Rapids and the line to Saginaw were restricted to a speed of eight miles per hour. The engineman and fireman were killed when the locomotive tipped off the track rounding the curve at a speed estimated to be at least fifteen miles per hour and probably higher.

Collisions with vehicles grew into a more serious problem as the number of automobiles increased. In September 1924 a Michigan Central passenger train struck and demolished an automobile that was stuck on the tracks near Kalamazoo. Debris from the car wedged under the engine, derailing it and the eleven-car train. The engineman died, and twenty-five passengers and two employees were injured. In August 1942 a Pere Marquette passenger train struck a car at Green Oak, the first station west of South Lyon. Part of the wreckage derailed the locomotive and five of the seven cars. The driver of the car was killed instantly, as were the engineman and fireman, while twenty-three passengers were injured. A Michigan Central collided with an automobile at Sibley in December 1944, resulting in two deaths and twenty-five more injured.

On 31 October 1945, just less than six months after the end of the war in Germany, one of Michigan's most regrettable vehicle collisions occurred. Many of the more than 7,000 prisoners of war held at Fort Custer were detailed to farms to overcome the shortage of agricultural workers. Late that day a truck was headed up Silberhorn Road carrying twenty-four German prisoners from the sugar beet fields back to their quarters at Blissfield. At the railroad crossing the driver apparently could not see to the east, pulled onto the crossing, and was struck by a westbound New York Central passenger train. Fourteen prisoners died instantly, and two more and their guard died soon after. The bodies of the sixteen prisoners were returned to Battle Creek and now rest in the German section of the Fort Custer National Cemetery.

The accident record for the interurban companies was quite good, with the exception of the Detroit United system, which went on in its appalling way. In September 1920 a rear-end collision at Ortonville killed four and injured twelve. A head-on collision west of Ann Arbor in June 1921 killed three and injured twenty-four. In July that year a westbound train pulled into the Warsaw siding west of Ann Arbor to meet an eastbound train. The conductor left the switch open for a following second section of his train. Apparently the second section had braking problems, went into the siding, and smashed into the rear of the first section. The collision caused three passengers' deaths and twenty-four injuries; two of those injured died later. Another rear-end collision in June 1923 killed one and injured fifteen. In December 1924 a train running at normal speed struck a truck trailer in Wyandotte, which resulted in five deaths and ten more injured, all on the train. This was followed in August 1925 by a head-on collision killing one and injuring seventeen. This was followed a year later, in September 1926, by the DUR's most serious accident, a head-on collision at Monroe that caused ten deaths and injuries to thirty-six more.

By this time the DUR was in such poor financial shape that it had no money to install any kind of signal system that might reduce the likelihood of either head-on or rear-end collisions. In March 1928 the second section of a westbound DUR train collided with an eastbound train at Austin siding, a short distance west of Wayne. The crew of the eastbound train overlooked its orders to meet the other at Austin. The two trains were moving at low speeds when the two cars struck head-on, but the result was the death of one passenger and the injury of twenty-five riders. The DUR's last serious accident occurred at Ortonville in June 1929. A northbound freight train went into the siding to allow a following passenger train to pass it. Before the conductor could reset the switch to the main track, the passenger train came up, rolled into the siding, and struck the rear of the freight train. Although no one died as a result, sixty passengers and an employee were injured.

SOURCE

U.S. Interstate Commerce Commission, Report of Accident Investigation, various
   reports individually printed.

World War II

The wars in Europe and Asia began larger in the late 1930s and started to lift America's economy, and, as a result, U.S. railroads emerged out of the slump of the severe depression that had lasted nearly ten years. As the economy built up steam the railroads benefited from the increases in war matériel freight shipments to both continents. The revenues in 1940 were $4.3 billion and the best since 1930, and in 1941 they increased by another $1 billion. America did not enter hostilities officially until December 1941, after the attack on Pearl Harbor, but the amount of freight hauled by railroads increased almost 20 percent in 1939, in 1940 by another 10 percent, and in 1941 by another 25 percent to an all-time record of 513 billion ton-miles. The peak war year was 1944, when the rails moved 785 billion ton-miles, a record not ever matched again.

There was no time to prepare for mobilization. Of the investments made in the 1920s, and after nearly a decade of skimping and saving during the Depression, tracks, buildings, cars, and locomotives were run down or worn out. But as traffic increased the railroads took on the challenge and moved it. In 1940 President Franklin Delano Roosevelt named Ralph Budd, president of the Chicago, Burlington & Quincy, to be the nation's transportation commissioner, and later to be director of transportation to coordinate the different forms of transportation. After Pearl Harbor the Office of Defense Transportation was created to continue Budd's program on a formal basis, and Joseph Eastman was named its director. By using this approach the government avoided the need to take over railroad operations as it had done during World War I.

From Pearl Harbor to V-J Day, U.S. railroads handled 97 percent of all domestic troop movements and 90 percent of all domestic military supplies and equipment. More than forty-three million soldiers and sailors were moved in 115,000 troop trains. It may not have been the most pleasant travel circumstances for the troops, but the job got done. In addition to the military needs, gasoline and tire rationing took travelers out of their automobiles and into trains. Passenger-miles were five times as great in 1944 as in 1940. This was done while the government charged a 15 percent wartime excise tax to discourage civilian travel.

The government placed few restrictions on travel during the war. For the traveler, the greatest nuisance was crowded trains, and the principal difficulty was finding sleeping-car space, but no trains were dropped from the schedules because of the war effort. Michigan's summer season trains ran to northern Michigan through the 1942 season, then did not run again until 1946. Late in the war a few sleeping-car routes shorter than 200 miles were dropped. In Michigan this affected the Chicago–Grand Rapids and Chicago-Muskegon runs on the Pere Marquette. The Grand Trunk Western's Detroit-Muskegon sleeper survived only because its 199.9-mile ran was rounded up to 200 miles.

Located just west of Battle Creek on the Michigan Central, Fort Custer, Michigan's largest army base, was roused from its tranquil state and made into a basic training post for the army. In five years it saw a constant stream of troop trains to move some 300,000 inductees who passed through it. For a time after the war it served as a separation post. Railroad stations in some larger cities acquired a Red Cross

HOW YOU CAN HELP

Rail travel in wartime is definitely not "as usual." Like all railroads, Pere Marquette is engaged in the biggest double-barrelled job in its history . . . handling increased civilian travel, at the same time carrying military traffic of total war.

People in war industries are traveling more . . . on necessary business. More folks are riding trains since war denied them new cars and tires. Troops are moving in greater and greater numbers. Increased war tempo demands increased essential travel. So, sometimes you won't find a railroad journey as simple and comfortable as it used to be . . . or as we should like it to be, as war needs come first. By following these suggestions, you'll be making travel easier for yourself . . . and, at the same time, you'll be serving your Uncle Sam.

Here are some hints that will help your country and yourself

☆ Travel during mid-week, rather than on congested week-ends.

☆ Plan your trip in advance; purchase your railroad and Pullman tickets in advance, preferably at our city ticket office, and avoid delay at station.

☆ If your trip is postponed, immediate cancellation of your reservation will make room for someone else.

☆ When your customary Pullman space is not available, accept other accommodations or use coach service.

☆ Travel "light"; there's no room on crowded trains for superfluous luggage.

☆ Buy round-trip tickets — save time for yourself and the ticket seller.

☆ Don't waste transportation; avoid unnecessary travel — buy War Bonds instead.

WARTIME DINING CAR SERVICE

More diners . . . but no more dining cars.

More meals to serve . . . but less of many important foods to go around.

That is the wartime dining car situation.

With no additional dining cars being built . . . with some of our present cars busy serving the armed forces . . . the number available for our greatly increased passenger traffic will remain limited for the duration.

At the same time, many of our chefs, stewards and waiters . . . hard men to replace . . . have exchanged their New York Central uniforms for those of Uncle Sam.

That is why most dining cars and crews must now do double wartime duty.

That is why some peacetime niceties are omitted . . . why meals are simplified to speed service . . . and why menus are planned to make the most of rationed foods.

From now till Victory we will go on serving you to the best of our ability. In the meantime, thanks for your aid and understanding in today's difficult situation.

NEW YORK CENTRAL

USO building. These temporary wooden buildings, painted white and trimmed in red, were staffed with volunteers who met each train and provided traveling soldiers with coffee and doughnuts.

Detroit's automobile industry retooled itself. Almost overnight its output changed to military vehicles, combat vehicles, tanks, aircraft, aircraft parts, marine equipment, guns, artillery, and engines of all sorts. Ford Motor Company built the mammoth Willow Run plant, which by mid-1942 had 42,000 men and women at work, and produced 8,685 B-24 bombers, more than came from any other factory in the nation. Other war matériel came from Flint, Grand Rapids, Kalamazoo, Bay City, Lansing, Muskegon, and a good many smaller towns. K rations came from Kellogg in Battle Creek, and Dow Chemical in Midland produced wartime chemicals.

By war's end over 600,000 Michigan men and women served in the

Two advertisements in railroad timetables that appeared during World War II.

Author's collection.

armed forces. Despite labor shortages, strikes, and a race riot in Detroit, Michigan was at the forefront of what made America the "Arsenal of Democracy."

SOURCES

Dunbar, Willis F. *Michigan: A History of the Wolverine State*. Grand Rapids, Mich.: W. B. Eerdmans, 1970.

Stover, John F. *American Railroads*. Chicago: University of Chicago Press, 1961.

The Waning Years, 1945–1976

The End of the Line?

World War II changed American society profoundly. The automobile became a necessity. A new house in the suburbs, new kinds of businesses, and the increased desire for higher education all characterized the postwar years, but are outside the scope of this work. The railroads turned to an overhaul of their physical plant after years of wartime stress. They designed new and more powerful higher-speed steam locomotives. They ordered new freight cars of all varieties and also a large fleet of new passenger cars. Between 1948 and 1953 the railroads spent more than $1 billion annually, about three-quarters of it for new equipment and the remainder for track and buildings. This was done in expectation of a return of the good times they had enjoyed before 1930.

But after spending nearly $10 billion in the eight years after the war the hoped-for profits did not appear. Net profits for the year 1954 were no higher than those earned in the best year during the war, and at the same time the rails' share of national freight traffic hauled dropped below 50 percent for the first time in history. Revenue ton-miles of freight were down about 10 percent although revenues were up by about one-third. Passenger traffic dropped off after the war, and the costs of the service increased, at least by the formula of the Interstate Commerce Commission (ICC). The first imperative for the railroads to improve their financial condition was to get operating costs under control. Companies began a wholesale conversion to diesel-electric locomotives, to replace ancient, old, and modern steam locomotives. This represented the largest share of the capital costs incurred for equipment. As will be seen below, the changeover began in earnest in 1946 and was substantially complete by the early 1960s.

Unneeded real estate went on the block. Employment remained steady, but salary and benefit costs increased by nearly one-third. The ICC continued to delay rate increases that the roads thought crucial and allowed abandonment nationwide of only about 4,000 miles of the most marginal of lines. Under these restraints the rails could only watch as their share of intercity freight continued to drop as trucking companies doubled their volume. Oil traffic went to pipelines; livestock went to trucks. Newer high-value commodities went almost exclusively by truck and much of that in company-owned fleets.

For rail passenger service the future was especially bleak. Travel dropped by a third in 1946 from the year before and another third the next year. Every year after, with one exception, fewer riders took the train. Airlines, supported by federal and local tax financing, became the preferred mode for long-distance travelers. Automobiles completely took away the short-distance market. The interstate highway system, begun in the early 1950s and financed by the taxpayers under the guise of a national defense project, made the demise of the passenger train a certainty. The railroads' investment in new cars and trains brought them nothing, for by the mid-1960s ridership had sunk to 20 percent of the level of twenty years earlier. To protect themselves the railroads began dropping trains as quickly as they could. The ICC response to this was predictable: it began regulating passenger train service quality and discontinuances. The result was drawn-out hearings that changed no public attitudes and only delayed the inevitable.

Freight rate increases helped to maintain profitability, but net income stalled at about $1 billion per year until the early 1950s; then it began to slide. The rails' return on investment shrunk to around 3 percent, barely half the level even the ICC believed was desirable. There appeared to be only three ways out of the financial problems the railroads faced: holding companies, mergers, and sharp reductions in labor costs. Pioneered by Ben W. Heineman of the Chicago & North Western, the holding company was a revolutionary concept for the rail industry in the mid-1950s. He created Northwest Industries, put the railroad into it, then went out shopping for other businesses. Once the holding company concept eventually passed regulatory muster, other roads began to adopt it. Mergers have been a way of life for railroads, but in the late 1950s the pace accelerated. After laborious hearings the ICC approved the Chesapeake & Ohio's control of the Baltimore & Ohio in 1963. The next year the Norfolk & Western took over the Wabash and the Nickel Plate to greatly enlarge its system. In 1967 the Atlantic Coast Line and the Seaboard Air Line joined to become the Seaboard Coast Line. In 1968 the largest merger ever took place. Ten years after the first discussions and five and one-half years after the ICC began

Roll in luxury on

The PERE MARQUETTES

The *Pere Marquette*s were introduced on 10 August 1946. With specially designed "Sleepy Hollow" coach seats assigned by reservation, and no tipping allowed in the diner-lounge, the trains were an instant success.

Author's collection.

its hearings, the New York Central and Pennsylvania Railroads finally merged to become Penn Central. In 1970 a still larger one was consummated: the Great Northern, the Northern Pacific, the Burlington, and the Spokane, Portland & Seattle merged to form the Burlington Northern. The Seaboard Coast Line acquired several other southern roads. Only one road took aggressive moves to reduce labor costs. The Florida East Coast began running freight trains with small crews and no cabooses, was struck by the brotherhoods, and then continued to operate with non-union employees.

Getting rid of the losses from passenger train operations was finally accomplished in May 1971 when the government-sponsored Amtrak took over intercity service. But even removing these losses did not strengthen the railroads to any great extent. One spotlight on this problem came in June 1970 when Penn Central went bankrupt. In short order it was followed by the Ann Arbor, the Lehigh Valley, the Erie-Lackawanna, and the Rock Island line. Whatever failings on whatever side contributed to these downfalls, Washington finally took notice. At last the federal government was convinced that there was a severe financial problem that affected every American railroad to some extent.

In 1976 the government formed Conrail out of pieces of Penn Central and several other bankrupt eastern carriers. For the first time in history Conrail was allowed a solution to the one of the major problems that had brought down its constituents. It was acknowledged that there were too many branch lines hauling too little freight and that there were too many duplicating main lines. Since it did not have to get ICC approval, Conrail pruned these ruthlessly and in so doing laid the groundwork for a new approach to railroading in the United States.

SOURCES

Dunbar, Willis F. *All Aboard! A History of Railroads in Michigan*. Grand Rapids,
     Mich.: W. B. Eerdmans, 1969.

Saunders, Richard. *The Railroad Mergers and the Coming of Conrail*. Westport,
     Conn.: Greenwood, 1978.

Stover, John F. *American Railroads*. Chicago: University of Chicago Press, 1961.

The Situation in Michigan

In his history of Michigan railroads Willis Dunbar describes the period after World War II in a chapter entitled "The Iron Horse Wheezes and Expires." Although a somewhat overdramatic title, it does convey much of the feeling about the future of railroads when it was written in 1969. At that time the railroad industry had been in decline for almost forty years, since the early 1930s. World War II brought a spike of prosperity, but the decline resumed soon after the war's end. Nationally, and in Michigan as well, freight traffic, train miles, miles of road, and profits declined, and passenger traffic plummeted.

At the end of 1945 Michigan had 6,954 miles of rail lines. Since its peak in 1908 the state's total had dropped 23 percent from a high of 9,059 miles, an average of about 55 miles each year. With the grudging permission of the ICC roads abandoned another 446 miles over the next twenty years, to bring the 1965 total to 6,408 miles. After 1968 the pace accelerated, and another 574 miles was pulled up by 1975, which

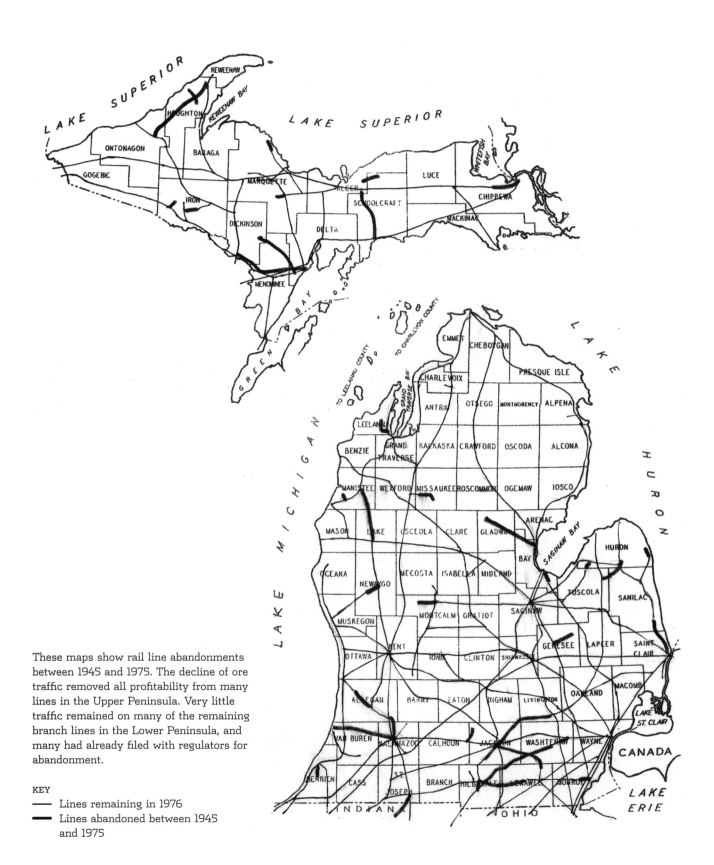

These maps show rail line abandonments between 1945 and 1975. The decline of ore traffic removed all profitability from many lines in the Upper Peninsula. Very little traffic remained on many of the remaining branch lines in the Lower Peninsula, and many had already filed with regulators for abandonment.

KEY
—— Lines remaining in 1976
━━ Lines abandoned between 1945 and 1975

reduced Michigan's total to 5,834 miles of rail line. This represented a further loss of 16 percent of the state's 1945 railroad mileage. The Upper Peninsula was more severely affected, with mileage dropping 23 percent from 1,700 to 1,300 between 1945 and 1975.

Between 1945 and 1959 a little more than 200 miles of Lower Peninsula trackage was abandoned. In 1956 the Grand Trunk Western removed its eighteen-mile Cass City–Bad Axe branch. The Manistee & Northeastern took up its branch from Hatchs to Cedar City in 1954. The Chesapeake & Ohio removed the line between Baldwin and Kaleva in 1956, eliminating its expensive high bridge over the Manistee River. The New York Central resumed its elimination of marginal branches with the 1953 removal of seven miles between Monroe and Ida, and in 1958 the Vienna Junction–Hallett, Ohio, line that provided access to North Toledo Yard, and ten miles between Baroda and St. Joseph. That same year the NYC completed a major line upgrading; parts of three branches were connected together to form a through route between Jackson, a major Michigan yard, and Elkhart, Indiana, the site of the NYC's sophisticated new Robert R. Young yard. The Indiana yard brought in and concentrated traffic that had been spread over a number of other yards. In Michigan this resulted in the almost complete closing of the Niles yard when through freight trains were diverted through Elkhart. This left the Detroit-Chicago main line with only a minimum level of local freight service west of Kalamazoo. This much-reduced amount of traffic made the second main track west of Kalamazoo unnecessary. Within a few years this part of the Michigan Central's original Detroit-Chicago main line was made single track.

Another 200 miles of lines were removed between 1960 and 1970. The Pennsylvania took up its Harbor Springs branch in 1962 and in 1964 sold all of its Missaukee branch to the Cadillac & Lake City as a tourist line. The Chesapeake & Ohio removed its line between White Cloud and Fremont in 1963. The New York Central abandoned its line between Sturgis and Shipshewana, Indiana, and the section between Jackson and Manchester in 1960. In 1961 two sections of the Ypsilanti branch were torn up, from Bridgewater to Brooklyn and from Cement City to North Adams. The Pinconning-Gladwin branch was taken up in 1962, and also a short section of the Detroit–Bay City line between Munger and Bay City, severing the direct route to Bay City. The line between Manchester and Clinton came out in 1964. In a major move that year the New York Central and Pennsylvania filed petitions with the ICC to abandon their respective lines from Bay City and Cedar

BUFFALO—DETROIT—CHICAGO (Union Station)

LOCAL TIME	17 Daily	371 Daily	355 Daily	357 Except Sat&Sun. H	351 Daily	Miles	LOCAL TIME	14 Daily	356 Daily	52 Daily	374 Except Sat&Sun. H	52 Daily	376 Daily
	AM	AM	AM	PM	PM			PM	PM	PM	AM	AM	PM
BUFFALO (Penn Cent. Sta.) (ET) Lv	3.15	4.35			4.55	0	CHICAGO (Union Sta.) (CT) Lv	1.05	4.00	11.05			
Fort Erie (Can. EDT) "		5.05			5.25	6	Englewood "	R 1.23	R 4.18	A 11.55			
Welland "	L 4.06	5.40			5.49	26	Gary (See Note M) "		A 4.53	12.29			
Waterford "					F 6.41	56	Michigan City (CT) "	2.28		1.08			
Tillsonburg "					F 7.04	92	Niles (ET) "	3.10	6.02	1.21			
St. Thomas "	5.46				7.35	105	Dowagiac "			T 1.33			
Ridgetown "					F 8.18	116	Decatur "			T 1.42			
Windsor (Can. EDT) "	7.30				9.28	124	Lawton "						
DETROIT (ET) Ar	6.45				8.45	141	Kalamazoo "	4.06	6.55	2.19			
DETROIT Lv	7.25		11.10	5.15	10.30	164	Battle Creek "	4.32	7.22	T 2.54			
Ypsilanti "				5.45	L 11.01	189	Albion "			T 3.19			
Ann Arbor "	8.06		11.53	Ar 6.10	11.16	209	Jackson "	5.20	8.12	3.50			
Jackson "	8.50		12.38		12.15	247	Ann Arbor "	6.10	9.00	4.30	6.45		
Albion "	9.15				1.11	255	Ypsilanti "			4.40	6.55		
Battle Creek "	9.43		1.28		2.20	283	DETROIT Ar	7.00	9.55	5.30	7.40		
Kalamazoo "	10.13		1.59			283	DETROIT Lv	7.30				7.45	
Lawton "	J 10.40					286	Windsor (Can. EDT) "	8.40				8.55	
Decatur "	J 10.51					352	Ridgetown "					N 9.53	
Dowagiac "						395	St. Thomas "	10.15				10.35	
Niles (ET) "	11.10		2.54		3.29	420	Tillsonburg "					X 11.22	11.10
Michigan City (CT) "						442	Waterford "					12.17	11.45
Gary (See Note M) "	P 12.25				P 4.50	496	Welland "	B 11.56				12.48	
Englewood "	D 1.05		D 4.45		D 5.25	528	Fort Erie (Can. EDT) "	D 12.27				1.25	12.30
CHICAGO (Union Sta.) (CT) Ar	1.20		5.05		5.45	535	BUFFALO (Penn Cent. Sta.) (ET) Ar	1.07					
	PM	AM	PM	PM	AM			AM	PM	AM	AM	PM	AM

Springs to Mackinaw City. After several years of deliberations the ICC rejected both requests. In 1967 the NYC took up the tracks between Hudson and Clayton on its Old Road, severing the original Michigan Southern main line from Toledo to Hillsdale and Elkhart, and as well abandoned that part of the Ypsilanti branch between Saline and Bridgewater. In 1968 the successor owner, Penn Central, removed the Albion-Springport branch. It followed this in 1969 with the sale of a remnant of the Ypsilanti branch between Pittsfield and Saline to the Ann Arbor Railroad, and then removed the remainder of the tracks between Pittsfield and Ypsilanti.

Between 1970 and 1976 the abandonment pace picked up. In 1972 the Chesapeake & Ohio took up its branch between Horton and Otisville, between Port Hope and Harbor Beach, and between Port Huron and Croswell. In 1973 it removed the tracks between Allegan and Hamilton and the next year those between Edmore and Lakeview. The former Manistee & Northeastern's short Onekama branch came out in 1972. In 1975 the Grand Trunk Western abandoned its Michigan Air Line branch between Lakeland and Jackson. The Cadillac & Lake City abandoned the branch into Falmouth in 1972 and from Round Lake to Lake City in 1975. Penn Central took up the tracks between Cement City and Brooklyn in 1970, and in 1972 sections of three lines: Hillsdale to Osseo, Hillsdale to North Adams, and Kalamazoo to Plainwell. In 1973 it removed six more short sections that totaled sixty-five miles: Adrian to Clayton, Haires

This June 1970 Penn Central timetable shows what little remained of the Detroit-Chicago service. The six-hour running times were hopeful at best since the line was plagued with numerous "slow orders" over track that deteriorated faster than Penn Central could find money to repair it.

Author's collection.

to Horton, Fort Wayne Junction to Bankers, a short piece in St. Joseph, Bach to Colling, and Kalamazoo to South Haven.

In the Upper Peninsula probably half of the nearly 600 miles of line abandoned was mining and lumbering branches. The Chicago & North Western built its 8.7-mile Marenisco branch in 1952 and abandoned it in 1962. In 1970 it took up the Felch Mountain branch, the Gibbs City branch, and the 52-mile Ore Line between Antoine and Escanaba, removing one track of what was in effect a double-track line between Iron Mountain and the ore docks at Escanaba. The Milwaukee Road removed all of its branch to Iron River and Crystal Falls in 1969. The Soo Line tore out the track between Raco and Sault Ste. Marie in 1961, on the former Duluth, South Shore & Atlantic branch. The Lake Superior & Ishpeming built the last major line construction in Michigan, an extension of 15.7 miles from Cusino to Sunrise Landing in 1957, used it for only a few years, then took it up in 1965. That same year it abandoned the 5 miles between Gwinn and Little Lake, the oldest part of its line. In 1963 it sold its Marquette–Big Bay branch to a new tourist line, the Marquette & Huron Mountain, which abandoned 16 of the 24 miles of that branch in 1967 and the remainder in 1982. Two roads were abandoned in their entirety. The Copper Range took up 31 miles of tracks between Hancock and Calumet in 1962, another 13 miles of branches in 1971, and in 1973 all the remaining 53 miles of road between Houghton and McKeever. The Manistique & Lake Superior abandoned all of its 38-mile line between Manistique and Doty in 1968. In connection with this move the Ann Arbor Railroad discontinued its Frankfort-Manistique car ferry service.

Michigan lost about 1,100 miles of railroad line between 1945 and 1975, but much of this trackage produced barely marginal revenues and profits, and generally had little impact on the affected freight service customers. At the same time, the trucks continued to draw freight from the rails. This was accompanied by the accelerated shrinkage of the heavy industries and the extractive industries that had characterized the Michigan economy. Some of them disappeared completely. Many smaller businesses in villages and towns closed or merged in the face of stronger competition from new and larger dealers. Coal, always an important share of freight tonnage, disappeared as a form of home heating. No amount of salesmanship or top-of-the-mark train service could restore a closed business that had been a mainstay of a branch. At the same time, there was much less need for that small-town fixture, the station agent, whose freight customers disappeared.

Railroads also changed an ages-old operating practice to take greater advantage of the flexibility of the diesel locomotive. Local freight trains that used to run through from terminal to terminal, based on the need for steam locomotives to reach the needed engine servicing facilities, now began to operate out of a home terminal only as far as there were cars to be handled and then returned to the home terminal. This approach left parts of lines with no trains running on them, and in turn allowed track maintenance to be stopped and weeds to grow up between the rails. With no trains to run over these pieces, the railroads made their case to the ICC that the section should be abandoned, and succeeded in winning ICC approval.

SOURCES

Dunbar, Willis F. *All Aboard! A History of Railroads in Michigan*. Grand Rapids,
    Mich.: W. B. Eerdmans, 1969.

U.S. Interstate Commerce Commission. *Finance Dockets*, various numbers.
    Washington, D.C.: Interstate Commerce Commission, various dates

Meints, Graydon M. *Michigan Railroad Lines*. East Lansing: Michigan State
    University Press, 2005.

Michigan Department of Transportation. Miscellaneous reports.

A New Way of Doing Things

For more than a hundred years the steam locomotive moved every train on every railroad. The only exceptions to this were a few electric operations in a few unique situations that developed in the twentieth century: high-density routes in the East, a few long river tunnels, a few city terminals, and a couple of Rocky Mountain routes. Electric operation was talked about widely, particularly in light of the perceived success of the interurban, but no installations were made after the Great Depression. Generally it was the substantial cost of installing a new system that stopped the movement; the onetime cost of wires, generators, and new locomotives was too much for railroad finances to absorb. One other innovation was the gasoline-powered single-unit railcar that began to appear on branch-line passenger trains in the 1920s. These were relatively slow and were rarely brought out onto the main line. At best these were a stopgap measure, and most disappeared during the Great Depression, although the concept enjoyed a brief revival with the introduction of the Budd Company's rail diesel car (RDC) on several branch lines in the 1950s and 1960s.

At the end of World War II there was a desperate need for new locomotives, and the railroads met it by heading in two directions. The industry applied its technological talents in attempts to improve the efficiency and capabilities of the steam locomotive. The result was such engines as the New York Central's *Niagara*-class, the Pennsylvania's T-1 high-speed long-distance passenger engine, and the Chesapeake & Ohio's coal-turbine. A host of mechanical improvements were installed to make as much of the steam locomotive as could be made. The steam locomotive was improved to its technological pinnacle by the late 1950s, reaching a plateau from which it could not be made more powerful, speedier, or more efficient. It continued to demand a vast supporting infrastructure of goods, facilities, and manpower, expenses that the railroads were increasingly unable to afford. Steamers demanded a special quality of water; carloads of coal for fuel had to be moved everywhere. Roundhouses for turning and storing engines when off the road or for basic maintenance and shops for mandatory heavier maintenance were required, all of which required staffing. And every engine pulling a train demanded two employees, an engineman and a fireman, while on stiff grades two engines were required. On the grades on the New York Central's branch from Bay City to Mackinaw City double-heading steam engines was the rule of the day.

Varieties of the diesel-electric locomotive, most often simply called a "diesel," had been around since 1925, but it was not until General Motors (GM) bought Electro-Motive Company in 1930 that development began. GM's plan was to develop diesel-powered applications for a variety of uses. It introduced the first prototype for main-line freight use in 1939, and it was only World War II that delayed the widespread adoption of the new motive power. The full history of the development of the diesel unfortunately is too long to relate here. The new steam engines that were developed, as advanced and photogenic as they were, paled when compared to the operating and cost advantages found in the diesel.

The railroads discovered the diesel's increased availability. It did not require extensive servicing at the end of each run; it made longer runs because of reduced refueling requirements; it had greater hauling capability that permitted longer and faster trains; the need for two steamers to pull heavier trains on grades was eliminated; it reduced track maintenance; it allowed reduced labor costs since no fireman

was needed; it had lower maintenance costs because there was no need for many of the specialized crafts demanded by the steam engine; its dynamic braking allowed the engine itself to provide braking for freight trains coming down grade; and it had greater reliability when compared to the aging steam engine fleet. In barely fifteen years, from 1945 to 1960, steam locomotives almost entirely disappeared from commercial railroad use. Through the efforts of a large number of devotees a few steam locomotives were saved, but only for museums and a few tourist lines. Michigan is fortunate to be the home of the Steam Railroad Institute, in Owosso, which has preserved and operates the Pere Marquette engine 1225. Sister engine 1223 is on static display at Grand Haven.

Soon after the end of World War II the New York Central introduced diesels to Michigan on its fastest Chicago-Detroit freight trains and then on its important passenger trains. As more diesels were delivered, they pushed the relatively new steamers out to branch-line service. The smallish Detroit & Mackinac replaced all its steamers with diesels

The New York Central introduced the Niagara-class locomotive in 1945 as the most sophisticated steam engine it ever designed. But it came to the rails at the same time that the road began to buy diesel-electric engines. Here is number 6007 at White Pigeon with Old Road local passenger train number 822 in the summer of 1954, a little more than a year before the train was discontinued and the engine scrapped.

Luvergne G. Isaac.

In the summer of 1940 the Grand Trunk Western operated with dignity, even to washing its streamlined locomotives. Here is number 6408 pulling train 17, the Inter-City Limited, headed west out of Lansing.

Emery Gulash photo, Sam Breck collection.

in 1948. The Pennsylvania Railroad replaced all of its Michigan steam engine operations between Fort Wayne and Mackinaw City with diesels in 1949, the first such complete division changeover by any major road. The Pere Marquette bought its first diesel in 1939 as a yard switching engine, and bought a few road passenger units in 1946 and freight units after its merger into the Chesapeake & Ohio in 1947; by early 1952 it had no steam engines left. The Duluth, South Shore & Atlantic went all-diesel in 1951. In 1957 both the New York Central and the Pennsylvania ended all steam operations.

In 1929 the Grand Trunk Western bought a gasoline-powered engine and assigned it to handle car ferry traffic at Milwaukee; in 1939 the GTW replaced it with diesel power, and eventually retired it in 1959. After the war the GTW began buying diesels to replace steamers as yard switch engines and in 1947 tried out a pair of freight road units. In the mid-1950s the GTW began buying road units for both freight and passenger service. Its steam operations came to an end on 27 March 1960, when it ran its last steam engine in regular service. This also is recorded as the last such run in the United States. Only special excursion runs and fan trips brought out steam locomotives after this date. In just fifteen years the revolution was complete.

Railroad cars changed as much as did the locomotives, as new types of cars were developed to better handle special commodities. Two new cars were the covered hopper car for grain, flour, and dry bulk products and the auto rack car, which carried new automobiles. Railcars of existing design became longer, up to eighty feet in contrast with the old standard forty-foot and extralong fifty-foot boxcar. Heavier loads could be moved as the carrying capacity of coal hopper cars increased from 70 to 110 tons. The longer trains that diesels could pull brought the development of stronger couplers. Higher speeds called for improved trucks with roller bearings, and these soon completely replaced the ages-old axle with brass bearings lubricated with oily waste. This change virtually eliminated a major source of running accidents, the "hot box" or burned journal.

Just as the telephone replaced the telegraph key, the radio provided improved communications. The need for miles of trackside telephone wire was eliminated. Supervisors used the radio to talk with trains on the road and now could issue new or revised instructions. The radio could notify management and approaching trains of any sort of emergency. Even the now anachronistic Teletype gained wider use. Trackside signals were spaced farther apart, and new indications were developed to allow more stopping room and higher train speeds. Traffic control systems (TCS) and centralized train control (CTC) were developed, which allowed a train dispatcher in a central office to set signals and switches over long stretches of track. In some cases it allowed roads to keep double-track capacity with only one track. Other roads took up third and fourth main tracks by using TCS in both directions on the two remaining tracks. Dispatchers always knew the position of trains rather than having to wait for a verbal report from a train order station. The rails used in the tracks were upgraded to heavier weights that were welded into 1,500-foot lengths. Using fewer joints to connect the rails end-to-end has reduced track wear.

These changes taken together brought an impressive improvement in one measurement of railroad performance: train speed between terminals. In the twenty years following World War II the speed increased by more than 20 percent, from sixteen miles per hour to just over twenty. The diesel contributed to this, but changes in freight service also were responsible. The railroads largely discontinued handling less-than-carload freight, a function that was labor and time intensive. As local and small-town industries consolidated and closed, there was less need for local freight runs and yard switching, and this allowed the roads to concentrate on longer trains hauling cars longer distances. At the same time, the truckers took away more kinds of freight from the railroads. Livestock traffic all but disappeared, accompanied by a good fraction of perishable fruit movements. The innovative unit train concentrated multiple carloads of freight into one group of cars that moved together from origin to destination. First applied to grain shipments in ten-car blocks, the approach soon expanded to all sorts of bulk products. Today the widest use is to move coal in solid trainloads in specially designed cars that can be inverted and dumped at delivery without uncoupling the cars. One other category of freight that has grown sharply for the railroads is intermodal traffic. This traffic embraces moving truck trailers and containers on specially designed cars. Truck trailers are received from one trucking company at origin, hauled by rail, then delivered to another trucker at the destination to be hauled to the consignee. Container traffic is loaded by special gantry crane onto railcars, then moved most often in unit trains to its destination, where it is loaded onto special truck trailers for delivery. A large share of container traffic originates overseas and is brought to the United States by ship, then transferred to rail at an American port.

The sum of these changes dramatically changed the need for railroad workers, which in the twenty years after World War II dropped in number by more than half, to just over 600,000. The end of the steam locomotive eliminated all need for several crafts, as well as the need for a fireman on the engine, although it took years of effort to persuade the brotherhoods to accept this change. Section gangs to maintain short territories of track were replaced by more sophisticated maintenance equipment in the hands of large mobile gangs that often worked in two shifts per day. More sophisticated signaling systems eliminated the need for towermen at most interlocked railroad crossings. When small-town freight traffic disappeared the station agent was no longer needed. Clerks of all varieties were eliminated when new records and accounting systems were put in place. In the thirty years between 1945 and 1975, the railroad became a much different place to work.

SOURCES

Armstrong, John H. *The Railroad: What It Is, What It Does.* 3rd ed. Omaha, Neb.: Simmons-Boardman Books, 1993.

Churella, Albert J. "Business Strategies and Diesel Development." *Railroad History*,
    special issue (2000). Other articles in this issue also are of merit.

Foss, Charles R. *Evening Before the Diesel*. Boulder, Colo.: Pruett Publishing, 1980.

McGonigal, Robert S., ed. "DieselVictory." *Classic Trains*, special edition 4, 2006.

Million, Arthur B., and Thomas W. Dixon Jr. *Pere Marquette Power*. Alderson, W.Va.:
    Chesapeake & Ohio Historical Society, 1984.

Stover, John F. *American Railroads*. Chicago: University of Chicago Press, 1961.

The End of an Era

At the end of World War II passenger trains ran about 18,600 miles in Michigan each day. The greatest share of this service, 15,900 miles, was in the Lower Peninsula, with only about 2,700 miles run in the Upper Peninsula. By 1955 these runs were down 45 percent to 11,400 train miles. By 1965 another 40 percent was dropped, and train miles were reduced to just under 6,800 per day. In 1971, on the eve of Amtrak taking over all passenger train service, Michigan had only 4,000 miles per day, barely 20 percent of the amount it had twenty-five years earlier.

The New York Central ran the most trains. In 1947 its Detroit-Chicago service had ten eastbound and nine westbound trains each day, with a Kalamazoo-Detroit round-tripper for good measure. Name trains were everywhere: the *Mercury*, the *Wolverine*, the *Twilight Limited*, the *North Shore Limited*, and the *Motor City Special* set the standard for service. The Detroit-Toledo line was second with seven each way led by the *Mercury* and several other runs through to Cleveland, the *Ponce de Leon* and the *Ohio Special* to Cincinnati, and through services to St. Louis and Columbus. The *Detroiter* and the *Empire State Express*, on overnight and daytime schedules, respectively, connected Detroit with Buffalo and New York City. Branch-line service was sparse, with two each way between Grand Rapids and Jackson making connections to Detroit, one between Bay City and Jackson with connections to Chicago, an overnight run between Detroit and Mackinaw City, and a round-trip run from Detroit to Bay City. The New York Central also ran two locals each way between Toledo and Elkhart through Adrian, Hillsdale, and Sturgis.

As soon as possible the New York Central started to upgrade and modernize its passenger train service. It speeded up some trains. It ordered new coaches and an assortment of dining, lounge, parlor, and observation cars. It bought a wide variety of new sleeping cars with roomettes, compartments, bedrooms, and drawing rooms replacing the archaic lower and upper berths. By 1950 nearly all the nonstreamlined cars were gone from the named through trains, although they were rolled out for special runs and heavy holiday traffic. For the 1947 summer season the NYC scheduled a new train, the *Michigan Timberliner*, which left Detroit Friday afternoons at 5:15 for a six-hour–forty-minute dash to Mackinaw City, and returned on Sunday afternoons. It carried car 1599, the only lunch-counter car in NYC's car fleet. But the hoped-for increase in passengers never came. The completion of toll roads in Indiana and Ohio accelerated the Detroit-Chicago service's loss to the automobile.

Chicago-Detroit service dropped to seven trains each way by 1950, with the eastbound Chicago–New York *North Shore Limited* off the schedule. The two remaining Detroit-Chicago locals came off in the winter of 1952–53. In April 1956 the experimental *Aerotrain* was introduced in an attempt to bring faster runs with lower-cost equipment. It had a running time of four hours twenty minutes with no stops between Chicago and Detroit. It was held to a maximum speed of eighty-five miles per hour, which was faster than the eighty miles per hour allowed to other trains. The test continued only until July, when the train was moved over to the Cleveland-Chicago service, but it lasted there only until October. The train was so light that track signal systems did not always work reliably, and the train gave its riders a rough ride as well. In April 1958 the *Chicago Mercury* disappeared from the timetable, leaving only five trains each way. In April 1966 the overnight Chicago-Buffalo train was ended, reducing the number to four. East of Detroit, the eastbound Detroit–New York overnight *Detroiter* was combined with the *Wolverine* in 1956 and in April 1959 the westbound run was as well. With this the *Detroiter* name disappeared. On the branches, single-unit railcars, called *Beeliners*, began to replace conventional trains. These cars, built by the Budd Company, were powered enough to be able to run at full track speeds. Some cars had special compartments for baggage and U.S. mail. In mid-1951 the daytime Detroit–Bay City round-trip was assigned a Budd car, speeded up by thirty-five minutes, and extended to Midland. In early 1952 the Jackson–Grand Rapids run was converted and speeded up by fifteen minutes. On both branches the cars could run at sixty-five miles per hour on straight track. The Grand Rapids car also was moved to Detroit in the afternoon to be able to return as a Detroit-Jackson commuter run. In early 1959 a *Beeliner* was put on the Bay City–Jackson night run, and in October the overnight Detroit–Mackinaw City train was replaced by a daytime *Beeliner*. The daylight Detroit–Bay

Announcing
SUMMER TRAIN SERVICE
to
Northern Michigan
VACATIONLANDS

Also

SPECIAL WEEKEND TRAIN

"The Michigan Timberliner"

Fully Air-Conditioned

Detroit 16, Mich.
Information and Reservations .... WOodward 5-7070
Ticket Offices: M. C. R. R. Terminal
3044 West Grand Blvd.
O. J. Steinhardt, Asst. Passr. Sales Mgr., M. C. R. R. Terminal .TAshmoo 5-7000

NORTHERN MICHIGAN SERVICES
Featuring the "Michigan Timberliner"

397 Fri. Only Note	396 Daily	393 Daily	Miles		394 Daily	392 Daily	396 Sun. Only Note
PM 5 01	PM 10 50	AM 8 05	0.0	Lv DETROIT......(EST) Ar	AM 6 45	PM 4 25	PM 11 30
5 09			0.0	Lv Woodward Ave.... .... Ar			11 10
6 29		8 30	15.6	Lv Warren............ Lv	E 6 01	3 57	10 46
		8 39	22.4	Lv Utica............ Lv	E 5 50		
5 46	c11 35	8 50	29.5	Lv Rochester......... Lv	E 5 39	3 40	10 28
		9 02	38.9	Lv Lake Orion....... Lv	E 5 26		
6 26	11 57	9 09	42.2	Lv Oxford........... Lv	5 19		9 49
	12 21	9 31	58.9	Lv Lapeer............ Lv	4 52		
	b12 31	9 41	67.6	Lv Columbiaville...... Lv	E 4 38		
		9 49	72.2	Lv Otter Lake........ Lv	E 4 31		
	b12 46	9 57	78.2	Lv Millington........ Lv	E 4 21		
6 56	12 54	10 05	84.8	Lv Vassar............ Lv	4 10	2 37	9 15
7 28	1 53	10 42	105.8	Ar SAGINAW (Gen. Ave.) Lv	3 35	3 00	9 00
7 53	2 30	11 12	119.6	Ar BAY CITY........ Lv	2 40	1 30	8 15
		11 17	0.0	Lv BAY CITY........ Ar		1 27	
		11 59	19.6	Ar Midland........... Lv		12 50	
8 00	2 55		0.0	Lv BAY CITY........ Ar	2 05		8 16
	3 31		18.9	Lv Pinconning....... Lv	1 25		
	3 47		27.7	Lv Standish......... Lv	1 10		
9 18	4 34		52.7	Lv West Branch...... Lv	12 35		
9 51	5 14		77.1	Lv Roscommon...... Lv	11 58		
10 13	5 45		92.4	Ar GRAYLING....... Lv	11 30		
			92.4	Lv GRAYLING....... Ar	11 25		
	D6 10		111.7	Lv Otsego Lake...... Lv	D 11 00		
10 50	6 25		119.2	Lv GAYLORD........ Lv	10 50		
11 02	6 40		127.7	Lv Vanderbilt....... Lv	10 39		
11 16	6 55		138.3	Lv Wolverine........ Lv	10 19		
11 41	7 15		148.4	Lv Indian River...... Lv	9 58		
	7 30		153.9	Lv Topinabee........ Lv	9 48		
11 52	7 45		160.4	Lv Mullet Lake....... Lv	9 37		
12 02	8 00		166.3	Lv Cheboygan....... Lv	9 22		
12 30	8 30		182.3	Ar MACKINAW CITY...(EST) Lv	9 05		
AM	AM	AM			PM	PM	PM

EXPLANATION OF REFERENCE MARKS

‡ Stops on signal to receive or discharge revenue passengers only.
† Stops daily except Sunday.
B Stops on signal to receive or discharge revenue passengers for or from Detroit.
C Stops on signal to discharge revenue passengers from Detroit and receive revenue passengers for Saginaw and beyond.
D Stops on signal to receive or discharge revenue passengers for or from Bay City and beyond.
E Stops on signal to discharge revenue passengers from Saginaw and beyond, or to receive revenue passengers for Detroit.

City round-trip was rescheduled to leave Detroit at 8:00 P.M., and the extension to Midland was dropped. These efforts to preserve branch-line service did not, however, succeed. The Toledo-Hillsdale-Elkhart train was discontinued in November 1956, ending a service between Toledo and Adrian that had begun in 1852 and with parts of it as early as 1836. In July 1959 the *Mercury* between Cleveland and Detroit was ended after more than twenty years as a pioneering New York Central streamliner service. It was replaced by a *Beeliner* that had come off the Jackson–Grand Rapids run that ended in April. In December 1959 the Bay City–Jackson run was discontinued. In 1960 the night run from Detroit to Bay City was taken off. The *Timberliner* made its last trip Labor Day weekend 1962. The next month the Detroit–Mackinaw City train was dropped north of Bay City, leaving only a daytime Detroit–Bay City round-trip. This was discontinued in late 1963, bringing the end to all New York Central branch-line service in Michigan.

The *Timberliner* was the New York Central's post–World War II attempt to lure new riders headed for their vacation homes in the northern Lower Peninsula. It ran summer weekends from 1947 through 1962. Printed on card stock, this 1947 pass-out was almost the only promotion the train received.

Author's collection.

In the December 1967 all train names disappeared from the New York Central timetable, reflecting its growing disillusion with passenger service as well as preparations for its merger with the Pennsylvania into Penn Central. In 1969 Penn Central discontinued one more Detroit-Chicago train, reducing the total to three each way. Service mirrored the company's financial condition, and went from bad to worse. A litany of late trains, dirty cars, and air-conditioning that did not work provided ample grist for the media mill. Amtrak's assumption of all passenger service in May 1971 came as a welcome relief.

The enthusiasm of the New York Central was also to be found on the Chesapeake & Ohio–controlled Pere Marquette. In August 1946 it started new runs named the *Pere Marquette*, with a pair of new streamlined trains between Detroit and Grand Rapids. These were the first streamlined trains put in service in the nation after World War II. With a morning and late-afternoon run in each direction they were immediately popular; the 152-mile run was made in 160 minutes. Tickets could be picked up on the train, meals were served, and no tipping was allowed. A third midday run soon was added, and then a Sunday late-evening run was put on. In 1948 the C&O extended the concept to its Grand Rapids–Chicago service, with two trains a day plus an overnight run each way. But by 1950 this was cut back to one round-trip a day plus the overnight service. By this time the Saginaw-Ludington train was gone. The two Detroit–Bay City trains were replaced by the streamlined *Queen of the Valley*, which left Saginaw each morning with an early-evening return from Detroit, but the newcomer lasted only one year. The midday and late-evening Detroit–Grand Rapids runs were then dropped. The Baldwin-Kaleva segment of the Grand Rapids–Petoskey line was abandoned in 1956 and the train rerouted through Manistee. This returned service to Manistee, which the Manistee & Northeastern had ended in 1949. In October 1962 the Petoskey–Traverse City leg was dropped, and Grand Rapids–Traverse City service ended in October 1966. In January 1969 the night Chicago–Grand Rapids run ended. When interstate highway I-96 was completed between Detroit and Grand Rapids in 1964, the end of the Detroit–Grand Rapids service was predicted, although it did last through 1970. Of all C&O Michigan service only one Grand Rapids–Chicago round-trip remained at the coming of Amtrak. The Chicago–Bay View summer train the *Resort Special* returned to the timetable in 1947, running daily except Saturday from Chicago and three times a week from Detroit. In 1949 it was cut back to three trips a week from Chicago and lost its connection to Detroit. By 1951

DETROIT · PONTIAC · DURAND · CHICAGO

READ DOWN   **READ UP**

991 ① Ex.Sat. & Sun.	993 ① Ex.Sat. & Sun.	987 ① Sat.	995 ① Ex.Sat. & Sun.	997 ① Ex.Sat. & Sun.	999 ① Ex.Fri. Sat. & Sun.	989 ① Fri.	169- 159 Daily	Mohawk 165 ③ Daily	TABLE 3 Eastern Standard Time	158- 168 Daily	Mohawk 164 ③ Daily	994 ① Ex.Sat. & Sun.	996 ① Ex.Sat. & Sun.	998 ① Ex Sun.	990 ① Ex.Sat. & Sun.	992 ① Ex.Sat. & Sun.
AM	PM	PM	PM	PM	PM	PM	PM	PM		PM	PM	AM	AM	AM	AM	PM
8.00	12.01	3.40	5.00	5.30	6.00	6.20	12.30	4.30	Lv Detroit.........................Ar	5.55	11.10	7.30	8.00	8.30	9.40	2.00
8.09	12.09	3.50	5.10	5.40	6.08	6.28	12.40	.....	Lv Milwaukee Jct.................Lv	5.46	.....	7.21	7.51	8.21	9.31	1.51
.....	.....	3.57	5.17	5.47	6.12	6.32	f12.45	.....	Lv Highland Park.................Lv	d 5.42	.....	7.14	7.44	8.14	.....	.....
f 8.24	f12.24	4.04	5.24	5.54	6.17	6.37	.....	.....	Lv Ferndale......................Lv	.....	.....	7.06	7.36	8.06	f 9.16	f1.36
.....	.....	4.06	5.26	5.56	6.19	6.39	.....	.....	Lv Pleasant Ridge................Lv	.....	.....	7.03	7.33	.....	.....	.....
8.30	12.30	4.10	5.30	6.00	6.21	6.41	12.55	4.51	Lv Royal Oak.....................Lv	5.35	10.42	7.00	7.30	8.00	9.10	1.30
f 8.35	f12.35	4.13	5.33	6.03	6.23	6.43	.....	.....	Lv Oakwood Blvd.................Lv	.....	.....	6.55	7.25	7.55	f 9.05	f1.25
8.40	12.40	4.22	5.42	6.12	6.30	6.50	1.01	4.55	Lv Birmingham....................Lv	5.29	10.38	6.49	7.19	7.50	9.00	1.20
		4.27	5.47	6.17	6.34	6.54	.....	.....	Lv Charing Cross.................Lv	.....	.....	f6.44	f7.14	7.45	.....	.....
		4.30	5.50	6.20	6.36	6.56	.....	.....	Lv Bloomfield Hills...............Lv	.....	.....	f6.42	f7.12	7.43	.....	.....
		4.40	6.00	6.30	6.45	7.05	1.13	5.06	Ar Pontiac.......................Lv	5.16	10.27	6.35	7.05	7.35	.....	.....
							1.15	5.08	Lv Pontiac.......................Ar	5.15	10.25					
							1.34	.....	Lv Holly.........................Lv	f 4.54	.....					
							1.39	.....	Lv Fenton........................Lv	f 4.49	.....					
							2.00	5.48	Ar Durand........................Lv	4.30	9.48					
							2.15	5.50	Lv Durand........................Ar	4.16	9.45					
							2.45	6.18	Ar Lansing.......................Lv	3.45	9.14					
							2.50	6.20	Lv Lansing.......................Ar	3.35	9.12					
							3.10	.....	Lv Charlotte.....................Lv	3.04	.....					
							3.37	7.01	Ar Battle Creek..................Lv	2.40	8.26					
							3.47	7.04	Lv Battle Creek..................Ar	2.30	8.23					
							4.10	.....	Lv Vicksburg.....................Lv	2.02	.....					
							4.28	.....	Lv Marcellus.....................Lv	f 1.45	.....					
							4.42	.....	Lv Cassopolis....................Lv	f 1.34	.....					
									Central Standard Time							
							4.05	7.11	Ar South Bend....................Lv	12.07	6.14					
							4.10	7.15	Lv South Bend....................Ar	12.01	6.11					
							4.58	.....	Lv Valparaiso....................Lv	11.22	.....					
							5.50	.....	Lv Chicago Lawn..................Lv	10.32	.....					
							6.15	9.10	Ar Chicago.......................Lv	10.10	4.30					
							PM	PM		AM	PM					

MOHAWK NEW FAST TRAIN

Lv. Detroit	4:30 PM EST
Lv. Royal Oak	4:51 PM EST
Lv. Birmingham	4:55 PM EST
Lv. Pontiac	5:08 PM EST
Ar. Chicago	9:10 PM CST

MOHAWK NEW FAST TRAIN

Lv. Chicago	4:30 PM CST
Ar. Pontiac	10:25 PM EST
Ar. Birmingham	10:38 PM EST
Ar. Royal Oak	10:42 PM EST
Ar. Detroit	11:10 PM EST

---

the summer train ran only Fridays from Chicago and Sundays from Bay View, a frequency that it retained until its last season of operation in 1957.

The Chesapeake & Ohio's *Sportsman* between Detroit and Newport News was made into a connection to its *George Washington* in 1963 and then changed to weekends only in late 1970. In 1965 the C&O-owned Baltimore & Ohio made its Detroit-Washington *Ambassador* a leg off its *Capitol Limited* and renamed it the *Capitol-Detroit*. On the Detroit-Cincinnati service it moved streamlined equipment onto the day run in the mid-1950s and renamed it the *Cincinnatian*. The overnight train to Cincinnati was discontinued in September 1967, the *Capitol-Detroit* was replaced by a bus in April 1969, and only the *Cincinnatian* remained until the Amtrak startup.

The Grand Trunk Western kept its service longer than might have been expected. It continued to run three Chicago–Port Huron–Toronto trains each way until 1967, when one was taken off. In October 1970 another train lost its Canadian leg. The remaining day train lasted until Amtrak began. In 1967 it inaugurated the *Mohawk* on a five-hour–forty-minute run between Detroit and Chicago, the first direct through train in the twentieth century on the GTW. This last valiant effort, certainly

The Grand Trunk Western's *Mohawk*, inaugurated in 1967, was the last effort to revive Detroit-Chicago service. The train lasted just four years—until the start of Amtrak. Its running time compared favorably with that offered by Penn Central's deteriorating service.

Author's collection.

ABOVE: The Wabash Railroad upgraded its Detroit–St. Louis day train around 1950 with newer equipment, added an observation car, and drew on the past for a new name—the *Wabash Cannon Ball*. This ad appeared in its September 1950 timetable.

Author's collection.

OPPOSITE: This regional timetable of the Pennsylvania Railroad showed only the Cincinnati-Michigan service. All of the trains shown in this 1 October 1945 schedule were gone within ten years.

Author's collection.

CINCINNATI, GRAND RAPIDS AND MACKINAW CITY

READ DOWN   READ UP

201-537	201-539 Ex. Sun.	511	501	Mls.		508 Ex. Sun.	502	510-506-200
PM	PM	AM	AM			PM	AM	PM
‡6.00	k6.00	....	†12.27	....	Lv. St. Louis (C.S.T.)....Mo. Ar.	....	¶5.45	q*1.20
‡7.30	k7.30	....	†11.30	....	" Louisville....Ky. "	....		*12.55
‡10.55	k10.55	....	†6.30	....	Lv. Indianapolis (C.S.T.)..Ind. Ar.	10.50		6.48
†12.11	§12.11	....	7.45	....	Ar. Richmond.... " Lv.	†9.28		*5.24
‡10.37	k10.37	....	†6.50	....	Lv. Columbus (E.S.T.)....Ohio Ar.	9.30		11.35
†12.17	§12.17	....	8.14	....	Lv. Dayton (E.S.T.)... " Ar.	8.02		7.37
12.15	12.15	....	8.02	....	Ar. Richmond (C.S.T.)..Ind. Lv.	*6.15		*5.40
‡11.40	k11.40	....	†8.55	.0	Lv. Cincinnati (E.S.T.)..Ohio Ar.	8.30		7.30
†12.28	§12.28	....	9.55	73.8	Ar. Richmond (C.S.T.)..Ind. Lv.	†5.50		*4.40
†12.40	§12.40	....	†10b15	73.8	Lv. Richmond....Ind. Ar.	†5h30		*4.30
......	......	....	10.27	82.7	" Fountain City.... " Lv.	5.18		......
......	......	....	10.37	89.1	" Lynn.... " "	5.07		......
......	......	....	10.51	98.3	" Winchester.... " "	4.47		......
......	......	....	11.05	106.8	" Ridgeville.... " "	4.36		......
......	......	....	11.22	117.0	" Portland.... " "	4.22		......
......	......	....	11.31	124.1	" Briant.... " "	4.09		......
......	......	....	11.40	128.0	" Geneva.... " "	4.00		......
......	......	....	11.53	132.6	" Berne.... " "	3.47		......
......	......	....	12.02	138.6	" Monroe.... " "	3.39		......
......	......	....	12.15	144.5	" Decatur.... " "	3.30		......
......	......	....	12.27	153.4	" Hoagland.... " "	3.17		......
2.52	2.52	....	†12h52	165.8	Ar. Ft. Wayne.... " Lv.	†2h55		*2.27
‡11.35	k11.35	11.30	....	....	Lv. Chicago (C.S.T.)....Ill. Ar.	4.40		7.40
11.50	11.50	11.45	....	....	" Englewood.... " "	d4.25		d7.23
†2.02	§2.02	1.58	....	....	Ar. Ft. Wayne....Ind. Lv.	2.00		*4.42
†3.40	§3.40	2.30	....	165.8	Lv. Ft. Wayne (C.S.T.)..Ind. Ar.	12.45		*1.23
......	......	2.49	....	177.9	" Huntertown.... " Lv.	f12.25		......
......	......	2.57	....	182.5	" La Otto.... " "	f12.15		......
......	......	3.04	....	187.4	" Avilla.... " "			......
4.30	4.30	3.14	....	194.0	" Kendallville.... " "	11 57		12.37
......	f4.43	3.29	....	201.1	" Rome City.... " "	11 38		e12.18
......	......	3.32	....	203.1	" Wolcottville.... " "	11 34		......
5.01	5.01	3.44	....	212.2	" La Grange.... " "	11 20		e12.02
5.11	f5.11	3.54	....	217.5	" Howe.... " "	11 09		e11.52
6.21	6.21	5.04	....	222.9	" Sturgis (E.S.T.)....Mich. "	11 59		12.41
......	......	f5.17	....	231.7	" Nottawa.... " "	11.43		......
......	......	5.27	....	237.9	" Mendon.... " "	11 32		......
6.59	6.59	5.40	....	246.8	" Vicksburg.... " "	11.20		12.06
7.35	7.35	6.10	....	259.2	" Kalamazoo.... " "	10.58		11.41
......	......	6.32	....	270.5	" Plainwell.... " "	f10.21		......
......	......	f6.42	....	277.0	" Martin.... " "	f10.10		......
......	......	f6.52	....	281.0	" Shelbyville.... " "	f10.00		......
8.22	......	7.04	....	286.8	" Wayland.... " "	9.50		......
......	......	f7.14	....	291.4	" Moline.... " "	f9.42		......
†8.55	§8.55	7.40	....	307.8	Ar. GRAND RAPIDS.... Lv.	9.15		*10.05
†9.20	......	....	....	307.8	Lv. GRAND RAPIDS....Mich. Ar.			†4.30
9.51				321.7	" Rockford.... " Lv.			3.56
10.05				329.0	" Cedar Springs.... " "			3.34
10.13				334.1	" Sand Lake.... " "			f3.22
f10.18				336.1	" Pierson.... " "			f3.16
10.30				341.7	" Howard City.... " "			3.07
10.42				348.1	" Morley.... " "			2.52
10.52				354.8	" Stanwood.... " "			f2.40
11.10				363.7	" Big Rapids.... " "			2.25
f11.18				369.2	" Paris.... " "			f2.10
11.34				376.5	" Reed City.... " "			1.59
11.55				389.0	" LeRoy.... " "			1.35
12.05				393.6	" Tustin.... " "			1.25
12.25				405.5	Ar.{ Cadillac....{Lv			1.05
12.45					Lv.{ ....{Ar			12.45
1.14				417.8	" Manton.... " Lv.			12.20
1.38				431.5	" Fife Lake.... " "			11.59
1.48				437.2	" So. Boardman.... " "			11.50
2.04				445.3	" Kalkaska.... " "			11.37
2.26				458.7	" Mancelona.... " "			11.15
2.36				465.2	" Alba.... " "			11.03
2.49				473.9	" Elmira.... " "			10.50
3.08				482.8	" Boyne Falls.... " "			10.32
3.20				490.0	" Walloon Lake.... " "			10.20
3.45				498.5	Ar.{ Petoskey....{Lv			9.59
3.45					Lv.{ ....{Ar			9.59
‡3.50				499.5	Ar. Bay View.... " Lv.			
‡3.59				503.8	Lv. Conway ♀.... " "			f9.39
f4.05				506.0	" Oden ♀.... " "			f9.34
4.10				508.7	" Alanson.... " "			9.27
f4.16				512.3	" Brutus.... " "			f9.21
4.24				516.4	" Pellston.... " "			9.14
4.36				522.4	" Levering.... " "			9.04
f4.45				526.5	" Carp Lake.... " "			8.57
†5.00				533.5	Ar. MACKINAW CITY.... " "			†8.45
......					Ar. MACKINAC ISLAND. " Lv.			
					(Steamer)			
PM	AM	PM	PM			AM	PM	AM

GRAND RAPIDS AND MUSKEGON

READ DOWN   READ UP

523 Ex. Sun.	521 Ex. Sun.	Mls.	EASTERN STANDARD TIME	522 Ex. Sun.	524 Ex. Sun.
PM	AM			PM	PM
h12.55	9.05	.0	Lv. GRAND RAPIDS...Mich. Ar.	h12.05	5.05
f1.30	9.40	17.2	" Conklin............. " Lv.	f11.29	4.28
f1.39	9.49	22.4	" Ravenna............. " "		4.18
.....	f9.57	27.2	" Sullivan............ " "		f4.08
h2.10	10.20	39.7	Ar.{MUSKEGON HGHTS / MUSKEGON (G.T.Sta.)} Lv.	h10.55	3.50
PM	AM			AM	PM

PETOSKEY AND HARBOR SPRINGS

READ DOWN   READ UP

Mls	EASTERN STANDARD TIME	PASSENGER SERVICE TEMPORARILY DISCONTINUED
.0	Lv. PETOSKEY....Mich. Ar.	
1.0	" Bay View.... " "	
6.7	" Wequetonsing... " "	
7.9	Ar. Harbor Springs. " Lv.	

CAR SERVICE

Nos. 201-537—Coach Service.

Nos. 510-506-200—Coach Service.

Reference Marks

* Daily.

§ Sunday only.

† Daily except Sunday.

‡ Daily except Saturday.

¶ Daily except Monday.

♀ Baggage should be checked to or from Alanson.

d Stops only to discharge passengers.

e Stops only on signal or notice to agent to receive passengers for Fort Wayne and beyond.

f Stops only on signal or notice to agent or conductor to receive or discharge passengers.

h Will not run November 22, December 25, 1945, January 1, May 30, July 4 and September 2, 1946.

k Saturday only.

q No coaches. Coach train—seats reserved—arrives St. Louis 1.35 p.m.

the last such attempt in Michigan, ended at the end of April 1971. The daytime Detroit-Muskegon train came off in 1959, and the night run went in 1960. Other branches had service by mixed trains that handled both freight and passengers, but all of these were gone by the mid-1950s.

In 1949 the Wabash dropped the three Detroit–Fort Wayne–Chicago trains run in conjunction with the Pennsylvania Railroad, but kept the two Detroit–St. Louis runs, renaming the day train in the early 1950s as the *Wabash Cannon Ball*. This train stayed until 1971, although the overnight run was gone by 1969. Other carriers did not keep their passenger trains long after World War II ended. The Ann Arbor ended its Toledo-Frankfort train in July 1950. The Detroit & Mackinac made one last attempt to keep service going by changing to a daytime Alpena–Bay City–Durand service that connected with Grand Trunk Western afternoon trains at Durand. This ended in March 1951 when it did not pay off.

All of the service on the Pennsylvania's Cincinnati–Fort Wayne–Grand Rapids–Cadillac–Mackinaw City line was gone by 1955, with the overnight Grand Rapids–Cincinnati train the last to go. The summers-only *Northern Arrow* ran through the 1961 season, and made its last run on 4 September. The Pennsylvania's service from Detroit to New York and Washington, D.C., ended in July 1959 when the *Red Arrow* made its last run.

Surprisingly, service in the Upper Peninsula lasted longer than might be expected, given the light traffic. The Soo Line's Twin Cities–Sault Ste. Marie overnight train ended in the late 1950s. The Duluth South Shore & Atlantic dropped its Marquette-Duluth overnight train in the early 1950s. In August 1955 it stopped moving passenger train cars across the Straits of Mackinac on the *Chief Wawatam* and at the same time replaced the day train between St. Ignace and Calumet with a Budd railcar between St. Ignace and Ishpeming. This run was shortened to Marquette not long after and ended in January 1958. The Milwaukee Road's daytime Chicago-Ontonagon *Chippewa* was upgraded with better equipment in 1948 and renamed the *Chippewa-Hiawatha*, but by 1954 its run was shortened to end at Channing, and was completely gone in 1959. The *Copper Country Limited*, the overnight Chicago-Calumet run in connection with the Duluth, South Shore & Atlantic, ended in early 1968.

The Chicago & North Western made a dramatic service improvement in January 1942 with the inauguration of the *Peninsula "400"* between Chicago and Ishpeming, going south in the morning and back in the evening. One set of streamlined equipment made each trip in seven hours twenty minutes, and completed an 800-mile round-trip every day. The last passenger trains in the Upper Peninsula were those of the Chicago & North Western. The *Iron and Copper Country Express* made an overnight run on the same route. An overnight Chicago-Escanaba train with a connection running to Iron River rounded out its service. The four Chicago-Duluth trains touched the western Upper Peninsula by backing into Ironwood. These were supplemented by the summers-only *Flambeau*, which ran weekends from Chicago to Ironwood. The overnight Chicago-Duluth run had a connecting train to Watersmeet. During the summer it added a daylight service into Watersmeet. In 1950 the daytime Duluth run was made over into a speedier *Flambeau "400."* Also that year came the end of service to Iron River. The overnight Escanaba train came off after 1955, and was followed by the overnight Duluth and Ishpeming runs. The *Peninsula "400"* and the *Flambeau "400"* were gone by 1970, the last of the Upper Peninsula passenger trains.

Mail contracts played an important part in keeping branch-line passenger trains running. When the post office began its campaign to end the contracts with railroads in the 1950s and early 1960s, and to transfer mail traffic to trucks and airplanes, the revenues from riders alone were inadequate to sustain the trains. When a railroad applied to discontinue a train, the Michigan Public Service Commission rarely could find any public need to support an order to keep the trains, and had no choice but to approve the discontinuance.

SOURCES

Chicago, Milwaukee, St. Paul & Pacific Railroad, public timetables, various dates.

Chicago & North Western Railway, public timetables, various dates.

Duluth, South Shore & Atlantic Railway, public timetables, various dates.

Dunbar, Willis F. *All Aboard! A History of Michigan Railroads.* Grand Rapids, Mich.: W. B. Eerdmans, 1969.

Grand Trunk Western Railway, public timetables, various dates.

New York Central Railroad, public timetables, various dates.

The Official Guide of the Railways. New York: National Railway Publication, various dates.

Pennsylvania Railroad, public timetables, various dates.

Pere Marquette Railway, public timetables, various dates.

Wabash Railway, public timetables, various dates.

The *Peninsula "400"* was the first of only two streamlined trains to serve the Upper Peninsula. This 1942 timetable ad of the Chicago & North Western announced the new service. The train lasted almost thirty years.

Author's collection.

Penn Central

On 1 November 1957 James M. Symes and Alfred E. Perlman stood together and announced that their companies were exploring a merger. As the presidents of the Pennsylvania and New York Central railroads, respectively, their study to make one prosperous company out of two bitter rivals was front-page news. The two men could hardly have been more different as reflections of their corporate cultures. The two roads had been aggressive competitors for a century; there were few major cities in the East and the Midwest that were not served by both roads. In a hundred years the Pennsylvania developed a somewhat more conservative management style, with its investments in other railroads providing it an important money stream. The New York Central was somewhat scrappier, more innovative and aggressive, but not by much. After World War II both roads began to experience a pressure on profits that followed from the national trend of reduced freight traffic. The problem, however, was even more severe for the eastern lines. Symes saw how the two roads overlapped with duplicated trackage, facilities, and services from one end of the line to the other, and came to believe that a merger could eliminate such redundancies. The resulting unified company would be stronger than either of the two components. Symes went first to NYC chairman Robert R. Young, who expressed interest and in turn brought Perlman into the discussions. After Young's suicide in January 1958, Perlman took over the discussions on behalf of the New York Central.

The first bump in the road came in 1959 when the Pennsylvania-controlled Norfolk & Western unexpectedly announced it would acquire the line of the paralleling Virginian Railroad. Perlman stopped negotiations, believing that Symes was trying to improve the Pennsylvania's position by allowing a subsidiary (the N&W) to acquire an important NYC connection (the Virginian). Perlman stopped meeting with Symes and started talking with the Chesapeake & Ohio, in which Young also had been intimately involved. In early 1960 the Norfolk & Western announced that it planned to acquire both the Wabash and the Nickel Plate roads. These two roads were more competitors of the NYC than of the Pennsylvania. In May Perlman learned that the Chesapeake & Ohio, apparently without telling him, had agreed to take over the Baltimore & Ohio. This was a move that would leave the NYC completely isolated. Perlman decided that the NYC should make its own bid for the B&O.

After a wild proxy battle the NYC came away with less than 40 percent of the votes. In October 1961 all Perlman could do was to go back to the Pennsylvania and try to resuscitate the merger talks. A downturn in 1960 and 1961 depressed revenues and profits for both roads and provided a new urgency and impetus for the talks. In January 1962 the two roads signed a merger agreement and in March filed it with the ICC. In October 1963 Symes retired from the Pennsylvania, although he stayed on as a director, and Stuart T. Saunders, president of the Norfolk & Western, was his handpicked successor. Saunders was viewed as the man who could get the merger done since he had led the N&W in acquiring three roads in the preceding four years.

Saunders introduced the idea that the Pennsylvania needed to diversify and that owning other, more profitable businesses would assure the profitability of the railroad. The Pennsy began to dabble. It was not long after Saunders's arrival that the Justice Department informed the company that it had objections to the NYC merger and that it would drop its opposition only if the Pennsy gave up control of the Norfolk & Western. This was a bitter pill for Saunders to swallow since the N&W was almost the only moneymaking Pennsy investment. He agreed to the sale, apparently in part because he wanted the merger at any price and in part because the N&W stock sale would give the Pennsy new cash for diversification. In 1964 he agreed to a labor protection agreement that would prove, after the merger, to be extremely expensive. Also he bowed to Attorney General Robert Kennedy's wishes and included the New York, New Haven & Hartford in the merger. The New Haven road was a bankrupt road with no good prospects for reorganization, but it was important to Kennedy because of the extensive service it provided in Massachusetts. With the Justice Department now bought off, the ICC approved the merger in April 1966, more than eight years after discussions began and more than four years after the merger was filed with the ICC. Several other roads sued to be included in the combined road, and it was not until January 1968 that the Supreme Court approved a merger that included only the New Haven road.

Saunders pulled out the throttle, and the Pennsylvania and New York Central were merged on 1 February 1968 to become Penn Central. Despite years of desultory planning efforts and conversations and meetings, no one seemed prepared for the actual event. A corporate hierarchy was put together, with Saunders as chairman and chief executive officer and Perlman as president and chief operating officer. The rest of the officer ranks were filled about equally from the two roads. Perlman was to run the railroad, and Saunders was responsible for everything else. The third most important man was David C. Bevan, vice president for finance, who came from the Pennsylvania. Reflecting the haste in which it was assembled, the management team broke down immediately. Saunders, Perlman, and Bevan rarely conferred. The Pennsylvania men disliked reporting to a superior from the New York Central, just as the NYC men chafed at reporting to an officer from the Pennsylvania. Often they went around their new supervisor to a superior higher up that they had worked with before the merger. It was a harbinger of things to come that at the ceremony Saunders was holding on the first hour of the merger day, Perlman was asleep in his private car with orders not to be disturbed. Another indicator of trouble was that Saunders worked out of the Pennsylvania's Philadelphia office and Perlman stayed in his old comfortable office in New York City.

Management conflict was far from the only problem. The two roads' computer systems could not talk to one another. Freight service fell apart; waybills to move cars and even for entire trains disappeared; trains were dispatched simply to get cars out of yards and put the problem somewhere else; accounting could not keep track of money until eventually no one knew how much belonged where. Customer loyalty evaporated. In 1969 and 1970 another business recession hit affecting the Northeast hardest, and Penn Central suffered severely. The company's diversification program yielded precious little money, and what it brought in the rail operations lost. The New Haven lost money from the day it was taken over. Penn Central was the largest passenger carrier in the United States, and those operations lost some $7 or $8 million each month. By 1970 Penn Central operations were losing $1 million a day. As revenues dropped the road's expenses continued to go up. The line began to defer maintenance of tracks and equipment and engines, then canceled as much as it could in a desperate attempt to save money. While Bevan beat the bushes to raise money in any way possible to keep the road afloat, Perlman's operations were strangled for a lack of it, and Saunders was sure everything would work out somehow. In what appears to be almost a deliberate campaign of deception, the information given to company directors and its lenders was, charitably put, misleading. Penn Central edged toward inevitable bankruptcy. Early in June 1970, with no notice, the board fired Saunders, Perlman, and Bevan. Two weeks later the road was in court filing for bankruptcy.

There is abundant responsibility to be distributed for the failure of Penn Central. It begins at the top with the isolation and lack of communication between Saunders, Perlman, Bevan, the other top officers, the directors, and the road's lenders. The rush to merger, after ICC approval, allowed no time to prepare for anything. What planning had been done proved worthless. The diversification program contributed nothing to the company's strength and probably contributed to its downfall. The expected savings from plant consolidations and labor reductions were never realized. The five-year delay, as the merger worked through the ICC and the Supreme Court, worsened it prospects. The economic bad times, the New Haven acquisition, the passenger operations, and the loss of U.S. mail revenue all played a part.

The Penn Central collapse was the largest of the failures of the eastern railroad network. The tiny Central of New Jersey preceded it in 1967. The Boston & Maine and the Lehigh Valley accompanied Penn Central in 1970; the Reading went under in 1971, the Erie-Lackawanna in 1972, and the Ann Arbor in 1973. The whole mess was dropped in the lap of Congress, for it to devise a way out of the chaos for which it was partially responsible.

SOURCES

Bryant, Keith L., Jr., ed. *Encyclopedia of American Business History and Biography: Railroads in the Age of Regulation, 1900–1980*. New York: Facts on File, 1988.

Daughen, Joseph R., and Peter Binzen. *The Wreck of the Penn Central*. Boston: Little, Brown, 1971.

U.S. Congress. House. Committee on Interstate and Foreign Commerce. *The Financial Collapse of the Penn Central Company*. 92nd Cong., 2nd sess. Washington, D.C., 1972.

U.S. Congress. Senate. Committee on Commerce. *The Penn Central and Other Railroads*. 92nd Cong., 2nd sess. Washington, D.C., 1972.

U.S. Department of Transportation. *Rail Service in the Midwest and Northeast Region*. Vol. 1. Washington, D.C.: Government Printing Office, 1974.

Amtrak Arrives

The collapse of the U.S. passenger train service began in the early 1950s and came as the result of the decline in ridership that began in the 1920s. Contrary to public opinion, the railroads had little to do with it; the impetus came from a variety of outside sources, foremost of which was the federal government. President Eisenhower had been impressed with the efficiency of Germany's autobahn, promoted the concept, and in 1956 signed the law to construct an interstate highway system that would link every large city in the United States and, incidentally, parallel every major rail passenger route in the country. Financed largely with federal taxes, this public works project worked severe damage on both rail passenger and rail freight service. The American love affair with the automobile made owners view train travel as inconvenient and expensive. Car travel cost no more for a family than for a single rider, and travelers in a car could leave at any time. In a fever to garner airline routes cities and counties built airports at public expense and then encouraged flights by charging user fees that barely covered the cost of operations and bond repayments. Railroads incurred identical expenses at their stations, but municipalities saw no inconsistency when they levied taxes on those stations to produce income.

By every measure passenger train ridership dropped sharply after World War II. Intercity passenger-miles dropped by a half between 1946 and 1951, and the number of passengers by even more. By the ICC formula, passenger trains just about broke even in 1946, with revenue of $3.67 and expenses of $3.68 for each mile a passenger train ran. These figures are slightly misleading since they include the frightfully expensive commuter train services in large cities. By 1951 revenue climbed to $4.08 per train-mile, but expenses were up to $5.48 per mile. Each year thereafter the picture grew darker. Some railroads thought the passenger train had no future and began dropping trains as rapidly as possible, but others held on believing there was a future in the business. As one route after another was dropped, travel became more and more difficult, and the public grew more and more disenchanted with the train service. The Transportation Act of 1958 took authority over train discontinuances from the states and transferred it to the ICC. That body established standards for train service and then presided over yet more undoing of the service network. Little public benefit came from the added delays of discontinuing a particular train.

The constant drain caused by a money-losing passenger service was brought into sharp focus by the situation at Penn Central. That line operated the nation's most extensive intercity passenger service, and although this was not the sole reason, the road was hemorrhaging money at a staggering rate. The railroads finally gave up their aversion to federal subsidies and headed to Washington for government help. Given the poor profit picture of the late 1960s, the health of the railroads was in peril without such assistance. The Senate, with Vance Hartke of

Indiana in the fore, began wrestling with the problem, encouraged by a rather small group of ardent advocates for continuing passenger trains.

A westbound Turboliner approaching Ann Arbor station in April 1975.

Sam Breck collection.

In early 1970 Penn Central petitioned the ICC to discontinue all of its passenger trains west of Buffalo, New York, and Harrisburg, Pennsylvania. Some said that it was move made in desperation, while others characterized it as a publicity ploy. Whichever it was, congressional thinking began to jell in the form of a government-subsidized semipublic corporation that would take over all intercity passenger service. When Penn Central went into bankruptcy in June 1970, the time for pondering was over, and Congress was forced to act. It created the National Railroad Passenger Corporation, better known as Amtrak, which on 1 May 1971 took over intercity passenger train operations on all but three roads.

The routes that Amtrak kept were a political patchwork quilt. Every representative, senator, and governor wanted another route in his or

Detroit-Chicago
Effective April 27, 1975

READ DOWN		Turbo Ex. Sun. #351	Turbo #353*	Turbo #355	Miles
City					
Detroit	Dp	7:00a	9:00a	5:00p	0
Ann Arbor		7:45a	9:45a	5:45p	36
Jackson		8:20a	10:25a	6:25p	74
Battle Creek		9:10a	11:20a	7:15p	119
Kalamazoo		9:40a	11:50a	7:45p	143
Niles (ET)		10:37a	12:45p	8:40p	190
Chicago	Ar	11:35a	1:40p	9:35p	279

Chicago-Detroit
Effective April 27, 1975

READ DOWN		Turbo #350	Turbo #352*	Turbo— Ex. Sat. #354
City				
Chicago	Dp	7:45a	4:10p	5:15p
Niles (ET)		10:35a	7:03p	8:10p
Kalamazoo		11:29a	8:00p	9:05p
Battle Creek		12:00n	8:30p	9:35p
Jackson		12:50p	9:25p	10:25p
Ann Arbor		1:30p	10:00p	11:00p
Detroit	Ar	2:25p	10:55p	11:55p

SERVICES. *NEW! Turboliner Service* — Chicago-Detroit. Light Meal and Beverage Service. Coach Service — Unreserved seats. Baggage Service — Checked hand baggage handled.
*Will operate with conventional equipment until May 15, 1975.
Connections at Chicago and Detroit with Amtrak's nationwide rail passenger service.

This April 1975 Amtrak timetable shows the inaugural service between Chicago and Detroit with its newly received Turboliner equipment.

Author's collection.

her home state, but the political enthusiasm behind Amtrak was so weak that no one was completely satisfied. About half of the nation's intercity passenger trains disappeared. In Michigan Amtrak cut Penn Central's three Detroit-Chicago runs to two. All service out of Detroit to New York City was discontinued. Chesapeake & Ohio trains from Grand Rapids to Chicago and Detroit were dropped, as were all runs out of Detroit to Toledo and points beyond. The *Wabash Cannon Ball* ran no more between Detroit and St. Louis. The Grand Trunk Western's service from Chicago to Detroit and Port Huron was ended, but with area government subsidy two commuter trains from Pontiac to Detroit were kept running.

Amtrak's start-up was less than auspicious. It was forced to use old locomotives and older cars cherry-picked from the existing fleet of railroad equipment. To the traveler, the new service appeared to be a continuation of the indifferent old service in the same cars from the same grimy stations. Citizen groups such as the Michigan Association of Railroad Passengers started lobbying for more trains as well as cleaning up some stations. With the enthusiastic support of Governor William Milliken, the *Blue Water* began a daily round-trip from Port Huron to Chicago in September 1974, running on a state subsidy. It featured brand-new "Turboliner" equipment—a set of cars with an engine and controls at each end allowing it to operate in either direction. The station stop in Lansing was moved to East Lansing, near the Michigan State University campus. Late in the year the *Niagara-Rainbow* between Detroit and Buffalo was added. It was integrated with Amtrak's New York City–Buffalo service and became a through train to New York City. In 1975 two more Turboliner sets provided new equipment for the Detroit-Chicago runs. With a new subsidy from the state of Michigan, a Jackson-Detroit commuter train called the *Michigan Executive* was started up. Also that year Amtrak built a new station at Port Huron for *Blue Water* passengers.

To the surprise of many, Amtrak was able to halt the slide in ridership on the trains it took over, a feat that the railroads had not been able to accomplish. But in its first five years it was not able to reverse the national trend to any meaningful degree. The OPEC-induced gasoline shortage in the early 1970s gave Amtrak a short-term increase in business, but no lasting benefit came from it. As the price of gasoline dropped, the new train riders went back to their cars.

SOURCES

American Association of Railroads. *Railroad Transportation: A Statistical Record.*
Washington, D.C.: American Association of Railroads, various years.

Amtrak, public timetables, various dates.

Michigan Association of Railroad Passengers. *Wolverine Mainliner,* various issues.

The Return of the Rails, 1976–2000

The Year of the Phoenix

When the nation's bicentennial opened in 1976, the future of the American railroad business could not have seemed gloomier. The litter of bankrupt roads with historic names was everywhere. In Michigan the Ann Arbor; the Chicago, Milwaukee, St. Paul & Pacific; and Penn Central were in the bankruptcy courts. The Rock Island and the reincarnated Erie and a good many other eastern roads were at the edge of collapse. Penn Central, the merger that brought together archrivals the Pennsylvania and the New York Central as a way to solve their problems, which then promptly fell into bankruptcy, was the most visible symbol of the problem. The federal government appeared unwilling to do anything to keep it alive. Other carriers, desperate in their scramble for some way to survive, also tried to merge their way to profitability.

The financial difficulties that were building up everywhere, the wide range of bankruptcies that extended into much of the nation, the passenger train service debacle that led to the formation of Amtrak, taken together, finally brought attention to the railroads' plight. Congress was forced, at long last, to realize that nearly a century of close, grinding regulation by the Interstate Commerce Commission (ICC) had brought the railroads dangerously close to their destruction as an industry. Not only was something needed, something different was demanded.

Amtrak to Date

Within five years of its start in 1971, Amtrak began to experience the problems that went with running a company that had an uncertain future and little popular support. Amtrak was brought into being as a political response to an unpopular issue raised by the clamor of a rather small group of passenger train service advocates. By 1976 the optimistic early days were over. The surge in traffic that came from the gasoline price increases in the early 1970s had disappeared, as people went back to their cars. While the Carter administration of the late 1970s had little enthusiasm for increasing Amtrak's funding to adequate levels, the successor Reagan administration went farther in the opposite direction by advocating an end to all federal assistance. The 1980s solidified these two opposing schools, the first questioning whether there was any need for rail passenger service in the United States, and the second holding to the wish for the service despite the worldwide demonstrated need for continuous government subsidies. Financial aid from the federal government was needed to start Amtrak, but it was given under the hopeful impression that there would not be an ongoing commitment. In 1976 new financial assistance and guarantees were needed to preserve freight service in the Northeast and to bring Conrail to life, which is discussed below. But this did not mute the chorus of objections to the continuing subsidies that some argued Amtrak would always need.

In 1975 professional railroader Paul Reistrup replaced Roger Lewis as Amtrak's president. Among the changes he instituted was the addition of a third midday train between Detroit and Chicago, and he followed it the next year with new Amfleet cars to replace two of the Detroit-Chicago Turboliners. By 1978 that part of the *Niagara-Rainbow* run between Buffalo and Detroit was dropped, a victim of a loss-reduction program. A completely new station in Dearborn was opened in 1978, providing the first convenient access for riders from the western suburbs of Detroit. The station in Kalamazoo was rehabilitated and renamed to be an intermodal center. The stations at Niles and Jackson were spruced up. In 1980 the Chicago-Detroit *Lake Cities* was extended to Toledo to make connections with the *Lake Shore Limited* to New York City and Boston. From the first this leg was hampered by the speed restrictions placed by several downriver municipalities; its running time was 110 minutes for a fifty-seven-mile trip. In September 1982 the *Blue Water Limited* was made into a through daytime run between Chicago and Toronto through Port Huron and renamed the *International*. The *Michigan Executive* was taken off in 1983, ending what had been a very modest commuter service from Jackson and Ann Arbor into Detroit. In March 1984 the state contracted with Amtrak and provided the subsidy needed to begin the *Pere Marquette*, which ran from Grand Rapids to Chicago each morning and returned each evening. This restored what had been one of the last Chesapeake & Ohio services in Michigan. In the summer of 1993

Amtrak extended the morning and evening Chicago-Detroit trains to run into Pontiac and later opened a new Detroit station at Woodward and Baltimore Avenues. This replaced a temporary building that had been used during the years since Amtrak moved out of the Michigan Central terminal. In 1995 the disappointing Detroit-Toledo leg of the *Lake Cities* was discontinued and replaced by an Ann Arbor–Detroit–Toledo bus. Although it was not an Amtrak service, the Pontiac-Detroit commuter service begun in 1931 by the Grand Trunk Western was continued after 1971 with two trains a day run under a contract with the Southeastern Michigan Transportation Authority. The trains made their final run in October 1983. This ended the oldest remaining continuously operated passenger train service in Michigan—between Detroit and Royal Oak, begun in July 1838.

In April 1976 Amtrak purchased the former Penn Central (nee Michigan Central) main line between Kalamazoo and Porter, Indiana. The United States Railway Association's *Final System Plan* recommended that Conrail not acquire the route for its freight operations. Its decision forced Amtrak to buy the line to preserve its Detroit-Chicago corridor service, but Conrail did agree to continue to provide local freight service. During the 1980s, and more so during the 1990s, the concept of important corridors of passenger service developed, with the Detroit-Chicago route near the top of the list of both midwestern and national planners. The state of Michigan, a high-speed rail association, several support and advocacy groups, and Amtrak all have studied the concept, and have made a number of improvements. Some highway crossings have been removed, gates and lights have been installed at many of the remaining road crossings, new sidings and a signaling system have been installed, and a global positioning system has been developed. The goal is to increase train speeds from the present 79 miles per hour to a hoped-for 120 miles per hour. A variety of state and federal agencies and Amtrak have funded such improvements. Several cities have bought and rehabilitated stations—Kalamazoo, Jackson, and Albion among them. The city of Battle Creek built a new train and bus terminal as part of its 1981 rail consolidation program, while Amtrak built new stations in Ann Arbor and Flint.

The national debate about Amtrak and its future has not quieted, much less been settled. Amtrak's opponents insist that the service should pay its own way, not expect government financial support, while holding that any experience in other countries is not germane to the United States. These people charge that the subsidies provide support for a

Chicago
Kalamazoo
Jackson

Detroit
Toledo

Port Huron
(Toronto)

Schedules Effective Apr. 28–Jun. 16 and Aug. 31–Oct. 26

▼READ DOWN   READ UP▲

354	352	364	350	km	Mi		Train Number		351	353	365	355	367
The Twilight Limited	The Lake Cities	Inter-national	The Wolver-ine				Train Name		The Wolver-ine	The Lake Cities	Inter-national	The Twilight Limited	Inter-national
Daily	Daily	Daily	Daily				Frequency of Operation		Daily	Daily	Ex Su	Daily	Su only
☕🍽	☕	⊠	☕				Type of Service		☕🍽	☕	⊠	☕	⊠
5 15P	2 05P	9 45A	8 30A	0	0	Dp	**(Conrail)** Chicago, IL -Union Sta. & (CDT)	Ar	12 20P	4 40P	5 59P	9 05P	10 47P
® 5 39P	® 2 29P	®10 09A	® 8 54A	25	16		Hammond-Whiting, IN ®		®11 40A	® 3 55P	® 5 22P	® 8 15P	®10 07P
6 24P				84	52		Michigan City, IN ● (CDT)		11 00A				
7 59P	4 47P	12 28P	11 17A	143	89		**(Amtrak)** Niles, MI (EDT)		11 25A	3 45P	5 12P	8 05P	9 57P
8 14P				163	101		Dowagiac, MI ●		11 10A				
8 44P	5 31P	1 14P	11 59A	220	137		**Kalamazoo, MI** &		10 35A	3 00P	4 25P	7 20P	9 10P
9 14P	6 01P	1 50P	12 29P	258 / 258	160 / 160	Ar / Dp	**(Grand Trunk Western)** Battle Creek, MI &	Dp / Ar	10 05A	2 25P	3 55P	6 50P	8 40P
		2 47P		333	207		**East Lansing, MI** (Lansing) &			2 40P			7 25P
		3 13P		381	237		Durand, MI ●			2 12P			6 57P
		3 38P		409	254		**Flint, MI**			1 52P			6 37P
		3 59P		439	273		Lapeer, MI ●			1 30P			6 15P
		5 00P		513	318	Ar	**Port Huron, MI**	Dp		12 45P			5 30P
	6 32P			298	185		**(Conrail)** Albion, MI ●			1 55P			
10 04P	6 57P		1 24P	331	205		**Jackson, MI** &		9 15A	1 30P		6 00P	
10 44P	7 37P		2 04P	390	243		**Ann Arbor, MI** &		8 35A	12 50P		5 20P	
D 11 19P	® 8 12P		® 2 39P	439	273		**Dearborn, MI** &		R 8 05A	®12 20P		® 4 50P	
11 45P	8 38P / 9 08P		3 00P	449 / 449	279 / 279	Ar / Dp	**Detroit, MI** -Amtrak Sta. &	Dp / Ar	7 45A	11 55A / 11 35A		4 30P	
	11 08P			542	337	Ar	**Toledo, OH** -Cntrl. Union Tml. & (EDT)	Dp		9 45A			
	48						Connecting Train Number			**49**			
	11 56P	To Toronto		542	337	Dp	Toledo, OH -Central Union Tml. &	Ar		9 04A	From Toronto		From Toronto
	1 54A			714	444	Ar	Cleveland, OH -Lakefront Sta. &	Dp		7 06A			
	5 08A			1017	632		Buffalo, NY -Depew Sta. &			3 48A			
	10 14A			1482	921		Albany-Rensselaer, NY &			10 48P			
	® 1 35P			1711	1063	Ar	New York, NY -Grand Central Tml. &	Dp		® 7 25P			
	3 35P			1804	1121	Ar	Boston, MA -South Sta. & (EDT)	Dp		5 15P			
®🔌		7 20P	®🔌			Dp	**(VIA Rail Canada, Inc.)** Windsor, ONT.	Ar			10 40A	®🔌	3 00P
		9 20P				Ar	London, ONT.	Dp			8 15A		1 00P
						Ar	Toronto, ONT. (EDT)	Dp					

Services

► **The Wolverine—The Twilight Limited**
Chicago-Detroit
Unreserved Coach Service
Food Service—Sandwiches, snacks and beverages.
Checked Baggage—Handled on Train Nos. 351 and 354 at all stations except Michigan City and Dowagiac.

► **The Lake Cities**
Chicago-Detroit-Toledo
Guaranteed connection at Toledo with **The Lake Shore Limited** to/from points east.
Unreserved Coach Service
Food Service—Chicago-Detroit—Sandwiches, snacks and beverages.
No Checked Baggage—Passengers may carry hand baggage on board.

► **International**
Chicago-Toronto
Unreserved Coach Service
Food Service—Tray meals, sandwiches, snacks and beverages.
No Checked Baggage—Passengers may carry hand baggage on board.

Chicago • Benton Harbor • Holland • Grand Rapids

Pere Mar-quette		◄ Train Name ►						Pere Mar-quette
® **370**		◄ Train Number ►						® **371**
Daily		◄ Days of Operation ►						Daily
®☕		◄ On Board Service ►						®☕
Read Down	Mile	▼				Symbol	▲	Read Up
5 20P	0	Dp	Chicago, IL–Union Sta.	(CT)		♿✳●	Ar	10 30A
7 37P	61		New Buffalo, MI	(ET)		○		10 05A
8 06P	89		St. Joseph-Benton Harbor, MI			○		9 36A
8 42P	116		Bangor, MI (South Haven)			○		8 59A
9 24P	151		Holland, MI			○		8 18A
10 21P	176	Ar	Grand Rapids, MI	(ET)		♿○	Dp	7 35A

Service on the Pere Marquette is financed in part through funds made available by the Michigan Department of Transportation. State supported trains are operated at the discretion of each state and their operation is dependent upon continued state financial support.

Chicago • Kalamazoo • Battle Creek • Port Huron • Detroit • Pontiac

350	364	352	354		◄ Train Number ►		351	353	365	355	367
Daily	Daily	Daily	Daily		◄ Days of Operation ►		Daily	Daily	Mo-Sa	Daily	Su
ⓑⓡ☕⊗	ⓑⓡ☕⊗	ⓑⓡ☕⊗	ⓑⓡ☕⊗		◄ On Board Service ►		ⓑⓡ☕⊗	ⓑⓡ☕⊗	ⓡ☕⊗	ⓡ☕⊗	ⓑⓡ☕⊗
8 40A	9 40A	2 10P	6 00P	Dp	Chicago, IL–Union Sta. (CT)	0 Ar	12 26P	3 35P	5 55P	10 09P	10 40P
9 07A		2 37P			Hammond-Whiting, IN	16		D 2 33P		D 9 19P	
		3 14P			Michigan City, IN (CT)	52		1 58P			
11 19A	12 15P	4 49P	8 37P		Niles, MI (South Bend) (ET)	89	11 23A	2 38P	4 58P	9 14P	9 43P
	12 27P		8 49P		Dowagiac, MI	102	11 08A		4 43P		9 28P
12 01P	1 01P	5 31P	9 22P		Kalamazoo, MI	138	10 39A	1 56P	4 14P	8 32P	8 59P
12 31P	1 36P	6 01P / [62]7 15P	9 52P / [62]10 40P	Ar / Dp	Battle Creek, MI	160 Dp / Ar	10 09A / [62]8 50A	1 26P / [62]11 35A	3 42P	8 02P	8 27P
	2 33P	[62]8 40P	[62]12 05A		East Lansing, MI	208	[62]7 30A	[62]10 15A	2 28P		7 23P
	3 09P				Durand, MI	238		1 51P	1 51P		6 46P
	3 38P	[62]9 40P	[62]1 00A	Dp	Flint, MI	256 Dp	[62]6 30A	[62]9 15A	1 25P		6 20P
	3 55P			Dp	Lapeer, MI	274 Dp			1 05P		6 00P
	4 50P			Ar	Port Huron, MI	319 Dp			12 20P		5 15P
		6 29P		Dp	Albion, MI	184		12 53P			
1 21P	To	6 53P	10 42P		Jackson, MI	205	9 14A	12 29P	From	7 07P	From
2 00P	Toronto	7 32P	11 21P		Ann Arbor, MI	243	8 38A	11 53A	Toronto	6 31P	Toronto
2 30P					Greenfield Village, MI	271		11 20A		5 58P	
[18]2 37P		[18] 8 07P	D11 52P		Dearborn, MI	273	[18] 8 03A	[18]11 16A		[18] 5 54P	
3 12P		8 38P	12 27A	Ar	Detroit, MI	281 Dp	7 42A	10 55A		5 33P	
3 16P		8 42P	12 31A	Dp			7 40A	10 53A		5 30P	
3 37P		9 03P	D12 51A		Royal Oak, MI	292	7 20A	10 35A		5 10P	
3 44P		9 10P	D12 58A		Birmingham, MI	296	7 13A	10 28A		5 03P	
4 10P		9 38P	1 25A	Ar	Pontiac, MI (ET)	304 Dp	7 00A	10 15A		4 50P	

For reservations and information, call 1-800-USA-RAIL or your travel agent, or visit www.amtrak.com on the Internet.

Amtrak is a registered service mark of the National Railroad Passenger Corporation.

Schedules subject to change without notice.

Chicago Grand Rapids — Pere Marquette

▼ READ DOWN 370						READ UP ▲ 371	373
Daily			Frequency of Operation			⑩ExSu	⑩Suonly
☕	km	Mi	Type of Service			☕	☕
			(Conrail)				
5 40P	0	0	Dp Chicago, IL -Union Sta. (CDT)		Ar	10 25A	4 25P
6 08P	25	16	Hammond-Whiting, IN (CDT)			9 43A	3 43P
			(Chesapeake & Ohio)				
7 57P	97	60	New Buffalo, MI (EDT)			9 54A	3 54P
8 27P	140	87	St. Joseph-Benton Harbor, MI			9 24A	3 24P
9 03P	185	115	Bangor, MI *(South Haven)*			8 49A	2 49P
9 44P	241	150	Holland, MI			8 11A	2 11P
10 35P	282	175	Grand Rapids, MI (EDT)			7 30A	1 30P

Services
► International
Chicago-Toronto
Unreserved Coach Service
Food Service—Tray meals, sandwiches, snacks and beverages.
No Checked Baggage—Passengers may carry hand baggage on board.

► Pere Marquette
Chicago-Grand Rapids
Unreserved Coach Service
Food Service—Sandwiches, snacks and beverages.
No Checked Baggage—Passengers may carry hand baggage on board.

Note:
Train Nos. 364, 365, 367, 370, 371, 373: service financed in part through a grant from the State of Michigan Department of Transportation. State supported trains are operated at the discretion of each state and are subject to discontinuance if a state withdraws its financial support.

THIS PAGE AND OPPOSITE: The service shown in Amtrak's April 1985 and October 2003 schedules changed very little over twenty years. The *International* has since been replaced by the *Blue Water Limited*, which makes a round-trip from Port Huron to Chicago each day.

Author's collection.

service that is used by only a marginally small group, and is a response to the advocacy efforts of an equally small group. Amtrak's supporters call up a variety of social and environmental advantages that train travel offers, as well as the need for such service by distinct segments of the populace. Another group of supporters is encouraging construction of an ultra-high-speed mass transit system in selected corridors, and holds up Japan's Bullet trains and France's TGV service and its European counterparts as models of what can be done.

Throughout its first thirty years Amtrak has been able to provide not much more than a skeleton network of service, a limit forced by its politically directed financial support. It has dropped some of its initial routes and started some new ones. California has become a leader in supporting new Amtrak service within that state. Special federal funding has allowing a much-improved northeast corridor service between Washington, D.C., New York City, and Boston, both in equipment and in train speeds. In its own defense Amtrak has been able to close some of the gap between its fare box income and its operating costs, but its critics continue to fault it for not paying all of its own way and expecting a continuing subsidy. Federal government policy, with direct and indirect subsidies, has actively supported all nonrail forms of intercity passenger transport throughout the twentieth century, and continues to do so in the twenty-first. But this truth has not persuaded Amtrak's critics or current politicians to face the need or the wisdom of a modern travel system that balances rail with all the other forms of transportation. This debate very likely will continue to be a political one, since it is unclear that Amtrak ever will be able to support itself financially and make itself independent. Each five-year anniversary of Amtrak prompts another book with some appreciation of what it has been able to accomplish and some cautious optimism about its future.

SOURCES

Amtrak, public timetables, various dates.

Michigan Association of Railroad Passengers. *Wolverine Mainliner* and *Wolverine Passenger* newsletters, various issues.

National Association of Railroad Passengers. *NARP News*, various issues.

Conrail Comes to Town

The bankrupt Penn Central limped through 1971 and 1972, kept alive only by infusions of cash from the federal government. There was some agreement that the road was too big and too important to be allowed to die, but no one could agree on how to keep it alive. Gradually the parties involved came to accept that many of Penn Central lines were so important that they had to be retained in some way. The alternatives came down to somehow reorganizing Penn Central in the same manner carriers had been for the last 100 years, or to chopping the company apart and allowing other roads to grab up any pieces they wanted. There were so many conflicting interests at the dock that any reorganization plan would likely be unacceptable to most of the parties. Liquidating Penn Central would preserve the most important service by new purchasers, but lines to some communities would be abandoned, and some lines torn up that once gone could never be rebuilt. One other alternative, nationalization, was trotted out, but the Nixon administration rejected that out of hand.

Judge John Fullam, in charge of the Penn Central reorganization proceedings, hired several quite competent trustees to manage the road while it was in bankruptcy. After two-and-a-half years of almost no progress, the judge brought matters to a head. Early in 1973 Fullam ordered that the trustees must file a reorganization plan with him by the end of June, or on 2 July he would order the company liquidated. The federal Department of Transportation (DOT), which up until now had kept a low profile in railroad matters, elbowed the ICC aside to take the lead for itself. It announced that Penn Central could be viable if most of its branch lines were pruned off, and that the ICC be kept from interfering in the revitalization the DOT wanted. Ironically, it was precisely this approach that Penn Central had used to support its merger application. Congress accepted the DOT's approach and rushed the 3R Act, the Regional Rail Reorganization Act of 1973, into law. This bill authorized creating the United States Railway Association (USRA) within the DOT, a new railroad company, as well as up to $1.5 billion of "off-budget" federal funding and loan guarantees to the new company. The Consolidated Rail Corporation, usually called Conrail, would acquire the lines USRA thought necessary. These lines would come principally from Penn Central, but also from other Eastern carriers if deemed vital. As a palliative the bill also provided federal support to

Sporting the Conrail logo, this is manifest freight DC-1 headed west out of Jackson in October 1976, en route to Elkhart, Indiana. The two trailing units still wear predecessor Penn Central's herald.

Douglas Leffler photo.

those states that chose to buy lines that Conrail did not take, as well as some support for other distressed roads and some for Amtrak.

The first result was DOT secretary Claude Brinegar's *Rail Service in the Midwest and Northeast Region*, released early in 1974. He concluded that 96 percent of all freight traffic in the study area could be retained while operating only 75 percent of rail lines. He said that the USRA should concentrate on high-volume interstate service and on local service, and that the financial viability of each should govern the Penn Central restructuring. Existing interstate routes ought to be consolidated to improve efficiency, and local service should be provided by only one carrier. Both the DOT and the ICC then went about formulating what Conrail should look like. In February 1975 the USRA released its first study, the *Preliminary System Plan*, for its design of Conrail. While the DOT worked in Washington conferring, it appears, mostly with bankers, lobbyists, and legislators, ICC's Rail Services Planning Office (RSPO) spent more than a year conducting hearings throughout the country. The DOT did acknowledge that it would consider the testimony taken by the RSPO in its final plan. When the USRA's *Final System Plan* was issued in July 1975, it looked very much like the preliminary plan, with the RSPO comments pasted in for good measure.

The validity of the analytical approach used by the USRA, and even the rationale for its approach, can be argued, but such a discussion is outside the scope of this work. For better or for worse, Conrail was a creation of the political forces at work at the time, in both houses of Congress and in the Nixon and Ford administrations. The result was a railroad that was Penn Central without many of its branch lines, particularly those with low traffic levels, and of some of intercity lines that were considered marginally profitable. To make its case about local service more solidly, the traffic levels for branches completely ignored any overhead movements and concentrated solely on local traffic generated. The *Preliminary System Plan* carried extended discussions about the service that had to be provided; the *Final System Plan* was almost exclusively a discussion of Conrail's finances. The ICC, correctly and traditionally, was concerned about service to communities and criticized the USRA for failing to provide what it considered adequate service. Such overly tender feelings by the ICC were part of the cause of the crisis that the USRA was created to solve, but the final decisions the USRA made when it created Conrail show considerably more concern about finances than about service.

Conrail took over operations on 1 April 1976. Of the 25,600 miles of line owned by the six bankrupt carriers that went into it, the new company operated about 15,000. Penn Central owned just under 1,700 miles of road in Michigan at the start-up of Conrail, and the Ann Arbor owned just under 300 miles, making a total of 1,975 miles. Of this Conrail took a little more than a third of Penn Central's lines, about 650 miles, and none of the Ann Arbor's. The principal routes were the Detroit-Kalamazoo main line; the Detroit-Toledo line; the branch from Jackson to Lansing; the line from Elkhart, Indiana, to Grand Rapids; the Air Line from Jackson to Three Rivers; the line from South Bend to Benton Harbor; and part of the New York Central's Old Road between Quincy and White Pigeon. To this basic network it added bits and pieces of other branches to retain specific shipper's traffic. To preserve its Detroit-Chicago route Amtrak bought the former main line between Kalamazoo and Porter, Indiana. The Grand Trunk Western bought the Ann Arbor's tracks between Durand and Ashley; the former Michigan Central line between Saginaw and Bay City, as well as the Bay City–Midland branch with a number of terminal lines in Saginaw and Bay City; and the former Pennsylvania line from Grand Rapids

Conrail tried to be rid of branches with sparse traffic, but it was not entirely successful since it did keep a Rives Junction–Eaton Rapids branch. Here is a Conrail westbound plodding through Onondaga in the late 1970s.

Sam Breck collection.

into Muskegon. The GTW also bought some scraps of trackage in such places as Owosso, Oxford, Lapeer, Charlotte, and Vicksburg to reach Penn Central's shippers who would otherwise have been abandoned. The Detroit & Mackinac bought a small piece of line in Bay City and the northern seventy miles of the Mackinaw branch, from south of Gaylord at Sallings to Mackinaw City. Nearly all of these sales were described and anticipated in the USRA's *Final System Plan*. The abandonment and sale of the remaining Penn Central and Ann Arbor lines are covered below.

Conrail had a difficult start. In the eight years and two months since the startup of Penn Central, little had gone right, and a great deal had gone wrong. Conrail inherited all of the problems and no advantages. Rid of most of the money-losing branches that were supposed to have brought down Penn Central, Conrail fared little better. Right from the start, to make matters worse, the new road was caught in the continuing decline of heavy industry in the Northeast that had so damaged Penn

Central. In 1980 L. Stanley Crane came from the Southern Railway to replace Richard Spence as Conrail's chief executive officer. Crane abandoned still more trackage, which in Michigan included the 1982 abandonments of the Jackson–Three Rivers line, the Benton Harbor branch, and the Eaton Rapids branch, as well as the eventual sale of several other short pieces. Crane also reduced the road's workforce by half and stepped up badly needed maintenance. All of this paid off in the second quarter of 1981 when Conrail posted its first profit. From then on Conrail remained in the black.

When Congress first formed the USRA and Conrail it had no clear idea about the eventual disposition of its creation. The *Final System Plan* included ten years of financial projections for Conrail, but did not discuss the future ownership of the road. In the Northeast Rail Services

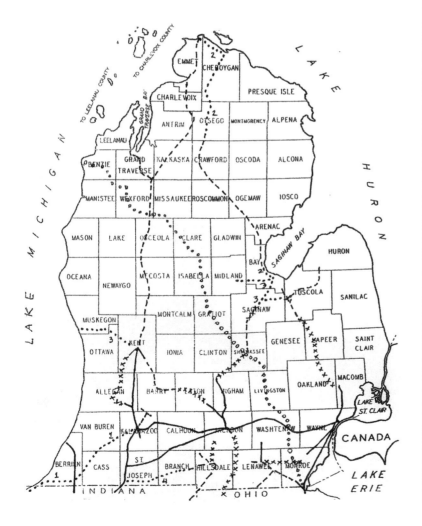

In 1976 Penn Central owned 1,680 miles of line in Michigan. At its breakup Conrail bought about 650 miles—38 percent of the total. Of the remainder, some was kept, some was sold to other roads, and the rest was abandoned.

KEY
—— PC lines sold to Conrail
- - PC lines to other roads
   1 to Amtrak
   2 to Detroit & Mackinac
   3 to Grand Trunk Western
   4 to others
••••• PC lines that were retained by PC and operated under a state subsidy
×××× PC lines abandoned
ᵒᵒᵒᵒ Ann Arbor line operated under a state subsidy

Act of 1981 Congress set 1984 as the date that the road should be sold to private ownership. Supporters of the sale claimed the government had no business doing what private enterprise could do, and that the proceeds would provide a welcome cash infusion against government deficits. Opponents claimed that the government had put $7 billion into Penn Central and Conrail, an expenditure that would largely be lost if the road were sold. The Reagan administration came down in favor of a sale and had the DOT assemble a list of potential buyers.

DOT secretary Elizabeth Dole found three serious buyers: the Norfolk Southern Railroad, J. W. Marriott leading a group of investors, and the Alleghany Corporation, which, when headed by Robert R. Young in the 1950s, had owned the New York Central. These were then joined by a group of Conrail officials who proposed buying the road and calling it an "employee purchase." Dole picked the Norfolk Southern as the most qualified of the prospects. Her choice brought a chorus of objectors. The Norfolk Southern first bid $1.2 billion for Conrail, and later raised that to $1.9 billion. The objectors considered this far too low, given the amount of money the government had put into the road. Congress made ready to hold investigations, CSX Corporation (the successor to the Chesapeake & Ohio) objected, and all sides threatened lawsuits against everybody. The Norfolk Southern withdrew its bid in August 1986.

The only reasonable course that now remained was for the government to sell its Conrail stock in a public offering. Despite Secretary Dole's objections, the government sold its 58,750,000 shares to the public in March 1987 at $28 a share, bringing a little over $1.6 billion to the federal treasury. Under Crane's management Conrail continued to grow in profitability, accomplished by holding expenses under strict control, by cutting the number of employees, and by shrinking its physical plant. In contrast to most other U.S. railroads, Conrail's freight traffic did not increase, in large part due to the continuing decline of the industrial base in its territory. In 1994 word leaked to the public that the Norfolk Southern was talking about a buyout with Conrail. Conrail stock jumped in price, but management announced it preferred to remain independent. At about the same time, two large mergers took place among the roads west of the Mississippi River. One of the new merged companies began talking about buying one of the eastern roads, and Conrail felt sure it was not the prospect.

Conrail management moved to defend itself, and in October 1996 announced it had agreed that CSX was to acquire the road. The deal worked out was to be $92.50 in stock and cash for each Conrail share, well over the current market price. Within days the Norfolk Southern fired back with its own offer of $100 per share, all of it in cash. In the ensuing publicity campaign neither suitor was able to persuade stockholders to give it a majority of the stock. The stalemate pushed the contest into the courts for a year and a half of suits, claims, and counterclaims. It became obvious that neither CSX nor the Norfolk Southern was going to gain the upper hand; they were forced to sit down to make a deal between themselves about how to divide up Conrail. The final agreement, bristling with conditions forced by every interested party, was approved by the Surface Transportation Board in June 1998. On 1 June 1999 Conrail was broken apart. The Norfolk Southern gained most of Conrail's lines in Michigan. In the greater Detroit area Conrail remained in existence as a jointly owned company, owning tracks for the mutual use of both roads.

SOURCES

Blaszak, Michael W. "Megamergers to the Far Horizon." *Trains* 57:4 (April 1997).

Daughen, Joseph R., and Peter Binzen. *The Wreck of the Penn Central*. Boston: Little, Brown, 1971.

Meints, Graydon M. *Michigan Railroad Lines*. East Lansing: Michigan State University Press, 2005.

Saunders, Richard. *The Railroad Mergers and the Coming of Conrail*. Westport, Conn.: Greenwood Press, 1978.

———. "Conrail." In *Encyclopedia of American Business History and Biography: Railroads in the Age of Regulation, 1900–1980*, ed. Keith L. Bryant Jr. New York: Facts on File, 1988.

U.S. Department of Transportation. *Rail Service in the Midwest and Northeast Region*. Washington, D.C.: Government Printing Office, 1974.

U.S. Interstate Commerce Commission. *Evaluation of the U.S. Railway Association's Preliminary System Plan*. Washington, D.C.: Government Printing Office, 1975.

United States Railway Association. *Preliminary System Plan*. 2 vols. Washington, D.C.: Government Printing Office, 1975.

———. *Final System Plan*. 2 vols. Washington, D.C.: Government Printing Office, 1975.

Michigan to the Rescue

Both of the USRA's reports, the *Preliminary System Plan* and the *Final System Plan*, anticipated that a large share of Penn Central's trackage would not be included in Conrail, and that some way had to be provided to allow other parties to continue those lines in operation. Both documents contained elaborate alternative proposals for the future of non-Conrail lines. Some of the stronger lines were to be offered to other carriers, many of which were accepted and sold, and are discussed below. In Michigan the remaining Penn Central lines were either to be abandoned or sustained by subsidy from the state.

In June 1974 the Michigan State Highway Department issued an elaborate *State of Michigan Action Plan*, which described in excruciating detail the planning process it would be using, but at the same time said almost nothing about railroads. A year later the state issued its *Michigan Railroad Plan, Phase I*. In a cover letter to the Federal Railroad Administration of the U.S. Department of Transportation, Governor William G. Milliken wrote that "it is even more essential that a balanced nationwide transportation system be provided to serve all states in such a manner as to provide for orderly economic and social development. Precipitous action at this time could result in the loss of major portions of our essential rail network. I cannot permit this to occur." This document spent more ink to describe how the state's planning and administrative process would work. When the *Michigan Railroad Plan, Phase II* was first released in December 1975, the state had made some decisions about which lines it wanted continued, with subsidy assistance from the federal government, and ten for which it would ask no subsidy. The state's final decisions appeared in June 1976 in a finalized *Michigan Railroad Plan, Phase II*.

The state of Michigan could not find contractors to operate several groups of lines and signed up Conrail to do so. Conrail owned the South Bend–Niles–Benton Harbor line, and agreed to serve both Dowagiac and Buchanan out of Niles without subsidy. The state wanted service maintained to towns between Kalamazoo and Dowagiac and between Michigan City and Buchanan, and Conrail took over this service under a state subsidy. The state also continued service on four Michigan Central lines out of Vassar, to Millington, to Caro and Colling, to Richville, and to Munger; Conrail handled this service until October 1977, when the newly formed Tuscola & Saginaw Bay took over the service. Conrail also provided service, under subsidy, from Grand Rapids to Vermontville, from Kalamazoo to Richland and Doster, and from Owosso to St. Charles, and several lines in the Adrian-Tecumseh-Clinton-Morenci area.

The first independent line to contract with the state was the Hillsdale County Railway. It proposed to operate several lines in

November 1975, and became a "designated operator" beginning in April 1976 for lines out of Hillsdale to Litchfield, Quincy, and south to Angola, Indiana. Michigan's agreement with the HCRC provided it with a track maintenance subsidy that was renewed annually. HCRC president John H. Marino assembled an experienced management and operating team that ran the sixty-mile line quite successfully. With two diesel locomotives and a road/rail switching engine the line offered daily (except Sunday) service that would pick up, deliver, and switch cars on demand. Its route to a connection with the Norfolk & Western (nee Wabash) at Steubenville, Indiana, supported by a subsidy from the state of Indiana, became its most valuable traffic connection, more so than that with Conrail at Quincy. In 1984 the state bought the Michigan trackage from Penn Central's trustees, and continues to own it to the present. The HCRC continued as an independent local operation until 1993, when it was sold to Indiana Northeastern, which continues to operate it.

An important goal of the state was to preserve service into the northern Lower Peninsula. The decision making involved the Ann Arbor Railroad line from Toledo to Frankfort, the Ann Arbor's car ferry operation across Lake Michigan, the former Michigan Central line from Bay City to Mackinaw City, and the Pennsylvania (nee Grand Rapids & Indiana) line from Grand Rapids, through Cadillac, to Traverse City and Mackinaw City. The railroad car ferry across the Straits of Mackinac, which Conrail also refused to take, connected the last two of these lines to the Soo Line at St. Ignace in the Upper Peninsula. Separate, but a part of the consideration, was the 1975 Chesapeake & Ohio (nee Pere Marquette) abandonment petition filed to abandon its line from Manistee to Petoskey. Any decision about the Ann Arbor car ferry route also had to take into account two other 1975 abandonment petitions, one by the C&O for all of its Lake Michigan car ferry routes out of Ludington to Kewaunee, Manitowoc, and Milwaukee, and another by the Grand Trunk Western to end its ferry service between Muskegon and Milwaukee.

The Michigan Northern's start was more difficult than that of the Hillsdale County. It was only a week before start-up that the state decided it would contract with Mark G. Campbell and the Michigan Northern's organizers. The company had trouble raising enough money to get under way, and the state had its own reservations about hiring an inexperienced group to operate a railroad. The decision may have come because the subsidy cost to hire Conrail would very likely be higher than the alternative. The Michigan Northern's situation was much different than that of the Hillsdale County. With almost 250 miles of line it had five times the mileage of the Hillsdale County, and following years of disinterested service by Penn Central it was moving barely half the traffic of the smaller company. The Northern Michigan started more frequent train service as it attempted to develop new traffic from its scanty shipper base, and tried to revitalize the overhead "bridge" traffic that the Straits of Mackinac car ferry brought across to it. Throughout 1976 and 1977 on-line freight traffic did not increase, despite the best efforts of Campbell and his successor, Elizabeth Andrus, and overhead traffic still remained minimal. In late 1977 Andrus decided that the MIGN could attract overhead movements if the road refused to participate in a recent ICC across-the-board rate increase, a maneuver called a "flag-out." This rate reduction worked. By May 1978 the *Chief Wawatam* and the MIGN were moving more than 600 southbound cars a month, up from less than ten a month a year earlier. The car ferry had to sail five days a week, often making two round-trips a day across the straits, to keep up with the rush of business. The MIGN thought this was the route to financial independence, but its success came at a price. As its revenues went up, so did its operating costs, and this increased the subsidy needed from the state. To handle two-and-a-half times as many cars the subsidy increased from $1.7 million per year to about $5 million per year. The subsidy for the *Chief Wawatam* rose from $655,000 per year to nearly $1.5 million per year to move the increased traffic. The state concluded that added manpower would be needed for the ferry to move additional traffic, with the result of still more subsidy increases.

The *Chief Wawatam* was also inextricably tied to the planning for the other line into northern Michigan, that of Penn Central (nee Michigan Central) from Bay City to Mackinaw City. The Grand Trunk Western agreed to buy all of Penn Central's lines in the Bay City area, including five miles of the Mackinaw branch as far as Kawkawlin. The state decided it would subsidize operations from Linwood, six miles north of Kawkawlin, to Sallings, about four miles south of Gaylord, and contracted with the Detroit & Mackinac as the designated operator. The D&M built a short line at Linwood to connect its own main line to the subsidy line. At the same time, the D&M bought the remainder of the Penn Central line between Gaylord and Mackinaw City as well as the short segment between Kawkawlin and Linwood. This combination of ownerships preserved service to the volume customers at Gaylord and Cheboygan, and also to the National Guard camp at Grayling.

The railroad car ferry *Chief Wawatam* was sixty-five years old, coal-fired and labor-intensive, and an expensive vessel to operate. The USRA's *Final System Plan* concluded that its operation was "irreversibly uneconomical and serves no function which cannot be provided better by all-rail routings," and refused to consider including it in Conrail operations. Although the ferry was needed to allow overhead freight movements to both the Michigan Northern and the D&M, the state thought there was little chance that traffic could be increased. Under an ICC order the Soo Line took control of ferry operations, and was replaced a few years later by the Detroit & Mackinac, with the support of a state subsidy.

Michigan's most difficult problem was what to do with the bankrupt Ann Arbor Railroad's line that extended from Toledo through Ann Arbor, Owosso, Mount Pleasant, and Cadillac, to Frankfort. Its Lake Michigan car ferries compounded the problem. The Grand Trunk Western bought a part of the line, between Durand and Ashley, which gave it all the traffic in Owosso as well as a line to its Greenville branch at Ashley. The section between Toledo and Ann Arbor, with the branch to the Ford Motor Company at Saline, had enough traffic to support continued operations, and that was the only section that the USRA considered retaining for Conrail. The remainder of the line, as far north as Mount Pleasant, had enough traffic to be considered for subsidy. North of that point the only station of importance was Yuma, which shipped sand for glass production to Toledo. The Lake Michigan car ferries to Kewaunee, Wisconsin, provided almost all the traffic beyond Yuma. From Kewaunee, the ferries carried a considerable amount of freight that was received from the Green Bay & Western. The USRA had not much more enthusiasm for this ferry run than it had for the Straits of Mackinac service, and recommended the entire route north of Ann Arbor not go into Conrail.

Rather than act rashly, the state bought the sections from Toledo to Ann Arbor and from Ashley to Cadillac, hired Conrail to begin subsidized operations over the entire Toledo-Frankfort route, continued one of the car ferries, and considered rehabilitating a second one. In October 1977 the state transferred operations from Conrail to Vincent Malanaphy's newly formed Michigan Interstate Railway. By dropping Conrail the state hoped to halt a continuing decline in car ferry traffic, which the state thought Conrail caused by soliciting freight to move via Chicago and its own rails rather than over Lake Michigan. In November 1978 Malanaphy also began a flag-out on certain types of freight in an attempt to boost cross-lake traffic. Despite challenges by several railroads, the flag-out stayed in effect, and nearly double the traffic moved on the car ferry traffic in both directions. Reopening the cross-lake route to Manitowoc, with its connections to the Chicago & North Western and the Soo Line, contributed to the increase.

In October 1977 the Lenawee County Railroad, founded and headed by John Marino of the Hillsdale County, replaced a part of Conrail subsidy operations. At first it connected with Conrail at Lenawee Junction to handle freight into the city of Adrian, but the next year began serving the Grosvenor-Morenci line. In February 1979 the LCRC bought a former Detroit, Toledo & Ironton line between Leaf and Bimo, which provided a better route between Adrian and the Morenci line. In 1982 Conrail announced that it planned to abandon its line between Ottawa Lake and Clinton; the state bought the line between Lenawee Junction and the DT&I crossing at Riga and assigned this to the LCRC. At the same time, it abandoned most of the line between Grosvenor and Weston due to damage to the River Raisin bridge. The operation was no particular success, leading the state to cancel the LCRC's designated operator contract in September 1990.

Toward the end of the 1970s Michigan began to face a recession in its industrial base, led by the automobile industry, and a squeeze on tax revenues. The state was forced to cut back on its subsidy programs for railroads. The first to go was the small service out of Kalamazoo to Richland and Doster. The hoped-for traffic failed to materialize, and the cost of maintenance was expected to go up. The subsidy ended in 1978 and the line torn up. In July 1979 the state ended Conrail's subsidized operation of the former Michigan Central line between Bowen, southeast of Grand Rapids, and Vermontville, and reassigned it to the Kent, Barry, Eaton Connecting Railway. The state was proud that it had located a minority-owned firm as contractor, but traffic remained at dismally low levels. In 1982 the subsidy to operate between Caledonia and Vermontville was ended, and the next year it was ended on the rest of the line. When the service stopped the line was torn up.

SOURCES

Cady, Ron. "Michigan Metamorphosis." *Trains* 47:10 (October 1987).

Keefe, Kevin P. "How Michigan Got into the Railroad Business." *Trains* 36:12 (October 1976).

Meints, Graydon M. *Michigan Railroad Lines*. East Lansing: Michigan State University Press, 2005.

Michigan Department of State Highways and Transportation. *State of Michigan Action Plan*. Lansing: Michigan Department of State Highways and Transportation, 1974.

———. *Michigan Railroad Plan, Phase I, May 15, 1975; Michigan Railroad Plan, Phase 2, December 6, 1975;* and *Michigan Railroad Plan, Phase 2, June 1976*. Lansing: Michigan Department of State Highways and Transportation, 1975, 1976.

Abandonments Continue; Sales Begin

By 1976 Michigan had lost about one-third of its 1908 railroad trackage; the network shrank to a little more than 5,800 miles. The creation of Conrail in 1976 brought a new spate of abandonments and other changes. During the preceding eight years Penn Central aggressively tried to abandon trackage it considered marginal, but the ICC allowed it to shed only 30 miles of scraps and pieces in Michigan before it entered bankruptcy in 1970. This failed attempt was but one of the many savings that were never achieved and, in fact, were obstructed by a government agency. Conrail, given a luxury denied to Penn Central, selected only about 650 miles of Penn Central lines in Michigan for itself. Of its remaining 1,000 miles, a large chunk was sold to the Grand Trunk Western, and some smaller pieces to Amtrak and the Detroit & Mackinac. That left nearly 600 miles in Penn Central's hands, to be disposed of as it saw fit. Over the next sixteen years nearly all of this was sold or was abandoned after state attempts to have other roads operate lines under contract. Conrail did abandon some of the lines acquired in 1976, bringing Conrail trackage down to just under 400 miles in Michigan by 1999.

Even without the Conrail abandonments the Michigan network continued to shrink. In 1977 the Grand Trunk Western abandoned fifteen miles between Coopersville and Grand Haven and sold its Grand River bridge to the Chesapeake & Ohio. In 1983 it removed twenty-one miles from Middleton to Greenville, seven miles from Pigeon to Caseville, and ten miles from Lakeland to South Lyon. Also that year it traded its remaining line in Greenville to the Chesapeake & Ohio and acquired some trackage from the latter in Ionia. The next year the GTW took up seven miles of tracks between Middleton and Carson City, and sold the remaining twelve miles into Ashley to a group of shippers. It removed ten miles between Wixom and South Lyon and four miles between Sylvan Lake and Walled Lake, and sold the section between Wixom and Walled Lake to Coe Rail. In 1986 it abandoned fifty miles of road between Kings Mill and Pigeon. The GTW bought a number of lines in 1976 in an offer from the government for Penn Central trackage that Conrail would not take. It bought thirty-four miles between Durand and Ashley from the Ann Arbor's bankruptcy trustees and soon abandoned most of that road's trackage between Durand and Owosso. It bought thirty Penn Central miles from Walker to Muskegon, on which it had run on trackage rights since the 1930s; a line from Saginaw through Bay City to Midland; and a number of industrial spurs in Saginaw and Bay City. The GTW disposed of a large part of this purchase in September 1987 when it sold all of its Durand–Saginaw–Bay City–Midland and its Durand–Owosso–Ionia–Grand Rapids–Muskegon lines to the newly formed Central Michigan.

The Chesapeake & Ohio abandoned its nine-mile Elk Rapids and fourteen-mile Mt. Pleasant branches in 1979, nearly twenty-four miles from Montague north to Mears and Hart in 1981, and its line between Manistee and Bay View in 1982. Of this last line it sold the sections between Grawn and Williamsburg and between Charlevoix and Bay View to the state of Michigan, which planned to have some other road operate it under a subsidy program. In 1983 it abandoned its fourteen-mile branch between Portland and Ionia and sold its remaining trackage in Ionia to the Grand Trunk Western. In 1984 it took up seven miles from Kinde and Port Austin, and in 1986 seven miles from Eagle to Portland. In August 1984 the C&O sold its thirteen-mile Hartford–Paw Paw branch to the Southwestern Michigan Railroad, which began operations under the Kalamazoo, Lake Shore & Chicago name, and in 1986 abandoned the remaining fourteen miles between South Haven and Hartford. In December 1984 the C&O bought the eighteen-mile line of the Port Huron & Detroit that extended from Port Huron to Marine City. In 1977 the Boyne City sold its eight-mile line to Hollis Baker of Grand Rapids, who ended its common carrier status and operated it as a tourist road. In 1979 the Detroit, Toledo & Ironton took up two parts of its Napoleon, Ohio–Adrian–Tecumseh branch and left a piece in Adrian that became part of the Lenawee Country Railroad.

In 1976 the Milwaukee Road removed its line between Republic and Champion and in 1980 that between Channing and Republic. The Soo Line took up the remaining twenty-seven miles between Raco and Soo Junction in 1977. In 1978 the Soo Line abandoned the former Mineral Range main line between Hancock and Calumet. It took up the Rapid River branch to Eben Junction in 1979. It took out of service sixty-seven miles of the original DSS&A main line between Nestoria and Bergland in 1981, but the rails were left in place. In 1979 the Lake Superior & Ishpeming removed its lines between Marquette and Lawson and between Little Lake and Munising Junction. This left the road with only its major ore-hauling operation from the Marquette Range to its Presque Isle ore dock as well as an isolated section at Munising. Iron ore mining ended on the Gogebic Range and much of the Menominee Range by the 1970s. The Chicago & North Western abandoned all of its trackage west of Ishpeming in 1980 and between Marenisco and Hurley, Wisconsin, in 1981. In 1982 it took up its tracks between Iron Mountain and Watersmeet through Iron River, the Crystal Falls branch, and the line extending from Land O'Lakes, Wisconsin, through Watersmeet, to Marenisco. This ended all C&NW access to the iron mines in the Gogebic Range and in the western part of the Menominee Range.

By 1984, after most of the Penn Central and Conrail abandonments had been completed, Michigan's rail mileage was down to just under 4,700 miles, of which over 3,700 miles were in the Lower Peninsula and just over 900 miles above the Straits of Mackinac.

The Chesapeake & Ohio, which renamed itself as CSX Transportation in 1987 and by then was rid of its Lake Michigan car ferry operations, began to abandon sections of its Saginaw-Ludington line, beginning with the Clare-Evart segment and the next year the Evart-Baldwin part. These were part of the original Flint & Pere Marquette main line and among the oldest of CSX's Michigan lines.

The Soo Line removed the east end of the former Duluth, South Shore & Atlantic main line between St. Ignace and Trout Lake in 1986, which broke the rail connection that supported more than 100 years of car ferry service across the Straits of Mackinac. Equally sad was the end of all train service into the Keweenaw Peninsula in September 1992. Service over the last line, between Baraga and Lake Linden, which used the unique double-deck highway lift bridge between Houghton and Hancock, had dwindled to nearly nothing after the end of Calumet & Hecla mining and refining operations. After several unsuccessful attempts to revive the service, the Soo Line sold the line between Arnheim and Lake Linden to the state of Michigan, which kept the rails in place but ran no trains. The state was unable to interest either the Wisconsin Central or the Escanaba & Lake Superior in starting subsidized operations into the Keweenaw.

When the Wisconsin Central bought the Chicago & North Western lines in 1997 it decided the original Duluth, South Shore & Atlantic main line east of Marquette to Munising Junction was no longer needed. In

1999 the WCL abandoned those thirty-seven miles. The WCL also owned both the original C&NW main line and the Soo Line that paralleled it between Hermansville and a crossing north of Escanaba. The C&NW route had more business development along it; the WCL also abandoned the twenty-eight-mile Soo Line route in 1999.

The Chesapeake & Ohio abandoned its line through Traverse City in 1982, and also ended its lease of the Leelanau Transit, the owner of the Hatchs-Northport branch. This 24-mile road tried without success to operate as a tourist road. About 1995 it took up its tracks between Suttons Bay and Northport and a year later ended operations. Another northern Michigan tradition, the 3.4-mile Ludington & Northern, stopped hauling sand for its owner, the Sargent Sand Company, in the early 1990s; its tracks were finally taken up about 1997 after CSX had removed its branch in Ludington that connected to the L&N.

In 1987 the D&M moved its main line between Linwood and Pinconning over to the former Michigan Central Mackinaw branch tracks and abandoned its line along the Lake Huron shore. The Lake State Rail Corporation, which was formed by officers of the Detroit & Mackinac, bought all of the D&M lines in 1992. The state's designated operator contract for the former Penn Central Bay City–Gaylord line also was transferred to the LSRC. When the D&M first began providing designated operator service between Linwood and Sallings (south of Gaylord) in 1976 it also bought the remainder of the Penn Central line between Gaylord and Mackinaw City. When Straits of Mackinac car ferry service ended in 1986 no other traffic remained north of Cheboygan. The Cheboygan–Mackinaw City leg was taken up in 1989, as were forty miles of the original D&M line between Hawks and Cheboygan, a line that had seen little traffic for some years. When the paper mill at Cheboygan closed the last remaining important shipper there was gone; Lake State abandoned the forty-seven miles between Gaylord and Cheboygan in 1993. In 1998 Lake State took up the branch between Hillman Junction and Paxton.

The new century opening in 2000 found a Michigan rail network at its smallest since 1880. With just over 3,700 miles of road, the state's rail network was down to only 40 percent of its 1909 high-water level. About 2,900 miles were operated in the Lower Peninsula, while only 800 miles remained in the Upper Peninsula. Michigan is not unique in the loss of rail mileage, as other states, especially in the Midwest and Northeast, also experienced losses of like degree. On the whole, the network that now remains is in better physical condition and capable of bearing heavier traffic than it has been for many years. The loss of industry, manufacturing and extractive and agricultural, has occurred throughout the state and, in turn, has caused a substantial reduction in the demand for rail freight service. Finished automobiles, auto parts, and utility company unit coal trains are new sources of freight and do provide new strength to a few lines. This is a trend in industries that will continue over time. It is difficult to envision, however, any large increase in demand for rail freight service in Michigan on any except a few major trunk lines.

SOURCES

Michigan Department of Transportation, various reports and documents.

United States Railway Association. *Final System Plan.* 2 vols. Washington, D.C.:
    United States Railway Association, 1975.

New Rules Bring New Life

The early 1970s were dark days for American railroads and made clear that there could be no solution without federal involvement. Any remedy had to address the problems facing the rail freight haulers throughout the country as well as the larger situation presented by the bankruptcies of the Penn Central, Reading, Lehigh Valley, Erie-Lackawanna, and Ann Arbor. Congress created Amtrak and then the United States Railway Association, leading to the eventual creation of Conrail. The federal subsidies that accompanied the latter move were the first federal financial assistance given to any railroad since World War II, when the federal government provided scraps of financial support to keep a few roads operating.

The Northeast Rail Reorganization Act of 1981 allowed Conrail to drop all of the passenger service it operated, although by that time it was providing only commuter train service. Most of these commuter operations were in the Boston–New York–Washington, D.C., corridor and were taken over by state agencies or authorities, and by these means began to receive federal as well as state and municipal funding that had been largely denied to the individual railroads up to that time.

The passage of the Staggers Rail Act of 1980, named for the soon-to-retire Representative Harley O. Staggers (D-W.Va.), represented a complete change in the attitude of the federal government. Faced with a worsening economy the Carter administration hoped to stimulate the heavily regulated aviation and trucking industries by deregulating them. The Staggers Act brought this approach to the railroads. The railroads' regulator, the ICC, was the oldest of all such federal agencies. To many railroadmen it was the chief cause of the railroads' problems. Its micromanaging involvement in everything—such as accounting systems, stock and bond issuing, and line abandonment and construction—and its complete control over setting rates, were a smothering blanket. Its predictability and insularity were keynotes, while innovation and experimentation found a cold welcome at the ICC's door. An early 1960s Soo Line request to establish a multicar negotiated rate from Sault Ste. Marie was turned down. The Southern Railway's battle to offer reduced rates for grain movements in its large-capacity cars lasted throughout the late 1960s. The ICC's unimaginative involvement in deteriorating rail passenger service was fresh in the memory of all involved. Stagger's legislation removed a great deal of the commission's involvement in rate-making, while attempting to retain some degree of control over the charges for some commodities that were captive to rail movement. It set up provisions that allowed roads to add surcharges on certain shipments over unprofitable routes and branches. Most important, the law expressly allowed negotiated rates between a railroad and a shipper and exempted these from ICC regulation. Finally, the act liberalized the rules to make it easier to abandon lines, and also provided new options to transfer branch lines to local operators.

The Staggers Act was an unparalleled success. It allowed a freedom of action not seen in nearly eighty years. Permission to innovate encouraged railroad innovation. Contract rates brought out the unit train, which moves 10,000 tons of coal to power plants in 100-car trainloads. The railroads set up combination rates with ocean shipping lines to move trainloads of containers throughout the country. New short lines sprang up everywhere to provide service on branches that large carriers wanted to abandon as unprofitable. The steady shrinkage of the physical plant's capacity to handle trains stopped, new signal systems were installed, and in places second main tracks were put back in.

Although not a part of the legislative process, there was new progress in labor relations as the railroads worked out new agreements with the operating brotherhoods. The first was an agreement that allowed removal of the fireman on diesel locomotives. In the ensuing years certain work was transferred from employees to subcontractors; train wreck cleanup was given over to outside companies. The Regional Rail

Reorganization Act of 1973 made a dead letter of the few remaining state full-crew laws, a change that allowed reduced train crew size on freight trains. The railroads took this a step further by negotiating still more reductions in crew size. Eventually these allowed most freight trains to run without a caboose and with only two or at most three men in the engine cab. Amtrak passenger and most commuter rail trains now run with only one man in the engine cab. Most of the new short lines are not unionized, allowing still more economies because the traditional employee craft lines are ignored, a situation that does remain on the larger unionized roads.

As the Staggers Act ended much of the ICC's tight control over the railroads, it encouraged more calls for the abolition of the federal agency. That end came with the Interstate Commerce Commission Termination Act of 1995. The law shut down the 108-year-old regulatory body, ended some of its functions, and transferred other responsibilities to the newly created Surface Transportation Board (STB). The STB, a part of the U.S. Department of Transportation, is now the primary railroad regulatory agency, and has also some authority over intercity trucking companies, moving van companies, intercity bus companies, and some pipeline services. The STB is charged with resolving disputes over railroad rates and service and with reviewing proposed rail mergers. The STB has authority over rail line sales, construction, and abandonment. It also continues some of the statistics compilation that the ICC performed. The Federal Railroad Administration retains control over rail safety matters, transferred at its formation in 1966 from the ICC; control over federal financial assistance programs to railroads; and some Amtrak oversight.

In the twenty years after the new approach brought by the passage of the Staggers Act, the railroads have worked a revolution. The railroads have levels of profitability not seen in decades, and those profits have brought renewed investor confidence. The new freedom to innovate has brought successes and surprisingly few mistakes. Not every shipper has been pleased with the new climate or has retained every advantage gained under the ICC, but taken as a whole the business community has been well served with the railroads' improved strength.

SOURCES

Hilton, George W. "Staggers Rail Act of 1980." In *Railroads in the Age of Regulation: 1900–1980*. New York: Facts on File, 1988.

Martin, Albro. *Railroads Triumphant: The Growth, Rejection, and Rebirth of a Vital American Force.* New York: Oxford University Press, 1992.

New Companies with Old and New Names

In addition to the state of Michigan assuming a role in the railroad business, all of Michigan's rail companies acted on several fronts to improve profitability. One was to continue the long-standing practice of abandoning marginal lines, and a second was to hunt for other railroad companies to acquire. A third was to sell off marginal lines, lines that made little contribution to profits but were attractive to new, independent operators. A number of new companies, in addition to those named above, were formed to operate these unwanted branches.

The first of these companies was Coe Rail. Formed in 1984, it bought nine miles of track between Wixom and Walled Lake from the Grand Trunk Western and provided both freight service and passenger excursions. In March 1986 the Huron & Eastern bought more than 80 miles of Chesapeake & Ohio lines: between Croswell and Kinde, between Palms and Harbor Beach, and the Sandusky branch. The H&E added the former C&O Saginaw–Bad Axe and the Bay Port branches in 1988, expanding the road to 140 miles of line. In 1991 it became the state's designated operator of lines out of Vassar to Millington, Reese, and Caro, which had been the original core of the Tuscola & Saginaw Bay. In 1996 the H&E abandoned the 10 miles between Ruth and Harbor Beach.

In August 1986 the Southwestern Michigan Railroad bought the C&O line between Hartford and Paw Paw and operated it as the Kalamazoo, Lake Shore & Chicago, reviving a name that had died sixty years earlier. Its founder was Mark G. Campbell, who ten years earlier had been the first president of the Michigan Northern. In September 1987 the Central Michigan bought 225 miles of line from the Grand Trunk Western. The Central Michigan was formed by the owners of the Detroit & Mackinac, with Charles A. Pinkerton III at its head. This move expanded his operations to new areas of the state as well as improving the interchanges his D&M had with friendly railroads. The CM bought the GTW's Durand–Bay City and Durand–Grand Rapids lines, as well as the Grand Rapids–Muskegon line and the lines in the Saginaw, Bay City, and Midland areas that the GTW had bought from Penn Central.

Another classic name, Wisconsin Central, returned to Michigan in October 1987 when the newly formed company bought all of the Soo

Line system. The Canadian Pacific, the Soo Line's owner, acquired the lines of the bankrupt Milwaukee Road and wanted to dispose of the now-surplus Soo Line. Edward A. Burkhardt, former Chicago & North Western vice president of transportation, created Wisconsin Central, Ltd. (WCL) and was the guiding spirit of the new company. His conception of a regional railroad and the innovations in service he brought to the newly non-union company led to a much revitalized property. It regained business that had abandoned its rails years earlier, and it found new freight traffic. WCL began long-distance iron ore movements during the winter in amounts unseen in decades. Burkhardt formed a working relationship with the Canadian National, which gave that road a link between western Canada and the CN's Grand Trunk Western at Chicago. Eventually WCL bought the Algoma Central Railway, the road that extends north from Sault Ste. Marie, Ontario, and operates snow trains and excursions to Agawa Canyon. Burkhardt's acquisition fed new traffic across the International Bridge to his Michigan lines. When the Union Pacific bought the Chicago & North Western in April 1995 it had little desire to keep the lines in Michigan. Burkhardt made an offer and in January 1997 added nearly 200 miles of former C&NW trackage to a WCL subsidiary. Burkhardt's road now owned about three-quarters of all the rail mileage in the Upper Peninsula.

In December 1987 Mid-Michigan bought two parts of the C&O's "Turkey Trail," from Paines to Elwell and from Elmdale to Greenville; the next year the C&O removed the connecting piece between Elwell and Greenville through Edmore. In 1988 the Alanson & Petoskey began a tourist operation between those points on tracks leased from Penn Central. It continued running for only about four years. In 1989 a group of shippers along Conrail's Sturgis-Quincy line bought the thirty-mile section to preserve it when Conrail threatened abandonment, after running no trains since 1984. The shippers hired the Michigan Southern to operate trains for them.

In 1989 the Central Michigan began its own downsizing program. It removed its line from Walker into Muskegon and in December 1989 sold a short section west of Walker to the Coopersville & Marne, which otherwise would have been isolated. In 1990 the CM sold the remainder of its trackage in Muskegon to a new short line, the Michigan Shore. After an extended attempt to revive traffic the Central Michigan took up its tracks between Owosso and Ionia in 1991. This left the Ionia–Grand Rapids section isolated from the rest of the system, and this section was finally sold to the Grand Rapids Eastern in July 1993. Rail-Tex Corporation, a national operator of short-line railroads, owns the Michigan Shore and the Grand Rapids Eastern as well as the Mid-Michigan.

The Adrian & Blissfield started operating the state-owned line between Riga and Adrian in December 1990. It began to supplement its basic freight service with passenger excursions and a dinner train operating out of Blissfield. In January 1999 two A&B subsidiaries bought short sections of line from the Grand Trunk Western: three miles went to the Charlotte Southern and two-and-a-half miles to the Detroit Connecting in those cities. In June 1999 a third, the Lapeer Industrial, bought one mile in Lapeer. The Charlotte Southern also operates a dinner train, while the latter two are entirely industrial operations.

In 1995 the West Michigan Railroad, a subsidiary of Pioneer Railcorp., bought the Kalamazoo, Lake Shore & Chicago line from Hartford to Paw Paw. The KLS&C was forced out of business after it tried to replace a dinner train operation that moved with little notice from the KLS&C to Coe Rail. In February 1997 the Grand Trunk Western sold part of the Detroit, Toledo & Ironton line it had bought in 1983. The line south of the Ann Arbor Railroad crossing at Diann was sold to the Indiana & Ohio. The GTW kept the section between Detroit and Diann to continue its access to the Ford Motor Company Rouge plant complex.

SOURCES

News articles from the *Chesapeake and Ohio Historical Magazine, Michigan Railfan, North Western Lines,* and *Soo Line.*

Rails Across the Lakes

The Lake Michigan railcar ferries provided an alternative for freight traffic between Michigan and the Northwest to avoid Chicago, an area that at the beginning of the twentieth century caused considerable delays to movements. By the 1960s these delays were less often the case; new operating techniques had removed many of the bottlenecks. At the same time, railroads developed larger freight cars that could carry heavier loads and moved them in longer trains. Most of the boats were coal-fired, all were labor-intensive and generally could handle no more than twenty-four freight cars on a trip. The Chesapeake & Ohio considered them more a detriment to good service than an asset. Since World War II car ferry traffic levels slowly eroded. In the late 1960s the

C&O attempted to boost passenger use of the ferries but after this met
with only modest success; it decided to rid itself of them completely.
It sold off several boats and in March 1975 applied to the ICC to end
all ferry service. The resulting melee resulted in the C&O offering the
ferries and docks to anyone who would take them, but no takers came
forward. Three years later the ICC granted some relief. Its decided to
allow the Ludington-Milwaukee service to end, which came in 1980, and
to Manitowoc in 1982, but required the C&O to continue the Ludington-
Kewaunee route. The C&O offered to sell its boats and docks to the
states of Michigan and Wisconsin, but they could not find the money.
In 1983 Ludington businessman Glen Bowden headed up a group that
bought the three remaining ferries for $1 each. His Michigan-Wisconsin
Transportation made a valiant effort to keep going by using only the
City of Midland and keeping the *Spartan* and the *Badger* in reserve. The
company finally ran out of money in November 1990, ending the ferry

The Pere Marquette's *Spartan*, one of the
last of the Lake Michigan ferries built.
Still docked at Ludington, it provides
parts for its sister ship the *Badger*, which
still sails.

Sam Breck collection.

service. In 1991 a new angel appeared: Charles Conrad of Holland bought the three ferries and spent $1.5 million to rehabilitate the *Badger*. His Lake Michigan Car Ferry Service began summer-season sailings from Ludington in 1992. In its first year it carried 115,000 passengers; it also carries automobiles but no freight cars. Changing the Wisconsin port from Kewaunee to Manitowoc brought new riders. After several seasons its popularity shows no sign of waning.

The state of Michigan was directly involved in continuing the Ann Arbor's Lake Michigan car ferry service as well as that at the Straits of Mackinac. These were considered important routes for the areas served, and the straits ferry connected the two peninsulas as well. The Grand Trunk Western applied in 1975 to end its Muskegon-Milwaukee freight car ferry service; it had stopped carrying passengers in 1971. After three years of studies, hearings, and legal maneuvers, and over the protests of both states, it was over. The *City of Milwaukee* made its last trip in October 1978 and, now owned by the state, moved to Frankfort to supplement the Ann Arbor service. In 1973, when the Ann Arbor declared bankruptcy, its ferry, the *Arthur K. Atkinson*, broke its crankshaft, leaving only the *Viking* to handle all traffic. The Ann Arbor dropped its Frankfort-Manitowoc route and kept only the service to Kewaunee. The state repaired the *Atkinson*, and the increased traffic from the rate flag-out kept the ferries busy. But when the ferry's operator, Michigan Interstate, stopped operations because of its disagreement with the state, the ferries also stayed in port. When it was settled the car ferries did not resume sailing. By 1999 only the *City of Milwaukee* remained at Frankfort, an attraction to some and a public nuisance to others.

At the Straits of Mackinac the *Chief Wawatam* enjoyed a sudden short burst of business in the late 1970s, then settled down to one trip a week. It cost more money keeping it in port between trips than was spent to make a crossing. The state grew increasingly unhappy at the cost of this subsidy, and in October 1984 the *Chief* made its last crossing. It spent several years docked at the railroad pier in Mackinaw City while officials tried to figure out some use for it. The final insult came when the *Chief* was cut down to a barge while keeping its original name.

SOURCES

Michigan Department of Transportation, various reports and documents.

Zimmerman, Karl. *Lake Michigan's Railroad Car Ferries*. Andover, N.J.: Andover Junction Publications, 1993.

Old Rails, New Riders

The Michigan Central last carried passengers between Kalamazoo and South Haven in 1937 on a mixed train that hauled both freight and people. Sixty years later there were more people on the line in a week than probably rode in a month or two when the train was running. With the rails gone the route became the Kal-Haven trail, and walkers and bicyclists are the travelers. The idea came from similar projects in adjoining states, particularly in Wisconsin. Promoted as a Bicentennial project, and opposed by a good many adjoining property owners, it has lived up to all the hopes of its first supporters to become Michigan's oldest "rail-to-trail" undertaking. The state bought the right-of-way from Penn Central after it had removed the rails and ties in 1976. The clapboard-sided depot in Bloomingdale became a local museum.

The success of the Kal-Haven trail has led to more. The Paint Creek trail north of Rochester is on a part of the Michigan Central's Detroit–Bay City line that was abandoned in 1976. The Lakeland trail is on the Grand Trunk Western line between Pinckney and Stockbridge. The abandonment of the Chesapeake & Ohio (nee Pere Marquette) line between Montague and Hart provided another trail route. The newest and longest—over ninety miles—is the White Pine trail between Comstock Park and Cadillac on the former Grand Rapids & Indiana grade. The Upper Peninsula is crisscrossed with trails good for hikes in summer and snowmobiles in winter. Among the longest is the State Line trail, extending 107 miles from Wakefield through Watersmeet to Stager. Connecting trails extend to Land O'Lakes, Gibbs City, and Crystal Falls. The Haywire trail uses the grade of the Manistique & Lake Superior between Manistique and Shingleton. Many of the abandoned grades of the Copper Range are used: McKeever to Houghton, a branch to Freda, Hancock to Calumet, and Mohawk to Gay.

The Huckleberry Central Railroad operates in a Genesee County park northeast of Flint. It uses some of the grade of the Pere Marquette's former Flint-Fostoria branch for a narrow-gauge train that uses an engine from the Denver & Rio Grande Western. The Southern Michigan Railroad Society at Clinton offers its line to Raisin Center for weekend excursions for track speeders, the motorized riding machines used by section crews when maintaining tracks.

Sprinkled across the state are several of a new railroad service. The dinner train attempts to recapture the period ambiance of exceptional

One innovative—and very popular—program to reuse abandoned railroad routes is "rails-to-trails." Hikers and bicyclists are enthusiastic supporters. In the Lower Peninsula several hundred miles have been prepared for this new use, and many more have been proposed.

dining while riding a train. The *Star Clipper*, the first to start up in Michigan, began operating from Paw Paw on the Kalamazoo, Lake Shore & Chicago about 1987. It ran there for several years until it moved to Walled Lake and began running on Coe Rail. Other such ventures were the Grand Traverse Dinner Train which runs east from Traverse City on former Pere Marquette tracks; the Coopersville & Marne; the Adrian & Blissfield running out of Blissfield; and the Charlotte dinner train operated by an A&B subsidiary out of Charlotte.

Each year several rail excursions run in Michigan with a few of them pulled by a steam locomotive. A dedicated and hard-working group from Michigan State University began in 1970 to restore Pere Marquette locomotive 1225 to running condition. After years of effort they reached their goal, and now under the auspices of the Steam Railroading Institute at Owosso, the engine pulls a few special excursion runs each year.

Other trips, pulled by diesel locomotives, are offered with Tuscola & Saginaw Bay lines as host for many of them.

The Twenty-First Century

A catalog of proposals developed as part of a movement broadly called "deregulation." After the concept was applied to the trucking industry and to the airlines in the late 1970s, it gradually was brought to the railroads. They were given more freedom, as privately owned companies, to develop their own practices to gain added profitability. The concept of railroads as a public utility remained, but with it was the understanding that deregulation provided a means of allowing the freedom needed to meet and compete with other forms of transport. The creation of Amtrak was one early step, followed five years later by the formation of Conrail. In Michigan, the state adopted an ambitious program to preserve freight service scheduled to disappear with Conrail's start-up. Michigan's program was more ambitious than that of any other state. In scope it was larger than the internal improvements program that was begun in 1836. Radical new federal legislation delivered new freedom to set rates, and, eventually, the deadening hand of the ICC was removed.

The sum of the efforts over the last thirty years—by the railroads, by Congress, and by the states—has brought success. The railroads have rediscovered an ability to provide service and to compete and have it yield a profit. But this came at a cost. Many miles of track have been removed as a part of "rationalizing" the physical plant, with Michigan experiencing more of it than many states. Many employees lost their jobs, had their work rules altered, and were forced to move to new work locations. Some towns that counted railroadmen as a large category of their residents now have to look hard to find a handful. Freight service to small towns often has suffered, much of it the result of many community industries moving out or closing down, reducing the need to run trains. Much of the "bridge" freight traffic that moved through Michigan as it crossed the country has been rerouted, with only one route remaining. There are no more Great Lakes car ferries to bring across freight to move through Michigan.

In the final analysis the railroad's resuscitation has been a success. An industry that many were sure was ready for burial is now much more prosperous. Railroad companies, large national and small regional ones, now book profits. Calls for subsidy from the federal government are muted, and demands for government ownership are little heard. Surely, today's railroad looks different than it did thirty years ago, than fifty years ago, and certainly so than a hundred years ago. The wail of a steam locomotive whistle is rarely heard, and the branch-line passenger train is gone. The click of the Morse telegraph and the small-town depot agent and the written train order are evidences of a past that will not return. Entire workers' crafts have disappeared. The wave of the brakeman from the platform of a caboose is hard to find. Yet despite all of this change, the railroad is still here and still doing what the Erie & Kalamazoo did on its first run in the pioneering days of 1836.

Afterword

This narrative relates the beginnings, growth, and maturity of a vital and fascinating Michigan industry that extends over nearly two centuries. I began writing this near the beginning of the new millennium, and with each passing year it becomes clearer that Michigan's railroads have played an important, even critical, role in the state's development, in a process that began before Michigan became a state and extended for nearly the next 100 years. For whatever reason, the railroad's place in Michigan's growth is sometimes ignored, occasionally misunderstood, and often underestimated. But plainly put, Michigan would not and could not have developed into what it has become without its railroads. The iron highway, often built in advance of American settlement, brought with it many new communities and shaped the development of every one of its major cities. In ways unimagined only a decade or two before the rails came, early Michiganders saw settlement and movement and intercommunication made speedier as well as easier and less expensive. Industry of every kind, from agriculture to automobiles, from logging to heavy manufacturing, was aided by an iron horse that helped it to develop and enabled it to grow to large size.

Michigan's railroad saga is full of unexpected turns of events and of unusual people. There are upstanding enterprises, a few embarrassments, and some outright frauds. Some men struggled against heavy odds to build a line, while a few others simply fleeced their investors. There are heroes and scalawags. There are business successes and corporate failures. The events told here have such strength that there has been no need for embellishment, or even to color anything favorably. It is always tempting for a historian to consider that a particular activity is socially desirable and that another is repugnant. I have tried to resist this allure and to have this story unfold with candor and without bias. Regretfully, I have had to relate the events only in their essentials. In the research for this work, in itself a far more stimulating undertaking than I believed possible, fascinating details and intriguing detours came up that called out to be included, but the demands of space have prevailed and forced limits. I have tried throughout, however, to weave the complex history of the railroad business into the broader fabric of Michigan's society and industry and to place it against the backdrop of the national scene. It is unfortunate that many railroad devotees overlook the essential fact that railroads do not exist in a vacuum, but act in the warp and woof of personal and economic life. To this day, despite a somewhat diminished role, the railroads remain an important part of the state's industrial community and of its society.

I thought it necessary that this narrative include not only significant events but also the important participants. These are the men whose role is often given only the most fleeting mention, but more often who are completely unnoticed. In many fields of history the reader expects to learn as much about the actors as their actions, but unfortunately this is not usually the case in much of what we have today that passes for railroad history. A few plutocrats, such as the Vanderbilts or J. P. Morgan, come immediately to mind, but most railroad men toil in far more modest but not less important situations. Many writers have yielded to the temptation to give the company the credit for its acts. The truth of the matter is that a man or group of men within the company decided there should be the act. It was such men, deliberating and deciding, that inform the corporate acts that shape nearly every event in this narrative. My regret is that I have not been able to do full or even partial justice to most of those who appear herein, nor have I been able to describe in them the vitality and substance that they deserve. Along with such corporate leaders are many others who made their own contribution, fully as important as those who are included, and who have been left unmentioned. Some personal research has developed a list of more than 8,000 executives, directors, officers, managers, and supervisors who were affiliated with Michigan railroads during just the nineteenth century. This is a wide field of opportunity for the student of railroad history.

A work of this sort poses one particular problem on which I must comment. Most corporate historians have the ease of being able to take one enterprise from conception, through its existence, and then bring it to its conclusion. In a field so broad and diverse as railroad history, with so many simultaneous strands of events occurring in so many places, the choice of an appropriate narrative form is a difficult one. It proved easiest for me, and it is the technique I have used herein, to take several decades, often a period that extended from one financial or political upheaval to the next, and present the full range of events by all participants for the period. This has the advantage of covering a wide range of contemporaneous events in one section, but it brings with it a considerable disadvantage. The narrative of any one company must be split into several parts, and these appear in different parts of the work. The alternative to this approach is to keep each company's complete narrative together, then treat the next company, then the next. But this puts on the reader the additional burden of bringing together the events by the different participants in one period of time. Since many of the railroad companies covered herein already have been favored with their own individual histories, it seemed less important to keep each corporate narrative as a unit. However, the presentation by periods that I have used does not lend itself well to all types of events. Railroad wrecks, for one example, do not vary much in character. The improvements to cars and locomotives took place over a span of at least 100 years, and some would say still longer if the diesel-electric engine is taken into account, making it difficult to categorize into particular periods. The kind of work done by the men on the ground today is much like it has been throughout the entire saga of railroading. Using a writer's prerogative, I have assigned some of these topics to one place when it seemed appropriate, while others I have divided and presented in separate periods as they occurred.

As have so many historians before me, I have relied heavily on the research and writing of a great many other workers in pertinent fields. The bibliography shows the extent of this debt. In addition to the cited works about railroads, there are other studies that have helped to form a general understanding of the backdrop of state and national economic and political events for the narrative in the foreground. I include at the end of each chapter a few of the most valuable sources of information. But I would suggest that readers keep near them a few works that I had always close at hand. Willis Dunbar's *All Aboard! A History of Michigan Railroads*, his *Michigan: A History of the Wolverine State*, and George N. Fuller's *Michigan: A Centennial History* have been constant and reliable sources of information. The annual reports of Michigan's commissioner of railroads provide a wealth of financial detail between 1872 and the early 1900s, and the narrative observations in these reports give the reader wide windows on the period. Thomas C. Cochran and William Miller's *The Age of Enterprise* provides a perspective on national economic and financial conditions and events that usually is missing from most railroad studies. John F. Stover's *American Railroads* is a readable, reliable, and valuable survey of American railroad history from its earliest days down to the present. One other work has to be mentioned: the Michigan Railroad Commission's *Aids, Gifts, Grants and Donations to Railroads Including Outline of Development and Successions in Titles to Railroads in Michigan*, but often simply called *Aids, Gifts and Grants*, is invaluable, and every student should give effusive thanks to Edmund A. Calkins for his labors. This worthwhile little book is difficult to locate in libraries, and expensive to buy when it can be found. With no disrespect to Calkins, this writer's *Michigan Railroads and Railroad Companies* and *Michigan Railroad Lines* add data that is not to be found elsewhere and also supplement and carry forward Calkins's work.

In addition to bibliographic material, I have relied extensively on the advice, direction, and assistance of many others. Le Roy Barnett and Sam Breck freely shared their enthusiasm and counsel about the history of the railroad business, and particularly about Michigan lines. Paul Trap, William McKnight, and Evan Garrett provided encouragement and technical information. This study has been strengthened by the photographs and other illustrations that have been loaned freely by many willing contributors. Librarians in a number of cities across the state have been most helpful in finding and obtaining reference material, and they deserve more thanks than they usually get. My publisher, Michigan State University Press; its directors, Fred Bohm (now retired) and Gabriel Dotto; and its senior editor, Julie Loehr, have supported the development of this book from its beginning. My sincere thanks to every member of the Press staff that worked so diligently to bring this work to completion.

I must acknowledge and dedicate this book to my late parents, Dewey and Bertha Meints, one of whom enjoyed and one of whom tolerated my enthusiasm for railroads. Most important of all, without the constant encouragement and support of my wife, Gerlinde, and my children, Cynthia and Richard, this trip would not have started, much less reached its destination.

Bibliography

American Association of Railroads. *Consolidation of Railroads.* Washington, D.C.: American Association of Railroads, 1945.

———. *Railroad Transportation: A Statistical Record.* Washington, D.C.: American Association of Railroads, various years.

The American Railway: Its Construction, Development, Management, and Appliances. New York: Charles Scribner's Sons, 1897. Reprint, New York: Arno Press, 1976.

Amtrak, public timetables, various dates.

Anderson, Jim, and Dwayne Anderson. "Unseen Wonder of the World: The St. Clair Railroad Tunnel." *Chronicle* 19:2 (Summer 1983).

Armstrong, John H. *The Railroad: What It Is, What It Does.* 3rd ed. Omaha, Neb.: Simmons-Boardman Books, 1993.

Bajema, Carl Jay. "The First Logging Railroads in the Great Lakes Region." *Forest & Conservation History* 35 (April 1991).

Bald, F. Clever. *Michigan in Four Centuries.* New York: Harper & Row, 1961.

Barnett, Le Roy. "Detroit, Mackinac & Marquette." *SOO* 12:4 (October 1990), 13:1 (January 1991).

Barton, Richard H. "A History of Railroad Regulation in Michigan." Master's thesis, Michigan State University, 1948.

Baxter, Albert. *History of the City of Grand Rapids, Michigan.* New York: Munsell, 1891.

Beal, Junius E. "The Beginnings of Interurbans." *Michigan Pioneer & Historical Collections* 35 (1907). Lansing, Mich.: Wynkoop, Hallenbeck, Crawford, 1907.

Blaszak, Michael W. "Megamergers to the Far Horizon." *Trains* 57:4 (April 1997).

Bliss, A. N. "Federal Land Grants for Internal Improvements in the State of Michigan." *Michigan Pioneer & Historical Collections* 7 (1886). Lansing, Mich.: Thorp & Godfrey, 1886.

Blois, John T. *1838 Gazeteer of the State of Michigan.* Detroit: Sydney L. Rood, 1838. Reprint, Knightstown, Ind.: Bookmark, 1979.

Blum, Albert A., and Dan Georgakas. *Michigan Labor and the Civil War.* Lansing: Michigan Civil War Centennial Observance Commission, 1964.

Boyum, Burton H. *The Saga of Iron Mining in Michigan's Upper Peninsula*. Marquette, Mich.: John M. Longyear, 1983.

———. "Superior Copper and Iron." In *A Most Superior Land: Life in the Upper Peninsula of Michigan*. Lansing, Mich.: Two Peninsula Press, 1983.

Brock, Thomas D. "Paw Paw versus the Railroads." *Michigan History* 39:2 (June 1955).

Brooks, John Wood. *Report on the Merits of the Michigan Central Railroad, as an Investment for Eastern Capitalists*. Detroit: Charles Willcox, 1846.

Bruce, Robert V. *1877: Year of Violence*. Indianapolis: Bobbs-Merrill, 1959.

Bryant, Keith L., Jr., ed. *Encyclopedia of American Business History and Biography: Railroads in the Age of Regulation, 1900–1980*. New York: Facts on File, 1988.

Buley, R. Carlyle. *The Old Northwest*. 2 vols. Bloomington: Indiana University Press, 1951.

Burger, Henry F. "Building the Ann Arbor Railroad." *Ann Arbor Railroad Technical & Historical Association Newsletter* 3 (1984): 4–6, 2 (1985): 9–11.

Burgess, George H., and Miles C. Kennedy. *Centennial History of the Pennsylvania Railroad Company, 1846–1946*. Philadelphia: Pennsylvania Railroad, 1949.

Burgtorf, Frances D. *Chief Wawatam: The Story of a Hand-Bomber*. Cheboygan, Mich.: author, 1976.

Burton, Robert E. "Car Ferry from Northport: Broken Link to the Upper Peninsula." *Michigan History* 51:1 (Spring 1967).

Bush, George. *Future Builders*. New York: McGraw-Hill, 1973.

Cady, Ron. "Michigan Metamorphosis." *Trains* 47:12 (October 1987).

Carter, Clarence E., ed. *Territorial Papers of the United States*. 17 vols. Washington, D.C.: Government Printing Office, 1934–1950.

Ceasar, Ford Stevens. *The Great Northern Ghost*. Lansing, Mich.: Wellman, 1980.

———. *The Lamp Road*. Lansing, Mich.: Wellman, 1983.

Chicago & North Western Railway, public timetables, various dates.

Churella, Albert J. "Business Strategies and Diesel Development." *Railroad History*, special issue (2000). Other articles in this issue also are of merit.

Cochrane, Thomas C., and William Miller. *The Age of Enterprise*. Rev. ed. New York: Harper & Row, 1961.

Comstock, Oliver C. "Internal Improvements." *Michigan Pioneer and Historical Collections* 1 (1875).

Cook, Richard J., Sr. *New York Central's Mercury*. Lynchburg, Va.: TLC Publishing, 1991.

Corliss, Carlton J. *The Day of Two Noons*. Washington, D.C.: Association of American Railroads, 1941.

———. *Main Line of Mid-America*. New York: Creative Age, 1950.

Cousins, G. R., and Paul Maximuke. "The Station That Looks Like a Hotel."

Trains, August 1978.

———. "The Ceremony Was 61 Years Too Late." *Trains*, September 1978.

Currie, A. W. *The Grand Trunk Railroad of Canada*. Toronto: University of Toronto Press, 1957.

Daughen, Joseph R., and Peter Binzen. *The Wreck of the Penn Central*. Boston: Little, Brown, 1971.

DeLand, Charles V. *History of Jackson County*. Indianapolis: B. F. Bowen, 1903.

Dickens, Laurie C. *Wreck on the Wabash*. Blissfield, Mich.: Made For Ewe, 2001.

Dickenson, John M. *To Build a Canal: Sault Ste. Marie, 1853–1854, and After.* Columbus: Ohio State University Press, 1981.

Dodge, (Mrs.) Frank P. "Marking the Terminus of the Erie and Kalamazoo Railroad." *Michigan Pioneer & Historical Collections* 38. Lansing, Mich.: Wynkoop, Hallenbeck, Crawford, 1912.

Dodge, Roy L. *Michigan Ghost Towns*. 3 vols. AuTrain, Mich.: Avery Studios, various years.

Donaldson, Thomas. *The Public Domain: Its History, with Statistics*. Washington, D.C.: Government Printing Office, 1884.

Drutchas, Geoffrey G. "A Capital Design." *Michigan History* 86:2 (March–April 2002).

Due, John F. "The Rise and Decline of the Midwest Interurban." *Railroad Magazine* 61:4 (September 1953).

Dunbar, Willis F. *Michigan through the Centuries*. 2 vols. New York: Lewis Historical Publishing, 1955.

———. *All Aboard! A History of Railroads in Michigan*. Grand Rapids, Mich.: W. B. Eerdmans, 1969.

———. *Michigan: A History of the Wolverine State*. Grand Rapids, Mich.: W. B. Eerdmans, 1970.

Durant, Samuel W. *History of Kalamazoo County, Michigan*. Philadelphia: Everts & Abbott, 1880.

Durocher, Aurele A. "The Duluth, South Shore and Atlantic Railway Company." *(Railway & Locomotive Historical Society) Bulletin* No. 111 (October 1964).

Eckert, Kathryn Bishop. *Buildings of Michigan*. New York: Oxford University Press, 1993.

Elliott, Frank N. *When the Railroad Was King*. Lansing: Michigan Historical Commission, 1966.

Ellis, Franklin. *History of Berrien and Van Buren Counties*. Philadelphia: D. W. Ensign, 1880.

———. *History of Shiawassee and Clinton Counties*. Philadelphia: D. W. Ensign, 1880.

Farmer, Silas. *History of Detroit and Wayne County and Early Michigan*. 3rd ed. Detroit: Silas Farmer, 1890. Reprint, Detroit: Gale Research, 1969.

Foner, Philip S. *History of the Labor Movement in the United States.* 4 vols. New York: International Publishers, 1947–1965.

Foss, Charles R. *Evening Before the Diesel.* Boulder, Colo.: Pruett Publishing, 1980.

Frederickson, Arthur C., and Lucy F. Frederickson. *Early History of the Ann Arbor Carferries.* Frankfort, Mich.: Patriot Publishing, 1949.

———. *Pictorial History of the C&O Train and Auto Ferries.* Rev. ed. Ludington, Mich.: Lakeside, 1955.

Frimodig, David M. "The $2,000,000 Ride." In *A Most Superior Land: Life in the Upper Peninsula of Michigan.* Lansing, Mich.: Two Peninsula Press, 1983.

Fuller, George N. *Economic and Social Beginnings of Michigan.* Lansing: Wynkoop, Hallenbeck, Crawford, 1916.

———. *Michigan: A Centennial History.* 2 vols. Chicago: Lewis Publishing, 1939.

Gaertner, John. "The Gogebic Range." *SOO* 18:1 (Winter 1996), 18:2 (Spring 1996), 18:3 (Summer 1996), 18:4 (Fall 1996).

———. *Duluth, South Shore & Atlantic Railway: A History of the Lake Superior District's Pioneer Iron Ore Hauler.* Bloomington: Indiana University Press, 2009.

Galloway, Joseph A. *Interurban Trails.* Toledo: Eastern Ohio Chapter, National Railway Historical Society, n.d.

Garrett, Evan. "The Ann Arbor Comes to Ann Arbor." *Ann Arbor Railroad Technical & Historical Association Newsletter* 6 (1984): 4, 10–12.

Gilpin, Alec R. *The Territory of Michigan, 1805–1837.* East Lansing: Michigan State University Press, 1970.

Ginger, Ray. *The Bending Cross: A Biography of Eugene Victor Debs.* New Brunswick, N.J.: Rutgers University Press, 1949.

Gould, Lucius E. "The Passing of the Old Town." *Michigan Pioneer & Historical Collections* 30 (1906). Lansing, Mich.: Wynkoop, Hallenbeck, Crawford, 1906.

Grand Trunk Railway, public timetables, various dates.

Grant, H. Roger, and Charles W. Bohi. *The Country Railroad Station in America.* Sioux Falls, S.D.: Center of Western Studies, 1988.

Grodinsky, Julius. *Jay Gould: His Business Career, 1867–1892.* Philadelphia: University of Pennsylvania Press, 1957.

Hague, Wilbur E., and Kirk F. Hise. *The Detroit, Monroe & Toledo Short Line Railway.* Forty Fort, Pa.: Harold E. Cox, 1986.

Harlow, Alvin F. *Steelways of New England.* New York: Creative Age Press, 1946.

———. *The Road of the Century.* New York: Creative Age Press, 1947.

Hatcher, Harlan. *A Century of Iron and Men.* Indianapolis: Bobbs-Merrill, 1950.

Hedrick, Ulysses P. *The Land of the Crooked Tree.* New York: Oxford University Press, 1948.

Hedrick, Wilbur O. "The History of Railroad Taxation in Michigan." Ph.D. diss., University of Michigan, 1909.

Henning, William H. *Detroit, Its Trolleys and Interurbans*. Fraser, Mich.: Michigan Transit Museum, 1976.

Hilton, George W. *The Great Lakes Car Ferries*. Berkeley, Calif.: Howell-North, 1962.

———. "Staggers Rail Act of 1980." In *Railroads in the Age of Regulation: 1900–1980*. New York: Facts on File, 1988.

———. *American Narrow Gauge Railroads*. Stanford, Calif.: Stanford University Press, 1990.

———. *Lake Michigan Passenger Steamers*. Stanford, Calif.: Stanford University Press, 2002.

Hilton, George W., and John F. Due. *The Electric Interurban Railways in America*. Stanford, Calif.: Stanford University Press, 1960.

Hines, Walker D. *War History of American Railroads*. New Haven, Conn.: Yale University Press, 1928.

Hirschfield, Charles. "The Great Railroad Conspiracy." *Michigan History* 36:2 (June 1952).

———. *The Great Railroad Conspiracy*. East Lansing: Michigan State University Press, 1953.

History of Jackson County. Chicago: Inter-state Publishing, 1881.

History of Saginaw County, Michigan. Chicago: Chas. C. Chapman, 1881.

Holbrook, Stewart H. *Holy Old Mackinaw*. New York: McMillan, 1938.

———. *The Story of American Railroads*. New York: Crown, 1947.

Hoogenboom, Ari A., and Olive Hoogenboom. *A History of the ICC: From Panacea to Palliative*. New York: W. W. Norton, 1976.

Hopper, A. B., and T. Kearney. *Canadian National Railways: Synoptical History . . . as of December 31, 1960*. Montreal: Canadian National Railways, 1962.

Hungerford, Edward. *Men and Iron: The History of New York Central*. New York: Thomas Y. Crowell, 1938.

———. *Men of Erie*. New York: Random House, 1946.

Husband, Joseph. *The History of the Pullman Car*. 1917. Reprint, Grand Rapids, Mich.: Black Letter Press, 1974.

Hutchins, Jere C. *Jere C. Hutchins: A Personal Story*. Detroit: author, 1938.

Inglis, James G. *Northern Michigan Handbook for Traveler's, 1898*. Petoskey, Mich.: George E. Sprang, 1898. Reprint, Grand Rapids, Mich.: Black Letter Press, 1974.

Ivey, Paul Wesley. *The Pere Marquette Railroad: An Historical Study of the Growth and Development of One of Michigan's Most Important Railway Systems*. Lansing: Michigan Historical Commission, 1919. Reprint, Grand Rapids, Mich.: Black Letter Press, 1970.

Johnson, Paul. *A History of the American People*. New York: HarperCollins, 1997.

Johnston, Marie. "The Building of the Grand Rapids and Indiana Railroad."

Indiana Magazine of History 41 (1945).

Kaminski, Edward S. *American Car & Foundry Company: A Centennial History, 1899–1999.* Wilton, Calif.: Signature Press, 1999.

Keefe, Kevin P. "How Michigan Got into the Railroad Business." *Trains* 36:12 (October 1976).

Keenan, Hudson. "America's First Successful Logging Railroad." *Michigan History* 44:3 (September 1960).

Kirkpatrick, Frank A. "The Saginaw, Tuscola & Huron: An Early Railroad of the Thumb Peninsula." *Michigan History* 52:2 (Summer 1968).

Kleiman, Jeff. *The Rise and Fall of the CSCRR: A Short History of a Short-Lived Railroad.* Grand Rapids, Mich.: Friends of the Public Museum, 1992.

Kolko, Gabriel. *Railroads and Regulation, 1877–1916.* Princeton, N.J.: Princeton University Press, 1965.

Lacey, Robert. *Ford, the Men and the Machine.* Boston: Little, Brown, 1986.

Lake Shore & Michigan Southern Railway, public timetables, various dates.

Lane, Wheaton J. *Commodore Vanderbilt: An Epic of the Steam Age.* New York: Alfred A. Knopf, 1942.

Lee, Robert E. "The Streetcar Lines of Grand Rapids." *Michigan History* 46:1 (March 1962).

Leech, C. A. "Deward: A Lumberman's Ghost Town." *Michigan History* 28:1 (Spring 1944).

Lenderink, A. Rodney. "The Electric Interurban Railway in Kalamazoo County." *Michigan History* 43:1 (March 1959).

Lewis, Martin D. *Lumberman from Flint: The Michigan Career of Henry H. Crapo.* Detroit: Wayne State University Press, 1958.

Leyendecker, Liston E. *Palace Car Prince: A Biography of George Mortimer Pullman.* Niwot: University Press of Colorado, 1992.

Marks, Joseph J. *Effects of the Civil War on Michigan Farming.* Lansing: Michigan Civil War Centennial Observance Committee, 1965.

Marshall, Albert P. *The "Real McCoy" of Ypsilanti.* Ypsilanti, Mich.: Marlan, 1989.

Martin, Albro. *Enterprise Denied.* New York: Columbia University Press, 1971.

———. *Railroads Triumphant: The Growth, Rejection, and Rebirth of a Vital American Force.* New York: Oxford University Press, 1992.

Massie, Larry. "Depot Dreams and Jerkwater Schemes." *Michigan History* 77:6 (November–December 1993).

Maybee, Rolland H. *Michigan's White Pine Era, 1840–1900.* Lansing: Michigan Department of State, 1976.

McAdoo, William G. *Crowded Years.* New York: Houghton Mifflin, 1931.

McCaleb, Walter F. *Brotherhood of Railroad Trainmen....* New York: Albert Boni, 1936.

McClintock, William R., Jr. "Early Railroad Regulation in Michigan: 1850–1863." Ph.D. diss., University of Wyoming, 1976.

McGonigal, Robert S., ed. "DieselVictory." *Classic Trains*, special edition 4 (2006).

McLellan, David, and Bill Warrick. *The Lake Shore & Michigan Southern Railway*. Polo, Ill.: Transportation Trail, 1989.

McLeod, Richard. "History of the Wisconsin and Michigan Railway." *(Railway & Locomotive Historical Society) Bulletin* No. 118 (April 1968).

Meints, Graydon M. *Michigan Railroads and Railroad Companies*. East Lansing: Michigan State University Press, 1992.

———. "Race to Chicago." *Railroad History* No. 183 (Autumn 2000).

———. "Overwhelmed with Good Fortune." *Railroad History* No. 188 (Spring 2003).

———. *Michigan Railroad Lines*. East Lansing: Michigan State University Press, 2005.

Men of Ohio in Nineteen Hundred. Cleveland, Ohio: Benesch Art Publishing, 1901.

Merk, George P. "A Profile of Courage." *Michigan History* 87:1 (January–February 2003).

Michigan. *First Annual Report of the Commissioner of Railroads*. Lansing: W. S. George, 1874. (Covers the year 1872)

———. *Fourth Annual Report of the Commissioner of Railroads*. Lansing: W. S. George, 1876. (Covers the year 1875)

———. *Thirteenth Annual Report of the Commissioner of Railroads*. Lansing: W. S. George, 1885. (Covers the year 1884)

———. *Nineteenth Annual Report of the Commissioner of Railroads*. Lansing: Robert Smith, 1891. (Covers the year 1890)

———. *Twenty-First Annual Report of the Commissioner of Railroads*. Lansing: Robert Smith, 1893. (Covers the year 1892)

———. *Twenty-Fourth Annual Report of the Commissioner of Railroads*. Lansing: Robert Smith, 1896. (Covers the year 1895)

———. *Twenty-Fifth Annual Report of the Commissioner of Railroads*. Lansing: Robert Smith, 1898. (Covers the year 1896)

Michigan Association of Railroad Passengers. *Wolverine Mainliner* and *Wolverine Passenger*, various issues.

Michigan Central Railroad, public timetables, various dates.

Michigan Department of State Highways and Transportation. *State of Michigan Action Plan*. Lansing: Michigan Department of State Highways and Transportation, 1974.

———. *Michigan Railroad Plan, Phase I, May 15, 1975; Michigan Railroad Plan, Phase 2, December 6, 1975;* and *Michigan Railroad Plan, Phase 2, June 1976*. Lansing: Michigan Department of State Highways and Transportation, 1975, 1976.

Michigan Department of Transportation. *150 Years of Michigan's Railroad History*. Lansing: Michigan Department of Transportation, 1987.

Michigan Historical Commission. *Michigan Biographies*. 2 vols. Lansing: Michigan Historical Commission, 1924.

Michigan Legislature. *Acts of the Legislature*, various years. Lansing, Mich.: various publishers.

Michigan Pathfinder Guide, December 1915. Detroit: Pathfinder, 1915.

Michigan Railroad Commission. *Aids, Gifts, Grants and Donations to Railroads . . .* Lansing, Mich.: Wynkoop, Hallenbeck, Crawford, 1919.

Michigan Railway Guide, June 1909. Detroit: John R. Wood, 1909.

Miller, George H. *Railroads and the Granger Laws*. Madison: University of Wisconsin Press, 1971.

Miller, William J. "The Detroit, Bay City & Western Railroad . . ." *Michigan Railfan* 50:2 (February 1989).

Million, Art. "Wreck at East Paris." *Pere Marquette Rails* No. 14. (2002).

Million, Arthur B., and Thomas W. Dixon Jr. *Pere Marquette Power*. Alderson, W.Va.: Chesapeake & Ohio Historical Society, 1984.

Monette, Clarence J. *The Copper Range Railroad*. Lake Linden, Mich.: author, 1989.

———. *The Mineral Range Railroad*. Lake Linden, Mich.: author, 1993.

———. *Keweenaw Central Railroad and the Crestview Resort*. Calumet, Mich.: Greenlee Publishing, 1997.

Morison, Samuel Eliot. *The Oxford History of the American People*. New York: Oxford University Press, 1965.

Murdoch, Angus. *Boom Copper: The Story of the First U.S. Mining Boom*. 1943. Reprint, Calumet, Mich.: Roy W. Drier and Louis G. Koepel, 1964.

National Association of Railroad Passengers. *NARP News*, various issues.

Neimann, Linda, and Lina Bertucci. *Railroad Voices*. Stanford, Calif.: Stanford University Press, 1998.

New York Central Railroad, public timetables, various dates.

The Official Guide of the Railways. New York: National Railway Publication, various dates.

O'Geran, Graeme. *A History of the Detroit Street Railways*. Detroit: Conover Press, 1931.

Parks, Robert J. *Democracy's Railroads*. Port Washington, N.Y.: Kennikat, 1972.

Pearson, Henry G. *An American Railroad Builder: John Murray Forbes*. New York: Houghton Mifflin, 1911.

Pennsylvania Railroad, public timetables, various dates.

Percival, John J. "Railroads in Ottawa County." *Michigan Pioneer & Historical Collections* 9 (1886). Lansing, Mich.: Thorp & Godfrey, 1886.

Pere Marquette Railroad, also Railway, public timetables, various dates.

Peters, John Douglas, and Vincent G. Robinson. *Detroit: Freight Cars Before Automobiles*. Belleville, Mich.: Treasure Press, 2005.

Peterson, William R. *The View from Courthouse Hill*. Philadelphia: Dorrance, 1972.

Pletz, William C. "The Railroad That Went No Place." *Inside Track* 10:5 (November–December 1979), 11:1 (January–February 1980).

Potter, Janet Greenstein. *Great American Railroad Stations*. New York: John Wiley & Sons, 1996.

Progressive Men of Northern Ohio. Cleveland, Ohio: Plain Dealer Publishing, 1906.

Quaife, Milo M., and Sidney Glazer. *Michigan: From Primitive Wilderness to Industrial Commonwealth*. New York: Prentice-Hall, 1948.

Rector, William G. "Railroad Logging in the Lake States." *Michigan History* 36:4 (December 1952).

———. *Log Transportation in the Lake States Lumber Industry*. Glendale, Calif.: Arthur H. Clark, 1953.

Rehor, John A. *The Nickel Plate Story*. Milwaukee: Kalmbach, 1965.

Reimann, Lewis C. *When Pine Was King*. Ann Arbor, Mich.: Northwoods Publishers, 1952.

Reinhardt, Richard, ed. *Workin' on the Railroad*. Palo Alto, Calif.: American West, 1970.

Reutter, Mark, ed. "The Diesel Revolution." *Railroad History*, special issue (2000).

Riddering, Don. "The Great Salem Wreck." *(Salem Area Historical Society) Historical Monograph* 1 (May 1987).

Riggs, Henry E. *The Ann Arbor Railroad Fifty Years Ago*. Toledo, Ohio: Ann Arbor RR, 1947. Reprint, Ann Arbor, 1991.

Rohe, Randall. "Tramways and Pole Railroads: An Episode in the Technological History of the Great Lakes Lumber Era." *Upper Midwest History* 5 (1985).

Romig, Walter. *Michigan Place Names*. Grosse Pointe, Mich.: author, n.d.

Rubenstein, Bruce A., and Lawrence E. Ziewacz. *Michigan: A History of the Great Lakes State*. Arlington Heights, Ill.: Forum Press, 1981.

Saunders, Richard. *The Railroad Mergers and the Coming of Conrail*. Westport, Conn.: Greenwood, 1978.

———. *Merging Lines: American Railroads, 1900–1970*. DeKalb: Northern Illinois University Press, 2001.

———. *Main Lines: Rebirth of the North American Railroads, 1970–2002*. DeKalb: Northern Illinois University Press, 2003.

Schramm, Jack E., and William H. Henning. *Detroit's Street Railways*. Vol. 1, *City Lines 1863–1922*. Chicago: Central Electric Railfans' Association, 1978.

———. *When Eastern Michigan Rode the Rails, Book 2*. Glendale, Calif.: Interurban Press, 1986.

Schramm, Jack E., William H. Henning, and Richard R. Andrews. *When Eastern*

Michigan Rode the Rails, Book 1. Glendale, Calif.: Interurban Press, 1984.

——. *When Eastern Michigan Rode the Rails, Book 3*. Glendale, Calif.: Interurban Press, 1988.

——. *When Eastern Michigan Rode the Rails, Book 4*. Polo, Ill.: Transportation Trails, 1994.

Seavoy, Ronald E. "Borrowed Laws to Speed Development: Michigan, 1835–1863." *Michigan History* 59:1–2 (Spring–Summer 1975).

Sell, Bob, and Jim Findlay. *The Teeter & Wobble*. Blissfield, Mich.: authors, 1993.

Shaw, Robert B. "Railroad Accidents and Passenger Safety." *Railroad History* No. 184 (Spring 2001).

Simons, Richard S., and Francis H. Parker. *Railroads of Indiana*. Bloomington: Indiana University Press, 1997.

Specht, Ray. "Milwaukee, Lake Shore & Western." *(Railway & Locomotive Historical Society) Bulletin* No. 121 (October 1969).

——. "The Milwaukee & Northern." *(Railway & Locomotive Historical Society) Bulletin* No. 121 (October 1969).

Stennett, William H. *Yesterday and Today: A History of the Chicago and North Western Railway System*. 3rd ed. Chicago: n.p., 1910.

Stevens, G. R. *Canadian National Railways: Sixty Years of Trial and Error, 1836–1896*. 2 vols. Toronto: Clark, Irwin, 1960, 1962.

Stover, John F. *American Railroads*. Chicago: University of Chicago Press, 1961.

Stromquist, Shelton. *A Generation of Boomers*. Urbana: University of Illinois Press, 1987.

Stroup, Donald. "Boom to Bankruptcy: The Story of the Manistee and Northeastern Railroad." Master's thesis, Western Michigan University, 1965. (Also published in abridged form as *The Life and Death of a Railroad, The Manistee and Northeastern* [Lansing: Michigan Historical Commission, 1964])

Swartz, William. "The Wabash Railroad." *Railroad History* No. 133 (Fall 1975).

Taylor, George R., and Irene D. Neu. *The American Railroad Network, 1861–1890*. Cambridge, Mass.: Harvard University Press, 1956.

Tennant, Robert D., Jr. *Canada Southern Country*. Erin, Ont.: Boston Mills Press, 1991.

Thornton, W. Neil. *High Iron along the Huron Shore*. Tawas City, Mich.: Printer's Devil Press, 1982.

Trap, Paul. "The Detroit and Pontiac Railroad." *Railroad History* No. 168 (Spring 1993).

Travelers Official Guide of the Railway and Steam Navigation Lines. Reprint of June 1893 issue.

Travelers Official Rail Way Guide of the United States and Canada. Reprints of June 1868 and June 1869 issues.

Trostel, Scott D. *Detroit, Toledo and Iron Railroad: Henry Ford's Railroad*. Fletcher, Ohio: Cam-Tech Publishing, 1988.

———. *Henry Ford: When I Ran the Railroad*. Fletcher, Ohio: Cam-Tech Publishing, 1989.

Uhelski, John M., and Robert M. Uhelski. *An Inventory of the Railroad Depots in the State of Michigan*. Crete, Nebr.: Railroad Station Historical Society, 1979.

U.S. Congress. House. Committee on Interstate and Foreign Commerce. *The Financial Collapse of the Penn Central Company*. 92nd Cong., 2nd sess. Washington, D.C., 1972.

U.S. Congress. Senate. Committee on Commerce. *The Penn Central and Other Railroads*. 92nd Cong., 2nd sess. Washington, D.C., 1972.

U.S. Department of the Interior, Heritage Conservation and Recreation Service, Historic American Engineering Record. *The Upper Peninsula of Michigan: An Inventory of Historic Engineering and Industrial Sites*, by Charles K. Hyde and Diane B. Abbott. Washington, D.C., 1978.

U.S. Department of the Interior, National Park Service, Historic American Engineering Record. *The Lower Peninsula of Michigan: An Inventory of Historic Engineering and Industrial Sites*, by Charles K. Hyde and Diane B. Abbott. Washington, D.C., 1976.

U.S. Department of Transportation. *Rail Service in the Midwest and Northeast Region*. Washington, D.C.: Government Printing Office, 1974.

U.S. Interstate Commerce Commission. *Annual Reports*. Washington, D.C.: Government Printing Office, various years.

———. *Evaluation of the U.S. Railway Association's Preliminary System Plan*. Washington, D.C.: Government Printing Office, 1975.

———. *Finance Docket No. 6833*. Washington, D.C.: Interstate Commerce Commission, n.d.

———. *Valuation Docket No. 127*. Washington, D.C.: Interstate Commerce Commission, 1924.

United States Railway Association. *Preliminary System Plan*. 2 vols. Washington, D.C.: Government Printing Office, 1975.

———. *Final System Plan*. 2 vols. Washington, D.C.: Government Printing Office, 1975.

Utley, Henry M., and Byron M. Cutcheon. *Michigan as a Province, Territory and State, the Twenty-Sixth Member of the Federal Union*. New York: Publishing Society of Michigan, 1906.

van Reken, Donald L. *The Interurban Era in Holland, Michigan*. Holland, Mich.: author, 1981.

———. *The Railroads of Holland, Michigan*. 2 vols. Holland, Mich.: author, 1997, 1998.

Waggoner, Clark, ed. *History of the City of Toledo and Lucas County, Ohio.* New York and Toledo: n.p., 1888.

Wakefield, Lawrence, and Lucille Wakefield. *Sail and Rail: A Narrative History of Transportation in Western Michigan.* Grand Rapids, Mich.: W. B. Eerdmans, 1980. Reprint, Holt, Mich.: Thunder Bay Press, 1996.

Wakeman, George L. "My Story of the Detroit and Mackinac Railway." Unpublished manuscript, Michigan Historical Collections, University of Michigan, Ann Arbor.

Weber, Thomas. *The Northern Railroads in the Civil War, 1861–1865.* New York: King's Crown Press, 1952. Reprint, Bloomington: Indiana University Press, 1999.

Weeks, George. *Stewards of the State: The Governors of Michigan.* Ann Arbor: Historical Society of Michigan, 1987.

Westmeyer, Russell E. *Economics of Transportation.* Englewood Cliffs, N.J.: Prentice-Hall, 1952.

"When U.S. Took Over the Railroads." *Railroad Magazine* 24:5 (October 1938).

White, John H., Jr. *The American Railroad Passenger Car.* Baltimore: Johns Hopkins University Press, 1978.

———. *The American Railroad Freight Car: From the Wood-Car Era to the Coming of Steel.* Baltimore: Johns Hopkins University Press, 1993.

———. *American Locomotives: An Engineering History, 1830–1880.* Rev. ed. Baltimore: Johns Hopkins University Press, 1997.

White, Peter. "The Iron Region of Lake Superior." *Michigan Pioneer & Historical Collections* 8 (1885). Lansing, Mich.: Thorp & Godfrey, 1886.

Williams, Ralph D. *The Honorable Peter White.* Cleveland: Penton, 1907.

Wilner, Frank N. *The Amtrak Story.* Omaha, Neb.: Simmons-Boardman, 1994.

Wing, Talcott E. *History of Monroe County.* New York: Munsell, 1890.

Woodford, Frank R., and Arthur M. Woodford. *All Our Yesterdays.* Detroit: Wayne State University Press, 1969.

Wyllie, Cleland B. "How the Grand Trunk Got to Chicago." Unpublished manuscript, n.d. Bentley Historical Library, University of Michigan.

Zimmerman, Karl. *Lake Michigan's Railroad Car Ferries.* Andover, N.J.: Andover Junction Publications, 1993.

Zink, Maximillian A., and George Krambles, eds. *Electric Railways of Michigan, Bulletin 103.* Chicago: Central Electric Railfans' Association, 1959.

———. *Electric Railways of Indiana, Bulletin 104.* Chicago: Central Electric Railfans' Association, 1960.

Index